Quantum Chemistry

VALUES OF SOME PHYSICAL CONSTANTS

Constant	Symbol	Value
Avogadro's number	N_0	6.02205×10^{23} mol^{-1}
Proton charge	e	1.60219×10^{-19} C
Planck's constant	h $\hbar$	6.62618×10^{-34} J$\cdot$s 1.05459×10^{-34} J$\cdot$s
Speed of light in vacuum	c	2.997925×10^{8} m$\cdot$s^{-1}
Atomic mass unit	amu	1.66056×10^{-27} kg
Electron rest mass	m_e	9.10953×10^{-31} kg
Proton rest mass	m_p	1.67265×10^{-27} kg
Boltzmann constant	k_B	1.38066×10^{-23} J$\cdot$K^{-1} 0.69509 cm^{-1}
Molar gas constant	R	8.31441 J$\cdot$K$^{-1}\cdot$mol^{-1}
Permittivity of a vacuum	ε_0 $4\pi\varepsilon_0$	8.854188×10^{-12} C$^2\cdot$s$^2\cdot$kg$^{-1}\cdot$m^{-3} 1.112650×10^{-10} C$^2\cdot$s$^2\cdot$kg$^{-1}\cdot$m^{-3}
Rydberg constant (infinite nuclear mass)	R_∞	2.179914×10^{-23} J 1.097373 cm^{-1}
First Bohr radius	a_0	5.29177×10^{-11} m
Bohr magneton	μ_B	9.27409×10^{-24} J$\cdot$T^{-1}
Stefan-Boltzmann constant	σ	5.67032×10^{-8} J$\cdot$m$^{-2}\cdot$K$^{-4}\cdot$s^{-1}

CONVERSION FACTORS FOR ENERGY UNITS

	joule	kJ$\cdot$mol^{-1}	eV	au	cm^{-1}	Hz
1 joule $= 1$		6.022×10^{20}	6.242×10^{18}	2.2939×10^{17}	5.035×10^{22}	1.509×10^{33}
1 kJ$\cdot$mol^{-1} $= 1.661 \times 10^{-21}$		1	1.036×10^{-2}	3.089×10^{-4}	83.60	2.506×10^{12}
1 eV $= 1.602 \times 10^{-19}$		96.48	1	3.675×10^{-2}	8065	2.418×10^{14}
1 au $= 4.359 \times 10^{-18}$		2625	27.21	1	2.195×10^{5}	6.580×10^{15}
1 cm^{-1} $= 1.986 \times 10^{-23}$		1.196×10^{-2}	1.240×10^{-4}	4.556×10^{-6}	1	2.998×10^{10}
1 Hz $= 6.626 \times 10^{-34}$		3.990×10^{-13}	4.136×10^{-15}	1.520×10^{-16}	3.336×10^{-11}	1

SOME MATHEMATICAL FORMULAS

$$\sin \alpha \sin \beta = \tfrac{1}{2} \cos (\alpha - \beta) - \tfrac{1}{2} \cos (\alpha + \beta)$$

$$\cos \alpha \cos \beta = \tfrac{1}{2} \cos (\alpha - \beta) + \tfrac{1}{2} \cos (\alpha + \beta)$$

$$\sin \alpha \cos \beta = \tfrac{1}{2} \sin (\alpha + \beta) + \tfrac{1}{2} \sin (\alpha - \beta)$$

$$\sin (\alpha \pm \beta) = \sin \alpha \cos \beta \pm \cos \alpha \sin \beta$$

$$\cos (\alpha \pm \beta) = \cos \alpha \cos \beta \mp \sin \alpha \sin \beta$$

$$e^{\pm i\theta} = \cos \theta \pm i \sin \theta$$

$$\cos \theta = \frac{e^{i\theta} + e^{-i\theta}}{2}$$

$$\sin \theta = \frac{e^{i\theta} - e^{-i\theta}}{2i}$$

$$f(x) = f(a) + f'(a)(x - a) + \frac{1}{2!} f''(a)(x - a)^2 + \frac{1}{3!} f'''(a)(x - a)^3 + \cdots$$

$$e^x = 1 + x + \frac{x^2}{2!} + \frac{x^3}{3!} + \frac{x^4}{4!} + \cdots$$

$$\cos x = 1 - \frac{x^2}{2!} + \frac{x^4}{4!} - \frac{x^6}{6!} + \cdots$$

$$\sin x = x - \frac{x^3}{3!} + \frac{x^5}{5!} - \frac{x^7}{7!} + \cdots$$

$$\frac{1}{1 - x} = 1 + x + x^2 + x^3 + x^4 + \cdots \qquad x^2 < 1$$

$$(1 \pm x)^n = 1 \pm nx + \frac{n(n - 1)}{2!} x^2 \pm \frac{n(n - 1)(n - 2)}{3!} x^3 + \cdots \qquad x^2 < 1$$

$$\int_0^\infty x^n e^{-ax} dx = \frac{n!}{a^{n+1}} \qquad (n \text{ positive integer})$$

$$\int_0^\infty e^{-ax^2} dx = \left(\frac{\pi}{4a}\right)^{1/2}$$

$$\int_0^\infty x^{2n} e^{-ax^2} dx = \frac{1 \cdot 3 \cdot 5 \cdots (2n - 1)}{2^{n+1} a^n} \left(\frac{\pi}{a}\right)^{1/2} \qquad (n \text{ positive integer})$$

$$\int_0^\infty x^{2n+1} e^{-ax^2} dx = \frac{n!}{2a^{n+1}} \qquad (n \text{ positive integer})$$

$$\int_0^a \sin \frac{n\pi x}{a} \sin \frac{m\pi x}{a} dx = \int_0^a \cos \frac{n\pi x}{a} \cos \frac{m\pi x}{a} dx = \frac{a}{2} \delta_{nm}$$

Quantum Chemistry

Donald A McQuarrie

Viva Books

New Delhi | Mumbai | Chennai | Kolkata | Bengaluru | Hyderabad | Kochi | Guwahati

First Indian Edition 2003
Reprinted 2005, 2007, 2008, 2010, 2011, 2013, 2014, 2015, 2016, 2018

VIVA BOOKS PRIVATE LIMITED

- 4737/23 Ansari Road, Daryaganj, New Delhi 110 002
  E-mail: vivadelhi@vivagroupindia.net, Tel. 42242200
- 76, Service Industries, Shirvane, Sector 1, Nerul, Navi Mumbai 400 706
  E-mail: vivamumbai@vivagroupindia.net, Tel. 27721273, 27721274
- Megh Towers, Old No. 307, New No. 165, Poonamallee High Road, Maduravoyal
  Chennai - 600 095, E-mail: vivachennai@vivagroupindia.net, Tel. 23780991, 23780992
- B-103, Jindal Towers, 21/1A/3 Darga Road, Kolkata 700 017
  E-mail: vivakolkata@vivagroupindia.net, Tel. 22836381, 22816713
- 7, Sovereign Park Apartments, 56-58, K. R. Road, Basavanagudi, Bengaluru 560 004
  E-mail: vivabangalore@vivagroupindia.net, Tel. 26607409, 26607410
- 101-102 Mughal Marc Aptt., 3-4-637 to 641, Narayanguda, Hyderabad 500 029
  E-mail: vivahyderabad@vivagroupindia.net, Tel. 27564481, 27564482
- First Floor, Beevi Towers, SRM Road, Kaloor, Kochi 682 018, Kerala
  E-mail: vivakochi@vivagroupindia.net, Tel: 0484-2403055, 2403056
- 232, GNB Road, Beside UCO Bank, Silpukhuri, Guwahati 781 003
  E-mail: vivaguwahati@vivagroupindia.net, Tel: 0361-2666386

Published by arrangement with
University Science Books
55 D Gate Five Road
Sausalito, CA 94965
USA

Photo Credits
Chapter-opening photos

Chapter 1	Courtesy of Deric Bownds and Stan Carlson, University of Wisconsin
Chapter 2	Education Development Center Inc. Newton, Massachussetts
Chapter 3	AIP Niels Bohr Library and Photo Pfaundler, Innsbruck, Austria
Chapter 4	Oregon Museum of Science and Industry, Portland, Oregon
Chapter 5	Smithsonian Institution Photo No. 75-3966.
Chapter 6	Courtesy of Hervey E. White, Dept. of Physics, University of California, Berkley
Chapter 7	From *Molecular Spectra and Molecular Structure*, 2nd Revised Edition, by G. Herzberg (New York Dover Publications, 1944)
Chapter 8	From Fig. 4.6 in *General College Chemistry*, 6th Edition, by Charles W. Keenan, Donald C. Kleinfelter and Lesse H. Wood. Copyright © 1980 by Charles W. Keenan, Donald C. Kleinfelter and Jesse H. Wood. Permission of Haper and Row, Publishers Inc.
Chapter 9	From *Chemical Principles*, 4th Edition by Williams Masterton and Emil Slowinski. Copyright © 1977 by WB Saunders Co. Reprinted by permission of Holt, Rinehart and Winston, CBS College Publishing
Chapter 10	Courtesy of National Research Council of Canada

Text Photo

Pages 5, 23 : Courtesy of Professor J.B. Loeb, Berkley, California
Page 9, 36, 84, 99 (photo by P. Eherenfest Jr) 293, 299, 320, 344, 379: AIP Niels Bohr Library
Page 16: *From Molecular Spectra and Molecular Structure,* 2nd Rev Ed. by G. Herzsberg (New York, Dover Publications)
Page 63: Bay Stark
Page 141: Reproduced by permission of *Institute Internationaux de Physique et de Chimie,* (Solvay) Brussels, Belgium
Page 239: Museum Boerhaave, Leiden Nederland
Page 358: Courtesy of University of Chicago
Page 413: *Velag Chemie*

ISBN : 978-81-309-1894-5

Published by Vinod Vasishtha for Viva Books Private Limited, 4737/23, Ansari Road, Daryaganj New Delhi - 110 002. Printed and bound by Raj Press, R-3 Inderpuri, New Delhi - 110 012.

Preface

THIS BOOK has evolved from the notes
that I developed while teaching the quantum chemistry part of physical chemistry for a number of years at Indiana University. I have included more material
than can easily be covered in a one-semester course in recognition of the
preferences of individual instructors. I have taught most of this material
regularly at the junior level, but the text would also be suitable for a senior-
level course in quantum chemistry. The mathematics background required
of the students is simply one year of calculus, with no knowledge of differential
equations. Most of the necessary mathematical techniques are developed
within the text.

The first chapter is a discussion of the historical development of quantum
mechanics from Planck to Schrödinger. I have used this chapter not only to
present the historical development of quantum mechanics, but also to introduce several classical mechanical concepts that are required for any discussion
of quantum mechanics. Chapter 2 is a digression on the classical wave equation. This chapter introduces some elementary differential equations and the
method of separation of variables, but more importantly it illustrates the
relationship between the mathematical solution of a problem and its physical
interpretation. The concepts of standing waves, traveling waves, normal modes,
and the superposition of normal modes are developed. Chapter 3 presents
the Schrödinger equation and its application to a one-dimensional particle in
a box. Many of the procedures of quantum mechanics are developed informally
and intuitively using the simplicity of the particle-in-a-box results as a guide.
A formal set of postulates is not presented until Chapter 4, after the student
has acquired some concrete experience with quantum-mechanical problems
in Chapter 3. Chapter 5 presents the harmonic oscillator, and Chapter 6
presents several exactly solvable three-dimensional problems such as the rigid
rotator and the hydrogen atom. After pointing out that we cannot go beyond
the hydrogen atom without resorting to some systematic approximate procedures, we develop both perturbation theory and the variational method in
Chapter 7. Chapter 8 discusses atoms and Chapter 9 discusses molecules.
Lastly, Chapter 10 presents the applications and the results of previous chapters to molecular spectroscopy. Chapter 10 concludes with a fairly detailed

discussion of the Born-Oppenheimer Approximation, time-dependent perturbation theory, and the derivation of selection rules.

One of the pedagogical features of the text is the inclusion of many worked examples in each chapter. In addition there are about 30 problems at the end of each chapter with the solutions to all the numerical problems given at the back of the book. Furthermore, the chapters have been written such that any advanced material appears in the final sections of a chapter, so that this material may be easily passed over. This applies particularly to Chapters 4, 5, 8, and 10.

Physical chemistry textbook authors nowadays face a dilemma concerning units. There is a strong trend toward the use of SI units, and I have given in to this as much as possible. For example, energies are expressed in terms of joules, and distances are expressed in terms of picometers instead of angstroms. Nevertheless, the spectroscopic unit of wave number (cm^{-1}) is used throughout, and electron volts are used frequently. One disadvantage of SI units is the annoying feature of $4\pi\varepsilon_0$ which must be included in Coulomb's law. When we switch to atomic units in Chapter 8, however, this factor is absorbed into the atomic units and effectively disappears.

Many people have contributed to the writing of this book. I particularly would like to thank Atilla Szabo for many stimulating and helpful discussions on teaching quantum chemistry to undergraduates. I would also like to thank David Case, James Copeland, William Fink, Kenneth Hedberg, Charles Palke, Peter Rock, Donald Rogers, and Donald Truhlar for reading portions of the manuscript and making many helpful suggestions. I would also like to thank Joseph Ledbetter for reading the galleys and checking the solutions to all the problems; Elaine Rock for typing a beautiful manuscript; Greg Hubit for overseeing the development of this project in a most efficient and competent manner; and my publisher, Bruce Armbruster, for encouraging me to complete this project and for being a helpful and considerate agent and friend. Lastly, I would like to thank my wife, Carole, for reading much of the manuscript and galleys, for helping with the index, and for finally believing that quantum chemistry is not so bad after all.

Contents

1 Historical Background   3

1-1   J. J. Thomson Was the Discoverer of the Electron   4

1-2   Blackbody Radiation Could Not Be Explained by Classical Physics   5

1-3   Planck Used a Quantum Hypothesis to Derive the Blackbody Radiation Law   7

1-4   Einstein Explained the Photoelectric Effect with a Quantum Hypothesis   12

1-5   The Vibrations of Atoms in Crystals Are Quantized   15

1-6   The Hydrogen Atomic Spectrum Consists of Several Series of Lines   16

1-7   The Rydberg Formula Accounts for All the Lines in the Hydrogen Atomic Spectrum   19

1-8   Angular Momentum Is a Fundamental Quantity of Rotating Systems   21

1-9   Bohr Assumed That the Angular Momentum of the Electron in a Hydrogen Atom Is Quantized   22

1-10   The Electronic Mass Should Be Replaced by a Reduced Mass in the Bohr Theory   27

1-11   de Broglie Postulated That Matter Has Wavelike Properties   30

1-12   de Broglie Waves Are Observed Experimentally   33

1-13   The de Broglie Formula Gives an Alternative Interpretation of Bohr's First Postulate   34

1-14   The Heisenberg Uncertainty Principle States That It Is Not Possible to Specify Both the Position and the Momentum of a Particle Simultaneously with Infinite Precision   36

2 The Wave Equation   47

2-1   The One-Dimensional Wave Equation Describes the Motion of a Vibrating String   48

2-2   The Wave Equation Can Be Solved by the Method of Separation of Variables   49

2-3   Some Differential Equations Have Oscillatory Solutions   52

2-4   The General Solution to the Wave Equation Is a Superposition of Normal Modes   54

2-5   A Vibrating Membrane Is Described by a Two-Dimensional Wave Equation   58

3 *The Schrödinger Equation and Some Simple Applications* 77

3-1 The Schrödinger Equation Is the Equation for the Wave Function of a Particle 78

3-2 The Schrödinger Equation Can Be Formulated as an Eigenvalue Problem 79

3-3 Classical-Mechanical Quantities Are Represented by Linear Operators in Quantum Mechanics 82

3-4 Wave Functions Have a Probabilistic Interpretation 83

3-5 The Energy of a Particle in a Box Is Quantized 85

3-6 Wave Functions Are Normalized 88

3-7 The Variance Is a Measure of the Spread of a Distribution About Its Mean 89

3-8 A Continuous Probability Distribution May Be Pictured as a Unit Mass Distributed Continuously Along an Axis 92

3-9 The Average Momentum of a Particle in a Box Is Zero 95

3-10 A Particle in a One-Dimensional Box Is Equally Likely to Be Moving in Either Direction 97

3-11 The Uncertainty Principle Says That $\sigma_p \sigma_x > \hbar/2$ 98

4 *The Postulates and General Principles of Quantum Mechanics* 113

4-1 The State of a System Is Completely Specified by Its Wave Function 113

4-2 Quantum-Mechanical Operators Represent Classical-Mechanical Variables 116

4-3 The Time Dependence of Wave Functions Is Governed by the Time-Dependent Schrödinger Equation 120

4-4 Quantum-Mechanical Operators Must Be Hermitian Operators 123

4-5 The Eigenfunctions of Hermitian Operators Are Orthogonal 126

4-6 A Fourier Series Is an Expansion in Terms of an Orthonormal Set 129

4-7 The Probability of Obtaining a Certain Value of an Observable in a Measurement Is Given by a Fourier Coefficient 133

4-8 Many Operators Do No Commute 135

4-9 The Commutator of Two Operators Plays a Central Role in the Uncertainty Principle 138

5 *The Harmonic Oscillator* 153

5-1 A Harmonic Oscillator Obeys Hooke's Law 153

5-2 The Energy of a Harmonic Oscillator Is Conserved 155

5-3 The Equation for a Harmonic-Oscillator Model of a Diatomic Molecule Contains the Reduced Mass of the Molecule 158

5-4 The Harmonic-Oscillator Approximation Results from the Expansion of an Internuclear Potential Around Its Minimum 160

5-5 The Energy Levels of a Quantum-Mechanical Harmonic Oscillator Are $E_n = \hbar\omega(n + \frac{1}{2})$ with $n = 0, 1, 2, \ldots$ 162

5-6   The Harmonic Oscillator Accounts for the Infrared Spectrum of a
      Diatomic Molecule   163
5-7   The Harmonic-Oscillator Wave Functions Involve Hermite
      Polynomials   165
5-8   Hermite Polynomials Are Either Even or Odd Functions   168
5-9   The Average Kinetic Energy Is Equal to the Average Potential
      Energy of a Harmonic Oscillator   170
5-10 The Amplitude of a Quantum-Mechanical Harmonic Oscillator
      Can Exceed Its Classical Value   173
5-11 The Asymptotic Solution of the Harmonic-Oscillator Schrödinger
      Equation Is exp $(-\alpha x^2/2)$ 175
5-12 Hermite's Differential Equation Can Be Solved by the Series
      Method   177
5-13 There Are Many Relations Among Hermite Polynomials   181

6   Three-Dimensional Systems   **195**

6-1   The Problem of a Particle in a Three-Dimensional Box Is a Simple
      Extension of the One-Dimensional Case   195
6-2   If a Hamiltonian Is Separable, Then Its Eigenfunctions Are
      Products of Simpler Eigenfunctions   199
6-3   The Laplacian Operator Can Be Expressed in a Variety of
      Coordinate Systems   203
6-4   The Energy Levels of a Rigid Rotator Are $E = \hbar^2 l(l + 1)/2I$ 206
6-5   The Rigid Rotator Is a Model for a Rotating Diatomic Molecule   210
6-6   The Wave Functions of a Rigid Rotator Are Called Spherical
      Harmonics   212
6-7   The Operators Corresponding to the Three Components of
      Angular Momentum Do Not Commute with Each Other   217
6-8   The Schrödinger Equation for the Hydrogen Atom Can Be Solved
      Exactly   221
6-9 s Orbitals Are Spherically Symmetric   225
6-10 There Are Three p Orbitals for Each Value of the Principal
      Quantum Number   230
6-11 The Energy Levels of a Hydrogen Atom Are Split by a Magnetic
      Field   237
6-12 The Schrödinger Equation for the Helium Atom Cannot Be Solved
      Exactly   242

7   Approximate Methods   **255**

7-1   Perturbation Theory Expresses the Solution to One Problem in
      Terms of Another Problem That Has Been Solved Previously   255
7-2   Perturbation Theory Consists of a Set of Successive Corrections to
      an Unperturbed Problem   257
7-3   The Variational Method Provides an Upper Bound to the Ground-
      State Energy of a System   262
7-4   A Trial Function That Depends Linearly on the Variational
      Parameters Leads to a Secular Determinant   266

7-5   The Secular Determinant Simplifies If the Trial Function Is a
      Linear Combination of Orthonormal Functions   269
7-6   Terms in a Trial Function That Correspond to Progressively
      Higher Energies Contribute Progressively Less to the
      Ground-State Energy   274
7-7   Trial Functions Can Be Linear Combinations of Functions That
      Also Contain Variational Parameters   275

8   *Atoms*   **287**

8-1   Atomic and Molecular Calculations Are Expressed in Atomic Units   287
8-2   Both Perturbation Theory and the Variational Method Can Yield
      Excellent Results for Helium   290
8-3   Hartree-Fock Equations Are Solved by the Self-Consistent Field
      Method   294
8-4   An Electron Has An Intrinsic Spin Angular Momentum   298
8-5   Wave Functions Must Be Antisymmetric in the Interchange of
      Any Two Electrons   301
8-6   Antisymmetric Wave Functions Can Be Represented by Slater
      Determinants   303
8-7   The Hartree-Fock Method Uses Antisymmetric Wave Functions   307
8-8   Hartree-Fock Calculations Give Good Agreement with
      Experimental Data   309
8-9   A Term Symbol Gives a Detailed Description of an Electron
      Configuration   313
8-10 Hund's Rules Are Used to Determine the Term Symbol of the
      Ground Electronic State   319
8-11 Atomic Term Symbols Are Used to Describe Atomic Spectra   320
8-12 Russell-Saunders Coupling Is Most Useful for Light Atoms   327

9   *Molecules*   **343**

9-1   The Born-Oppenheimer Approximation Simplifies Molecular
      Hamiltonian Operators   343
9-2   The Valence-Bond Treatment of a Hydrogen Molecule Was the
      First Successful Description of a Chemical Bond   345
9-3   The Valence-Bond Energy of H_2 Is Given in Terms of a Coulomb
      Integral, an Exchange Integral, and an Overlap Integral   347
9-4   The Exchange Integral Accounts for the Stability of the Chemical
      Bond in H_2 350
9-5   The Two States of H_2 Given by the Heitler-London Theory Are a
      Singlet State and a Triplet State   354
9-6   The Simple Molecular-Orbital Treatment of H_2^+ Yields a Bonding
      Orbital and an Antibonding Orbital   358
9-7   The Simple Valence-Bond Theory Ignores Ionic Terms and the
      Simple Molecular-Orbital Theory Overemphasizes Ionic Terms   363
9-8   Valence-Bond Theory plus Ionic Terms Are Formally Identical
      with Molecular-Orbital Theory with Configuration Interaction   366
9-9   Molecular Orbitals Can Be Ordered According to Their Energies   369

9-10 Molecular-Orbital Theory Predicts That Diatomic Helium Does Not Exist   373

9-11 Molecular Electron Configurations Are Obtained by Placing Electrons into Molecular Orbitals in Accord with the Pauli Exclusion Principle   374

9-12 Photoelectron Spectra Demonstrate the Existence of Molecular Orbitals   377

9-13 Molecular-Orbital Theory Correctly Predicts That Oxygen Molecules Are Paramagnetic and That Diatomic Neon Does Not Exist   379

9-14 An SCF-LCAO-MO Wave Function Is a Molecular Orbital That Is Formed from a Linear Combination of Atomic Orbitals Where the Coefficients Are Determined by a Self-Consistent Field Method   381

9-15 The Electronic States of Diatomic Molecules Are Designated by Molecular Term Symbols   387

9-16 It Is Possible to Calculate Molecular Properties to a High Degree of Accuracy   390

9-17 The Valence-Bond Theory Has a Nice Relation to Lewis Formulas   394

9-18 sp Hybrid Orbitals Are Equivalent and Are Directed 180° from Each Other   398

9-19 sp^2 Hybrid Orbitals Are Equivalent, Lie in a Plane, and Are Directed 120° from Each Other   401

9-20 sp^3 Hybrid Orbitals Are Directed Toward the Vertices of a Regular Tetrahedron   405

9-21 Conjugated Hydrocarbons and Aromatic Hydrocarbons Can Be Treated by a π-Electron Approximation   409

9-22 The Energies in Hückel Molecular-Orbital Theory Are Expressed in Terms of an Empirical Parameter β 411

9-23 Butadiene Is Stabilized by a Delocalization Energy   415

9-24 The Coefficients in Hückel Molecular Orbitals Can Be Used to Calculate Charge Distributions and Bond Orders   419

10 Molecular Spectroscopy   **437**

10-1 Different Regions of the Electromagnetic Spectrum Are Used to Investigate Different Molecular Processes   439

10-2 A Rigid Rotator Is the Simplest Model of Molecular Rotation   439

10-3 The Harmonic Oscillator Is the Simplest Model of Molecular Vibrations   442

10-4 Most Diatomic Molecules Are in the $n = 0$ Vibrational State at Room Temperature   443

10-5 Rotational Transitions Accompany Vibrational Transitions   445

10-6 The Intensities of the Lines in the P and R Branches in a Vibration-Rotation Spectrum Are Explained by a Rotational Boltzmann Distribution   448

10-7 The Lines in a Rotational Spectrum Are Not Equally Spaced   449

10-8 Overtones Are Observed in Vibrational Spectra   452

10-9 Vibration-Rotation Interaction Accounts for the Unequal Spacing of the Lines in the P Branch and R Branch of a Vibration-Rotation Spectrum   455

10-10   The Vibrations of Polyatomic Molecules Are Represented by Normal Coordinates   457

10-11   Electronic Spectra Contain Both Vibrational and Rotational Information   460

10-12   The Born-Oppenheimer Approximation Factors a Molecular Wave Function into an Electronic Part and a Nuclear Part   469

10-13   The Schrödinger Equation for Nuclear Motion Can Be Factored Approximately into a Rotational Part and a Vibrational Part   470

10-14   Selection Rules Are Derived from Time-Dependent Perturbation Theory   472

10-15   The Selection Rule in the Rigid Rotator Approximation Is $\Delta J = \pm 1$ 475

10-16   The Harmonic-Oscillator Selection Rule Is $\Delta n = \pm 1$ 476

10-17   The Selection Rule in Electronic Spectroscopy Is Less Restrictive Than for Pure Rotational or Vibrational Spectroscopy   478

10-18   The Franck-Condon Principle Predicts the Relative Intensities of Vibronic Transitions   479

A   *Derivation of the Classical Wave Equation*   *491*

B   *Complex Numbers*   *494*

Solutions to Problems   *500*

Index   *512*

Quantum Chemistry

Quantum Chemistry

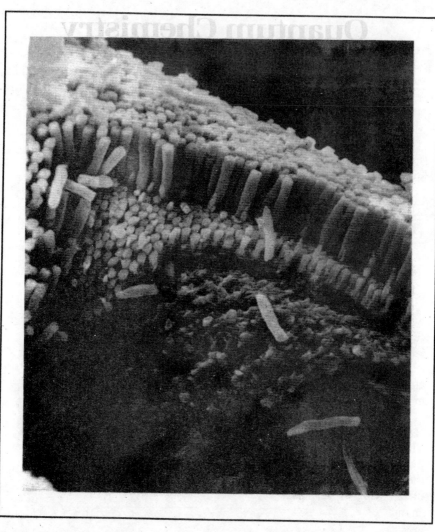

A scanning electron micrograph of retinal rod cells, which are photoreceptors in the retina. Rod cells contain light-sensitive compounds that absorb photons. When photons are absorbed, the rod cells transmit an electrical signal to the optic nerve. A rod cell can respond to the absorption of a single photon, and as few as six photons can produce a visual perception.

1

Historical Background

TOWARD the end of the nineteenth century, many physicists felt that all the principles of physics had been discovered and little remained but to clear up a few minor problems and to improve experimental methods in order to "investigate the next decimal place." This attitude was somewhat justified by the great advances in physics that had been made up to that time. Newton's mechanics had been brought to a high degree of both practical and theoretical sophistication by the work of Lagrange and Hamilton, resulting in the mathematical theory of elasticity and hydrodynamics. The equivalence of heat and mechanical work had been demonstrated clearly by the experiments of Count Rumford and Joule, and Carnot had formulated the second law of thermodynamics. This work was followed by Gibbs's complete development of thermodynamics, which is presented in essentially unchanged form in every physical chemistry course today. The kinetic theory of gases and statistical mechanics were formulated to a great degree of refinement by Maxwell, Boltzmann, and Gibbs, giving us, for example, the Maxwell-Boltzmann distribution of molecular speeds and its consequences in chemical kinetics. The field of optics also saw great advances as a result of the early work of Young and Fresnel on interference phenomena, resulting in a general acceptance of the wave theory over the corpuscular theory of light. A controversy over whether light is wavelike or corpuscular-like had been raging since the days of Newton, who had proposed the corpuscular theory, and Huygens, who had proposed the wave theory. The first half of the nineteenth century was an intensely active period for discovery of electric and magnetic effects, best exemplified by the brilliant career of Michael Faraday and the complete unification of many diverse experimental observations by Maxwell. Not only did Maxwell's prediction of the electromagnetic nature of light unify the fields of optics and electricity and magnetism, but its subsequent experimental demonstration by Hertz in 1887 appeared to be a final blow to the corpuscular theory of light.

The body of these accomplishments is now considered to be the development of what we now call "classical physics." Little was it realized in this justifiably heady era of success that physics was about to enter a period of profound discovery and growth whose effects have filtered not only into the fields of chemistry, biology, and engineering but into technology and politics as well. The early twentieth century saw the birth of the theory of relativity and of quantum mechanics. The first, due to Einstein alone, completely altered our ideas of space and time and is an extension of classical physics to the region of high velocities and astronomical distances. Quantum mechanics, on the other hand, was developed over several decades by many people and is an extension of classical physics to subatomic, atomic, and molecular sizes and distances. Relativity theory and quantum theory constitute what is now called *modern physics*. Although relativity theory has played a profound role in our everyday life through the concept of the equivalence of mass and energy and its manifestation through nuclear energy, it has not yet played an important role in the field of chemistry. Quantum mechanics, however, in dealing in the atomic and molecular region has played a very important role in chemistry, so much so that an introductory course in quantum mechanics and its applications to chemistry, often called *quantum chemistry*, is an integral part of any chemistry curriculum. Let us go back now to the complacent final years of the nineteenth century and see just what were the events that shook the world of physics so.

1-1   *J. J. Thomson Was the Discoverer of the Electron*

In the late 1800s, glassblowing technique had reached the point where it became possible to seal metal electrodes into glass tubes and then evacuate these tubes to very low pressures. Using such an apparatus, called a *Crooke's tube*, one could apply a voltage across the electrodes and study the effect of lowering the gas pressure. Before evacuation of the sealed tube, an increase of voltage results in a spark passing between the electrodes. As the pressure is lowered, the sparking is replaced by a luminous beam between the electrodes. In 1897, the British physicist J. J. Thomson demonstrated that the beam that leaves the cathode, the so-called *cathode rays*, consists of a beam of negatively charged discrete particles. By balancing this beam between an electric and magnetic field, Thomson was able to measure the charge-to-mass ratio of these particles, the currently accepted value being 1.7588×10^{11} coulombs/ kilogram ($C \cdot kg^{-1}$). Thomson also estimated the charge on the electron by utilizing the observation by C. T. R. Wilson (of the Wilson cloud chamber) that a charged particle acts as a nucleus around which water vapor condenses.

J. J. Thomson (Joseph John) (1856–1940) studied engineering at Owens College, where he developed an interest in the sciences. In 1876 he went to Cambridge University on a scholarship and remained there for the rest of his life. In 1884 he succeeded Lord Rayleigh as the Cavendish Professor of Physics and director of the Cavendish Laboratory. Thomson was an excellent teacher and administrator. Seven Nobel Prize winners trained under Thomson at the Cavendish. In 1919 he resigned his directorship in favor of Ernest Rutherford, in part because of his lack of sympathy for the new physics of Niels Bohr. Thomson was awarded the Nobel Prize in physics in 1906 and was knighted in 1908.

Thus by performing an early version of the famous oil drop experiment of Millikan, Thomson calculated the charge on the electron to be about 1×10^{-19} C and its mass to be about 6×10^{-31} kg. Although Thomson's charge-to-mass measurement was quite accurate, his determination of the charge itself was in error by about 50%. Consequently, his calculation of the electronic mass was in error by about 50%. Nevertheless, he did show that an electron was much lighter than the lightest atom and so showed that an electron was a *subatomic particle*. A little over 10 years later, the American physicist R. A. Millikan refined the determination of the electronic charge, obtaining 1.60×10^{-19} C versus the modern value of 1.6022×10^{-19} C. (A list of physical constants is given inside the front cover.)

Although these experiments did not lead immediately to the realization of the inadequacy of classical physics, the discovery of the electron, and the discovery of X rays by Röentgen in 1895 and radioactivity by Becquerel in 1896, showed the atom was far more complex than had previously been thought. It was a major challenge to classical physics to provide a structure for the atom, but this was a challenge to which classical physics never rose.

1-2   *Blackbody Radiation Could Not Be Explained by Classical Physics*

The series of experiments that revolutionized the concepts of physics had to do with the radiation given off by material bodies when they are heated. We all know, for instance, that when the burner of a stove is heated, it first turns a dull red and progressively becomes more and more red as the temperature increases. We also know that as a body is heated even further, the radiation becomes white and even becomes blue as the temperature becomes higher and higher. Thus we see that there is a continual shift of the color of a heated body from the red through the white and into the blue as it is heated to a higher and higher temperature. In terms of frequency, the radiation emitted goes from a lower frequency to a higher frequency as the temperature increases, because red is in a lower frequency region of the spectrum than is blue. The exact frequency spectrum emitted by the body depends on the particular body itself, but an *ideal body*, one that absorbs and emits all frequencies, is called a *blackbody* and serves as an idealization for any radiating material. The radiation emitted by a blackbody is called *blackbody radiation*.

A plot of the intensity of blackbody radiation versus frequency for several temperatures is given in Figure 1-1. Many theoretical physicists tried to derive expressions consistent with the experimental intensity versus frequency curves shown in Figure 1-1, but they were all unsuccessful. In fact, the expression

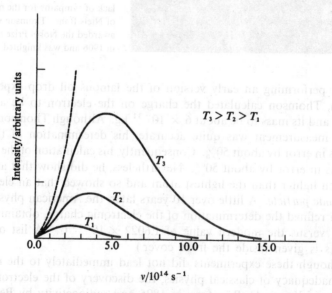

Figure 1-1. Spectral distribution of the intensity of blackbody radiation as a function of frequency for several temperatures. The intensity is given in arbitrary units. The dashed line is the prediction of classical physics. As the temperature increases, the maximum shifts to higher frequencies and the total radiated energy (the area under each curve) increases greatly. Note that the horizontal axis is labeled by $v/10^{14}$ s^{-1}. This notation means that the dimensionless numbers on that axis are frequencies divided by 10^{14} s^{-1}. Symbolically, we write that the frequency, for example, is

$$\frac{v}{10^{14}\ \text{s}^{-1}} = 2.00$$

or that $v = 2.00 \times 10^{14}$ s^{-1}. We shall use this notation to label columns in tables and axes in figures because of its unambiguous nature and algebraic convenience.

that is derived according to the laws of nineteenth century physics is

$$\rho(v, T)\,dv = \frac{8\pi kT}{c^3}\,v^2\,dv \qquad (1\text{-}1)$$

where $\rho(v, T)\,dv$ is the density of radiative energy between the frequency v and $v + dv$ and has units of joules/cubic meter ($J \cdot m^{-3}$). The quantity k is the *Boltzmann constant;* that is, the ideal gas constant R divided by Avogadro's number, T is the absolute temperature, and c is the speed of light. Equation 1-1 is due to Rayleigh and Jeans and is called the *Rayleigh-Jeans law.* The dashed line in Figure 1-1 shows the prediction of the Rayleigh-Jeans law. It can be seen that the Rayleigh-Jeans law reproduces the experimental data at low frequencies. At high frequencies, however, the Rayleigh-Jeans law diverges as v^2. Because the frequency increases going into the ultraviolet region, this divergence was termed the *ultraviolet catastrophe.* We have here a phenomenon that classical physics was unable to explain theoretically. This was the first such phenomenon to occur in physics and, therefore, is of great historical interest. One might think that Rayleigh and Jeans had simply made a mistake or had misapplied some of the ideas of physics; but many people had reproduced the equation of Rayleigh and Jeans, and by all means this equation is correct according to the physics of the time. This was a somewhat disconcerting result and many people wrestled with a theoretical explanation of blackbody radiation.

1-3 *Planck Used a Quantum Hypothesis to Derive the Blackbody Radiation Law*

The first person to offer a successful explanation of blackbody radiation was the German physicist Max Planck in 1900. Like Rayleigh and Jeans before him, Planck assumed that the radiation emitted by the body was due to the oscillations of the electrons in the constituent particles of the material body. These electrons were pictured to oscillate in an atom much like electrons oscillate in an antenna to give off radio waves. In the case of the atomic antennae, however, the oscillations occur at a much higher frequency and hence we find frequencies in the visible, infrared, and ultraviolet regions rather than in the radio-wave region of the spectrum. Implicit in the derivation of Rayleigh and Jeans is the assumption that the energies of the electronic oscillators responsible for the emission of the radiation could have any value whatsoever. This assumption, in fact, is one of the basic assumptions of classical physics, namely, that physically observable variables can take on a continuum of values. Planck had the great insight to realize that he had to break away from this mode of thinking in order to derive an expression that would reproduce experimental data like those shown in Figure 1-1. Planck made the revolutionary assumption that the energies of the oscillators had to be proportional to an integral multiple of the frequency or, in an equation, that $\varepsilon = nhv$, where n is an integer, h is a proportionality constant, and v is the frequency. Using statistical thermodynamic arguments, Planck was able to derive the equation

$$\rho(v, T)\, dv = \frac{8\pi h v^3}{c^3} \frac{dv}{e^{hv/kT} - 1} \tag{1-2}$$

All the symbols except h in Eq. 1-2 have the same meaning as in Eq. 1-1. The only adjustable constant in Eq. 1-2 is h. Planck was able to show that this equation gives excellent agreement with the experimental data for all frequencies and temperatures if h has the value 6.626×10^{-34} joule-seconds (J·s). This constant is one of the most famous and fundamental constants of physics and is now called *Planck's constant*. Equation 1-2 is known as *Planck's distribution law* for blackbody radiation. For small frequencies, Eq. 1-1 and 1-2 become identical (Problem 4), but the Planck distribution does not diverge at large frequencies and, in fact, looks like the curves in Figure 1-1.

EXAMPLE 1-1

Show that $\rho(v, T)\, dv$ in both Eqs. 1-1 and 1-2 has units of energy per unit volume, joules per cubic meter.

Solution: For the Rayleigh-Jeans law (Eq. 1-1),

$$\rho(v, T)\, dv = \frac{8\pi kT}{c^3}\, v^2\, dv$$

$$\sim \frac{(\mathrm{J \cdot K^{-1}})(\mathrm{K})}{(\mathrm{m \cdot s^{-1}})^3}\, (\mathrm{s^{-1}})^2(\mathrm{s^{-1}}) = \mathrm{J \cdot m^{-3}}$$

For the Planck distribution (Eq. 1-2),

$$\rho(v, T)\, dv = \frac{8\pi h v^3}{c^3} \frac{dv}{e^{hv/kT} - 1}$$

$$\sim \frac{(\mathrm{J \cdot s})(\mathrm{s^{-1}})^3}{(\mathrm{m \cdot s^{-1}})^3}\, (\mathrm{s^{-1}}) = \mathrm{J \cdot m^{-3}}$$

Thus we see that $\rho(v, T)\, dv$ is an energy density.

EXAMPLE 1-2

Equation 1-2 expresses Planck's radiation law in terms of frequency. Express Planck's radiation law in terms of wavelength λ.

Solution: Because v and λ are related by $\lambda v = c$, $dv = -c\, d\lambda/\lambda^2$. If we substitute $dv = -c\, d\lambda/\lambda^2$ into Eq. 1-2, we obtain

$$\rho'(\lambda, T)\, d\lambda = \frac{8\pi hc}{\lambda^5} \frac{d\lambda}{e^{hc/\lambda kT} - 1} \tag{1-3}$$

The quantity $\rho'(\lambda, T)\, d\lambda$ is the energy density between λ and $\lambda + d\lambda$. Equation 1-3 is plotted in Figure 1-2.

Max Planck (1858–1947) showed early talent in both music and science. He received his Ph.D. at the University of Munich in 1879 in theoretical physics. In 1888 he was appointed director of the Institute of Theoretical Physics, which was formed for him, at the University of Berlin. Planck was president of the Kaiser Wilhelm Society, later renamed the Max Planck Society, from 1930 until 1937 when he was forced to retire by the Nazi government. Planck was awarded the Nobel Prize in physics in 1918. Planck's personal life was clouded by tragedy. His two daughters died in childbirth, one son died in World War I, and another son was executed in World War II for his part in the attempt to assassinate Hitler in 1944.

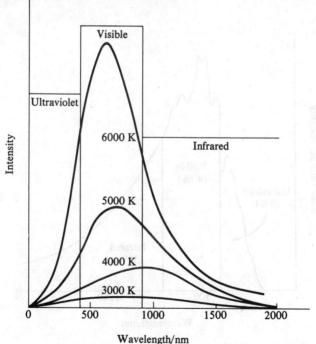

Figure 1-2. The distribution of the intensity of the radiation emitted by a blackbody versus wavelength for various temperatures. As the temperature increases, the total radiation emitted (the area under each curve) increases greatly.

We can use Eq. 1-3 to derive an empirical relationship that was known at the time (and still is) as the *Wien displacement law*. The Wien displacement law says that if λ_{max} is the wavelength at which $\rho'(\lambda, T)$ is a maximum, then

$$\lambda_{max}T = 2.90 \times 10^{-3}\ \text{m} \cdot \text{K} \tag{1-4}$$

By differentiating $\rho'(\lambda, T)$ with respect to λ, one can show that (Problem 5)

$$\lambda_{max}T = \frac{hc}{4.965k} \tag{1-5}$$

in accord with the Wein displacement law. Using the modern values of h, c, and k given inside the front cover, one obtains $2.90 \times 10^{-3}\ \text{m} \cdot \text{K}$ for the right-hand side of Eq. 1-5, in excellent agreement with the experimental value.

The theory of blackbody radiation is used regularly in astronomy to estimate the surface temperatures of stars. Figure 1-3 shows the electromagnetic spectrum of the sun measured at the earth's upper atmosphere. A comparison of Figure 1-3 with Figure 1-2 suggests that the solar spectrum can be approximated as a blackbody at around 6000 K. If we estimate λ_{max} from Figure 1-3 to be 500 nm, then the Wein displacement law (Eq. 1-4) gives

$$T = \frac{2.90 \times 10^{-3}\ \text{m} \cdot \text{K}}{500 \times 10^{-9}\ \text{m}} = 5800\ \text{K}$$

The star Sirius, which appears blue, has a surface temperature of about 11,000 K. (cf. Problem 7)

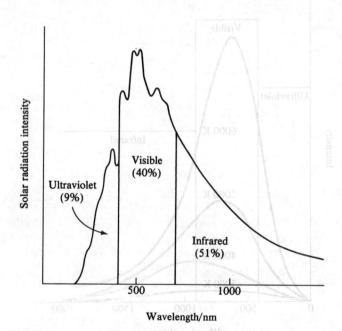

Figure 1-3. The electromagnetic spectrum of the sun as measured in the upper atmosphere of the earth. A comparison of this figure with Figure 1-2 shows that the sun's surface radiates as a blackbody at a temperature about 6000 K.

Equation 1-2 can be used to derive another law that was known at the time. It can be shown by thermodynamic arguments that the total energy radiated per unit area per unit time from a blackbody is given by

$$R = \frac{c}{4} E_V = \sigma T^4 \qquad (1\text{-}6)$$

where E_V is the total radiation energy density. Equation 1-6 is known as the *Stefan-Boltzmann law* and σ is known as the *Stefan-Boltzmann constant.* The experimental value of σ is $5.6697 \times 10^{-8} \, \text{J} \cdot \text{m}^{-2} \cdot \text{K}^{-4} \cdot \text{s}^{-1}$. Note that the units of σ are consistent with Eq. 1-6.

EXAMPLE 1-3

Planck's distribution of blackbody radiation gives the energy density between v and $v + dv$. Integrate the Planck distribution over all frequencies and compare the result to Eq. 1-6.

Solution: The integral of Eq. 1-2 over all frequencies is

$$E_V = \int_0^\infty \rho(v, T)\, dv = \frac{8\pi h}{c^3} \int_0^\infty \frac{v^3 \, dv}{e^{hv/kT} - 1} \qquad (1\text{-}7)$$

If we use the fact that

$$\int_0^\infty \frac{x^3 \, dx}{e^x - 1} = \frac{\pi^4}{15}$$

then we obtain

$$E_V = \frac{8\pi h}{c^3} \left(\frac{kT}{h} \right)^4 \int_0^\infty \frac{x^3 \, dx}{e^x - 1}$$

$$= \frac{8\pi^5 k^4 T^4}{15 h^3 c^3} \qquad (1\text{-}8)$$

By comparing this result to the Stefan-Boltzmann law (Eq. 1-6), we see that

$$\sigma = \frac{2\pi^5 k^4}{15 h^3 c^2} \qquad (1\text{-}9)$$

Using the values of k, h, and c given inside the front cover, the calculated value of σ is $5.670 \times 10^{-8} \, \text{J} \cdot \text{m}^{-2} \cdot \text{K}^{-4} \cdot \text{s}^{-1}$, in excellent agreement with the experimental value. Certainly Planck's derivation of the blackbody distribution law was an impressive feat. Nevertheless, Planck's derivation and, in particular, Planck's assumption that the energies of the oscillators have to be an integral multiple of hv was not accepted by most physicists at the time and was considered to be simply an ad hoc derivation. It was felt that in time a satisfactory classical derivation would be found. In a sense, Planck's derivation was little more than a curiosity. Just a few years later, however, in 1905, Einstein used the very same idea to explain the *photoelectric effect*.

1-4   *Einstein Explained the Photoelectric Effect with a Quantum Hypothesis*

In 1886 and 1887, while Heinrich Hertz was carrying out the experiments that confirmed Maxwell's theory of the electromagnetic nature of light, Hertz discovered that ultraviolet light causes electrons to be emitted from a metallic surface. The ejection of electrons from the surface of a metal by radiation is called the *photoelectric effect.* Two experimental observations of the photo-electric effect are in stark contrast with the classical wave theory of light. It turns out that the kinetic energy of the ejected electrons is independent of the intensity of the incident radiation. According to classical physics, electro-magnetic radiation is an electric field oscillating perpendicular to its direction of propagation, and the intensity of the radiation is proportional to the square of the electric field. As the intensity increases, so does the amplitude of the oscillating electric field. The electrons at the surface of the metal oscillate along with the field and so, as the intensity (amplitude) increases, the electrons oscillate more violently and eventually break away from the surface with a kinetic energy that depends on the amplitude (intensity) of the field. This nice classical picture is at complete variance with the experimental observations. Furthermore, this classical picture predicts that the photoelectric effect should occur for any frequency of the light as long as the intensity is sufficiently intense. The experimental fact, however, is that there is a *threshold frequency* v_0 charac-teristic of the metallic surface, below which no electrons are ejected. Above v_0, the kinetic energy of the ejected electrons is proportional to the frequency v, an embarrassing contradiction of classical theory.

Before going on to discuss Einstein's nonclassical explanation of the photoelectric effect, we shall first discuss how one can measure the kinetic energies of electrons. If the electrons are directed toward a negatively charged electrode, then they will slow down because they are working against the electrical potential. If the potential is continously increased, the electrons eventually will be stopped completely, and the potential needed to do this is called the *stopping potential.* At the stopping potential, the initial kinetic energy of the electrons is equal to the potential energy or, in an equation,

$$\tfrac{1}{2}mv^2 = -eV_s \qquad\qquad (1\text{-}10)$$

where V_s is the stopping potential. Realize that e is a negative number and that the right-hand side of Eq. 1-10 is positive. The experimental results of the photoelectric effect are customarily presented as a plot of stopping potential (essentially kinetic energy of the ejected electrons) versus frequency as shown in Figure 1-4.

In order to explain these results, Einstein appealed to Planck's hypothesis but extended it in an important way. Recall that Planck had applied his energy quantization concept, $\Delta\varepsilon = hv$, to the emission and absorption mech-anism of the atomic electronic oscillators. Planck believed that once the light energy was emitted, it behaved like a classical wave. Einstein proposed instead that the radiation itself existed as small packets of energy, $\varepsilon = hv$, which are

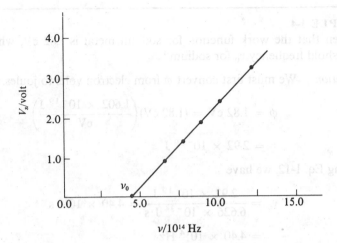

Figure 1-4. The stopping potential versus frequency for electrons ejected by ultraviolet radiation from the surface of sodium metal. The threshold frequency here is 4.40×10^{14} Hz (s^{-1}).

now known as *photons*. Using a simple conservation-of-energy argument, Einstein showed that the kinetic energy of the ejected electrons ($\frac{1}{2}mv^2$) is equal to the energy of the incident radiation ($h\nu$) minus the minimum energy required to remove an electron from the surface of the particular metal (ϕ). In an equation,

$$\tfrac{1}{2}mv^2 = h\nu - \phi \qquad (1\text{-}11)$$

where ϕ, called the *work function* of the metal, is similar to an ionization energy. The left-hand side of Eq. 1-11 cannot be negative, and so Eq. 1-11 predicts that $h\nu \geq \phi$. The minimum frequency that will eject an electron is just the frequency required to overcome the work function of the metal, and so we see that there is a threshold frequency ν_0, given by

$$h\nu_0 = \phi \qquad (1\text{-}12)$$

Using Eqs. 1-10 and 1-12, we can write Eq. 1-11 as

$$-eV_s = h\nu - h\nu_0 \qquad (1\text{-}13)$$

This equation shows that a plot of V_s versus ν should be linear, in complete agreement with the data in Figure 1-4, and that the slope of the line should be $h/-e$.

Before we can discuss Eq. 1-13 numerically, we must consider the units involved. It is customary to express the work function ϕ in energy units of electron volts (eV). One electron volt is the energy that a particle with the same charge as an electron (or a proton) picks up when it falls through a potential drop of one volt. If you recall that (1 coulomb) × (1 volt) = 1 joule, then

$$1 \text{ eV} = (1.602 \times 10^{-19} \text{ C})(1 \text{ V})$$
$$= 1.602 \times 10^{-19} \text{ J}$$

EXAMPLE 1-4

Given that the work function for sodium metal is 1.82 eV, what is the threshold frequency v_0 for sodium?

Solution: We must first convert ϕ from electron volts to joules.

$$\phi = 1.82 \text{ eV} = (1.82 \text{ eV})\left(\frac{1.602 \times 10^{-19} \text{ J}}{\text{eV}}\right)$$

$$= 2.92 \times 10^{-19} \text{ J}$$

Using Eq. 1-12, we have

$$v_0 = \frac{2.92 \times 10^{-19} \text{ J}}{6.626 \times 10^{-34} \text{ J}\cdot\text{s}} = 4.40 \times 10^{14} \text{ s}^{-1}$$

$$= 4.40 \times 10^{14} \text{ Hz}$$

In the last line here, we have introduced the unit hertz (Hz) for per second (s^{-1}).

EXAMPLE 1-5

When lithium is irradiated with light, one finds a stopping potential of 1.83 V for $\lambda = 3000$ Å and 0.80 V for $\lambda = 4000$ Å. From these data and the known charge on the electron, calculate (a) Planck's constant, (b) the threshold potential, and (c) the work function of lithium.

Solution:
(a) From Eq. 1-13, we write

$$-e(V_1 - V_2) = h(v_1 - v_2) = hc\left(\frac{1}{\lambda_1} - \frac{1}{\lambda_2}\right)$$

$$-e(1.03 \text{ V}) = (2.49 \times 10^{14} \text{ Hz})h$$

$$\frac{h}{-e} = \frac{1.03 \text{ V}}{2.49 \times 10^{14} \text{ Hz}} = 4.14 \times 10^{-15} \text{ J}\cdot\text{s}\cdot\text{C}^{-1}$$

$$h = (4.14 \times 10^{-15} \text{ J}\cdot\text{s}\cdot\text{C}^{-1})(1.602 \times 10^{-19} \text{ C})$$

$$= 6.63 \times 10^{-34} \text{ J}\cdot\text{s}$$

(b) Using the $\lambda = 3000$ Å data, we have

$$(1.602 \times 10^{-19} \text{ C})(1.83 \text{ V}) = \frac{hc}{3.00 \times 10^{-7} \text{ m}} - hv_0$$

from which we find that $v_0 = 5.57 \times 10^{14}$ Hz.
(c) Using Eq. 1-12,

$$\phi = hv_0 = 3.69 \times 10^{-19} \text{ J} = 2.30 \text{ eV}$$

Using the known value of e, Einstein obtained a value of h in close agreement with Planck's value deduced from the blackbody radiation formula. This surely was a fantastic result since the whole business of energy quantization was quite mysterious and not at all well accepted by the scientific community of the day. Nevertheless here, in two very different sets of experiments, blackbody radiation and the photoelectric effect, the very same quantization constant h, arose naturally. Perhaps there was something to all this after all.

1-5   *The Vibrations of Atoms in Crystals Are Quantized*

Just 2 years later, in 1907, Einstein added another notch of respectability to the energy-quantization concept. You may have learned the law of Dulong and Petit in general chemistry. This law states that the specific heat of an atomic solid times the atomic mass is approximately 25 J. A more fundamental, but equivalent, version of the law of Dulong and Petit says that the molar heat capacity at constant volume C_V is equal to $3R$, where R is the molar gas constant, $8.314\,\mathrm{J\cdot K^{-1}\cdot mol^{-1}}$. This is the standard classical result for the heat capacity of one mole of atoms vibrating about their equilibrium lattice positions. The experimental molar heat capacity, however, looks like that shown in Figure 1-5. The classical result is seen to occur at high temperatures, but C_V decreases and goes to zero as the temperature is lowered. These low-temperature heat capacities are quite contrary to classical theory. Einstein assumed that the oscillations of the atoms about their equilibrium lattice positions are quantized

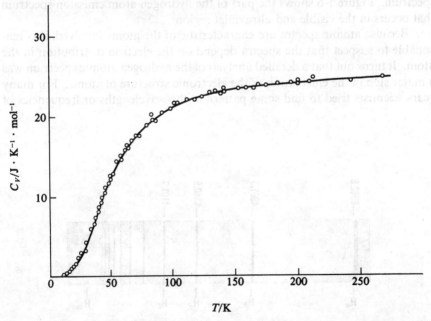

Figure 1-5. The molar heat capacity at constant volume of metallic silver as a function of temperature. Classical physics is unable to predict the shape of this curve and predicts that C_V is equal to $25\,\mathrm{J\cdot K^{-1}\cdot mol^{-1}}$ at all temperatures. The decrease of C_V with decreasing temperature requires a quantum-theoretical explanation.

according to the formula $\varepsilon = nh\nu$, or $\Delta\varepsilon = h\nu$. With this assumption, Einstein was able to achieve excellent agreement with the data shown in Figure 1-5 by using only the vibrational frequency ν as an adjustable parameter. Once again the formula $\Delta\varepsilon = h\nu$ showed itself. It is important to realize in this case, however, that it is the *mechanical* vibrations of the atoms that are subject to quantization. Previously it was the oscillations of electrons within atoms or radiation itself, both being obscure enough that one could tolerate unconventional ideas; but the vibrations of the atoms in a crystal are well modeled by a network of masses and springs; to have these vibrations be subject to the same quantization condition was indeed provocative.

1-6 *The Hydrogen Atomic Spectrum Consists of Several Series of Lines*

The next significant occurrence on our road to the development of quantum mechanics is Bohr's theory of the structure of the hydrogen atom, but before discussing this let us review a little bit of atomic spectroscopy. It was known for some time that every atom, when subjected to high temperatures or an electrical discharge, emits electromagnetic radiation of characteristic frequencies or that each atom has a characteristic *emission spectrum*. Because the emission spectra of atoms consist of only certain frequencies, the spectra are called *line spectra*. Hydrogen, the lightest and simplest atom, has the simplest spectrum. Figure 1-6 shows the part of the hydrogen atom emission spectrum that occurs in the visible and ultraviolet region.

Because atomic spectra are characteristic of the atoms involved, it is reasonable to suspect that the spectra depend on the electron distribution in the atom. It turns out that a detailed analysis of the hydrogen atomic spectrum was a major step in the elucidation of the electronic structure of atoms. For many years scientists tried to find some pattern in the wavelengths or frequencies of

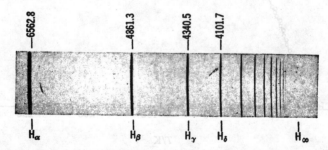

Emission spectrum of the hydrogen atom in the visible and near ultraviolet region. H_∞ gives the position of the series limit. [From *Molecular Spectra and Molecular Structure*, 2nd Revised Edition, by G. Herzberg (New York: Dover Publications, 1944.)]

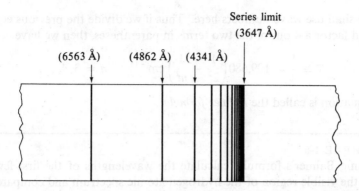

Figure 1-6. Emission spectrum of the hydrogen atom in the visible and the near ultraviolet region, showing that the emission spectrum of atomic hydrogen is a line spectrum. The wavelengths of the lines are given in units of angstroms ($\text{Å} = 10^{-10}$ m).

the lines in the atomic hydrogen spectrum and finally, in 1885, an amateur Swiss scientist Johann Balmer showed that a plot of the frequency of the lines versus $1/n^2$ is a linear plot. This is shown in Figure 1-7. In particular, Balmer showed that

$$v = 8.2202 \times 10^{14}\left(1 - \frac{4}{n^2}\right) \text{Hz}$$

where $n = 3, 4, 5, \ldots$. It is customary nowadays to write this equation in terms of the quantity $1/\lambda$ instead of v. Reciprocal wavelength is denoted by $\bar{v}$. The standard units used for $\bar{v}$ in spectroscopy are cm^{-1}, called *wave numbers*. Although wave number is not an SI unit, its use is so prevalent in spectroscopy

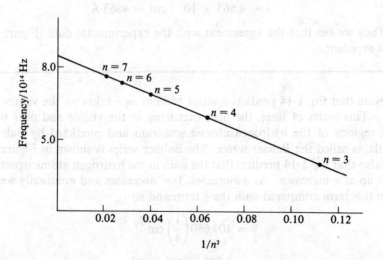

Figure 1-7. A plot of frequency versus $1/n^2$ ($n = 3, 4, 5, \ldots$) for the series of lines of the hydrogen atom spectrum that occurs in the visible and near ultraviolet regions. The actual spectrum is shown in Figure 1-6. The linear nature of this plot leads directly to Eq. 1-14.

that we shall use wave numbers here. Thus if we divide the previous equation by c and factor a 4 out of the two terms in parentheses, then we have

$$\bar{\nu} \equiv \frac{1}{\lambda} = 109{,}680 \left(\frac{1}{2^2} - \frac{1}{n^2} \right) \text{cm}^{-1} \qquad n = 3, 4, \ldots \qquad (1\text{-}14)$$

This equation is called the *Balmer formula*.

EXAMPLE 1-6

Using Balmer's formula, calculate the wavelengths of the first few lines of the visible region of the hydrogen atomic spectrum and compare them to the experimental values given in Figure 1-6.

Solution: The first line is obtained by setting $n = 3$, in which case we have

$$\bar{\nu} = 109{,}680 \left(\frac{1}{2^2} - \frac{1}{3^3} \right) \text{cm}^{-1}$$

$$= 1.523 \times 10^4 \text{ cm}^{-1}$$

and

$$\lambda = 6.564 \times 10^{-5} \text{ cm} = 6564 \text{ Å}$$

The next line is obtained by setting $n = 4$, and so

$$\bar{\nu} = 109{,}680 \left(\frac{1}{2^2} - \frac{1}{4^2} \right) \text{cm}^{-1}$$

$$= 2.056 \times 10^4 \text{ cm}^{-1}$$

and

$$\lambda = 4.863 \times 10^{-5} \text{ cm} = 4863 \text{ Å}$$

Thus we see that the agreement with the experimental data (Figure 1-6) is excellent.

Note that Eq. 1-14 predicts a series of lines as n takes on the values 3, 4, 5, ... This series of lines, the ones occurring in the visible and near ultraviolet regions of the hydrogen atomic spectrum and predicted by Balmer's formula, is called the *Balmer series*. The Balmer series is shown in Figure 1-6. Note also that Eq. 1-14 predicts that the lines in the hydrogen atomic spectrum bunch up as n increases. As n increases, $1/n^2$ decreases and eventually we can ignore this term compared with the $\frac{1}{4}$ term and so

$$\bar{\nu} = 109{,}680 \left(\frac{1}{4} \right) \text{cm}^{-1}$$

$$= 2.742 \times 10^4 \text{ cm}^{-1}$$

or

$$\lambda = 3647 \text{ Å}$$

in excellent agreement with the data in Figure 1-6. This is essentially the last line in the Balmer series and is called the *series limit*.

As we have just said, the Balmer series occurs in the visible and near ultraviolet regions. There are lines in the hydrogen atomic spectrum in other regions; in fact, there are series of lines similar to the Balmer series in the ultraviolet and in the infrared region (cf. Figure 1-8).

1-7   *The Rydberg Formula Accounts for All the Lines in the Hydrogen Atomic Spectrum*

The Swiss spectroscopist Johannes Rydberg accounted for all the lines in the hydrogen atomic spectrum by generalizing the Balmer formula to

$$\bar{v} = 109{,}680\left(\frac{1}{n_1^2} - \frac{1}{n_2^2}\right) \text{cm}^{-1} \qquad (n_2 > n_1) \tag{1-15}$$

where both n_1 and n_2 are integers but n_2 is always greater than n_1. Equation 1-15 is called the *Rydberg formula*. Note that the Balmer series is recovered if we let $n_1 = 2$. The other series are obtained by letting n_1 be $1, 3, 4, \ldots$. The names associated with these various series are given in Figure 1-8 and Table 1-1. The constant appearing in Eq. 1-15 is called the *Rydberg constant* and it is common to see Eq. 1-15 written as

$$\bar{v} = R_H\left(\frac{1}{n_1^2} - \frac{1}{n_2^2}\right) \tag{1-16}$$

where R_H is the Rydberg constant. The modern value of the Rydberg constant is 109,677.57 cm^{-1} and is one of the most accurately known physical constants.

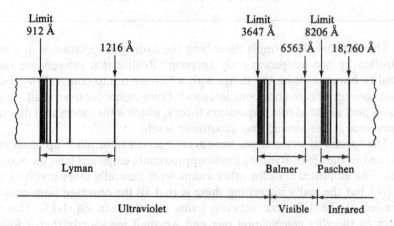

Figure 1-8. A schematic representation of the various series in the hydrogen atomic spectrum. The Lyman series lies in the ultraviolet region, the Balmer lies in the visible region, and the others lie in the infrared region (see Table 1-1).

TABLE 1-1

The First Five Series of Lines Making Up the Hydrogen Atomic Spectrum.
The terms, *near infrared* **and** *far infrared*, **denote the part of the infrared region of the**
spectrum that is near to and far from the visible region, respectively.

Name	n_1	n_2	Region of electromagnetic spectrum
Lyman	1	2, 3, 4, ...	Ultraviolet
Balmer	2	3, 4, 5, ...	Visible
Paschen	3	4, 5, 6, ...	Near infrared
Bracket	4	5, 6, 7, ...	Infrared
Pfund	5	6, 7, 8, ...	Far infrared

EXAMPLE 1-7

Calculate the wavelength of the second line in the Paschen series and show that this line lies in the near infrared, that is, in the infrared region near the visible.

Solution: In the Paschen series, $n_1 = 3$ and $n_2 = 4, 5, 6, ...$ according to Table 1-1. Thus the second line in the Paschen series is given by setting $n_1 = 3$ and $n_2 = 5$ in Eq. 1-15:

$$\bar{v} = 109{,}680 \left(\frac{1}{3^2} - \frac{1}{5^2} \right) \text{cm}^{-1}$$

$$= 7.799 \times 10^3 \text{ cm}^{-1}$$

and

$$\lambda = 1.282 \times 10^{-4} \text{ cm} = 12{,}820 \text{ Å}$$

The fact that the formula describing the hydrogen spectrum is in a sense controlled by two integers is truly amazing. Realize that integers are rather special to humans, being the things with which we use to count. Why should a hydrogen atom care about our integers? Once again, soon we shall see that integers play a special role in quantum theory, which is the theory that describes phenomena at the atomic and subatomic level.

The spectra of other atoms were also observed to be made up of series of lines, and in the 1890s Rydberg found approximate empirical laws for many of them. The empirical laws for other atoms were generally more involved than Eq. 1-15 but the really interesting thing is that all the observed lines could be expressed as the difference between terms like those in Eq. 1-15. This was known as the *Ritz combination rule* and we shall see shortly that it follows immediately from our modern view of atomic structure. At the time, however, it was just an empirical rule waiting for a theoretical explanation.

1-8 *Angular Momentum Is a Fundamental Property of Rotating Systems*

The theoretical explanation of the atomic spectrum of hydrogen was to come from a young Dane named Niels Bohr. In 1911, the New Zealand physicist Ernest Rutherford, based upon the α-particle scattering experiments of his colleagues Hans Geiger and Ernest Marsden, had proposed the nuclear model of the atom. Bohr was working in Rutherford's laboratory at the time and saw how to incorporate this new viewpoint of the atom and the quantization condition of Planck into a successful theory of the hydrogen atom. Before discussing this, however, we must have a digression on classical mechanics because Bohr's model of the hydrogen atom deals with some classical mechanical ideas of circular motion.

Linear momentum is given by mv and is usually denoted by the symbol p. Now consider a particle rotating in a plane about a fixed center as in Figure 1-9. Let v_{rot} be the frequency of rotation (cycles/second). The velocity of the particle, then, is $v = 2\pi r v_{rot} = r\omega_{rot}$, where $\omega_{rot} \equiv 2\pi v_{rot}$ has units of radians/second and is called the *angular velocity*. The kinetic energy of the revolving particle is

$$K = \tfrac{1}{2}mv^2 = \tfrac{1}{2}mr^2\omega^2 = \tfrac{1}{2}I\omega^2 \tag{1-17}$$

where the quantity $I = mr^2$ is the *moment of inertia*. By comparing the first and the last expressions for the kinetic energy in Eq. 1-17, we can make the correspondences $\omega \leftrightarrow v$ and $I \leftrightarrow m$, where ω and I are angular quantities and v and m are linear quantities. According to this correspondence, there should be a quantity $I\omega$ corresponding to the linear momentum mv, and in fact the quantity l, defined by

$$l = I\omega = (mr^2)\left(\frac{v}{r}\right) = mvr \tag{1-18}$$

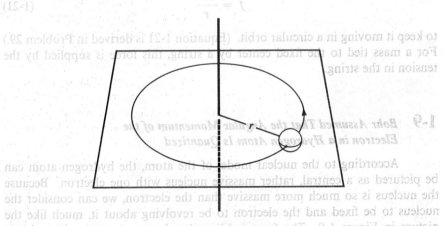

Figure 1-9. The rotation of a single particle about a fixed point.

TABLE 1-2

The Correspondences Between Linear Systems and Rotating Systems

	Type of motion	
Linear		*Angular*
Mass (m)		Moment of inertia (I)
Speed (v)		Angular speed (ω)
Momentum ($p = mv$)		Angular momentum ($l = I\omega$)
Kinetic energy $\left(K = \dfrac{mv^2}{2} = \dfrac{p^2}{2m} \right)$		Rotational kinetic energy $\left(K = \dfrac{I\omega^2}{2} = \dfrac{l^2}{2I} \right)$

is called the *angular momentum* and is a fundamental quantity associated with rotating systems, just as linear momentum is a fundamental quantity in linear systems.

Kinetic energy can be written in terms of momentum. For a linear system, we have

$$K = \frac{mv^2}{2} = \frac{(mv)^2}{2m} = \frac{p^2}{2m} \tag{1-19}$$

and, for a rotating system,

$$K = \frac{I\omega^2}{2} = \frac{(I\omega)^2}{2I} = \frac{l^2}{2I} \tag{1-20}$$

The correspondences between linear systems and rotating systems are given in Table 1-2.

Recall from general physics that a particle revolving around a fixed point as in Figure 1-9 experiences an outward acceleration, and requires an inward force

$$f = \frac{mv^2}{r} \tag{1-21}$$

to keep it moving in a circular orbit. (Equation 1-21 is derived in Problem 29.) For a mass tied to the fixed center by a string, this force is supplied by the tension in the string.

1-9 *Bohr Assumed That the Angular Momentum of the Electron in a Hydrogen Atom Is Quantized*

According to the nuclear model of the atom, the hydrogen atom can be pictured as a central, rather massive nucleus with one electron. Because the nucleus is so much more massive than the electron, we can consider the nucleus to be fixed and the electron to be revolving about it, much like the picture in Figure 1-9. The force holding the electron in a circular orbit is

supplied by the coulombic force of attraction between the proton and the
electron. If we equate Coulomb's force law $(e^2/4\pi\varepsilon_0 r^2)$ with Eq. 1-21, then
we have

$$\frac{e^2}{4\pi\varepsilon_0 r^2} = \frac{mv^2}{r} \tag{1-22}$$

where ε_0 is the permittivity of free space and is equal to 8.85419×10^{-12} coulomb^2/newton-meter^2 (C$^2\cdot$N$^{-1}\cdot$m^{-2}). The occurrence of the factor
$4\pi\varepsilon_0$ in Coulomb's law is a result of using SI units.

We are tacitly assuming here that the electron is revolving around the
fixed nucleus in a circular orbit of radius r. Classically, however, because the
electron is constantly being accelerated according to Eq. 1-21, it should emit
electromagnetic radiation and lose energy just as electrons accelerated in an
antenna. Consequently, classical physics predicts that an electron revolving
around a nucleus will lose energy and spiral into the nucleus, and so a stable
orbit for the electron is classically forbidden. It was Bohr's great contribution
to make two nonclassical assumptions. The first of these was to assume the
existence of stationary electron orbits, in defiance of classical physics. He then
specified these orbits by invoking a quantization condition, and in this case he
assumed that the angular momentum of the electron must be quantized according to

$$l = mvr = n\hbar \qquad n = 1, 2, \ldots \tag{1-23}$$

where $\hbar$ (called *h-bar*) is equal to $h/2\pi$ and occurs often in quantum mechanics.

Solving this equation for v and substituting into Eq. 1-22, we obtain

$$r = \frac{4\pi\varepsilon_0 \hbar^2 n^2}{me^2} \qquad n = 1, 2, \ldots \qquad (1\text{-}24)$$

Thus we see that the radii of the allowed orbits, or *Bohr orbits*, are *quantized*. According to this picture, the electron can move around the nucleus only in circular orbits with radii given by Eq. 1-24. The orbit with the smallest radius is the orbit with $n = 1$:

$$r = \frac{4\pi(8.85419 \times 10^{-12}\ \mathrm{C^2 \cdot N^{-1} \cdot m^{-2}})(1.055 \times 10^{-34}\ \mathrm{J \cdot s})^2}{(9.110 \times 10^{-31}\ \mathrm{kg})(1.602 \times 10^{-19}\ \mathrm{C})^2}$$

$$= 5.29 \times 10^{-11}\ \mathrm{m} = 52.9\ \mathrm{pm} = 0.529\ \text{Å} \qquad (1\text{-}25)$$

The radius of the first Bohr orbit is often denoted by a_0.

The total energy of the electron is equal to the sum of its kinetic energy and potential energy. The potential energy of an electron and a proton separated by a distance r is

$$U(r) = -\frac{e^2}{4\pi\varepsilon_0 r} \qquad (1\text{-}26)$$

The negative sign here indicates that the proton and electron attract each other; their energy is less than it is when they are infinitely separated $[U(\infty) = 0]$. The total energy of the electron in a hydrogen atom is

$$E = \frac{1}{2}mv^2 - \frac{e^2}{4\pi\varepsilon_0 r} \qquad (1\text{-}27)$$

Using Eq. 1-22 to eliminate the mv^2 in the kinetic energy term, Eq. 1-27 becomes

$$E = \frac{1}{2}\left(\frac{e^2}{4\pi\varepsilon_0 r}\right) - \frac{e^2}{4\pi\varepsilon_0 r}$$

$$= -\frac{e^2}{8\pi\varepsilon_0 r}$$

The only allowed values of r are those given by Eq. 1-24, and so if we substitute Eq. 1-24 into the previous equation, then we find that the only allowed energies are

$$E_n = -\frac{me^4}{8\varepsilon_0^2 h^2}\frac{1}{n^2} \qquad n = 1, 2, \ldots \qquad (1\text{-}28)$$

The negative sign in this equation indicates that the energy states are bound states; the energies given by Eq. 1-28 are less than when the proton and electron are infinitely separated. Note that $n = 1$ in Eq. 1-28 corresponds to the state of lowest energy. This is called the *ground-state energy*. At ordinary temperatures, hydrogen atoms, as well as most other atoms and molecules, will be found almost exclusively in their ground electronic state. The states of higher energy are called *excited states* and are generally unstable with respect to the ground state. An atom or a molecule in an excited state will usually relax back

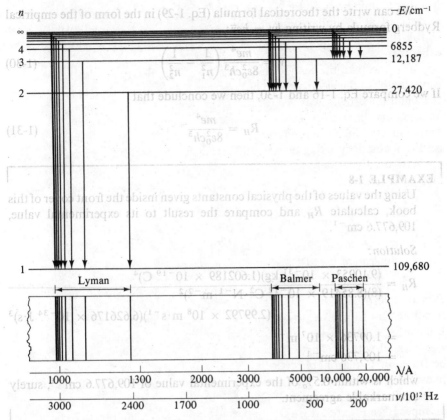

Figure 1-10. The energy-level diagram for the hydrogen atom, showing how transitions from higher states into some particular state lead to the observed spectral series for hydrogen.

to the ground state and give off the energy as electromagnetic radiation (see Figure 1-10).

We can display the energies given by Eq. 1-28 in an energy-level diagram like that in Figure 1-10. Note that the energy levels merge as $n \rightarrow \infty$. Bohr assumed that the observed spectrum of the hydrogen atom is due to transitions from one allowed energy state to another, and so

$$\Delta E = \frac{me^4}{8\varepsilon_0^2 h^2}\left(\frac{1}{n_1^2} - \frac{1}{n_2^2}\right) = h\nu \qquad (1\text{-}29)$$

Setting $\Delta E = h\nu$ is called the *Bohr frequency condition* and is the basic assumption that as the electron falls from one level to another, the energy evolved is given off as a photon of energy $E = h\nu$. Figure 1-10 groups the various transitions that occur according to the final state into which the electron falls. We can see, then, that the various observed spectral series arise in a natural way from the Bohr model. The Lyman series occurs when electrons that are excited to higher levels relax to the $n = 1$ state, that the Balmer series occurs when excited electrons fall back into the $n = 2$ state, and so on.

We can write the theoretical formula (Eq. 1-29) in the form of the empirical Rydberg formula by writing $hv = hc\bar{v}$:

$$\bar{v} = \frac{me^4}{8\varepsilon_0^2 ch^3}\left(\frac{1}{n_1^2} - \frac{1}{n_2^2}\right) \tag{1-30}$$

If we compare Eq. 1-16 and 1-30, then we conclude that

$$R_H = \frac{me^4}{8\varepsilon_0^2 ch^3} \tag{1-31}$$

EXAMPLE 1-8

Using the values of the physical constants given inside the front cover of this book, calculate R_H and compare the result to its experimental value, 109,677.6 cm^{-1}.

Solution:

$$R_H = \frac{(9.10953 \times 10^{-31}\ \text{kg})(1.602189 \times 10^{-19}\ \text{C})^4}{(8)(8.85419 \times 10^{-12}\ \text{C}^2 \cdot \text{N}^{-1} \cdot \text{m}^{-2})^2}$$

$$(2.99792 \times 10^8\ \text{m} \cdot \text{s}^{-1})(6.626176 \times 10^{-34}\ \text{J} \cdot \text{s})^3$$

$$= 1.09736 \times 10^7\ \text{m}^{-1}$$

$$= 109,736\ \text{cm}^{-1}$$

which is within 0.5% of the experimental value of 109,677.6 cm^{-1}, surely a remarkable agreement.

EXAMPLE 1-9

Calculate the ionization energy of the hydrogen atom.

Solution: The ionization energy *IE* is the energy required to take the electron from the ground state to the first unbound state, which is obtained by letting $n_2 = \infty$ in Eq. 1-30. Thus we write

$$IE = R_H\left(\frac{1}{1^2} - \frac{1}{\infty^2}\right)$$

or

$$IE = R_H = 109,680\ \text{cm}^{-1}$$

$$= 2.179 \times 10^{-18}\ \text{J}$$

$$= 13.6\ \text{eV}$$

Note that we have expressed the energy in units of wave numbers (cm^{-1}). This is not strictly a unit of energy, but because of the simple relation between wave number and energy, $\varepsilon = hc\bar{v}$, one often does express energy in this way (cf. Problem 1).

1-10   *The Electronic Mass Should Be Replaced by a Reduced Mass in the Bohr Theory*

In deriving Eqs. 1-24 and 1-28, we have assumed that because the proton is so much more massive than the electron, we can regard the proton as being a fixed center around which the electron revolves. It is not really necessary to make this assumption. Consider the general case of two masses rotating about each other as shown in Figure 1-11. The center of mass of this system is fixed and each of these masses will be rotating about that point. The center of mass lies along the line joining their centers and is defined through the condition

$$m_1 r_1 = m_2 r_2 \tag{1-32}$$

where r_1 and r_2 are defined in Figure 1-11. The distance between the particles is

$$r = r_1 + r_2 \tag{1-33}$$

Using Eqs. 1-32 and 1-33, simple algebra shows that

$$r_1 = \frac{m_2}{m_1 + m_2} r \quad \text{and} \quad r_2 = \frac{m_1}{m_1 + m_2} r \tag{1-34}$$

The total kinetic energy is

$$K = \tfrac{1}{2} m_1 v_1^2 + \tfrac{1}{2} m_2 v_2^2 \tag{1-35}$$

Now if ω is the angular velocity of the two masses about the fixed center of mass, then

$$v_1 = r_1 \omega \quad \text{and} \quad v_2 = r_2 \omega \tag{1-36}$$

If we substitute Eqs. 1-36 into Eq. 1-35, then we obtain

$$
\begin{aligned}
K &= \tfrac{1}{2} m_1 r_1^2 \omega^2 + \tfrac{1}{2} m_2 r_2^2 \omega^2 \\
&= \tfrac{1}{2} (m_1 r_1^2 + m_2 r_2^2) \omega^2 \\
&= \tfrac{1}{2} I \omega^2
\end{aligned}
\tag{1-37}
$$

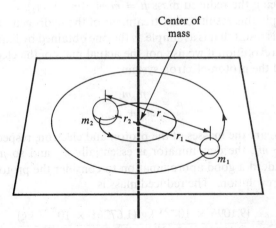

Figure 1-11. Two masses rotating about their center of mass. The center of mass lies along the line joining the two masses and is given by the condition $r_1 m_1 = r_2 m_2$, where r_1 and r_2 is the distance of m_1 and m_2, respectively, from the center of mass.

where

$$I = m_1 r_1^2 + m_2 r_2^2 \tag{1-38}$$

and is called the *moment of inertia* of the system. Using Eq. 1-34 in Eq. 1-38 for I, we find that I can be written as

$$I = \left(\frac{m_1 m_2}{m_1 + m_2}\right) r^2 \tag{1-39}$$

The factor $m_1 m_2/(m_1 + m_2)$ has units of mass and occurs often in problems involving two masses interacting along their line of center; this quantity is called the *reduced mass* μ;

$$\mu = \frac{m_1 m_2}{m_1 + m_2} \tag{1-40}$$

Using Eq. 1-40, we can write Eq. 1-39 in the form

$$I = \mu r^2 \tag{1-41}$$

In Eq. 1-35, both masses are rotating about the center of mass of the system as in Figure 1-11. Recall that in Figure 1-9 we had one mass revolving about a fixed point, and in that case I was given by

$$I = mr^2 \tag{1-42}$$

A comparison of Eqs. 1-41 and 1-42 allows us to give a useful interpretation of reduced mass, one that we shall use several times throughout the book. Equation 1-41 means that we can treat the two-body system with masses m_1 and m_2 revolving about each other as simply one body of mass μ revolving about the other one fixed in position, that is, with an infinite mass. This is an extremely important and useful result regarding two-body systems. We have reduced the two-body problem to a one-body problem, the effective mass of the one body being the reduced mass $\mu = m_1 m_2/(m_1 + m_2)$.

We can apply this result to our treatment of the hydrogen atom. We can obtain a rigorous result that is as simple as the one obtained by fixing the proton at the center of revolution if we use not the actual mass of the electron but the reduced mass of the proton-electron system:

$$\mu = \frac{m_p m_e}{m_p + m_e} \tag{1-43}$$

where m_p and m_e are the masses of the proton and electron, respectively. Note that since $m_p \gg m_e$, the denominator is essentially m_p and so $\mu \approx m_e$. This says that it is indeed a good approximation to consider the proton to be fixed at the center of revolution. The reduced mass is

$$\mu = \frac{(9.1096 \times 10^{-31} \text{ kg})(1.67261 \times 10^{-27} \text{ kg})}{(9.1096 \times 10^{-31} + 1.67261 \times 10^{-27}) \text{ kg}}$$

$$= 0.9995 m_e = 9.1046 \times 10^{-31} \text{ kg} \tag{1-44}$$

Equation 1-31 for the Rydberg constant now reads

$$R_H = \frac{\mu e^4}{8\varepsilon_0^2 ch^3} \tag{1-45}$$

and now one calculates R_H to be 109,681 cm^{-1} instead of 109,737 cm^{-1} (Problem 18). Recall that the accepted experimental value is 109,677.6 cm^{-1}.

In spite of its algebraic simplicity, the Bohr theory gives a very nice picture of the hydrogen atom. It can also be directly applied to any hydrogen-like ion such as He$^+$ and Li^{2+} consisting of one electron around a nucleus. It is a simple matter to extend the above results to these ions. Instead of starting with Eq. 1-22, we realize that the charge on the nucleus is Ze instead of just e and write

$$\frac{Ze^2}{4\pi\varepsilon_0 r^2} = \frac{\mu v^2}{r} \tag{1-46}$$

Everything else now follows directly and eventually we have (Problem 19)

$$\bar{v} = \frac{Z^2 e^4 \mu}{8\varepsilon_0^2 ch^3}\left(\frac{1}{n_1^2} - \frac{1}{n_2^2}\right) \tag{1-47}$$

or simply

$$\bar{v} = Z^2 \bar{v}_H \tag{1-48}$$

where $\bar{v}_H$ is $\Delta E/hc$ for the hydrogen atom (cf. Eq. 1-29).

EXAMPLE 1-10

Calculate the radius of the first Bohr orbit for He$^+$.

Solution: By eliminating v between Eq. 1-23 and 1-46, we find

$$r = \frac{\varepsilon_0 h^2 n^2}{Z\pi\mu e^2}$$

Note that this reduces to Eq. 1-24 when $Z = 1$. If we let $Z = 2$ and $n = 1$, we find

$$r = \frac{(8.854 \times 10^{-12}\ \text{C}^2\cdot\text{J}^{-1}\cdot\text{m}^{-1})(6.626 \times 10^{-34}\ \text{J}\cdot\text{s})^2}{2(3.1416)(9.110 \times 10^{-31}\ \text{kg})(1.602 \times 10^{-19}\ \text{C})^2}$$

$$= 2.65 \times 10^{-11}\ \text{m} = 26.5\ \text{pm} = 0.265\ \text{Å}$$

One spectacular success of the Bohr theory was the correct assignment of some solar spectral lines due to He$^+$. These lines were previously thought to be due to atomic hydrogen and to be anomalous because they did not fit the Rydberg formula (cf. Problem 20). In spite of a number of successes and the beautiful simplicity of the Bohr theory, it could not be extended successfully even to a two-electron system such as helium. Furthermore, even for simple systems such as hydrogen, it was never able to explain the spectra that arise when a magnetic field is applied to the system, nor was it able to predict the intensities of the spectral lines. In spite of ingenious efforts by Bohr, he was never able to extend the theory to explain such phenomena.

1-11 *de Broglie Postulated That Matter Has Wavelike Properties*

Although we have an intriguing partial insight into the electronic structure of atoms, there is something missing. To explore this further, let us go back to a discussion of the nature of light.

Scientists have always had trouble describing the nature of light. In many experiments light shows a definite wavelike character, but there are many other experiments in which light seems to behave as a stream of photons. The dispersion of white light into its spectrum by a prism is an example of the first type of experiment and the photoelectric effect is an example of the second. Because light appears to be wavelike in some instances and particlelike

Louis de Broglie (b. 1892) studied history as an undergraduate in the early 1910's. His interest turned to science as a result of his assignment to radio communications in World War I. Undecided on a career, he worked with his brother, Maurice, who had built his own private laboratory for X-ray research. de Broglie received his Dr. Sc. from the University of Paris in 1924. He was professor of theoretical physics at the University of Paris from 1932 until his retirement in 1962. de Broglie was awarded the Nobel Prize in physics in 1929.

in others, this is referred to as the *wave-particle duality of light*. In 1924, a young French scientist named Louis de Broglie reasoned that if light can display this wave-particle duality, then matter, which certainly appears to be particlelike, might also display wavelike properties under certain conditions. This is a rather strange proposal at first sight, but it does suggest a nice symmetry in nature. Certainly if light can be particlelike at times, why should matter not be wavelike at times?

de Broglie was able to put his idea into a quantitative scheme. Einstein had shown from relativity theory that the momentum of a photon is (Problem 28)

$$p = \frac{h}{\lambda}$$

de Broglie argued that both light *and* matter obey the equation

$$\lambda = \frac{h}{p} \tag{1-49}$$

This equation predicts that a particle of mass m moving with a velocity v will have a *de Broglie wavelength* given by $\lambda = h/mv$.

EXAMPLE 1-11

Calculate the de Broglie wavelength for a baseball (5 oz) traveling at 90 mph.

Solution: Five ounces corresponds to

$$m = (5 \text{ oz})\left(\frac{1 \text{ lb}}{16 \text{ oz}}\right)\left(\frac{0.454 \text{ kg}}{1 \text{ lb}}\right) = 0.14 \text{ kg}$$

and 90 mph corresponds to

$$v = \left(90 \frac{\text{mi}}{\text{hr}}\right)\left(\frac{1610 \text{ m}}{\text{mi}}\right)\left(\frac{\text{hr}}{3600 \text{ s}}\right) = 40 \text{ m·s}^{-1}$$

The momentum of the baseball is

$$p = mv = (0.14 \text{ kg})(40 \text{ m·s}^{-1})$$
$$= 5.6 \text{ kg·m·s}^{-1}$$

The de Broglie wavelength is

$$\lambda = \frac{h}{p} = \frac{6.626 \times 10^{-34} \text{ J·s}}{5.6 \text{ kg·m·s}^{-1}} = 1.2 \times 10^{-34} \text{ m}$$

This is a ridiculously small wavelength.

We see from Example 1-11 that the de Broglie wavelength of the baseball is so small as to be completely undetectable and of no practical consequence.

The reason for this is the large value of *m*. What if we calculate the de Broglie wavelength of an electron instead of a baseball?

EXAMPLE 1-12

Calculate the de Broglie wavelength of an electron traveling at 1% of the speed of light.

Solution: The mass of an electron is 9.11×10^{-31} kg. One percent of the speed of light is

$$v = (0.01)(3.00 \times 10^8 \text{ m} \cdot \text{s}^{-1}) = 3.00 \times 10^6 \text{ m} \cdot \text{s}^{-1}$$

The momentum of the electron is given by

$$p = mv = (9.11 \times 10^{-31} \text{ kg})(3.00 \times 10^6 \text{ m} \cdot \text{s}^{-1})$$
$$= 2.73 \times 10^{-24} \text{ kg} \cdot \text{m} \cdot \text{s}^{-1}$$

The de Broglie wavelength of this electron is

$$\lambda = \frac{h}{p} = \frac{6.626 \times 10^{-34} \text{ J} \cdot \text{s}}{2.73 \times 10^{-24} \text{ kg} \cdot \text{m} \cdot \text{s}^{-1}} = 2.43 \times 10^{-10} \text{ m}$$

$$= 243 \text{ pm} = 2.43 \text{ Å}$$

This wavelength is of atomic dimensions.

EXAMPLE 1-13

Through what potential must an electron initially at rest fall in order that $\lambda = 10^{-10}$ m (1 Å)?

Solution: The momentum associated with this wavelength is

$$p = \frac{h}{\lambda} = \frac{6.626 \times 10^{-34} \text{ J} \cdot \text{s}}{10^{-10} \text{ m}} = 6.626 \times 10^{-24} \text{ kg} \cdot \text{m} \cdot \text{s}^{-1}$$

The energy of an electron with this momentum is

$$E = \frac{1}{2} mv^2 = \frac{p^2}{2m} = \frac{(6.626 \times 10^{-24} \text{ kg} \cdot \text{m} \cdot \text{s}^{-1})^2}{2 \times 9.11 \times 10^{-31} \text{ kg}} = 2.41 \times 10^{-17} \text{ J}$$

Recalling that 1 eV = 1.602×10^{-19} J, the energy is 150 eV, and hence the voltage through which the electron must fall is 150 V.

The wavelengths of the electrons in Examples 1-12 and 1-13 correspond to the wavelength of X rays. Thus, although Eq. 1-49 is of trivial consequence for a macroscopic object like a baseball, it predicts that electrons can be observed to act like X rays. The wavelengths of some other moving objects are given in Table 1-3.

TABLE 1-3
The de Broglie Wavelengths of Various Moving Objects

Particle	Mass/kg	Velocity/m·s^{-1}	Wavelength/pm
Electron accelerated through 100 V	9.11×10^{-31}	5.9×10^{6}	120
Electron accelerated through 10,000 V	9.29×10^{-31}	5.9×10^{7}	12
α particle ejected from radium	6.68×10^{-27}	1.5×10^{7}	6.6×10^{-3}
22-caliber rifle bullet	1.9×10^{-3}	3.2×10^{2}	1.1×10^{-21}
Golf ball	0.045	30	4.9×10^{-22}
Baseball	0.140	25	1.9×10^{-22}

1-12 *de Broglie Waves Are Observed Experimentally*

When a beam of X rays is directed at a crystalline substance, the beam is scattered in a definite manner characteristic of the atomic structure of the crystalline substance. This phenomenon is called *X-ray diffraction* and is due to the fact that the interatomic spacings in the crystal are about the same as the wavelength of the X rays. The X-ray diffraction pattern from an aluminum foil is shown in Figure 1-12(a). Right beside it is an electron diffraction pattern

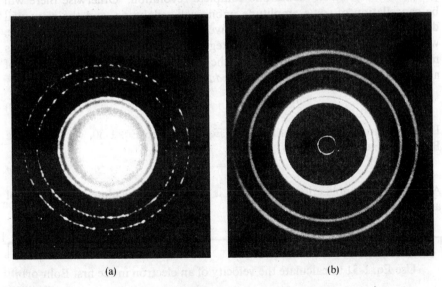

(a)   (b)

Figure 1-12. (a) The X-ray diffraction pattern of aluminum foil. (b) The electron diffraction pattern of aluminum foil. The similarity of these two patterns shows that electrons can behave like X rays and display wavelike properties. (From PSCC Physics film, "Matter Waves," Education Development Center, Inc., Newton, Mass.)

from an aluminum foil [Figure 1-12(b)] that results when a beam of electrons is directed at a similar aluminum foil. The similarity of the two patterns shows that both X rays and electrons do indeed behave similarly in these experiments.

The wavelike property of electrons is used in electron microscopes. The wavelengths of the electrons can be controlled through an applied voltage, and the small de Broglie wavelengths attainable offer a more precise probe than an ordinary light microscope. In addition, in contrast to electromagnetic radiation of similar wavelengths (X rays and UV), the electron beam can be readily focused by using electric and magnetic fields. Electron microscopes are now used routinely in chemistry and biology to investigate atomic and molecular structures.

1-13   *The de Broglie Formula Gives an Alternative Interpretation of Bohr's First Postulate*

Not only has de Broglie's hypothesis the practical application of electron microscopy, but it was also a key step in our understanding of atomic structure. It can be used to give a simple, physical argument for the quantized Bohr orbits. As the electron revolves around the proton, it has a wavelength λ associated with it. This situation is shown in Figure 1-13. For the orbit to be stable, it is reasonable to assume that the wave must "match," or be in phase, as the electron makes one complete revolution. Otherwise there will be cancellation of some amplitude upon each revolution, and the wave will disappear (see Figure 1-13). For the wave pattern around an orbit to be stable, we are led to the condition that an integral number of complete wavelengths must fit around the circumference of the orbit. Because the circumference of a circle is $2\pi r$, we have the *quantum condition*

$$2\pi r = n\lambda \qquad n = 1, 2, 3, \ldots \tag{1-50}$$

If we substitute de Broglie's relation (Eq. 1-49) into Eq. 1-50, we obtain the Bohr quantization condition

$$mvr = n\hbar \tag{1-51}$$

An interesting application of Eq. 1-51 is to use it to calculate the velocity of an electron in a Bohr orbit.

EXAMPLE 1-14

Use Eq. 1-51 to calculate the velocity of an electron in the first Bohr orbit.

Solution: If we solve Eq. 1-51 for v, we find

$$v = \frac{n\hbar}{mr}$$

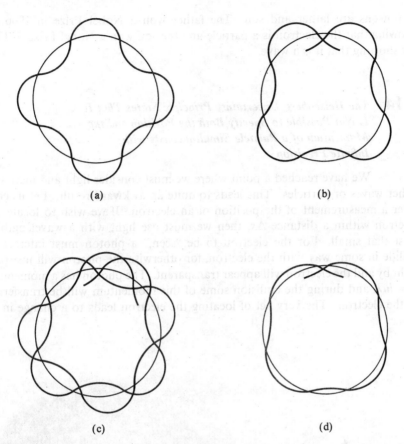

(a) (b)

(c) (d)

Figure 1-13. An illustration of matching and mismatching de Broglie waves traveling in Bohr orbits. If the wavelengths of the de Broglie waves are such that an integral number of them fit around the circle, then they match after a complete revolution (a). If a wave does not match after a complete revolution, cancellation will result and the wave will progressively disappear (b–d).

For the first Bohr orbit, $n = 1$, and the radius is given by Eq. 1-24. If we substitute $n = 1$ and Eq. 1-24 into the previous equation for v, we find

$$v = \frac{1.055 \times 10^{-34} \text{ J} \cdot \text{s}}{(9.11 \times 10^{-31} \text{ kg})(5.29 \times 10^{-11} \text{ m})}$$

$$= 2.19 \times 10^{6} \text{ m} \cdot \text{s}^{-1}$$

Note that this is almost 1% of the speed of light, a very large speed.

An interesting aside in the concept of the wave-particle duality of matter is that it was J. J. Thomson who first showed in 1895 that the electron was a subatomic particle and G. P. Thomson who was one of the first to show experimentally in 1926 that the electron could act as a wave. These two

Thomsons are father and son. The father won a Nobel Prize in 1906 for showing that the electron is a particle and the son won a Nobel Prize in 1937 for showing that it is a wave.

1-14　*The Heisenberg Uncertainty Principle States That It Is Not Possible to Specify Both the Position and the Momentum of a Particle Simultaneously with Infinite Precision*

We have reached a point where we must consider light and matter as either waves or particles. This leads to quite an awkward result. Let us consider a measurement of the position of an electron. If we wish to locate the electron within a distance Δx, then we must use light with a wavelength at least that small. For the electron to be "seen," a photon must interact or collide in some way with the electron, for otherwise the photon will just pass right by and the electron will appear transparent. The photon has a momentum $p = h/\lambda$, and during the collision some of this momentum will be transferred to the electron. The very act of locating the electron leads to a change in its

Werner Heisenberg (1901–1976) received his Ph.D. in physics from the University of Munich in 1923. He then spent a year working with Max Born at Göttingen and three years with Niels Bohr in Copenhagen. He was professor of physics at the University of Leipzig from 1927 to 1941. During World War II, Heisenberg was in charge of German research on the atomic bomb. After the war he was named director of the Max Planck Institute for Physics in Göttingen. Heisenberg was an ardent anti-communist and was involved in street brawls in his youth. He was also an accomplished mountain climber. Heisenberg was awarded the Nobel Prize in physics in 1932.

momentum. If we wish to locate the electron more accurately, we must use light with a smaller wavelength. Consequently, the photons in the light beam will have greater momentum because of the relation $p = h/\lambda$. Because some of the photon's momentum must be transferred to the electron in the process of locating it, the momentum change of the electron becomes greater.

A careful analysis of this process was carried out by the German physicist Werner Heisenberg in the mid-1920s and he showed that it is not possible to determine exactly how much momentum is transferred to the electron. This means that if we wish to locate an electron to within a region Δx, then this causes an uncertainty in the momentum of the electron. Heisenberg was able to show that if Δp is the uncertainty in the momentum of the electron, then

$$\Delta x\, \Delta p \approx h \tag{1-52}$$

Equation 1-52 is called *Heisenberg's Uncertainty Principle* and is a fundamental principle of nature. The Uncertainty Principle states that if we wish to locate any particle to within a distance Δx, then we automatically introduce an uncertainty in the momentum of the particle that is given by Eq. 1-52. It is important to realize that this uncertainty is not due to poor measurement or poor experimental technique but is a fundamental property of the act of measurement itself.

The following two examples demonstrate the numerical consequences of the Uncertainty Principle.

EXAMPLE 1-15

Calculate the uncertainty in the position of a baseball thrown at 90 mph if we measure its velocity to a millionth of 1%.

Solution: According to Example 1-11, a baseball traveling at 90 mph has a momentum of 5.6 kg·m·s^{-1}. A millionth of 1% of this is $5.6 \times 10^{-8} \text{ kg·m·s}^{-1}$, and so

$$\Delta p = 5.6 \times 10^{-8} \text{ kg·m·s}^{-1}$$

The uncertainty in the position of the baseball is

$$\Delta x = \frac{h}{\Delta p} = \frac{6.625 \times 10^{-34} \text{ J·s}}{5.6 \times 10^{-8} \text{ kg·m·s}^{-1}}$$

$$= 1.2 \times 10^{-26} \text{ m}$$

This is a completely inconsequential distance.

EXAMPLE 1-16

What is the uncertainty in momentum if we wish to locate an electron within an atom, say, so that Δx is approximately 50 pm?

Solution:

$$\Delta p = \frac{h}{\Delta x} = \frac{6.626 \times 10^{-34} \text{ J} \cdot \text{s}}{50 \times 10^{-12} \text{ m}}$$

$$= 1.3 \times 10^{-23} \text{ kg} \cdot \text{m} \cdot \text{s}^{-1}$$

Because $p = mv$ and the mass of an electron is 9.11×10^{-31} kg, this value of Δp corresponds to

$$\Delta v = \frac{\Delta p}{m} = \frac{1.3 \times 10^{-23} \text{ kg} \cdot \text{m} \cdot \text{s}^{-1}}{9.11 \times 10^{-31} \text{ kg}}$$

$$= 1.4 \times 10^{7} \text{ m} \cdot \text{s}^{-1}$$

This is a very large uncertainty in the speed.

These two examples show that although the Heisenberg Uncertainty Principle is of no consequence for everyday, macroscopic bodies, it has very important consequences in dealing with atomic and subatomic particles. This is similar to the conclusion we drew for the application of the de Broglie relation between wavelength and momentum.

We have stated above that the Uncertainty Principle leads us to an awkward result. Recall that Bohr assumed that the electron in the hydrogen atom revolves around the proton in certain circular orbits of radii r. This implies that $\Delta r = 0$. The Uncertainty Principle states, however, that it is not possible to know that $\Delta r = 0$ without a total uncertainty in the (angular) momentum. Yet Bohr's primary quantum hypothesis was that the angular momentum is an integral multiple of $\hbar$. Fortunately, at about this time a new, more general quantum theory was presented that is consistent with the Uncertainty Principle. In addition, we shall see that this new theory is applicable to all atoms and molecules and forms the basis for our understanding of atomic and molecular structure. This theory is due to Schrödinger and forms the central topic of this book.

Summary

Toward the end of the nineteenth century, several experiments were done that were unable to be explained theoretically. Two of the most famous of these experiments are blackbody radiation and the photoelectric effect. The explanation of these experiments required a drastic break from the theoretical ideas of the time. Max Planck was able to derive theoretical equations for blackbody radiation only by introducing an ad hoc assumption that energy could be emitted from a heated body only in discrete little packets, or quanta. Five years later Einstein explained the photoelectric effect by assuming that electromagnetic radiation itself is quantized and that it consists of a beam of photons. Both Planck and Einstein used the same equation, $E = h\nu$, to derive their results. These theories were the first theories ever to introduce some sort of quantum condition and are the forerunners of modern quantum theory.

In 1914, Niels Bohr used another ad hoc quantum condition to formulate a model of the hydrogen atom that was in beautiful accord with the line spectrum of atomic hydrogen. The Bohr theory yields quantized orbits and quantized energy levels for the electron in a hydrogen atom. In spite of the great success of the Bohr theory, it could not be extended even to helium. The reason for the deficiency of the Bohr theory became clearer in the mid-1920s. The Heisenberg Uncertainty Principle, which is a fundamental, general principle of nature, was proposed in 1926. The Bohr model of the hydrogen atom was shown to be inconsistent with the Uncertainty Principle; it is not possible to specify both the orbit and the angular momentum of an electron in a hydrogen atom simultaneously, as Bohr had done.

The stage for the next advance was set by de Broglie, who argued that particles have wavelike properties and that the wavelike properties of atomic and subatomic particles play a key role in a description of the behavior of these particles. An equation that governs the behavior of atomic and subatomic particles was proposed by Schrödinger in 1925, and we shall discuss the Schrödinger equation in Chapter 3.

Terms That You Should Know

cathode rays	series limit
blackbody radiation	Rydberg formula
Boltzmann constant	Rydberg constant
Rayleigh-Jeans law	Ritz combination rule
ultraviolet catastrophe	moment of inertia
Planck's distribution law	angular momentum
Wien displacement law	Coulomb's law
Stefan-Boltzmann law	Bohr orbit
Stefan-Boltzmann constant	ground state
photoelectric effect	excited state
threshold frequency	Bohr frequency condition
stopping potential	reduced mass
photons	wave-particle duality
work function	de Broglie wavelength
line spectra	angstrom unit
wave number	quantum condition
Balmer formula	Heisenberg Uncertainty Principle
Balmer series	

Problems

1. Radiation in the ultraviolet region of the electromagnetic spectrum is usually described in terms of wavelength, λ, and is given in angstrom units $(1 \text{ Å} = 10^{-10} \text{ m})$ or nanometers (10^{-9} m). Calculate v, $\bar{v}$, and ε for ultraviolet radiation with $\lambda = 2000$ Å and compare your results to Figure 1-14.

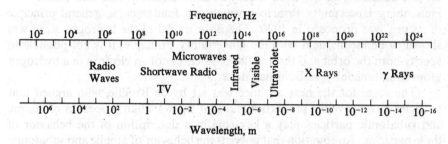

Figure 1-14. The regions of electromagnetic radiation.

2. Radiation in the infrared region is often expressed in terms of wave numbers, $\bar{v} = 1/\lambda$. A typical value of $\bar{v}$ in this region is 10^3 cm^{-1}. Calculate v, λ, and ε for radiation with $\bar{v} = 10^3 \text{ cm}^{-1}$ and compare your results to those in Figure 1-14.

3. Past the infrared region, in the direction of lower energies, is the microwave region. In this region radiation is usually characterized by its frequency v, expressed in units of megahertz (MHz), where the unit, hertz (Hz), is a cycle per second. A typical microwave frequency is 2.0×10^4 MHz. Calculate $\bar{v}$, λ, and ε for this radiation and compare your results to Figure 1-14.

4. Planck's principal assumption was that the energies of the electronic oscillators can have only the values $\varepsilon = nhv$ and that $\Delta\varepsilon = hv$. As $v \to 0$, then $\Delta\varepsilon \to 0$ and ε is essentially continuous. Thus we should expect the nonclassical Planck distribution to go over to the classical Rayleigh-Jeans distribution at low frequencies, where $\Delta\varepsilon \to 0$. Show that Eq. 1-2 reduces to Eq. 1-1 as $v \to 0$ (recall that $e^x = 1 + x + (x^2/2!) + \cdots$).

5. Before Planck's theoretical work on blackbody radiation, Wien showed empirically that

$$\lambda_{max}T = 2.90 \times 10^{-3} \text{ m·K}$$

where λ_{max} is the wavelength at which the blackbody spectrum has its maximum value at a particular temperature T. This expression is called the *Wien displacement law;* derive it from Planck's theoretical expression for the blackbody distribution by differentiating Eq. 1-3 with respect to λ. *Hint:* Set $hc/\lambda_{max}kT = x$ and derive the intermediate result $e^{-x} + (x/5) = 1$. This cannot be solved analytically but must be solved numerically. Solve this by iteration on a hand calculator and show that $x = 4.965$ is the solution.

6. At what wavelength does the maximum in the energy-density distribution function for a blackbody occur if (a) $T = 300$ K? (b) $T = 3000$ K? (c) $T = 10,000$ K?

7. Sirius, one of the hottest known stars, has approximately a blackbody spectrum with $\lambda_{max} = 2600$ Å. Estimate the surface temperature of Sirius.

8. The temperature of the fireball in a thermonuclear explosion can reach temperatures of about 10^7 K. What value of λ_{max} does this correspond to? In what region of the spectrum is this found (cf. Figure 1-14)?

9. Using the values of k, h, and c given inside the front cover, calculate the value of the Stefan-Boltzmann constant and compare it to the experimental value, 5.670×10^{-8} J·m^{-2}·K^{-4}·s^{-1}.

10. Following Planck, we can use the equations of the theory of blackbody radiation to determine Avogadro's number, whose value was not known very accurately in 1900. Using the experimental values of $\lambda_{max}T$ and of the Stefan-Boltzmann constant and the fact that $c = 2.998 \times 10^8$ m·s^{-1} (the value of c was known accurately in 1900), calculate the values of h and the Boltzmann constant k. Recall that the k is equal to the molar gas constant R divided by Avogadro's number. Now, using the experimental value of R (8.314 J·K^{-1}·mol^{-1}), determine the value of Avogadro's number.

11. Given that the work function of chromium is 4.40 eV, calculate the kinetic energy of electrons emitted from a chromium surface when it is irradiated with ultraviolet radiation of wavelength 2000 Å. What is the stopping potential for these electrons?

12. When a clean surface of silver is irradiated with light of wavelength 230 nm, the stopping potential of the ejected electrons is found to be 0.80 V. Calculate the work function and the threshold frequency of silver.

13. Show that the Lyman series occurs between 912 Å and 1216 Å, that the Balmer series occurs between 3640 Å and 6563 Å, and that the Paschen series occurs between 8210 Å and 18,760 Å. Identify the spectral regions to which these wavelengths correspond.

14. Show that Planck's constant has dimensions of angular momentum.

15. What is the wavelength and frequency of electromagnetic radiation having an energy of 1 Rydberg (a Rydberg is equal to 109,680 cm^{-1}). Convert 1 Rydberg to electron volts and to kilojoules/mole (kJ·mol^{-1}).

16. Calculate the reduced mass of a nitrogen molecule in which both nitrogen atoms have an atomic mass of 14.00. Do the same for a hydrogen chloride molecule in which the chlorine atom has an atomic mass of 34.97. Hydrogen has an atomic mass of 1.008.

17. We shall learn when we study molecular spectroscopy that heteronuclear diatomic molecules absorb radiation in the microwave region and that one determines directly the so-called rotational constant of the molecule, defined by

$$B = \frac{h}{4\pi^2 I}$$

where I is the moment of inertia of the molecule. Given that $B = 3.13 \times 10^5$ MHz for HCl^{35}, calculate the internuclear separation for HCl^{35}. The atomic mass of H and Cl^{35} are 1.008 and 34.97, respectively.

18. Use Eq. 1-45 to calculate the Rydberg constant and compare your result to the experimental value, 109,678 cm^{-1}.

19. Derive the Bohr formula for $\bar{v}$ for a nucleus of atomic number Z.

20. The series in the He^+ spectrum that corresponds to the set of transitions where the electron falls from a higher level into the $n = 4$ state is called the *Pickering series* and is an important series in solar astronomy. Derive the formula for the wavelengths of the observed lines in this series. In what region of the spectrum does it occur?

21. Using the Bohr theory, calculate the ionization energy (in electron volts) of singly ionized helium.

22. A proton and a negatively charged μ meson (called a *muon*) can form a short-lived species called a *mesonic atom*. The charge of a muon is the same as that on an electron and the mass of a muon is 207 m_e. Assume that the Bohr theory can be applied to such a mesonic atom and calculate the ground-state energy, the radius of the first Bohr orbit, and the energy and frequency associated with the $n = 1$ to $n = 2$ transition in a mesonic atom.

23. Calculate the de Broglie wavelength for (a) an electron with a kinetic energy of 100 eV, (b) a proton with a kinetic energy of 10^5 eV, and (c) an electron in the first Bohr orbit of a hydrogen atom.

24. Calculate (a) the wavelength and kinetic energy of an electron in a beam of electrons accelerated by a voltage increment of 100 V and (b) the kinetic energy of an electron having a de Broglie wavelength of 2.00 Å.

25. Through what potential must a proton initially at rest fall so that $\lambda = 10^{-10}$ m (1 Å)?

26. Calculate the energy and wavelength associated with an α particle that has fallen through a potential difference of 4.0 V.

27. Show that the speed of an electron in the nth Bohr orbit is $v = e^2/2\varepsilon_0 nh$. Calculate v for the first few Bohr orbits.

28. In this problem we shall derive the equation for the momentum of a photon, $p = h/\lambda$. You might have expected the momentum of a photon to be zero because the mass of a photon is zero, but you must remember that a photon

travels at the speed of light and that we must consider its relativistic mass. For this problem, we must accept one formula from the special theory of relativity. The mass of a particle varies with its velocity according to

$$m = \frac{m_0}{[1 - (v^2/c^2)]^{1/2}} \tag{1-53}$$

where m_0, the mass as $v \to 0$, is called the *rest mass* of the particle. If we assume that the motion takes place in the x direction, the momentum is mv_x, and so

$$p_x = \frac{m_0 v_x}{[1 - (v_x^2/c^2)]^{1/2}} \tag{1-54}$$

Note that even though $m_0 = 0$ for a photon, p_x is not necessarily zero because $v_x = c$, and so $p_x \approx 0/0$, an indeterminate form. Recall that force F is equal to the rate of change of momentum or that

$$F = \frac{dp}{dt} \tag{1-55}$$

This is just Newton's second law. Kinetic energy can be defined as the work that is required to accelerate a particle from rest to some final velocity v. Because work is the integral of force times distance, the kinetic energy can be expressed as

$$K = \int_{v=0}^{v=v} F \, dx \tag{1-56}$$

where we have dropped the x subscripts for convenience. Equation 1-56 can be manipulated as

$$K = \int_{v=0}^{v=v} F \, dx = \int_{v=}^{v=v} \frac{dp}{dt} \frac{dx}{dt} dt = \int_{v=0}^{v=v} v \frac{dp}{dt} dt$$

$$= \int_{v=0}^{v=v} v \frac{d(mv)}{dt} dt = \int_{v=0}^{v=v} v \, d(mv) \tag{1-57}$$

Remember now that m in these last two integrals is *not* constant but is a function of v through Eq. 1-53. Note that if m were a constant, as it is in nonrelativistic (or classical) mechanics, then $K = \frac{1}{2}mv^2$, the classical result. Now substitute Eq. 1-53 into Eq. 1-57 to obtain

$$K = m_0 c^2 \left\{ \frac{1}{[1 - (v^2/c^2)]^{1/2}} - 1 \right\} \tag{1-58}$$

To obtain this result, you need the standard integral

$$\int \frac{x \, dx}{(ax^2 + b)^{3/2}} = -\frac{1}{a(ax^2 + b)^{1/2}}$$

Show that Eq. 1-58 reduces to the classical result as $v/c \to 0$. By combining Eq. 1-53 and 1-58, show that K can be written as

$$K = (m - m_0)c^2 \tag{1-59}$$

This equation is interpreted by considering mc^2 to be the total energy E of the particle and m_0c^2 to be the rest energy of the particle, so that

$$E = K + m_0c^2 \tag{1-60}$$

Lastly now, eliminate v in favor of p by using Eqs. 1-54 and 1-58, and show that

$$(K + m_0c^2)^2 = (pc)^2 + (m_0c^2)^2$$

and, using Eq. 1-60, write this as

$$E = [(pc)^2 + (m_0c^2)^2]^{1/2} \tag{1-61}$$

which is our desired equation and a fundamental equation of the special theory of relativity. In the case of a photon, $m_0 = 0$ and $E = pc$. But E also equals $h\nu$ according to the quantum theory and so we have $pc = h\nu$ or, finally, $p = h/\lambda$.

29. In this problem we shall prove that the inward force required to keep a mass revolving around a fixed center is $f = mv^2/r$. To do this, let us look at the velocity and the acceleration of a revolving mass. Referring to Figure 1-15, we see that

$$|\Delta \mathbf{r}| \approx \Delta s = r\,\Delta\theta \tag{1-62}$$

if $\Delta\theta$ is small enough that the arc length Δs and the vector difference $|\Delta \mathbf{r}| = |\mathbf{r}_2 - \mathbf{r}_1|$ are the same. In this case, then

$$v = \lim_{\Delta t \to 0} \frac{\Delta s}{\Delta t} = r \lim_{\Delta t \to 0} \frac{\Delta\theta}{\Delta t} = r\omega \tag{1-63}$$

If ω and r are constant, $v = r\omega$ is constant, and because acceleration is $\lim_{t \to 0}(\Delta v/\Delta t)$, we might wonder if there is any acceleration. The

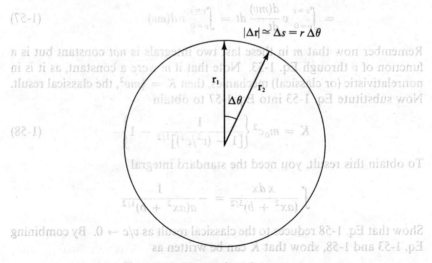

Figure 1-15. Diagram for defining angular velocity.

answer is most definitely *yes* because velocity is a vector quantity and the direction of **v**, which is the same as Δ**r**, is constantly changing even though its magnitude is not. To calculate this acceleration, draw a figure like Figure 1-15 but expressed in terms of v instead of r. From the figure, show that

$$\Delta v = |\Delta \mathbf{v}| = v\,\Delta\theta \tag{1-64}$$

is in direct analogy with Eq. 1-62, and show that the particle experiences an acceleration given by

$$a = \lim_{\Delta t \to 0} \frac{\Delta v}{\Delta t} = v \lim_{\Delta t \to 0} \frac{\Delta\theta}{\Delta t} = v\omega \tag{1-65}$$

Thus we see that the particle experiences an acceleration and requires an inward force equal to $ma = mv\omega = mv^2/r$ to keep it moving in its circular orbit.

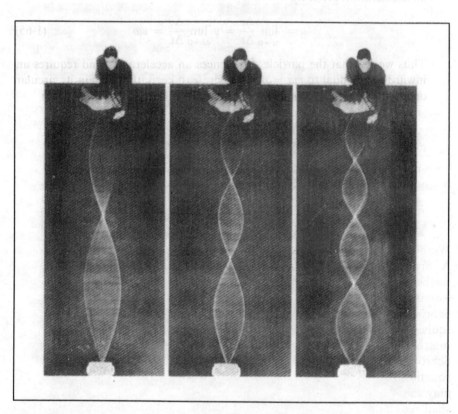

Standing waves can be set up in a string by shaking one end of the string at the correct frequency.

2

The
Wave
Equation

IN 1925 both Erwin Schrödinger and Werner Heisenberg independently formulated a general quantum theory. At first sight the two methods appeared to be different because Heisenberg's method is formulated in terms of matrices whereas Schrödinger's method is formulated in terms of partial differential equations. Just a year later, however, Schrödinger was able to show that the two formulations are mathematically equivalent. Because most students of physical chemistry are not familiar with matrix algebra, it is customary to present quantum theory according to Schrödinger's formulation, the central feature of which is a partial differential equation now known as the *Schrödinger equation*. Partial differential equations may sound no more comforting than matrix algebra, but it turns out that we shall require only elementary calculus to treat them. The wave equation of classical physics describes various wave phenomena such as a vibrating string, a vibrating drum head, ocean waves, and acoustic waves. Not only does the classical wave equation provide a physical background to the Schrödinger equation, but, in addition, the mathematics involved in solving the classical wave equation are central to any discussion of quantum mechanics. Most students of physical chemistry do not have much experience with classical wave equations, and so this chapter consists of a discussion of this topic. In particular, we shall solve the standard problem of a vibrating string because not only is the method of solution of this problem similar to the method we shall use to solve the Schrödinger equation, but it also gives us an excellent opportunity to relate the mathematical solution of a problem to the physical

47

nature of the problem. Many of the problems at the end of the chapter illustrate the connection between physical problems and the mathematics developed in the chapter.

2-1   *The One-Dimensional Wave Equation Describes the Motion of a Vibrating String*

Consider a uniform string stretched between two fixed points as shown in Figure 2-1. The displacement of the string from its equilibrium horizontal position is called its *amplitude*. If we let $u(x, t)$ be the amplitude of the string, then it is shown in Appendix A that $u(x, t)$ satisfies the equation

$$\frac{\partial^2 u}{\partial x^2} = \frac{1}{v^2}\frac{\partial^2 u}{\partial t^2} \tag{2-1}$$

where v is the speed with which a disturbance moves along the string. Equation 2-1 is the *classical wave equation*. Equation 2-1 is a *partial differential equation* because the unknown, $u(x, t)$ in this case, occurs in partial derivatives. The variables x and t are said to be the *independent variables* and $u(x, t)$, which depends on x and t, is said to be the *dependent variable*. Equation 2-1 is a *linear partial differential equation* because $u(x, t)$ and its derivatives appear only to the first power and there are no cross terms.

In addition to having to satisfy Eq. 2-1, the amplitude $u(x, t)$ must also satisfy certain physical conditions as well. Because the ends of the string are held fixed, the amplitude at these two points is always zero, and so we have the requirement that

$$u(0, t) = 0 \qquad u(l, t) = 0 \qquad \text{(for all } t) \tag{2-2}$$

These two conditions are called *boundary conditions* because they specify $u(x, t)$ at the boundaries. Generally, a partial differential equation must be solved subject to certain boundary conditions, the nature of which will be apparent on physical grounds.

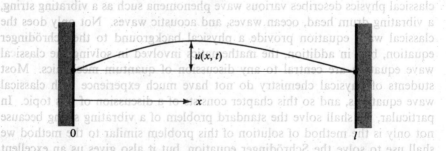

Figure 2-1. A vibrating string whose ends are fixed at 0 and l. The amplitude of the vibration at position x and time t is $u(x, t)$.

2-2 The Wave Equation Can Be Solved by the Method of Separation of Variables

The classical wave equation, as well as the Schrödinger equation and many other partial differential equations that arise in physics, can be solved readily by a method called *separation of variables*. We shall use the problem of a vibrating string to illustrate this method.

The key step in the method of separation of variables is to assume that $u(x, t)$ factors into a function of x only times a function of t only or that

$$u(x, t) = X(x)T(t) \tag{2-3}$$

If we substitute Eq. 2-3 into Eq. 2-1, then we obtain

$$T(t)\frac{d^2X}{dx^2} = \frac{1}{v^2} X(x)\frac{d^2T}{dt^2} \tag{2-4}$$

Now we divide by $u(x, t) = X(x)T(t)$ and obtain

$$\frac{1}{X(x)}\frac{d^2X}{dx^2} = \frac{1}{v^2 T(t)}\frac{d^2T}{dt^2} \tag{2-5}$$

The left-hand side of Eq. 2-5 is a function of x only and the right-hand side is a function of t only. Because x and t are independent variables, each side of Eq. 2-5 can be varied independently. The only way for the equality of the two sides to be preserved under any variation of x and t is that each side be equal to a constant. If we let this constant be k then we can write

$$\frac{1}{X(x)}\frac{d^2X}{dx^2} = k \tag{2-6}$$

$$\frac{1}{v^2 T(t)}\frac{d^2T}{dt^2} = k \tag{2-7}$$

where k is called the *separation constant* and will be determined later. Equations 2-6 and 2-7 can be written as

$$\frac{d^2X}{dx^2} - kX(x) = 0 \tag{2-8}$$

$$\frac{d^2T}{dt^2} - kv^2 T(t) = 0 \tag{2-9}$$

Equations 2-8 and 2-9 are called *ordinary differential equations* (as opposed to partial differential equations) because the unknowns, $X(x)$ and $T(t)$ in this case, occur as ordinary derivatives. Both of these differential equations are linear because the unknowns and their derivatives appear only to the first power. Furthermore, the coefficients of every term involving the unknowns in these equations are constants, being 1 and $-k$ in Eq. 2-8 and 1 and $-kv^2$ in Eq. 2-9. These equations are called *linear differential equations with constant coefficients* and are quite easy to solve, as we shall see.

The value of k in Eqs. 2-8 and 2-9 is yet to be determined. We do not know right now whether k is positive, negative, or even zero. Let us first assume that $k = 0$. In this case, Eqs. 2-8 and 2-9 can be integrated immediately to find

$$X(x) = a_1 x + b_1 \tag{2-10}$$

$$T(t) = a_2 t + b_2 \tag{2-11}$$

where the a's and b's are just integration constants, which can be determined by using the boundary conditions given in Eq. 2-2. In terms of $X(x)$ and $T(t)$, the boundary conditions are

$$u(0, t) = X(0)T(t) = 0 \tag{2-12}$$

and

$$u(l, t) = X(l)T(t) = 0 \tag{2-13}$$

Because $T(t)$ certainly does not vanish for all t, we must have that

$$X(0) = 0 \qquad X(l) = 0 \tag{2-14}$$

This is how the boundary conditions affect $X(x)$. Going back to Eq. 2-10, we conclude that the only way to satisfy Eq. 2-14 is for $a_1 = b_1 = 0$, which means that $X(x) = 0$ and that $u(x, t) = 0$ for all x. This is called a *trivial solution* to Eq. 2-1 and is of no interest.

Let's look at Eqs. 2-8 and 2-9 for $k \neq 0$. Both equations are of the form

$$\frac{d^2 y}{dx^2} - ky(x) = 0 \tag{2-15}$$

where k is a positive or negative constant. A specific example of a case in which k is positive is the equation

$$\frac{d^2 y}{dx^2} - 4y(x) = 0 \tag{2-16}$$

To solve this type of differential equation, a linear one with constant coefficients, we let $y(x) = e^{\alpha x}$ where α is to be determined. Substituting $e^{\alpha x}$ into Eq. 2-16, we find

$$(\alpha^2 - 4)y(x) = 0$$

To have a nontrivial solution, $\alpha^2 - 4$ must equal zero, and so

$$\alpha = \pm 2$$

Thus there are two solutions: $y(x) = e^{2x}$ and e^{-2x}. It is an easy exercise to prove that

$$y(x) = c_1 e^{2x} + c_2 e^{-2x}$$

(where c_1 and c_2 are constants) is also a solution. Note that the highest derivative in Eq. 2-16 is a second derivative, which implies that in some sense we are performing two integrations when we find its solution. When we do two integrations, we always obtain two constants of integration. The solution we have found has two constants, c_1 and c_2, and so this suggests that this is the most general solution.

The solution of other ordinary differential equations with constant coefficients is best illustrated by examples.

EXAMPLE 2-1

Solve the equation

$$\frac{d^2y}{dx^2} - 3\frac{dy}{dx} + 2y = 0$$

Solution: If we substitute $y(x) = e^{\alpha x}$ into this differential equation, then we obtain

$$\alpha^2 y - 3\alpha y + 2y = 0$$

$$\alpha^2 - 3\alpha + 2 = 0$$

$$(\alpha - 2)(\alpha - 1) = 0$$

or that $\alpha = 1$ and 2. The two solutions are $y(x) = e^x$ and $y(x) = e^{2x}$, and the general solution is

$$y(x) = c_1 e^x + c_2 e^{2x}$$

Prove this by substituting back into the original equation.

EXAMPLE 2-2

Solve the equation in Example 2-1 subject to the two conditions $y(0) = 0$ and $y'(0) = -1$. [$y'(0)$ denotes the first derivative of $y(x)$ at $x = 0$.]

Solution: The general solution is

$$y(x) = c_1 e^x + c_2 e^{2x}$$

The two conditions that are given allow us to evaluate c_1 and c_2 and hence find a particular solution. Putting $x = 0$ into $y(x)$ and $x = 0$ into dy/dx gives

$$y(0) = c_1 + c_2 = 0$$

$$y'(0) = c_1 + 2c_2 = -1$$

Solving these two equations simultaneously gives $c_1 = 1$ and $c_2 = -1$, and so

$$y(x) = e^x - e^{2x}$$

satisfies not only the differential equation, but also the two conditions as well.

2-3 *Some Differential Equations Have Oscillatory Solutions*

In the differential equations that we have solved up to now, the values of α in $e^{\alpha x}$ have been real. In many cases, α will be imaginary. Consider the differential equation

$$\frac{d^2 y}{dx^2} + y(x) = 0$$

If we let $y(x) = e^{\alpha x}$, then we have

$$(\alpha^2 + 1)y(x) = 0$$

or that

$$\alpha = \pm i$$

where, by definition, the quantity i obeys the equation $i^2 = -1$. Complex numbers occur frequently in quantum mechanics, and they are reviewed in Appendix B. The general solution to the previous differential equation is then

$$y(x) = c_1 e^{ix} + c_2 e^{-ix}$$

It is easy to verify that this is a solution to the differential equation.

Although the above solution is correct, it is usually more convenient to rewrite expressions like e^{ix} or e^{-ix} using *Euler's formula* (Appendix B), which is

$$e^{\pm i\theta} = \cos \theta \pm i \sin \theta$$

If we substitute Euler's formula into the above solution, then we find

$$y(x) = c_1(\cos x + i \sin x) + c_2(\cos x - i \sin x)$$
$$= (c_1 + c_2) \cos x + (ic_1 - ic_2) \sin x$$

But $c_1 + c_2$ and $ic_1 - ic_2$ are also just constants, and if we call them c_3 and c_4, respectively, then we can write

$$y(x) = c_3 \cos x + c_4 \sin x$$

instead of

$$y(x) = c_1 e^{ix} + c_2 e^{-ix}$$

These two forms for $y(x)$ are equivalent.

EXAMPLE 2-3
    Prove that

$$y(x) = A \cos x + B \sin x$$

(where A and B are constants), is a solution to the differential equation

$$\frac{d^2 y}{dx^2} + y(x) = 0$$

Solution: The first derivative of $y(x)$ is

$$\frac{dy}{dx} = -A \sin x + B \cos x$$

and the second derivative is

$$\frac{d^2y}{dx^2} = -A \cos x - B \sin x$$

Therefore, we see that

$$\frac{d^2y}{dx^2} + y(x) = 0$$

or that $y(x) = A \cos x + B \sin x$ is a solution of the differential equation

$$\frac{d^2y}{dx^2} + y(x) = 0$$

The next example is important and one whose general solution should be learned.

EXAMPLE 2-4

Solve the equation

$$\frac{d^2x}{dt^2} + \omega^2 x(t) = 0$$

Subject to the initial conditions $x(0) = A$ and $x'(0) = 0$.

Solution: In this case, we find $\alpha = \pm i\omega$ and

$$x(t) = c_1 e^{i\omega t} + c_2 e^{-i\omega t}$$

or

$$x(t) = c_3 \cos \omega t + c_4 \sin \omega t$$

Now

$$x(0) = c_3 = A$$

and

$$x'(0) = \omega c_4 = 0$$

implying that $c_4 = 0$ and that the particular solution we are seeking is

$$x(t) = A \cos \omega t$$

This solution is plotted in Figure 2-2. Note that it oscillates cosinusiodally in time, with an amplitude A. The wavelength of the oscillation is 2π and the frequency v is given by (see Problem 3)

$$v = \frac{\omega}{2\pi}$$

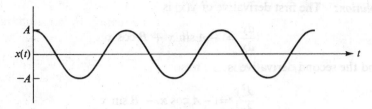

Figure 2-2. A plot of $x(t) = A \cos \omega t$, the solution to the problem in Example 2-4. The amplitude is A, the wavelength is 2π, and the frequency is $\omega/2\pi$.

2-4   *The General Solution to the Wave Equation Is a Superposition of Normal Modes*

Let us assess where we are now. We have obtained Eqs. 2-8 and 2-9 by applying the method of separation of variables to the wave equation. We have already shown that if the separation constant k is zero, then only a trivial solution results. Now let us assume that k is positive. To this end, write k as β^2, where β is real. This assures that k is positive because it is the square of a real number. In the case $k = \beta^2$, the general solution to Eq. 2-8 is

$$X(x) = c_1 e^{\beta x} + c_2 e^{-\beta x}$$

It is easy to show that the only way to satisfy the boundary conditions (Eq. 2-14) is for $c_1 = c_2 = 0$, and so once again we find only a trivial solution.

Let us hope then that assuming k to be negative gives us something interesting. If we set $k = -\beta^2$, then k is negative if β is real. In this case Eq. 2-8 is

$$\frac{d^2 X}{dx^2} + \beta^2 X(x) = 0$$

Referring to Example 2-4, we see that the general solution can be written as

$$X(x) = A \cos \beta x + B \sin \beta x$$

The boundary conditions that $X(0) = 0$ implies that $A = 0$. The condition at the boundary at $x = l$ says that

$$X(l) = B \sin \beta l = 0 \tag{2-17}$$

There are two ways for Eq. 2-17 to be satisfied. One is that $B = 0$, but this along with the fact that $A = 0$ yields a trivial solution. The other way to satisfy Eq. 2-17 is to require that $\sin \beta l = 0$. Because $\sin \theta = 0$ when $\theta = 0$, $\pi, 2\pi, 3\pi, \ldots$ Eq. 2-17 implies that

$$\beta l = n\pi \qquad n = 1, 2, 3, \ldots \tag{2-18}$$

where we have omitted the $n = 0$ case because this also produces a trivial solution. Equation 2-18 determines the parameter β and hence the separation constant $k = -\beta^2$. So far then we have that

$$X(x) = B \sin \frac{n\pi x}{l} \qquad (2\text{-}19)$$

Remember that we have Eq. 2-9 to solve also. Equation 2-9 can be written as

$$\frac{d^2 T(t)}{dt^2} + \beta^2 v^2 T(t) = 0 \qquad (2\text{-}20)$$

where we have found previously that $\beta = n\pi/l$. Referring to Example 2-4 again, the general solution is

$$T(t) = D \cos \omega_n t + E \sin \omega_n t \qquad (2\text{-}21)$$

where $\omega_n = \beta v = n\pi v/l$. We have no conditions to specify D and E, and so the amplitude $u(x, t)$ is (cf. Eq. 2-3)

$$u(x, t) = X(x)T(t)$$

$$= \left(B \sin \frac{n\pi x}{l} \right)(D \cos \omega_n t + E \sin \omega_n t)$$

$$= (F \cos \omega_n t + G \sin \omega_n t) \sin \frac{n\pi x}{l} \qquad n = 1, 2, \ldots$$

where we have let $F = DB$ and $G = EB$. Because there is a $u(x, t)$ for each integer n and because the values of F and G may depend on n, we should write $u(x, t)$ as

$$u_n(x, t) = (F_n \cos \omega_n t + G_n \sin \omega_n t) \sin \frac{n\pi x}{l} \qquad n = 1, 2, \ldots \qquad (2\text{-}22)$$

Because each $u_n(x, t)$ is a solution to Eq. 2-1, their sum is also a solution of Eq. 2-1 and is, in fact, the general solution. Therefore, we have

$$u(x, t) = \sum_{n=1}^{\infty} (F_n \cos \omega_n t + G_n \sin \omega_n t) \sin \frac{n\pi x}{l} \qquad (2\text{-}23)$$

It is easy to verify that Eq. 2-23 is a solution to Eq. 2-1 by substituting it directly into Eq. 2-1. Problem 5 shows that $F \cos \omega t + G \sin \omega t$ can be written in the equivalent form, $A \cos (\omega t + \phi)$, where A and ϕ are constants that are expressible in terms of F and G (cf. Problem 5). The quantity A is the amplitude of the wave and ϕ is called the *phase angle*. Using this relation, we can write Eq. 2-23 in the form

$$u(x, t) = \sum_{n=1}^{\infty} A_n \cos (\omega_n t + \phi_n) \sin \frac{n\pi x}{l} \equiv \sum_{n=1}^{\infty} u_n(x, t) \qquad (2\text{-}24)$$

Equation 2-24 has a nice physical interpretation. Each $u_n(x, t)$ is called a *normal mode* and the time dependence of each normal mode represents harmonic motion of frequency

$$v_n = \frac{\omega_n}{2\pi} = \frac{vn}{2l} \tag{2-25}$$

where we have used the fact that $\omega_n = \beta v = n\pi v/l$ (cf. Eq. 2-21). The spatial dependence of the first few terms in Eq. 2-24 is shown in Figure 2-3. The first term, $u_1(x, t)$, called the *fundamental mode* or *first harmonic*, represents a cosinusoidal (harmonic) time dependence of frequency $v/2l$ of the motion depicted in Figure 2-3(a). The *second harmonic* or *first overtone*, $u_2(x, t)$, vibrates harmonically with frequency v/l and looks like the motion depicted in Figure 2-3(b). Note that the midpoint of this harmonic is fixed at zero for all t. Such a point is called a *node*, a concept that arises in quantum mechanics as well. Note also that the second harmonic oscillates with twice the frequency of the first harmonic. Figure 2-3(c) shows that the *third harmonic* or *second overtone* has two nodes. It is easy to continue and show that the number of nodes is equal to $n - 1$ (Problem 11).

The waves shown in Figure 2-3 are called *standing waves* because the positions of the nodes are fixed in time. Between the nodes, the string oscillates

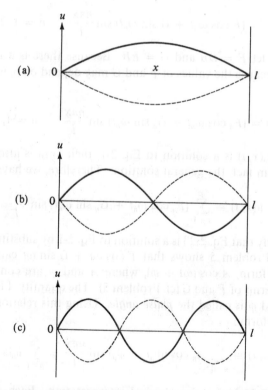

Figure 2-3. The first three normal modes of a vibrating string. Note that each normal mode is a standing wave and that the nth harmonic has n − 1 nodes.

up and down. A standing wave is a superposition of traveling waves. We can see this mathematically by considering only the first harmonic,

$$u_1(x, t) = A_1 \cos \omega_1 t \sin \frac{\pi x}{l} \qquad (2\text{-}26)$$

where, for convenience, we have set $\phi_1 = 0$. Using the trigonometric identity

$$\sin \alpha \cos \beta = \tfrac{1}{2} \sin(\alpha + \beta) + \tfrac{1}{2} \sin(\alpha - \beta) \qquad (2\text{-}27)$$

and Eq. 2-25 for ω_1, Eq. 2-26 becomes

$$u_1(x, t) = \frac{A_1}{2} \sin \left(\frac{\pi x}{l} + \frac{\pi v t}{l} \right) + \frac{A_1}{2} \sin \left(\frac{\pi x}{l} - \frac{\pi v t}{l} \right)$$

$$= \frac{A_1}{2} \sin \left[\frac{\pi}{l}(x + vt) \right] + \frac{A_1}{2} \sin \left[\frac{\pi}{l}(x - vt) \right] \qquad (2\text{-}28)$$

The wavelength of the first harmonic is $\lambda = 2l$ [cf. Figure 2-3(a)], and so Eq. 2-28 can be written as

$$u_1(x, t) = \frac{A_1}{2} \sin \left[\frac{2\pi}{\lambda}(x + vt) \right] + \frac{A_1}{2} \sin \left[\frac{2\pi}{\lambda}(x - vt) \right] \qquad (2\text{-}29)$$

Each of the terms in Eq. 2-29 represents a *traveling wave*. If we look at some position x and let t vary, the first term in Eq. 2-29 would appear to be a wave of wavelength λ and frequency $v = v/\lambda$, traveling to the left. The second term in Eq. 2-29 would be a similar wave traveling to the right. Thus, we see that a standing wave is the superposition of two similar traveling waves, traveling in opposite directions.

It is instructive to consider a simple case in which $u(x, t)$ consists of only the first two harmonics and is of the form (cf. Eq. 2-24)

$$u(x, t) = \cos \omega_1 t \sin \frac{\pi x}{l} + \frac{1}{2} \cos \left(\omega_2 t + \frac{\pi}{2} \right) \sin \frac{2\pi x}{l} \qquad (2\text{-}30)$$

Equation 2-30 is illustrated in Figure 2-4. The left-hand side of Figure 2-4 shows the time dependence of each mode separately. Notice that $u_2(x, t)$ has gone through one complete oscillation in the time depicted while $u_1(x, t)$ has gone through only one-half cycle, nicely illustrating that $\omega_2 = 2\omega_1$. The right-hand side of Figure 2-4 shows the sum of the two harmonics, or the actual motion of the string, as a function of time. It is interesting to see how a superposition of the standing waves in the left-hand side of the figure yields the traveling wave in the right-hand side.

The decomposition of any complicated, general wave motion into a sum or a superposition of normal modes is a fundamental property of oscillatory behavior and follows from the fact that the wave equation is a linear equation. Equation 2-24 is an example of a *Fourier series*, a concept that plays a particularly important role in the analysis of vibrational motion. The two sets of constants in Eq. 2-24, the A_n and ϕ_n, can all be determined from the initial displacement and motion of the string. (We shall learn to do this in Chapter 4.)

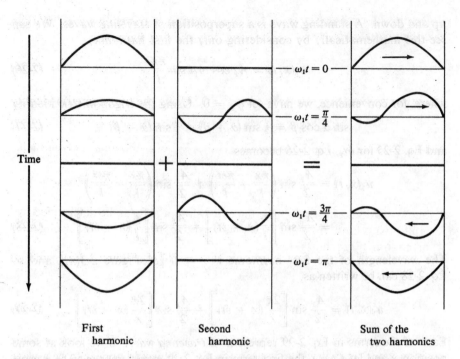

Time

First   Second   Sum of the
harmonic   harmonic   two harmonics

Figure 2-4. An illustration of how two standing waves can combine to give a traveling wave. In both parts, time increases downward. The left-hand portion shows the independent motion of the first two harmonics. Both harmonics are standing waves; the first harmonic goes through half a cycle and the second harmonic goes through one complete cycle in the time shown. The right-hand side shows the sum of the two harmonics. The sum is not a standing wave. As shown, the sum is a traveling wave that travels back and forth between the fixed ends. The traveling wave has gone through one-half a cycle in the time shown.

The set of A's and ϕ's for a string plucked in the middle, say, differ from those for a string plucked somewhere else, and therefore $u(x, t)$, and so the subsequent motion of the string, will depend on its initial conditions.

Our path from the wave equation to its solution was fairly long because we had to learn to solve a certain class of ordinary differential equations on the way. The overall procedure is actually straightforward, and to illustrate this, in Section 2.5, we shall solve the problem of a vibrating rectangular membrane, a two-dimensional problem.

2-5 *A Vibrating Membrane Is Described by a Two-Dimensional Wave Equation*

The generalization of Eq. 2-1 to two dimensions is

$$\frac{\partial^2 u}{\partial x^2} + \frac{\partial^2 u}{\partial y^2} = \frac{1}{v^2}\frac{\partial^2 u}{\partial t^2} \tag{2-31}$$

where $u = u(x, y, t)$ and x, y, and t are the independent variables. We shall apply this equation to a rectangular membrane whose entire perimeter is clamped. By referring to the geometry in Figure 2-5, the boundary conditions that $u(x, y, t)$ must satisfy because its four edges are clamped are

$$u(0, y) = u(a, y) = 0$$
$$\text{(for all } t)\tag{2-32}$$
$$u(x, 0) = u(x, b) = 0$$

By applying the method of separation of variables to Eq. 2-31, we assume that $u(x, y, t)$ can be written as the product of a spatial part and a temporal part or that

$$u(x, y, t) = F(x, y)\, T(t)\tag{2-33}$$

We substitute Eq. 2-33 into Eq. 2-31 and divide by $F(x, y)T(t)$ to find

$$\frac{1}{v^2 T(t)}\frac{d^2 T}{dt^2} = \frac{1}{F(x, y)}\left(\frac{\partial^2 F}{\partial x^2} + \frac{\partial^2 F}{\partial y^2}\right)\tag{2-34}$$

The right-hand side of Eq. 2-34 is a function of x and y only and the left-hand side is a function of t only. This can be so only if both sides are equal to a constant. Anticipating that the separation constant will be negative as it was in the previous sections, we write it as $-\beta^2$ and obtain the two separate equations

$$\frac{d^2 T}{dt^2} + v^2\beta^2 T(t) = 0\tag{2-35}$$

and

$$\frac{\partial^2 F}{\partial x^2} + \frac{\partial^2 F}{\partial y^2} + \beta^2 F(x, y) = 0\tag{2-36}$$

Equation 2-36 is still a partial differential equation. To solve it, we once again use separation of variables. Substitute $F(x, y) = X(x)Y(y)$ into Eq. 2-36

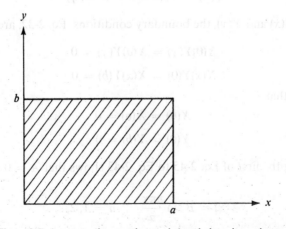

Figure 2-5. A rectangular membrane clamped along its perimeter.

and divide by $X(x)Y(y)$ to obtain

$$\frac{1}{X(x)}\frac{d^2 X}{dx^2} + \frac{1}{Y(y)}\frac{d^2 Y}{dy^2} + \beta^2 = 0 \qquad (2\text{-}37)$$

Again we argue that because x and y are independent variables, the only way that this equation can be valid is that

$$\frac{1}{X(x)}\frac{d^2 X}{dx^2} = -p^2 \qquad (2\text{-}38)$$

and

$$\frac{1}{Y(y)}\frac{d^2 Y}{dy^2} = -q^2 \qquad (2\text{-}39)$$

where p^2 and q^2 are separation constants, which according to Eq. 2-37 must satisfy

$$p^2 + q^2 = \beta^2 \qquad (2\text{-}40)$$

Equations 2-38 and 2-39 can be rewritten as

$$\frac{d^2 X}{dx^2} + p^2 X(x) = 0 \qquad (2\text{-}41)$$

$$\frac{d^2 Y}{dy^2} \pm q^2 Y(y) = 0 \qquad (2\text{-}42)$$

Equation 2-31, a partial differential equation in three independent variables, has been reduced to three ordinary differential equations (Eqs. 2-35, 2-41, and 2-42), each of which is exactly of the form discussed in Example 2-4. The solutions to Eqs. 2-41 and 2-42 are

$$X(x) = A \cos px + B \sin px \qquad (2\text{-}43)$$

and

$$Y(y) = C \cos qy + D \sin qy \qquad (2\text{-}44)$$

In terms of $X(x)$ and $Y(y)$, the boundary conditions, Eq. 2-32, are

$$X(0)Y(y) = X(a)Y(y) = 0$$

$$X(x)Y(0) = X(x)Y(b) = 0$$

which imply that

$$X(0) = X(a) = 0$$

$$Y(0) = Y(b) = 0 \qquad (2\text{-}45)$$

Applying the first of Eq. 2-45 to Eq. 2-43 shows that $A = 0$ and $pa = n\pi$, so that

$$X(x) = B \sin \frac{n\pi x}{a} \qquad n = 1, 2, \ldots \qquad (2\text{-}46)$$

In exactly the same manner, we find that $C = 0$ and $qb = m\pi$, where $m = 1, 2, \ldots$, and so

$$Y(y) = D \sin \frac{m\pi y}{b} \qquad m = 1, 2, \ldots \qquad (2\text{-}47)$$

Recalling that $p^2 + q^2 = \beta^2$, we see that

$$\beta_{nm} = \pi \left(\frac{n^2}{a^2} + \frac{m^2}{b^2} \right)^{1/2} \qquad \begin{array}{l} n = 1, 2, 3, \ldots \\ m = 1, 2, 3, \ldots \end{array} \qquad (2\text{-}48)$$

where we have subscripted β to emphasize that it depends on the two integers n and m.

Finally now we solve Eq. 2-35 for the time dependence. The solution to Eq. 2-35 is

$$T_{nm}(t) = E_{nm} \cos \omega_{nm} t + F_{nm} \sin \omega_{nm} t \qquad (2\text{-}49)$$

where

$$\omega_{nm} = v\beta_{nm}$$

$$= v\pi \left(\frac{n^2}{a^2} + \frac{m^2}{b^2} \right)^{1/2} \qquad (2\text{-}50)$$

According to Problem 5, Eq. 2-49 can be written as

$$T_{nm}(t) = G_{nm} \cos (\omega_{nm} t + \phi_{nm}) \qquad (2\text{-}51)$$

The complete solution to Eq. 2-31 is

$$u(x, y, t) = \sum_{n=1}^{\infty} \sum_{m=1}^{\infty} u_{nm}(x, y, t)$$

$$= \sum_{n=1}^{\infty} \sum_{m=1}^{\infty} A_{nm} \cos (\omega_{nm} t + \phi_{nm}) \sin \frac{n\pi x}{a} \sin \frac{m\pi y}{b} \qquad (2\text{-}52)$$

As in the one-dimensional case of a vibrating string, we see that the general vibrational motion of a rectangular drum can be expressed as a superposition of normal modes, $u_{nm}(x, y, t)$. Some of these modes are those shown in Figure 2-6. Note that in this two-dimensional problem we obtain *nodal lines*. In two-dimensional problems, the nodes are lines, as compared to points in one-dimensional problems.

Figure 2-6 shows the normal modes for a case in which $a \neq b$. It is interesting to look at the case in which $a = b$. The frequencies of the normal modes are given by Eq. 2-50. When $a = b$ in Eq. 2-50, we have

$$\omega_{nm} = \frac{v\pi}{a} (n^2 + m^2)^{1/2} \qquad (2\text{-}53)$$

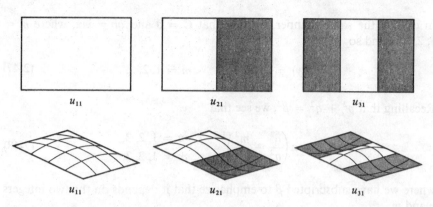

Figure 2-6. The first few normal modes of a rectangular membrane with shaded and clear sections having opposite sinusoidal displacements as indicated.

We see from Eq. 2-53 that $\omega_{12} = \omega_{21} = 5^{1/2}v\pi/a$ in this case; yet the normal modes $u_{12}(x, y, t)$ and $u_{21}(x, y, t)$ are not the same, as seen from Figure 2-7. What we have here is an example of what is called a *degeneracy*, and we say that the frequency $\omega_{12} = \omega_{21}$ is *doubly degenerate* or *twofold degenerate*. Note that the phenomenon of degeneracy arises because of the symmetry that is introduced when $a = b$. This can be seen easily by comparing the modes u_{12} and u_{21} in Figures 2-6 and 2-7. It can be seen from Eq. 2-53 that there will be at least a twofold degeneracy when $m \neq n$ because $m^2 + n^2 = n^2 + m^2$. We shall see that the concept of degeneracy arises in quantum mechanics also.

This chapter has been a discussion of the wave equation and its solutions. We shall see in Chapter 3 that we shall use all the mathematical methods that

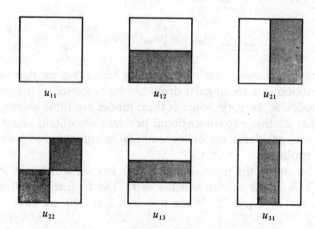

Figure 2-7. The normal modes of a square membrane, illustrating the occurrence of degeneracy in this system. The normal modes u_{12} and u_{21} have different orientations but the same frequency, given by Eq. 2-53. The same is true for the normal modes u_{13} and u_{31}.

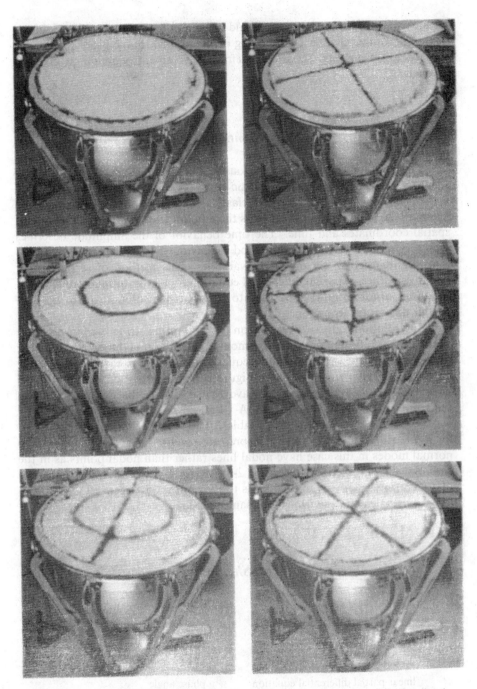

Powder that is sprinkled on a vibrating drumhead will collect at the nodes, where the vibrations are the weakest. The above photographs illustrate six of the normal modes of a circular drumhead.

we have developed here and so it would be helpful to do many of the problems at the end of this chapter before going on. A number of the problems involve physical problems and serve as a refresher or an introduction to classical mechanics.

Summary

The equation that describes various wave phenomena such as a vibrating string, a vibrating drum head, acoustic waves, and other oscillatory behavior is the classical wave equation. The classical wave equation is a linear partial differential equation whose solution is the amplitude of a wave as a function of spatial coordinates and time. The time behavior of the amplitude describes vibratory motion. A standard method of solving the classical wave equation is by the method of separation of variables. The method of separation of variables reduces a partial differential equation to a set of ordinary differential equations, whose solutions are used to construct the solution to the original partial differential equation.

The solution of the wave equation for a vibrating string is expressed as a summation of normal modes, or harmonics. Each normal mode is a standing wave that oscillates with a certain frequency. In addition, each normal mode has a certain number of nodes (see Figure 2-3). A summation of two or more normal modes leads to a traveling wave, that is, a wave that propagates along the string, as shown in Figure 2-4. A vibrating membrane is described by a wave equation with two spatial variables. The solution of the wave equation for a vibrating membrane also is expressed in terms of normal modes. The normal modes in this case have nodal lines rather than nodal points as in the case of a vibrating string (see Figure 2-6). A study of the allowed frequencies of a vibrating square membrane leads to the concept of degeneracy. Two different normal modes can have the same frequency.

Terms That You Should Know

classical wave equation	separation constant
partial differential equation	ordinary differential equation
independent variable	trivial solution
dependent variable	Euler's formula
linear partial differential equation	phase angle
amplitude	normal mode
boundary condition	fundamental mode
separation of variables	first harmonic

second harmonic   traveling wave

first overtone   Fourier series

standing wave   nodal line

node   degeneracy

Problems

1. Find the general solutions of the following differential equations.

(a) $\dfrac{d^2y}{dx^2} - 4\dfrac{dy}{dx} + 3y = 0$ (b) $\dfrac{d^2y}{dx^2} + 6\dfrac{dy}{dx} = 0$

(c) $\dfrac{dy}{dx} + 3y = 0$ (d) $\dfrac{d^2y}{dx^2} + 2\dfrac{dy}{dx} - y = 0$

(e) $\dfrac{d^2y}{dx^2} - 3\dfrac{dy}{dx} + 2y = 0$

2. Solve the following differential equations.

(a) $\dfrac{d^2y}{dx^2} - 4y = 0$ $y(0) = 2;\;\; y'(0) = 4$

(b) $\dfrac{d^2y}{dx^2} - 5\dfrac{dy}{dx} + 6y = 0$ $y(0) = -1;\;\; y'(0) = 0$

(c) $\dfrac{dy}{dx} - 2y = 0$ $y(0) = 2$

3. Prove that $x(t) = \cos \omega t$ oscillates with a frequency $v = \omega/2\pi$. Prove that $x(t) = A \cos \omega t + B \sin \omega t$ oscillates with the same frequency.

4. Solve the following differential equations.

(a) $\dfrac{d^2x}{dt^2} + \omega^2 x(t) = 0$ $x(0) = 0;\;\; x'(0) = v_0$

(b) $\dfrac{d^2x}{dt^2} + \omega^2 x(t) = 0$ $x(0) = A;\;\; x'(0) = v_0$

Prove in both cases that $x(t)$ oscillates with frequency $\omega/2\pi$.

5. The general solution to the differential equation

$$\frac{d^2x}{dt^2} + \omega^2 x(t) = 0$$

is

$$x(t) = c_1 \cos \omega t + c_2 \sin \omega t$$

It is often convenient to write this solution in the equivalent form

$$x(t) = A \sin (\omega t + \phi)$$

or

$$x(t) = B \cos (\omega t + \Psi)$$

Show that all three of these expressions for $x(t)$ are equivalent. Derive equations for A and ϕ in terms of c_1 and c_2 and for B and Ψ in terms of c_1 and c_2. Show that all three forms of $x(t)$ oscillate with frequency $\omega/2\pi$. *Hint:* Use the trigonometric identities

$$\sin (\alpha + \beta) = \sin \alpha \cos \beta + \cos \alpha \sin \beta$$

$$\cos (\alpha + \beta) = \cos \alpha \cos \beta - \sin \alpha \sin \beta$$

6. In all the differential equations that we have discussed so far, the values of the exponents α that we have found have been either real or purely imaginary. Let us consider a case in which α turns out to be complex. Consider the equation

$$y'' + 2y' + 10y = 0$$

If we substitute $y(x) = e^{\alpha x}$ into this, we find that $\alpha^2 + 2\alpha + 10 = 0$ or that $\alpha = -1 \pm 3i$. The general solution is

$$y(x) = c_1 e^{(-1+3i)x} + c_2 e^{(-1-3i)x}$$
$$= c_1 e^{-x} e^{3ix} + c_2 e^{-x} e^{-3ix}$$

Show that $y(x)$ can be written in the equivalent form

$$y(x) = e^{-x}(c_3 \cos 3x + c_4 \sin 3x)$$

Thus we see that complex values of the α's lead to trigonometric solutions modulated by an exponential factor. Solve the following equations.

(a) $y'' + 2y' + 2y = 0$
(b) $y'' - 6y' + 25y = 0$
(c) $y'' + 2\beta y' + (\beta^2 + \omega^2)y = 0$
(d) $y'' + 4y' + 5y = 0$ $y(0) = 1; \quad y'(0) = -3$

7. This problem develops the idea of a classical harmonic oscillator. Consider a mass m attached to a spring as shown in Figure 2-8. Let the relaxed or undistorted length of the spring be x_0. Hooke's law says that the force acting on the mass m is $f = -k(x - x_0)$, where k is a constant that is characteristic of the spring and is called the *force constant* of the spring. Note that the minus sign indicates the direction of the force: upward if $x > x_0$ (extended) and downward if $x < x_0$ (compressed). The momentum of the mass is

$$p = m \frac{dx}{dt} = m \frac{d(x - x_0)}{dt}$$

Newton's second law says that the rate of change of momentum is equal to a force

$$\frac{dp}{dt} = f$$

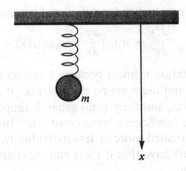

Figure 2-8. A body of mass m connected to a wall by a spring.

Because $p = mv$,

$$\frac{dp}{dt} = m\frac{dv}{dt} = m\frac{d^2x}{dt^2}$$

for fixed mass, and so we have

$$m\frac{d^2x}{dt^2} = f$$

Replacing $f(x)$ by Hooke's law, we find

$$m\frac{d^2x}{dt^2} = -k(x - x_0)$$

Upon letting $\xi = x - x_0$ be the displacement of the spring from its undistorted length, then

$$m\frac{d^2\xi}{dt^2} + k\xi = 0$$

Given that the mass starts at $x = x_0$ with an initial velocity v_0, show that the displacement is given by

$$\xi(t) = v_0\left(\frac{m}{k}\right)^{1/2} \sin\left[\left(\frac{k}{m}\right)^{1/2} t\right]$$

Interpret and discuss this solution. What does the motion look like? What is the frequency? What is the amplitude?

8. Modify Problem 7 to the case where the mass is moving through a viscous medium with a viscous force proportional to but opposite the velocity. Show that the equation of motion is

$$m\frac{d^2\xi}{dt^2} + \gamma\frac{d\xi}{dt} + k\xi = 0$$

where γ is the viscous drag coefficient. Solve this equation and discuss the behavior of $\xi(t)$ for various relative values of m, γ, and k. This system is called a *damped harmonic oscillator*.

9. Consider the linear second-order differential equation

$$\frac{d^2y}{dx^2} + a_1(x)\frac{dy}{dx} + a_0(x)y(x) = 0$$

Note that this equation is linear because y and its derivatives appear only to the first power and there are no cross terms. It does not have constant coefficients, however, and there is no general, simple method for solving it like there is if the coefficients were constants. In fact, each equation of this type must be treated more or less individually. Nevertheless, because it is linear, we must have that if $y_1(x)$ and $y_2(x)$ are two solutions, then a linear combination,

$$y(x) = c_1y_1(x) + c_2y_2(x)$$

where c_1 and c_2 are constants, is also a solution. Prove this.

10. We shall see in Chapter 3 that the Schrödinger equation for a particle of mass m that is constrained to move freely along a line between 0 and a is

$$\frac{d^2\psi}{dx^2} + \left(\frac{8\pi^2mE}{h^2}\right)\psi(x) = 0$$

with the boundary condition

$$\psi(0) = \psi(a) = 0$$

In this equation, E is the energy of the particle and $\psi(x)$ is its wave function. Solve this differential equation for $\psi(x)$, apply the boundary conditions, and show that the energy can have only the values

$$E_n = \frac{n^2h^2}{8ma^2} \qquad n = 1, 2, 3, \ldots$$

or that the energy is quantized.

11. Prove that the number of nodes for a vibrating string clamped at both ends is $n - 1$ for the nth harmonic.

12. Prove that

$$y(x, t) = A \sin\left[\frac{2\pi}{\lambda}(x - vt)\right]$$

is a wave of wavelength λ and frequency $v = v/\lambda$ traveling to the right with a velocity v.

13. Prove that $u_n(x, t)$, the nth normal mode of a vibrating string (Eq. 2-24), can be written as the superposition of two similar traveling waves traveling in opposite directions. Let $\phi_n = 0$ in Eq. 2-24.

14. Consider the temperature in a long, thin, uniform, homogeneous bar or wire of length l that is oriented along the x axis and is perfectly insulated laterally, so that heat flows in the x direction only. Then the temperature

T depends only on x and t, and the equation that governs the temperature is the so-called one-dimensional heat equation

$$\frac{\partial T}{\partial t} = \kappa^2 \frac{\partial^2 T}{\partial x^2}$$

where $\kappa^2 = K/\sigma\rho$, K is the thermal conductivity, σ is the specific heat, and ρ is the density of the bar.

Consider the case in which the ends of the bar are kept at zero temperature, so that

$$T(0, t) = T(l, T) = 0$$

Show that the solution to this problem is

$$T(x, t) = \sum_{n=1}^{\infty} B_n e^{-\lambda_n^2 t} \sin \frac{n\pi x}{l}$$

where $\lambda_n = \kappa n\pi/l$.

Incidentally, even though there is an infinite number of unknown constants in this solution, it is possible to find all of them if we are given the initial temperature profile within the bar, that is, if we are given $T(x, 0)$ (cf. Problem 22 in Chapter 4).

15. Sketch the normal modes of a vibrating rectangular membrane and show that they look like those shown in Figure 2-6.

16. This problem is the extension of Problem 10 to two dimensions. In this case, the particle is constrained to move freely over the surface of a rectangle of sides a and b. The Schrödinger equation for this problem is

$$\frac{\partial^2 \psi}{\partial x^2} + \frac{\partial^2 \psi}{\partial y^2} + \left(\frac{8\pi^2 mE}{h^2}\right)\psi(x, y) = 0$$

with the boundary conditions

$$\psi(0, y) = \psi(a, y) = 0 \qquad \text{for all } y, \quad 0 \leq y \leq b$$
$$\psi(x, 0) = \psi(x, b) = 0 \qquad \text{for all } x, \quad 0 \leq x \leq a$$

Solve this equation for $\psi(x, y)$, apply the boundary conditions, and show that the energy is quantized according to

$$E_{n_x n_y} = \frac{n_x^2 h^2}{8ma^2} + \frac{n_y^2 h^2}{8mb^2} \qquad \begin{array}{l} n_x = 1, 2, 3, \ldots \\ n_y = 1, 2, 3, \ldots \end{array}$$

17. Extend Problems 10 and 16 to three dimensions, where a particle is constrained to move freely throughout a rectangular box of sides a, b, and c. The Schrödinger equation for this system is

$$\frac{\partial^2 \psi}{\partial x^2} + \frac{\partial^2 \psi}{\partial y^2} + \frac{\partial^2 \psi}{\partial z^2} + \left(\frac{8\pi^2 mE}{h^2}\right)\psi(x, y, z) = 0$$

and the boundary conditions are that $\psi(x, y, z)$ vanishes over all the surfaces of the box.

Many problems in classical mechanics can be reduced to the problem of solving a differential equation with constant coefficients (cf. Problems 7 and 8). The basic starting point is Newton's second law, which says that the rate of change of momentum is equal to the force acting on a body. Momentum p equals mv, and so if the mass is constant, then in one dimension we have

$$\frac{dp}{dt} = m\frac{dv}{dt} = m\frac{d^2x}{dt^2} = f \tag{2-54}$$

If we are given the force as a function of x, then Eq. 2-54 is a differential equation for $x(t)$, which is called the *trajectory of the particle*. Going back to the simple harmonic oscillator discussed in Problem 7, if we let x be the displacement of the mass from its equilibrium position, then Hooke's law says that $f(x) = -kx$, and the differential equation corresponding to Newton's second law is

$$\frac{d^2x}{dt^2} + kx(t) = 0$$

a differential equation that we have seen several times.

Problems 18–23 illustrate some other applications of differential equations to classical mechanics.

18. Consider a body falling freely from a height x_0 according to Figure 2-9. If we neglect air resistance or viscous drag, the only force acting upon the body is the gravitational force mg. Using the coordinates in Figure 2-9, mg acts in the same direction as x and so the differential equation corre-

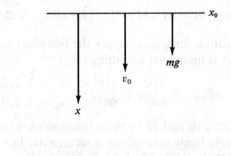

Figure 2-9. A coordinate system for a body falling from a height x_0.

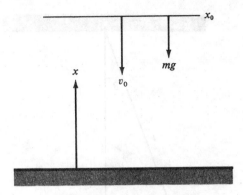

Figure 2-10. Another coordinate system for a body falling from a height x_0.

sponding to Newton's second law is

$$m\frac{d^2x}{dt^2} = mg$$

This can be readily integrated twice to obtain

$$x(t) = \tfrac{1}{2}gt^2 + v_0t + x_0$$

where x_0 and v_0 are the initial values of x and v. According to Figure 2-9, $x_0 = 0$ and so

$$x(t) = \tfrac{1}{2}gt^2 + v_0t$$

If the particle is just dropped, $v_0 = 0$ and so

$$x(t) = \tfrac{1}{2}gt^2$$

Discuss this solution.

Now do the same problem using Figure 2-10 as the definition of the various quantities involved and show that although the equations may look different from those above, they say exactly the same thing because the picture we draw to define the direction of x, v_0, and mg does not affect the falling body.

19. Derive an equation for the maximum height that a body will reach if it is shot straight upward with a velocity v_0. Refer to Figure 2-10 but realize that in this case v_0 points upward. How long will it take for the body to return to earth?

20. Consider a simple pendulum as shown in Figure 2-11. We let the length of the pendulum be l and assume that all the mass of the pendulum is concentrated at its end as shown in Figure 2-11. A physical example of this might be a mass suspended by a string. We assume that the motion of the pendulum is set up such that it oscillates within a plane so that we have a problem in plane polar coordinates. Let the distance along the arc in the figure describe the motion of the pendulum, so that its momentum

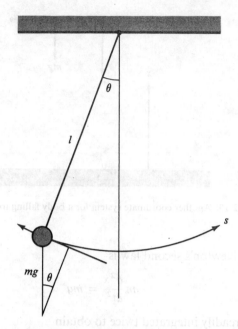

Figure 2-11. The coordinate system describing an oscillating pendulum.

is $m\, ds/dt = ml\, d\theta/dt$ and its rate of change of momentum is $ml\, d^2\theta/dt^2$. Show that the component of force in the direction of motion is $-mg \sin \theta$, where the minus sign occurs because the direction of this force is opposite to that of the angle θ. Show that the equation of motion is

$$ml\frac{d^2\theta}{dt^2} = -mg \sin \theta$$

Now assume that the motion takes place only through very small angles and show that the motion becomes that of a simple harmonic oscillator. What is the natural frequency of this harmonic oscillator? *Hint:* $\sin \theta \approx \theta$ for small values of θ.

21. Consider the motion of a pendulum like that in Problem 20 but swinging in a viscous medium. Suppose that the viscous force is proportional to but oppositely directed to its velocity; that is,

$$f_{\text{viscous}} = -\lambda \frac{ds}{dt} = -\lambda l \frac{d\theta}{dt}$$

where λ is a viscous drag coefficient. Show that, for small angles, Newton's equation is

$$ml\frac{d^2\theta}{dt^2} + \lambda l \frac{d\theta}{dt} + mg\theta = 0$$

Show that there is no harmonic motion if

$$\lambda^2 > \frac{4m^2 g}{l}$$

Does it make physical sense that the medium can be so viscous that the pendulum undergoes no harmonic motion?

22. Consider two pendulums of equal lengths and masses that are connected by a harmonic spring, that is, by a spring that obeys Hooke's law. This system is shown in Figure 2-12. Assuming that the motion takes place in a plane, show that the equations of motion for this system are

$$m\frac{d^2 x}{dt^2} = -m\omega_0^2 x - k(x - y)$$

$$m\frac{d^2 y}{dt^2} = -m\omega_0^2 y - k(y - x)$$

where ω_0 is the natural vibrational frequency of each isolated pendulum [i.e., $\omega_0 = (g/l)^{1/2}$] and k is the force constant of the connecting spring. In order to solve these two simultaneous differential equations, assume that the two pendulums swing harmonically and so try

$$x(t) = Ae^{i\omega t} \qquad y(t) = Be^{i\omega t}$$

Substitute these into the two differential equations and show that we find

$$\left(\omega^2 - \omega_0^2 - \frac{k}{m}\right)A = \frac{k}{m}B$$

$$\left(\omega^2 - \omega_0^2 - \frac{k}{m}\right)B = -\frac{k}{m}A$$

Now we have two simultaneous linear homogeneous algebraic equations for the two amplitudes A and B. The determinant of the coefficients must

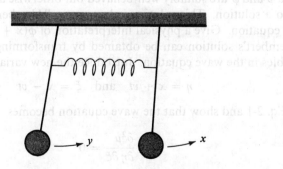

Figure 2-12. Two pendulums coupled by a spring that obeys Hooke's law.

vanish in order for there to be a nontrivial solution. Show that this condition gives

$$\left(\omega^2 - \omega_0^2 - \frac{k}{m}\right)^2 = \left(\frac{k}{m}\right)^2$$

or that there are two natural frequencies for this system; namely,

$$\omega_1^2 = \omega_0^2 \quad \text{and} \quad \omega_2^2 = \omega_0^2 + \frac{2k}{m}$$

Interpret the motion associated with these frequencies by substituting ω_1^2 and ω_2^2 back into the two equations for A and B. The motion associated with these values of A and B are called *normal modes* and any complicated, general motion of this system can be written as a linear combination of these normal modes. Notice that there are two coordinates (x and y) in this problem and two normal modes. We say that this problem has *two degrees of freedom*. We shall see in Chapter 10 that the complicated vibrational motion of molecules can be resolved into a linear combination of natural, or normal, modes.

23. Problem 22 can be solved by introducing center-of-mass and relative coordinates (cf. Section 5-3). Add and subtract the differential equations for $x(t)$ and $y(t)$ and then introduce the new variables

$$\eta = x + y \quad \text{and} \quad \xi = x - y$$

Show that the differential equations for η and ξ are independent. Solve each one and compare your results to Problem 22.

24. Equation 2-29 suggests that $\sin\left[2\pi(x + vt)/\lambda\right]$ and $\sin\left[2\pi(x - vt)/\lambda\right]$ are solutions of the one-dimensional wave equation. Prove that

$$u(x, t) = A \sin\left[\frac{2\pi}{\lambda}(x + vt)\right] + B \sin\left[\frac{2\pi}{\lambda}(x - vt)\right]$$

is a solution to the wave equation. Now prove that

$$u(x, t) = \phi(x + vt) + \psi(x - vt)$$

where ϕ and ψ are suitably well-behaved but otherwise arbitrary functions, is also a solution. This solution is known as d'Alembert's solution of the wave equation. Give a physical interpretation of $\phi(x + vt)$ and $\psi(x - vt)$. D'Alembert's solution can be obtained by transforming the independent variables in the wave equation. Introduce the new variables

$$\eta = x + vt \quad \text{and} \quad \xi = x - vt$$

into Eq. 2-1 and show that the wave equation becomes

$$\frac{\partial^2 u}{\partial \eta \, \partial \xi} = 0$$

This form of the wave equation can be solved by two successive integrations. The first integration gives

$$\frac{\partial u}{\partial \eta} = f(\eta)$$

where $f(\eta)$ is an arbitrary function of η only. Show that a second integration gives

$$u(\eta, \xi) = \int f(\eta)\, d\eta + \psi(\xi)$$

$$= \phi(\eta) + \psi(\xi)$$

or

$$u(x, t) = \phi(x + vt) + \psi(x - vt)$$

Erwin Schrödinger was born in Vienna, Austria, in 1887 and died there in 1961. Schrödinger received his Ph.D. in theoretical physics in 1910 from the University of Vienna. He remained at the university, where his teaching duties included supervising a large physics laboratory course. During World War I he was an officer in fortress artillery, and still he found time to study Einstein's papers on relativity. In 1927 Schrödinger succeeded Max Planck at the University of Berlin at Planck's request. In 1933 Schrödinger left Berlin because of his opposition to Hitler and Nazi policies, and returned to Austria in 1936. After the invasion of Austria by Germany, Schrödinger was forcibly removed from his professorship. Concerned scientists helped him go to Dublin, Ireland, to the Institute of Advanced Studies, which was created for him. He remained in Dublin for seventeen years and then returned to his native Austria and beloved Alps. His influential book, What Is Life?, *caused a number of physicists to become interested in biology. Schrödinger shared the Nobel Prize for physics with P. A. M. Dirac in 1933.*

3

The Schrödinger Equation and Some Simple Applications

THE SCHRÖDINGER EQUATION is our
fundamental equation of quantum mechanics. The solutions to the Schrödinger
equation are called *wave functions*. We shall see that a wave function gives a
complete description of any system. In this chapter, we shall present and discuss
the version of the Schrödinger equation that does not contain time as a variable.
Solutions to this time-independent Schrödinger equation are called *stationary-
state wave functions* because they are independent of time. Many problems of
interest to chemists can be treated by using only stationary-state wave functions.
We shall not consider any time dependence until Chapter 10, where we shall
discuss molecular spectroscopy.

In this chapter, we present the time-independent Schrödinger equation
and then apply it to a free particle of mass m that is restricted to lie along a
one-dimensional interval of length a. This system is called a *particle in a box*
and the calculation of its properties is the standard introductory problem in
quantum mechanics. The particle-in-a-box problem is a simple, yet very instructive, problem. In the course of discussing this problem, we shall introduce
the probabilistic interpretation of wave functions. This will lead us to a digression on some basic ideas of probability, which we shall then use to illustrate
the application of the Uncertainty Principle to a particle in a box.

77

3-1 *The Schrödinger Equation Is the Equation for the Wave Function of a Particle*

We cannot derive the Schrödinger equation anymore than we can derive Newton's laws, and Newton's second law, $f = ma$, in particular. We shall regard the Schrödinger equation to be a fundamental postulate, or axiom of quantum mechanics, just as Newton's laws are fundamental postulates of classical mechanics. Even though we cannot derive the Schrödinger equation, we can at least show that it is plausible and perhaps even trace Schrödinger's original line of thought. We finished Chapter 1 with a discussion of matter waves, arguing that matter has wavelike character, as well as its obvious particlelike character. As one story goes, at a meeting at which this new idea of matter waves was being discussed, someone mentioned that if indeed matter does posses wavelike properties, then there must be some sort of wave equation that governs them.

Let us start with the classical one-dimensional wave equation for simplicity:

$$\frac{\partial^2 u}{\partial x^2} = \frac{1}{v^2}\frac{\partial^2 u}{\partial t^2} \tag{3-1}$$

We have seen in Chapter 2 that Eq. 3-1 can be solved by the method of separation of variables and that $u(x, t)$ can be written as the product of a function of x and a harmonic or sinusoidal function of time. We shall express the temporal part as $\cos \omega t$ (cf. Eq. 2-24) and write $u(x, t)$ as

$$u(x, t) = \psi(x) \cos \omega t \tag{3-2}$$

Because $\psi(x)$ is the spatial factor of the amplitude, $u(x, t)$, we shall call $\psi(x)$ the *spatial amplitude* of the wave. If we substitute Eq. 3-2 into Eq. 3-1, we obtain an equation for the spatial amplitude $\psi(x)$,

$$\frac{d^2\psi}{dx^2} + \frac{\omega^2}{v^2}\,\psi(x) = 0 \tag{3-3}$$

We now introduce the idea of de Broglie matter waves into Eq. 3-3. The total energy of a particle is the sum of its kinetic energy and potential energy,

$$E = \frac{p^2}{2m} + U(x) \tag{3-4}$$

where $U(x)$ is the potential energy. If we solve Eq. 3-4 for the momentum p, then we find

$$p = \{2m[E - U(x)]\}^{1/2} \tag{3-5}$$

According to the de Broglie formula, the wavelength λ associated with this momentum is h/p, and so using Eq. 3-5 for p gives

$$\lambda = \frac{h}{p} = \frac{h}{\{2m[E - U(x)]\}^{1/2}} \tag{3-6}$$

The factor ω^2/v^2 in Eq. 3-3 can be written in terms of λ because $\omega = 2\pi v$ and

$v\lambda = v$. Putting all this together, we have

$$\frac{\omega^2}{v^2} = \frac{4\pi^2 v^2}{v^2} = \frac{4\pi^2}{\lambda^2} = \frac{2m[E - U(x)]}{\hbar^2}$$

Substituting this into Eq. 3-3, we find

$$\frac{d^2\psi}{dx^2} + \frac{2m}{\hbar^2}[E - U(x)]\psi(x) = 0 \qquad\qquad (3\text{-}7)$$

This is the famous *Schrödinger equation*, a differential equation for $\psi(x)$ for a particle of mass m moving in a potential field described by $U(x)$. The exact nature of $\psi(x)$ is vague at this point, but in some sense it is a measure of the amplitude of the matter wave and is called the *wave function* of the particle. Equation 3-7 does not contain time and is called the *time-independent Schrödinger equation*. The wave functions obtained from Eq. 3-7 are called *stationary-state wave functions*. Although there is a more general Schrödinger equation that contains a time dependence (Section 4-3), we shall see throughout the book that a great number of problems of chemical interest can be described in terms of stationary-state wave functions.

Equation 3-7 can be rewritten in the form

$$-\frac{\hbar^2}{2m}\frac{d^2\psi}{dx^2} + U(x)\psi(x) = E\psi(x) \qquad\qquad (3\text{-}8)$$

This is a particularly nice way to write the Schrödinger equation when we introduce the idea of an operator in Section 3-2.

3-2   *The Schrödinger Equation Can Be Formulated as an Eigenvalue Problem*

An *operator* is a symbol that tells you to do something to whatever follows the symbol. For example, we can consider dy/dx to be the d/dx operator operating on the function $y(x)$. Some other examples are SQRT (take the square root of what follows), $\int_0^1$, 3 (multiply by 3), and $\partial/\partial y$. Clearly the operator and the *operand* (the function on which the operator acts) must be compatible; the operation and the result must be mathematically well-defined. We shall usually denote an operator by a capital letter with a carat over it. Thus we write

$$g(x) = \hat{A}f(x)$$

to indicate that the operator $\hat{A}$ operates on $f(x)$ to give a new function $g(x)$.

EXAMPLE 3-1

Perform the following operations.

(a) $\hat{A}(2x)$, $\hat{A} = \dfrac{d^2}{dx^2}$

(b) $\hat{A}(x^2)$, $\hat{A} = \dfrac{d^2}{dx^2} + 2\dfrac{d}{dx} + 3$

(c) $\hat{A}(xy^3)$, $\hat{A} = \dfrac{\partial}{\partial y}$

Solution:

(a) $\hat{A}(2x) = \dfrac{d^2}{dx^2}(2x) = 0$

(b) $\hat{A}(x^2) = \dfrac{d^2}{dx^2}x^2 + 2\dfrac{d}{dx}x^2 + 3x^2 = 2 + 4x + 3x^2$

(c) $\hat{A}(xy^3) = \dfrac{\partial}{\partial y}xy^3 = 3xy^2$

In quantum mechanics, we deal only with *linear operators*. An operator is said to be linear if

$$\hat{A}[c_1 f_1(x) + c_2 f_2(x)] = c_1\hat{A}f_1(x) + c_2\hat{A}f_2(x) \tag{3-9}$$

where c_1 and c_2 are (possibly complex) constants. Clearly the "differentiate" and "integrate" operators are linear because

$$\frac{d}{dx}[c_1 f_1(x) + c_2 f_2(x)] = c_1\frac{df_1}{dx} + c_2\frac{df_2}{dx}$$

and

$$\int [c_1 f_1(x) + c_2 f_2(x)]\,dx = c_1\int f_1(x)\,dx + c_2\int f_2(x)\,dx$$

The "square" operator, SQR, on the other hand, is nonlinear because

$$\text{SQR}[c_1 f_1(x) + c_2 f_2(x)] = c_1^2 f_1^2(x) + c_2^2 f_2^2(x) + 2c_1 c_2 f_1(x)f_2(x)$$
$$\neq c_1 f_1^2(x) + c_2 f_2^2(x)$$

as it must in order to satisfy Eq. 3-9.

EXAMPLE 3-2

Determine whether the following operators are linear or nonlinear.

(a) $\hat{A}f(x) = \text{SQRT}\, f(x)$
(b) $\hat{A}f(x) = x^2 f(x)$

Solution:

(a) $\hat{A}[c_1 f_1(x) + c_2 f_2(x)] = [c_1 f_1(x) + c_2 f_2(x)]^{1/2}$
$$\neq c_1 f_1^{1/2}(x) + c_2 f_2^{1/2}(x)$$

and so SQRT is a nonlinear operator.

(b) $\hat{A}[c_1 f_1(x) + c_2 f_2(x)] = x^2[c_1 f_1(x) + c_2 f_2(x)]$
$$= c_1 x^2 f_1(x) + c_2 x^2 f_2(x)$$
$$= c_1 \hat{A} f_1(x) + c_2 \hat{A} f_2(x)$$

and so x^2 (multiply by x^2) is a linear operator.

A problem that occurs frequently is the following: Given $\hat{A}$, find a function $\phi(x)$ *and* a constant a such that

$$\hat{A}\phi(x) = a\phi(x) \qquad (3\text{-}10)$$

Note that the result of operating on the function $\phi(x)$ by $\hat{A}$ is simply to give $\phi(x)$ back again, only multiplied by a constant factor. Clearly $\hat{A}$ and $\phi(x)$ have a very special relationship with respect to each other. The function $\phi(x)$ is called an *eigenfunction* of the operator $\hat{A}$, and a is called an *eigenvalue*. The problem of determining $\phi(x)$ and a for a given $\hat{A}$ is called an *eigenvalue problem*.

EXAMPLE 3-3

Show that $e^{\alpha x}$ is an eigenfunction of the operator $\hat{D}^n$ (differentiate with respect to x n times). What is the eigenvalue?

Solution: We differentiate $e^{\alpha x}$ n times and obtain

$$\hat{D}^n e^{\alpha x} = \frac{d^n}{dx^n} e^{\alpha x} = \alpha^n e^{\alpha x}$$

and so the eigenvalue is α^n.

Operators can be imaginary or complex quantities. We shall see that the x component of the momentum can be represented in quantum mechanics by an operator of the form

$$\hat{P}_x = -i\hbar \frac{\partial}{\partial x} \qquad (3\text{-}11)$$

EXAMPLE 3-4

Show that e^{ikx} is an eigenfunction of the momentum operator, $\hat{P}_x = -i\hbar \, \partial/\partial x$. What is the eigenvalue?

Solution: We apply $\hat{P}_x$ to e^{ikx} and find

$$\hat{P}_x e^{ikx} = -i\hbar \frac{\partial}{\partial x} e^{ikx} = \hbar k e^{ikx}$$

and so we see that e^{ikx} is an eigenfunction and $\hbar k$ is an eigenvalue of the momentum operator.

Let us go back to Eq. 3-8. We can write the left-hand side of Eq. 3-8 in the form

$$\left[-\frac{\hbar^2}{2m}\frac{d^2}{dx^2} + U(x)\right]\psi(x) = E\psi(x) \tag{3-12}$$

If we denote the operator in brackets by $\hat{H}$, then Eq. 3-12 is

$$\hat{H}\psi(x) = E\psi(x) \tag{3-13}$$

We have formulated the Schrödinger equation as an eigenvalue problem. The operator $\hat{H}$,

$$\hat{H} = -\frac{\hbar^2}{2m}\frac{d^2}{dx^2} + U(x) \tag{3-14}$$

is called the *Hamiltonian operator. The wave function is an eigenfunction and the energy is an eigenvalue of the Hamiltonian operator.* This suggests a correspondence between the Hamiltonian operator and the energy. We shall see that such correspondences of operators and classical-mechanical variables are fundamental to the formalism of quantum mechanics.

3-3 *Classical-Mechanical Quantities Are Represented by Linear Operators in Quantum Mechanics*

If $U(x) = 0$ in Eq. 3-14, the energy is all kinetic energy and so we define a kinetic energy operator according to

$$\hat{K} = -\frac{\hbar^2}{2m}\frac{d^2}{dx^2} \tag{3-15}$$

Furthermore, classically, $K = p^2/2m$, and so we conclude that

$$\hat{P}^2 = -\hbar^2\frac{d^2}{dx^2} \tag{3-16}$$

We can interpret the operator $\hat{P}^2$ by considering the case of two operators acting sequentially, as in $\hat{A}\hat{B}f(x)$. In cases like this, we apply each operator in turn, working from right to left. Thus

$$\hat{A}\hat{B}f(x) = \hat{A}[\hat{B}f(x)] = \hat{A}h(x)$$

where $h(x) = \hat{B}f(x)$. Once again we require that all the indicated operations be compatible. If $\hat{A} = \hat{B}$, we have $\hat{A}\hat{A}f(x)$ and denote this as $\hat{A}^2f(x)$. Note that $\hat{A}^2f(x) \neq [\hat{A}f(x)]^2$ for arbitrary $f(x)$.

EXAMPLE 3-5

Given $\hat{A} = d/dx$ and $\hat{B} = x^2$ (multiply by x^2), show (a) that $\hat{A}^2f(x) \neq [\hat{A}f(x)]^2$ and (b) that $\hat{A}\hat{B}f(x) \neq \hat{B}\hat{A}f(x)$ for arbitrary $f(x)$.

Solution:

(a)
$$\hat{A}^2 f(x) = \frac{d}{dx}\left(\frac{df}{dx}\right) = \frac{d^2 f}{dx^2}$$

$$[\hat{A}f(x)]^2 = \left(\frac{df}{dx}\right)^2 \neq \frac{d^2 f}{dx^2}$$

for arbitrary $f(x)$.

(b)
$$\hat{A}\hat{B}f(x) = \frac{d}{dx}[x^2 f(x)] = 2xf(x) + x^2 \frac{df}{dx}$$

$$\hat{B}\hat{A}f(x) = x^2 \frac{df}{dx} \neq \hat{A}\hat{B}f(x)$$

for arbitrary $f(x)$.

We see from this last case that the order of the application of operators must be specified. If $\hat{A}$ and $\hat{B}$ are such that

$$\hat{A}\hat{B}f(x) = \hat{B}\hat{A}f(x)$$

for any compatible $f(x)$, the two operators are said to *commute*. The two operators in this example, however, do not commute. Prove to yourself that the two operators d/dx and 2 (multiply by 2) do commute.

The operator $\hat{P}^2$ in Eq. 3-15 can be factored as

$$\hat{P}^2 = -\hbar^2 \frac{d^2}{dx^2} = \left(-i\hbar \frac{d}{dx}\right)\left(-i\hbar \frac{d}{dx}\right)$$

Note that this is consistent with Eq. 3-11.

3-4 *Wave Functions Have a Probabilistic Interpretation*

In this section we shall study the case of a free particle of mass m constrained to lie along the x axis between $x = 0$ and $x = a$. This is called the *problem of a particle in a one-dimensional box* (cf. Figure 3-1). It is mathematically a fairly simple problem, so it is possible to study the solutions in

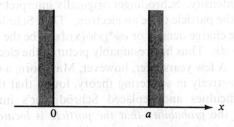

Figure 3-1. The geometry of the problem of a particle in a one-dimensional box.

Max Born (1882–1970) studied mathematics and physics at Breslau, Heidelberg, Zurich, and Göttingen, where he received his Ph.D. in 1907. In 1917 he was appointed professor at the University of Berlin to relieve Max Planck of his teaching duties. In 1921, Born returned to Göttingen, which became a center of theoretical physics. Wolfgang Pauli and Werner Heisenberg were both assistants to Born at Göttingen. In 1933 Born left Germany because of Hitler's rise to power. In 1936 he obtained a position at the University of Edinburgh, where he remained until his retirement in 1953. Although Born became a British subject, he returned to Göttingen after his retirement. Born was awarded the Nobel Prize for physics in 1954.

great detail and to extract and discuss their physical consequences, which carry over to more complicated problems. In addition, we shall see that this simple model has at least a crude application to the π electrons in a linear conjugated hydrocarbon.

The terminology *free particle* means that the particle experiences no potential energy or that $U(x) = 0$. If we set $U(x) = 0$ in Eq. 3-7, we see that the Schrödinger equation for a free particle in a one-dimensional box is

$$\frac{d^2\psi}{dx^2} + \frac{2mE}{\hbar^2}\,\psi(x) = 0 \qquad 0 \leq x \leq a \qquad (3\text{-}17)$$

The particle is restricted to the region $0 \leq x \leq a$ and so cannot be found outside this region (cf. Figure 3-1). In order to implement the condition that the particle is restricted to the region $0 \leq x \leq a$, we must formulate an interpretation of the wave function $\psi(x)$. We have said that $\psi(x)$ represents the amplitude of the particle in some sense. Because the intensity of a wave is the square of the magnitude of the amplitude (cf. Problem 3-30), we can write that the "intensity of the particle" is proportional to $\psi^*(x)\psi(x)$, where the asterisk here denotes a complex conjugate (cf. Appendix B). The problem lies in just what we mean by intensity. Schrödinger originally interpreted it in the following way. Suppose the particle to be an electron. Then Schrödinger considered $e\psi^*(x)\psi(x)$ to be the charge density or $e\psi^*(x)\psi(x)\,dx$ to be the amount of charge between x and $x + dx$. Thus he presumably pictured the electron to be spread all over the region. A few years later, however, Max Born, a German physicist who was working actively in scattering theory, found that this interpretation led to logical difficulties and replaced Schrödinger's interpretation with $\psi^*(x)\psi(x)\,dx$ being the *probability that the particle is located between x and $x + dx$*. Born's view is now generally accepted.

Because the particle is restricted to the region $(0, a)$, the probability that the particle is found outside the region $(0, a)$ is zero. Consequently, we shall require that $\psi(x) = 0$ outside the region $0 \leq x \leq a$. This is mathematically how we restrict the particle to the region $(0, a)$. Furthermore, because $\psi(x)$ is a measure of the position of the particle, we shall require that $\psi(x)$ be a continuous function. If $\psi(x) = 0$ outside the interval $0 \leq x \leq a$ and is a continuous function, then

$$\psi(0) = \psi(a) = 0 \tag{3-18}$$

These are boundary conditions that are imposed onto the problem.

3-5 *The Energy of a Particle in a Box Is Quantized*

The general solution of Eq. 3-17 is (cf. Example 2-4)

$$\psi(x) = A \cos kx + B \sin kx$$

with

$$k = \frac{(2mE)^{1/2}}{\hbar} \tag{3-19}$$

The first boundary condition requires that $\psi(0) = 0$, which implies immediately that $A = 0$. The second boundary condition gives us that

$$\psi(a) = B \sin ka = 0 \tag{3-20}$$

We reject the obvious choice that $B = 0$ because this yields a trivial solution, $\psi(x) = 0$, for all x. The other choice is that

$$ka = n\pi \qquad n = 1, 2, \ldots \tag{3-21}$$

(compare all this to Eqs. 2-17 through 2-19). By using Eq. 3-19 for k, we find that

$$E_n = \frac{h^2 n^2}{8ma^2} \qquad n = 1, 2, \ldots \tag{3-22}$$

Thus, the energy turns out to have only the discrete values given by Eq. 3-22 and no other values. The energy of the particle is said to be *quantized* and the integer n is called a *quantum number*. Note that the quantization arises rather naturally from the boundary conditions. We seem to have gone beyond the stage of Planck and Bohr where quantum numbers are introduced in an ad hoc manner. The natural occurrence of quantum numbers was an exciting feature of the Schrödinger equation, and, in the introduction to the first of his now famous series of four papers published in 1926, Schrödinger says.

> In this communication I wish to show that the usual rules of quantization can be replaced by another postulate (the Schrödinger equation) in which there occurs no mention of whole numbers. Instead, the introduction of integers arises in the same natural way as, for example, in a vibrating string, for which the number of nodes is integral. The new conception can be generalized, and I believe that it penetrates deeply into the true nature of the quantum rules.

The wave function corresponding to E_n is

$$\psi_n(x) = B \sin kx$$

$$= B \sin \frac{n\pi x}{a} \qquad n = 1, 2, \ldots \qquad (3\text{-}23)$$

We shall determine the constant B shortly. These wave functions are plotted in Figure 3-2. They look just like the standing waves set up in a vibrating

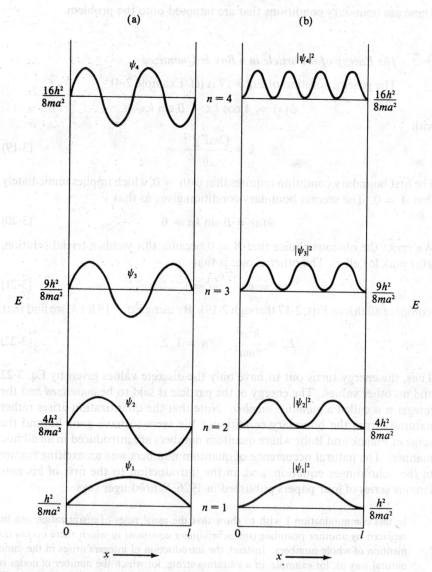

Figure 3-2. The energy levels, wave functions (a) and probability densities (b) for the particle in a box.

string (cf. Figure 2-2, Problem 8). Note that the energy increases with the number of nodes.

The model of a particle in a one-dimensional box has been applied to the π electrons in linear conjugated hydrocarbons. Consider butadiene, $H_2C=CH-CH=CH_2$, which has four π electrons. Although butadiene, like all polyenes, is not a linear molecule, we shall assume for simplicity that the π electrons in butadiene move along a straight line whose length can be estimated as equal to two $C=C$ bond lengths, or 2×1.35 Å, plus one $C-C$ bond, or 1.54 Å, plus the distance of a carbon atom radius at each end, or another 1.54 Å, for a total of 5.78 Å. According to Eq. 3-22, the energy states are given by

$$E_n = \frac{n^2 h^2}{8ma^2} \qquad n = 1, 2, \ldots$$

But the Pauli Exclusion Principle (which we shall discuss later but is assumed here to be known from general chemistry) says that each of these states can hold only two electrons (with opposite spins) and so the four π electrons fill the first two levels as shown in Figure 3-3. The energy of the first excited state of this system of four π electrons is that having one electron elevated to the $n = 3$ state (cf. Figure 3-3), and the energy to make a transition from the $n = 2$ state to the $n = 3$ state is

$$\Delta E = \frac{h^2}{8ma^2} (3^2 - 2^2)$$

The mass m is that of an electron and the width of the box is given above to be 5.78 Å, or 5.78×10^{-10} m. Therefore

$$\Delta E = \frac{(6.626 \times 10^{-34} \text{ J·s})^2 5}{8(9.110 \times 10^{-31} \text{ kg})(5.78 \times 10^{-10} \text{ m})^2} = 9.02 \times 10^{-19} \text{ J}$$

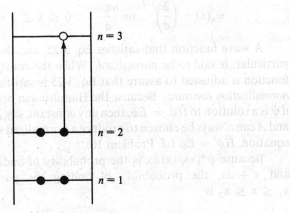

Figure 3-3. The free-electron model energy-level scheme for butadiene.

and

$$\bar{v} = 4.54 \times 10^4 \text{ cm}^{-1}$$

Butadiene has an absorption at $4.61 \times 10^4 \text{ cm}^{-1}$, and so we see that this very simple model, called the *free-electron model*, is somewhat successful (cf. Problem 9).

3-6   *Wave Functions Are Normalized*

According to the Born interpretation,

$$\psi_n^*(x)\psi_n(x)\,dx = B^*B \sin^2 \frac{n\pi x}{a}\,dx \qquad (3\text{-}24)$$

is the probability that the particle is located between x and $x + dx$. Because the particle is restricted to the region $(0, a)$, it is certain to be found there and so the probability that the particle lies between 0 and a is unity. The probability that the particle lies between 0 and a is given by

$$\int_0^a \psi_n^*(x)\psi_n(x)\,dx = 1 \qquad (3\text{-}25)$$

If we substitute Eq. 3-24 into Eq. 3-25, we find that

$$|B|^2 \int_0^a \sin^2 \frac{n\pi x}{a}\,dx = 1 \qquad (3\text{-}26)$$

We let $n\pi x/a$ be z in Eq. 3-26 to obtain

$$\int_0^a \sin^2 \frac{n\pi x}{a}\,dx = \frac{a}{n\pi} \int_0^{n\pi} \sin^2 z\,dz = \frac{a}{n\pi}\left(\frac{n\pi}{2}\right) = \frac{a}{2} \qquad (3\text{-}27)$$

Therefore, $B^2(a/2) = 1$, $B = (2/a)^{1/2}$, and

$$\psi_n(x) = \left(\frac{2}{a}\right)^{1/2} \sin \frac{n\pi x}{a} \qquad 0 \le x \le a \quad n = 1, 2, 3, \ldots \qquad (3.28)$$

A wave function that satisfies Eq. 3-25, and the one given by Eq. 3-28 in particular, is said to be *normalized*. When the constant that multiplies a wave function is adjusted to assure that Eq. 3-25 is satisfied, the constant is called a *normalization constant*. Because the Hamiltonian operator is a linear operator, if ψ is a solution to $\hat{H}\psi = E\psi$, then any constant, say A, times ψ is also a solution and A can always be chosen to produce a normalized solution to the Schrödinger equation, $\hat{H}\psi = E\psi$ (cf. Problem 10).

Because $\psi^*(x)\psi(x)\,dx$ is the probability of finding the particle between x and $x + dx$, the probability of finding the particle within the interval $x_1 \le x \le x_2$ is

$$\text{Prob}\{x_1 \le x \le x_2\} = \int_{x_1}^{x_2} \psi^*(x)\psi(x)\,dx \qquad (3\text{-}29)$$

EXAMPLE 3-6

Calculate the probability that a particle in a one-dimensional box of length a is found to be between 0 and $a/2$.

Solution: The probability that the particle will be found between 0 and $a/2$ is

$$\text{Prob} = \int_0^{a/2} \psi^*(x)\psi(x)\, dx = \frac{2}{a}\int_0^{a/2} \sin^2 \frac{n\pi x}{a}\, dx$$

If we let $n\pi x/a$ be z, then we find

$$\text{Prob} = \frac{2}{n\pi}\int_0^{n\pi/2} \sin^2 z\, dz = \frac{2}{n\pi}\left.\left|\frac{x}{2} - \frac{\sin 2x}{4}\right.\right|_0^{n\pi/2}$$

$$= \frac{2}{n\pi}\left(\frac{n\pi}{4} - \frac{\sin n\pi}{4}\right) = \frac{1}{2} \quad \text{(for all } n)$$

Thus the probability that the particle lies in one-half of the interval $(0, a)$ is $\frac{1}{2}$.

We can also calculate averages and standard deviations, and this leads us to the next topic, which is a disgression on probability.

3-7   *The Variance Is a Measure of the Spread of a Distribution About Its Mean*

Consider some experiment, such as the tossing of a coin or the rolling of a die, which has n possible outcomes, each with probability f_j, where $j = 1, 2, \ldots, n$. If the experiment is repeated indefinitely, we intuitively expect that

$$f_j = \lim_{N \to \infty} \frac{N_j}{N} \quad j = 1, 2, \ldots, n \tag{3-30}$$

where N_j is the number of times that the event j occurs and N is the total number of repetitions of the experiment. Because $0 \le N_j \le N$, f_j must satisfy the condition

$$0 \le f_j \le 1 \tag{3-31}$$

When $f_j = 1$, we say that the event j is a certainty and when $f_j = 0$, we say that it is impossible. In addition, because

$$\sum_{j=1}^{n} N_j = N$$

we have the normalization condition,

$$\sum_{j=1}^{n} f_j = 1 \tag{3-32}$$

Suppose now that some number x_j is associated with the outcome j. Then we define the *average* of x or the *expectation value* of x to be

$$\bar{x} \equiv \langle x \rangle = \sum_{j=1}^{n} x_j f_j = \sum_{j=1}^{n} x_j f(x_j) \tag{3-33}$$

where in the last term we have used the expanded notation $f(x_j)$, meaning the probability of realizing the number x_j.

EXAMPLE 3-7

Suppose we are given the following data

x	$f(x)$
1	0.20
3	0.25
4	0.55

Calculate the average value of x.

Solution: Using Eq. 3-33, we have

$$\langle x \rangle = (1)(0.20) + (3)(0.25) + (4)(0.55) = 3.15$$

EXAMPLE 3-8

Suppose you are involved in a game in which you win a dollar if a coin comes up heads and you lose a dollar if it comes up tails. Calculate your expected winnings in this game.

Solution: In this case, $f_j = \frac{1}{2}$ for $j = 1$ and 2. If we let $j = 1$ be heads and $j = 2$ be tails, then $x_1 = +1$ and $x_2 = -1$. Our expectation, then, is

$$\langle x \rangle = \sum_{j=1}^{2} x_j f_j = \frac{1}{2} \sum_{j=1}^{2} x_j = 0$$

as you might have guessed.

It is helpful to interpret a probability distribution like f_j as a distribution of a unit mass along the x axis in a discrete manner such that f_j is the amount of mass or the fraction of mass located at the point x_j. This interpretation is shown in Figure 3-4. According to this interpretation, the average value of x is the center of mass of this system. Another quantity of importance is

$$\langle x^2 \rangle = \sum_{j=1}^{n} x_j^2 f_j \tag{3-34}$$

This is called the *second moment* of the distribution $\{f_j\}$ and is analogous to the moment of inertia.

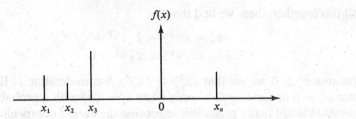

Figure 3-4. The discrete probability frequency function or probability density, $f(x)$.

EXAMPLE 3-9

Calculate the second moment of the data given in Example 3-7.

Solution: Using Eq. 3-34, we have

$$\langle x^2 \rangle = (1)^2(0.20) + (3)^2(0.25) + (4)^2(0.55) = 11.25$$

Note from Examples 3-7 and 3-9 that $\langle x^2 \rangle \neq \langle x \rangle^2$. This is a general result that we shall prove below.

A physically more interesting quantity than $\langle x^2 \rangle$ is the *second central moment*, or the *variance*, defined by

$$\sigma_x^2 = \langle (x - \langle x \rangle)^2 \rangle = \sum_{j=1}^{n} (x_j - \langle x \rangle)^2 f_j \qquad (3\text{-}35)$$

As the notation suggests, we shall denote the square root of the quantity in Eq. 3-35 by σ_x. By thinking about the summation in Eq. 3-35, we can see that σ_x^2 will be large if x_j is likely to differ from $\langle x \rangle$, because in that case $(x_j - \langle x \rangle)$ and so $(x_j - \langle x \rangle)^2$ will be large for the significant values of f_j. On the other hand, σ_x^2 will be small if x_j is not likely to differ from $\langle x \rangle$, or if the x_j cluster around $\langle x \rangle$, because then $(x_j - \langle x \rangle)^2$ will be small for the significant values of f_j. Thus we see that the variance is a measure of the spread of the distribution about its mean.

Equation 3-35 shows that σ_x^2 is a sum of positive terms, and so $\sigma_x^2 \geq 0$. Furthermore,

$$\sigma_x^2 = \sum_{j=1}^{n} (x_j - \langle x \rangle)^2 f_j = \sum_{j=1}^{n} (x_j^2 - 2\langle x \rangle x_j + \langle x \rangle^2) f_j$$

$$= \sum_{j=1}^{n} x_j^2 f_j - 2 \sum_{j=1}^{n} \langle x \rangle x_j f_j + \sum_{j=1}^{n} \langle x \rangle^2 f_j$$

The first term here is just $\langle x^2 \rangle$ (cf. Eq. 3-34). To evaluate the second and third terms, it is important to realize that $\langle x \rangle$, the average of x_j, is just a number and so can be factored out of the summations, leaving a summation of the form $\sum x_j f_j$ in the second term and $\sum f_j$ in the third term. This first summation is $\langle x \rangle$ by definition and the second is unity because of normalization. Putting all this together, then, we find that

$$\sigma_x^2 = \langle x^2 \rangle - 2\langle x \rangle^2 + \langle x \rangle^2$$
$$= \langle x^2 \rangle - \langle x \rangle^2 \geq 0 \tag{3-36}$$

Because $\sigma_x^2 \geq 0$, we see that $\langle x^2 \rangle \geq \langle x \rangle^2$. A consideration of Eq. 3-35 shows that $\sigma_x^2 = 0$ or $\langle x^2 \rangle = \langle x \rangle^2$ only when $x_j = \langle x \rangle$ with a probability of one, a case that is not really probabilistic because the event j occurs all the time.

3-8   *A Continuous Probability Distribution May Be Pictured As a Unit Mass Distributed Continuously Along an Axis*

So far we have considered only discrete distributions. It turns out that continuous distributions are more important for our purposes. It is convenient to use the unit mass analogy. Consider a unit mass to be distributed continuously along the x axis, or along some interval on the x axis. We define linear mass density $\rho(x)$ by

$$dm = \rho(x)\,dx$$

where dm is the fraction of the mass lying between x and $x + dx$. By analogy, then, we say that the probability that some quantity x, such as the position of a particle in a box, lies between x and $x + dx$ is

$$\text{Prob}\,\{x, x + dx\} = f(x)\,dx \tag{3-37}$$

and that

$$\text{Prob}\,\{a \leq x \leq b\} = \int_a^b f(x)\,dx \tag{3-38}$$

In the mass analogy, $\text{Prob}\,\{a \leq x \leq b\}$ is the fraction of mass that lies in the interval $a \leq x \leq b$. The normalization condition is

$$\int_{-\infty}^{\infty} f(x)\,dx = 1 \tag{3-39}$$

Following Eqs. 3-33 through 3-35, we have the definitions

$$\langle x \rangle = \int_{-\infty}^{\infty} x f(x)\,dx \tag{3-40}$$

$$\langle x^2 \rangle = \int_{-\infty}^{\infty} x^2 f(x)\,dx \tag{3-41}$$

and

$$\sigma_x^2 = \int_{-\infty}^{\infty} (x - \langle x \rangle)^2 f(x)\,dx \tag{3-42}$$

EXAMPLE 3-10

Perhaps the simplest continuous distribution is the so-called uniform distribution, where

$$f(x) = \text{constant} = A \qquad a \leq x \leq b$$
$$= 0 \qquad\qquad\qquad \text{otherwise}$$

Show that A must equal $1/(b - a)$. Evaluate $\langle x \rangle$, $\langle x^2 \rangle$, σ_x^2, and σ_x for this distribution.

Solution: Because $f(x)$ must be normalized,

$$\int_a^b f(x)\,dx = 1 = A \int_a^b dx$$

$$= A(b - a)$$

and so $A = 1/(b - a)$ and

$$f(x) = \frac{1}{b - a} \qquad a \le x \le b$$

$$= 0 \qquad\qquad \text{otherwise}$$

The mean of x is given by

$$\langle x \rangle = \int_a^b x f(x)\,dx = \frac{1}{b - a} \int_a^b x\,dx$$

$$= \frac{b^2 - a^2}{2(b - a)} = \frac{b + a}{2}$$

and the second moment of x is

$$\langle x^2 \rangle = \int_a^b x^2 f(x)\,dx = \frac{1}{b - a} \int_a^b x^2\,dx = \frac{b^3 - a^3}{3(b - a)}$$

$$= \frac{b^2 + ab + a^2}{3}$$

Lastly, the variance is given by Eq. 3-36, and so

$$\sigma_x^2 = \langle x^2 \rangle - \langle x \rangle^2 = \frac{(b - a)^2}{12}$$

and

$$\sigma_x = \frac{(b - a)}{\sqrt{12}}$$

EXAMPLE 3-11

The most commonly occurring continuous probability distribution is the Gaussian, or normal, distribution, given by

$$f(x)\,dx = ce^{-x^2/2a^2}\,dx \qquad -\infty \le x \le \infty$$

Find c, $\langle x \rangle$, σ^2, and σ.

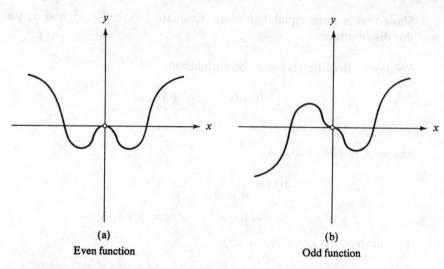

Figure 3-5. (a) An even function, $y(x) = y(-x)$. (b) An odd function, $y(x) = -y(-x)$.

Solution: The constant c is determined by normalization,

$$\int_{-\infty}^{\infty} f(x)\,dx = 1 = c \int_{-\infty}^{\infty} e^{-x^2/2a^2}\,dx = c(2\pi a^2)^{1/2}$$

or $c = 1/(2\pi a^2)^{1/2}$. The mean of x is given by

$$\langle x \rangle = \int_{-\infty}^{\infty} x f(x)\,dx = (2\pi a^2)^{-1/2} \int_{-\infty}^{\infty} x e^{-x^2/2a^2}\,dx$$

This integral can be evaluated by inspection if we recognize the odd-even property of the integrand. Recall that a function $y(x)$ is odd if $y(x) = -y(-x)$. The graph of an odd function looks like that shown in Figure 3-5(b). The integral of an odd function between the symmetric limits $-A$ and $+A$ is zero because the area on one side of the y axis cancels the area on the other side. The integrand in the expression for $\langle x \rangle$ is $x e^{-x^2/2a^2}$. This is an odd function, and so $\langle x \rangle = 0$.

The variance of x is given by

$$\sigma^2 = \langle x^2 \rangle - \langle x \rangle^2 = (2\pi a^2)^{-1/2} \int_{-\infty}^{\infty} x^2 e^{-x^2/2a^2}\,dx$$

The integrand in this case is even because $y(x) = x^2 e^{-x^2/2a^2} = y(-x)$. The graph of an even function is symmetric across the y axis [cf. Figure 3-5(a)] and so

$$\sigma^2 = 2(2\pi a^2)^{-1/2} \int_{0}^{\infty} x^2 e^{-x^2/2a^2}\,dx$$

This integral can be evaluated with the use of integral tables (see also Problem 15 in Chapter 5), and the result is that

$$\sigma^2 = \frac{2}{(2\pi a^2)^{1/2}} \frac{(2\pi a^2)^{1/2} a^2}{2} = a^2$$

and

$$\sigma = a$$

The variance of a normal distribution is the parameter that appears in the exponential. A Gaussian distribution function is written as

$$f(x)\,dx = (2\pi\sigma^2)^{-1/2}e^{-x^2/2\sigma^2}\,dx$$

With this brief introduction to probability theory, we are ready to go back to the particle in a one-dimensional box.

3-9   *The Average Momentum of a Particle in a Box Is Zero*

Because $\psi^*(x)\psi(x)\,dx$ has a probabilistic interpretation, we can use wave functions to calculate average values and variances. Using the example of a particle in a box, we see that

$$f(x)\,dx = \frac{2}{a}\sin^2\frac{n\pi x}{a}\,dx \qquad 0 \le x \le a$$

$$= 0 \qquad\qquad\qquad \text{otherwise} \qquad\qquad (3\text{-}43)$$

is the probability that the particle is found between x and $x + dx$. These probabilities are plotted in Figure 3-2. The average value of x, or the mean position of the particle, is

$$\langle x \rangle = \frac{2}{a}\int_0^a x\sin^2\frac{n\pi x}{a}\,dx \qquad\qquad (3\text{-}44)$$

This integral, as well as several others that we need, is discussed in **Problem 15** and equals $a^2/4$. Therefore (see **Problem 16**)

$$\langle x \rangle = \frac{a}{2} \qquad \text{(for all } n\text{)} \qquad\qquad (3\text{-}45)$$

This is the physically expected result because the particle sees nothing except the walls at $x = 0$ and $x = a$, and so by symmetry $\langle x \rangle$ must be $a/2$.

We can calculate the spread about $\langle x \rangle$ by calculating σ_x^2. First we calculate $\langle x^2 \rangle$, which is

$$\langle x^2 \rangle = \frac{2}{a}\int_0^a x^2\sin^2\frac{n\pi x}{a}\,dx$$

$$= \left(\frac{a}{2\pi n}\right)^2\left(\frac{4\pi^2 n^2}{3} - 2\right) \qquad\qquad (3\text{-}46)$$

The variance of x is

$$\sigma_x^2 = \langle x^2 \rangle - \langle x \rangle^2 = \left(\frac{a}{2\pi n}\right)^2\left(\frac{\pi^2 n^2}{3} - 2\right)$$

and so

$$\sigma_x = \frac{a}{2\pi n} \left(\frac{\pi^2 n^2}{3} - 2 \right)^{1/2} \tag{3-47}$$

We shall see that σ_x is directly involved in the Heisenberg Uncertainty Principle.

A problem arises if we wish to calculate the average energy or momentum because they are represented by differential operators. Recall that the energy and momentum operators are

$$\hat{H} = -\frac{\hbar^2}{2m} \frac{d^2}{dx^2} + U(x)$$

and

$$\hat{P} = -i\hbar \frac{d}{dx}$$

The problem is that we must decide whether the operator works on $\psi^*(x)\psi(x)$ or on $\psi(x)$ or $\psi^*(x)$ alone. To determine this, let us go back to the Schrödinger equation in operator notation

$$\hat{H}\psi_n(x) = E_n\psi_n(x) \tag{3-48}$$

If we multiply this equation from the left by $\psi_n^*(x)$ and integrate over all values of x, we obtain

$$\int \psi_n^*(x)\hat{H}\psi_n(x)\,dx = E_n \int \psi_n^*(x)\psi_n(x)\,dx$$

$$= E_n \tag{3-49}$$

where the last step follows because $\psi_n(x)$ is normalized. Equation 3-49 suggests that we sandwich the operator between ψ^* and ψ in order to calculate the average value of the physical quantity associated with that operator. We shall set this up as a formal postulate in Chapter 4, but what we are assuming is that

$$\langle s \rangle = \int \psi^* \hat{S} \psi \, dx \tag{3-50}$$

where $\hat{S}$ is the quantum-mechanical operator associated with the physical quantity s, and $\langle s \rangle$ is the average value of s in the state described by the wave function ψ. For example, the average momentum of a particle in a box in the state described by $\psi_n(x)$ is

$$\langle p \rangle = \int_0^a \left[\left(\frac{2}{a} \right)^{1/2} \sin \frac{n\pi x}{a} \right] \left(-i\hbar \frac{d}{dx} \right) \left[\left(\frac{2}{a} \right)^{1/2} \sin \frac{n\pi x}{a} \right] dx \tag{3-51}$$

Notice that the operator is sandwiched in between ψ_n^* and ψ_n and so operates only on ψ_n because only ψ_n lies to the right of the operator. We did not have to worry about this when we calculated $\langle x \rangle$ above because the position operator $\hat{X}$ is simply the "multiply by x" operator and it makes no difference where we put it in the integrand in Eq. 3-50.

If we simplify Eq. 3-51, then we find

$$\langle p \rangle = -i\hbar \frac{2\pi n}{a^2} \int_0^a \sin \frac{n\pi x}{a} \cos \frac{n\pi x}{a} \, dx$$

By consulting either a table of integrals or Problem 18, we find that this integral is equal to zero, and so

$$\langle p \rangle = 0 \tag{3-52}$$

3-10   A Particle in a One-Dimensional Box Is Equally Likely to Be Moving in Either Direction

It is interesting to look at the result given by Eq. 3-52 in more depth. If we operate on the particle-in-a-box wave functions by the momentum operator (Eq. 3-11), then we find

$$\hat{P}\psi_n(x) = \hat{P}\left(\frac{2}{a}\right)^{1/2} \sin \frac{n\pi x}{a} = -i\hbar \frac{d}{dx}\left(\frac{2}{a}\right)^{1/2} \sin \frac{n\pi x}{a}$$

$$= -i\hbar n\pi \left(\frac{2}{a^3}\right)^{1/2} \cos \frac{n\pi x}{a}$$

Note that this is *not* an eigenvalue equation. Therefore, the particle-in-a-box wave functions are not eigenfunctions of the momentum operator. We interpret this by saying that the particle does not have a definite momentum. We can explore this interpretation by writing the particle-in-a-box wave functions in terms of complex exponentials by using Euler's formula (Appendix B):

$$\sin \theta = \frac{e^{i\theta} - e^{-i\theta}}{2i} \tag{3-53}$$

If we substitute Eq. 3-53 into Eq. 3-28, then we obtain

$$\psi_n(x) = \frac{1}{i(2a)^{1/2}}\left(e^{in\pi x/a} - e^{-in\pi x/a}\right) \tag{3-54}$$

It is easy to show that $e^{\pm in\pi x/a}$ are eigenfunctions of $\hat{P}$ and, in particular, that

$$\hat{P}e^{\pm in\pi x/a} = \pm \frac{n\pi\hbar}{a} e^{\pm in\pi x/a} \tag{3-55}$$

Therefore,

$$\hat{P}\psi_n(x) = \frac{1}{i(2a)^{1/2}}\left(\frac{n\pi\hbar}{a} e^{in\pi x/a} + \frac{n\pi\hbar}{a} e^{-in\pi x/a}\right) \tag{3-56}$$

If we multiply Eq. 3-56 by the complex conjugate of Eq. 3-54 and integrate, then we obtain

$$\langle p \rangle = \frac{1}{2a}\int_0^a \left(\frac{n\pi\hbar}{a} + \frac{n\pi\hbar}{a} e^{-2in\pi x/a} - \frac{n\pi\hbar}{a} e^{2in\pi x/a} - \frac{n\pi\hbar}{a}\right) dx \tag{3-57}$$

The two integrals involving the exponential functions vanish because

$$e^{\pm 2in\pi x/a} = \cos \frac{2\pi n x}{a} \pm i \sin \frac{2\pi n x}{a}$$

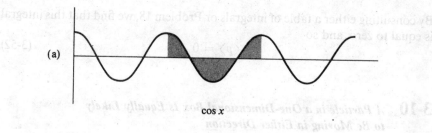

(a)

$\cos x$

(b)

$\sin x$

Figure 3-6. An illustration of the fact that the integrals of $\cos x$ and $\sin x$ vanish if the limits of integration extend over complete cycles.

and so

$$\int_0^a e^{\pm 2in\pi x/a}\, dx = \int_0^a \cos \frac{2\pi nx}{a}\, dx \pm i \int_0^a \sin \frac{2\pi nx}{a}\, dx = 0$$

because these last two integrals go over complete cycles of the cosine and sine (cf. Figure 3-6 and Problem 20).

Returning to Eq. 3-57, then, we see that

$$\langle p \rangle = \frac{1}{2}\left(\frac{n\pi h}{a}\right) + \frac{1}{2}\left(-\frac{n\pi h}{a}\right) = 0 \qquad (3\text{-}58)$$

We have written this equation the way we have to emphasize the following interpretation. The average momentum is zero, not because the particle has zero momentum but because the wave function $\psi_n(x)$ is a superposition of two momentum eigenfunctions, one with definite momentum $+n\pi\hbar/a$ and the other with definite momentum $-n\pi\hbar/a$. The factors of $\frac{1}{2}$ in Eq. 3-58 mean that the probability that the particle has momentum $+n\pi\hbar/a$ or $-n\pi\hbar/a$ is $\frac{1}{2}$, averaging out to zero. We shall develop this interpretation in some detail in Chapter 4.

3-11 *The Uncertainty Principle Says That $\sigma_p\sigma_x > \hbar/2$*

Now let us calculate the variance of the momentum, $\sigma_p^2 = \langle p^2 \rangle - \langle p \rangle^2$ of a particle in a box. To calculate $\langle p^2 \rangle$, we use

$$\langle p^2 \rangle = \int_0^a \psi_n^*(x)\hat{P}^2\psi_n(x)\, dx \qquad (3\text{-}59)$$

Werner Heisenberg and Niels Bohr dining in Copenhagen in 1934.

and remember that $\hat{P}^2$ means apply $\hat{P}$ twice in succession. Using Eq. 3-16

$$\langle p^2 \rangle = \int_0^a \left[\left(\frac{2}{a}\right)^{1/2} \sin\frac{n\pi x}{a} \right] \left(-\hbar^2 \frac{d^2}{dx^2} \right) \left[\left(\frac{2}{a}\right)^{1/2} \sin\frac{n\pi x}{a} \right] dx$$

$$= \frac{2n^2\pi^2\hbar^2}{a^3} \int_0^a \sin\frac{n\pi x}{a} \sin\frac{n\pi x}{a}\, dx$$

$$= \frac{n^2\pi^2\hbar^2}{a^2} \tag{3-60}$$

The square root of this is called the *root-mean-square momentum*. Note how Eq. 3-60 is consistent with the equation

$$\langle E \rangle = \left\langle \frac{p^2}{2m} \right\rangle = \frac{\langle p^2 \rangle}{2m} = \frac{n^2 h^2}{8ma^2}$$

Using Eq. 3-52 and 3-60, we see that

$$\sigma_p^2 = \frac{n^2\pi^2\hbar^2}{a^2}$$

and

$$\sigma_p = \frac{n\pi\hbar}{a} \tag{3-61}$$

Because the variance σ^2, and hence σ, is a measure of the spread of a distribution about its mean value, we can interpret σ as a measure of the uncertainty involved in any measurement. For the case of a particle in a box, we have been able to evaluate σ_x and σ_p explicitly in Eqs. 3-47 and 3-61. We interpret these quantities as the uncertainty involved when we measure the position or the momentum of the particle, respectively. We expect to obtain a distribution of measured values because the position of the particle is given by the probability distribution, Eq. 3-29.

Equation 3-61 shows that the uncertainty in a measurement of p is inversely proportional to a. Thus, the more we try to localize the particle, the greater is the uncertainty in its momentum. The uncertainty in the position of the particle is directly proportional to a (Eq. 3-47), which simply means that the larger the region over which the particle can be found, the greater is the uncertainty in its position. A particle that can range over the entire x axis ($-\infty < x < \infty$) is called a *free particle*. In the case of a free particle, $a \rightarrow \infty$ in Eq. 3-61 and there is no uncertainty in the momentum. The momentum of a free particle has a definite value (see Problem 31). The uncertainty in the position, however, is infinite. Thus, we see that there is a reciprocal relation between the uncertainty in momentum and position. If we take the product of σ_x and σ_p, then we have

$$\sigma_x \sigma_p = \frac{\hbar}{2}\left(\frac{\pi^2 n^2}{3} - 2\right)^{1/2} \tag{3-62}$$

The value of the square-root term here is greater than unity for all n and so

$$\sigma_x \sigma_p > \frac{\hbar}{2} \tag{3-63}$$

Equation 3-63 is the Heisenberg Uncertainty Principle. We have been able to derive Eq. 3-63 explicitly here because the mathematical manipulations for a particle in a box are fairly simple. We shall prove the Uncertainty Principle in general in Chapter 4.

Let us try to summarize what we have learned here concerning the Uncertainty Principle. A free particle has a definite momentum, but its position is completely indefinite. When we localize a particle by restricting it to a region of length a, it no longer has a definite momentum, and the spread in its momentum is given by Eq. 3-61. If we let the length a of the region go to zero, so that we have localized the particle precisely, so that there is no uncertainty in its position, then Eq. 3-61 shows that there is an infinite uncertainty in the momentum. The Uncertainty Principle says that the product of the two uncertainties is of the order of Planck's constant.

We have used the simple case of a particle in a box to illustrate some of the general principles and results of quantum mechanics. In Chapter 4 we shall present and discuss a set of postulates that we shall use throughout the remainder of the book.

Summary

The Schrödinger equation is a partial differential equation whose solution is a wave function, which for one particle is denoted by $\psi(x, y, z)$. The wave function of a particle has the physical interpretation that $\psi^*(x, y, z)\psi(x, y, z)\,dx\,dy\,dz$ is the probability that the particle is found in the volume element $dx\,dy\,dz$ located at the point (x, y, z). The Schrödinger equation is the quantum-mechanical analog of Newton's equation. The Schrödinger equation presented in this chapter does not contain time and is called the *time-independent Schrödinger equation*. The wave functions obtained from the time-independent Schrödinger equation are called *stationary-state wave functions*. We shall use only stationary-state wave functions throughout most of this book.

The Schrödinger equation is usually presented as an eigenvalue problem, with the operator being the Hamiltonian operator and the eigenvalues being the allowed energies of the system. The eigenfunctions of the Hamiltonian operator are the wave functions of the system. Operators and eigenvalue problems play a central role in quantum mechanics. Classical mechanical quantities are represented by linear operators in quantum mechanics. The eigenvalues of these operators are the allowed values of the corresponding classical mechanical quantity.

A number of the general principles of quantum mechanics can be illustrated by means of a particle in a box. The problem of a particle in a box is a relatively easy problem to solve exactly and to obtain simple expressions for the wave functions and the allowed energies. The discrete, quantized energy levels for a particle in a box arise naturally from the boundary conditions imposed on the Schrödinger equation for this system. We can use the wave functions of a particle in a box to illustrate explicitly the Heisenberg Uncertainty Principle. In doing so, we calculate the average values and the variances of the position and the momentum of a particle in a box. The average value and the variance of a quantity are key parameters in the measurement of that quantity.

Terms That You Should Know

Schrödinger equation	linear operator
wave function	eigenfunction
time-independent Schrödinger equation	eigenvalue
stationary-state wave functions	eigenvalue problem
operator	Hamiltonian operator
operand	commuting operators

quantum number   second moment

free-electron model   central moment

normalized wave function   variance

normalization constant   particle in a box

average   free particle

expectation value

Problems

1. Evaluate $g = \hat{A}f$ where $\hat{A}$ and f are given below.

$\hat{A}$	f
(a) SQRT	x^4
(b) $\dfrac{d^3}{dx^3} + x^3$	e^{-ax}
(c) $\displaystyle\int_0^1 dx$	$x^3 - 2x + 3$
(d) $\dfrac{\partial^2}{\partial x^2} + \dfrac{\partial^2}{\partial y^2} + \dfrac{\partial^2}{\partial z^2}$	$x^3 y^2 z^4$

2. Determine whether the following operators are linear or nonlinear.

   (a) $\hat{A}f(x) = \text{SQR } f(x)$ [square $f(x)$]
   (b) $\hat{A}f(x) = f^*(x)$ [form the complex conjugate of $f(x)$]
   (c) $\hat{A}f(x) = 0$ [multiply $f(x)$ by zero]
   (d) $\hat{A}f(x) = [f(x)]^{-1}$ [take the reciprocal of $f(x)$]
   (e) $\hat{A}f(x) = f(0)$ [evaluate $f(x)$ at $x = 0$]
   (f) $\hat{A}f(x) = \ln f(x)$ [take the logarithm of $f(x)$]

3. In each case, show that $f(x)$ is an eigenfunction of the operator given
   Find the eigenvalue.

$\hat{A}$	$f(x)$
(a) $\dfrac{d^2}{dx^2}$	$\cos \omega x$
(b) $\dfrac{d}{dt}$	$e^{i\omega t}$
(c) $\dfrac{d^2}{dx^2} + 2\dfrac{d}{dx} + 3$	e^{ax}
(d) $\dfrac{\partial}{\partial y}$	$x^2 e^{6y}$

4. Show that $(\cos ax)(\cos by)(\cos cz)$ is an eigenfunction of the operator,

$$\nabla^2 = \frac{\partial^2}{\partial x^2} + \frac{\partial^2}{\partial y^2} + \frac{\partial^2}{\partial z^2}$$

which is called the *Laplacian operator*.

5. Write out the operator $\hat{A}^2$ for $\hat{A} =$

(a) $\dfrac{d^2}{dx^2}$ (b) $\dfrac{d}{dx} + x$ (c) $\dfrac{d^2}{dx^2} - 2x\dfrac{d}{dx} + 1$

Hint: Be sure to include $f(x)$ before carrying out the operations.

6. Determine whether or not the following pairs of operators commute.

	$\hat{A}$	$\hat{B}$
(a)	$\dfrac{d}{dx}$	$\dfrac{d^2}{dx^2} + 2\dfrac{d}{dx}$
(b)	x	$\dfrac{d}{dx}$
(c)	SQR	SQRT
(d)	$\dfrac{\partial}{\partial x}$	$\dfrac{\partial}{\partial y}$

7. In ordinary algebra, $(P + Q)(P - Q) = P^2 - Q^2$. Expand $(\hat{P} + \hat{Q})(\hat{P} - \hat{Q})$. Under what condition do we find the same result as in the case of ordinary algebra?

8. If we operate on the particle-in-a-box wave functions (Eq. 3-23) with the momentum operator, Eq. 3-11, we find

$$\hat{P}B \sin \frac{n\pi x}{a} = -i\hbar \frac{i}{dx}\left(B \sin \frac{n\pi x}{a}\right)$$

$$= -\frac{i\hbar n\pi}{a} B \cos \frac{n\pi x}{a}$$

Note that this is *not* an eigenvalue equation, and so we say that the momentum of a particle in a box does not have a fixed, definite value. Although the particle does not have a definite momentum, we can use the classical equation $E = p^2/2m$ to define formally some sort of effective momentum. Using Eq. 3-22 for E, show that $p = nh/2a$ and that the de Broglie wavelengths associated with these momenta are $\lambda = h/p = 2a/n$. Show that this last equation says that an integral number of half-wavelengths fit into the box or that Figure 3-2 corresponds to standing de Broglie waves or matter waves.

9. In Section 3-5 we applied the equations for a particle in a box to the π electrons in butadiene. This simple model is called the *free-electron model*.

Using the same argument, show that the length of hexatriene can be estimated to be 8.67 Å. Show that the first electronic transition is predicted to occur at 2.8×10^4 cm^{-1}. (Realize that there are six π electrons in hexatriene.)

10. Prove that if $\psi(x)$ is a solution to the Schrödinger equation, then any constant times $\psi(x)$ is also a solution.

11. Using the following table

x	$f(x)$
-6	0.05
-2	0.15
0	0.50
1	0.10
3	0.05
4	0.10
5	0.05

calculate $\langle x \rangle$ and $\langle x^2 \rangle$, and show that $\sigma^2 > 0$.

12. A discrete probability distribution that is commonly used in statistics is the Poisson distribution:

$$f_n = \frac{\lambda^n}{n!} e^{-\lambda} \qquad n = 0, 1, 2, \ldots$$

Prove that f_n is normalized. Evaluate $\langle n \rangle$ and $\langle n^2 \rangle$ and show that $\sigma^2 > 0$. Recall that

$$e^x = \sum_{n=0}^{\infty} \frac{x^n}{n!}$$

13. An important continuous distribution is the exponential distribution

$$p(x)\,dx = ce^{-\lambda x}\,dx \qquad 0 \leq x < \infty$$

Evaluate c, $\langle x \rangle$, σ^2, and the probability that $x \geq a$.

14. Without using a table of integrals, show that all the odd moments of a Gaussian distribution are zero. Using a table of integrals, or the results derived in Problem 15 in Chapter 5, calculate $\langle x^4 \rangle$ for a Gaussian distribution.

15. Using a table of integrals, show that

$$\int_0^a \sin^2 \frac{n\pi x}{a}\,dx = \frac{a}{2}$$

$$\int_0^a x \sin^2 \frac{n\pi x}{a}\,dx = \frac{a^2}{4}$$

$$\int_0^a x^2 \sin^2 \frac{n\pi x}{a}\,dx = \left(\frac{a}{2\pi n}\right)^3 \left(\frac{4\pi^3 n^3}{3} - 2n\pi\right)$$

All of these integrals can be evaluated from

$$I(\beta) \equiv \int_0^a e^{\beta x} \sin^2 \frac{n\pi x}{a} \, dx$$

Show that the above integrals are given by $I(0)$, $I'(0)$, and $I''(0)$, respectively, where the primes denote differentiation with respect to β. Using a table of integrals, evaluate $I(\beta)$ and then the above three integrals by differentiation.

16. Show that

$$\langle x \rangle = \frac{a}{2}$$

for all the states of a particle in a box. Is this result physically reasonable?

17. Show that

$$\sigma_x = (\langle x^2 \rangle - \langle x \rangle^2)^{1/2}$$

for a particle in a box is less than a, the width of the box, for any value of n. If σ_x is the uncertainty in the position of the particle, could σ_x ever be larger than a?

18. Using the trigonometric identity,

$$\sin 2\theta = 2 \sin \theta \cos \theta$$

show that

$$\int_0^a \sin \frac{n\pi x}{a} \cos \frac{n\pi x}{a} \, dx = 0$$

19. Using Eq. 3-15 for $\hat{K}$ and Eq. 3-60 for $\langle p^2 \rangle$, show that

$$E = \frac{n^2 h^2}{8ma^2}$$

20. Prove that

$$\int_0^a e^{\pm i2\pi nx/a} \, dx = 0 \qquad n \neq 0$$

21. We can use the Uncertainty Principle for a particle in a box to argue that free electrons cannot exist in a nucleus. Before the discovery of the neutron, one might have thought that a nucleus of atomic number Z and mass number A is made up of A protons and $A - Z$ electrons, that is, just enough electrons such that the net nuclear charge is $+Z$. Such a nucleus would have an atomic number Z and mass number A. In this problem we shall use Eq. 3-61 to *estimate* the energy of an electron confined to a region of nuclear size. The diameter of a typical nucleus is about 10^{-14} m. Substitute $a = 10^{-14}$ m into Eq. 3-61 and show that σ_p is

$$\sigma_p = 3 \times 10^{-20} \text{ kg·m·s}^{-1}$$

Show that

$$E = \frac{\sigma_p^2}{2m} = 5 \times 10^{-10} \text{ J}$$

$$\approx 3000 \text{ MeV}$$

where millions of electron volts (MeV) is the common nuclear physics unit of energy. It is observed experimentally that electrons emitted from nuclei as β radiation have energies of only a few MeV, which is far less than the energy we have calculated above. Argue then that there can be no free electrons in nuclei because they should be ejected with much higher energies than are found experimentally.

22. Using the trigonometric identity

$$\sin \alpha \sin \beta = \tfrac{1}{2}\cos(\alpha - \beta) - \tfrac{1}{2}\cos(\alpha + \beta)$$

Show that the particle-in-a-box wave functions (Eq. 3-28) satisfy the relation

$$\int_0^a \psi_n^*(x)\psi_m(x)\,dx = 0 \qquad m \neq n$$

(The asterisk in this case is superfluous because the functions are real.) If a set of functions satisfies the above integral condition, we say that the set is *orthogonal* and, in particular, that $\psi_m(x)$ is orthogonal to $\psi_n(x)$. If, in addition, the functions are normalized, we say that the set is *orthonormal*.

23. Prove that the set of functions

$$\psi_n(x) = a^{-1/2}e^{in\pi x/a} \qquad n = 0, \pm 1, \pm 2, \ldots$$

is orthonormal (cf. Problem 22) over the interval $(0, a)$. A compact way to express orthonormality in the $\psi_n(x)$ is to write

$$\int_0^a \psi_m^*(x)\psi_n(x)\,dx = \delta_{nm}$$

The symbol δ_{nm} is called a *Kroenecker delta* and is defined by

$$\delta_{nm} = 1 \qquad \text{if } m = n$$
$$= 0 \qquad \text{if } m \neq n$$

24. In problems dealing with a particle in a box, one often needs to evaluate integrals of the type

$$\int_0^a \sin\frac{n\pi x}{a}\sin\frac{m\pi x}{a}\,dx \quad \text{and} \quad \int_0^a \cos\frac{n\pi x}{a}\cos\frac{m\pi x}{a}\,dx$$

Integrals like these are easy to evaluate if you convert the trigonometric functions to complex exponentials by using the identities (see Appendix B)

$$\cos\theta = \frac{e^{i\theta} + e^{-i\theta}}{2} \quad \text{and} \quad \sin\theta = \frac{e^{i\theta} - e^{-i\theta}}{2i}$$

and then realize that the set of functions

$$\psi_n(x) = a^{-1/2}e^{in\pi x/a} \qquad n = 0, \pm 1, \pm 2, \ldots$$

is orthonormal on the interval $(0, a)$ (Problem 23). Show that

$$\int_0^a \sin\frac{n\pi x}{a}\sin\frac{m\pi x}{a}\,dx = \int_0^a \cos\frac{n\pi x}{a}\cos\frac{m\pi x}{a}\,dx = \frac{a}{2}\delta_{nm}$$

where δ_{nm} is the Kroenecker delta, defined in Problem 23.

25. Show that the set of functions

$$\phi_n(\theta) = (2\pi)^{-1/2}e^{in\theta} \qquad 0 \le \theta \le 2\pi$$

is orthonormal (Problem 22); that is,

$$\int_0^{2\pi} \phi_m^*\phi_n \, d\theta = 1 \qquad m = n$$
$$= 0 \qquad m \neq n$$

26. The Schrödinger equation for a particle of mass m constrained to move on a circle of radius a is

$$-\frac{\hbar^2}{2I}\frac{d^2\psi}{d\theta^2} = E\psi(\theta) \qquad 0 \le \theta \le 2\pi$$

where $I = ma^2$ is the moment of inertia and θ is the angle that describes the position of the particle around the ring. Show that the solutions to this equation are

$$\psi(\theta) = Ae^{in\theta}$$

where $n = (2IE)^{1/2}/\hbar$. Argue that the appropriate boundary condition is $\psi(\theta) = \psi(\theta + 2\pi)$ and use this to show that

$$E = \frac{n^2\hbar^2}{2I} \qquad n = 0, \pm 1, \pm 2, \ldots$$

Show that the normalization constant A is $(2\pi)^{-1/2}$. Discuss how you might use these results for a free-electron model of benzene.

27. Set up the problem of a particle in a box with its walls located at $-a$ and $+a$. Show that the energies are equal to those of a box with walls located at 0 and $2a$. (These may be obtained from the results that we derived in the chapter simply by replacing a by $2a$.) Show, however, that the wave functions are not the same and are given by

$$\psi_n(x) = \frac{1}{2a^{1/2}} \sin \frac{n\pi x}{a} \qquad n \text{ even}$$
$$= \frac{1}{2a^{1/2}} \cos \frac{n\pi x}{a} \qquad n \text{ odd}$$

Does it bother you that the wave functions seem to depend on whether the walls are located at $\pm a$ or 0 and $2a$? Surely the particle knows only that it has a region of length $2a$ to move in and cannot be affected by where you place the origin for the two sets of wave functions. What does this tell you? Do you think that any experimentally observable properties depend on where you choose to place the origin of the x axis? Show that $\sigma_x\sigma_p > \hbar/2$, exactly as we obtained in Section 3-11.

28. We can use the wave functions of Problem 27 to illustrate some fundamental symmetry properties of wave functions. Show that the wave functions are alternately symmetric and antisymmetric or even and odd with respect to the operation $x \rightarrow -x$, which is a reflection through the $x = 0$ line. This symmetry property of the wave function is a consequence of the symmetry of the Hamiltonian, as we shall now show. Schrödinger's equation may be written as

$$\hat{H}(x)\psi_n(x) = E_n\psi_n(x)$$

Reflection through the $x = 0$ line gives $x \rightarrow -x$ and so

$$\hat{H}(-x)\psi_n(-x) = E_n\psi_n(-x)$$

Now show that $\hat{H}(x) = \hat{H}(-x)$ (i.e., that $\hat{H}$ is symmetric), and so show that

$$\hat{H}(x)\psi_n(-x) = E_n\psi_n(-x)$$

Thus we see that $\psi_n(-x)$ is also an eigenfunction of $\hat{H}$ belonging to the same eigenvalue E_n. Now, if there is only one eigenfunction associated with each eigenvalue (we call this a *nondegenerate case*), then argue that $\psi_n(x)$ and $\psi_n(-x)$ must differ only by a multiplicative constant [i.e., that $\psi_n(-x) = c\psi_n(x)$]. By applying the inversion operation again to this equation, show that $c = \pm 1$ and that all the wave functions must be either even or odd with respect to reflection through the $x = 0$ line because the Hamiltonian is symmetric. Thus, we see that the symmetry of the Hamiltonian influences the symmetry of the wave functions.

   Very often the symmetry properties of a wave function are sufficient to learn a great deal about the system. For example, we shall learn in Chapter 10 that the intensity of the spectral line that results from a transition of one state to another is given in terms of an integral like

$$\int_{-a}^{a} \psi_n(x)x\psi_m(x)\,dx$$

Using only the symmetry properties of the above wave functions, show that transitions to and from levels separated by $|n - m| = 2, 4, 6, \ldots$ have zero intensity or, in other words, are not allowed. This calculation is an example of how the symmetry of the wave functions, and hence of only the Hamiltonian, have directly observable consequences. One does not even have to solve the Schrödinger equation. A general study of symmetry uses group theory and this example is actually an elementary application of group theory to quantum-mechanical problems. There are many nice applications of group theory in quantum chemistry, particularly in inorganic chemistry.

29. For a particle moving in a one-dimensional potential well, the mean value of x is $x = a/2$, and the mean square deviation $\sigma^2 = (a^2/12)[1 - (6/\pi^2 n^2)]$. Show that as n becomes very large, this value agrees with the classical

value. The classical value is obtained by saying that the classical probability distribution is uniform, that is, by saying that

$$p(x)\,dx = \frac{1}{a}\,dx \qquad 0 \le x \le a$$

$$= 0 \qquad \text{otherwise}$$

30. This problem shows that the intensity of a wave is proportional to the square of its amplitude. Figure 3-7 illustrates the geometry of a vibrating string. Because the velocity at any point of the string is $\partial u/\partial t$, the kinetic energy of the entire string is

$$K = \int_0^l \frac{1}{2}\rho\left(\frac{\partial u}{\partial t}\right)^2 dx$$

where ρ is the linear mass density of the string (Appendix A). The potential energy is found by considering the increase of length of the small arc *PQ* of length *ds* in Figure 3-7. The segment of the string along that arc has increased its length from *dx* to *ds*. Therefore, the potential energy associated with this increase is

$$U = \int_0^l T(ds - dx)$$

where T is the tension in the string. Using the fact that $(ds)^2 = (dx)^2 + (du)^2$, show that

$$U = \int_0^l T\left\{\left[1 + \left(\frac{\partial u}{\partial x}\right)^2\right]^{1/2} - 1\right\} dx$$

Using the fact that $(1 + x)^{1/2} \approx 1 + (x/2)$ for small x, show that

$$U = \frac{1}{2}T\int_0^l \left(\frac{\partial u}{\partial x}\right)^2 dx$$

for small displacements.

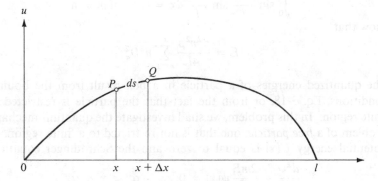

Figure 3-7. A vibrating string.

The total energy of the vibrating string is the sum of K and U and so

$$E = \frac{\rho}{2} \int_0^l \left(\frac{\partial u}{\partial t}\right)^2 dx + \frac{T}{2} \int_0^l \left(\frac{\partial u}{\partial x}\right)^2 dx$$

We showed in Chapter 2 (Eq. 2-24) that the nth normal mode can be written in the form

$$u_n(x, t) = D_n \cos(\omega_n t + \phi_n) \sin \frac{n\pi x}{l}$$

where $\omega_n = v n \pi / l$. Using this equation, show that

$$K_n = \frac{\pi^2 v^2 n^2 \rho}{4l} D_n^2 \sin^2(\omega_n t + \phi_n)$$

$$U_n = \frac{\pi^2 n^2 T}{4l} D_n^2 \cos^2(\omega_n t + \phi_n)$$

Using the fact that $v = (T/\rho)^{1/2}$, show that

$$E_n = \frac{\pi^2 v^2 n^2 \rho}{4l} D_n^2$$

Note that the total energy, or intensity, is proportional to the square of the amplitude. Although we have shown this only for the case of a vibrating string, it is a general result and shows that the intensity of a wave is proportional to the square of the amplitude. If we had carried everything through in complex exponential notation instead of sines and cosines, then we would have found that E_n is proportional to $|D_n|^2$ instead of just D_n^2.

Generally, there are many normal modes present at the same time, and the complete solution is

$$u(x, t) = \sum_{n=1}^{\infty} D_n \cos(\omega_n t + \phi_n) \sin \frac{n\pi x}{l}$$

Using the fact that (cf. Problem 22)

$$\int_0^l \sin \frac{m\pi x}{l} \sin \frac{n\pi x}{l} dx = 0 \qquad \text{if } m \neq n$$

show that

$$E = \frac{\pi^2 v^2 \rho}{4l} \sum_{n=1}^{\infty} n^2 D_n^2$$

31. The quantized energies of a particle in a box result from the boundary conditions, Eq. 3-18, or from the fact that the particle is restricted to a finite region. In this problem, we shall investigate the quantum-mechanical problem of a *free particle*, one that is not restricted to a finite region. The potential energy $U(x)$ is equal to zero and the Schrödinger equation is

$$\frac{d^2\psi}{dx^2} + \frac{2mE}{\hbar^2} \psi(x) = 0 \qquad -\infty < x < \infty$$

Note that the particle can lie anywhere along the x axis in this problem. Show that the two solutions of this Schrödinger equation are (cf. Example 2-4)

$$\psi_1(x) = A_1 e^{i(2mE)^{1/2}x/\hbar} = A_1 e^{ikx}$$
$$\psi_2(x) = A_2 e^{-i(2mE)^{1/2}x/\hbar} = A_2 e^{-ikx}$$

where

$$k = \frac{(2mE)^{1/2}}{\hbar} \tag{3-32}$$

Show that if E is allowed to take on negative values, then the wave functions become unbounded for large x. Therefore, we shall require that the energy, E, be a positive quantity. We saw in our discussion of the Bohr atom that negative energies correspond to bound states and that positive energies correspond to unbound states, and so our requirement that E be positive is consistent with the picture of a free particle.

To get a physical interpretation of the states that $\psi_1(x)$ and $\psi_2(x)$ describe, operate on $\psi_1(x)$ and $\psi_2(x)$ with the momentum operator $\hat{P}$, Equation (3-11), and show that

$$\hat{P}\psi_1 = -i\hbar \frac{d\psi_1}{dx} = \hbar k \psi_1$$

and

$$\hat{P}\psi_2 = -i\hbar \frac{d\psi_2}{dx} = -\hbar k \psi_2$$

Notice that these are eigenvalue equations. Our interpretation of these two equations is that $\psi_1(x)$ describes a free particle with fixed momentum $\hbar k$ and that $\psi_2(x)$ describes a free particle with fixed momentum $-\hbar k$. Thus $\psi_1(x)$ describes a particle moving to the right and $\psi_2(x)$ describes one moving to the left, both with a fixed momentum. Notice also that there are no restrictions on k, and so the particle can have any value of momentum. Now show that

$$E = \frac{\hbar^2 k^2}{2m}$$

Notice that the energy is not quantized; the energy of the particle can have any positive value in this case because there are no boundaries associated with this problem.

Lastly, show that $\psi_1^*(x)\psi_1(x) = A_1^* A_1 = |A_1|^2 = $ constant and that $\psi_2^*(x)\psi_2(x) = A_2^* A_2 = |A_2|^2 = $ constant. Discuss this result in terms of the probabilistic interpretation of $\psi^*\psi$. Also discuss the application of the Uncertainty Principle to this problem. What are σ_p and σ_x?

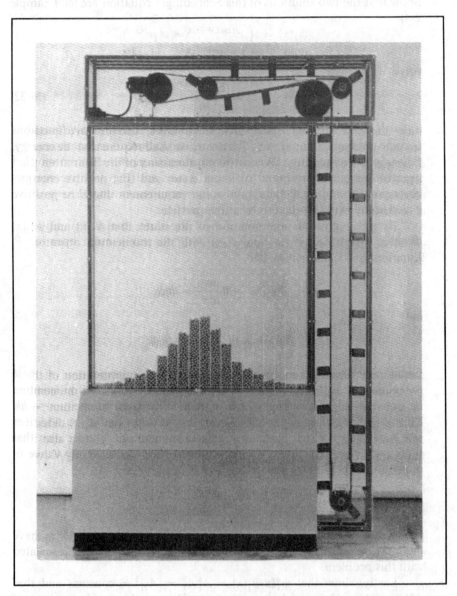

The mechanical device shown above is called a Galton board, after Sir Francis Galton, who constructed the first one. As the balls fall down past the series of obstacles, they collect at the bottom of the board in a distribution that approximates a Gaussian distribution.

4

The Postulates
and General Principles
of Quantum Mechanics

UP TO NOW we have made a number of conjectures concerning the formulation of quantum mechanics. For example; we have been led to suspect that the variables of classical mechanics are represented in quantum mechanics by operators. These operate on wave functions to give the average or expected results of measurements according to Eq. 3-50. In this chapter we shall formalize the various conjectures that we have made in Chapter 3 as a set of postulates and then discuss some general theorems that follow from these postulates. This is similar to setting up a set of axioms in geometry and then logically deducing the consequences of these axioms. The ultimate test of whether the axioms or postulates are sensible is to compare the end results to experimental data. As one gains experience and insight in an area, one can propose more abstract and economical postulates, but here we shall present a fairly elementary set that will suffice for all the systems that we shall discuss in this book and for almost all systems of interest in chemistry. The mathematical level of some of the latter sections of this chapter is somewhat higher than in most of the book. Sections 4-1 through 4-5, however, are sufficient for an introductory course.

4-1 *The State of a System Is Completely Specified by Its Wave Function*

Classical mechanics deals with quantities called *dynamical variables*, such as position, momentum, angular momentum, and energy. A measurable

113

dynamical variable is called an *observable*. The classical-mechanical state of a one-body system at any particular time is specified completely by the three position coordinates (x, y, z) and the three momenta or velocities (v_x, v_y, v_z) at that time. The time evolution of the system is governed by Newton's equations,

$$m\frac{d^2x}{dt^2} = F_x, \qquad m\frac{d^2y}{dt^2} = F_y, \qquad m\frac{d^2z}{dt^2} = F_z \qquad (4\text{-}1)$$

where F_x, F_y, and F_z are the components of the force, $\mathbf{F}(x, y, z)$. Realize that generally each force component depends on x, y, and z. To emphasize this, we write

$$m\frac{d^2x}{dt^2} = F_x(x, y, z), \qquad m\frac{d^2y}{dt^2} = F_y(x, y, z), \qquad m\frac{d^2z}{dt^2} = F_z(x, y, z) \quad (4\text{-}2)$$

Note that each of these equations is a second-order equation, and so there will be two integration constants from each one. We can choose the integration constants to be the initial positions and velocities and write them as x_0, y_0, z_0, v_{x0}, v_{y0}, and v_{z0}. The solutions to Eq. 4-2 are $x(t)$, $y(t)$, and $z(t)$, which describe the position of the particle as a function of time. The position of the particle depends not only on the time but also on the initial conditions. To emphasize this, we write the solutions to Eq. 4-2 as

$$x(t) = x(t; x_0, y_0, z_0, v_{x0}, v_{y0}, v_{z0})$$
$$y(t) = y(t; x_0, y_0, z_0, v_{x0}, v_{y0}, v_{z0})$$
$$z(t) = z(t; x_0, y_0, z_0, v_{x0}, v_{y0}, v_{z0})$$

We can write these three equations in vector notation:

$$\mathbf{r}(t) = \mathbf{r}(t; \mathbf{r}_0, \mathbf{v}_0)$$

The vector $\mathbf{r}(t)$ describes the position of the particle as a function of time; $\mathbf{r}(t)$ is called the *trajectory* of the particle. Classical mechanics provides a method for calculating the trajectory of a particle in terms of the forces acting upon the particle through Newton's equations, Eqs. 4-2.

If there are N particles in the system, then it takes $3N$ coordinates and $3N$ velocities to specify the state of the system. There are $3N$ second-order differential equations and hence $3N$ initial positions and $3N$ initial velocities. The trajectory of the system is the position of each of the N particles in the system as a function of time and as a function of the initial conditions. An N-body system may be mathematically more complicated than a one-body system, but no new concepts need to be introduced.

Thus we see that in classical mechanics we can specify the state of a system by giving $3N$ positions and $3N$ velocities or momenta. We should suspect immediately that this is not going to be so in quantum mechanics because the Uncertainty Principle tells us that we cannot specify or determine the position and momentum of a particle simultaneously with infinite precision. The Uncertainty Principle is of no practical importance for macroscopic bodies, and so classical mechanics is a perfectly adequate prescription for macroscopic bodies; but for small bodies such as electrons, atoms, and molecules the consequences of the Uncertainty Principle are far from negligible and so the classical-mechanical picture is not valid. This leads us to our first postulate of quantum mechanics:

Postulate 1

The state of a quantum-mechanical system is completely specified by a function $\Psi(\mathbf{r}, t)$ that depends on the coordinates of the particle and on the time. This function, called the wave function or the state function, has the important property that $\Psi^*(\mathbf{r}, t)\Psi(\mathbf{r}, t)\,dx\,dy\,dz$ is the probability that the particle lies in the volume element $dx\,dy\,dz$, located at $\mathbf{r}$, at the time t.

If there is more than one particle, say two, then we write $\Psi^*(\mathbf{r}_1, \mathbf{r}_2, t)\Psi(\mathbf{r}_1, \mathbf{r}_2, t)$ $dx_1\,dy_1\,dz_1\,dx_2\,dy_2\,dz_2$ for the probability that particle 1 lies in the volume element $dx_1\,dy_1\,dz_1$ at $\mathbf{r}_1$ and that particle 2 lies in the volume element $dx_2\,dy_2\,dz_2$ at $\mathbf{r}_2$ at the time t. Postulate 1 says that the state of a quantum-mechanical system such as two electrons is completely specified by this function and that nothing else is required.

Because the square of the wave function has a probabilistic interpretation, it must satisfy certain physical requirements. For example, a wave function must be normalized, so that in the case of one particle, for simplicity, we have

$$\iiint_{-\infty}^{\infty} \Psi^*(\mathbf{r}, t)\Psi(\mathbf{r}, t)\,dx\,dy\,dz = 1 \tag{4-3}$$

for all time. The limits of the integral here symbolically mean over all possible values of x, y, and z. For the specific case of a particle in a box, the limits are $(0, a)$. It is convenient to abbreviate Eq. 4-3 by letting $dx\,dy\,dz = d\tau$ and to write

$$\int_{-\infty}^{\infty} \Psi^*(\mathbf{r}, t)\Psi(\mathbf{r}, t)\,d\tau = 1 \tag{4-4}$$

with the understanding that this is really a triple integral.

A milder condition than Eq. 4-4 is that the wave function must be able to be normalized. This can be so only if the integral in Eq. 4-3 is finite. If this is the case, we say that $\Psi(\mathbf{r}, t)$ is *quadratically integrable* or *square integrable* (cf. Problem 1). In addition to being normalized or at least normalizable, we also require that $\Psi(\mathbf{r}, t)$ and its first derivative be single-valued, continuous, and finite (cf. Problem 2). We summarize these requirements by saying that $\Psi(\mathbf{r}, t)$ must be well-behaved.

EXAMPLE 4-1

Determine whether each of the following functions is acceptable or not as a state function over the indicated intervals.

(a) e^{-x} $(0, \infty)$

(b) e^{-x} $(-\infty, \infty)$

(c) $\sin^{-1} x$ $(-1, 1)$

(d) $\dfrac{\sin x}{x}$ $(0, \infty)$

(e) $e^{-|x|}$ $(-\infty, \infty)$

Solution:

(a) Acceptable; e^{-x} is single-valued, continuous, finite, and quadratically integrable over the interval $(0, \infty)$.

(b) Not acceptable; e^{-x} cannot be normalized over the interval $(-\infty, \infty)$ because e^{-x} diverges as $x \to -\infty$.

(c) Not acceptable; $\sin^{-1} x$ is a multivalued function. For example,

$$\sin^{-1} 1 = \frac{\pi}{2}, \frac{\pi}{2} + 2\pi, \frac{\pi}{2} + 4\pi, \text{etc.}$$

(d) Acceptable; realize that $\sin x/x$ is finite at $x = 0$.

(e) Not acceptable; the first derivative of $e^{-|x|}$ is not continuous at $x = 0$.

4-2   *Quantum-Mechanical Operators Represent Classical-Mechanical Variables*

Postulate 2

To every observable in classical mechanics there corresponds an operator in quantum mechanics.

We have seen some examples of the correspondence between observables and operators in Chapter 3. These correspondences are collected in Table 4-1.

The only new entry in Table 4-1 is that for the angular momentum, which requires some comment. In Section 1-8, we discussed circular motion in some detail. In that particular case, the angular momentum l is given by $l = mvr$. Just like linear momentum, however, angular momentum is actually a vector quantity. If a particle is at some point $\mathbf{r}$ and has momentum $\mathbf{p}$, then its angular momentum is defined by $\mathbf{l} = \mathbf{r} \times \mathbf{p}$ (cf. Problems 3 through 7 for a review of vector algebra). Recall that a vector cross product like this is defined to be a vector of magnitude $|\mathbf{r}| |\mathbf{p}| \sin \theta$ where $|\mathbf{r}|$ and $|\mathbf{p}|$ denote the magnitudes of $\mathbf{r}$ and $\mathbf{p}$, respectively, and where θ is the angle between $\mathbf{r}$ and $\mathbf{p}$. The direction of $\mathbf{l}$ is perpendicular to the plane formed by $\mathbf{r}$ and $\mathbf{p}$ and is directed as a right-hand screw would advance as $\mathbf{r}$ is rotated into $\mathbf{p}$. The components of $\mathbf{l}$ are given by (cf. Problem 4)

$$l_x = yp_z - zp_y$$
$$l_y = zp_x - xp_z \qquad (4\text{-}5)$$
$$l_z = xp_y - yp_x$$

TABLE 4-1
Classical-Mechanical Observables
and Their Corresponding Quantum-Mechanical Operators

Observable		Operator	
Name	*Symbol*	*Symbol*	*Operation*
Position	x	$\hat{X}$	Multiply by x
	$\mathbf{r}$	$\hat{R}$	Multiply by $\mathbf{r}$
Momentum	p_x	$\hat{P}_x$	$-i\hbar \dfrac{\partial}{\partial x}$
	$\mathbf{p}$	$\hat{P}$	$-i\hbar \left(\mathbf{i} \dfrac{\partial}{\partial x} + \mathbf{j} \dfrac{\partial}{\partial y} + \mathbf{k} \dfrac{\partial}{\partial z} \right)$
Kinetic energy	K_x	$\hat{K}_x$	$-\dfrac{\hbar^2}{2m} \dfrac{\partial^2}{\partial x^2}$
	K	$\hat{K}$	$-\dfrac{\hbar^2}{2m} \left(\dfrac{\partial^2}{\partial x^2} + \dfrac{\partial^2}{\partial y^2} + \dfrac{\partial^2}{\partial z^2} \right)$
Potential energy	$U(x)$	$U(\hat{x})$	Multiply by $U(x)$
	$U(x, y, z)$	$U(\hat{x}, \hat{y}, \hat{z})$	Multiply by $U(x, y, z)$
Total energy	E	$\hat{H}$	$-\dfrac{\hbar^2}{2m} \left(\dfrac{\partial^2}{\partial x^2} + \dfrac{\partial^2}{\partial y^2} + \dfrac{\partial^2}{\partial z^2} \right)$
			$+ U(x, y, z)$
Angular momentum	$l_x = yp_z - zp_y$	$\hat{L}_x$	$-i\hbar \left(y \dfrac{\partial}{\partial z} - z \dfrac{\partial}{\partial y} \right)$
	$l_y = zp_x - xp_z$	$\hat{L}_y$	$-i\hbar \left(z \dfrac{\partial}{\partial x} - x \dfrac{\partial}{\partial z} \right)$
	$l_z = xp_y - yp_x$	$\hat{L}_z$	$-i\hbar \left(x \dfrac{\partial}{\partial y} - y \dfrac{\partial}{\partial x} \right)$

Note that the operators given in Table 4-1 can be obtained from Eq. 4-5 by letting the momenta assume their operator equivalent.

We shall see in the following that the operators in Table 4-1 and any other operators that we shall use must have certain special properties. They are all clearly linear operators (cf. Eq. 3-9), but they also satisfy a more subtle condition that is discussed in Section 4-4.

Our third postulate follows.

Postulate 3

In any measurement of the observable associated with the operator $\hat{A}$, the only values that will ever be observed are the eigenvalues a, which satisfy the eigenvalue equation

$$\hat{A}\Psi = a\Psi \qquad (4\text{-}6)$$

Generally, an operator will have a set of eigenfunctions and eigenvalues, and we indicate this by writing

$$\hat{A}\Psi_n = a_n\Psi_n \tag{4-7}$$

Thus in any experiment designed to measure the observable corresponding to $\hat{A}$, the only values we find are $a_1, a_2, a_3, \ldots$. The set of eigenvalues $\{a_n\}$ of an operator $\hat{A}$ is called the *spectrum* of $\hat{A}$.

As a specific example, consider the measurement of the energy. The operator corresponding to the energy is the Hamiltonian operator, and its eigenvalue equation is

$$\hat{H}\Psi_n = E_n\Psi_n \tag{4-8}$$

This is just the Schrödinger equation. The solution of this equation gives the Ψ_n and E_n. For the case of a particle in a box, $E_n = n^2h^2/8ma^2$. Postulate 3 says that if we measure the energy of a particle in a box, we shall find one of these energies and no others.

Notice that the Schrödinger equation is just one of many possible eigenvalue equations because there is one for each possible operator. Equation 4-8 is the most important and most famous one, however, because the energy spectrum of a system is one of its most important properties. Because of the equation $\Delta E = h\nu$, we see that the experimentally observed spectrum of the system is intimately related to the mathematical spectrum. This is the motivation for calling the set of eigenvalues of an operator its *spectrum* and this is also why the Schrödinger equation is a special eigenvalue equation.

The particle in a box is a bound system, and for bound systems the spectrum is discrete. For an unbound system, the spectrum is continuous (see Problem 31 on p. 110). For other systems, such as a particle in a box with finite walls (cf. Figure 4-1), the spectrum can have both discrete and continuous parts. The energies below U_0 in Figure 4-1 are discrete and those with $E > U_0$ are continuous.

If a system is in a state described by Ψ_n, an eigenfunction of $\hat{A}$, then a measurement of the observable corresponding to $\hat{A}$ will yield the value a_n and

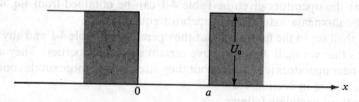

Figure 4-1. A potential well with a finite potential. The potential energy $U(x)$ that describes the system illustrated in this figure is

$$U(x) = 0 \qquad 0 < x < a$$
$$= U_0 \qquad x < 0 \quad \text{and} \quad x > a$$

As the value of U_0 increases, the system becomes a particle in a box because the large potential U_0 restricts the particle to lie within the well between 0 and a.

only a_n. It is important to realize, however, that the $\{\Psi_n\}$ are very special functions and it is possible that a system will not be in one of these states. Postulate 1 does not say that a system must be in a state described by an eigenfunction. Any suitably well-behaved function is a possible wave function or state function. What, then, if we measure the energy of a system that is in a state described by Ψ that is not an eigenfunction of $\hat{H}$? Indeed our observed value will be one of the values E_n, but which one it will be cannot be predicted with certainty. In fact, if we were to measure the energy of each member of a collection of similarly described systems, all in the state described by Ψ, then we would observe a distribution of energies, but each member of this distribution will be one of the energies E_n. This leads us to our fourth postulate.

Postulate 4

If a system is in a state described by a normalized wave function Ψ, then the average value of the observable corresponding to $\hat{A}$ is given by

$$\langle a \rangle = \int_{-\infty}^{\infty} \Psi^* \hat{A} \Psi \, d\tau \tag{4-9}$$

According to Postulate 4, if we were to measure the energy of each member of a collection of similarly prepared systems, each described by Ψ, then the average of the observed values is given by Eq. 4-9 with $\hat{A} = \hat{H}$.

EXAMPLE 4-2

Suppose that a particle in a box is in the state

$$\Psi(x) = \left(\frac{30}{a^5}\right)^{1/2} x(a - x) \qquad 0 \le x \le a$$

$$= 0 \qquad\qquad\qquad \text{otherwise}$$

Note that $\Psi(x)$ is not an eigenfunction for a particle in a box. Sketch $\Psi(x)$ versus x and then show that $\Psi(x)$ is normalized. Then calculate the average energy associated with this state.

Solution: The normalization integral of $\Psi(x)$ is elementary,

$$\frac{30}{a^5} \int_0^a x^2 (a - x)^2 \, dx = 1$$

According to Eq. 4-9, the average energy associated with this state is

$$\langle E \rangle = \int_0^a \Psi^*(x) \hat{H} \Psi(x) \, dx = \int_0^a \Psi^*(x) \left(-\frac{\hbar^2}{2m} \frac{d^2}{dx^2} \right) \Psi(x) \, dx$$

$$= -\frac{15 \hbar^2}{ma^5} \int_0^a x(a - x) \left(\frac{d^2}{dx^2} x(a - x) \right) dx$$

$$= \frac{30 \hbar^2}{ma^5} \int_0^a x(a - x) \, dx = \frac{5 \hbar^2}{ma^2} = \frac{5 \hbar^2}{4 \pi^2 ma^2}$$

Note that this value is not one of the energy eigenvalues of a particle in a box (Eq. 3-22). Which one is it closest to? Which eigenfunction (Eq. 3-28) is $\Psi(x)$ most similar to? Does this result seem sensible?

Suppose that Ψ just happens to be an eigenfunction of $\hat{A}$; that is, suppose that $\Psi = \Psi_n$ where

$$\hat{A}\Psi_n = a_n\Psi_n$$

Then

$$\langle a \rangle = \int_{-\infty}^{\infty} \Psi_n^* \hat{A}\Psi_n \, d\tau = \int_{-\infty}^{\infty} \Psi_n^* a_n \Psi_n \, d\tau = a_n \int_{-\infty}^{\infty} \Psi_n^* \Psi_n \, d\tau = a_n \quad (4\text{-}10)$$

Furthermore, if $\hat{A}\Psi_n = a_n\Psi_n$, then

$$\hat{A}^2\Psi_n = \hat{A}(\hat{A}\Psi_n) = \hat{A}(a_n\Psi_n) = a_n(\hat{A}\Psi_n) = a_n^2\Psi_n$$

and so

$$\langle a^2 \rangle = \int_{-\infty}^{\infty} \Psi_n^* \hat{A}^2\Psi_n \, d\tau = a_n^2 \quad (4\text{-}11)$$

From Eq. 4-10 and 4-11 we see that the variance of the measurements gives

$$\sigma_a^2 = \langle a^2 \rangle - \langle a \rangle^2 = a_n^2 - a_n^2 = 0 \quad (4\text{-}12)$$

Thus, as Postulate 3 says, the only value that we measure is the value a_n. Often, however, the system is not in a state described by an eigenfunction and one measures a distribution of values whose average is given by Postulate 4.

4-3   The Time Dependence of Wave Functions Is Governed by the Time-Dependent Schrödinger Equation

We need one more postulate. Notice that the wave function in Postulate 1 contains time explicitly. This is something that we have not considered before. Except for this one thing, we have tacitly used all the given postulates in Chapter 3 and so all our discussion so far should be fairly familiar. Now we must discuss the time dependence of wave functions. The time dependence of wave functions is governed by the time-dependent Schrödinger equation. We cannot derive the time-dependent Schrödinger equation, any more than we can derive Newton's equation. It is difficult to try to justify the form of the time-dependent Schrödinger equation without using some arguments that are beyond the level of this book, and so we shall simply postulate its form and then show that it is consistent with the time-independent Schrödinger equation.

Postulate 5

The wave function or state function of a system evolves in time according to the time-dependent Schrödinger equation

$$\hat{H}\Psi(x, t) = i\hbar \frac{\partial \Psi}{\partial t} \quad (4\text{-}13)$$

Postulate 5 is the only one of the postulates presented here that we did not use in Chapter 3 and that should be new. For most systems, $\hat{H}$ does not contain time explicitly, and in this case we can apply the method of separation of variables and write

$$\Psi(x, t) = \psi(x)f(t)$$

If we substitute this into Eq. 4-13 and divide both sides by $\psi(x)f(t)$, we obtain

$$\frac{1}{\psi(x)} \hat{H}\psi(x) = \frac{i\hbar}{f(t)} \frac{df}{dt} \qquad (4\text{-}14)$$

If $\hat{H}$ does not contain time explicitly, then the left-hand side in Eq. 4-14 is a function of x only and the right-hand side is a function of t only, and so both sides must equal a constant. If we denote the separation constant by E, then Eq. 4-14 gives

$$\hat{H}\psi(x) = E\psi(x) \qquad (4\text{-}15)$$

and

$$\frac{df}{dt} = -\frac{i}{\hbar} Ef(t) \qquad (4\text{-}16)$$

The first of these two equations is what we have been calling the *Schrödinger equation*. In view of Eq. 4-13, Eq. 4-15 is often called the *time-independent Schrödinger equation*.

Equation 4-16 can be integrated immediately to give

$$f(t) = e^{-iEt/\hbar}$$

and so $\Psi(x, t)$ is of the form

$$\Psi(x, t) = \psi(x)e^{-iEt/\hbar} \qquad (4\text{-}17)$$

If we use the relation $E = h\nu = \hbar\omega$, we can write Eq. 4-17 as

$$\Psi(x, t) = \psi(x)e^{-i\omega t} \qquad (4\text{-}18)$$

It is interesting to note that Eq. 4-18 oscillates harmonically in time and is characteristic of wave motion. Yet the time-dependent Schrödinger equation does *not* have the same form as a classical wave equation. The Schrödinger equation has a first derivative in time, whereas the classical wave equation (Eq. 2-1) has a second derivative in time. Nevertheless, the Schrödinger equation does have wavelike solutions, which is one reason why quantum mechanics is sometimes called *wave mechanics*.

There is a set of solutions to Eq. 4-15, and so we write Eq. 4-17 as

$$\Psi_n(x, t) = \psi_n(x)e^{-iE_nt/\hbar} \qquad (4\text{-}19)$$

If the system happens to be in one of the eigenstates given by Eq. 4-19, then

$$\Psi_n^*(x, t)\Psi_n(x, t)\,dx = \psi_n^*(x)\psi_n(x)\,dx \qquad (4\text{-}20)$$

Thus, the probability density and the averages calculated from Eq. 4-19 are independent of time, and the $\psi_n(x)$ are called *stationary-state* wave functions. Stationary states are of central importance in chemistry. For example, in later chapters we shall represent an atom or a molecule by a set of stationary energy states and express the spectroscopic properties of the system in terms of transitions from one stationary state to another. The Bohr model of the hydrogen atom is a simple illustration of this idea.

EXAMPLE 4-3

We shall learn in Chapter 5 that a vibrating diatomic molecule can be well approximated as a harmonic oscillator (cf. Problem 7, p. 67) and that the quantum-mechanical treatment of a harmonic oscillator gives a set of stationary energy states with energies

$$E_n = \hbar \left(\frac{k}{\mu}\right)^{1/2} \left(n + \frac{1}{2}\right) \qquad n = 0, 1, 2, \ldots$$

where k is the force constant of the molecule and μ is its reduced mass. Given that transitions can occur only between adjacent states, show that there is only one frequency absorbed:

$$\nu = \frac{1}{2\pi}\left(\frac{k}{\mu}\right)^{1/2}$$

The observed frequency is 2160 cm^{-1} for $^{12}C^{16}O$. Calculate the force constant of $^{12}C^{16}O$.

Solution: Absorption occurs for transitions from the state n to the state $n + 1$ (adjacent states). The energy difference is

$$\Delta E = E_{n+1} - E_n = \hbar\left(\frac{k}{\mu}\right)^{1/2}\left[\left(n + 1 + \frac{1}{2}\right) - \left(n + \frac{1}{2}\right)\right]$$

$$= \hbar\left(\frac{k}{\mu}\right)^{1/2}$$

Using the fact that $\Delta E = h\nu$ and $\hbar = h/2\pi$, we have

$$\nu = \frac{1}{2\pi}\left(\frac{k}{\mu}\right)^{1/2}$$

The reduced mass of $^{12}C^{16}O$ is given by

$$\mu = \frac{(12.0)(16.0)}{28.0}(1.66 \times 10^{-27}\text{ kg}) = 1.14 \times 10^{-26}\text{ kg}$$

Using the fact that $\nu = c\bar{\nu}$, we find that the force constant

$$k = \mu(2\pi c\bar{\nu})^2 = (1.14 \times 10^{-26}\text{ kg})[2\pi(3.00 \times 10^8\text{ m·s}^{-1})(2.16 \times 10^5\text{ m}^{-1})]^2$$
$$= 1.89 \times 10^3\text{ N·m}^{-1}$$

It is important to realize that a system is not generally in a state described by a wave function of the form of Eq. 4-19. The general solution to Eq. 4-13 is a superposition of Eq. 4-19:

$$\Psi(x, t) = \sum_n c_n \psi_n(x) e^{-iE_n t/\hbar} \tag{4-21}$$

For simplicity, let us consider a case in which $\Psi(x, t)$ is a summation of only two terms:

$$\Psi(x, t) = c_1 \psi_1(x) e^{-iE_1 t/\hbar} + c_2 \psi_2(x) e^{-iE_2 t/\hbar}$$

The probability density in this case is

$$
\begin{aligned}
\Psi^*(x, t)\Psi(x, t) = &\left[c_1^* \psi_1^*(x) e^{iE_1 t/\hbar} + c_2^* \psi_2^*(x) e^{iE_2 t/\hbar} \right] \\
& \times \left[c_1 \psi_1(x) e^{-iE_1 t/\hbar} + c_2 \psi_2(x) e^{-iE_2 t/\hbar} \right] \\
= & |c_1|^2 \psi_1^*(x)\psi_1(x) + |c_2|^2 \psi_2^*(x)\psi_2(x) \\
& + c_1^* c_2 \psi_1^*(x)\psi_2(x) \exp\left[\frac{i(E_1 - E_2)t}{\hbar} \right] \\
& + c_2^* c_1 \psi_2^*(x)\psi_1(x) \exp\left[\frac{i(E_2 - E_1)t}{\hbar} \right]
\end{aligned}
$$

The third and fourth terms here contain time explicitly, and so $\Psi^*(x, t)\Psi(x, t)$ is not independent of time. In this case, we do not have a stationary state.

In general, we form $\Psi^*(x, t)\Psi(x, t)$ using Eq. 4-21 (cf. Problem 12 for a lesson on double summations) and obtain

$$
\begin{aligned}
\Psi^*(x, t)\Psi(x, t) &= \left[\sum_n c_n^* \psi_n^*(x) e^{iE_n t/\hbar} \right]\left[\sum_m c_m \psi_m(x) e^{-iE_m t/\hbar} \right] \\
&= \sum_n |c_n|^2 \psi_n^*(x)\psi_n(x) + \sum_n \sum_{m \neq n} c_n^* c_m \psi_n^*(x)\psi_m(x) \exp\left[\frac{i(E_n - E_m)t}{\hbar} \right]
\end{aligned}
\tag{4-22}
$$

The terms in the second summation here contain time explicitly and so we see that, in the general case, we do not have a stationary state.

4-4 Quantum-Mechanical Operators Must Be Hermitian Operators

Table 4-1 contains a list of some commonly occurring quantum-mechanical operators. We stated previously that these operators must have certain properties. We noticed that they all are linear, and this is one require-ment that we impose. A more subtle requirement arises if we consider Pos-tulate 3, which says that, in any measurement of the observable associated with the operator $\hat{A}$, the only values that are ever observed are the eigenvalues of $\hat{A}$. We have seen, however, that wave functions and operators generally are complex quantities, but certainly the eigenvalues must be real quantities if they are to correspond to the result of experimental measurement. In an equation, we have

$$\hat{A}\psi = a\psi \tag{4-23}$$

where $\hat{A}$ and ψ may be complex but a must be real. We shall insist, then, that quantum-mechanical operators have only real eigenvalues. Clearly this places a certain restriction on the operator $\hat{A}$.

To see what this restriction is, we multiply Eq. 4-23 from the left by ψ^* and integrate to obtain

$$\int \psi^* \hat{A} \psi \, dx = a \int \psi^* \psi \, dx = a \qquad (4\text{-}24)$$

Now we take the complex conjugate of Eq. 4-23,

$$\hat{A}^* \psi^* = a^* \psi^* = a \psi^* \qquad (4\text{-}25)$$

where the equality $a^* = a$ recognizes that a is real. Multiply Eq. 4-25 from the left by ψ and integrate:

$$\int \psi \hat{A}^* \psi^* \, dx = a \int \psi \psi^* \, dx = a \qquad (4\text{-}26)$$

Equating the left-hand sides of Eqs. 4-24 and 4-26 gives

$$\int \psi^* \hat{A} \psi \, dx = \int \psi \hat{A}^* \psi^* \, dx \qquad (4\text{-}27)$$

The operator $\hat{A}$ must satisfy Eq. 4-27 to assure that its eigenvalues be real. An operator that satisfies Eq. 4-27 for *any well-behaved function* is called a *Hermitian operator*. Thus, we can write the definition of a Hermitian operator as an operator that satisfies

$$\int_{-\infty}^{\infty} f^* \hat{A} f \, dx = \int_{-\infty}^{\infty} f \hat{A}^* f^* \, dx \qquad (4\text{-}28)$$

where $f(x)$ is any well-behaved function. Hermitian operators have real eigenvalues. Postulate 2 should be modified to read as follows:

Postulate 2'

> To every observable in classical mechanics there corresponds a linear, Hermitian operator in quantum mechanics.

All the operators in Table 4-1 are Hermitian. How do you determine if an operator is Hermitian? Consider the operator $\hat{A} = d/dx$. Does $\hat{A}$ satisfy Eq. 4-28? Let us substitute $\hat{A} = d/dx$ into Eq. 4-28 and integrate by parts:

$$\int_{-\infty}^{\infty} f^* \frac{d}{dx} f \, dx = \int_{-\infty}^{\infty} f^* \frac{df}{dx} \, dx = \left.\vphantom{\int} f^* f \right|_{-\infty}^{\infty} - \int_{-\infty}^{\infty} f \frac{df^*}{dx} \, dx$$

For a wave function to be normalizable, it must vanish at infinity, and so the first term on the right-hand side here is zero. Therefore, we have

$$\int_{-\infty}^{\infty} f^* \frac{d}{dx} f \, dx = -\int_{-\infty}^{\infty} f \frac{d}{dx} f^* \, dx$$

For an arbitrary function $f(x)$, d/dx does *not* satisfy Eq. 4-28 and so is *not* Hermitian.

Let us consider the momentum operator $\hat{P} = -i\hbar d/dx$. Substitution into Eq. 4-28 and integration by parts give

$$\int_{-\infty}^{\infty} f^* \left(-i\hbar \frac{d}{dx} \right) f \, dx = -i\hbar \int_{-\infty}^{\infty} f^* \frac{df}{dx} \, dx$$

$$= +i\hbar \int_{-\infty}^{\infty} f \frac{df^*}{dx} \, dx$$

and

$$\int_{-\infty}^{\infty} f\hat{P}^* f^* \, dx = \int_{-\infty}^{\infty} f \left(-i\hbar \frac{d}{dx} \right)^* f^* \, dx = i\hbar \int_{-\infty}^{\infty} f \frac{df^*}{dx} \, dx$$

Thus, we see that $\hat{P}$ does, indeed, satisfy Eq. 4-28. Therefore, the momentum operator is a Hermitian operator.

EXAMPLE 4-4

Prove that the kinetic energy operator is Hermitian.

$$\hat{K} = -\frac{\hbar^2}{2m} \frac{d^2}{dx^2}$$

Solution: As always, we shall assume that f vanishes at infinity. Thus, following the procedure of integrating by parts twice,

$$-\frac{\hbar^2}{2m} \int_{-\infty}^{\infty} f^* \frac{d^2 f}{dx^2} \, dx = -\frac{\hbar^2}{2m} \left. f^* \frac{df}{dx} \right|_{-\infty}^{\infty} + \frac{\hbar^2}{2m} \int_{-\infty}^{\infty} \frac{df^*}{dx} \frac{df}{dx} \, dx$$

$$= \left. \frac{\hbar^2}{2m} \frac{df^*}{dx} f \right|_{-\infty}^{\infty} - \frac{\hbar^2}{2m} \int_{-\infty}^{\infty} \frac{d^2 f^*}{dx^2} f \, dx$$

and so we see that

$$\int_{-\infty}^{\infty} f^* \left(-\frac{\hbar^2}{2m} \frac{d^2}{dx^2} \right) f \, dx = \int_{-\infty}^{\infty} f \left(-\frac{\hbar^2}{2m} \frac{d^2}{dx^2} \right) f^* \, dx$$

$$= \int_{-\infty}^{\infty} f \left(-\frac{\hbar^2}{2m} \frac{d^2}{dx^2} \right)^* f^* \, dx$$

Thus, Eq. 4-28 is satisfied, and the kinetic energy operator is Hermitian.

The definition of a Hermitian operator that is given by Eq. 4-28 is not the most general definition. A more general definition of a Hermitian operator is

$$\int_{-\infty}^{\infty} g^* \hat{A} f \, dx = \int_{-\infty}^{\infty} f \hat{A}^* g^* \, dx \tag{4-29}$$

where f and g are any two well-behaved functions. We shall use this definition quite often. It so happens that it is possible to prove that Eq. 4-29 follows from Eq. 4-28 and so the definition Eq. 4-28 suffices if you know this. Problem 15 leads you through the proof.

4-5   *The Eigenfunctions of Hermitian Operators Are Orthogonal*

We have been led naturally to the definition and use of Hermitian operators by requiring that quantum-mechanical operators have real eigenvalues. Not only are the eigenvalues of Hermitian operators real, but their eigenfunctions satisfy a rather special condition also. Consider the two eigenvalue equations

$$\hat{A}\psi_n = a_n\psi_n \qquad \hat{A}\psi_m = a_m\psi_m \qquad (4\text{-}30)$$

We multiply the first of Eq. 4-30 by ψ_m^* and integrate; then we take the complex conjugate of the second, multiply by ψ_n, and integrate to obtain

$$\int_{-\infty}^{\infty} \psi_m^* \hat{A}\psi_n \, dx = a_n \int_{-\infty}^{\infty} \psi_m^* \psi_n \, dx$$

$$\int_{-\infty}^{\infty} \psi_n \hat{A}^* \psi_m^* \, dx = a_m^* \int_{-\infty}^{\infty} \psi_n \psi_m^* \, dx \qquad (4\text{-}31)$$

By subtracting Eqs. 4-31, we obtain

$$\int_{-\infty}^{\infty} \psi_m^* \hat{A}\psi_n \, dx - \int_{-\infty}^{\infty} \psi_n \hat{A}^* \psi_m^* \, dx = (a_n - a_m^*) \int_{-\infty}^{\infty} \psi_m^* \psi_n \, dx$$

Because $\hat{A}$ is Hermitian, the left-hand side here is zero, and so we have

$$(a_n - a_m^*) \int_{-\infty}^{\infty} \psi_m^* \psi_n \, dx = 0 \qquad (4\text{-}32)$$

There are two possibilities to consider in Eq. 4-32: $n = m$ and $n \neq m$. When $n = m$, the integral is unity by normalization and so we have

$$a_n = a_n^* \qquad (4\text{-}33)$$

which is just another proof that the eigenvalues are real.

When $n \neq m$, we have

$$(a_n - a_m) \int_{-\infty}^{\infty} \psi_m^* \psi_n \, dx = 0 \qquad m \neq n \qquad (4\text{-}34)$$

Now if the system is nondegenerate, $a_n \neq a_m$, and

$$\int_{-\infty}^{\infty} \psi_m^* \psi_n \, dx = 0 \qquad n \neq m \qquad (4\text{-}35)$$

A set of eigenfunctions that satisfies the condition in Eq. 4-35 is said to be *orthogonal*. We have just proved that the eigenfunctions of a Hermitian operator are orthogonal, at least for a nondegenerate system. The particle in a box is a nondegenerate system. The wave functions for this system are (Eq. 3-28)

$$\psi_n(x) = \left(\frac{2}{a}\right)^{1/2} \sin \frac{n\pi x}{a} \qquad n = 1, 2, \ldots \qquad (4\text{-}36)$$

It is easy to prove that these functions are orthogonal if one uses the trigonometric identity

$$\sin \alpha \sin \beta = \tfrac{1}{2} \cos (\alpha - \beta) - \tfrac{1}{2} \cos (\alpha + \beta) \tag{4-37}$$

Then

$$\frac{2}{a} \int_0^a \sin \frac{n\pi x}{a} \sin \frac{m\pi x}{a} dx = \frac{1}{a} \int_0^a \cos \frac{(n-m)\pi x}{a} dx - \frac{1}{a} \int_0^a \cos \frac{(n+m)\pi x}{a} dx \tag{4-38}$$

Because n and m are integers, both integrands on the right-hand side of Eq. 4-38 are of the form $\cos (N\pi x/a)$ where N is an integer. Consequently, both integrals go over complete cycles of the cosine and equal zero if $m \neq n$. Thus, we see that

$$\frac{2}{a} \int_0^a \sin \frac{n\pi x}{a} \sin \frac{m\pi x}{a} dx = 0 \qquad m \neq n \tag{4-39}$$

The wave functions of a particle in a box are orthogonal.

When $n = m$ in Eq. 4-38, the integrand of the first integral on the right-hand side of Eq. 4-38 is unity because $\cos 0 = 1$. The second integral on the right-hand side of Eq. 4-38 vanishes and so we have that

$$\frac{2}{a} \int_0^a \sin^2 \frac{n\pi x}{a} dx = 1 \tag{4-40}$$

or that the particle-in-a-box wave functions are normalized. A set of functions that are both normalized and orthogonal to each other is called an *orthonormal* set. We can express the condition of orthonormality by writing

$$\int_{-\infty}^{\infty} \psi_j^* \psi_i \, dx = \delta_{ij} \tag{4-41}$$

where

$$\delta_{ij} = \begin{cases} 1 & i = j \\ 0 & i \neq j \end{cases} \tag{4-42}$$

The symbol δ_{ij} occurs frequently and is called the *Kroenecker delta* (cf. Problem 18).

EXAMPLE 4-5

According to Problem 26 on p. 107 the eigenfunctions of a particle constrained to move on a circular ring of radius a are

$$\psi_m(\theta) = (2\pi)^{-1/2} e^{im\theta} \qquad m = 0, \pm 1, \pm 2, \ldots$$

where θ describes the angular position of the particle about the ring. Clearly $0 \leq \theta \leq 2\pi$. Prove that these eigenfunctions form an orthonormal set.

Solution: To prove that a set of functions forms an orthonormal set, we must show that they satisfy Eq. 4-41. To see if they do satisfy Eq. 4-41, we have

$$\int_0^{2\pi} \psi_m^*(\theta)\psi_n(\theta)\, d\theta = \frac{1}{2\pi}\int_0^{2\pi} e^{-im\theta}e^{in\theta}\, d\theta$$

$$= \frac{1}{2\pi}\int_0^{2\pi} e^{i(n-m)\theta}\, d\theta$$

$$= \frac{1}{2\pi}\int_0^{2\pi} \cos(n-m)\theta\, d\theta + \frac{i}{2\pi}\int_0^{2\pi} \sin(n-m)\theta\, d\theta$$

For $n \neq m$, the final two integrals vanish because they are over complete cycles of the cosine and sine. For $n = m$, the last integral vanishes because $\sin 0 = 0$ and the next to last gives 2π because $\cos 0 = 1$. Thus

$$\int_0^{2\pi} \psi_m^*(\theta)\psi_n(\theta)\, d\theta = \delta_{mn}$$

and the $\psi_m(\theta)$ form an orthonormal set.

When we proved that the eigenfunctions of a Hermitian operator are orthogonal, we assumed that the system was nondegenerate. For simplicity, let us consider the case in which two states, described by ψ_1 and ψ_2, have the same eigenvalue a_1. By referring to Eq. 4-34, we see that it does not follow that ψ_1 and ψ_2 are orthogonal, because $a_1 = a_2$. The two eigenvalue equations are

$$\hat{A}\psi_1 = a_1\psi_1 \quad \hat{A}\psi_2 = a_1\psi_2$$

Now let us consider a linear combination of ψ_1 and ψ_2, say, $\phi = c_1\psi_1 + c_2\psi_2$. Then

$$\hat{A}\phi = \hat{A}(c_1\psi_1 + c_2\psi_2) = c_1\hat{A}\psi_1 + c_2\hat{A}\psi_2$$
$$= a_1c_1\psi_1 + a_1c_2\psi_2 = a_1(c_1\psi_1 + c_2\psi_2)$$
$$= a_1\phi$$

Thus, we see that if ψ_1 and ψ_2 describe a twofold degenerate state with eigenvalue a_1, then any linear combination of ψ_1 and ψ_2 is also an eigenfunction with eigenvalue a_1. It is convenient to choose two linear combinations of ψ_1 and ψ_2, call them ϕ_1 and ϕ_2, such that

$$\int_{-\infty}^{\infty} \phi_1^*\phi_2\, dx = 0$$

To see how to do this in practice, we choose

$$\phi_1 = \psi_1 \quad \text{and} \quad \phi_2 = \psi_2 + c\psi_1$$

where ψ_1 and ψ_2 are normalized and c is a constant to be determined. We choose c such that ϕ_1 and ϕ_2 are orthogonal:

$$\int_{-\infty}^{\infty} \phi_1^*\phi_2\, dx = \int_{-\infty}^{\infty} \psi_1^*(\psi_2 + c\psi_1)\, dx$$
$$= \int_{-\infty}^{\infty} \psi_1^*\psi_2\, dx + c = 0$$

If c is chosen to be

$$c = -\int_{-\infty}^{\infty} \psi_1^* \psi_2 \, dx$$

then ϕ_1 and ϕ_2 will be orthogonal. [This procedure can be generalized to the case of n functions and is called the *Schmidt orthogonalization procedure* (cf. Problem 19.)] So even if there is a degeneracy, we can construct the eigenfunctions of a Hermitian operator such that they are orthogonal and say that they form an orthonormal set, Eq. 4-41.

EXAMPLE 4-6

This example illustrates the Schmidt orthogonalization procedure. The set of functions 1 and x is not orthonormal over the interval $0 \le x \le 1$. Use the Schmidt orthogonalization procedure to construct an orthonormal set from these two functions.

Solution: Let $\phi_1(x) = 1$. This function is normalized over $(0, 1)$ because

$$\int_0^1 \phi_1^2(x) \, dx = 1$$

Now let

$$\phi_2(x) = x + c_1\phi_1(x) = x + c_1$$

and require that

$$\int_0^1 \phi_1(x)\phi_2(x) \, dx = \int_0^1 (x + c_1) \, dx = \tfrac{1}{2} + c_1 = 0$$

Therefore, $\phi_2(x) = x - \tfrac{1}{2}$ is orthogonal to $\phi_1(x)$. To normalize $\phi_2(x)$, we multiply $\phi_2(x)$ by N_2 and require that N_2 satisfy the condition

$$N_2^2 \int_0^1 \phi_2^2(x) \, dx = N_2^2 \int_0^1 (x - \tfrac{1}{2})^2 \, dx = N_2^2 \left(\tfrac{1}{12}\right) = 1$$

Therefore, $N_2 = (12)^{1/2}$ and

$$\phi_2(x) = (12)^{1/2} (x - \tfrac{1}{2})$$

The two functions $\phi_1(x)$ and $\phi_2(x)$ are orthonormal over the interval $(0, 1)$. For more than two functions, the procedure is a straightforward generalization.

4-6   *A Fourier Series Is an Expansion in Terms of an Orthonormal Set*

The concept of an orthonormal set is extremely useful in many branches of physics and chemistry. Consider a fairly arbitrary function $f(x)$. We assume that if $\{\psi_n(x)\}$ is some orthonormal set defined over the same interval as $f(x)$ and satisfying the same boundary conditions as $f(x)$, then it is possible to write $f(x)$ as

$$f(x) = \sum_{n=1}^{\infty} c_n \psi_n(x) \qquad (4\text{-}43)$$

A set of functions such as the $\psi_n(x)$ here is said to be *complete* if Eq. 4-43 holds for a suitably arbitrary function $f(x)$. It is generally difficult to prove completeness and in practice one usually assumes that the orthonormal set associated with some Hermitian operator is complete. If we multiply both sides of Eq. 4-43 by $\psi_m^*(x)$ and integrate, then we find

$$\int_{-\infty}^{\infty} \psi_m^*(x) f(x)\, dx = \sum_{n=1}^{\infty} c_n \int_{-\infty}^{\infty} \psi_m^*(x)\psi_n(x)\, dx = \sum_{n=1}^{\infty} c_n \delta_{mn} = c_m \qquad (4\text{-}44)$$

The last equality in Eq. 4-44 follows from the fact that $\delta_{mn} = 0$ for every term in the summation except for the one term in which $m = n$, and then $\delta_{mn} = 1$ (Problem 18). Equation 4-44 gives us a simple formula for the coefficients in the expansion, Eq. 4-43,

$$c_n = \int_{-\infty}^{\infty} \psi_n^*(x) f(x)\, dx \qquad (4\text{-}45)$$

The expansion of a function in terms of an orthonormal set as in Eq. 4-43 is an important and useful technique in many branches of physics. We can illustrate the procedure by considering a particle in a box. In Example 4-2, we calculated the average energy of a particle in a box if it is in the state described by the wave function $(30/a^5)^{1/2}x(a - x)$. Let us expand this function in terms of the orthonormal complete set of eigenfunctions of a particle in a box. If we substitute Eq. 3-28 for $\psi_n(x)$ into Eq. 4-43, then we obtain

$$f(x) = \left(\frac{2}{a}\right)^{1/2} \sum_{n=1}^{\infty} c_n \sin \frac{n\pi x}{a} \qquad 0 \le x \le a \qquad (4\text{-}46)$$

Equation 4-45 gives

$$c_n = \left(\frac{2}{a}\right)^{1/2} \int_0^a f(x) \sin \frac{n\pi x}{a}\, dx \qquad (4\text{-}47)$$

In our case,

$$f(x) = \left(\frac{30}{a^5}\right)^{1/2} x(a - x) \qquad 0 \le x \le a \qquad (4\text{-}48)$$

If we substitute Eq. 4-48 into Eq. 4-47, then we find

$$c_n = \left(\frac{60}{a^6}\right)^{1/2} \int_0^a x(a - x) \sin \frac{n\pi x}{a}\, dx$$

$$= \left(\frac{60}{a^6}\right)^{1/2} \left[2\left(\frac{a}{n\pi}\right)^3 (1 - \cos n\pi) \right]$$

$$= \frac{4(15)^{1/2}}{\pi^3 n^3} [1 - (-1)^n]$$

Therefore, we find that

$$c_n = \begin{cases} \dfrac{8(15)^{1/2}}{\pi^3 n^3} & \text{for odd values of } n \\ 0 & \text{for even values of } n \end{cases} \tag{4-49}$$

Problem 21 explains why $c_n = 0$ for even values of n. In Section 4-7, we shall show that c_n^2 is the probability that we obtain the energy $E_n = n^2 h^2 / 8 m a^2$ if we measure the energy of a particle in a box described by the wave function given by Eq. 4-48. The expansion of a function in terms of an orthonormal set is called a *Fourier expansion* or a *Fourier series*. Because Eq. 4-46 contains only sine functions, it is called a *Fourier sine series*. The coefficients c_n in the expansion are called *Fourier coefficients*. Fourier series occur frequently in both classical mechanics and quantum mechanics. Example 4-7 illustrates the application of Fourier series to a vibrating string.

EXAMPLE 4-7

The general solution to a vibrating string fixed at both ends is given by Eq. 2-23:

$$u(x, t) = \sum_{n=1}^{\infty} (F_n \cos \omega_n t + G_n \sin \omega_n t) \sin \frac{n\pi x}{l} \tag{4-50}$$

This was as far as we took the solution because at that time we did not know how to determine the F_n's and G_n's. We can determine them now. Suppose we are given the initial deflection, or profile, of the string and its initial velocity. In terms of $u(x, t)$, these are $u(x, 0)$ and $(\partial u / \partial t)_{t=0}$. As a specific example, let us suppose that the string is plucked from the middle as in Figure 4-2. The equation for $u(x, 0)$ is

$$u(x, 0) = \begin{cases} \dfrac{2k}{l} x & 0 \le x \le \dfrac{l}{2} \\ \dfrac{2k}{l}(l - x) & \dfrac{l}{2} \le x \le l \end{cases} \tag{4-51}$$

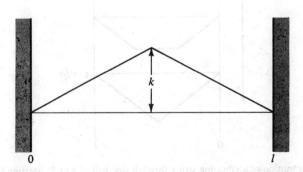

Figure 4-2. The initial profile of a vibrating string that is plucked in the middle.

If we hold the string as in Figure 4-2 and simply let it go, then its initial velocity is zero, or

$$\left(\frac{\partial u}{\partial t}\right)_{t=0} = 0 \qquad \text{for all } x$$

Use the initial conditions to determine $u(x, t)$ in Eq. 4-50 completely.

Solution: If we let $t = 0$ in Eq. 4-50, then we see that

$$u(x, 0) = \sum_{n=1}^{\infty} F_n \sin \frac{n\pi x}{l} \qquad (4\text{-}52)$$

If we evaluate $(\partial u/\partial t)$ at $t = 0$, then we find

$$\left(\frac{\partial u}{\partial t}\right)_{t=0} = \sum_{n=1}^{\infty} G_n \omega_n \sin \frac{n\pi x}{l}$$

Because $(\partial u/\partial t)_{t=0} = 0$ for all x, then all the G_n must equal zero. This leaves only the F_n to be determined. Equation 4-52 is essentially the same

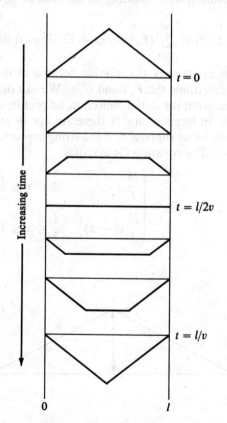

Figure 4-3. The motion of a vibrating string through one-half of a cycle, starting from rest at the profile shown at $t = 0$.

form as Eq. 4-46, and so the F_n can be found by using Eq. 4-45. For this case,

$$F_n = \frac{2}{l} \int_0^l u(x, 0) \sin \frac{n\pi x}{l} dx$$

where $u(x, 0)$ is given by Eq. 4-51. By carrying out the integrations, we find

$$F_n = \frac{8k}{n^2 \pi^2} \sin \frac{n\pi}{2}$$

Substituting this result along with the fact that all the G_n's $= 0$ into Eq. 4-50 gives

$$u(x, t) = \frac{8k}{\pi^2} \left(\frac{1}{1^2} \sin \frac{\pi x}{l} \cos \frac{\pi vt}{l} - \frac{1}{3^2} \sin \frac{3\pi x}{l} \cos \frac{3\pi vt}{l} + \cdots \right)$$

as the complete solution. Figure 4-3 shows this solution through one-half of a cycle of the motion. This is just one of many applications of Fourier series in classical mechanics (cf. Problem 22).

4-7   *The Probability of Obtaining a Certain Value of an Observable in a Measurement Is Given by a Fourier Coefficient*

Postulate 3 says that the only values of the observable corresponding to $\hat{A}$ that one obtains in a measurement are the eigenvalues of $\hat{A}$. Postulate 4 tells us how to calculate the average in a series of measurements:

$$\langle a \rangle = \int_{-\infty}^{\infty} \Psi^*(x, t)\hat{A}\Psi(x, t) dx \tag{4-53}$$

If $\Psi(x, t)$ is an eigenstate of $\hat{A}$, then we observe only one value of a; but in the general case, when we carry out a series of measurements, we observe a distribution of the set of possible results $\{a_n\}$, whose average is given by Eq. 4-53. A natural question to ask is: If the system is in a state described by $\Psi(x, t)$, then what is the probability of obtaining the particular result a_n in a single measurement? To answer this question, we consider a measurement of the energy, so that $\hat{A} = \hat{H}$ and $\langle a \rangle = \langle E \rangle$ in Eq. 4-53. Now we substitute Eq. 4-21 for $\Psi(x, t)$ into Eq. 4-53 and find

$$\langle E \rangle = \int_{-\infty}^{\infty} \Psi^*(x, t)\hat{H}\Psi(x, t) dx$$

$$= \int_{-\infty}^{\infty} \left[\sum_n c_n^* \psi_n^*(x) e^{iE_n t/\hbar} \right] \hat{H} \left[\sum_m c_m \psi_m(x) e^{-iE_m t/\hbar} \right] dx$$

$$= \sum_n \sum_m c_n^* c_m \exp\left[\frac{i(E_n - E_m)t}{\hbar} \right] \int_{-\infty}^{\infty} \psi_n^*(x)\hat{H}\psi_m(x) dx \tag{4-54}$$

If we use the fact that $\hat{H}\psi_m(x) = E_m\psi_m(x)$, Eq. 4-54 becomes

$$\langle E \rangle = \sum_n \sum_m c_n^* c_m E_m \exp\left[\frac{i(E_n - E_m)t}{\hbar}\right] \int_{-\infty}^{\infty} \psi_n^*(x)\psi_m(x)\,dx \qquad (4\text{-}55)$$

The integral here is equal to the Kroenecker delta δ_{nm}, and so Eq. 4-55 becomes

$$\langle E \rangle = \sum_n \sum_m c_n^* c_m E_m \exp\left[\frac{i(E_n - E_m)t}{\hbar}\right]\delta_{nm}$$

or

$$\langle E \rangle = \sum_n c_n^* c_n E_n = \sum_n |c_n|^2 E_n \qquad (4\text{-}56)$$

Recall that the average of a set of energies is defined as (Eq. 3-33)

$$\langle E \rangle = \sum_n p_n E_n \qquad (4\text{-}57)$$

where p_n is the probability of observing the value E_n. By comparing Eqs. 4-56 and 4-57, we see that we can interpret $|c_n|^2$ as the probability of observing E_n when carrying out a measurement on the system, or

$$\text{probability of observing } E_n = |c_n|^2 \qquad (4\text{-}58)$$

Suppose the system is in an energy eigenstate, say $\psi_1(x)$, so that $\hat{H}\psi_1(x) = E_1\psi_1(x)$. Then all the c_n's are zero, except for c_1, which is equal to unity. According to Eq. 4-58, the probability of observing E_1 is unity, in agreement with Postulate 3. Example 4-8 illustrates the case where the system is not in an energy eigenstate.

EXAMPLE 4-8

Consider the system discussed in Example 4-2. We have a particle in a box that is described by the wave function

$$f(x) = \left(\frac{30}{a^5}\right)^{1/2} x(a - x) \qquad 0 \le x \le a$$

Calculate the probability that if we were to measure the energy of the particle, the value $E_n = n^2 h^2/8ma^2$ would result. Show that the sum of these probabilities is unity. Using these probabilities, calculate $\langle E \rangle$ and compare the result to the value found in Example 4-2.

Solution: The energy eigenfunctions of a particle in a box are $(2/a)^{1/2} \sin(n\pi x/a)$. According to Eq. 4-58, we must determine the Fourier coefficients $\{c_n\}$ in the expansion

$$f(x) = \left(\frac{2}{a}\right)^{1/2} \sum_{n=1}^{\infty} c_n \sin\frac{n\pi x}{a} \qquad (4\text{-}46)$$

In Section 4-6, we showed that (Eq. 4-46 through 4-49)

$$c_n = \begin{cases} \dfrac{8(15)^{1/2}}{\pi^3 n^3} & \text{if } n \text{ is odd} \\ \\ 0 & \text{if } n \text{ is even} \end{cases} \qquad (4\text{-}49)$$

The probability of observing the energy $n^2 h^2 / 8ma^2$ is

$$\text{probability of observing } E_n = |c_n|^2 = \begin{cases} \dfrac{960}{\pi^6 n^6} & \text{if } n \text{ is odd} \\ \\ 0 & \text{if } n \text{ is even} \end{cases} \qquad (4\text{-}59)$$

To show that these probabilities sum to unity, we must show that

$$\sum_{n=1}^{\infty} c_n^2 = \frac{960}{\pi^6} \sum_{n \text{ odd}} \frac{1}{n^6} \overset{?}{=} 1 \qquad (4\text{-}60)$$

The summation here is of the form

$$\lambda(s) = \sum_{k=0}^{\infty} (2k + 1)^{-s} \qquad (4\text{-}61)$$

where $s = 6$. Values of $\lambda(s)$ can be found in many handbooks (for example, the CRC Handbook), and $\lambda(6) = \pi^6/960$. If we use this value in Eq. 4-60, then we find that

$$\sum_{n=1}^{\infty} c_n^2 = 1$$

The average energy is given by Eq. 4-56:

$$\langle E \rangle = \sum_{n=1}^{\infty} c_n^2 E_n = \sum_{n \text{ odd}} \left(\frac{960}{\pi^6 n^6} \right) \left(\frac{n^2 h^2}{8ma^2} \right)$$

$$= \frac{120 h^2}{m \pi^6 a^2} \sum_{n \text{ odd}} \frac{1}{n^4} \qquad (4\text{-}62)$$

The value of the summation here is $\lambda(4)$ in Eq. 4-61, and reference to a handbook gives $\lambda(4) = \pi^4/96$. If we substitute this value into Eq. 4-62, then we find

$$\langle E \rangle = \frac{5 h^2}{4 \pi^2 m a^2}$$

which is exactly the value we obtained in Example 4-2 by another method.

4-8   Many Operators Do Not Commute

When two operators act sequentially on a function, as in $\hat{A}\hat{B}f(x)$, we apply each operator in turn, working from right to left:

$$\hat{A}\hat{B}f(x) = \hat{A}[\hat{B}f(x)] = \hat{A}h(x)$$

where $h(x) = \hat{B}f(x)$. An important difference between operators and ordinary algebraic quantities is that operators do not necessarily *commute*. If

$$\hat{A}\hat{B}f(x) = \hat{B}\hat{A}f(x) \quad \text{(commutative)} \quad (4\text{-}63)$$

for arbitrary $f(x)$, then $\hat{A}$ and $\hat{B}$ are said to *commute*. If

$$\hat{A}\hat{B}f(x) \neq \hat{B}\hat{A}f(x) \quad \text{(noncommutative)} \quad (4\text{-}64)$$

for arbitrary $f(x)$, then $\hat{A}$ and $\hat{B}$ do not commute. For example, if $\hat{A} = d/dx$ and $\hat{B} = x$ (multiply by x), then

$$\hat{A}\hat{B}f(x) = \frac{d}{dx}\left[xf(x)\right] = f(x) + x\frac{df}{dx}$$

and

$$\hat{B}\hat{A}f(x) = x\frac{d}{dx}f(x) = x\frac{df}{dx}$$

Therefore, $\hat{A}\hat{B}f(x) \neq \hat{B}\hat{A}f(x)$, and $\hat{A}$ and $\hat{B}$ do not commute. In this particular case, we have

$$\hat{A}\hat{B}f(x) - \hat{B}\hat{A}f(x) = f(x) \quad (4\text{-}65)$$

or

$$(\hat{A}\hat{B} - \hat{B}\hat{A})f(x) = \hat{I}f(x)$$

where we have introduced the identity operator $\hat{I}$, which simply multiplies $f(x)$ by unity. Because $f(x)$ is arbitrary, we can write Eq. 4-65 as an operator equation by suppressing $f(x)$ on both sides of the equation to give

$$\hat{A}\hat{B} - \hat{B}\hat{A} = \hat{I} \quad (4\text{-}66)$$

Realize that an operator equality like this is valid only if it is true for all $f(x)$. The combination of $\hat{A}$ and $\hat{B}$ appearing in Eq. 4-66 occurs often and is called the *commutator*, $[\hat{A}, \hat{B}]$, of $\hat{A}$ and $\hat{B}$:

$$[\hat{A}, \hat{B}] = \hat{A}\hat{B} - \hat{B}\hat{A} \quad (4\text{-}67)$$

If $[\hat{A}, \hat{B}]f(x) = 0$ for all $f(x)$ on which the commutator acts, then we write that $[\hat{A}, \hat{B}] = 0$ and we say that $\hat{A}$ and $\hat{B}$ commute.

EXAMPLE 4-9

Let $\hat{A} = d/dx$ and $\hat{B} = x^2$. Evaluate the commutator $[\hat{A}, \hat{B}]$.

Solution: We let $\hat{A}$ and $\hat{B}$ act upon an arbitrary function $f(x)$:

$$\hat{A}\hat{B}f(x) = \frac{d}{dx}\left[x^2 f(x)\right] = 2xf(x) + x^2\frac{df}{dx}$$

$$\hat{B}\hat{A}f(x) = x^2\frac{d}{dx}f(x) = x^2\frac{df}{dx}$$

By subtracting these two results, we obtain

$$(\hat{A}\hat{B} - \hat{B}\hat{A})f(x) = 2xf(x)$$

Because, and only because, $f(x)$ is arbitrary, we write

$$[\hat{A}, \hat{B}] = 2x\hat{I}$$

When evaluating a commutator, it is essential to include a function $f(x)$ as we have done; otherwise we can find a spurious result. To this end, note well that

$$[\hat{A}, \hat{B}] = \hat{A}\hat{B} - \hat{B}\hat{A} = \frac{d}{dx}x^2 - x^2\frac{d}{dx}$$

$$\neq 2x - x^2\frac{d}{dx}$$

a result that is obtained by forgetting to include the function $f(x)$. Such errors will not occur if an arbitrary function $f(x)$ is included from the outset.

EXAMPLE 4-10

For a one-dimensional system, the momentum operator is (Eq. 3-11)

$$\hat{P}_x = -i\hbar\frac{d}{dx}$$

and the position operator is

$$\hat{X} = x \quad \text{(multiply by } x\text{)}$$

Evaluate $[\hat{P}_x, \hat{X}]$.

Solution: We let $[\hat{P}_x, \hat{X}]$ act upon an arbitrary function $f(x)$:

$$[\hat{P}_x, \hat{X}]f(x) = \hat{P}_x\hat{X}f(x) - \hat{X}\hat{P}_xf(x)$$

$$= -i\hbar\frac{d}{dx}[xf(x)] + xi\hbar\frac{d}{dx}f(x)$$

$$= -i\hbar f(x) - i\hbar x\frac{df}{dx} + i\hbar x\frac{df}{dx}$$

$$= -i\hbar f(x)$$

Because $f(x)$ is arbitrary, we write this result as

$$[\hat{P}_x, \hat{X}] = -i\hbar\hat{I} \tag{4-68}$$

where $\hat{I}$ is the unit operator (the multiply-by-one operator). We shall see in Section 4-9 that because $\hat{P}_x$ and $\hat{X}$ do not commute, the momentum and the position of a particle cannot be determined simultaneously with infinite precision.

4-9   *The Commutator of Two Operators Plays a Central Role in the Uncertainty Principle*

Suppose that two operators $\hat{A}$ and $\hat{B}$ have the same set of eigenfunctions, so that we have

$$\hat{A}\phi_n = a_n\phi_n \qquad \hat{B}\phi_n = b_n\phi_n \qquad (4\text{-}69)$$

Equations 4-69 imply that the quantities corresponding to $\hat{A}$ and $\hat{B}$ have simultaneously sharply defined values. According to Eq. 4-69, the values that we observe are a_n and b_n. We shall prove that if two operators have the same set of eigenfunctions, then they necessarily commute. To prove this, we must show that

$$[\hat{A}, \hat{B}]f(x) = 0 \qquad (4\text{-}70)$$

for an arbitrary function $f(x)$. We can expand $f(x)$ in terms of the complete set of eigenfunctions of $\hat{A}$ and $\hat{B}$ and write

$$f(x) = \sum_n c_n\phi_n(x)$$

If we substitute this expansion into Eq. 4-70, then we obtain

$$[\hat{A}, \hat{B}]f(x) = \sum_n c_n[\hat{A}, \hat{B}]\phi_n(x)$$
$$= \sum_n c_n(a_nb_n - b_na_n)\phi_n(x) = 0 \qquad (4\text{-}71)$$

Because $f(x)$ is arbitrary, $[\hat{A}, \hat{B}] = 0$. Thus, we see that $\hat{A}$ and $\hat{B}$ commute because they have the same eigenfunctions.

The converse is also true; if $\hat{A}$ and $\hat{B}$ commute, then they have a mutual set of eigenfunctions. Let the eigenvalue equations of $\hat{A}$ and $\hat{B}$ be (we are dropping the subscript n for simplicity)

$$\hat{A}\phi_a = a\phi_a \qquad \hat{B}\phi_b = b\phi_b \qquad (4\text{-}72)$$

Because $\hat{A}$ and $\hat{B}$ commute, we have

$$[\hat{A}, \hat{B}]\phi_a = 0 = \hat{A}\hat{B}\phi_a - \hat{B}\hat{A}\phi_a$$
$$= \hat{A}(\hat{B}\phi_a) - a(\hat{B}\phi_a) = 0$$

and so

$$\hat{A}(\hat{B}\phi_a) = a(\hat{B}\phi_a) \qquad (4\text{-}73)$$

Equation 4-73 implies that $\hat{B}\phi_a$ is an eigenfunction of $\hat{A}$. If the system is nondegenerate, there is only one eigenfunction ϕ_a for each eigenvalue a, and so Eq. 4-73 says that

$$\hat{B}\phi_a = (\text{constant})\phi_a \qquad (4\text{-}74)$$

But Eq. 4-74 says that ϕ_a is an eigenfunction of $\hat{B}$ as well as an eigenfunction of $\hat{A}$. Because the system is nondegenerate, there is only one eigenfunction of $\hat{B}$ for each eigenvalue b and so Eq. 4-74 implies that ϕ_a and ϕ_b are the same. Thus we see that if $\hat{A}$ and $\hat{B}$ commute, then they have the same set of eigenfunctions; and because they have mutual eigenfunctions, the observables corresponding to $\hat{A}$ and $\hat{B}$ have simultaneously sharply defined values. We have proved this only in this case in which there is no degeneracy, but by using an argument similar to that following Example 4-5 one can prove that the above conclusions are valid even for a degenerate system.

If operators do not commute, then their corresponding observable quantities do not have simultaneously well-defined values, and in fact we shall prove that

$$\sigma_A^2 \sigma_B^2 \geq -\frac{1}{4}\left(\int \psi^*[\hat{A}, \hat{B}]\psi \, dx \right)^2 \tag{4-75}$$

where σ_A^2 and σ_B^2 are

$$\sigma_A^2 = \int \psi^*(\hat{A} - \langle a \rangle)^2 \psi \, dx \tag{4-76}$$

$$\sigma_B^2 = \int \psi^*(\hat{B} - \langle b \rangle)^2 \psi \, dx \tag{4-77}$$

and ψ is a suitably behaved state function. Before we prove Eq. 4-75, let us see how to use it in the case where $\hat{A}$ and $\hat{B}$ are the momentum and position operators. In this case (cf. Eq. 4-68),

$$[\hat{A}, \hat{B}] = [\hat{P}_x, \hat{X}] = -i\hbar\hat{I} \tag{4-78}$$

If we substitute this into Eq. 4-75, then we find

$$\sigma_p^2 \sigma_x^2 \geq -\frac{1}{4}\left[\int \psi^*(-i\hbar)\psi \, dx \right]^2$$

or

$$\sigma_p^2 \sigma_x^2 \geq -\frac{1}{4}(-i\hbar)^2 = \frac{\hbar^2}{4}$$

By taking the square root of both sides, we have

$$\sigma_p \sigma_x \geq \frac{\hbar}{2} \tag{4-79}$$

which is the Heisenberg Uncertainty Principle for momentum and position.

We shall now prove Eq. 4-75. This is the last topic in this chapter, and so you can finish this chapter at this point if you are willing to accept Eq. 4-75. For our proof we need to use a famous inequality called the *Schwartz inequality*, which says that if $f(x)$ and $g(x)$ are arbitrary functions, then

$$\left[\int f^*(x)f(x) \, dx \right]\left[\int g^*(x)g(x) \, dx \right] \geq \frac{1}{4}\left\{ \int [f^*(x)g(x) + f(x)g^*(x)] \, dx \right\}^2 \tag{4-80}$$

The proof of the Schwartz inequality is developed in Problem 29. We now let

$$f(x) = (\hat{A} - \langle a \rangle)\psi(x) \qquad g(x) = i(\hat{B} - \langle b \rangle)\psi(x) \tag{4-81}$$

where $\psi(x)$ is a suitably behaved state function. If we substitute Eq. 4-81 into Eq. 4-80, then the two terms on the left-hand side are

$$\int (\hat{A} - \langle a \rangle)^*\psi^*(x)(\hat{A} - \langle a \rangle)\psi(x) \, dx \tag{4-82}$$

and

$$\int i^*(\hat{B} - \langle b \rangle)^*\psi^*(x)i(\hat{B} - \langle b \rangle)\psi(x) \, dx \tag{4-83}$$

If $\hat{A}$ and $\hat{B}$ are Hermitian, then so are $\hat{A} - \langle a \rangle$ and $\hat{B} - \langle b \rangle$ (Problem 14). Therefore, Eqs. 4-82 and 4-83 can be written in the form (cf. Problem 16)

$$\int \psi^*(x)(\hat{A} - \langle a \rangle)^2 \psi(x)\, dx = \sigma_A^2 \tag{4-84}$$

and

$$\int \psi^*(x)(\hat{B} - \langle b \rangle)^2 \psi(x)\, dx = \sigma_B^2 \tag{4-85}$$

Now let us look at the right-hand side of Eq. 4-80. Under the substitution of Eq. 4-81, the right-hand side of Eq. 4-80 becomes

$$\frac{1}{4}\left[i \int (\hat{A} - \langle a \rangle)^* \psi^*(x)(\hat{B} - \langle b \rangle)\psi(x)\, dx - i \int (\hat{B} - \langle b \rangle)^* \psi^*(x)(\hat{A} - \langle a \rangle)\psi(x)\, dx \right]^2$$

Using the Hermitian property of $\hat{A} - \langle a \rangle$ and $\hat{B} - \langle b \rangle$ once again, we find

$$-\frac{1}{4}\left[\int \psi^*(x)(\hat{A} - \langle a \rangle)(\hat{B} - \langle b \rangle)\psi(x)\, dx - \int \psi^*(x)(\hat{B} - \langle b \rangle)(\hat{A} - \langle a \rangle)\psi(x)\, dx \right]^2$$

$$= -\frac{1}{4}\left\{ \int \psi^*(x)[\hat{A}\hat{B} - \langle a \rangle \hat{B} - \hat{A}\langle b \rangle + \langle a \rangle\langle b \rangle \right.$$

$$\left. - \hat{B}\hat{A} + \langle b \rangle \hat{A} + \hat{B}\langle a \rangle - \langle a \rangle\langle b \rangle]\psi(x)\, dx \right\}^2$$

Because $\langle a \rangle$ and $\langle b \rangle$ are just numbers, most of these terms cancel and we are left with simply

$$-\frac{1}{4}\left\{ \int \psi^*(x)[\hat{A}\hat{B} - \hat{B}\hat{A}]\psi(x)\, dx \right\}^2 = -\frac{1}{4}\left\{ \int \psi^*(x)[\hat{A}, \hat{B}]\psi(x)\, dx \right\}^2$$

Putting all this together gives

$$\sigma_A^2 \sigma_B^2 > -\frac{1}{4}\left\{ \int \psi^*(x)[\hat{A}, \hat{B}]\psi(x)\, dx \right\}^2$$

which was to be proved.

Summary

Just as geometry is built upon a set of axioms, quantum mechanics is built upon a set of postulates. The ultimate test of the soundness of the postulates is a comparison of the predictions derived from the postulates to experimental data. The postulates that we have set up in this chapter are:

Postulate 1

The state of a quantum-mechanical system is completely specified by a function $\Psi(\mathbf{r}, t)$ that depends on the coordinates of the particles and on the time. This function, called the wave function *or the* state function, *has the important property that $\Psi^*(\mathbf{r}, t)\Psi(\mathbf{r}, t)\, dx\, dy\, dz$ is the probability that the particle lies in the volume element $dx\, dy\, dz$, located at $\mathbf{r}$, at the time t.*

R. H. FOWLER

A. PICCARD E. HENRIOT ED. HERZEN TH. DE DONDER E. SCHRÖDINGER W. PAULI W. HEISENBERG L. BRILLOUIN

P. EHRENFEST   E. VERSCHAFFELT

P. DEBYE M. KNUDSEN W. L. BRAGG H. A. KRAMERS P. A. M. DIRAC A. H. COMPTON L. V. DE BROGLIE M. BORN

N. BOHR

I. LANGMUIR M. PLANCK MADAME CURIE H. A. LORENTZ A. EINSTEIN P. LANGEVIN CH. E. GUYE C. T. R. WILSON

O. W. RICHARDSON

ABSENT: SIR W. H. BRAGG, MM. H. DESLANDRES AND E. VAN AUBEL

The participants at the 1927 Solvay Conference. Solvay conferences were established by the Belgian chemist and industrialist, Ernest Solvay, who became wealthy through his patent for the production of sodium carbonate (Solvay process). Solvay conferences dealt with the leading scientific problems of the time, and only the most prominent European physicists attended, as can be seen from the above photograph.

Postulate 2

To every observable in classical mechanics there corresponds a linear, Hermitian operator in quantum mechanics.

Postulate 3

In any measurement of the observable associated with the operator $\hat{A}$, the only values that will ever be observed are the eigenvalues a, which satisfy the eigenvalue equation

$$\hat{A}\Psi = a\Psi$$

Postulate 4

If a system is in a state described by a normalized wave function Ψ, *then the average value of the observable corresponding to* $\hat{A}$ *is given by*

$$\langle a \rangle = \int_{-\infty}^{\infty} \Psi^* \hat{A} \Psi \, d\tau$$

Postulate 5

The wave function or state function of a system evolves in time according to the time-dependent Schrödinger equation

$$\hat{H}\Psi(x, t) = i\hbar \frac{\partial \Psi}{\partial t}$$

Most of this chapter consists of proving a number of formal, general results that we shall use throughout the rest of the book. For example, we proved that the eigenvalues of a Hermitian operator are real. Postulate 3 says that the eigenvalues of quantum-mechanical operators are the values that are obtained in a measurement of the variable corresponding to that operator. The fact that measured quantities are real quantities requires that the operators of quantum mechanics be Hermitian. We also showed that the eigenfunctions of a Hermitian operator form an orthonormal set. In Chapters 5 and 6 we shall see several specific examples in which the wave functions that we obtain form an orthonormal set. We concluded this chapter with a discussion of the theory of measurement in quantum mechanics. A particularly interesting result is the formal connection between the Uncertainty Principle and the commutator of two operators (Eq. 4-75). The relation between two experimentally measured quantities and the commutator of their corresponding operators is a magnificent feat of abstraction and human intelligence.

Terms That You Should Know

dynamical variable	orthogonal functions
observable	orthonormal set
trajectory	Kroenecker delta
wave function	Schmidt orthogonalization
state function	Fourier series
quadratically integrable	Fourier coefficients
square integrable	commuting operators
spectrum of an operator	commutator
time-dependent Schrödinger equation	mutual eigenfunctions
stationary-state wave function	Schwartz inequality
Hermitian operator	

Problems

1. Which of the following functions are normalizable over the indicated intervals?

(a) e^{-x^2} $(-\infty, \infty)$ (b) e^x $(0, \infty)$
(c) $e^{i\theta}$ $(0, 2\pi)$ (d) $\sinh x$ $(0, \infty)$
(e) xe^{-x} $(0, \infty)$

Normalize those that can be normalized.

2. Determine whether the following functions are acceptable or not as a state function over the indicated intervals:

(a) $\dfrac{1}{x}$ $(0, \infty)$ (b) $e^{-2x} \sinh x$ $(0, \infty)$

(c) $(1 - x^2)^{-1}$ $(-1, 1)$ (d) $e^{-x} \cos x$ $(0, \infty)$
(e) $\tan^{-1} x$ $(0, \infty)$

3. Consider two vectors $\mathbf{v}_1 = 2\mathbf{i} - \mathbf{j} + 3\mathbf{k}$ and $\mathbf{v}_2 = \mathbf{i} + 2\mathbf{j} + \mathbf{k}$, where $\mathbf{i}$, $\mathbf{j}$, and $\mathbf{k}$ are unit vectors pointing along the positive x, y, and z axes, respectively. Recall that the dot product of two vectors $\mathbf{a}$ and $\mathbf{b}$ is given by

$$\mathbf{a} \cdot \mathbf{b} = |\mathbf{a}| |\mathbf{b}| \cos \theta$$

where $|\ \ |$ denotes the length of a vector and θ is the angle between $\mathbf{a}$ and $\mathbf{b}$. Using this definition of a dot product, show that $\mathbf{i} \cdot \mathbf{i} = \mathbf{j} \cdot \mathbf{j} = \mathbf{k} \cdot \mathbf{k} = 1$ and that $\mathbf{i} \cdot \mathbf{j} = \mathbf{i} \cdot \mathbf{k} = \mathbf{j} \cdot \mathbf{k} = 0$. Now show that a dot product is also given by

$$\mathbf{a} \cdot \mathbf{b} = a_x b_x + a_y b_y + a_z b_z$$

Find the dot product of $\mathbf{v}_1$ and $\mathbf{v}_2$. Why is the length of a vector equal to $(\mathbf{a} \cdot \mathbf{a})^{1/2}$? Find the lengths of $\mathbf{v}_1$ and $\mathbf{v}_2$. Find the angle between $\mathbf{v}_1$ and $\mathbf{v}_2$. Show that $\mathbf{a} \cdot \mathbf{b} = 0$ if $\mathbf{a}$ is perpendicular to $\mathbf{b}$.

4. Recall that the cross product of two vectors $\mathbf{a} \times \mathbf{b}$ is a vector of magnitude $|\mathbf{a}| |\mathbf{b}| \sin \theta$ (θ is the angle between $\mathbf{a}$ and $\mathbf{b}$) and that its direction is that which a right-hand screw would travel as $\mathbf{a}$ is rotated into $\mathbf{b}$. Show that $\mathbf{i} \times \mathbf{i} = \mathbf{j} \times \mathbf{j} = \mathbf{k} \times \mathbf{k} = 0$ and that $\mathbf{i} \times \mathbf{j} = \mathbf{k}, \mathbf{i} \times \mathbf{k} = -\mathbf{j}$, and $\mathbf{j} \times \mathbf{k} = \mathbf{i}$, where $\mathbf{i}$, $\mathbf{j}$, and $\mathbf{k}$ are defined in Problem 3. Using all this, show that $\mathbf{a} \times \mathbf{b}$ is given by

$$\mathbf{a} \times \mathbf{b} = \begin{vmatrix} \mathbf{i} & \mathbf{j} & \mathbf{k} \\ a_x & a_y & a_z \\ b_x & b_y & b_z \end{vmatrix}$$

Show that

$$\mathbf{a} \times \mathbf{b} = (a_y b_z - a_z b_y)\mathbf{i} + (a_z b_x - a_x b_z)\mathbf{j} + (a_x b_y - a_y b_x)\mathbf{k}$$

and that

$$\mathbf{a} \times \mathbf{b} = -\mathbf{b} \times \mathbf{a}$$

Show that $\mathbf{a} \times \mathbf{a} = 0$. Find the cross product of the two vectors in Problem 3. Find the angle between them.

5. If the components of a vector depend on some parameter, say time, then the derivative of the vector is

$$\frac{d\mathbf{a}}{dt} = \frac{da_x}{dt}\mathbf{i} + \frac{da_y}{dt}\mathbf{j} + \frac{da_z}{dt}\mathbf{k}$$

Show that

$$\frac{d}{dt}(\mathbf{a} \cdot \mathbf{b}) = \frac{d\mathbf{a}}{dt} \cdot \mathbf{b} + \mathbf{a} \cdot \frac{d\mathbf{b}}{dt}$$

$$\frac{d}{dt}(\mathbf{a} \times \mathbf{b}) = \frac{d\mathbf{a}}{dt} \times \mathbf{b} + \mathbf{a} \times \frac{d\mathbf{b}}{dt}$$

6. Using the results of Problem 5, prove that

$$\mathbf{a} \times \frac{d\mathbf{a}}{dt} + \frac{d\mathbf{a}}{dt} \times \mathbf{a} = 0$$

(*Hint:* Start with $d/dt\,(\mathbf{a} \times \mathbf{a}) = 0$). Also prove that

$$\mathbf{a} \times \frac{d^2\mathbf{a}}{dt^2} = \frac{d}{dt}\left(\mathbf{a} \times \frac{d\mathbf{a}}{dt}\right)$$

7. In vector notation, Newton's equations for a single particle are

$$m\frac{d^2\mathbf{r}}{dt^2} = \mathbf{F} = \mathbf{F}(x, y, z)$$

By operating on this equation from the left by $\mathbf{r} \times$ and using the results from Problem 6, show that

$$m\frac{d}{dt}\left(\mathbf{r} \times \frac{d\mathbf{r}}{dt}\right) = \mathbf{r} \times \mathbf{F}$$

Because the momentum $\mathbf{p}$ is defined by

$$\mathbf{p} = m\frac{d\mathbf{r}}{dt}$$

then the previous equation reads

$$\frac{d}{dt}(\mathbf{r} \times \mathbf{p}) = \mathbf{r} \times \mathbf{F}$$

This last equation is the form of Newton's equations for a rotating system and shows the origin of the definition of angular momentum as $\mathbf{r} \times \mathbf{p}$. Notice that the angular momentum is conserved if $\mathbf{r} \times \mathbf{F} = 0$. Can you identify $\mathbf{r} \times \mathbf{F}$? Show that the formula $\mathbf{r} \times \mathbf{p}$ for angular momentum reduces to *mvr* for circular motion. What is the direction of $\mathbf{l} = \mathbf{r} \times \mathbf{p}$ in the case of circular motion?

8. Calculate $\sigma_E^2 = \langle E^2 \rangle - \langle E \rangle^2$ for a particle in a box in the state described by

$$\Psi(x) = \left(\frac{630}{a^9}\right)^{1/2} x^2(a - x)^2 \qquad 0 \leq x \leq a$$

9. Consider a free particle constrained to move over the rectangular region $0 \leq x \leq a, 0 \leq y \leq b$ (cf. Figure 4-4). We call this system a particle in a two-dimensional box. The energy eigenfunctions of this system are

$$\psi_{n_x,n_y}(x, y) = \left(\frac{4}{ab}\right)^{1/2} \sin \frac{n_x \pi x}{a} \sin \frac{n_y \pi y}{b} \qquad \begin{array}{l} n_x = 1, 2, 3, \ldots \\ n_y = 1, 2, 3, \ldots \end{array}$$

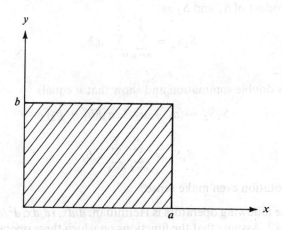

Figure 4-4. The geometry associated with a particle in a two-dimensional box.

The Hamiltonian operator for this system is

$$\hat{H} = -\frac{\hbar^2}{2m}\left(\frac{\partial^2}{\partial x^2} + \frac{\partial^2}{\partial y^2}\right)$$

Show that if the system is in one of its eigenstates, then

$$\sigma_E^2 = \langle E^2 \rangle - \langle E \rangle^2 = 0$$

10. The momentum operator in two dimensions is

$$\hat{P} = -i\hbar\left(\mathbf{i}\frac{\partial}{\partial x} + \mathbf{j}\frac{\partial}{\partial y}\right)$$

Using the wave functions given in Problem 9, calculate $\langle p \rangle$ and then

$$\sigma_p^2 = \langle p^2 \rangle - \langle p \rangle^2$$

Compare your result to σ_p^2 in the one-dimensional case.

11. Suppose that a particle in a two-dimensional box (cf. Problem 9) is in the state

$$\psi(x, y) = \frac{30}{(a^5 b^5)^{1/2}} x(a - x)y(b - y)$$

Show that $\psi(x, y)$ is normalized, and then calculate $\langle E \rangle$ associated with the state described by $\psi(x, y)$.

12. Consider two simple summations:

$$S_1 = \sum_{n=1}^{3} a_n \qquad S_2 = \sum_{n=1}^{2} b_n$$

It is important to realize that in writing the product of S_1 and S_2 as a double summation it is necessary to use two different summation indices and to write the product of S_1 and S_2 as

$$S_1 S_2 = \sum_{n=1}^{3} \sum_{m=1}^{2} a_n b_m$$

Expand this double summation and show that it equals

$$S_1 S_2 = (a_1 + a_2 + a_3)(b_1 + b_2)$$

Show that

$$S_1 S_2 \neq \sum_{n=1}^{3} \sum_{n=1}^{2} a_n b_n$$

Does this notation even make sense?

13. Which of the following operators is Hermitian: d/dx, $i\,d/dx$, d^2/dx^2, $i\,d^2/dx^2$, $x\,d/dx$, and x? Assume that the functions on which these operators operate are appropriately well-behaved at infinity.

14. Show that if $\hat{A}$ is Hermitian, then $\hat{A} - \langle a \rangle$ is Hermitian. Show that the sum of two Hermitian operators is Hermitian.

15. To prove that Eq. 4-29 follows from Eq. 4-28, let $\psi = f$ and g in Eq. 4-27:

$$\int f^* \hat{A} f \, dx = \int f \hat{A}^* f^* \, dx$$

and

$$\int g^* \hat{A} g \, dx = \int g \hat{A}^* g^* \, dx$$

Now let $\psi = c_1 f + c_2 g$ where c_1 and c_2 are arbitrary complex constants:

$$\int (c_1^* f^* + c_2^* g^*) \hat{A}(c_1 f + c_2 g) \, dx = \int (c_1 f + c_2 g) \hat{A}^*(c_1^* f^* + c_2^* g^*) \, dx$$

If we expand both sides and use the first two equations, then we find

$$c_1^* c_2 \int f^* \hat{A} g \, dx + c_2^* c_1 \int g^* \hat{A} f \, dx = c_1 c_2^* \int f \hat{A}^* g^* \, dx + c_1^* c_2 \int g \hat{A}^* f^* \, dx$$

Rearrange this into

$$c_1^* c_2 \int (f^* \hat{A} g - g \hat{A}^* f^*) \, dx = c_1 c_2^* \int (f \hat{A}^* g^* - g^* \hat{A} f) \, dx$$

Notice that the two sides of this equation are complex conjugates of each other. If $z = x + iy$ and $z = z^*$, then show that this implies that z is real. Thus both sides of this equation are real. But because c_1 and c_2 are arbitrary complex constants, the only way for both sides to be real is for both integrals to equal zero. Show that this implies Eq. 4-29.

16. Show that if $\hat{A}$ is Hermitian, then

$$\int \hat{A}^*\psi^*\hat{B}\psi \, dx = \int \psi^*\hat{A}\hat{B}\psi \, dx$$

Hint: Use Eq. 4-29.

17. Show that the set of functions $\{(2/a)^{1/2} \cos (n\pi x/a)\}$, $n = 0, 1, 2, \ldots$, is orthonormal over the interval $0 \le x \le a$.

18. Prove that if δ_{nm} is the Kroenecker delta

$$\delta_{nm} = \begin{cases} 1 & n = m \\ 0 & n \ne m \end{cases}$$

then

$$\sum_{n=1}^{\infty} c_n \delta_{nm} = c_m$$

and

$$\sum_n \sum_m a_n b_m \delta_{nm} = \sum_n a_n b_n$$

These results will be used frequently.

19. Given the three polynomials $f_0(x) = a_0$, $f_1(x) = a_1 + b_1 x$, and $f_2(x) = a_2 + b_2 x + c_2 x^2$, find the constants such that the f's form an orthogonal set over the interval $0 \le x \le 1$.

20. Using the orthogonality of the set $\{\sin (n\pi x/a)\}$ over the interval $0 \le x \le a$, show that if

$$f(x) = \sum_{n=1}^{\infty} b_n \sin \frac{n\pi x}{a}$$

then

$$b_n = \frac{2}{a} \int_0^a f(x) \sin \frac{n\pi x}{a} \, dx \qquad n = 1, 2, \ldots$$

Use this to show that the Fourier expansion of $f(x) = x$, $0 \le x \le a$, is

$$x = \frac{2a}{\pi} \sum_{n=1}^{\infty} \frac{(-1)^{n+1}}{n} \sin \frac{n\pi x}{a}$$

21. Show that $\sin (n\pi x/a)$ is an even function of x about $a/2$ if n is odd and is an odd function about $a/2$ if n is even. Use this result to show that the c_n in Eq. 4-49 are zero for even values of n.

22. In Problem 14 on p. 69 we found that the temperature in a long, thin, uniform bar or wire of length l, oriented along the x axis and perfectly insulated laterally, whose temperature is kept at $0°C$ at $x = 0$ and $x = l$ is

$$T(x, t) = \sum_{n=1}^{\infty} B_n e^{-\lambda_n^2 t} \sin \frac{n\pi x}{l}$$

where $\lambda_n = \kappa n\pi/l$ where κ is a constant related to the thermal conductivity, specific heat, and density of the bar. We were not able to determine the B_n in Chapter 2 because we had not learned about Fourier series. Now suppose that the initial temperature is

$$T(x, 0) = \begin{cases} x & 0 < x < \dfrac{l}{2} \\[2ex] l - x & \dfrac{l}{2} < x < l \end{cases}$$

as shown in Figure 4-5. Show that

$$B_n = 0 \qquad n \text{ even}$$

$$= \frac{4l}{n^2 \pi^2} \qquad n = 1, 5, 9, \ldots$$

$$= -\frac{4l}{n^2 \pi^2} \qquad n = 3, 7, 11, \ldots$$

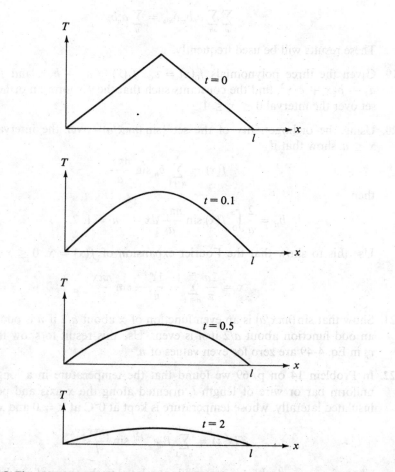

Figure 4-5. The temperature profile in a rod as a function of time starting with the profile shown at $t = 0$.

so that the temperature in the bar at any time t is

$$T(x, t) = \frac{4l}{\pi^2} \left[e^{-(\kappa\pi/l)^2 t} \sin \frac{\pi x}{l} - \frac{1}{9} e^{-(3\kappa\pi/l)^2 t} \sin \frac{3\pi x}{l} + \cdots \right]$$

This solution is plotted in Figure 4-5 for several values of t.

23. In Section 4-8, we considered a measurement of only the energy. In this problem we shall consider the measurement of some other quantity, say a. First expand $\Psi(x, t)$ in Eq. 4-53 in terms of the eigenfunctions of $\hat{A}$:

$$\Psi(x, t) = \sum C_m(t)\phi_m(x)$$

where

$$\hat{A}\phi_m(x) = a_m\phi_m(x)$$

Note that the expansion coefficients are functions of time. Show that

$$C_m(t) = \int_{-\infty}^{\infty} \phi_m^*(x)\Psi(x, t) \, dx$$

Now use Eq. 4-21 for $\Psi(x, t)$ and show that

$$C_m(t) = \sum_n c_n e^{-iE_n t/\hbar} \int_{-\infty}^{\infty} \phi_m^*(x)\psi_n(x) \, dx$$

Now suppose that the initial state function of the system $\Psi(x, 0)$ is an eigenfunction of $\hat{A}$, say $\phi_k(x)$. Show that

$$C_m(0) = \delta_{mk}$$

and that the probability

$$P_m(0) = |C_m(0)|^2 = \delta_{mk}$$

which says that we observe the value a_k with certainty at $t = 0$. Now show that if $\hat{A}$ and $\hat{H}$ have different eigenfunctions, then the probability of observing the value a_k loses its sharpness for $t > 0$ and that other eigenvalues of $\hat{A}$ will be observed at later times. What happens if $\hat{A}$ and $\hat{H}$ have a mutual set of eigenfunctions?

24. Evaluate the commutator $[\hat{A}, \hat{B}]$, where $\hat{A}$ and $\hat{B}$ are given below.

	$\hat{A}$	$\hat{B}$
(a)	$\dfrac{d^2}{dx^2}$	x
(b)	$\dfrac{d}{dx} - x$	$\dfrac{d}{dx} + x$
(c)	$\int_0^x dx'$	$\dfrac{d}{dx}$
(d)	$\dfrac{d^2}{dx^2} - x$	$\dfrac{d}{dx} + x^2$

25. Referring to Table 4-1 for the operator expressions for angular momentum, show that

$$[\hat{L}_x, \hat{L}_y] = i\hbar\hat{L}_z$$

$$[\hat{L}_y, \hat{L}_z] = i\hbar\hat{L}_x$$

and that

$$[\hat{L}_z, \hat{L}_x] = i\hbar\hat{L}_y$$

(Do you see a pattern here to help remember these commutation relations?)
   Defining

$$\hat{L}^2 = \hat{L}_x^2 + \hat{L}_y^2 + \hat{L}_z^2$$

show that $\hat{L}^2$ commutes with each component separately.

26. Show that if the operators $\hat{A}$ and $\hat{B}$ are Hermitian, then

$$\int \phi_1^* \hat{A}\hat{B}\phi_2 \, dx = \int \phi_2 (\hat{B}\hat{A}\phi_1)^* \, dx$$

Show that if $\hat{A}$ and $\hat{B}$ are Hermitian, then $\hat{A}\hat{B}$ is Hermitian if and only if $\hat{A}$ and $\hat{B}$ commute.

27. We can define functions of operators through their Taylor series. For example, we define the operator $\exp(\hat{S})$ by

$$e^{\hat{S}} = \sum_{n=0}^{\infty} \frac{(\hat{S})^n}{n!}$$

Under what conditions does the equality

$$e^{\hat{A}+\hat{B}} \overset{?}{=} e^{\hat{A}} e^{\hat{B}}$$

hold?

28. If an operator $\hat{A}$ commutes with a Hamiltonian $\hat{H}$, then $\hat{A}$ and $\hat{H}$ share a mutual set of eigenfunctions. Using the results of Problem 23, discuss the implications of $[\hat{A}, \hat{H}] = 0$ on the measurement of A.

29. In this problem we shall prove the Schwartz inequality, which says that if f and g are two suitably well-behaved functions, then

$$\left(\int f^* f \, dx \right)\left(\int g^* g \, dx \right) \geq \frac{1}{4}\left[\int (f^*g + fg^*) \, dx \right]^2$$

Show that an equivalent way of writing this is

$$\left(\int |f|^2 \, dx \right)\left(\int |g|^2 \, dx \right) \geq \left| \int f^*g \, dx \right|^2$$

and that f and g may be interchanged on the right-hand side. In order to prove the Schwartz inequality, we start with

$$\int (f + \lambda g)^*(f + \lambda g) \, dx \geq 0$$

where λ is an arbitrary complex number. Expand this to find

$$|\lambda|^2 \int g^*g\, dx + \lambda^* \int f^*g\, dx + \lambda \int fg^*\, dx + \int f^*f\, dx \geq 0$$

This inequality must be true for any complex λ and, in particular, choose

$$\lambda = -\frac{\int g^*f\, dx}{\int g^*g\, dx} = -\frac{\left(\int gf^*\, dx\right)^*}{\int g^*g\, dx}$$

Show that this choice of λ gives the Schwartz inequality:

$$\left(\int f^*f\, dx\right)\left(\int g^*g\, dx\right) \geq \left|\int f^*g\, dx\right|^2$$

30. Starting with

$$\langle x \rangle = \int \Psi^*(x, t)\, x\, \Psi(x, t)\, dx$$

and the time-dependent Schrödinger equation, show that

$$\frac{d\langle x \rangle}{dt} = \int \Psi^* \frac{i}{\hbar}(\hat{H}x - x\hat{H})\Psi\, dx$$

Given that

$$\hat{H} = -\frac{\hbar^2}{2m}\frac{d^2}{dx^2} + U(x)$$

show that

$$[\hat{H}, x] = \hat{H}x - x\hat{H} = -2\frac{\hbar^2}{2m}\frac{d}{dx}$$

$$= -\frac{\hbar^2}{m}\frac{i}{\hbar}\hat{P}_x = -\frac{i\hbar}{m}\hat{P}_x$$

Finally, substitute this into the equation for $d\langle x\rangle/dt$ to show that

$$\frac{d\langle x \rangle}{dt} = \frac{\langle P_x \rangle}{m}$$

Interpret this result.

31. Generalize the results of Problem 30 and show that if F is any dynamical quantity, then

$$\frac{d\langle F \rangle}{dt} = \int \Psi^* \frac{i}{\hbar}(\hat{H}\hat{F} - \hat{F}\hat{H})\Psi\, dx$$

Use this equation to show that

$$\frac{d\langle P_x \rangle}{dt} = \left\langle -\frac{dU}{dx}\right\rangle$$

Interpret this result. This last equation is known as *Ehrenfest's theorem*.

A Foucault pendulum is used to demonstrate the rotation of the Earth. It is called a Foucault pendulum because it was first used by Jean Foucault, who in 1852 suspended a 28-kilogram iron ball on a 67-meter steel wire from the dome of the Pantheon in Paris. He started the pendulum swinging and drew a line on the floor beneath the swing of the pendulum. After a period of time, the line on the floor was no longer under the swing of the pendulum. The pendulum remains faithful to its original arc with respect to space, while the Earth (and the floor) rotates under the pendulum. Most science museums have a Foucault pendulum.

5

The Harmonic Oscillator

THE VIBRATION of a diatomic molecule can be described by a harmonic oscillator. In this chapter we shall first study a classical harmonic oscillator and then present and discuss the energies and the corresponding wave functions of a quantum-mechanical harmonic oscillator. We shall use the quantum-mechanical energies to describe the infrared spectrum of a diatomic molecule and learn how to determine molecular force constants and vibrational amplitudes.

Although the Schrödinger equation for a harmonic oscillator can be solved exactly, it is a fairly lengthy mathematical procedure. Because it is not necessary to go through the details of solving the Schrödinger equation to be able to understand and use the results, they are simply presented and used in the first 10 sections. The details of solving the Schrödinger equation are not discussed until Sections 5-11 through 5-13. These last sections may be skipped by anyone not interested in the mathematical details of solving the Schrödinger equation.

5-1 *A Harmonic Oscillator Obeys Hooke's Law*

Consider a mass m connected to a wall by a spring as shown in Figure 5-1. Suppose further that there is no gravitational force acting on m so that the only force is due to the spring. If we let l_0 be the equilibrium, or undistorted, length of the spring, then the force must be some function of the displacement

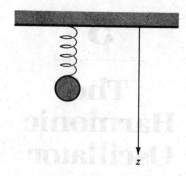

Figure 5-1. A mass connected to a wall by a spring. If the force acting upon the mass is directly proportional to the displacement of the spring from its undistorted length, then the force law is called *Hooke's law.*

of the spring from its equilibrium length. Let this displacement be denoted by x, so that $x = z - l_0$. The simplest assumption that we can make about the force on m as a function of the displacement is to assume that the force is directly proportional to the displacement and to write

$$f = -k(z - l_0) = -kx \qquad (5\text{-}1)$$

The negative sign indicates that the force is downward in Figure 5-1 if the spring is compressed ($z < l_0$) and is upward if the spring is stretched ($z > l_0$). Equation 5-1 is called *Hooke's law* and the proportionality constant k is called the *force constant* of the spring. A small value of k implies a weak or loose spring, and a large value of k implies a stiff spring.

Newton's equation with a Hooke's law force is

$$m \frac{d^2z}{dt^2} = -k(z - l_0) \qquad (5\text{-}2)$$

If we let $x = z - l_0$, then $d^2z/dt^2 = d^2x/dt^2$ and

$$m \frac{d^2x}{dt^2} + kx = 0 \qquad (5\text{-}3)$$

According to Section 2-3, the general solution to this equation is (Problem 1)

$$x(t) = A \sin \upsilon t + B \cos \omega t \qquad (5\text{-}4)$$

where

$$\omega = \left(\frac{k}{m}\right)^{1/2} \qquad (5\text{-}5)$$

EXAMPLE 5-1

Show that Eq. 5-4 can be written in the form

$$x(t) = C \sin (\omega t + \phi) \qquad (5\text{-}6)$$

Solution: The easiest way to prove this is to write

$$\sin(\omega t + \phi) = \sin \omega t \cos \phi + \cos \omega t \sin \phi$$

and substitute this into Eq. 5-6 to obtain

$$x(t) = C \cos \phi \sin \omega t + C \sin \phi \cos \omega t$$
$$= A \sin \omega t + B \cos \omega t$$

where

$$A = C \cos \phi \qquad B = C \sin \phi$$

Equation 5-6 shows that the displacement oscillates sinusoidally, or *harmonically*, with a natural frequency $\omega = (k/m)^{1/2}$. In Eq. 5-6, C is the *amplitude* of the vibration and ϕ is the phase angle.

Suppose that initially we stretch the spring to a length z_0 so that its initial displacement is $x_0 = z_0 - l_0$ and then let go. The initial velocity in this case is zero and so from Eq. 5-4 we have

$$x(0) = x_0 = B$$

$$\left(\frac{dx}{dt}\right)_{t=0} = 0 = A\omega$$

These two equations imply that $A = 0$ and $B = x_0$ in Eq. 5-4, and so

$$x(t) = x_0 \cos \omega t \tag{5-7}$$

The displacement versus time is plotted in Figure 5-2, which shows that the mass oscillates back and forth between x_0 and $-x_0$ with a frequency ω radians/sec, or $v = \omega/2\pi$ cycles/sec. The quantity x_0 is called the *amplitude* of the vibration.

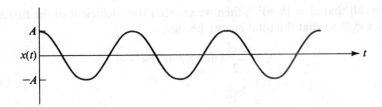

Figure 5-2. An illustration of the displacement of a harmonic oscillator versus time.

5-2   *The Energy of a Harmonic Oscillator Is Conserved*

Let us look at the total energy of a harmonic oscillator. The force is given by Eq. 5-1. Recall that a force can be expressed as a derivative of a potential energy or that

$$f(x) = -\frac{dU}{dx} \tag{5-8}$$

so that the potential energy is

$$U(x) = -\int f(x)\,dx + \text{constant} \tag{5-9}$$

Using Eq. 5-1 for $f(x)$, we see that

$$U(x) = \frac{k}{2}x^2 + \text{constant} \tag{5-10}$$

The constant term here is an arbitrary constant that can be used to fix the zero of energy. If we choose the potential energy of the system to be zero when the spring is undistorted ($x = 0$), then we have

$$U(x) = \frac{k}{2}x^2 \tag{5-11}$$

for the potential energy associated with a simple harmonic oscillator.

The kinetic energy is

$$K = \frac{1}{2}m\left(\frac{dz}{dt}\right)^2 = \frac{1}{2}m\left(\frac{dx}{dt}\right)^2 \tag{5-12}$$

Using Eq. 5-7 for $x(t)$, we see that

$$K = \tfrac{1}{2}m\omega^2 x_0^2 \sin^2 \omega t \tag{5-13}$$

and

$$U = \tfrac{1}{2}kx_0^2 \cos^2 \omega t \tag{5-14}$$

Both K and U are plotted in Figure 5-3. The total energy is

$$E = K + U$$

$$= \frac{1}{2}m\omega^2 x_0^2 \sin^2 \omega t + \frac{k}{2}x_0^2 \cos^2 \omega t$$

If we recall that $\omega = (k/m)^{1/2}$, then we see that the coefficient of the first term here is $kx_0^2/2$, so that the total energy becomes

$$E = \frac{kx_0^2}{2}(\sin^2 \omega t + \cos^2 \omega t)$$

$$= \frac{kx_0^2}{2} \tag{5-15}$$

Thus we see that the total energy is a constant and, in particular, is equal to the potential energy at its largest displacement, where the kinetic energy is zero. Figure 5-3 shows how the total energy is distributed between the kinetic energy and the potential energy. Each oscillates in time between zero and its maximum value but in such a way that their sum is always a constant. We say that the total energy is conserved and that the system is a *conservative system*.

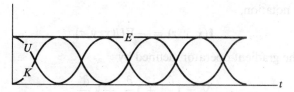

Figure 5-3. The kinetic energy (curve labeled K) and the potential energy (curve labeled U) of a harmonic oscillator as a function of time. The total energy is the horizontal curve labeled E. This curve is the sum of K and U.

EXAMPLE 5-2

Using the more general equation

$$x(t) = C \sin (\omega t + \phi)$$

prove that the total energy of a harmonic oscillator is

$$E = \frac{k}{2} C^2$$

Solution:

$$E = K + U = \frac{1}{2} m \left(\frac{dx}{dt}\right)^2 + \frac{1}{2} kx^2$$

$$= \frac{m}{2} \omega^2 C^2 \cos^2 (\omega t + \phi) + \frac{k}{2} C^2 \sin^2 (\omega t + \phi)$$

Using the fact that $\omega^2 = k/m$, we have

$$E = \frac{k}{2} C^2 [\cos^2 (\omega t + \phi) + \sin^2 (\omega t + \phi)] = \frac{k}{2} C^2$$

The concept of a conservative system is important and is worth discussing in more detail. For a system to be conservative, the force must be derivable from a potential energy function that is a function of only the spatial coordinates describing the system. In the case of a simple harmonic oscillator, $U(x)$ is given by Eq. 5-11 and the force is given by Eq. 5-8. For a single particle in three dimensions, we would have $U = U(x, y, z)$ and

$$f_x(x, y, z) = -\frac{\partial U}{\partial x}$$

$$f_y(x, y, z) = -\frac{\partial U}{\partial y}$$

$$f_z(x, y, z) = -\frac{\partial U}{\partial z}$$

or, in vector notation,

$$\mathbf{f}(x, y, z) = -\nabla U(x, y, z) \tag{5-16}$$

where ∇ is the gradient operator, defined by

$$\nabla = \mathbf{i}\frac{\partial}{\partial x} + \mathbf{j}\frac{\partial}{\partial y} + \mathbf{k}\frac{\partial}{\partial z} \tag{5-17}$$

To prove that Eq. 5-16 implies that the system is conservative, consider the one-dimensional case for simplicity. In this case, Newton's equation is

$$m\frac{d^2x}{dt^2} = -\frac{dU}{dx} \tag{5-18}$$

If we integrate both sides of this equation, then the right-hand side becomes

$$\int -\frac{dU}{dx}\,dx = -U(x) + \text{constant} \tag{5-19}$$

and the left-hand side becomes

$$\int m\frac{d^2x}{dt^2}\,dx = m\int \frac{d^2x}{dt^2}\frac{dx}{dt}\,dt = \frac{m}{2}\int \frac{d}{dt}\left(\frac{dx}{dt}\right)^2 dt = \frac{m}{2}\left(\frac{dx}{dt}\right)^2 + \text{constant} \tag{5-20}$$

By equating Eq. 5-19 and 5-20, we find that

$$\frac{m}{2}\left(\frac{dx}{dt}\right)^2 + U(x) = \text{constant} \tag{5-21}$$

or that the total energy is conserved. Thus we see that if the force can be expressed as the derivative of a potential energy that is a function of the spatial coordinates only, then the system is conservative (Problem 5).

5-3   *The Equation for a Harmonic-Oscillator Model of a Diatomic Molecule Contains the Reduced Mass of the Molecule*

We are going to see later that the simple harmonic oscillator is a good model for a vibrating diatomic molecule. A diatomic molecule, however, does not look like the system pictured in Figure 5-1 but more like two masses connected by a spring as in Figure 5-4. In this case we have two equations of motion, one for each mass:

$$m_1\frac{d^2z_1}{dt^2} = k(z_2 - z_1 - l_0) \tag{5-22}$$

$$m_2\frac{d^2z_2}{dt^2} = -k(z_2 - z_1 - l_0) \tag{5-23}$$

Note that if $z_2 - z_1 > l_0$, the spring is stretched and so the force on mass m_1 is toward the right and that on mass m_2 is toward the left. This is why the force

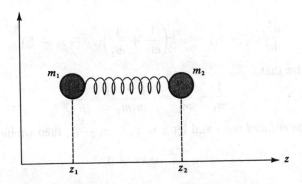

Figure 5-4. Two masses connected by a spring, which is a model that is used to describe the vibrational motion of a diatomic molecule.

term in Eq. 5-22 is positive and that in Eq. 5-23 is negative. Note also that the force on m_1 is equal and opposite to the force on m_2, as it should be according to Newton's third law, action and reaction.

If we add Eq. 5-22 and 5-23, then we find

$$m_1 \frac{d^2 z_1}{dt^2} + m_2 \frac{d^2 z_2}{dt^2} = 0$$

or

$$\frac{d^2}{dt^2} (m_1 z_1 + m_2 z_2) = 0 \qquad (5\text{-}24)$$

This last form suggests that we introduce a *center-of-mass coordinate*

$$Z = \frac{m_1 z_1 + m_2 z_2}{M} \qquad (5\text{-}25)$$

where $M = m_1 + m_2$, and we write Eq. 5-24 in the form

$$M \frac{d^2 Z}{dt^2} = 0 \qquad (5\text{-}26)$$

This shows that the center of mass moves uniformly in time with a constant momentum.

The motion of the two-mass or two-body system in Figure 5-4 must depend only the *relative* separation of the two masses, or upon the *relative coordinate*

$$z = z_2 - z_1 \qquad (5\text{-}27)$$

If we divide Eq. 5-22 by m_1 and Eq. 5-23 by m_2 and subtract Eq. 5-22 from Eq. 5-23, then we find

$$\frac{d^2 z_2}{dt^2} - \frac{d^2 z_1}{dt^2} = -\frac{k}{m_2} (z_2 - z_1 - l_0) - \frac{k}{m_1} (z_2 - z_1 - l_0)$$

or

$$\frac{d^2}{dt^2}(z_2 - z_1) = -k\left(\frac{1}{m_1} + \frac{1}{m_2}\right)(z_2 - z_1 - l_0)$$

If we recognize that

$$\frac{1}{m_1} + \frac{1}{m_2} = \frac{m_1 + m_2}{m_1 m_2} = \frac{1}{\mu}$$

where μ is the *reduced mass* and let $x = z_2 - z_1 - l_0$, then we have

$$\mu \frac{d^2 x}{dt^2} + kx = 0 \qquad\qquad (5\text{-}28)$$

Equation 5-28 is an important and physical result. If we compare Eq. 5-28 to Eq. 5-3, we see that Eq. 5-28 is the same except for the substitution of the reduced mass μ. Thus the two-body system in Figure 5-4 can be treated as easily as the one-body problem in Figure 5-1 by using the reduced mass of the two-body system. In particular, the motion of the system is governed by Eq. 5-6, but with $\omega = (k/\mu)^{1/2}$. We have seen this type of result before in Section 1-10 when we studied the Bohr atom. Generally, if the potential energy depends on only the *relative* distance between two bodies, then one can introduce relative coordinates such as $z_2 - z_1$ and reduce the two-body problem to a one-body problem. This important and useful theorem of classical mechanics is discussed in Problems 6 and 7.

5-4   *The Harmonic-Oscillator Approximation Results from the Expansion of an Internuclear Potential Around Its Minimum*

Before we go on to discuss the quantum-mechanical treatment of a harmonic oscillator, we should discuss just how good an approximation it is for a vibrating diatomic molecule. The internuclear potential for a diatomic molecule is illustrated in Figure 5-5. Notice that the curve is quite asymmetric. The potential is zero at the equilibrium position $z = l_0$, where l_0 is the bond length of the molecule. The potential energy curve rises steeply to the left of the point $z = l_0$, indicating the difficulty of pushing the two nuclei closer together. The curve to the right-hand side of the equilibrium position rises initially but then levels off. The potential energy at large separations is essentially the bond energy. The dashed line shows the potential $\frac{1}{2}k(z - l_0)^2$ associated with Hooke's law. We see from this figure that the harmonic-oscillator approximation is satisfactory near the bottom of the potential well, or for small values of the displacement $x = z - l_0$. Although the harmonic oscillator unrealistically allows the displacement to vary from $-\infty$ to $+\infty$, these large displacements produce potential energies that are so large that they do not often occur in practice. Therefore, we might expect that the harmonic oscillator will be a good approximation for vibrations with small amplitudes. We shall discuss this in a more quantitative manner later.

We can put the previous discussion into mathematical terms by considering the Taylor expansion of the potential energy $U(z)$ about the equilib-

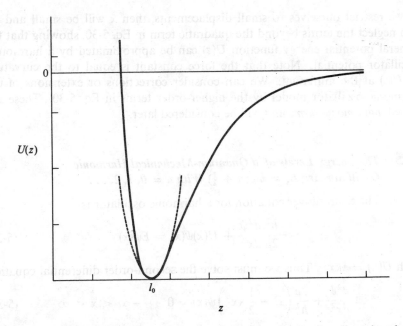

Figure 5-5. The internuclear potential energy versus internuclear distance for a diatomic molecule. The dashed line is the harmonic-oscillator potential.

rium bond length $z = l_0$. The first few terms in this expansion are

$$U(z) = U(l_0) + \left(\frac{dU}{dz}\right)_{z=l_0} (z - l_0) + \frac{1}{2!} \left(\frac{d^2U}{dz^2}\right)_{z=l_0} (z - l_0)^2$$
$$+ \frac{1}{3!} \left(\frac{d^3U}{dz^3}\right)_{z=l_0} (z - l_0)^3 + \cdots \qquad (5\text{-}29)$$

The first term here is a constant and depends on where we choose the zero of energy. Either we can set $U(l_0)$ equal to zero and relate $U(z)$ to this convention or, what amounts to the same thing, we can bring $U(l_0)$ to the left-hand side of Eq. 5-29 and consider only the difference $U(z) - U(l_0)$, or $\Delta U(z)$. The second term on the right-hand side of Eq. 5-29 involves the quantity $(dU/dz)_{z=l_0}$. Because the point $z = l_0$ is the minimum of the potential energy curve, dU/dz vanishes there and so there is no linear term in the displacement in Eq. 5-29. Note that dU/dz is essentially the force acting between the two nuclei and the fact that dU/dz vanishes at $z = l_0$ means that the force acting between the nuclei is zero at this point. This is why $z = l_0$ is called the *equilibrium bond length*.

If we denote $(d^2U/dz^2)_{z=l_0}$ by k and $(d^3U/dz^3)_{z=l_0}$ by γ, then Eq. 5-29 becomes

$$\Delta U(z) = \tfrac{1}{2}k(z - l_0)^2 + \tfrac{1}{6}\gamma(z - l_0)^3 + \cdots$$
$$= \tfrac{1}{2}kx^2 + \tfrac{1}{6}\gamma x^3 + \cdots \qquad (5\text{-}30)$$

If we restrict ourselves to small displacements, then x will be small and we can neglect the terms beyond the quadratic term in Eq. 5-30, showing that the general potential energy function $U(z)$ can be approximated by a harmonic-oscillator potential. Note that the force constant is equal to the curvature of $U(z)$ at the minimum. We can consider corrections or extensions of the harmonic-oscillator model by the higher-order terms in Eq. 5-30. These are called *anharmonic terms* and will be considered later.

5-5   *The Energy Levels of a Quantum-Mechanical Harmonic Oscillator Are $E_n = \hbar\omega(n + \frac{1}{2})$ With $n = 0, 1, 2, \ldots$*

The Schrödinger equation for a harmonic oscillator is

$$-\frac{\hbar^2}{2\mu}\frac{d^2\psi}{dx^2} + U(x)\psi(x) = E\psi(x) \tag{5-31}$$

with $U(x) = \frac{1}{2}kx^2$. Thus we must solve the second-order differential equation

$$\frac{d^2\psi}{dx^2} + \frac{2\mu}{\hbar^2}\left(E - \frac{1}{2}kx^2\right)\psi(x) = 0 \qquad -\infty < x < \infty \tag{5-32}$$

This differential equation, however, does not have constant coefficients and so we cannot use the method that we developed in Section 2-2. In fact, when a differential equation does not have constant coefficients, there is no simple, general technique for solving it and each case must be studied individually. We shall present the details of the solution of this equation in the latter sections of this chapter, but here we shall simply present and discuss the solutions.

When Eq. 5-32 is solved, it turns out that well-behaved, finite solutions can be obtained only if the energy is restricted to the quantized values

$$E_n = \hbar\left(\frac{k}{\mu}\right)^{1/2}\left(n + \frac{1}{2}\right)$$

$$= \hbar\omega\left(n + \frac{1}{2}\right) = h\nu\left(n + \frac{1}{2}\right) \qquad n = 0, 1, 2, \ldots \tag{5-33}$$

where

$$\omega = \left(\frac{k}{\mu}\right)^{1/2} \tag{5-34}$$

and

$$\nu = \frac{1}{2\pi}\left(\frac{k}{\mu}\right)^{1/2} \tag{5-35}$$

The energies are plotted in Figure 5-6. Note that the energy levels are equally spaced, with a separation $\hbar\omega$ or $h\nu$. This is a property peculiar to the quadratic potential of a harmonic oscillator. Note also that the energy of the ground state, the state with $n = 0$, is $\frac{1}{2}h\nu$ and is not zero as the lowest classical energy is. This is called the *zero-point energy* of the harmonic oscillator and is a direct result of the Uncertainty Principle. The energy of a harmonic oscillator can be written in the form $(p^2/2\mu) + (kx^2/2)$ and so we see that a zero value for

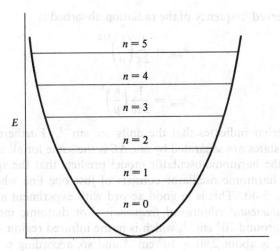

Figure 5-6. The energy levels of a quantum-mechanical harmonic oscillator.

the energy would require that both p and x or, more precisely, the expectation values of $\hat{P}^2$ and $\hat{X}^2$ be simultaneously zero, in violation of the Uncertainty Principle.

5-6 *The Harmonic Oscillator Accounts for the Infrared Spectrum of a Diatomic Molecule*

The harmonic oscillator is a standard problem in quantum mechanics because it is a good approximation for a vibrating molecule. We shall discuss molecular spectroscopy in Chapter 10, but here we shall discuss the spectroscopic predictions of a harmonic oscillator. According to Eq. 5-33, the vibrational energy levels of a diatomic molecule are given by

$$E_n = \hbar \left(\frac{k}{\mu}\right)^{1/2} \left(n + \frac{1}{2}\right) \qquad n = 0, 1, 2, \ldots \qquad (5\text{-}36)$$

A diatomic molecule can make a transition from one vibrational energy state to another by absorbing or emitting electromagnetic radiation whose observed frequency satisfies the Bohr frequency condition

$$\Delta E = h\nu_{\text{obs}} \qquad (5\text{-}37)$$

We shall prove in Chapter 10 that the harmonic-oscillator model allows transitions between adjacent energy states only, so that we have the condition that $\Delta n = \pm 1$. Such a condition is called a *selection rule*.

For absorption to occur, $\Delta n = +1$ and so

$$\Delta E = E_{n+1} - E_n = \hbar \left(\frac{k}{\mu}\right)^{1/2} \qquad (5\text{-}38)$$

Thus, the observed frequency of the radiation absorbed is

$$v_{obs} = \frac{1}{2\pi}\left(\frac{k}{\mu}\right)^{1/2} \tag{5-39}$$

or

$$\bar{v}_{obs} = \frac{1}{2\pi c}\left(\frac{k}{\mu}\right)^{1/2} \tag{5-40}$$

where the overbar indicates that the units are cm^{-1}. Furthermore, because all the energy states are separated by $\hbar\omega$, ΔE is the same for all allowed transitions and so the harmonic-oscillator model predicts that the spectrum associated with a harmonic oscillator consists of just one line whose frequency is given by Eq. 5-40. This is in good accord with experiment and this line is called the *fundamental vibrational frequency*. For diatomic molecules, these lines occur at around 10^3 cm^{-1}, which is in the infrared region. For example, for $H^{35}Cl$, $\bar{v}_{obs}$ is about 2.90×10^3 cm^{-1} and so, according to Eq. 5-40, the force constant of $H^{35}Cl$ is

$$k = (2\pi c\bar{v}_{obs})^2 \mu$$

$$= [2\pi(3.00 \times 10^8 \text{ m·s}^{-1})(2.90 \times 10^5 \text{ m}^{-1})]^2 \left(\frac{35}{36}\right)(1.66 \times 10^{-27} \text{ kg})$$

$$= 4.82 \times 10^2 \text{ N·m}^{-1}$$

EXAMPLE 5-3

The infrared spectrum of $^{75}Br^{19}F$ consists of an intense line at 380 cm^{-1}. Calculate the force constant of $^{75}Br^{19}F$.

Solution: The force constant is given by

$$k = (2\pi c\bar{v}_{obs})^2 \mu$$

The reduced mass is

$$\mu = \frac{(75)(19)}{(75 + 19)}(1.66 \times 10^{-27}) = 2.52 \times 10^{-26} \text{ kg}$$

and so

$$k = [2\pi(3.00 \times 10^8 \text{ m·s}^{-1})(3.8 \times 10^4 \text{ m}^{-1})]^2(2.52 \times 10^{-26} \text{ kg})$$

$$= 129 \text{ kg·s}^{-2} = 129 \text{ N·m}^{-1}$$

Force constants for diatomic molecules generally are of the order of 10^2 $N·m^{-1}$ (cf. Problems 9 and 10). Table 5-1 lists the fundamental vibrational frequencies and the force constants of some diatomic molecules. We shall also see in Chapter 10 not only that must $\Delta n = \pm 1$ in the harmonic-oscillator model but that the dipole moment of the molecule must change as the molecule vibrates. Thus the harmonic-oscillator model predicts that HCl

TABLE 5-1

The Fundamental Vibrational Frequencies and the Force Constants of Some Diatomic Molecules

Molecule	$\bar{v}/cm^{-1}$	$k/N \cdot m^{-1}$
H_2	4159	520
D_2	2990	530
$H^{35}Cl$	2886	482
$H^{79}Br$	2559	385
$H^{127}I$	2230	293
$^{35}Cl^{35}Cl$	556	320
$^{79}Br^{79}Br$	321	240
$^{127}I^{127}I$	213	170
$^{16}O^{16}O$	1556	1140
$^{14}N^{14}N$	2331	2260
$^{12}C^{16}O$	2143	1870
$^{14}N^{16}O$	1876	1550
$^{23}Na^{23}Na$	158	170
$^{23}Na^{35}Cl$	378	120
$^{39}K^{35}Cl$	278	80

absorbs in the infrared but that N_2 does not. We shall see that this is in good agreement with experiment. There are, indeed, deviations from the harmonic-oscillator model, but we shall see not only that they are fairly small but that we can systematically introduce corrections and extensions.

5-7   *The Harmonic-Oscillator Wave Functions Involve Hermite Polynomials*

The wave functions corresponding to the E_n are nondegenerate and are given by

$$\psi_n(x) = N_n H_n(\alpha^{1/2}x)e^{-\alpha x^2/2} \tag{5-41}$$

where

$$\alpha = \left(\frac{k\mu}{\hbar^2}\right)^{1/2} \tag{5-42}$$

the normalization constant N_n is

$$N_n = \frac{1}{(2^n n!)^{1/2}}\left(\frac{\alpha}{\pi}\right)^{1/4} \tag{5-43}$$

and the $H_n(\alpha^{1/2}x)$ are polynomials called *Hermite polynomials*. The first few Hermite polynomials are listed in Table 5-2 and are plotted in Figure 5-7. Note that $H_n(\xi)$ is an nth-degree polynomial in ξ.

Although we have not solved Eq. 5-32 (we do this in the latter sections of the chapter for anyone who wishes to carry out the solution), we can at least show that the functions given by Eq. 5-41 are solutions to Eq. 5-32. For example, let us consider $\psi_0(x)$, which according to Eq. 5-41 and Table 5-2 is

$$\psi_0(x) = \left(\frac{\alpha}{\pi}\right)^{1/4} e^{-\alpha x^2/2}$$

Substitute this into Eq. 5-32 with $E_0 = \frac{1}{2}\hbar\omega$ to obtain

$$\frac{d^2\psi_0}{dx^2} + \frac{2\mu}{\hbar^2}\left(E_0 - \frac{1}{2}kx^2\right)\psi_0(x) = 0$$

$$\left(\frac{\alpha}{\pi}\right)^{1/4}(\alpha^2 x^2 e^{-\alpha x^2/2} - \alpha e^{-\alpha x^2/2}) + \frac{2\mu}{\hbar^2}\left(\frac{\hbar\omega}{2} - \frac{kx^2}{2}\right)\left(\frac{\alpha}{\pi}\right)^{1/4} e^{-\alpha x^2/2} = 0$$

or

$$(\alpha^2 x^2 - \alpha) + \left(\frac{\mu\omega}{\hbar} - \frac{\mu k}{\hbar^2}x^2\right) = 0$$

Using the facts that $\alpha = (k\mu/\hbar^2)^{1/2}$ and $\omega = (k/\mu)^{1/2}$, we see that everything cancels in the above expression. Thus, $\psi_0(x)$ is a solution to Eq. 5-32. Problem 11 involves proving explicitly that $\psi_1(x)$ and $\psi_2(x)$ are solutions of Eq. 5-32.

We can also show explicitly that the $\psi_n(x)$ are normalized or that N_n given by Eq. 5-43 is the normalization constant.

EXAMPLE 5-4

Show that $\psi_0(x)$ and $\psi_1(x)$ are normalized.

Solution: According to Eq. 5-41 and 5-43 and Table 5-2,

$$\psi_0(x) = \left(\frac{\alpha}{\pi}\right)^{1/4} e^{-\alpha x^2/2} \quad \text{and} \quad \psi_1(x) = \left(\frac{\alpha}{4\pi}\right)^{1/4}(2\alpha^{1/2}x)e^{-\alpha x^2/2}$$

Then

$$\int_{-\infty}^{\infty} \psi_0^2(x)\,dx = \left(\frac{\alpha}{\pi}\right)^{1/2}\int_{-\infty}^{\infty} e^{-\alpha x^2}\,dx = \left(\frac{\alpha}{\pi}\right)^{1/2}\left(\frac{\pi}{\alpha}\right)^{1/2} = 1$$

and

$$\int_{-\infty}^{\infty} \psi_1^2(x)\,dx = 2\alpha\left(\frac{\alpha}{\pi}\right)^{1/2}\int_{-\infty}^{\infty} x^2 e^{-\alpha x^2}\,dx = 2\alpha\left(\frac{\alpha}{\pi}\right)^{1/2}\left[\frac{1}{2\alpha}\left(\frac{\pi}{\alpha}\right)^{1/2}\right] = 1$$

The integrals here are given inside the front cover of this book, and they are evaluated in Problem 15 also.

TABLE 5-2
The First Few Hermite Polynomials

$H_0(\xi) = 1$	$H_1(\xi) = 2\xi$
$H_2(\xi) = 4\xi^2 - 2$	$H_3(\xi) = 8\xi^3 - 12\xi$
$H_4(\xi) = 16\xi^4 - 48\xi^2 + 12$	$H_5(\xi) = 32\xi^5 - 160\xi^3 + 120\xi$

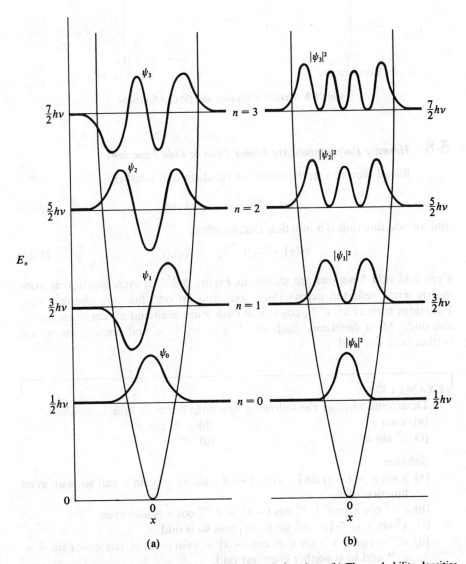

Figure 5-7. (a) The normalized harmonic-oscillator wave functions. (b) The probability densities for a harmonic oscillator.

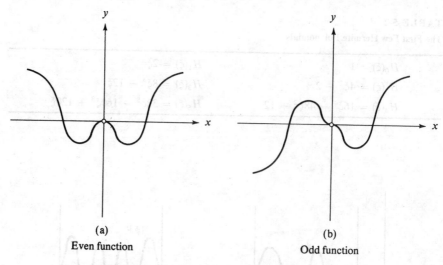

(a)   (b)

Even function   Odd function

Figure 5-8. Graphs of (a) even and (b) odd functions.

5-8   *Hermite Polynomials Are Either Even or Odd Functions*

Recall that an even function is a function that satisfies

$$f(x) = f(-x) \qquad \text{(even)} \tag{5-44}$$

and an odd function is a function that satisfies

$$f(x) = -f(-x) \qquad \text{(odd)} \tag{5-45}$$

Even and odd functions are shown in Figure 5-8. An even function is symmetric when reflected across the y axis and an odd function changes sign. Functions such as x^2, e^{-x^2}, $\cos x$, and $\cosh x$ are even and x^3, $\sin x$, and xe^{-x^2} are odd. Most functions, such as e^x, $x + x^2$, $\ln x$, and $\sin x + \cos x$, are neither even nor odd.

EXAMPLE 5-5

Determine whether the following functions are even, odd, or neither.
(a) $x \sin x$ (b) $e^{-x^2} \cos x$
(c) $x^2 \sin x$ (d) e^{ix}

Solution:
(a) $x \sin x = (-x) \sin(-x) = (-x)(-\sin x) = x \sin x$ and so is an even function of x.
(b) $e^{-x^2} \cos x = e^{-(-x)^2} \cos(-x) = e^{-x^2} \cos x$ is also even.
(c) $x^2 \sin x = -[(-x)^2 \sin(-x)]$ and so is odd.
(d) $e^{ix} = \cos x + i \sin x \neq \cos(-x) + i \sin(-x) = \cos x - i \sin x = e^{-ix}$ and so is neither even nor odd.

Note that the product of two even or two odd functions is an even function and the product of an even and an odd function is odd.

The Hermite polynomials are even or odd functions.

EXAMPLE 5-6

Show that the Hermite polynomials $H_n(\xi)$ are even if n is even and odd if n is odd.

Solution: Using Table 5-2,

$H_0(\xi) = 1$ is even.

$H_1(\xi) = 2\xi = -2(-\xi) = -H_1(-\xi)$ and so is odd.

$H_2(\xi) = 4\xi^2 - 2 = 4(-\xi)^2 - 2 = H_2(-\xi)$ is even.

$H_3(\xi) = 8\xi^3 - 12\xi = -[8(-\xi)^3 - 12(-\xi)] = -H_3(-\xi)$ and so is odd.

The even-odd property of a function is a rather special and important property. Figure 5-8(b) shows that if $f(x)$ is an odd function, then

$$\int_{-A}^{A} f(x)\,dx = 0 \qquad f(x) \text{ odd} \tag{5-46}$$

because the areas on each side of the y axis cancel. This is a useful property. According to Eq. 5-41, the harmonic-oscillator wave functions are

$$\psi_n(x) = N_n H_n(\alpha^{1/2}x)e^{-\alpha x^2/2}$$

Because the $\psi_n(x)$ are even when n is an even integer and odd when n is an odd integer, $\psi_n^2(x)$ is an even function for any value of n. According to Eq. 5-46 then, integrals of the sort

$$\int_{-\infty}^{\infty} \psi_n(x)x\psi_n(x)\,dx = 0 \tag{5-47}$$

because the integrand is an odd function for any value of n. We shall use such symmetry arguments rather often.

We can appeal to the general results of Chapter 4 to argue that the harmonic-oscillator wave functions are orthogonal. The energy eigenvalues are nondegenerate and so we have that

$$\int_{-\infty}^{\infty} \psi_n(x)\psi_m(x)\,dx = 0 \qquad m \neq n$$

or, more explicitly, that

$$\int_{-\infty}^{\infty} H_n(\alpha^{1/2}x)H_m(\alpha^{1/2}x)e^{-\alpha x^2}\,dx = 0 \qquad m \neq n$$

EXAMPLE 5-7

Show explicitly that $\psi_0(x)$ and $\psi_1(x)$ are orthogonal.

Solution:

$$\psi_0(x) = N_0 e^{-\alpha x^2/2} \qquad \psi_1(x) = N_1(2\alpha^{1/2}x)e^{-\alpha x^2/2}$$

and so

$$\int_{-\infty}^{\infty} \psi_1(x)\psi_0(x)\,dx = 2\alpha^{1/2}N_0N_1 \int_{-\infty}^{\infty} xe^{-\alpha x^2}\,dx = 0$$

because the integrand is an odd function of x. Note that the even-odd property of the Hermite polynomials guarantees that $\psi_n(x)$ and $\psi_m(x)$ are orthogonal whenever n is even and m is odd. This property cannot be used to prove that $\psi_0(x)$ and $\psi_2(x)$ are orthogonal.

Problem 14 has you verify that the harmonic oscillator wave functions are orthogonal for a few other cases.

5-9   *The Average Kinetic Energy Is Equal to the Average Potential Energy of a Harmonic Oscillator*

We can use the wave functions to calculate expectation values. For example, the average displacement is

$$\langle x \rangle = \int_{-\infty}^{\infty} \psi_n(x)x\psi_n(x)\,dx \qquad (5\text{-}48)$$

But this is zero according to Eq. 5-47, and so

$$\langle x \rangle = 0 \qquad (5\text{-}49)$$

which says that the average internuclear separation is the equilibrium bond length l_0.

The average momentum is given by

$$\langle p \rangle = \int_{-\infty}^{\infty} \psi_n(x)\left(-i\hbar\frac{d}{dx}\right)\psi_n(x)\,dx \qquad (5\text{-}50)$$

The derivative of an odd (even) function is even (odd), and so this integral vanishes because the integrand is the product of an odd and even function and hence is overall odd. Thus we have that $\langle p \rangle = 0$.

We can use $\langle x^2 \rangle$ and $\langle p^2 \rangle$ to discuss the Uncertainty Principle. We need some of the relations involving Hermite polynomials that are developed in Section 5-13 to do this in general, but here at least we can evaluate $\langle x^2 \rangle$ and $\langle p^2 \rangle$ for the first few quantum states. For example, for the state $n = 0$, we have that

$$\psi_0(x) = \left(\frac{\alpha}{\pi}\right)^{1/4} e^{-\alpha x^2/2} \qquad (5\text{-}51)$$

and so (cf. Problem 15 for the evaluation of the necessary integral)

$$\langle x^2 \rangle = \left(\frac{\alpha}{\pi}\right)^{1/2} \int_{-\infty}^{\infty} x^2 e^{-\alpha x^2} \, dx$$

$$= \left(\frac{\alpha}{\pi}\right)^{1/2} \left[\frac{1}{2\alpha}\left(\frac{\pi}{\alpha}\right)^{1/2}\right] = \frac{1}{2\alpha}$$

$$= \frac{1}{2}\frac{\hbar}{(\mu k)^{1/2}} \tag{5-52}$$

EXAMPLE 5-8

Evaluate $\langle x^2 \rangle$ for the $n = 1$ state.

Solution: For the state $n = 1$, we have

$$\psi_1(x) = \left(\frac{\alpha}{4\pi}\right)^{1/4} (2\alpha^{1/2}x)e^{-\alpha x^2/2}$$

and so

$$\langle x^2 \rangle = 4\alpha\left(\frac{\alpha}{4\pi}\right)^{1/2} \int_{-\infty}^{\infty} x^4 e^{-\alpha x^2} \, dx$$

$$= 4\alpha\left(\frac{\alpha}{4\pi}\right)^{1/2} \left[\frac{3}{4\alpha^2}\left(\frac{\pi}{\alpha}\right)^{1/2}\right]$$

$$= \frac{3}{2\alpha} = \frac{3}{2}\frac{\hbar}{(\mu k)^{1/2}}$$

These two results for $\langle x^2 \rangle$ suggest that

$$\langle x^2 \rangle = \frac{\hbar}{(\mu k)^{1/2}}\left(n + \frac{1}{2}\right) \tag{5-53}$$

which is a correct conjecture (cf. Problem 16).

We can calculate $\langle p^2 \rangle$ for the $n = 0$ and $n = 1$ states just as easily. Using $\psi_0(x)$, we have

$$\langle p^2 \rangle = \left(\frac{\alpha}{\pi}\right)^{1/2} \int_{-\infty}^{\infty} e^{-\alpha x^2/2}\left(-\hbar^2\frac{d^2}{dx^2}\right)e^{-\alpha x^2/2} \, dx$$

$$= \hbar^2\left(\frac{\alpha}{\pi}\right)^{1/2} \int_{-\infty}^{\infty} (\alpha - \alpha^2 x^2)e^{-\alpha x^2} \, dx$$

$$= \hbar^2\left(\frac{\alpha}{\pi}\right)^{1/2} \left\{\alpha\left(\frac{\pi}{\alpha}\right)^{1/2} - \alpha^2\left[\frac{1}{2\alpha}\left(\frac{\pi}{\alpha}\right)^{1/2}\right]\right\}$$

$$= \frac{\hbar^2\alpha}{2} = \frac{\hbar(\mu k)^{1/2}}{2} \tag{5-54}$$

EXAMPLE 5-9

Evaluate $\langle p^2 \rangle$ for the $n = 1$ state.

Solution: Using $\psi_1(x)$ from Example 5-8, we have

$$\langle p^2 \rangle = \left(\frac{\alpha}{4\pi}\right)^{1/2} \int_{-\infty}^{\infty} (2\alpha^{1/2}x)e^{-\alpha x^2/2}\left(-\hbar^2\frac{d^2}{dx^2}\right)(2\alpha^{1/2}xe^{-\alpha x^2/2})\,dx$$

$$= -4\alpha\hbar^2\left(\frac{\alpha}{4\pi}\right)^{1/2}\int_{-\infty}^{\infty}(\alpha^2 x^4 - 3\alpha x^2)e^{-\alpha x^2}\,dx$$

$$= -4\alpha\hbar^2\left(\frac{\alpha}{4\pi}\right)^{1/2}\left\{\alpha^2\left[\frac{3}{4\alpha^2}\left(\frac{\pi}{\alpha}\right)^{1/2}\right] - 3\alpha\left[\frac{1}{2\alpha}\left(\frac{\pi}{\alpha}\right)^{1/2}\right]\right\}$$

$$= \frac{3}{2}\hbar^2\alpha = \frac{3\hbar(\mu k)^{1/2}}{2} \tag{5-55}$$

Once again we correctly guess the general result to be

$$\langle p^2 \rangle = \hbar(\mu k)^{1/2}(n + \tfrac{1}{2}) \tag{5-56}$$

Using Eqs. 5-53 and 5-56, we see that

$$\sigma_p^2\sigma_x^2 = \langle p^2 \rangle\langle x^2 \rangle = \hbar^2(n + \tfrac{1}{2})^2$$

or that

$$\sigma_p\sigma_x = \hbar(n + \tfrac{1}{2})$$

Thus we have that

$$\sigma_p\sigma_x \geq \frac{\hbar}{2} \tag{5-57}$$

in accord with the Heisenberg Uncertainty Principle.

Equations 5-53 and 5-56 also show us that

$$\langle K \rangle = \left\langle \frac{p^2}{2\mu} \right\rangle = \frac{1}{2\mu}\langle p^2 \rangle = \frac{\hbar}{2}\left(\frac{k}{\mu}\right)^{1/2}\left(n + \frac{1}{2}\right)$$

$$= \frac{\hbar\omega}{2}\left(n + \frac{1}{2}\right) = \frac{E_n}{2} \tag{5-58}$$

and that

$$\langle U(x) \rangle = \left\langle \frac{kx^2}{2} \right\rangle = \frac{k}{2}\langle x^2 \rangle = \frac{\hbar}{2}\left(\frac{k}{\mu}\right)^{1/2}\left(n + \frac{1}{2}\right)$$

$$= \frac{\hbar\omega}{2}\left(n + \frac{1}{2}\right) = \frac{E_n}{2} \tag{5-59}$$

On the average then the total energy in any state is equally distributed between the kinetic energy and the potential energy. Problem 4 shows that this is true classically as well.

5-10   *The Amplitude of a Quantum-Mechanical Harmonic*
          Oscillator Can Exceed Its Classical Value

We can use the harmonic-oscillator wave functions to illustrate an interesting phenomenon that we have not yet encountered. The probability that the displacement of a harmonic oscillator in its ground state lies between x and $x + dx$ is given by

$$P(x)\,dx = \psi_0^2(x)\,dx = \left(\frac{\alpha}{\pi}\right)^{1/2} e^{-\alpha x^2}\,dx \tag{5-60}$$

The energy of the oscillator in its ground state is $(\hbar/2)(k/\mu)^{1/2}$. The greatest displacement that this oscillator can have classically is its amplitude, where all its energy is potential energy and so (cf. Eq. 5-15)

$$\frac{kA^2}{2} = \frac{\hbar}{2}\left(\frac{k}{\mu}\right)^{1/2}$$

or

$$A = \left[\frac{\hbar}{(k\mu)^{1/2}}\right]^{1/2} = \frac{1}{\alpha^{1/2}} \tag{5-61}$$

According to Eq. 5-60, however, there is a nonzero probability that the displacement of the oscillator will exceed this classical value. This probability is given by

$$\int_{-\infty}^{-\alpha^{-1/2}} P(x)\,dx + \int_{\alpha^{-1/2}}^{\infty} P(x)\,dx = 2\int_{\alpha^{-1/2}}^{\infty} P(x)\,dx$$

$$= 2\left(\frac{\alpha}{\pi}\right)^{1/2} \int_{\alpha^{-1/2}}^{\infty} e^{-\alpha x^2}\,dx \tag{5-62}$$

$$= \frac{2}{\pi^{1/2}} \int_{1}^{\infty} e^{-z^2}\,dz$$

where in going across the first equality we have recognized that $P(x)$ is an even function of x. The integral here cannot be evaluated in closed form but occurs so frequently in a number of different fields (such as the kinetic theory of gases and statistics) that it is well-tabulated under the name *complementary error function*, erfc(x), which is defined as

$$\text{erfc}(x) = \frac{2}{\pi^{1/2}} \int_{x}^{\infty} e^{-z^2}\,dz \tag{5-63}$$

By referring to tables, it can be found that the probability that the displacement of the molecule will exceed its classical amplitude is 0.16.

This feature is characteristic of quantum-mechanical systems and is responsible for the phenomenon called the *tunnel effect*, where the system is said to have tunneled into a classically forbidden region. This is thought to be important in problems involving classically insurmountable potential barriers such as α radioactivity, field emission of electrons from metals, the doublet inversion in the ammonia molecule, and some proton transfer reactions in solution.

We see then that although a classical harmonic oscillator has a fixed amplitude, a quantum-mechanical harmonic oscillator does not. We can, however, use $\langle x^2 \rangle$ as a measure of the square of the amplitude, and, in particular, we can use the square root of $\langle x^2 \rangle$, the root-mean-square value of x,

$$A_{\mathrm{rms}} \equiv x_{\mathrm{rms}} = \langle x^2 \rangle^{1/2} \tag{5-64}$$

as a measure of the amplitude. We can use all these ideas now to learn about the vibrational amplitudes in diatomic molecules. We have seen above that the vibrational spectrum of a diatomic molecule consists of just one line in the infrared region of the spectrum and that the frequency of this line is given by (cf. Eq. 5-40)

$$\bar{\nu}_{\mathrm{obs}} = \frac{1}{2\pi c} \left(\frac{k}{\mu} \right)^{1/2} \tag{5-65}$$

According to Eq. 5-52, the amplitude in the ground vibrational state is

$$A_{\mathrm{rms}} \equiv x_{\mathrm{rms}} = \left(\frac{\hbar}{2(\mu k)^{1/2}} \right)^{1/2} \tag{5-66}$$

We can eliminate k from this expression by using Eq. 5-65 to obtain

$$A_{\mathrm{rms}} = \left(\frac{\hbar}{4\pi c \bar{\nu}_{\mathrm{obs}} \mu} \right)^{1/2} \tag{5-67}$$

Because the reduced mass is derivable from the chemical formula of the diatomic molecule, one can calculate $\langle x^2 \rangle^{1/2}$ given $\bar{\nu}_{\mathrm{obs}}$. For example, for $H^{35}Cl$, $\bar{\nu}_{\mathrm{obs}}$ is 2.95×10^3 cm^{-1}, and so Eq. 5-67 gives

$$A_{\mathrm{rms}} = \left[\frac{1.055 \times 10^{-34} \text{ J} \cdot \text{s}}{4\pi(3.00 \times 10^8 \text{ m} \cdot \text{s}^{-1})(2.95 \times 10^5 \text{ m}^{-1})(35/36)(1.66 \times 10^{-27} \text{ kg})} \right]^{1/2}$$

$$= 7.67 \times 10^{-12} \text{ m} = 7.67 \text{ pm}$$

The bond length of HCl is 127 pm, and so we can see that the root-mean-square amplitude is only about 5% of the bond length. This is typical for diatomic molecules (cf. Problem 18).

EXAMPLE 5-10

The fundamental vibrational frequency of $H^{75}Br$ is 2.63×10^3 cm^{-1} and l_0 is 141 pm. Calculate the root-mean-square displacement in the ground state and compare your result to l_0.

Solution: Equation 5-67 is

$$A_{rms} = \left(\frac{\hbar}{4\pi c \overline{v}_{obs}\mu}\right)^{1/2}$$

$$= \left[\frac{1.055 \times 10^{-34}\,\text{J}\cdot\text{s}}{4\pi(3.00 \times 10^8\,\text{m}\cdot\text{s}^{-1})(2.63 \times 10^5\,\text{m}^{-1})(75/76)(1.66 \times 10^{-27}\,\text{kg})}\right]^{1/2}$$

$$= 8.06\,\text{pm}$$

Comparing this with the bond length, 141 pm, shows that A_{rms} is less than 6% of l_0.

Thus far we have not solved the Schrödinger equation for a harmonic oscillator. Instead, we have simply presented and discussed the harmonic-oscillator energy levels and the corresponding wave functions. In particular, we have applied the results to a vibrating diatomic molecule and have shown how to use infrared spectroscopy to determine molecular force constants and vibrational amplitudes. In the remainder of this chapter, we shall discuss the solution to the Schrödinger equation, Eq. 5-32, and then derive some general properties of Hermite polynomials. For those readers who do not wish to learn all the mathematical details of solving Eq. 5-32, they can proceed directly to Chapter 6 because the material to be presented here will not be used later. Many people believe, however, that it is important to solve at least one quantum-mechanical model in detail to understand how the discrete energy levels arise and how a set of wave functions is generated.

5-11   The Asymptotic Solution of the Harmonic-Oscillator Schrödinger Equation Is exp $(-\alpha x^2/2)$

Here we shall present a set of substitutions that converts Eq. 5-32 into a differential equation that is not difficult to solve by anyone who has some experience with differential equations. It so happens that Eq. 5-32 itself is rather awkward to solve and the manipulations presented here are standard in any discussion of the quantum-mechanical harmonic oscillator. First, let

$$\lambda = \frac{2\mu E}{\hbar^2} \quad \text{and} \quad \alpha^2 = \frac{k\mu}{\hbar^2} = \left(\frac{2\pi\mu v}{\hbar}\right)^2 \tag{5-68}$$

so that the Schrödinger equation becomes

$$\frac{d^2\psi}{dx^2} + (\lambda - \alpha^2 x^2)\psi(x) = 0 \tag{5-69}$$

It might be tempting to let $\alpha x = \xi$ in this equation, but this would not simplify things because there are two powers of x in the second-derivative term $d^2\psi/dx^2$.

To find a substitution that does simplify things, divide Eq. 5-69 through by a parameter c to find

$$\frac{d^2\psi}{c\, dx^2} + \left(\frac{\lambda}{c} - \frac{\alpha^2}{c}x^2\right)\psi(x) = 0$$

In order that x be multiplied by the same parameter in both terms of this equation, we must have that $c = \alpha^2/c$ or that $c = \alpha$. This makes the coefficient of x^2 be α in both terms and so suggests that we let

$$\xi = \alpha^{1/2}x = \left(\frac{k\mu}{\hbar^2}\right)^{1/4} x \qquad (5\text{-}70)$$

in Eq. 5-69. This substitution gives the simplified form

$$\frac{d^2\psi}{d\xi^2} + \left(\frac{\lambda}{\alpha} - \xi^2\right)\psi(\xi) = 0 \qquad (5\text{-}71)$$

(cf. Problem 19 for an alternative method to derive this result).

Again we point out that Eq. 5-71 does not have constant coefficients. Generally speaking, a good place to start is to look for any values of the independent variable, ξ in this case, that lead to infinity. Such a point here is $\xi = \infty$, and so this tells us that we should look at large values of ξ first. For large values of ξ, we can neglect λ/α compared to ξ^2 and Eq. 5-71 becomes

$$\frac{d^2\psi}{d\xi^2} - \xi^2\psi(\xi) = 0 \qquad \text{(large } \xi) \qquad (5\text{-}72)$$

We still cannot solve this equation because the coefficient ξ^2 is not a constant, but if it were, then $\psi(\xi) = e^{\pm\xi^2}$ would be the solution. It is easy to verify that this is not a solution to Eq. 5-72 for large values of ξ, but it does suggest trying something like

$$\psi(\xi) = e^{\beta\xi^2} \qquad (5\text{-}73)$$

where β is a parameter to be determined. If we substitute this into Eq. 5-72, we find

$$2\beta e^{\beta\xi^2} + 4\beta^2\xi^2 e^{\beta\xi^2} - \xi^2 e^{\beta\xi^2} = 0$$

or

$$[\xi^2(4\beta^2 - 1) + 2\beta]e^{\beta\xi^2} = 0$$

Because ξ is very large, we can ignore the second term in the brackets and see that $\beta = \pm\frac{1}{2}$ does indeed give us a solution of Eq. 5-71 for large values of ξ. Because $\psi(\xi)$ is a wave function, we reject the $\beta = +\frac{1}{2}$ value because this would give us a wave function that diverges as $e^{\xi^2/2}$ as $\xi \to \infty$. Thus we see that

$$\psi(\xi) = e^{-\xi^2/2} \qquad (5\text{-}74)$$

is an asymptotic solution to Eq. 5-71.

EXAMPLE 5-11

Verify that $\psi(\xi) = e^{-\xi^2/2}$ is an asymptotic solution to Eq. 5-71.

Solution: By asymptotic solution, we mean a solution that is valid only for large values of ξ. Substituting $e^{-\xi^2/2}$ into Eq. 5-71 gives

$$\xi^2 e^{-\xi^2/2} - e^{-\xi^2/2} + \left(\frac{\lambda}{\alpha} - \xi^2\right)e^{-\xi^2/2} \overset{?}{=} 0$$

$$\left[\xi^2 - 1 + \left(\frac{\lambda}{\alpha} - \xi^2\right)\right]e^{-\xi^2/2} \overset{?}{=} 0$$

For large values of ξ, the -1 and λ/α can be neglected in the brackets and we see that $\psi(\xi)$ is an asymptotic solution to Eq. 5-71.

We now assume that the complete solution to Eq. 5-71 is of the form

$$\psi(\xi) = H(\xi)e^{-\xi^2/2} \tag{5-75}$$

where $H(\xi)$ is a function to be determined. If we substitute Eq. 5-75 into Eq. 5-71, we find (Problem 21)

$$\frac{d^2H}{d\xi^2} - 2\xi\frac{dH}{d\xi} + \left(\frac{\lambda}{\alpha} - 1\right)H(\xi) = 0 \tag{5-76}$$

This differential equation is called *Hermite's equation*. It certainly may not be obvious, but Eq. 5-76 is much easier to solve than Eq. 5-71 (cf. Problem 30). The identification of the asymptotic form of $\psi(\xi)$ and its extraction in the form of Eq. 5-75 generally leads to great simplification. The standard and general method for solving Eq. 5-76 is the so-called *series method*.

It is interesting to note that Eq. 5-76 arises in the treatment of the scattering of electromagnetic radiation from a parabolic reflector and had been studied and solved years earlier by the French mathematician Charles Hermite and was known in the mathematical literature as Hermite's equation. Prior to his formulation of quantum mechanics in 1925, Schrödinger's previous research was in the area of such classical problems as the scattering of radiation from various geometrical surfaces and he was already familiar with Hermite's equation and the properties of its solutions. We shall see that a number of quantum-mechanical problems lead to such "name" differential equations that were well studied and reported upon prior to the development of quantum mechanics.

5-12 Hermite's Differential Equation Can Be Solved by the Series Method

In this section we shall solve Hermite's differential equation, Eq. 5-76, and discuss the properties of its acceptable solutions, the Hermite polynomials. We shall see that the Hermite polynomials satisfy a number of interrelationships, much like those that exist among the ordinary trigonometric functions.

We shall solve Eq. 5-76 by the *series method*. We first write $H(\xi)$ as a power series in ξ:

$$H(\xi) = a_0 + a_1\xi + a_2\xi^2 + \cdots$$

$$\frac{dH}{d\xi} = a_1 + 2a_2\xi + 3a_3\xi^2 + \cdots \qquad (5\text{-}77)$$

$$\frac{d^2H}{d\xi^2} = 1 \cdot 2a_2 + 2 \cdot 3a_3\xi + 3 \cdot 4a_4\xi^2 + \cdots$$

If we substitute these into Eq. 5-76 and collect like powers of ξ, then we obtain

$$\left[1 \cdot 2a_2 + \left(\frac{\lambda}{\alpha} - 1 \right)a_0 \right] + \left[2 \cdot 3a_3 + \left(\frac{\lambda}{\alpha} - 1 - 2 \right)a_1 \right]\xi$$

$$+ \left[3 \cdot 4a_4 + \left(\frac{\lambda}{\alpha} - 1 - 2 \cdot 2 \right)a_2 \right]\xi^2$$

$$+ \left[4 \cdot 5a_5 + \left(\frac{\lambda}{\alpha} - 1 - 2 \cdot 3 \right)a_3 \right]\xi^3 + \cdots = 0 \qquad (5\text{-}78)$$

For this series to vanish for all values of ξ, each of the coefficients must vanish separately:

$$1 \cdot 2a_2 + \left(\frac{\lambda}{\alpha} - 1 \right)a_0 = 0$$

$$2 \cdot 3a_3 + \left(\frac{\lambda}{\alpha} - 1 - 2 \right)a_1 = 0$$

$$3 \cdot 4a_4 + \left(\frac{\lambda}{\alpha} - 1 - 2 \cdot 2 \right)a_2 = 0 \qquad (5\text{-}79)$$

$$4 \cdot 5a_5 + \left(\frac{\lambda}{\alpha} - 1 - 2 \cdot 3 \right)a_3 = 0$$

or, generally, that

$$(n + 1)(n + 2)a_{n+2} + \left(\frac{\lambda}{\alpha} - 1 - 2n \right)a_n = 0 \qquad n = 0, 1, 2, \ldots \quad (5\text{-}80)$$

This type of formula is a standard result of the series solution method of solving differential equations and is called a *recursion formula*. It gives one coefficient in the series expansion of $H(\xi)$ in terms of a previous coefficient. In particular, Eq. 5-80 is called a *two-term recursion formula*. If a_0 and a_1 are taken to be arbitrary, Eq. 5-80 gives two independent sets of coefficients and hence two independent solutions:

$$H_{even}(\xi) = a_0 + a_2\xi^2 + a_4\xi^4 + \cdots$$

$$H_{odd}(\xi) = a_1\xi + a_3\xi^3 + a_5\xi^5 + \cdots \qquad (5\text{-}81)$$

where we have subscripted $H(\xi)$ according to whether the series contains even or odd powers of ξ. Remember that Hermite's differential equation is second order and so there should be two independent solutions.

We can use Eq. 5-80 to solve for the a_{2n} in terms of a_0 and the a_{2n+1} in terms of a_1. The first few of these relations are

$$a_2 = -\frac{1}{2 \cdot 1}\left(\frac{\lambda}{\alpha} - 1\right)a_0 \tag{5-82}$$

$$a_4 = -\frac{1}{3 \cdot 4}\left(\frac{\lambda}{\alpha} - 1 - 2 \cdot 2\right)a_2$$

$$= \frac{1}{4!}\left(\frac{\lambda}{\alpha} - 1\right)\left(\frac{\lambda}{\alpha} - 1 - 2 \cdot 2\right)a_0 \tag{5-83}$$

and

$$a_3 = -\frac{1}{2 \cdot 3}\left(\frac{\lambda}{\alpha} - 1 - 2\right)a_1 \tag{5-84}$$

$$a_5 = -\frac{1}{4 \cdot 5}\left(\frac{\lambda}{\alpha} - 1 - 2 \cdot 3\right)a_3$$

$$= \frac{1}{5!}\left(\frac{\lambda}{\alpha} - 1 - 2\right)\left(\frac{\lambda}{\alpha} - 1 - 2 \cdot 3\right)a_1 \tag{5-85}$$

and so forth. Note that this procedure is giving us one solution as a power series in even powers of ξ and another in odd powers of ξ, that is, an even or an odd solution.

We must investigate the behavior of these power series for large values of ξ to assure that these solutions qualify as acceptable wave functions. For large values of ξ, the high powers of ξ or, that is, large values of n dominate the power series for $H(\xi)$. Recall that the convergence of a power series is related to the ratio of successive coefficients, or to a_{n+2}/a_n in this case. Because we are concerned with large values of n, we note from Eq. 5-80 that

$$\left|\frac{a_{n+2}}{a_n}\right| \rightarrow \frac{2n}{n^2} = \frac{2}{n} \quad \text{as} \quad n \rightarrow \infty \tag{5-86}$$

But the series expansion of e^{ξ^2} is

$$e^{\xi^2} = 1 + \xi^2 + \frac{\xi^4}{2!} + \frac{\xi^6}{3!} + \cdots + \frac{\xi^n}{(n/2)!} + \cdots$$

and so if we denote the coefficient of ξ^n by b_n, then we see that

$$\frac{b_{n+2}}{b_n} = \frac{(n/2)!}{[(n/2) + 1]!} = \frac{1}{n/2} = \frac{2}{n} \tag{5-87}$$

A comparison of Eq. 5-86 and 5-87 shows that both series behave in the same way or that the power series that we have found for the $H(\xi)$ go as e^{ξ^2} for large values of ξ. This behavior is quite unacceptable, however, since according to Eq. 5-75 the harmonic-oscillator wave functions are $\psi(\xi) = H(\xi)e^{-\xi^2/2}$, and so $\psi(\xi)$ would diverge as $e^{+\xi^2/2}$ as $\xi \to \infty$. To avoid this difficulty, we must choose values of λ/α in Eq. 5-80 such that the a_n equal zero after a certain number of terms so that we have polynomial solutions instead of power series. It is easy to see from Eq. 5-80 that this can be achieved by setting

$$\frac{\lambda}{\alpha} - 1 - 2n = 0 \qquad n = 0, 1, 2, \ldots \tag{5-88}$$

If we substitute the definitions of λ and α (Eq. 5-68) into Eq. 5-88, then we find that

$$E_n = \hbar\left(\frac{k}{\mu}\right)^{1/2}\left(n + \frac{1}{2}\right) = \hbar\omega\left(n + \frac{1}{2}\right) = h\nu\left(n + \frac{1}{2}\right) \tag{5-89}$$

We have subscripted E with an n to indicate that there is a set of quantized energies. The quantization in this case arises by requiring that $\psi(\xi)$ be well-behaved as $\xi \to \infty$.

If we let $(\lambda/\alpha) - 1$ equal $2n$ in Eqs. 5-82 and 5-83, then we obtain

$$a_2 = -\frac{2na_0}{1\cdot 2}$$

$$a_4 = \frac{(2n)(2n-4)}{4!}a_0$$

It is a simple exercise to continue this argument and show that (Problem 26)

$$H_n(\xi) = a_0\left[1 - \frac{2n}{2!}\xi^2 + \frac{2^2n(n-2)}{4!}\xi^4 - \frac{2^3n(n-2)(n-4)}{6!}\xi^6 + \cdots\right] \quad (n \text{ even}) \tag{5-90}$$

Similarly, using Eqs. 5-84, 5-85, and so forth, we find that

$$H_n(\xi) = a_1\left[\xi - \frac{2(n-1)}{3!}\xi^3 + \frac{2^2(n-1)(n-3)}{5!}\xi^5 - \cdots\right] \quad (n \text{ odd}) \tag{5-91}$$

Because n is an even integer in Eq. 5-90 or an odd integer in Eq. 5-91, each of these series truncates, yielding a polynomial. It is customary to choose a_0 and a_1 such that the coefficient of the highest power of ξ, that is, ξ^n, is 2^n. Thus we finally write

$$H_n(\xi) = (-1)^{n/2}\frac{n!}{(n/2)!}$$

$$\times\left[1 - \frac{2n}{2!}\xi^2 + \frac{2^2n(n-2)}{4!}\xi^4 - \frac{2^3n(n-2)(n-4)}{6!}\xi^6 + \cdots\right] \quad (n \text{ even}) \tag{5-92}$$

and

$$H_n(\xi) = (-1)^{(n-1)/2} \frac{2(n!)}{[(n-1)/2]!}$$

$$\times \left[\xi - \frac{2(n-1)}{3!} \xi^3 + \frac{2^2(n-1)(n-3)}{5!} \xi^5 - \cdots \right] \qquad (n \text{ odd}) \quad (5\text{-}93)$$

It is easy to show that these two formulas reproduce the explicit expressions given in Table 5-2.

5-13   *There Are Many Relations Among Hermite Polynomials*

An equivalent and more useful definition of the Hermite polynomials is

$$H_n(\xi) = (-1)^n e^{\xi^2} \frac{d^n}{d\xi^n} e^{-\xi^2} \qquad (5\text{-}94)$$

EXAMPLE 5-12

Show that Eq. 5-94 generates the Hermite polynomials by using it to generate $H_0(\xi)$, $H_1(\xi)$, and $H_2(\xi)$.

Solution: If we let $n = 0$, we have

$$H_0(\xi) = e^{\xi^2} e^{-\xi^2} = 1$$

Letting $n = 1$,

$$H_1(\xi) = (-1)e^{\xi^2} \frac{d}{d\xi} e^{-\xi^2} = (-1)e^{\xi^2}(-2\xi e^{-\xi^2}) = 2\xi$$

Letting $n = 2$,

$$H_2(\xi) = e^{\xi^2} \frac{d^2}{d\xi^2} e^{-\xi^2} = e^{\xi^2}(-2 + 4\xi^2)e^{-\xi^2} = 4\xi^2 - 2$$

If we differentiate both sides of Eq. 5-94 with respect to ξ, we obtain

$$\frac{dH_n(\xi)}{d\xi} = (-1)^n 2\xi e^{\xi^2} \frac{d^n e^{-\xi^2}}{d\xi^n} + (-1)^n e^{\xi^2} \frac{d^{n+1} e^{-\xi^2}}{d\xi^{n+1}}$$

$$= 2\xi H_n(\xi) - H_{n+1}(\xi) \qquad (5\text{-}95)$$

This gives us a useful derivative formula for the $H_n(\xi)$. By a repeated application of this formula, we obtain

$$\frac{d^2 H_n(\xi)}{d\xi^2} = 2H_n(\xi) + 2\xi[2\xi H_n(\xi) - H_{n+1}(\xi)] - [2\xi H_{n+1}(\xi) - H_{n+2}(\xi)]$$

$$= 2(1 + 2\xi^2)H_n(\xi) - 4\xi H_{n+1}(\xi) + H_{n+2}(\xi) \qquad (5\text{-}96)$$

If we substitute Eqs. 5-95 and 5-96 into Hermite's equation, Eq. 5-76 with $(\lambda/\alpha) - 1$ replaced by $2n$, then we find

$$H_{n+2}(\xi) - 2\xi H_{n+1}(\xi) + 2(n+1)H_n(\xi) = 0$$

or, equivalently, by replacing n by $n-1$ everywhere,

$$H_{n+1}(\xi) - 2\xi H_n(\xi) + 2nH_{n-1}(\xi) = 0 \tag{5-97}$$

Equation 5-97 is a *recursion formula* for the $H_n(\xi)$.

EXAMPLE 5-13

Show explicitly that the first few Hermite polynomials satisfy the recursion formula, Eq. 5-97.

Solution: To do this, we shall use the recursion formula to generate Hermite polynomials starting with $H_0(\xi)$ and $H_1(\xi)$. Setting $n=1$ in Eq. 5-97, we have

$$H_2(\xi) = 2\xi H_1(\xi) - 2H_0(\xi)$$

Substituting $H_0(\xi) = 1$ and $H_1(\xi) = 2\xi$ into this equation gives

$$H_2(\xi) = 4\xi^2 - 2$$

Now let $n=2$ in Eq. 5-97:

$$H_3(\xi) = 2\xi H_2(\xi) - 4H_1(\xi)$$
$$= 2\xi(4\xi^2 - 2) - 4(2\xi) = 8\xi^3 - 12\xi$$

With $n=3$, we have

$$H_4(\xi) = 2\xi H_3(\xi) - 6H_2(\xi)$$
$$= 2\xi(8\xi^3 - 12\xi) - 6(4\xi^2 - 2)$$
$$= 16\xi^4 - 48\xi^2 + 12$$

By combining Eq. 5-97 with Eq. 5-95, we find

$$\frac{dH_n(\xi)}{d\xi} = 2nH_{n-1}(\xi) \tag{5-98}$$

Formulas like Eq. 5-97 and 5-98 can be used to evaluate integrals involving Hermite polynomials in general. For example, consider

$$\langle \xi \rangle = \alpha^{-1/2} \int_{-\infty}^{\infty} \psi_n(\xi)\xi\psi_n(\xi)\,d\xi \tag{5-99}$$

We have shown earlier that this integral is equal to zero because of the even-odd character of the $\psi_n(\xi)$, but let us show this using Eq. 5-97. Equation 5-99 is

$$\langle \xi \rangle = \alpha^{-1/2} N_n^2 \int_{-\infty}^{\infty} H_n(\xi)\xi H_n(\xi)e^{-\xi^2}\,d\xi \tag{5-100}$$

According to Eq. 5-97,

$$\xi H_n(\xi) = nH_{n-1}(\xi) + \tfrac{1}{2}H_{n+1}(\xi) \qquad (5\text{-}101)$$

and when this substituted into Eq. 5-100, we have

$$\langle \xi \rangle = \alpha^{-1/2}\, nN_n^2 \int_{-\infty}^{\infty} H_n(\xi)H_{n-1}(\xi)e^{-\xi^2}\,d\xi + \alpha^{-1/2}\frac{N_n^2}{2}\int_{-\infty}^{\infty} H_n(\xi)H_{n+1}(\xi)e^{-\xi^2}\,d\xi$$

But both of these integrals are equal to zero because of orthogonality. Notice that we did not have to know the form of the Hermite polynomials.

This example did not give us anything new because we could have evaluated $\langle \xi \rangle$ by symmetry. Let us consider the more difficult case

$$\langle \xi^2 \rangle = \alpha^{-1/2}\, N_n^2 \int_{-\infty}^{\infty} H_n(\xi)\xi^2 H_n(\xi)e^{-\xi^2}\,d\xi \qquad (5\text{-}102)$$

We apply Eq. 5-101 two times and write

$$\xi^2 H_n(\xi) = n\xi H_{n-1}(\xi) + \tfrac{1}{2}\xi H_{n+1}(\xi)$$
$$= n[(n-1)H_{n-2}(\xi) + \tfrac{1}{2}H_n(\xi)] + \tfrac{1}{2}[(n+1)H_n(\xi) + \tfrac{1}{2}H_{n+2}(\xi)]$$

When we substitute this into Eq. 5-102, the terms involving $H_{n-2}(\xi)$ and $H_{n+2}(\xi)$ vanish by orthogonality, and we are left with simply

$$\langle \xi^2 \rangle = \alpha^{-1/2}\,(n + \tfrac{1}{2})N_n^2 \int_{-\infty}^{\infty} H_n(\xi)\xi^2 H_n(\xi)e^{-\xi^2}\,d\xi$$
$$= n + \tfrac{1}{2}$$

because of normalization. Because $\xi = \alpha^{1/2}x$, we have that

$$\langle x^2 \rangle = \frac{1}{\alpha}\langle \xi^2 \rangle = \frac{\hbar}{(\mu k)^{1/2}}\left(n + \frac{1}{2}\right)$$

in agreement with Eq. 5-53. The evaluation of $\langle p \rangle$ and $\langle p^2 \rangle$ by this method is left to Problem 28.

This section was a digression on the mathematical properties of the harmonic-oscillator wave functions and on the Hermite polynomials in particular. It was meant to show just how much one can deduce about the solutions even though they are defined formally by truncated infinite series. In a real sense, we have developed a set of relationships among the Hermite polynomials much like those among the ordinary trigonometric functions. A number of quantum-mechanical problems involve solving a rather complicated differential equation like Hermite's equation and then deriving general properties of those solutions much like we have done in this section for the Hermite polynomials. Each set of solutions has a generating formula (Eq. 5-94) and recursion formulas (Eqs. 5-95, 5-97 and 5-98). In later chapters we shall not derive all of these types of relations but shall simply present them since this involves a mathematical digression like this section. The general procedure is much the same, however.

Summary

A harmonic oscillator is a good approximate model for the vibrational motion of a diatomic molecule. In this chapter, first we reviewed the development of a classical harmonic oscillator and showed that a classical harmonic oscillator vibrates sinusoidally (harmonically) with a frequency that depends on the reduced mass and on the force constant of the spring connecting the two masses. The harmonic-oscillator approximation results from a Taylor expansion of an internuclear potential energy function about its minimum. The leading term in such an expansion is a harmonic-oscillator potential and the higher-order terms in the expansion are called *anharmonic terms*. For vibrations of small amplitude, the anharmonic terms are small relative to the harmonic-oscillator term, and the harmonic oscillator serves as a satisfactory approximation.

The quantum-mechanical treatment of a harmonic oscillator gives a set of equally spaced energies, with $E_n = \hbar(k/\mu)^{1/2}(n + \frac{1}{2})$, $n = 0, 1, 2, \ldots$, and $\Delta E = \hbar(k/\mu)^{1/2}$. This model predicts that the vibrational spectrum of a diatomic molecule consists of a single line in the infrared region, in good agreement with experiment. The frequency of the line gives the force constant of the molecule.

The wave functions of a harmonic oscillator involve Hermite polynomials. The harmonic-oscillator wave functions can be used to calculate average vibrational properties of a diatomic molecule. For example, we showed that the average displacement of a harmonic oscillator is zero and that its average kinetic energy and its average potential energy are equal. We also calculated root-mean-square amplitudes of vibration and showed that there is a certain nonzero probability that its amplitude exceed its classical value. In Sections 5-11 through 5-13, we solved the Schrödinger equation for a harmonic oscillator in detail and derived a number of general properties of Hermite polynomials and the relations among them.

Terms That You Should Know

Hooke's law	zero-point energy
force constant	Hermite polynomials
harmonic motion	odd function
amplitude	even function
conservative system	tunnel effect
center-of-mass coordinate	root-mean-square amplitude
relative coordinate	asymptotic solution
reduced mass	Hermite's equation
Taylor expansion	series method
anharmonic terms	recursion formula
fundamental vibrational frequency	two-term recursion formula

Problems

1. Verify that $x(t) = A \sin \omega t + B \cos \omega t$ $[\omega = (k/m)^{1/2}]$ solves Newton's equation for a harmonic oscillator.

2. Verify that $x(t) = C \sin (\omega t + \phi)$ solves Newton's equation for a harmonic oscillator.

3. The general solution for the classical harmonic oscillator is $x(t) = C \sin (\omega t + \phi)$. Show that the displacement oscillates between $+C$ and $-C$ with a frequency ω radians/sec or $v = \omega/2\pi$ cycles/sec. What is the period of the oscillations; that is, how long does it take to undergo 1 cycle?

4. From Problem 3 we see that the period of a harmonic vibration is $\tau = 1/v$. The average of the kinetic energy over 1 cycle is given by

$$\langle K \rangle = \frac{1}{\tau} \int_0^\tau \frac{m \omega^2 C^2}{2} \cos^2 (\omega t + \phi) \, dt$$

Show that $\langle K \rangle = E/2$ where E is the total energy. Show also that $\langle U \rangle = E/2$, where the instantaneous potential energy is given by

$$U = \frac{k C^2}{2} \sin^2 (\omega t + \phi)$$

Interpret the result $\langle K \rangle = \langle U \rangle$.

5. Consider a freely falling body, that is, one in which the only force is the gravitational force mg. Using the coordinate system shown in Figure 5-9(a), show that the sum of the instantaneous kinetic energy and potential energy is a constant. Note that the kinetic energy increases with time but that the potential energy decreases with time such that their sum is always a constant. Do the same for the geometry illustrated in Figure 5-9(b).

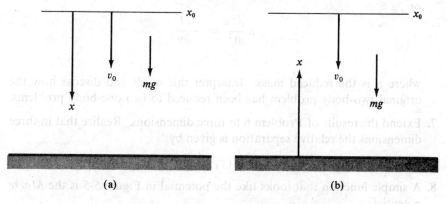

Figure 5-9. Two coordinate systems for a freely falling body.

6. Consider two masses m_1 and m_2 in one dimension, interacting through a potential that depends only on their relative separation $(x_1 - x_2)$ so that

$U(x_1, x_2) = U(x_1 - x_2)$. Given that the force acting upon the jth particle is $f_j = -(\partial U / \partial x_j)$, show that $f_1 = -f_2$, What law is this?

Newton's equations for m_1 and m_2 are

$$m_1 \frac{d^2 x_1}{dt^2} = -\frac{\partial U}{\partial x_1} \qquad m_2 \frac{d^2 x_2}{dt^2} = -\frac{\partial U}{\partial x_2}$$

Now introduce center-of-mass and relative coordinates by

$$X = \frac{m_1 x_1 + m_2 x_2}{M} \qquad x = x_1 - x_2$$

Solve for x_1 and x_2 to obtain

$$x_1 = X + \frac{m_2}{M} x \qquad x_2 = X - \frac{m_1}{M} x$$

Show that Newton's equations in these coordinates are

$$m_1 \frac{d^2 X}{dt^2} + \frac{m_1 m_2}{M} \frac{d^2 x}{dt^2} = -\frac{\partial U}{\partial x}$$

and

$$m_2 \frac{d^2 X}{dt^2} - \frac{m_1 m_2}{M} \frac{d^2 x}{dt^2} = +\frac{\partial U}{\partial x}$$

Now add these two equations to find

$$M \frac{d^2 X}{dt^2} = 0$$

Interpret this result. Now divide the first equation by m_1 and the second by m_2 and subtract to obtain

$$\frac{d^2 x}{dt^2} = -\left(\frac{1}{m_1} + \frac{1}{m_2} \right) \frac{\partial U}{\partial x}$$

or

$$\mu \frac{d^2 x}{dt^2} = -\frac{\partial U}{\partial x}$$

where μ is the reduced mass. Interpret this result and discuss how the original two-body problem has been reduced to two one-body problems.

7. Extend the results of Problem 6 to three dimensions. Realize that in three dimensions the relative separation is given by

$$r_{12} = [(x_1 - x_2)^2 + (y_1 - y_2)^2 + (z_1 - z_2)^2]^{1/2}$$

8. A simple function that looks like the potential in Figure 5-5 is the *Morse potential*:

$$U(x) = D_e (1 - e^{-\beta x})^2$$

where x is the displacement of the bond from its equilibrium position and D_e is the value of $U(x)$ at large separations. Expand $U(x)$ in a Taylor series about $x = 0$ to obtain

$$U(x) = D_e\beta^2 x^2 - D_e\beta^3 x^3 + \cdots$$

Given that $D_e = 7.31 \times 10^{-19}$ J·molecule^{-1} and $\beta = 1.82 \times 10^{10}$ m^{-1} for HCl, calculate the force constant of HCl. Plot the Morse potential for HCl and plot the corresponding harmonic oscillator potential on the same graph (cf. Figure 5-5).

9. In the infrared spectrum of H^{79}Br there is an intense line at 2.60×10^3 cm^{-1}. Calculate the force constant of H^{79}Br and the period of vibration of H^{79}Br.

10. The force constant of ^{79}Br^{79}Br is 240 N·m^{-1}. Calculate the fundamental vibrational frequency and the zero-point energy of ^{79}Br^{79}Br.

11. Verify that $\psi_1(x)$ and $\psi_2(x)$ given by Eqs. 5-41 and 5-43 and Table 5-2 satisfy the Schrödinger equation for a harmonic oscillator.

12. Prove that the product of two even functions is even, that the product of two odd functions is even, and that the product of an even and an odd function is odd.

13. Prove that the derivative of an even (odd) function is odd (even).

14. Show explicitly that $\psi_0(\xi)$ is orthogonal to $\psi_1(\xi)$, $\psi_2(\xi)$, and $\psi_3(\xi)$ and that $\psi_1(\xi)$ is orthogonal to $\psi_2(\xi)$ and $\psi_3(\xi)$.

15. To normalize the harmonic-oscillator wave functions and to calculate various expectation values, one must be able to evaluate integrals of the form

$$I_n(a) = \int_{-\infty}^{\infty} x^{2n} e^{-ax^2}\, dx \qquad n = 0, 1, 2, \ldots$$

One can simply either look them up in a table of integrals or continue this problem. First show that

$$I_n(a) = 2 \int_0^{\infty} x^{2n} e^{-ax^2}\, dx$$

The case $n = 0$ can be handled by the following trick. Show that the square of $I_0(a)$ can be written in the form

$$I_0^2(a) = 4 \int_0^{\infty} \int_0^{\infty} dx\, dy\, e^{-a(x^2 + y^2)}$$

Now convert to plane polar coordinates, letting

$$r^2 = x^2 + y^2$$

$$dx\, dy = r\, dr\, d\theta$$

and showing that the appropriate limits of integration are $0 \le r < \infty$ and $0 \le \theta \le \pi/2$. Show that this gives

$$I_0^2(a) = 4 \int_0^{\pi/2} d\theta \int_0^{\infty} dr\, r e^{-ar^2}$$

which is elementary and gives

$$I_0^2(a) = 4 \cdot \frac{\pi}{2} \cdot \frac{1}{2a} = \frac{\pi}{a}$$

or that

$$I_0(a) = \left(\frac{\pi}{a}\right)^{1/2}$$

Now prove that the $I_n(a)$ may be obtained by repeated differentiation of $I_0(a)$ with respect to a and, in particular, that

$$\frac{d^n I_0(a)}{da^n} = (-1)^n I_n(a)$$

Use this result and the fact that $I_0(a) = (\pi/a)^{1/2}$ to generate $I_1(a)$, $I_2(a)$, and so forth.

16. Show that

$$\langle x^2 \rangle = \int_{-\infty}^{\infty} \psi_2(x) x^2 \psi_2(x)\, dx = \frac{5}{2} \frac{\hbar}{(\mu k)^{1/2}}$$

for a harmonic oscillator.

17. Show that

$$\langle p^2 \rangle = \int_{-\infty}^{\infty} \psi_2(x) \hat{P}^2 \psi_2(x)\, dx = \tfrac{5}{2}\hbar(\mu k)^{1/2}$$

for a harmonic oscillator.

18. Using the fundamental vibrational frequencies of some diatomic molecules given below, calculate the root-mean-square displacement in the $n = 0$ state and compare it to the equilibrium bond length (also given below).

Molecule	$\bar{\nu}/cm^{-1}$	l_0/pm
H_2	4.33×10^3	74
$^{35}Cl^{35}Cl$	5.60×10^2	199
$^{14}N^{14}N$	2.35×10^3	110

19. Convert Eq. 5-69 to dimensionless form by letting $x = \beta\xi$ (β undetermined at this point), multiplying through by β^2 so that the coefficient of the second-derivative term is unity, and finally choosing β such that the coefficient of ξ^2 is also unity.

20. Verify that $e^{\pm\xi^2}$ is not an asymptotic solution to Eq. 5-71.

21. Substitute $\psi(\xi) = H(\xi)e^{-\xi^2/2}$ into Schrödinger's equation and show that the equation for $H(\xi)$ is Hermite's equation.

22. Show that $H_0(\xi) = 1$, $H_1(\xi) = 2\xi$, $H_2(\xi) = 4\xi^2 - 2$, and $H_3(\xi) = 8\xi^3 - 12\xi$ are solutions to Hermite's differential equation by substituting them directly into Hermite's equation (Eq. 5-76) with $(\lambda/\alpha) - 1 = 2n$.

23. Substitute $H(\xi) = a_0 + a_1\xi + a_2\xi^2 + \cdots$ into Hermite's differential equation, equate the coefficient of each power of ξ to zero, and show that

$$(n + 1)(n + 2)a_{n+2} + \left(\frac{\lambda}{\alpha} - 1 - 2n \right)a_n = 0$$

24. Referring to Problem 23, show that

$$\left| \frac{a_{n+2}}{a_n} \right| \to \frac{2}{n} \quad \text{as} \quad n \to \infty$$

25. Prove that setting

$$\frac{\lambda}{\alpha} - 1 - 2n = 0$$

truncates the power series for the $H(\xi)$ so that they become polynomials.

26. By setting $(\lambda/\alpha) - 1 - 2n = 0$ in Eqs. 5-82 through 5-85, derive explicit expressions for the Hermite polynomials.

27. In Section 5-13, a number of general relations between the Hermite polynomials and their derivatives are derived. Some of these are

$$\frac{dH_n(\xi)}{d\xi} = 2\xi H_n(\xi) - H_{n+1}(\xi)$$

$$H_{n+1}(\xi) - 2\xi H_n(\xi) + 2nH_{n-1}(\xi) = 0$$

$$\frac{dH_n(\xi)}{d\xi} = 2nH_{n-1}(\xi)$$

Such connecting relations are called *recursion formulas*. Verify these formulas explicitly using the first few Hermite polynomials given in Table 5-2.

28. Use the recursion formula for the Hermite polynomials to show that $\langle p \rangle = 0$ and $\langle p^2 \rangle = \hbar(\mu k)^{1/2}(n + \frac{1}{2})$. *Hint:* Remember that the momentum operator involves a differentiation with respect to x, not ξ.

29. This problem is similar to Problem 3-28. Show that the fact that the harmonic-oscillator wave functions are alternately even and odd functions of x is a direct result of the fact that the Hamiltonian operator obeys $\hat{H}(x) = \hat{H}(-x)$.

   Define a reflection operator $\hat{R}$ by

$$\hat{R}u(x) = u(-x)$$

Show that $\hat{R}$ is linear and that it commutes with $\hat{H}(x)$. Show furthermore that the eigenvalues of $\hat{R}$ are ± 1. What are its eigenfunctions? Show that the harmonic-oscillator wave functions are eigenfunctions of $\hat{R}$.

Note that they are eigenfunctions of both $\hat{H}$ and $\hat{R}$. What does this say about the eigenfunctions of $\hat{H}$ and $\hat{R}$?

30. Show that the power series method yields a three-term recursion formula if it is applied to Eq. 5-71 directly. Three-term recursion formulas are usually awkward and this is why it is necessary to separate the asymptotic behavior of $\psi(\xi)$ and to convert the differential equation into Hermite's equation, which yields a two-term recursion formula (cf. Eq. 5-80).

31. Figure 5-10 compares the probability distribution associated with $\psi_{10}(\xi)$ to the classical distribution. This problem illustrates what is meant by the classical distribution. Consider

$$x(t) = A \sin(\omega t + \phi)$$

which can be written as

$$\omega t = \sin^{-1}\left(\frac{x}{A}\right) - \phi$$

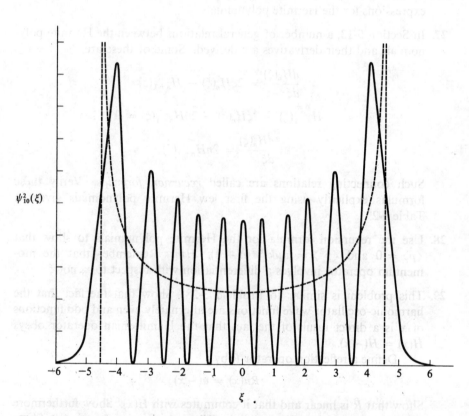

Figure 5-10. The probability distribution function of a harmonic oscillator in the $n = 10$ state. The dashed line is that for a classical harmonic oscillator with the same energy.

Now

$$dt = \frac{\omega^{-1}\,dx}{\sqrt{A^2 - x^2}}$$

This gives the time that the oscillator spends between x and $x + dx$. Since one period of motion is $2\pi/\omega$, show that the fraction of time that the oscillator spends between x and $x + dx$ is

$$f(t)\,dt = \frac{dx}{2\pi\sqrt{A^2 - x^2}}$$

Interpreting this as a probability, and remembering that $-A \le x \le A$, show that this is normalized. Plot this and compare it to the dashed line in Figure 5-10.

32. We solved Hermite's differential equation by the series method because the coefficients are not constants and this method works generally. It might be instructive to use the series method to solve the familiar equation

$$y'' + k^2 y = 0$$

because we know already that its solution is $A \cos kx + B \sin kx$. First write $y(x)$ as a power series:

$$y(x) = a_0 + a_1 x + a_2 x^2 + a_3 x^3 + \cdots$$

Substitute this into the differential equation, collect like powers of x, and set the coefficient of each power of x equal to zero to obtain

$$2a_2 + k^2 a_0 = 0 \qquad (x^0)$$
$$6a_3 + k^2 a_1 = 0 \qquad (x^1)$$
$$12a_4 + k^2 a_2 = 0 \qquad (x^2)$$
$$20a_5 + k^2 a_3 = 0 \qquad (x^3)$$

or, in general, for the coefficient of x^{n-2},

$$n(n-1)a_n + k^2 a_{n-2} = 0 \qquad n \ge 2$$

This is the recursion formula for this problem. Show that it gives the odd-indexed a's in terms of a_1 and the even-indexed a's in terms of a_0, giving two separate solutions. Show that

$$y(x) = a_0\left(1 - \frac{k^2 x^2}{2!} + \frac{k^4 x^4}{4!} - \frac{k^6 x^6}{6!} + \cdots\right)$$
$$+ a_1\left(x - \frac{k^2 x^3}{3!} + \frac{k^4 x^5}{5!} - \frac{k^6 x^7}{7!} + \cdots\right)$$

Letting $a_1' = a_1/k$, show that $y(x)$ becomes

$$y(x) = a_0 C(kx) + a_1' S(kx)$$

where

$$C(\xi) = 1 - \frac{\xi^2}{2!} + \frac{\xi^4}{4!} - \frac{\xi^6}{6!} + \cdots$$

and

$$S(\xi) = \xi - \frac{\xi^3}{3!} + \frac{\xi^5}{5!} - \frac{\xi^7}{7!} + \cdots$$

You should know that $C(\xi)$ and $S(\xi)$ are just the power series of the sine and the cosine, but let us assume that we do not know anything about these functions. Use these formal power series definitions to prove that

$$dS/d\xi = C(\xi)$$
$$dC/d\xi = -S(\xi)$$
$$e^{i\xi} = C(\xi) + iS(\xi)$$
$$C^2(\xi) + S^2(\xi) = 1$$
$$S(2\xi) = 2S(\xi)C(\xi)$$
$$S^2(\xi) = \tfrac{1}{2}[1 - C(2\xi)]$$

You may not be facile enough with manipulating power series to prove these in general, but you can at least prove each relation term by term in the expansion and then guess the general result. Note how this problem compares to the discussion of Hermite's equation and to the generation and evaluation of the Hermite polynomials.

33. It is interesting to note that Hermite polynomials were used in mathematical statistics before the advent of quantum mechanics. As you may know, the most important probability density is the Gaussian, or normal, distribution,

$$\phi(z)\,dz = (2\pi\sigma^2)^{-1/2} \exp\left[-\frac{(z - \langle z\rangle)^2}{2\sigma^2}\right] dz$$

where $\langle z\rangle$ and σ^2 are the mean and variance, respectively. Many distributions, although not exactly normal, do approximate a normal distribution in some sense. There is a systematic expansion of an arbitrary distribution about a normal distribution. Such an expansion has found a number of physical applications and is called a *Gram-Charlier series*. Let $f(z)$ be some probability density that looks to be somewhat normal and let $\phi(z)$ be a normal distribution. Without loss of generality, let the variable be taken to be a standardized variable $x = (z - \langle z\rangle)/\sigma$, that is, one with zero mean and unit variance. Show that in terms of this new variable x the normal distribution becomes

$$\phi(x)\,dx = (2\pi)^{-1/2}e^{-x^2/2}\,dx$$

Then we can write

$$f(x) = \phi(x) + c_1\phi'(x) + \left(\frac{c_2}{2!}\right)\phi''(x) + \left(\frac{c_3}{3!}\right)\phi'''(x) + \cdots$$

But the nth derivative of $e^{-x^2/2}$ is the generating function for a certain type of Hermite polynomials:

$$He_n(x) = (-1)^n e^{x^2/2} \left(\frac{d^n}{dx^n}\right) e^{-x^2/2}$$

so that the equation for $f(x)$ becomes

$$f(x) = e^{-x^2/2}[a_0 He_0(x) + a_1 He_1(x) + a_2 He_2(x) + \cdots]$$

which is simply an expansion of $f(x)$ in a set of orthogonal polynomials because

$$\int_{-\infty}^{\infty} e^{-x^2/2} He_m(x) He_n(x)\, dx = (2\pi)^{1/2} n! \delta_{mn}$$

Show that the coefficients a_j in the expansion of $f(x)$ can be determined by multiplying both sides by $He_j(x)$, integrating over all x, and using the orthonormality relation to find

$$a_j = [(2\pi)^{1/2} j!]^{-1} \int_{-\infty}^{\infty} He_j(x) f(x)\, dx$$

Show that the first few coefficients are

$$a_0 = (2\pi)^{-1/2} \int_{-\infty}^{\infty} He_0(x) f(x)\, dx$$

$$= (2\pi)^{-1/2} \int_{-\infty}^{\infty} f(x)\, dx = (2\pi)^{-1/2}$$

$$a_1 = (2\pi)^{-1/2} \int_{-\infty}^{\infty} He_1(x) f(x)\, dx$$

$$= (2\pi)^{1/2} \int_{-\infty}^{\infty} x f(x)\, d(x) = 0$$

$$a_2 = [2(2\pi)^{1/2}]^{-1} \int_{-\infty}^{\infty} He_2(x) f(x)\, dx$$

$$= [2(2\pi)^{1/2}]^{-1} \int_{-\infty}^{\infty} (x^2 - 1) f(x)\, dx = 0$$

a_1 and a_2 are zero because x has been taken to be a standardized variable; that is, $\langle x \rangle = 0$ and $\sigma^2 = 1$. The equation for $f(x)$ becomes

$$f(x) = (2\pi)^{-1/2} e^{-x^2/2} + e^{-x^2/2} \sum_{n=3}^{\infty} a_n He_n(x)$$

which is the form usually presented as the Gram-Charlier series. The leading term is a normal distribution and the remaining terms represent deviations of $f(x)$ from normal behavior. For example,

$$(2\pi)^{1/2} 3! a_3 = \langle x^3 \rangle$$

$$(2\pi)^{1/2} 4! a_4 = \langle x^4 \rangle - 3$$

both of which are zero for a Gaussian distribution. It should be pointed out that this expansion is mathematically valid for only a fairly small class of functions, but often physical grounds can be argued for its use.

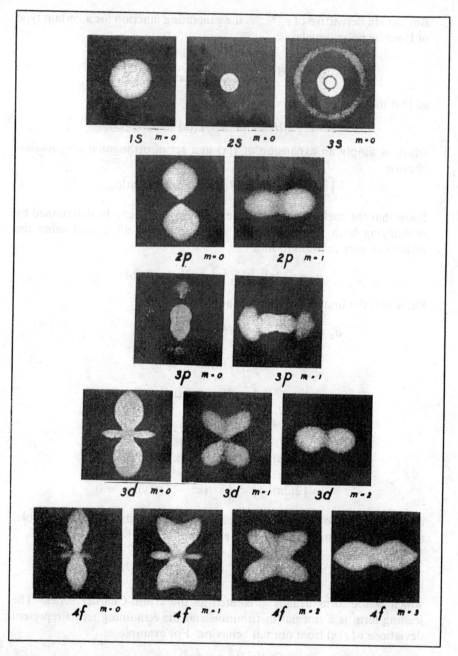

An illustration of electron probability densities in various states of the hydrogen atom. The chance that the electron will be found in a certain region is proportional to the brightness of the cloud in that region.

6

Three-Dimensional Systems

UP TO NOW we have discussed only systems that can be described by one spatial coordinate, that is, one-dimensional systems. In this chapter, we shall study some systems that require two or three spatial coordinates for their description. In Section 6-1 we shall discuss a particle confined to a three-dimensional box. Then in Section 6-4 we shall discuss a rigid rotator, which is the standard model for a rotating diatomic or linear molecule. The treatment of a rigid rotator leads naturally to a discussion of the properties of angular momentum in quantum-mechanical systems and finally to the simplest, and yet prototype, atomic system, the hydrogen atom. Most readers are probably already familiar with the quantum-mechanical results and properties of the hydrogen atom from general chemistry.

6-1 *The Problem of a Particle in a Three-Dimensional Box Is a Simple Extension of the One-Dimensional Case*

The simplest three-dimensional system is the three-dimensional version of a particle in a box. In this case, the particle is confined to lie within a rectangular parallelepiped with sides of lengths a, b, and c (Figure 6-1). The Schrödinger equation for this system is the three-dimensional extension of Eq. 3-17.

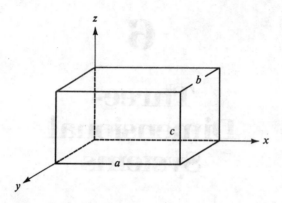

Figure 6-1. A rectangular parallelepiped of sides a, b, and c. In the problem of a particle in a three-dimensional box, the particle is restricted to lie within the region shown above.

$$-\frac{\hbar^2}{2m}\left(\frac{\partial^2\psi}{\partial x^2} + \frac{\partial^2\psi}{\partial y^2} + \frac{\partial^2\psi}{\partial z^2}\right) = E\psi(x, y, z) \qquad \begin{matrix} 0 \le x \le a \\ 0 \le y \le b \\ 0 \le z \le c \end{matrix} \qquad (6\text{-}1)$$

The wave function $\psi(x, y, z)$ satisfies the boundary condition that it vanishes at the walls of the box, and so

$$\psi(0, y, z) = \psi(a, y, z) = 0 \qquad \text{for all } y \text{ and } z$$
$$\psi(x, 0, z) = \psi(x, b, z) = 0 \qquad \text{for all } x \text{ and } z \qquad (6\text{-}2)$$
$$\psi(x, y, 0) = \psi(x, y, c) = 0 \qquad \text{for all } x \text{ and } y$$

We shall use the method of separation of variables to solve Eq. 6-1. We write

$$\psi(x, y, z) = X(x)Y(y)Z(z) \qquad (6\text{-}3)$$

Substitute Eq. 6-3 into Eq. 6-1, and then divide through by $\psi = XYZ$ to obtain

$$-\frac{\hbar^2}{2m}\frac{X''}{X} - \frac{\hbar^2}{2m}\frac{Y''}{Y} - \frac{\hbar^2}{2m}\frac{Z''}{Z} = E \qquad (6\text{-}4)$$

Each of the three terms on the left-hand side of Eq. 6-4 is a function of only x, y, or z. Therefore, each term must equal a constant for Eq. 6-4 to be valid for all values of x, y, or z. Thus we can write Eq. 6-4 as

$$E_x + E_y + E_z = E \qquad (6\text{-}5)$$

where E_x, E_y, and E_z are constants and where

$$-\frac{\hbar^2}{2m}\frac{X''}{X} = E_x$$

$$-\frac{\hbar^2}{2m}\frac{Y''}{Y} = E_y \qquad (6\text{-}6)$$

and

$$-\frac{\hbar^2}{2m}\frac{Z''}{Z} = E_z$$

From Eq. 6-2, the boundary conditions associated with Eq. 6-6 are that

$$X(0) = X(a) = 0$$

$$Y(0) = Y(b) = 0 \qquad\qquad (6\text{-}7)$$

and

$$Z(0) = Z(c) = 0$$

Thus, we see that Eqs. 6-6 and 6-7 are the same as for the one-dimensional case of a particle in a box (cf. Section 3-4). Following the same development as in Section 3-5, we obtain

$$X(x) = A_x \sin\frac{n_x\pi x}{a} \qquad n_x = 1, 2, 3, \ldots$$

$$Y(y) = A_y \sin\frac{n_y\pi y}{b} \qquad n_y = 1, 2, 3, \ldots \qquad (6\text{-}8)$$

and

$$Z(z) = A_z \sin\frac{n_z\pi z}{c} \qquad n_z = 1, 2, 3, \ldots$$

According to Eq. 6-3, the solution to Eq. 6-1 is

$$\psi(x, y, z) = A_x A_y A_z \sin\frac{n_x\pi x}{a} \sin\frac{n_y\pi y}{b} \sin\frac{n_z\pi z}{c} \qquad (6\text{-}9)$$

with n_x, n_y, and n_z independently assuming the values $1, 2, 3, \ldots$. The normalization constant $A_x A_y A_z$ is found from the equation

$$\int_0^a dx \int_0^b dy \int_0^c dz\,\psi^*(x, y, z)\psi(x, y, z) = 1 \qquad (6\text{-}10)$$

Problem 1 shows that

$$A_x A_y A_z = \left(\frac{8}{abc}\right)^{1/2} \qquad (6\text{-}11)$$

Thus, the wave functions of a particle in a three-dimensional box are

$$\psi_{n_x n_y n_z}(x, y, z) = \left(\frac{8}{abc}\right)^{1/2} \sin\frac{n_x\pi x}{a} \sin\frac{n_y\pi y}{b} \sin\frac{n_z\pi z}{c} \qquad \begin{aligned} n_x &= 1, 2, 3, \ldots \\ n_y &= 1, 2, 3, \ldots \\ n_z &= 1, 2, 3, \ldots \end{aligned} \quad (6\text{-}12)$$

If we substitute Eq. 6-12 into Eq. 6-1, we obtain

$$E_{n_x n_y n_z} = \frac{h^2}{8m}\left(\frac{n_x^2}{a^2} + \frac{n_y^2}{b^2} + \frac{n_z^2}{c^2}\right) \qquad \begin{aligned} n_x &= 1, 2, 3, \ldots \\ n_y &= 1, 2, 3, \ldots \\ n_z &= 1, 2, 3, \ldots \end{aligned} \quad (6\text{-}13)$$

Equation 6-13 is the three-dimensional extension of Eq. 3-22.

We should expect by symmetry that the average position of a particle in a box is at the center of the box, but we can show this by direct calculation.

EXAMPLE 6-1

Show that the average position of a particle confined to the region shown in Figure 6-1 is the point $(a/2, b/2, c/2)$.

Solution: The position operator in three dimensions is

$$\hat{\mathbf{R}} = \hat{X}\mathbf{i} + \hat{Y}\mathbf{j} + \hat{Z}\mathbf{k}$$

and the average position is given by

$$\langle \mathbf{r} \rangle = \int_0^a dx \int_0^b dy \int_0^c dz\, \psi^*(x, y, z)\hat{\mathbf{R}}\psi(x, y, z)$$

$$= \mathbf{i}\langle x \rangle + \mathbf{j}\langle y \rangle + \mathbf{k}\langle z \rangle$$

Let us evaluate $\langle x \rangle$ first. Using Eq. 6-12, we have

$$\langle x \rangle = \left[\left(\frac{2}{a} \right) \int_0^a x \sin^2 \frac{n_x \pi x}{a}\, dx \right]\left[\left(\frac{2}{b} \right) \int_0^b \sin^2 \frac{n_y \pi y}{b}\, dy \right]$$

$$\times \left[\left(\frac{2}{c} \right) \int_0^c \sin^2 \frac{n_z \pi z}{c}\, dz \right]$$

The second and third integrals here are unity by the normalization condition of a particle in a one-dimensional box (Eq. 3-28). The first integral is just $\langle x \rangle$ for a particle in a one-dimensional box. Referring to Eq. 3-45, we see that $\langle x \rangle = a/2$. The calculations for $\langle y \rangle$ and $\langle z \rangle$ are similar, and so we see that

$$\langle \mathbf{r} \rangle = \frac{a}{2}\mathbf{i} + \frac{b}{2}\mathbf{j} + \frac{c}{2}\mathbf{k}$$

Thus the average position of the particle is the center of the box.

In a similar manner, we should expect from the case of a particle in a one-dimensional box that the average momentum of a particle in a three-dimensional box is zero. The momentum operator in three dimensions is

$$\hat{\mathbf{P}} = -i\hbar \left(\mathbf{i}\frac{\partial}{\partial x} + \mathbf{j}\frac{\partial}{\partial y} + \mathbf{k}\frac{\partial}{\partial z} \right) \tag{6-14}$$

and so

$$\langle \mathbf{p} \rangle = \int_0^a dx \int_0^b dy \int_0^c dz\, \psi^*(x, y, z)\hat{\mathbf{P}}\psi(x, y, z)$$

It is a straightforward exercise to show that $\langle \mathbf{p} \rangle = 0$ (cf. Problem 2).

An interesting feature of a particle in a three-dimensional box occurs when the sides of the box are equal. In this case, $a = b = c$ in Eq. 6-13, and so

$$E_{n_x n_y n_z} = \frac{h^2}{8ma^2}(n_x^2 + n_y^2 + n_z^2) \tag{6-15}$$

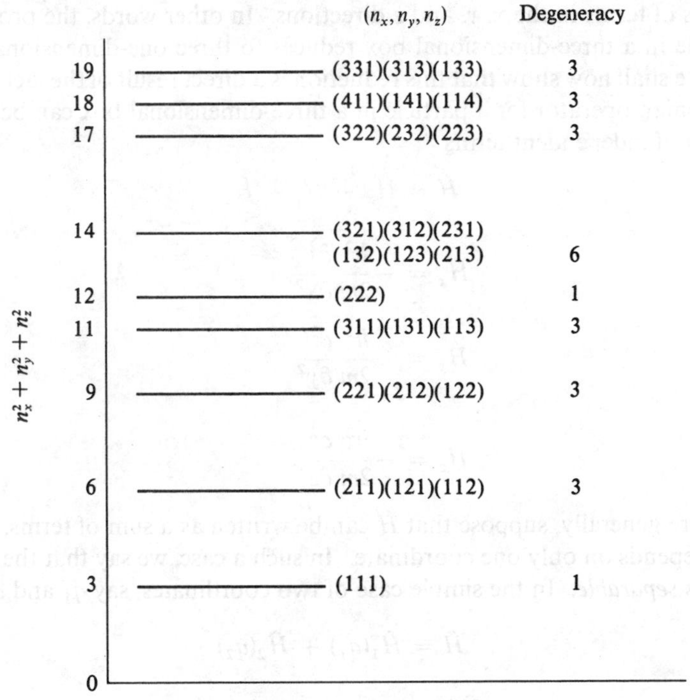

	(n_x, n_y, n_z)	Degeneracy
19	———— (331)(313)(133)	3
18	———— (411)(141)(114)	3
17	———— (322)(232)(223)	3
14	———— (321)(312)(231) (132)(123)(213)	6
12	———— (222)	1
11	———— (311)(131)(113)	3
9	———— (221)(212)(122)	3
6	———— (211)(121)(112)	3
3	———— (111)	1
0		

(y-axis label: $n_x^2 + n_y^2 + n_z^2$)

Figure 6-2. The energy levels for a particle in a box with $a = b = c$, showing the degeneracies.

The lowest level here, E_{111}, is nondegenerate, but the second level is threefold degenerate because

$$E_{211} = E_{121} = E_{112} = \frac{6h^2}{8ma^2}$$

Figure 6-2 shows the distribution of the first few energy levels of a particle in a cube. Note that the degeneracy occurs because of the symmetry introduced when the general rectangular box becomes a cube and that the degeneracy is "lifted" when the symmetry is destroyed by making the sides of different lengths. It is a general principle of quantum mechanics that degeneracies are the result of underlying symmetry and that degeneracies are lifted when the symmetry is broken. We shall see another example of this in Section 6-7.

6-2 *If a Hamiltonian Is Separable, Then Its Eigenfunctions Are Products of Simpler Eigenfunctions*

Note that according to Eq. 6-12, the wave functions for a particle in a three-dimensional box factor into products of wave functions for a particle in a one-dimensional box. In addition, Eq. 6-13 shows that the energy eigenvalues are sums of terms in the x, y, and z directions. In other words, the problem of a particle in a three-dimensional box reduces to three one-dimensional problems. We shall now show that this reduction is a direct result of the fact that the Hamiltonian operator for a particle in a three-dimensional box can be written as a sum of independent terms

$$\hat{H} = \hat{H}_x + \hat{H}_y + \hat{H}_z \tag{6-16}$$

where

$$\hat{H}_x = -\frac{\hbar^2}{2m}\frac{\partial^2}{\partial x^2}$$

$$\hat{H}_y = -\frac{\hbar^2}{2m}\frac{\partial^2}{\partial y^2}$$

and

$$\hat{H}_z = -\frac{\hbar^2}{2m}\frac{\partial^2}{\partial z^2}$$

More generally, suppose that $\hat{H}$ can be written as a sum of terms, each of which depends on only one coordinate. In such a case, we say that the Hamiltonian is *separable*. In the simple case of two coordinates, say q_1 and q_2, then

$$\hat{H} = \hat{H}_1(q_1) + \hat{H}_2(q_2) \tag{6-17}$$

with

$$\hat{H}\psi(q_1, q_2) = E\psi(q_1, q_2) \tag{6-18}$$

Now assume that $\psi(q_1, q_2) = \psi_1(q_1)\psi_2(q_2)$ where $\psi_1(q_1)$ and $\psi_2(q_2)$ are eigenfunctions of $\hat{H}_1$ and $\hat{H}_2$, respectively:

$$\hat{H}_1\psi_1(q_1) = E_1\psi_1(q_1)$$
$$\hat{H}_2\psi_2(q_2) = E_2\psi_2(q_2) \tag{6-19}$$

Substitute Eq. 6-19 into Eq. 6-18 to obtain

$$\hat{H}\psi(q_1, q_2) = (\hat{H}_1 + \hat{H}_2)\psi_1(q_1)\psi_2(q_2)$$
$$= \hat{H}_1\psi_1(q_1)\psi_2(q_2) + \hat{H}_2\psi_1(q_1)\psi_2(q_2)$$

Because $\hat{H}_1(q_1)$ operates upon only $\psi_1(q_1)$ and $\hat{H}_2(q_2)$ operates upon only $\psi_2(q_2)$, we can write

$$\hat{H}\psi(q_1, q_2) = \psi_2(q_2)\hat{H}_1\psi_1(q_1) + \psi_1(q_1)\hat{H}_2\psi_2(q_2)$$
$$= E_1\psi_1(q_1)\psi_2(q_2) + E_2\psi_1(q_1)\psi_2(q_2)$$
$$= (E_1 + E_2)\psi_1(q_1)\psi_2(q_2)$$
$$= E\psi(q_1, q_2)$$

In summary, then, we have shown that if

$$\hat{H}(q_1, q_2) = \hat{H}_1(q_1) + \hat{H}_2(q_2) \tag{6-20}$$

and

$$\hat{H}_1 \psi_1(q_1) = E_1 \psi_1(q_1) \quad \text{and} \quad \hat{H}_2 \psi_2(q_2) = E_2 \psi_2(q_2) \tag{6-21}$$

then $\psi(q_1, q_2)$ and E, which satisfy

$$\hat{H}\psi(q_1, q_2) = E\psi(q_1, q_2) \tag{6-22}$$

are given by

$$\psi(q_1, q_2) = \psi_1(q_1)\psi_2(q_2) \tag{6-23}$$

and

$$E = E_1 + E_2 \tag{6-24}$$

Thus, we see that if $\hat{H}$ is separable, that is, if $\hat{H}$ can be written as the sum of independent terms involving separate coordinates, then the eigenfunctions of $\hat{H}$ are the products of the eigenfunctions of $\hat{H}_1$ and $\hat{H}_2$ and the eigenvalues are the sums of the eigenvalues of $\hat{H}_1$ and $\hat{H}_2$. This important result provides a significant simplification because it reduces the original problem to several simpler problems. It is possible to generalize this result to the case where q_1 and q_2 are two independent sets of coordinates (cf. Problem 8).

EXAMPLE 6-2

Consider a two-dimensional harmonic oscillator, whose potential energy is

$$U(x, y) = \tfrac{1}{2}k_x x^2 + \tfrac{1}{2}k_y y^2$$

Derive the wave functions and energy levels of this system.

Solution: The Hamiltonian for this system is

$$\hat{H} = -\frac{\hbar^2}{2\mu}\left(\frac{\partial^2}{\partial x^2} + \frac{\partial^2}{\partial y^2}\right) + \frac{1}{2}k_x x^2 + \frac{1}{2}k_y y^2$$

and so $\hat{H}$ is of the form

$$\hat{H} = \hat{H}_1(x) + \hat{H}_2(y)$$

$$= \left(-\frac{\hbar^2}{2\mu}\frac{\partial^2}{\partial x^2} + \frac{1}{2}k_x x^2\right) + \left(-\frac{\hbar^2}{2\mu}\frac{\partial^2}{\partial y^2} + \frac{1}{2}k_y y^2\right)$$

Using the results in Eqs. 6-20 through 6-24 and the harmonic oscillator results in Chapter 5, we see that the energies are given by (cf. Eq. 5-33)

$$E = h v_x(n_x + \tfrac{1}{2}) + h v_y(n_y + \tfrac{1}{2}) \qquad \begin{aligned} n_x &= 0, 1, 2, \ldots \\ n_y &= 0, 1, 2, \ldots \end{aligned}$$

where

$$v_x = \frac{1}{2\pi}\left(\frac{k_x}{\mu}\right)^{1/2} \quad \text{and} \quad v_y = \frac{1}{2\pi}\left(\frac{k_y}{\mu}\right)^{1/2}$$

The wave functions are

$$\psi_{n_x n_y}(x, y) = \psi_{n_x}(x)\psi_{n_y}(y)$$

where $\psi_{n_x}(x)$ and $\psi_{n_y}(y)$ are the one-dimensional harmonic-oscillator wave functions given in Chapter 5 (Eq. 5-41)

$$\psi_{n_x}(x) = \left[\left(\frac{\alpha_x}{\pi}\right)^{1/2} \frac{1}{2^{n_x} n_x!}\right]^{1/2} H_{n_x}(\alpha_x^{1/2} x) e^{-\alpha_x x^2/2}$$

$$\psi_{n_y}(y) = \left[\left(\frac{\alpha_y}{\pi}\right)^{1/2} \frac{1}{2^{n_y} n_y!}\right]^{1/2} H_{n_y}(\alpha_y^{1/2} y) e^{-\alpha_y y^2/2}$$

where $\alpha_x = (\mu k_x)^{1/2}/\hbar$ and $\alpha_y = (\mu k_y)^{1/2}/\hbar$.

An important application of Eqs. 6-20 through 6-24 is to a system of two particles interacting through a potential energy that depends on only their relative separation. According to Section 5-3, if we let X, Y, and Z be the center-of-mass coordinates and x, y, and z be relative coordinates, then the total energy of the system can be written in the form

$$E = \frac{M}{2}(\dot{X}^2 + \dot{Y}^2 + \dot{Z}^2) + \frac{\mu}{2}(\dot{x}^2 + \dot{y}^2 + \dot{z}^2) + U(x, y, z) \quad (6\text{-}25)$$

where the dots over the coordinates signify time derivatives and where M is the total mass and μ is the reduced mass of the system. Equation 6-25 has the physical interpretation that the total energy is the sum of the kinetic energy of the center-of-mass motion, the kinetic energy of the relative motion, and the potential energy. We can write Eq. 6-25 in terms of momenta rather than velocities by introducing $P_x = M\dot{X}$, $p_x = \mu\dot{x}$, and so on to obtain

$$H = \frac{1}{2M}(P_X^2 + P_Y^2 + P_Z^2) + \frac{1}{2\mu}(p_x^2 + p_y^2 + p_z^2) + U(x, y, z) \quad (6\text{-}26)$$

The quantum-mechanical Hamiltonian operator corresponding to Eq. 6-26 is

$$\hat{H} = -\frac{\hbar^2}{2M}\left(\frac{\partial^2}{\partial X^2} + \frac{\partial^2}{\partial Y^2} + \frac{\partial^2}{\partial Z^2}\right) - \frac{\hbar^2}{2\mu}\left(\frac{\partial^2}{\partial x^2} + \frac{\partial^2}{\partial y^2} + \frac{\partial^2}{\partial z^2}\right) + U(x, y, z) \quad (6\text{-}27)$$

We see, then, that Eq. 6-27 can be written as

$$\hat{H} = \hat{H}_1(X, Y, Z) + \hat{H}_2(x, y, z) \quad (6\text{-}28)$$

where

$$\hat{H}_1 = -\frac{\hbar^2}{2M}\left(\frac{\partial^2}{\partial X^2} + \frac{\partial^2}{\partial Y^2} + \frac{\partial^2}{\partial Z^2}\right) \quad (6\text{-}29)$$

and

$$\hat{H}_2 = -\frac{\hbar^2}{2\mu}\left(\frac{\partial^2}{\partial x^2} + \frac{\partial^2}{\partial y^2} + \frac{\partial^2}{\partial z^2}\right) + U(x, y, z) \quad (6\text{-}30)$$

Consequently, the total wave function for this system factors into

$$\psi_{total}(X, Y, Z, x, y, z) = \psi_{trans}(X, Y, Z)\psi_{rel}(x, y, z) \quad (6\text{-}31)$$

and the total energy is

$$E_{total} = E_{trans} + E_{rel}$$

where *trans* stands for the translation of the center of mass and *rel* stands for relative motion.

The translational part represents just the free rectilinear motion of the center of mass and is of no interest. The interesting part is the relative motion, which is governed by the potential energy $U(x, y, z)$. The Schrödinger equation for the relative motion is

$$\left[-\frac{\hbar^2}{2\mu}\left(\frac{\partial^2}{\partial x^2} + \frac{\partial^2}{\partial y^2} + \frac{\partial^2}{\partial z^2}\right) + U(x, y, z)\right]\psi(x, y, z) = E\psi(x, y, z) \quad (6\text{-}32)$$

or

$$-\frac{\hbar^2}{2\mu}\nabla^2\psi + U\psi = E\psi \quad (6\text{-}33)$$

where ∇^2 is the *Laplacian operator*:

$$\nabla^2 = \frac{\partial^2}{\partial x^2} + \frac{\partial^2}{\partial y^2} + \frac{\partial^2}{\partial z^2} \quad (6\text{-}34)$$

We have dropped the subscript rel on E in Eq. 6-33 for convenience. Equation 6-33 is the equation that we solved for the harmonic-oscillator potential in Chapter 5.

6-3   The Laplacian Operator Can Be Expressed in a Variety of Coordinate Systems

The Laplacian operator ∇^2 occurs frequently in quantum mechanics. Equation 6-34 expresses ∇^2 in Cartesian coordinates. If the system has a center of symmetry, such as the hydrogen atom with a central proton and an electron around it, then it is more convenient to express ∇^2 in spherical coordinates. Therefore, it is necessary for us to be able to convert ∇^2 from Cartesian coordinates to spherical coordinates. The conversion of ∇^2 from Cartesian coordinates to some other system of coordinates requires that we use the chain rule of partial differentiation. For example, suppose we consider the conversion of ∇^2 from Cartesian coordinates to plane polar coordinates. The relation between these two coordinate systems is shown in Figure 6-3. Suppose that a function $f(r, \theta)$ depends on the polar coordinates r and θ. Then the chain rule of partial differentiation says that

$$\left(\frac{\partial f}{\partial x}\right)_y = \left(\frac{\partial f}{\partial r}\right)_\theta\left(\frac{\partial r}{\partial x}\right)_y + \left(\frac{\partial f}{\partial \theta}\right)_r\left(\frac{\partial \theta}{\partial x}\right)_y$$

and that

$$\left(\frac{\partial f}{\partial y}\right)_x = \left(\frac{\partial f}{\partial r}\right)_\theta\left(\frac{\partial r}{\partial y}\right)_x + \left(\frac{\partial f}{\partial \theta}\right)_r\left(\frac{\partial \theta}{\partial y}\right)_x \quad (6\text{-}35)$$

Example 6-3 illustrates the use of these equations.

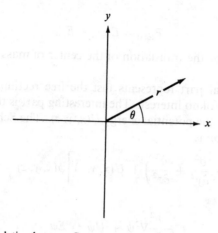

Figure 6-3. The relation between Cartesian coordinates and plane polar coordinates.

EXAMPLE 6-3

In plane polar coordinates (cf. Figure 6-3)

$$x = r \cos \theta \quad \text{and} \quad y = r \sin \theta \tag{1}$$

Evaluate $(\partial f/\partial x)_y$ and $(\partial f/\partial y)_x$, where $f(r, \theta)$ is given by

$$f(r, \theta) = e^{-\alpha r^2} \cos \theta \tag{2}$$

Solution: From Eq. 6-35, we write

$$\left(\frac{\partial f}{\partial x}\right)_y = \left(\frac{\partial f}{\partial r}\right)_\theta \left(\frac{\partial r}{\partial x}\right)_y + \left(\frac{\partial f}{\partial \theta}\right)_r \left(\frac{\partial \theta}{\partial x}\right)_y \tag{3}$$

To evaluate $(\partial r/\partial x)_y$ and $(\partial \theta/\partial x)_y$, we must use Eqs. 1 to find r and θ in terms of x and y. Note that

$$r^2 = x^2 + y^2 \quad \text{and} \quad \tan \theta = \frac{y}{x}$$

or that

$$r = (x^2 + y^2)^{1/2} \quad \text{and} \quad \theta = \tan^{-1}\left(\frac{y}{x}\right) \tag{4}$$

We are now ready to calculate $(\partial f/\partial x)_y$ from Eq. 3:

$$\left(\frac{\partial f}{\partial x}\right)_y = (-2\alpha r e^{-\alpha r^2} \cos \theta)\left(\frac{x}{r}\right) + (-e^{-\alpha r^2} \sin \theta)\left(-\frac{y}{x^2 + y^2}\right)$$

$$= -(2\alpha r e^{-\alpha r^2} \cos \theta)(\cos \theta) + (-e^{-\alpha r^2} \sin \theta)\left(-\frac{\sin \theta}{r}\right)$$

$$= \frac{e^{-\alpha r^2}}{r}(\sin^2 \theta - 2\alpha r^2 \cos^2 \theta)$$

Similarly,

$$\left(\frac{\partial f}{\partial y}\right)_x = \left(\frac{\partial f}{\partial r}\right)_\theta \left(\frac{\partial r}{\partial y}\right)_x + \left(\frac{\partial f}{\partial \theta}\right)_r \left(\frac{\partial \theta}{\partial y}\right)_x$$

$$= (-2\alpha r e^{-ar^2} \cos \theta)\left(\frac{y}{r}\right) + (-e^{-ar^2} \sin \theta)\left(\frac{x}{x^2 + y^2}\right)$$

$$= -(2\alpha r e^{-ar^2} \cos \theta)(\sin \theta) - (e^{-ar^2} \sin \theta)\left(\frac{\cos \theta}{r}\right)$$

$$= -\frac{e^{-ar^2}}{r} \sin \theta \cos \theta (1 + 2ar^2)$$

To convert ∇^2 to spherical coordinates, we need the equations that relate Cartesian coordinates and spherical coordinates. These relations are (cf. Figure 6-4)

$$x = r \sin \theta \cos \phi$$
$$y = r \sin \theta \sin \phi \qquad (6\text{-}36)$$
$$z = r \cos \theta$$

with $0 \le \theta \le \pi$, $0 \le \phi \le 2\pi$, and $0 \le r < \infty$. Consider some function $f(r, \theta, \phi)$. We can evaluate $(\partial f/\partial x)_{y,z}$ by using the extension of Eq. 6-35 to three dimensions. The extension of Eq. 6-35 to spherical coordinates is

$$\left(\frac{\partial f}{\partial x}\right)_{y,z} = \left(\frac{\partial f}{\partial r}\right)_{\theta,\phi} \left(\frac{\partial r}{\partial x}\right)_{y,z} + \left(\frac{\partial f}{\partial \theta}\right)_{r,\phi} \left(\frac{\partial \theta}{\partial x}\right)_{y,z} + \left(\frac{\partial f}{\partial \phi}\right)_{r,\theta} \left(\frac{\partial \phi}{\partial x}\right)_{y,z} \qquad (6\text{-}37)$$

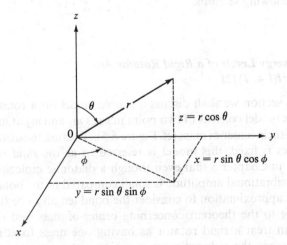

Figure 6-4. The spherical coordinate system, showing the relation between Cartesian coordinates (x, y, z) and spherical coordinates (r, θ, ϕ).

with a similar equation for the y and z derivatives. After evaluating all the partial derivatives in these equations and expressing the result explicitly in terms of the spherical coordinates r, θ, and ϕ, we must then take the second derivatives in order to obtain ∇^2 in spherical coordinates. It is convenient to write Eq. 6-37 as an operation on the function f:

$$\left(\frac{\partial}{\partial x}\right)_{y,z} f = \left[\left(\frac{\partial r}{\partial x}\right)_{y,z}\left(\frac{\partial}{\partial r}\right)_{\theta,\phi} + \left(\frac{\partial \theta}{\partial x}\right)_{y,z}\left(\frac{\partial}{\partial \theta}\right)_{r,\phi} + \left(\frac{\partial \phi}{\partial x}\right)_{y,z}\left(\frac{\partial}{\partial \phi}\right)_{r,\theta}\right] f$$

and so the second partial derivatives of f can be written as

$$\left(\frac{\partial^2 f}{\partial x^2}\right)_{y,z} = \left(\frac{\partial}{\partial x}\right)_{y,z}\left(\frac{\partial f}{\partial x}\right)_{y,z} = \left(\frac{\partial r}{\partial x}\right)_{y,z}\left[\left(\frac{\partial}{\partial r}\right)_{\theta,\phi}\left(\frac{\partial f}{\partial x}\right)_{y,z}\right]$$

$$+ \left(\frac{\partial \theta}{\partial x}\right)_{y,z}\left[\left(\frac{\partial}{\partial \theta}\right)_{r,\phi}\left(\frac{\partial f}{\partial x}\right)_{y,z}\right] + \left(\frac{\partial \phi}{\partial x}\right)_{y,z}\left[\left(\frac{\partial}{\partial \phi}\right)_{r,\theta}\left(\frac{\partial f}{\partial x}\right)_{y,z}\right]$$

with a similar equation for the y and z derivatives. One can see that this is a fairly lengthy algebraic process, and the conversion of the Laplacian operator from Cartesian coordinates to spherical coordinates is a long, tedious, standard problem that arises in every quantum-mechanics course and should be done once (and only once!) by any serious student. On the other hand, one can see how the process goes without the algebra by converting ∇^2 from two-dimensional Cartesian coordinates to plane polar coordinates. This conversion is done in detail in Problem 10. The final result for the more important case of spherical coordinates is

$$\nabla^2 = \frac{1}{r^2}\frac{\partial}{\partial r}\left(r^2\frac{\partial}{\partial r}\right)_{\theta,\phi} + \frac{1}{r^2 \sin\theta}\frac{\partial}{\partial \theta}\left(\sin\theta\frac{\partial}{\partial \theta}\right)_{r,\phi} + \frac{1}{r^2 \sin^2\theta}\left(\frac{\partial^2}{\partial \phi^2}\right)_{r,\theta} \quad (6\text{-}38)$$

We shall need this form of ∇^2 when we discuss the rigid rotator and the hydrogen atom in the following sections.

6-4 The Energy Levels of a Rigid Rotator Are $E = \hbar^2 l(l + 1)/2I$

In this section we shall discuss a simple model for a rotating diatomic molecule. The model consists of two point masses m_1 and m_2 at fixed distances r_1 and r_2 from their center of mass (cf. Figure 6-5). Because the distance between the two masses is fixed, this model is referred to as the *rigid rotator model*. We have seen in Chapter 5 that even though a diatomic molecule vibrates as it rotates, the vibrational amplitude is small compared to the bond length, and so it is a good approximation to consider the bond length to be fixed.

According to the theorem concerning center-of-mass and relative coordinates, we can treat a rigid rotator as having one mass fixed at the origin with another mass, the reduced mass μ, rotating about the origin at a fixed

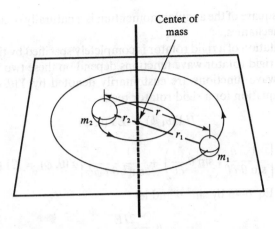

Figure 6-5. Two masses m_1 and m_2 shown rotating about their center of mass.

distance r. We discussed a rigid rotator classically in Section 1-8 and showed there that the energy of a rigid rotator is

$$K = \tfrac{1}{2} I \omega^2 \tag{6-39}$$

where ω is the angular velocity and I is the moment of inertia,

$$I = \mu r^2 \tag{6-40}$$

The angular momentum L is

$$L = I\omega \tag{6-41}$$

and the kinetic energy can be written in terms of L according to

$$K = \frac{L^2}{2I} \tag{6-42}$$

The Hamiltonian operator of a rigid rotator is just the kinetic energy operator, and using the correspondences between linear and angular systems given in Table 1-2, we can replace m by I in Table 4-1 and write

$$\hat{H} = -\frac{\hbar^2}{2I} \nabla^2 \qquad (r \text{ constant}) \tag{6-43}$$

Because one of the two masses of the rigid rotator is fixed at the origin, we shall express ∇^2 in spherical coordinates and so write $\hat{H}$ as (cf. Eq. (6-38))

$$\hat{H} = -\frac{\hbar^2}{2I} \left[\frac{1}{\sin\theta} \frac{\partial}{\partial\theta} \left(\sin\theta \frac{\partial}{\partial\theta} \right) + \frac{1}{\sin^2\theta} \frac{\partial^2}{\partial^2\phi} \right] \tag{6-44}$$

There is no term in $\hat{H}$ here involving the partial derivative with respect to r because r is fixed in the rigid rotator model. By comparing Eq. 6-44 with the classical expression, Eq. 6-42, we see that we can make the correspondence

$$\hat{L}^2 = -\hbar^2 \left[\frac{1}{\sin\theta} \frac{\partial}{\partial\theta} \left(\sin\theta \frac{\partial}{\partial\theta} \right) + \frac{1}{\sin^2\theta} \frac{\partial^2}{\partial\phi^2} \right] \tag{6-45}$$

Note that the square of the angular momentum is a naturally occurring operator in quantum mechanics.

The orientation of a rigid rotator is completely specified by the two angles θ and ϕ, and so rigid rotator wave functions depend on these two variables. The rigid rotator wave functions are customarily denoted by $Y(\theta, \phi)$, and so the Schrödinger equation for a rigid rotator reads

$$\hat{H} Y(\theta, \phi) = EY(\theta, \phi)$$

or

$$-\frac{\hbar^2}{2I}\left[\frac{1}{\sin\theta}\frac{\partial}{\partial\theta}\left(\sin\theta\frac{\partial}{\partial\theta}\right) + \frac{1}{\sin^2\theta}\frac{\partial^2}{\partial\phi^2}\right]Y(\theta, \phi) = EY(\theta, \phi) \qquad (6\text{-}46)$$

If we multiply Eq. 6-46 by $\sin^2\theta$ and let

$$\beta = \frac{2IE}{\hbar^2} \qquad (6\text{-}47)$$

we find the partial differential equation

$$\sin\theta\frac{\partial}{\partial\theta}\left(\sin\theta\frac{\partial Y}{\partial\theta}\right) + \frac{\partial^2 Y}{\partial\phi^2} + \beta\sin^2\theta Y = 0 \qquad (6\text{-}48)$$

To solve this partial differential equation, we use the method of separation of variables and let

$$Y(\theta, \phi) = \Theta(\theta)\Phi(\phi) \qquad (6\text{-}49)$$

If we substitute Eq. 6-49 into Eq. 6-48 and then divide by $\Theta(\theta)\Phi(\phi)$, we find

$$\frac{\sin\theta}{\Theta(\theta)}\frac{d}{d\theta}\left(\sin\theta\frac{d\Theta}{d\theta}\right) + \beta\sin^2\theta + \frac{1}{\Phi(\phi)}\frac{d^2\Phi}{d\phi^2} = 0 \qquad (6\text{-}50)$$

Because θ and ϕ are independent variables, we must have that

$$\frac{\sin\theta}{\Theta(\theta)}\frac{d}{d\theta}\left(\sin\theta\frac{d\Theta}{d\theta}\right) + \beta\sin^2\theta = m^2 \qquad (6\text{-}51)$$

and

$$\frac{1}{\Phi(\phi)}\frac{d^2\Phi}{d\phi^2} = -m^2 \qquad (6\text{-}52)$$

where m^2 is a constant. Note that Eqs. 6-51 and 6-52 add up to Eq. 6-50.

Equation 6-52 is relatively easy to solve, and its solutions are

$$\Phi(\phi) = A_m e^{im\phi} \quad \text{and} \quad \Phi(\phi) = A_{-m}e^{-im\phi} \qquad (6\text{-}53)$$

The requirement that $\Phi(\phi)$ be continuous is that

$$\Phi(\phi + 2\pi) = \Phi(\phi) \qquad (6\text{-}54)$$

By substituting Eq. 6-53 into Eq. 6-54, we see that

$$A_m e^{im(\phi + 2\pi)} = A_m e^{im\phi} \qquad (6\text{-}55)$$

and that

$$A_{-m}e^{-im(\phi + 2\pi)} = A_{-m}e^{-im\phi} \qquad (6\text{-}56)$$

Equations 6-55 and 6-56 together imply that

$$e^{\pm i2\pi m} = 1 \tag{6-57}$$

In terms of sines and cosines, Eq. 6-57 is

$$\cos(2\pi m) \pm i \sin(2\pi m) = 1$$

which implies that $m = 0, \pm 1, \pm 2, \ldots$, because $\cos 2\pi m = 1$ and $\sin 2\pi m = 0$ for $m = 0, \pm 1, \pm 2, \ldots$. Thus Eq. 6-53 can be written as one equation

$$\Phi_m(\phi) = A_m e^{im\phi} \qquad m = 0, \pm 1, \pm 2, \ldots \tag{6-58}$$

We can find A_m by requiring that the $\Phi_m(\phi)$ be normalized.

EXAMPLE 6-4
Determine the A_m in Eq. 6-58.

Solution: The A_m in Eq. 6-58 are determined by the requirement that the $\Phi_m(\phi)$ are normalized. The normalization condition is that

$$\int_0^{2\pi} d\phi \, \Phi_m^*(\phi)\Phi_m(\phi) = 1$$

Using Eq. 6-58 for the $\Phi_m(\phi)$, we have

$$|A_m|^2 \int_0^{2\pi} d\phi = 1$$

or

$$|A_m|^2 2\pi = 1$$

or

$$A_m = (2\pi)^{-1/2}$$

Thus, the normalized version of Eq. 6-58 is

$$\Phi_m(\phi) = \frac{1}{(2\pi)^{1/2}} e^{im\phi} \qquad m = 0, \pm 1, \pm 2, \ldots \tag{6-59}$$

The solution to Eq. 6-51, like the solution to Hermite's equation in Chapter 5, is obtained by the power series method. We shall not present all the details for the solution to Eq. 6-51, but when one does solve Eq. 6-51, it turns out naturally that β in Eq. 6-47 must obey the condition

$$\beta = l(l + 1) \qquad l = 0, 1, 2, \ldots \tag{6-60}$$

Using the definition of β, Eq. 6-60 is equivalent to

$$E_l = \frac{\hbar^2}{2I} l(l + 1) \qquad l = 0, 1, 2, \ldots \tag{6-61}$$

Once again, we obtain a set of discrete energy levels.

6-5   *The Rigid Rotator Is a Model for a Rotating Diatomic Molecule*

Equation 6-61 gives the allowed energies of a rigid rotator. We shall prove in Chapter 10 that electromagnetic radiation can cause a rigid rotator to undergo transitions from one state to another, and, in particular, we shall prove that transitions from only adjacent states are allowed or that

$$\Delta l = \pm 1 \qquad (6\text{-}62)$$

Equation 6-62 is called a *selection rule*. In addition to the requirement that $\Delta l = \pm 1$, the molecule must also possess a permanent dipole moment. In the case of absorption of electromagnetic radiation, the molecule goes from a state with a quantum number l to one with $l + 1$. The energy difference then is

$$\Delta E = E_{l+1} - E_l = \frac{\hbar^2}{2I}\left[(l + 1)(l + 2) - l(l + 1) \right]$$

$$= \frac{\hbar^2}{I}(l + 1) = \frac{h^2}{4\pi^2 I}(l + 1) \qquad (6\text{-}63)$$

The energy levels and the absorption transitions are shown in Figure 6-6.

Using the Bohr frequency condition $\Delta E = h\nu$, the frequencies at which the absorption transitions occur are

$$\nu = \frac{h}{4\pi^2 I}(l + 1) \qquad l = 0, 1, 2, \ldots \qquad (6\text{-}64)$$

The reduced mass of a diatomic molecule is typically around $10^{-25} - 10^{-26}$ kg, and a typical bond distance is around 10^{-10} m, and so the moment of inertia of a diatomic molecule typically is around $10^{-45} - 10^{-46}$ kg·m². Substituting $I = 5 \times 10^{-46}$ kg·m² into Eq. 6-64 gives that the absorption frequencies are around $2 \times 10^{10} - 10^{11}$ Hz (cf. Problem 12). By referring to Figure 1-14, we see that these frequencies lie in the microwave region. Consequently, rotational transitions of diatomic molecules occur in the microwave region, and the study of rotational transitions in molecules is called *microwave spectroscopy*.

It is common practice in microwave spectroscopy to write Eq. 6-64 as

$$\nu = 2B(l + 1) \qquad l = 0, 1, 2, \ldots \qquad (6\text{-}65)$$

where

$$B = \frac{h}{8\pi^2 I} \quad \text{(Hz)} \qquad (6\text{-}66)$$

is called the *rotational constant* of the molecule. It is also common practice to express the transition frequency in terms of wave numbers (cm^{-1}) rather than hertz (Hz). If we use the relation $\bar{\nu} = \nu/c$, then Eq. 6-64 becomes

$$\bar{\nu} = 2\bar{B}(l + 1) \qquad l = 0, 1, 2, \ldots \qquad (6.67)$$

where $\bar{B}$ is the rotational constant expressed in units of wave numbers

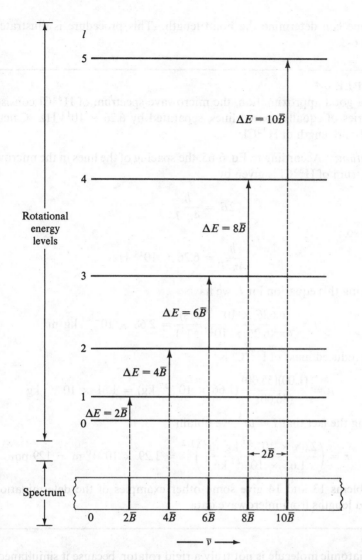

Figure 6-6. The energy levels and absorption transitions of a rigid rotator. The absorption transitions occur between adjacent levels, and so the absorption spectrum shown below the energy levels consists of a series of equally spaced lines. The quantity $\bar{B}$ in the figure is $h/8\pi^2 cI$ (Eq. 6-68).

$$\bar{B} = \frac{h}{8\pi^2 cI} \qquad (\text{cm}^{-1}) \qquad (6\text{-}68)$$

From either Eq. 6-65 or 6-67 we see that the rigid rotator model predicts that the microwave spectrum of a diatomic molecule consists of a series of equally spaced lines with a separation $2B$ Hz or $2\bar{B}$ cm^{-1} as shown in Figure 6-6. From the separation between the absorption frequencies, one can determine the rotational constant and hence the moment of inertia of the molecule. Furthermore, because $I = \mu r^2$, where r is the internuclear distance or bond length, one can determine the bond length. This procedure is illustrated in Example 6-5.

EXAMPLE 6-5

To a good approximation, the microwave spectrum of $H^{35}Cl$ consists of a series of equally spaced lines, separated by 6.26×10^{11} Hz. Calculate the bond length of $H^{35}Cl$.

Solution: According to Eq. 6-65, the spacing of the lines in the microwave spectrum of $H^{35}Cl$ is given by

$$2B = \frac{h}{4\pi^2 I}$$

and so

$$\frac{h}{4\pi^2 I} = 6.26 \times 10^{11} \text{ Hz}$$

Solving this equation for I, we have

$$I = \frac{(6.626 \times 10^{-34} \text{ J} \cdot \text{s})}{4\pi^2 (6.26 \times 10^{11} \text{ s}^{-1})} = 2.68 \times 10^{-47} \text{ kg} \cdot \text{m}^2$$

The reduced mass of $H^{35}Cl$ is

$$\mu = \frac{(1.00)(35.00)}{(36.00)} (1.66 \times 10^{-27} \text{ kg}) = 1.61 \times 10^{-27} \text{ kg}$$

Using the fact that $I = \mu r^2$, we obtain

$$r = \left(\frac{2.68 \times 10^{-47} \text{ kg} \cdot \text{m}^2}{1.61 \times 10^{-27} \text{ kg}} \right)^{1/2} = 1.29 \times 10^{-10} \text{ m} = 129 \text{ pm}$$

Problems 13 and 14 give some other examples of the determination of bond lengths from microwave data.

A diatomic molecule is not truly a rigid rotator, because it simultaneously vibrates, however small the amplitude. Consequently, we might expect that although the microwave spectrum of a diatomic molecule consists of a series of lines, their separation is not *exactly* constant. In Chapter 10, we shall learn how to correct for the fact that the bond is not exactly rigid.

6-6 *The Wave Functions of a Rigid Rotator Are Called Spherical Harmonics*

The wave functions of a rigid rotator are given by the solutions to Eq. 6-46. To solve Eq. 6-46, we assumed separation of variables and wrote $Y(\theta, \phi) = \Theta(\theta)\Phi(\phi)$ (Eq. 6-49). The resulting differential equation for $\Phi(\phi)$ (Eq. 6-52) is relatively easy to solve, and we showed that its solutions are

(Eq. 6-59)

$$\Phi_m(\phi) = \frac{1}{(2\pi)^{1/2}} e^{im\phi} \qquad m = 0, \pm1, \pm2, \ldots \qquad (6\text{-}59)$$

The differential equation for $\Theta(\theta)$, Eq. 6-51, is not easy to solve. It is convenient to let $x = \cos\theta$ and $\Theta(\theta) = P(x)$ in Eq. 6-51. Because $0 \le \theta \le \pi$, the range of x is $-1 \le x \le +1$. Under the change of variable, $x = \cos\theta$, Eq. 6-51 becomes (Problem 15)

$$(1 - x^2)\frac{d^2P}{dx^2} - 2x\frac{dP}{dx} + \left[l(l + 1) - \frac{m^2}{1 - x^2}\right]P(x) = 0 \qquad (6\text{-}69)$$

In Eq. 6-69 we have used the fact that $\beta = l(l + 1)$ (cf. Eq. 6-60). Equation 6-69 for $P(x)$ is called *Legendre's equation* and is a well-known equation in classical physics. It occurs in a variety of problems that are formulated in spherical coordinates. When the power series method of solution is applied to Eq. 6-69, the series must be truncated in order that the solutions be finite at $x = \pm1$. It is this truncation that yields Eq. 6-60. The solutions to Eq. 6-69 when $m = 0$ are called *Legendre polynomials* and are denoted by $P_l(x)$. Legendre polynomials arise in a number of physical problems. The first few Legendre polynomials are given in Table 6-1.

TABLE 6-1

The First Few Legendre Polynomials, Which Are the Solutions to Eq. 6-69 with $m = 0$.
The Subscript Indexing the Legendre Polynomials Is the Value of l in Eq. 6-69.

$$P_0(x) = 1$$
$$P_1(x) = x$$
$$P_2(x) = \tfrac{1}{2}(3x^2 - 1)$$
$$P_3(x) = \tfrac{1}{2}(5x^3 - 3x)$$
$$P_4(x) = \tfrac{1}{8}(35x^4 - 30x^2 + 3)$$

EXAMPLE 6-6

Prove that the first few Legendre polynomials satisfy Eq. 6-69 when $m = 0$.

Solution: Equation 6-69 with $m = 0$ is

$$(1 - x^2)\frac{d^2P_l}{dx^2} - 2x\frac{dP_l}{dx} + l(l + 1)P_l(x) = 0 \qquad (1)$$

The first Legendre polynomial $P_0(x) = 1$ is clearly a solution of Eq. 1 with $l = 0$. When we substitute $P_1(x) = x$ into Eq. 1, we obtain

$$-2x + 1(2)x = 0$$

and so $P_1(x)$ is a solution. For $P_2(x)$, Eq. 1 is

$$(1 - x^2)(3) - 2x(3x) + 2(3)[\tfrac{1}{2}(3x^2 - 1)] = (3 - 3x^2) - 6x^2 + (9x^2 - 3) = 0$$

Notice from Table 6-1 that $P_l(x)$ is an even function if l is even and an odd function if l is odd. The factors in front of the $P_l(x)$ are chosen such that $P_l(1) = 1$. In addition, although we shall not prove it, it can be shown generally that the $P_l(x)$ in Table 6-1 are orthogonal or that (Problem 18)

$$\int_{-1}^{1} dx\, P_l(x)P_n(x) = 0 \qquad l \neq n \tag{6-70}$$

Keep in mind here that the limits on x correspond to the natural, physical limits on $\theta(0$ to $\pi)$ in spherical coordinates because $x = \cos\theta$ (Problem 17). The Legendre polynomials are normalized by the general relation, which we simply present:

$$\int_{-1}^{1} dx\, [P_l(x)]^2 = \frac{2}{2l + 1} \tag{6-71}$$

Equation 6-71 shows that the normalization constant of $P_l(x)$ is $[(2l + 1)/2]^{1/2}$.

Although the Legendre polynomials arise only in the case $m = 0$, they are customarily studied first because the solutions for the $m \neq 0$ case, called *associated Legendre functions*, are defined in terms of the ordinary Legendre functions. If we denote the associated Legendre functions by $P_l^{|m|}(x)$, then their defining relation is

$$P_l^{|m|}(x) = (1 - x^2)^{|m|/2} \frac{d^m}{dx^m} P_l(x) \tag{6-72}$$

Note that only the magnitude of m is relevant here because the defining differential equation, Eq. 6-69, depends on only m^2. The first few associated Legendre functions are given in Table 6-2.

Before we go on to discuss a few of the properties of the associated Legendre functions, let us be sure to realize that it is θ and not x that is the variable of physical interest. Table 6-2 also lists the associated Legendre functions in

TABLE 6-2

The First Few Associated Legendre Functions $P_l^{|m|}(x)$

$$P_0^0(x) = 1$$
$$P_1^0(x) = x = \cos\theta$$
$$P_1^1(x) = (1 - x^2)^{1/2} = \sin\theta$$
$$P_2^0(x) = \tfrac{1}{2}(3x^2 - 1) = \tfrac{1}{2}(3\cos^2\theta - 1)$$
$$P_2^1(x) = 3x(1 - x^2)^{1/2} = 3\cos\theta\sin\theta$$
$$P_2^2(x) = 3(1 - x^2) = 3\sin^2\theta$$
$$P_3^0(x) = \tfrac{1}{2}(5x^3 - 3x) = \tfrac{1}{2}(5\cos^3\theta - 3\cos\theta)$$
$$P_3^1(x) = \tfrac{3}{2}(5x^2 - 1)(1 - x^2)^{1/2} = \tfrac{3}{2}(5\cos^2\theta - 1)\sin\theta$$
$$P_3^2(x) = 15x(1 - x^2) = 15\cos\theta\sin^2\theta$$
$$P_3^3(x) = 15(1 - x^2)^{3/2} = 15\sin^3\theta$$

terms of $\cos \theta$ and $\sin \theta$. Note that the factors $(1 - x^2)^{1/2}$ in Table 6-2 become $\sin \theta$ when the associated Legendre functions are expressed in the variable θ. Because $x = \cos \theta$, Eqs. 6-70 and 6-71 are

$$\int_{-1}^{1} P_l(x)P_n(x)\, dx = \int_0^{\pi} d\theta \sin \theta P_l(\cos \theta)P_n(\cos \theta) = \frac{2\delta_{ln}}{2l + 1} \tag{6-73}$$

Because the differential volume element in spherical coordinates is $d\tau = r^2 \sin \theta \, dr \, d\theta \, d\phi$, we see that the factor $\sin \theta \, d\theta$, in Eq. 6-73, is the "θ part" of $d\tau$ in spherical coordinates.

The associated Legendre functions satisfy the relation

$$\int_{-1}^{1} dx \, P_l^{|m|}(x)P_n^{|m|}(x) = \int_0^{\pi} d\theta \sin \theta P_l^{|m|}(\cos \theta)P_n^{|m|}(\cos \theta) = \frac{2}{(2l + 1)} \frac{(l + |m|)!}{(l - |m|)!} \delta_{ln} \tag{6-74}$$

Equation 6-74 can be used to show that the normalization constant of the associated Legendre functions is

$$N_{lm} = \left[\frac{(2l + 1)}{2} \frac{(l - |m|)!}{(l + |m|)!} \right]^{1/2} \tag{6-75}$$

EXAMPLE 6-7

Use Eq. 6-74 in both the x and θ variables and Table 6-2 to prove that P_1^1 and P_2^1 are orthogonal.

Solution: According to Eq. 6-74, we must prove that

$$\int_{-1}^{1} dx \, P_1^1(x)P_2^1(x) = 0$$

From Table 6-2, we have

$$\int_{-1}^{1} dx \left[(1 - x^2)^{1/2} \right] \left[3x(1 - x^2)^{1/2} \right] = 3 \int_{-1}^{1} dx \, x(1 - x^2) = 0$$

In terms of θ, we have from Eq. 6-74 and Table 6-2

$$\int_0^{\pi} d\theta \sin \theta (\sin \theta)(3 \cos \theta \sin \theta) = 3 \int_0^{\pi} d\theta \sin^3 \theta \cos \theta = 0$$

Returning to the original problem now, Eq. 6-46, the rigid rotator wave functions are $P_l^{|m|}(\cos \theta)\Phi_m(\phi)$. By referring to Eqs. 6-59 and 6-75, we see that the functions

$$Y_l^m(\theta, \phi) = \left[\frac{(2l + 1)}{4\pi} \frac{(l - |m|)!}{(l + |m|)!} \right]^{1/2} P_l^{|m|}(\cos \theta)e^{im\phi} \tag{6-76}$$

are solutions to Eq. 6-46. The $Y_l^m(\theta, \phi)$ form an orthonormal set

$$\int_0^{2\pi} d\phi \int_0^{\pi} d\theta \sin \theta \, Y_l^m(\theta, \phi)^* Y_n^k(\theta, \phi) = \delta_{nl}\delta_{mk} \tag{6-77}$$

Note that the $Y_l^m(\theta, \phi)$ are orthonormal with respect to $\sin \theta \, d\theta \, d\phi$ and not just $d\theta \, d\phi$. The factor $\sin \theta \, d\theta \, d\phi$ has a simple physical interpretation. The differential volume element in spherical coordinates is $r^2 \sin \theta \, dr \, d\theta \, d\phi$. If r is a constant, as it is in the case of a rigid rotator, and set equal to unity for convenience, then the spherical coordinate volume element becomes a surface element, $dA = \sin \theta \, d\theta \, d\phi$. If this surface element is integrated over θ and ϕ, we obtain 4π, the surface area of a sphere of unit radius. Thus, $\sin \theta \, d\theta \, d\phi$ is an area element on the surface of a sphere of unit radius. According to Eq. 6-77, the $Y_l^m(\theta, \phi)$ are orthonormal over a spherical surface and so are called *spherical harmonics*. The first few spherical harmonics are given in Table 6-3.

In summary, the Schrödinger equation for a rigid rotator is

$$\hat{H} Y_l^m(\theta, \phi) = \frac{\hbar^2 l(l + 1)}{2I} Y_l^m(\theta, \phi) \tag{6-78}$$

with $\hat{H}$ given by Eq. 6-44. Equation 6-45 shows that $\hat{H}$ and $\hat{L}^2$ differ only by the constant factor $2I$ for a rigid rotator, and so Eq. 6-78 is equivalent to

$$\hat{L}^2 Y_l^m(\theta, \phi) = \hbar^2 l(l + 1) Y_l^m(\theta, \phi) \tag{6-79}$$

Thus, we see that the spherical harmonics are also eigenfunctions of $\hat{L}^2$ and

---

TABLE 6-3
The First Few Spherical Harmonics

$$Y_0^0 = \frac{1}{(4\pi)^{1/2}}$$

$$Y_1^0 = \left(\frac{3}{4\pi}\right)^{1/2} \cos \theta$$

$$Y_1^1 = \left(\frac{3}{8\pi}\right)^{1/2} \sin \theta e^{i\phi}$$

$$Y_1^{-1} = \left(\frac{3}{8\pi}\right)^{1/2} \sin \theta e^{-i\phi}$$

$$Y_2^0 = \left(\frac{5}{16\pi}\right)^{1/2} (3 \cos^2 \theta - 1)$$

$$Y_2^1 = \left(\frac{15}{8\pi}\right)^{1/2} \sin \theta \cos \theta e^{i\phi}$$

$$Y_2^{-1} = \left(\frac{15}{8\pi}\right)^{1/2} \sin \theta \cos \theta e^{-i\phi}$$

$$Y_2^2 = \left(\frac{15}{32\pi}\right)^{1/2} \sin^2 \theta e^{2i\phi}$$

$$Y_2^{-2} = \left(\frac{15}{32\pi}\right)^{1/2} \sin^2 \theta e^{-2i\phi}$$

---

that the square of the angular momentum can have only the values given by

$$L^2 = \hbar^2 l(l + 1) \qquad l = 0, 1, 2, \ldots \qquad (6\text{-}80)$$

It turns out that angular momentum plays an important role in quantum mechanics as well as in classical mechanics, and we shall discuss angular momentum in Section 6-7.

6-7 *The Operators Corresponding to the Three Components of Angular Momentum Do Not Commute with Each Other*

Recall that the classical definition of angular momentum of a body about some origin is

$$\mathbf{L} = \mathbf{r} \times \mathbf{p} \qquad (6\text{-}81)$$

where $\mathbf{r}$ is the vector from the origin to the body and $\mathbf{p}$ is its momentum. In terms of components, Eq. 6-81 reads

$$L_x = yp_z - zp_y$$
$$L_y = zp_x - xp_z \qquad (6\text{-}82)$$
$$L_z = xp_y - yp_x$$

We form the corresponding quantum-mechanical operator by replacing the classical momentum by $-i\hbar\nabla$, and so Eq. 6-81 becomes

$$\hat{\mathbf{L}} = -i\hbar(\mathbf{r} \times \nabla) \qquad (6\text{-}83)$$

or

$$\hat{L}_x = -i\hbar\left(y\frac{\partial}{\partial z} - z\frac{\partial}{\partial y} \right)$$

$$\hat{L}_y = -i\hbar\left(z\frac{\partial}{\partial x} - x\frac{\partial}{\partial z} \right) \qquad (6\text{-}84)$$

$$\hat{L}_z = -i\hbar\left(x\frac{\partial}{\partial y} - y\frac{\partial}{\partial x} \right)$$

It is a straightforward, but somewhat tedious, exercise in partial differentiation to convert Eq. 6-84 into spherical coordinates to obtain

$$\hat{L}_x = -i\hbar\left(-\sin\phi\frac{\partial}{\partial\theta} - \cot\theta\cos\phi\frac{\partial}{\partial\phi} \right)$$

$$\hat{L}_y = -i\hbar\left(\cos\phi\frac{\partial}{\partial\theta} - \cot\theta\sin\phi\frac{\partial}{\partial\phi} \right) \qquad (6\text{-}85)$$

$$\hat{L}_z = -i\hbar\frac{\partial}{\partial\phi}$$

The last of these equations, the one for $\hat{L}_z$, turns out to be relatively simple. It is easy to see that $e^{im\phi}$ is an eigenfunction of $\hat{L}_z$ or that

$$\hat{L}_z(e^{im\phi}) = -i\hbar\frac{\partial}{\partial\phi}(e^{im\phi}) = m\hbar(e^{im\phi})$$

In terms of the functions $\Phi_m(\phi)$ introduced in Section 6-4, we see that

$$\hat{L}_z\Phi_m(\phi) = m\hbar\Phi_m(\phi) \qquad m = 0, \pm 1, \dots \qquad (6\text{-}86)$$

Furthermore, because $\hat{L}_z$ acts upon only ϕ, we also have that the spherical harmonics are eigenfunctions of $\hat{L}_z$:

$$\begin{aligned}\hat{L}_z Y_l^m(\theta, \phi) &= N_{lm}\hat{L}_z P_l^{|m|}(\cos\theta)e^{im\phi}\\ &= N_{lm}P_l^{|m|}(\cos\theta)\hat{L}_z e^{im\phi}\\ &= \hbar m Y_l^m(\theta, \phi)\end{aligned} \qquad (6\text{-}87)$$

Equation 6-87 shows that the only possible values that L_z can be observed to have are integral multiples of $\hbar$. Notice that $\hbar$ is a fundamental measure of angular momentum.

Equation 6-79 shows that the $Y_l^m(\theta, \phi)$ are eigenfunctions of $\hat{L}^2$ also, and so according to Section 4-10, it is possible to determine precise values of L^2 and L_z simultaneously. This implies that the operators $\hat{L}^2$ and $\hat{L}_z$ commute.

EXAMPLE 6-8

Prove that the operators $\hat{L}^2$ and $\hat{L}_z$ commute.

Solution: Using $\hat{L}^2$ from Eq. 6-45 and $\hat{L}_z$ from Eq. 6-85, we have

$$\begin{aligned}\hat{L}^2\hat{L}_z f &= -\hbar^2\left[\frac{1}{\sin\theta}\frac{\partial}{\partial\theta}\left(\sin\theta\frac{\partial}{\partial\theta}\right) + \frac{1}{\sin^2\theta}\frac{\partial^2}{\partial\phi^2}\right]\left(-i\hbar\frac{\partial f}{\partial\phi}\right)\\ &= i\hbar^3\left[\frac{1}{\sin\theta}\frac{\partial}{\partial\theta}\left(\sin\theta\frac{\partial^2 f}{\partial\theta\partial\phi}\right) + \frac{1}{\sin^2\theta}\frac{\partial^3 f}{\partial\phi^3}\right]\end{aligned}$$

and

$$\begin{aligned}\hat{L}_z\hat{L}^2 f &= \left(-i\hbar\frac{\partial}{\partial\phi}\right)\left\{-\hbar^2\left[\frac{1}{\sin\theta}\frac{\partial}{\partial\theta}\left(\sin\theta\frac{\partial f}{\partial\theta}\right) + \frac{1}{\sin^2\theta}\frac{\partial^2 f}{\partial\phi^2}\right]\right\}\\ &= i\hbar^3\left[\frac{1}{\sin\theta}\frac{\partial}{\partial\theta}\left(\sin\theta\frac{\partial^2 f}{\partial\phi\,\partial\theta}\right) + \frac{1}{\sin^2\theta}\frac{\partial^3 f}{\partial\phi^3}\right]\end{aligned}$$

where in writing the last line here we have recognized that $(\partial/\partial\phi)$ does not affect terms involving θ. Because

$$\left(\frac{\partial^2 f}{\partial\theta\,\partial\phi}\right) = \left(\frac{\partial^2 f}{\partial\phi\,\partial\theta}\right)$$

for any function well enough behaved to be a wave function, we see that

$$\hat{L}^2\hat{L}_z f = \hat{L}_z\hat{L}^2 f$$

or that

$$[\hat{L}^2, \hat{L}_z] = 0$$

because f is arbitrary.

It follows from Eq. 6-87 that

$$\hat{L}_z^2 Y_l^m(\theta, \phi) = m^2 \hbar^2 Y_l^m(\theta, \phi)$$

and because

$$\hat{L}^2 Y_l^m(\theta, \phi) = l(l + 1)\hbar^2 Y_l^m(\theta, \phi)$$

and

$$\hat{L}^2 = \hat{L}_x^2 + \hat{L}_y^2 + \hat{L}_z^2$$

then

$$(\hat{L}^2 - \hat{L}_z^2)Y_l^m(\theta, \phi) = (\hat{L}_x^2 + \hat{L}_y^2)Y_l^m(\theta, \phi) = [l(l + 1) - m^2]\hbar^2 Y_l^m(\theta, \phi) \quad (6\text{-}88)$$

Thus, the observed values of $L_x^2 + L_y^2$ are $[l(l + 1) - m^2]\hbar^2$; but because $L_x^2 + L_y^2$ is the sum of two squared terms, it cannot be negative, and so we have that

$$[l(l + 1) - m^2]\hbar^2 \geq 0$$

or that

$$l(l + 1) \geq m^2 \quad (6\text{-}89)$$

Equation 6-89 says that

$$|m| \leq l$$

or that the only possible values of the integer m are

$$m = 0, \pm 1, \pm 2, \ldots, \pm l \quad (6\text{-}90)$$

(This result might be familiar as the condition of the magnetic quantum number associated with the hydrogen atom.)

Equation 6-90 shows that there are $2l + 1$ values of m for each value of l, and because the energy depends only on l through Eq. 6-61,

$$E_l = \frac{\hbar^2}{2I} l(l + 1) \qquad l = 0, 1, 2, \ldots \quad (6\text{-}61)$$

we see that each energy level is $(2l + 1)$-fold degenerate. Let us look at the degeneracy in detail for the case of $l = 1$. Because $l = 1$, m can have only the values 0 and ± 1. Using the equations

$$\hat{L}^2 Y_1^m(\theta, \phi) = 2\hbar^2 Y_1^m(\theta, \phi)$$

and

$$\hat{L}_z Y_1^m(\theta, \phi) = m\hbar Y_1^m(\theta, \phi)$$

we see that

$$|L| \equiv (L^2)^{1/2} = \sqrt{2}\hbar$$

and

$$L_z = -\hbar, 0, +\hbar$$

Note that the maximum value of L_z is less than $|L|$, which implies that L_z cannot point in the same direction as L. This is illustrated in Figure 6-7, which shows L_z with a value $+\hbar$ and $|L|$ with its value $\sqrt{2}\hbar$. Now let us try to specify L_x and L_y. Problem 26 has you prove that $\hat{L}_x$, $\hat{L}_y$, and $\hat{L}_z$ commute with $\hat{L}^2$:

$$[\hat{L}^2, \hat{L}_x] = [\hat{L}^2, \hat{L}_y] = [\hat{L}^2, \hat{L}_z] = 0 \qquad (6\text{-}91)$$

but that they do not commute among themselves. In particular, we have

$$[\hat{L}_x, \hat{L}_y] = i\hbar\hat{L}_z$$
$$[\hat{L}_y, \hat{L}_z] = i\hbar\hat{L}_x \qquad (6\text{-}92)$$
$$[\hat{L}_z, \hat{L}_x] = i\hbar\hat{L}_y$$

Equations 6-91 and 6-92 imply that although it is possible to observe precise values of L^2 and L_z simultaneously, it is not possible to observe precise values of L_x and L_y simultaneously because they do not commute with each other. Even though L_x and L_y do not have precise values, they do, of course, have an average value, and Problem 27 shows that $\langle L_x \rangle = \langle L_y \rangle = 0$. These results are illustrated in Figure 6-7, which shows L_z with a value of $+\hbar$ and $|L|$ with a value of $\hbar\sqrt{2}$. A nice classical interpretation of these results is that L precesses about the z axis, mapping out the surface of the cone shown there. The average values of $\langle L_x \rangle$ and $\langle L_y \rangle$ are zero. This picture is in nice accord with the Uncertainty Principle: By specifying L_z exactly, we have a complete uncertainty in the angle ϕ associated with L_z.

Before leaving this section, we should address ourselves to the question: "What is so special about the z direction?" The answer is that there is nothing at all special about the z direction. We could have chosen either the x or y direction as the unique direction and all the above results would be the same,

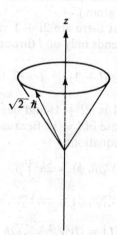

Figure 6-7. The $m = +1$ component of the angular momentum state, $l = 1$. The angular momentum describes a cone because the x and y components cannot be specified.

except for exchanging x or y for z. It is customary to choose the z direction because the expression for $\hat{L}_z$ in spherical coordinates is so much simpler than $\hat{L}_x$ or $\hat{L}_y$ (cf. Eq. 6-85). Clearly the rotating system does not know x from y from z and, in fact, this is why there is a $(2l + 1)$-fold degeneracy. If we were to apply a magnetic field to this system, then there would be a preferred direction, thus breaking the spherical symmetry and lifting the $(2l + 1)$-fold degeneracy. This broken symmetry results in the Zeeman effect, which we shall discuss in Chapter 7.

6-8   *The Schrödinger Equation for the Hydrogen Atom Can Be Solved Exactly*

We are finally ready to study the hydrogen atom, a problem of interest to chemists because it serves as the prototype for more complex atoms and, therefore, molecules. In addition, probably every chemistry student has studied the results of a quantum-mechanical treatment of the hydrogen atom in general chemistry, and here we shall see the familiar orbitals and their properties emerge from the Schrödinger equation.

As our model, we shall picture the hydrogen atom as a proton fixed at the origin and an electron of reduced mass μ interacting with the proton through a Coulombic potential (cf. Eq. 1-26):

$$U(r) = -\frac{e^2}{4\pi\varepsilon_0 r} \tag{6-93}$$

In Eq. 6-93, e is the charge on the proton, ε_0 is the permittivity of free space, and r is the distance between the electron and the proton. The factor $4\pi\varepsilon_0$ arises because we are using SI units. The model suggests that we use a spherical coordinate system with the proton at the origin. The Schrödinger equation for a hydrogen atom is

$$-\frac{\hbar^2}{2\mu}\nabla^2\psi(r, \theta, \phi) + U(r)\psi(r, \theta, \phi) = E\psi(r, \theta, \phi) \tag{6-94}$$

where ∇^2 is given by Eq. 6-38. Written out in full, Eq. 6-94 is

$$-\frac{\hbar^2}{2\mu}\left[\frac{1}{r^2}\frac{\partial}{\partial r}\left(r^2\frac{\partial\psi}{\partial r}\right) + \frac{1}{r^2\sin\theta}\frac{\partial}{\partial\theta}\left(\sin\theta\frac{\partial\psi}{\partial\theta}\right) + \frac{1}{r^2\sin^2\theta}\frac{\partial^2\psi}{\partial\phi^2}\right]$$

$$+ U(r)\psi(r, \theta, \phi) = E\psi(r, \theta, \phi) \tag{6-95}$$

At first sight, this partial differential equation looks exceedingly complicated. To bring Eq. 6-95 into a more manageable form, first multiply through by $2\mu r^2$ to obtain

$$-\hbar^2\frac{\partial}{\partial r}\left(r^2\frac{\partial\psi}{\partial r}\right) - \hbar^2\left[\frac{1}{\sin\theta}\frac{\partial}{\partial\theta}\left(\sin\theta\frac{\partial\psi}{\partial\theta}\right) + \frac{1}{\sin^2\theta}\frac{\partial^2\psi}{\partial\phi^2}\right]$$

$$+ 2\mu r^2[U(r) - E]\psi = 0$$

The second term here, the one containing all the θ and ϕ dependence, is nothing but $\hat{L}^2\psi$ according to Eq. 6-45. Thus we can write the Schrödinger equation in the form

$$-\hbar^2 \frac{\partial}{\partial r}\left(r^2 \frac{\partial \psi}{\partial r}\right) + \hat{L}^2\psi + 2\mu r^2[U(r) - E]\psi = 0 \qquad (6\text{-}96)$$

Notice now that if we consider the entire left-hand side of Eq. 6-96 to be an operator acting upon ψ, then this operator consists of a part that depends on only r (the first and third terms) and a part that depends on only θ and ϕ (the second term). According to Section 6-2, $\psi(r, \theta, \phi)$ factors into the product of a function that depends on only r and one that depends on only θ and ϕ. Furthermore, the θ, ϕ factor must be an eigenfunction of $\hat{L}^2$, which according to Eq. 6-79, we know to be the spherical harmonics $Y_l^m(\theta, \phi)$

$$\hat{L}^2 Y_l^m(\theta, \phi) = \hbar^2 l(l + 1) Y_l^m(\theta, \phi) \qquad (6\text{-}79)$$

Consequently, if we let

$$\psi(r, \theta, \phi) = R(r)Y_l^m(\theta, \phi) \qquad (6\text{-}97)$$

and use Eq. 6-79, Eq. 6-96 becomes

$$-\frac{\hbar^2}{2\mu r^2}\frac{d}{dr}\left(r^2 \frac{dR}{dr}\right) + \left[\frac{\hbar^2 l(l + 1)}{2\mu r^2} + U(r) - E\right]R(r) = 0 \qquad (6\text{-}98)$$

Equation 6-98 is called the *radial equation* for the hydrogen atom and is the only new equation that we have to study in order to have a complete solution to the hydrogen atom.

Notice that the square of the angular momentum is quantized and conserved in a central field, just as it is conserved classically in a central field. Equation 6-98 has the direct physical interpretation that the total energy E is the sum of a radial kinetic energy, an angular kinetic energy, and the potential energy. Equation 6-98 is an ordinary differential equation in r and must be solved by the series method like we outlined for the harmonic oscillator and the rigid rotator. The procedure is similar and one finds that in order that solutions be acceptable as the wave functions, the energy must be quantized according to

$$E_n = -\frac{\mu e^4}{8\varepsilon_0^2 h^2 n^2} \qquad n = 1, 2, \ldots \qquad (6\text{-}99)$$

If we introduce the Bohr radius from Section 1-9, $a_0 = \varepsilon_0 h^2/\pi\mu e^2$, then Eq. 6-99 becomes

$$E_n = -\frac{e^2}{8\pi\varepsilon_0 a_0 n^2} \qquad n = 1, 2, \ldots \qquad (6\text{-}100)$$

It is surely remarkable that these are the same energies obtained from the Bohr model of the hydrogen atom. Of course, the electron now is not restricted to sharply defined orbits but is described by its wave function.

In the course of solving Eq. 6-98, one finds not only that an integer n occurs naturally but that n must satisfy the condition that $n \geq l + 1$, which is usually written as

$$0 \leq l \leq n - 1 \qquad n = 1, 2, \ldots \qquad (6\text{-}101)$$

because the smallest possible value of l is zero. (Equation 6-101 should be familiar from general chemistry.) The solutions to Eq. 6-98 depend on two quantum numbers n and l and are given by

$$R_{nl}(r) = -\left[\frac{(n - l - 1)!}{2n[(n + l)!]^3}\right]^{1/2} \left(\frac{2}{na_0}\right)^{l + 3/2} r^l e^{-r/na_0} L_{n+l}^{2l+1}\left(\frac{2r}{na_0}\right) \qquad (6\text{-}102)$$

where the L_{n+l}^{2l+1} $(2r/na_0)$ are called *associated Laguerre functions*. The first few associated Laguerre functions are given in Table 6-4.

The functions given by Eq. 6-102 may look complicated, but notice that each one is just a polynomial multiplied by an exponential. The combinatorial factor in front assures that the $R_{nl}(r)$ are normalized with respect to an integration over r or that the $R_{nl}(r)$ satisfy

$$\int_0^\infty dr\, r^2 R_{nl}^*(r) R_{nl}(r) = 1$$

Note that the volume element here is $r^2\, dr$, which is the "r part" of the spherical coordinate volume element $r^2 \sin \theta\, dr\, d\theta\, d\phi$. The complete hydrogen atomic wave functions are

$$\psi_{nlm}(r, \theta, \phi) = R_{nl}(r) Y_l^m(\theta, \phi) \qquad (6\text{-}103)$$

The first few hydrogen atomic wave functions are given in Table 6-5. The normalization condition for hydrogen atomic wave functions is

$$\int_0^{2\pi} d\phi \int_0^\pi d\theta \sin \theta \int_0^\infty dr\, r^2 \psi_{nlm}^*(r, \theta, \phi) \psi_{nlm}(r, \theta, \phi) = 1 \qquad (6\text{-}104)$$

Because $\hat{H}$ is Hermitian, the ψ_{nlm} must also be orthogonal. The orthogonality condition is given by

$$\int_0^{2\pi} d\phi \int_0^\pi d\theta \sin \theta \int_0^\infty dr\, r^2 \psi_{nlm}^*(r, \theta, \phi) \psi_{n'l'm'}(r, \theta, \phi) = \delta_{nn'}\delta_{ll'}\delta_{mm'} \qquad (6\text{-}105)$$

TABLE 6-4
The First Few Associated Laguerre Functions

$n = 1; l = 0$	$L_1^1(x) = -1$	$x = 2r/a_0$
$n = 2; l = 0$	$L_2^1(x) = -2!(2 - x)$	$x = r/a_0$
$l = 1$	$L_3^3(x) = -3!$	
$n = 3; l = 0$	$L_3^1(x) = -3!(3 - 3x + \frac{1}{2}x^2)$	$x = 2r/3a_0$
$l = 1$	$L_4^3(x) = -4!(4 - x)$	
$l = 2$	$L_5^5(x) = -5!$	
$n = 4; l = 0$	$L_4^1(x) = -4!(4 - 6x + 2x^2 - \frac{1}{6}x^3)$	$x = r/2a_0$
$l = 1$	$L_5^3(x) = -5!(10 - 5x + \frac{1}{2}x^2)$	
$l = 2$	$L_6^5(x) = -6!(6 - x)$	
$l = 3$	$L_7^7(x) = -7!$	

TABLE 6-5

The Complete Hydrogenlike Atomic Wave Functions for $n = 1, 2,$ and 3. The Quantity Z Is the Atomic Number of the Nucleus, and $\sigma = Zr/a_0$, Where a_0 is the Bohr Radius.

$$n = 1; l = 0, m = 0 \qquad \psi_{100} = \frac{1}{\sqrt{\pi}}\left(\frac{Z}{a_0}\right)^{3/2} e^{-\sigma}$$

$$n = 2; l = 0, m = 0 \qquad \psi_{200} = \frac{1}{\sqrt{32\pi}}\left(\frac{Z}{a_0}\right)^{3/2}(2 - \sigma)e^{-\sigma/2}$$

$$l = 1, m = 0 \qquad \psi_{210} = \frac{1}{\sqrt{32\pi}}\left(\frac{Z}{a_0}\right)^{3/2}\sigma e^{-\sigma/2}\cos\theta$$

$$l = 1, m = \pm 1 \qquad \psi_{21\pm1} = \frac{1}{\sqrt{64\pi}}\left(\frac{Z}{a_0}\right)^{3/2}\sigma e^{-\sigma/2}\sin\theta e^{\pm i\phi}$$

$$n = 3; l = 0, m = 0 \qquad \psi_{300} = \frac{1}{81\sqrt{3\pi}}\left(\frac{Z}{a_0}\right)^{3/2}(27 - 18\sigma + 2\sigma^2)e^{-\sigma/3}$$

$$l = 1, m = 0 \qquad \psi_{310} = \frac{1}{81}\left(\frac{2}{\pi}\right)^{1/2}\left(\frac{Z}{a_0}\right)^{3/2}(6\sigma - \sigma^2)e^{-\sigma/3}\cos\theta$$

$$l = 1, m = \pm 1 \qquad \psi_{31\pm1} = \frac{1}{81\sqrt{\pi}}\left(\frac{Z}{a_0}\right)^{3/2}(6\sigma - \sigma^2)e^{-\sigma/3}\sin\theta e^{\pm i\phi}$$

$$l = 2, m = 0 \qquad \psi_{320} = \frac{1}{81\sqrt{6\pi}}\left(\frac{Z}{a_0}\right)^{3/2}\sigma^2 e^{-\sigma/3}(3\cos^2\theta - 1)$$

$$l = 2, m = \pm 1 \qquad \psi_{32\pm1} = \frac{1}{81\sqrt{\pi}}\left(\frac{Z}{a_0}\right)^{3/2}\sigma^2 e^{-\sigma/3}\sin\theta\cos\theta e^{\pm i\phi}$$

$$l = 2, m = \pm 2 \qquad \psi_{32\pm2} = \frac{1}{162\sqrt{\pi}}\left(\frac{Z}{a_0}\right)^{3/2}\sigma^2 e^{-\sigma/3}\sin^2\theta e^{\pm 2i\phi}$$

EXAMPLE 6-9

Show that the hydrogenlike atomic wave function ψ_{210} in Table 6-5 is normalized and that it is orthogonal to ψ_{200}.

Solution: The orthonormality condition is given by Eq. 6-105. Using ψ_{210} from Table 6-5,

$$\int_0^{2\pi} d\phi \int_0^{\pi} d\theta \sin\theta \int_0^{\infty} dr\, r^2 \left[\frac{1}{\sqrt{32\pi}}\left(\frac{Z}{a_0}\right)^{3/2}\left(\frac{Zr}{a_0}\right)e^{-Zr/2a_0}\cos\theta\right]^2$$

$$= \frac{1}{32\pi}\left(\frac{Z}{a_0}\right)^5 \int_0^{2\pi} d\phi \int_0^{\pi} d\theta \sin\theta \cos^2\theta \int_0^{\infty} dr\, r^4 e^{-Zr/a_0}$$

$$= \frac{1}{32\pi} \left(\frac{Z}{a_0}\right)^5 (2\pi)\left(\frac{2}{3}\right)\left[\left(\frac{a_0}{Z}\right)^5 24\right] = 1$$

and so ψ_{210} is normalized. To show that it is orthogonal to ψ_{200},

$$\int_0^{2\pi} d\phi \int_0^{\pi} d\theta \sin\theta \int_0^{\infty} dr\, r^2 \left[\frac{1}{\sqrt{32\pi}}\left(\frac{Z}{a_0}\right)^{3/2}\left(\frac{Zr}{a_0}\right)e^{-Zr/2a_0}\cos\theta\right]$$

$$\times \left[\frac{1}{\sqrt{32\pi}}\left(\frac{Z}{a_0}\right)^{3/2}\left(2 - \frac{Zr}{a_0}\right)e^{-Zr/2a_0}\right]$$

$$= \frac{1}{32\pi}\left(\frac{Z}{a_0}\right)^4 \int_0^{2\pi} d\phi \int_0^{\pi} d\theta \sin\theta\cos\theta \int_0^{\infty} dr\, r^3\left(2 - \frac{Zr}{a_0}\right)e^{-Zr/a_0}$$

The integral over θ here vanishes, and so we see that ψ_{210} and ψ_{200} are orthogonal.

6-9   s Orbitals Are Spherically Symmetric

The hydrogen atomic wave functions depend on three quantum numbers, n, l, and m. The quantum number n is called the *principal quantum number* and has the values 1, 2, ... The energy depends on only the principal quantum number through the equation $E_n = -e^2/8\pi\varepsilon_0 a_0 n^2$. The quantum number l is called the *angular momentum quantum number* and has the values 0, 1, ..., $n - 1$. The angular momentum of the electron about the proton is determined completely by l through $|L| = \hbar\sqrt{l(l + 1)}$. Note that the form of the radial wave functions depends on both n and l. It is customary to denote the value of l by a letter, with $l = 0$ being denoted by s, $l = 1$ by p, $l = 2$ by d, $l = 3$ by f, with higher values of l denoted by the alphabetic sequence following f. The origin of the letters s, p, d, f is historic and has to do with the designation of the observed spectral lines of atomic sodium. The letters s, p, d, and f stand for *sharp, principal, diffuse,* and *fundamental.* A wave function with $n = 1$ and $l = 0$ is called a $1s$ wave function; one with $n = 2$ and $l = 0$ a $2s$ wave function, and so on. The third quantum number m is called the *magnetic quantum number* and takes on the $2l + 1$ values $m = 0, \pm1, \pm2, \ldots, \pm l$. The z component of the angular momentum is determined completely by m through $L_z = m\hbar$. The quantum number m is called the magnetic quantum number because the energy of a hydrogen atom in a magnetic field depends on m. The $(2l + 1)$-fold degeneracy in the absence of a magnetic field is split into $2l + 1$ different energies in the presence of a magnetic field, and this splitting depends on the $2l + 1$ different values that m can have. This splitting is illustrated in Figure 6-8 and is discussed in detail in Section 6-11.

The complete hydrogen atomic wave functions depend on three variables and so it is difficult to plot them or to display them. It is common to consider

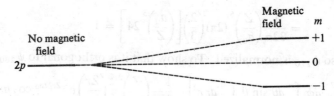

Figure 6-8. The splitting of the 2*p* state of a hydrogen atom in a magnetic field. We shall discuss this splitting in Section 6-11.

the radial and the angular parts separately. The state of lowest energy of a hydrogen atom is the 1*s* state. The radial function associated with the 1*s* state is ($Z = 1$)

$$R_{1s}(r) = \frac{2}{a_0^{3/2}} e^{-r/a_0}$$

As mentioned above, the radial wave functions are normalized with respect to integration over *r*, and so we have that

$$\int_0^\infty dr\, r^2 [R_{1s}(r)]^2 = \frac{4}{a_0^3} \int_0^\infty dr\, r^2 e^{-2r/a_0} = 1 \qquad (6\text{-}106)$$

From Eq. 6-106, we see that the probability that the electron lies between *r* and $r + dr$ is $[R_{nl}(r)]^2 r^2\, dr$, and plots of $r^2 R_{nl}^2(r)$ are shown in Figure 6-9. An important observation from the plots in Figure 6-9 is that the number of nodes in the radial function is equal to $n - l - 1$.

For the 1*s* state, the probability that the electron lies between *r* and $r + dr$ is

$$\text{Prob} = \frac{4}{a_0^3} r^2 e^{-2r/a_0}\, dr \qquad (6\text{-}107)$$

EXAMPLE 6-10

Calculate the probability that an electron described by a hydrogen atomic 1*s* wave function will be found within one Bohr radius of the nucleus.

Solution: The probability that the electron will be found within one Bohr radius of the nucleus is obtained by integrating Eq. 6-107 from 0 to a_0:

$$\text{Prob}\,(0 \le r \le a_0) = \frac{4}{a_0^3} \int_0^{a_0} dr\, r^2 e^{-2r/a_0}$$

$$= 4 \int_0^1 dx\, x^2 e^{-2x}$$

$$= 1 - 5e^{-2}$$

$$= 0.323$$

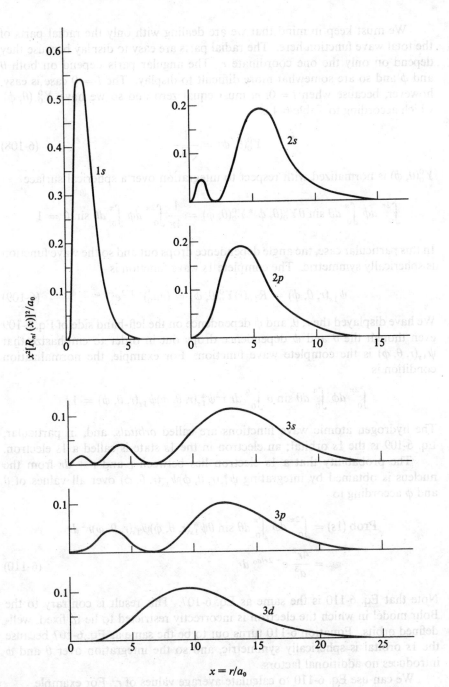

Figure 6-9. The probability densities $r^2[R_{nl}(r)]^2$ associated with the radial parts of the hydrogen atomic wave functions. The plots have been scaled by letting $x = r/a_0$ and plotting $x^2[R_{nl}(x)]^2/a_0$ versus x.

We must keep in mind that we are dealing with only the radial parts of the total wave function here. The radial parts are easy to display because they depend on only the one coordinate r. The angular parts depend on both θ and ϕ and so are somewhat more difficult to display. The $l = 0$ case is easy, however, because when $l = 0$, m must equal zero and so we have $Y_0^0(\theta, \phi)$, which according to Table 6-4 is

$$Y_0^0(\theta, \phi) = \frac{1}{\sqrt{4\pi}} \tag{6-108}$$

$Y_0^0(\theta, \phi)$ is normalized with respect to integration over a spherical surface

$$\int_0^{2\pi} d\phi \int_0^\pi d\theta \sin\theta\, Y_0^0(\theta, \phi)^* Y_0^0(\theta, \phi) = \frac{1}{4\pi} \int_0^{2\pi} d\phi \int_0^\pi d\theta \sin\theta = 1$$

In this particular case, the angle dependence drops out and so the wave function is spherically symmetric. The complete $1s$ wave function is

$$\psi_{1s}(r, \theta, \phi) = R_{10}(r) Y_0^0(\theta, \phi) = (\pi a_0^3)^{-1/2} e^{-r/a_0} \tag{6-109}$$

We have displayed the r, θ, and ϕ dependence on the left-hand side of Eq. 6-109 even though the θ and ϕ dependence drops out in order to emphasize that $\psi_{1s}(r, \theta, \phi)$ is the complete wave function. For example, the normalization condition is

$$\int_0^{2\pi} d\phi \int_0^\pi d\theta \sin\theta \int_0^\infty dr\, r^2 \psi_{1s}^*(r, \theta, \phi)\psi_{1s}(r, \theta, \phi) = 1$$

The hydrogen atomic wave functions are called *orbitals*, and, in particular, Eq. 6-109 is the $1s$ orbital; an electron in the $1s$ state is called a $1s$ electron.

The probability that a $1s$ electron lies between r and $r + dr$ from the nucleus is obtained by integrating $\psi_{1s}^*(r, \theta, \phi)\psi_{1s}(r, \theta, \phi)$ over all values of θ and ϕ according to

$$\text{Prob } (1s) = \int_0^{2\pi} d\phi \int_0^\pi d\theta \sin\theta\, \psi_{1s}^*(r, \theta, \phi)\psi_{1s}(r, \theta, \phi) r^2\, dr$$

$$= \frac{4r^2}{a_0^3} e^{-2r/a_0}\, dr \tag{6-110}$$

Note that Eq. 6-110 is the same as Eq. 6-107. This result is contrary to the Bohr model in which the electron is incorrectly restricted to lie in fixed, well-defined orbits. Equation 6-110 turns out to be the same as Eq. 6-107 because the $1s$ orbital is spherically symmetric, and so the integration over θ and ϕ introduces no additional factors.

We can use Eq. 6-110 to calculate average values of r. For example,

$$\langle r \rangle_{1s} = \frac{4}{a_0^3} \int_0^\infty r^3 e^{-2r/a_0}\, dr = \frac{3}{2} a_0 \tag{6-111}$$

The average potential energy is

$$\langle U(r) \rangle_{1s} = \int_0^{2\pi} d\phi \int_0^{\pi} d\theta \sin\theta \int_0^{\infty} dr\, r^2 \psi_{1s}^* \left(-\frac{e^2}{4\pi\varepsilon_0 r}\right) \psi_{1s}$$

$$= -\frac{e^2}{\pi\varepsilon_0 a_0^3} \int_0^{\infty} dr\, re^{-2r/a_0}$$

$$= -\frac{e^2}{4\pi\varepsilon_0 a_0} \tag{6-112}$$

It is interesting to note that

$$\langle U(r) \rangle = 2\langle E \rangle \tag{6-113}$$

Because $\langle K \rangle + \langle U \rangle = \langle E \rangle$, we have also that

$$\langle U \rangle = -2\langle K \rangle$$

and

$$\langle K \rangle = -\langle E \rangle \tag{6-114}$$

for this case. Although we have derived Eq. 6-114 only for the 1s state of the hydrogen atom, it is generally true for any system in which the potential energy is Coulombic. Equation 6-113 is called the *virial theorem* and is valid for all atoms and molecules. The virial theorem is proved in Problem 40.

Equation 6-110 can be used to determine the most probable distance of a 1s electron from the nucleus.

EXAMPLE 6-11
Show that the most probable value of r (r_{mp}) in a 1s state is a_0.

Solution: To determine the most probable value of r, we find the value of r that maximizes the probability density of r or that maximizes

$$f(r) = \frac{4r^2}{a_0^3} e^{-2r/a_0}$$

If we differentiate $f(r)$ and set the result equal to zero, we find that $r_{mp} = a_0$, the Bohr radius.

The next simplest orbital is the 2s orbital. A 2s orbital is given by

$$\psi_{2s}(r, \theta, \phi) = R_{20}(r) Y_0^0(\theta, \phi) \tag{6-115}$$

which is also spherically symmetric. In fact, because any s orbital will have the angular factor $Y_0^0(\theta, \phi)$, we see that s orbitals are generally spherically symmetric. By referring to Table 6-5, we see that

$$\psi_{2s}(r, \theta, \phi) = \frac{1}{\sqrt{32\pi}} \left(\frac{1}{a_0}\right)^{3/2} \left(2 - \frac{r}{a_0}\right) e^{-r/2a_0} \tag{6-116}$$

Remember that ψ_{2s} is normalized with respect to an integration over r, θ, and ϕ. The average value of r in the $2s$ state is (cf. Problem 32)

$$\langle r \rangle_{2s} = \int_0^{2\pi} d\phi \int_0^{\pi} d\theta \sin\theta \int_0^{\infty} dr\, r^2 \psi_{2s}^* r \psi_{2s} = 6a_0 \tag{6-117}$$

showing that a $2s$ electron is on the average a much greater distance from the nucleus than a $1s$ electron. In fact, using the general properties of the associated Laguerre polynomials, it is possible to show that $\langle r \rangle = \frac{3}{2}a_0 n^2$ for an ns electron. In addition, it is a straightforward exercise to show that $\langle U \rangle = 2\langle E \rangle$ for a $2s$ electron, in accord with the virial theorem (Problem 33).

6-10   *There Are Three p Orbitals for Each Value of the Principal Quantum Number*

When $l \neq 0$, the hydrogen atomic wave functions are not spherically symmetric; they depend on θ and ϕ. In this section, we shall concentrate on the angular parts of the hydrogen wave functions. Let us first consider states with $l = 1$, or p orbitals. Because $m = 0$ or ± 1 when $l = 1$, there are three p orbitals for each value of n. The angular part of the p orbitals is given by the three spherical harmonics, $Y_1^0(\theta, \phi)$ and $Y_1^{\pm 1}(\theta, \phi)$. The simplest of these spherical harmonics is

$$Y_1^0(\theta, \phi) = \left(\frac{3}{4\pi}\right)^{1/2} \cos\theta \tag{6-118}$$

which is readily shown to be normalized, because

$$\frac{3}{4\pi} \int_0^{2\pi} d\phi \int_0^{\pi} d\theta \sin\theta \cos^2\theta = \frac{3}{2} \int_0^{\pi} d\theta \sin\theta \cos^2\theta = \frac{3}{2} \int_{-1}^{1} dx\, x^2 = 1$$

In the last step, we let $\cos\theta = x$. It is customary to display $Y_1^0(\theta, \phi)$ in a *polar plot*. The polar plot of some function $f(\theta)$ is made on special graph paper, called *polar graph paper*. Polar graph paper consists of a central point with straight lines radiating outward every $5°$ or $10°$ (see Figure 6-10). To plot the function $f(\theta) = \cos\theta$, make a table of $f(\theta)$ versus θ such as

θ	$f(\theta) = \cos\theta$
$0°$	1.00
$20°$	0.94
$40°$	0.77
$60°$	0.50

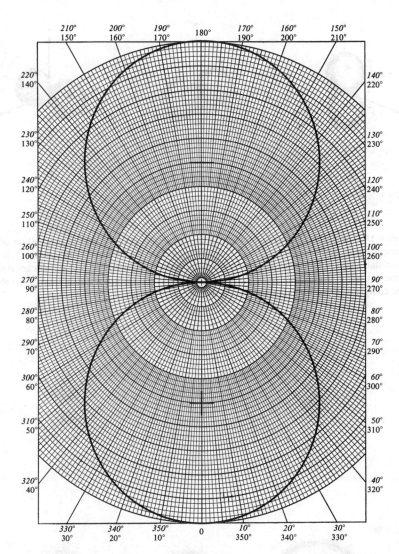

Figure 6-10. A polar plot of $f(\theta) = \cos\theta$. To construct such a plot, mark off the distance $f(\theta)$ along the radial line labeled by the angle θ.

and mark off the distance $f(\theta)$ along the radial line labeled by the angle θ. A polar plot of $f(\theta)) = \cos\theta$ is shown in Figure 6-10. A polar plot does not indicate the *shape* of an orbital but does show its direction or orientation. Figure 6-10 shows that $Y_1^0(\theta, \phi)$ is directed along the z axis (recall that $\theta = 0°$ and $\theta = 180°$ are directed along the z axis in a spherical coordinate system), and hence $Y_1^0(\theta, \phi)$ is called a p_z orbital.

Another common way to present the angular functions is as three-dimensional figures. Because $Y_1^0(\theta, \phi)$ turns out to be independent of ϕ, Y_1^0 is symmetric about the vertical axis in Figure 6-10. A three-dimensional plot of Y_1^0

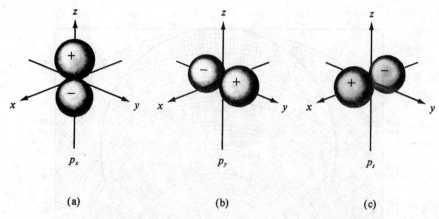

p_x

p_y

p_z

(a)

(b)

(c)

Figure 6-11. Three-dimensional polar plots of the angular part of the real representation of the hydrogen atomic wave functions for $l = 1$. These shapes are the familiar "tangent sphere" picture of p orbitals that are seen in many general chemistry books. Although tangent spheres are faithful representations of the angular parts of p orbitals, they are *not* a good representation of the shape of the complete orbital because the radial functions are not included here.

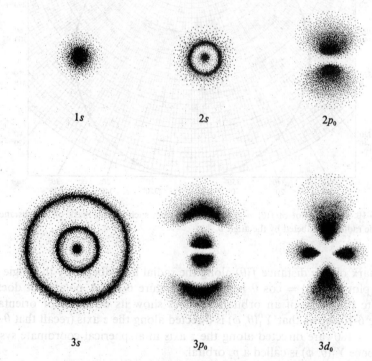

$1s$

$2s$

$2p_0$

$3s$

$3p_0$

$3d_0$

Figure 6-12. Probability density plots of some hydrogen atomic orbitals. The density of the dots represents the probability of finding the electron in that region.

is obtained by rotating the figure in Figure 6-10 about the z axis, the result of which is shown in Figure 6-11(a). Figure 6-11(a) is the familiar tangent sphere picture of a p orbital that is often presented in general chemistry texts. Although the tangent sphere picture represents the shape of the angular part of p orbitals, it is *not* a faithful representation of the shape of a p_z orbital because the radial functions are not included.

Because a complete wave function generally depends on three coordinates, it is difficult to display wave functions clearly. One useful and instructive way, however, is the following: The quantity $\psi^*\psi \, d\tau$ is the probability that the electron is located within the volume element $d\tau$. Thus, one can divide space into little volume elements and compute the average or some representative value of $\psi^*\psi$ within each volume element and then represent the value of $\psi^*\psi$ by the density of dots in a picture. Figure 6-12 shows such plots for several orbitals.

An alternate way to represent complete wave functions is as contour maps. Figure 6-13(a) shows a contour map for a $1s$ orbital. In each case, the nine contours shown enclose the $10\%, 20\%, \ldots, 90\%$ probability of finding the electron within each contour. Note that the contour maps appear as cross sections of the plots in Figure 6-12.

Figure 6-12 shows a $3d_0$ state along with the others. A $3d_0$ wave function is given by

$$\psi_{3d_0}(r, \theta, \phi) = R_{32}(r)Y_2^0(\theta, \phi) \tag{6-119}$$

where

$$Y_2^0(\theta, \phi) = \left(\frac{5}{16\pi}\right)^{1/2}(3\cos^2\theta - 1) \tag{6-120}$$

The angular part of ψ_{3d_0}, $Y_2^0(\theta, \phi)$, is presented as a polar plot in Figure 6-14. Because $R_{32}(r)$ in Eq. 6-119 has no nodes, the probability representations in Figures 6-12 and 6-13 are similar to the polar plot in Figure 6-14. When the radial function has nodes, however, the polar plot of the angular function does not faithfully represent the total orbital. A good example of this occurs for the $3p_0$ orbital, which is given by

$$\psi_{3p_0} = R_{31}(r)Y_1^0(\theta, \phi) \tag{6-121}$$

where the radial function $R_{31}(r)$ has one node. The difference in the shapes of the $3p_0$ and $2p_0$ orbitals in Figures 6-12 and 6-13 is due to the nodes in the radial function.

The angular functions with $m \neq 0$ are more difficult to represent pictorially because they not only depend on ϕ in addition to θ but are complex as well. In particular, the $l = 1$ states with $m \neq 0$ are

$$Y_1^{+1}(\theta, \phi) = \left(\frac{3}{8\pi}\right)^{1/2}\sin\theta e^{+i\phi} \tag{6-122}$$

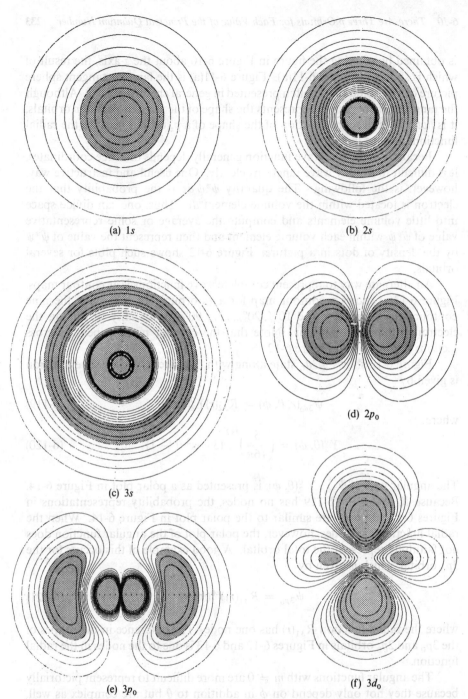

Figure 6-13. Probability contour maps for the hydrogen atomic orbitals. The nine contours shown in each case enclose the 10%, 20%, ..., 90% probability of finding the electron within each contour. The scale of the figure is indicated by hash marks: one mark corresponds to one Bohr radius a_0. Note that the different orbitals are presented on different scales. The shaded areas shown in each case indicates the highest 40% of the probability densities. [From G. Gerhold et al., Am. J. Phys. *40*, 998 (1972)]

234

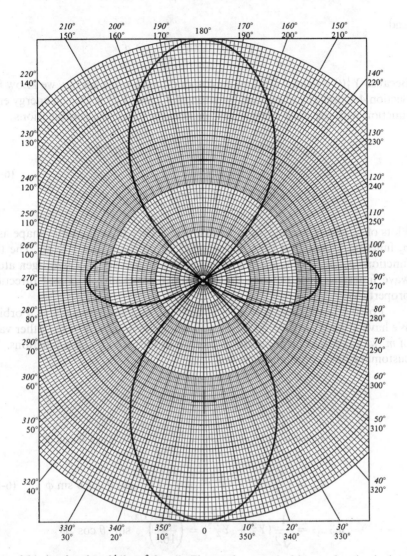

Figure 6-14. A polar plot of $\frac{1}{2}(3 \cos^2 \theta - 1)$. The angular part of a $3d_0$ wave function is given by Eq. 6-120. Because the angular part of a $3d_0$ orbital points along the z axis in a spherical coordinate system, a $3d_0$ wave function is often called a d_{z^2} orbital.

and

$$Y_1^{-1}(\theta, \phi) = \left(\frac{3}{8\pi}\right)^{1/2} \sin \theta e^{-i\phi}$$

The probability densities associated with $Y_1^{+1}(\theta, \phi)$ and $Y_1^{-1}(\theta, \phi)$ are the same because

$$|Y_1^{+1}(\theta, \phi)|^2 = \frac{3}{8\pi} \sin^2 \theta \qquad (6\text{-}123)$$

and

$$|Y_1^{-1}(\theta, \phi)|^2 = \frac{3}{8\pi} \sin^2 \theta$$

Because $Y_1^1(\theta, \phi)$ and $Y_1^{-1}(\theta, \phi)$ correspond to the same energy, we know from Section 4-5 that any linear combination of Y_1^1 and Y_1^{-1} is also an energy eigenfunction with the same energy. It is customary to use the combinations

$$p_x = \frac{1}{\sqrt{2}}(Y_1^1 + Y_1^{-1}) = \left(\frac{3}{4\pi}\right)^{1/2} \sin \theta \cos \phi$$

$$p_y = \frac{1}{\sqrt{2i}}(Y_1^1 - Y_1^{-1}) = \left(\frac{3}{4\pi}\right)^{1/2} \sin \theta \sin \phi$$

(6-124)

Plots of p_x and p_y are shown in Figure 6-11. They have the same shape as the p_z function except that they are directed along the x and y axes. The three functions p_x, p_y, and p_z are often used as the angular part of hydrogen atomic wave functions because they are real and have easily visualized directional properties.

For the $l = 2$ case, $m = 0, \pm 1$, and ± 2, and so there are five d orbitals. We have already considered the $m = 0$ value previously. For the other values of m, we take linear combinations like we did above for the p functions. The customary linear combinations are

$$d_{z^2} = Y_2^0 = \left(\frac{5}{16\pi}\right)^{1/2} (3 \cos^2 \theta - 1)$$

$$d_{xz} = \frac{1}{\sqrt{2}}(Y_2^1 + Y_2^{-1}) = \left(\frac{15}{4\pi}\right)^{1/2} \sin \theta \cos \theta \cos \phi$$

$$d_{yz} = \frac{1}{\sqrt{2i}}(Y_2^1 - Y_2^{-1}) = \left(\frac{15}{4\pi}\right)^{1/2} \sin \theta \cos \theta \sin \phi \qquad (6\text{-}125)$$

$$d_{x^2-y^2} = \frac{1}{\sqrt{2}}(Y_2^2 + Y_2^{-2}) = \left(\frac{15}{16\pi}\right)^{1/2} \sin^2 \theta \cos 2\phi$$

$$d_{xy} = \frac{1}{\sqrt{2i}}(Y_2^2 - Y_2^{-2}) = \left(\frac{15}{16\pi}\right)^{1/2} \sin^2 \theta \sin 2\phi$$

The angular parts of the five d orbitals are shown in Figure 6-15. Note that the last four orbitals given in Eqs. 6-125 differ only in their orientation. Figure 6-15 suggests the rationale of the notation of the d orbitals; d_{z^2} lies along the z axis, $d_{x^2-y^2}$ lies along the x and y axes; d_{xy} lies in the x-y plane; d_{xz} lies in the x-z plane, and d_{yz} lies in the y-z plane. Most chemists use the five d orbitals given by Eqs. 6-125 rather than the spherical harmonics, because the functions in Eqs. 6-125 are real and have convenient directional properties. The real representations of the hydrogen atomic wave functions are given in Table 6-6. The

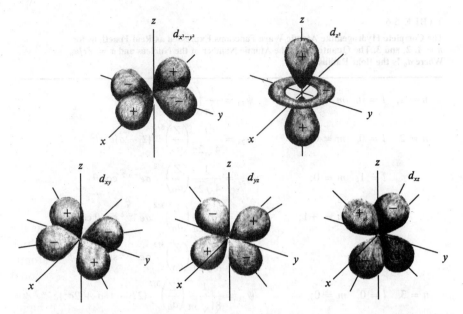

Figure 6-15. Three-dimensional polar plots of the angular part of the real representation of the hydrogen atomic wave functions for $l = 2$. Such plots show the directional character of these orbitals but are not good representations of the shape of these orbitals because the radial functions are not included.

functions in Table 6-6 are the linear combinations of the complex wave functions in Table 6-5. Both sets are equivalent, but chemists normally use the real functions in Table 6-6. We shall see in later chapters that molecular wave functions can be built out of atomic orbitals and if the atomic orbitals have a definite directional character, it is possible to use chemical intuition to decide which are the more important atomic orbitals to use to describe molecular orbitals.

6-11   *The Energy Levels of a Hydrogen Atom Are Split by a Magnetic Field*

In this section, we shall discuss a hydrogen atom in an external magnetic field. Before doing so, however, we shall review some facts and equations concerning magnetic dipoles and magnetic fields. The motion of an electric charge around a closed loop produces a magnetic dipole μ whose magnitude is given by

$$\mu = iA \qquad (6\text{-}126)$$

TABLE 6-6

The Complete Hydrogenlike Atomic Wave Functions Expressed as Real Functions for $n = 1$, 2, and 3. The Quantity Z Is the Atomic Number of the Nucleus and $\sigma = Zr/a_0$, Where a_0 Is the Bohr Radius.

$n = 1$, $l = 0$, $m = 0$;
$$\psi_{1s} = \frac{1}{\sqrt{\pi}}\left(\frac{Z}{a_0}\right)^{3/2} e^{-\sigma}$$

$n = 2$, $l = 0$, $m = 0$;
$$\psi_{2s} = \frac{1}{4\sqrt{2\pi}}\left(\frac{Z}{a_0}\right)^{3/2} (2 - \sigma)e^{-\sigma/2}$$

$l = 1$, $m = 0$;
$$\psi_{2p_z} = \frac{1}{4\sqrt{2\pi}}\left(\frac{Z}{a_0}\right)^{3/2} \sigma e^{-\sigma/2} \cos \theta$$

$l = 1$, $m = \pm 1$;
$$\psi_{2p_x} = \frac{1}{4\sqrt{2\pi}}\left(\frac{Z}{a_0}\right)^{3/2} \sigma e^{-\sigma/2} \sin \theta \cos \phi$$

$$\psi_{2p_y} = \frac{1}{4\sqrt{2\pi}}\left(\frac{Z}{a_0}\right)^{3/2} \sigma e^{-\sigma/2} \sin \theta \sin \phi$$

$n = 3$, $l = 0$, $m = 0$;
$$\psi_{3s} = \frac{1}{81\sqrt{3\pi}}\left(\frac{Z}{a_0}\right)^{3/2} (27 - 18\sigma + 2\sigma^2)e^{-\sigma/3}$$

$l = 1$, $m = 0$;
$$\psi_{3p_z} = \frac{\sqrt{2}}{81\sqrt{\pi}}\left(\frac{Z}{a_0}\right)^{3/2} \sigma(6 - \sigma)e^{-\sigma/3} \cos \theta$$

$l = 1$, $m = \pm 1$;
$$\psi_{3p_x} = \frac{\sqrt{2}}{81\sqrt{\pi}}\left(\frac{Z}{a_0}\right)^{3/2} \sigma(6 - \sigma)e^{-\sigma/3} \sin \theta \cos \phi$$

$$\psi_{3p_y} = \frac{\sqrt{2}}{81\sqrt{\pi}}\left(\frac{Z}{a}\right)^{3/2} \sigma(6 - \sigma)e^{-\sigma/3} \sin \theta \sin \phi$$

$l = 2$, $m = 0$;
$$\psi_{3d_{z^2}} = \frac{1}{81\sqrt{6\pi}}\left(\frac{Z}{a_0}\right)^{3/2} \sigma^2 e^{-\sigma/3}(3 \cos^2 \theta - 1)$$

$l = 2$, $m = \pm 1$;
$$\psi_{3d_{xz}} = \frac{\sqrt{2}}{81\sqrt{\pi}}\left(\frac{Z}{a_0}\right)^{3/2} \sigma^2 e^{-\sigma/3} \sin \theta \cos \theta \cos \phi$$

$$\psi_{3d_{yz}} = \frac{\sqrt{2}}{81\sqrt{\pi}}\left(\frac{Z}{a_0}\right)^{3/2} \sigma^2 e^{-\sigma/3} \sin \theta \cos \theta \sin \phi$$

$l = 2$, $m = \pm 2$;
$$\psi_{3d_{x^2 - y^2}} = \frac{1}{81\sqrt{2\pi}}\left(\frac{Z}{a_0}\right)^{3/2} \sigma^2 e^{-\sigma/3} \sin^2 \theta \cos 2\phi$$

$$\psi_{3d_{xy}} = \frac{1}{81\sqrt{2\pi}}\left(\frac{Z}{a_0}\right)^{3/2} \sigma^2 e^{-\sigma/3} \sin^2 \theta \sin 2\phi$$

where i is the current in amperes (coulombs/second) and A is the area of the loop in square meters. If we consider a circular loop for simplicity, then

$$i = \frac{qv}{2\pi r} \tag{6-127}$$

where v is the velocity of the charge q and r is the radius of the circle. Substituting

Pieter Zeeman (1865–1943) studied at the University of Leiden as an assistant to Hendrick Lorentz and received his Ph.D. in 1893. In 1897 he went to the University of Amsterdam, where he remained until his retirement in 1935. Zeeman succeeded van der Waals as director of the Physical Institute in 1908. In 1923 he became director of the newly created Laboratorium Physica, which was later renamed the Zeeman Laboratory. Zeeman was known as an excellent experimentalist. He shared the Nobel Prize for physics in 1902 with Lorentz.

Eq. 6-127 and $A = \pi r^2$ into Eq. 6-126 gives

$$\mu = \frac{qrv}{2} \qquad (6\text{-}128)$$

More generally, if the orbit is not circular, then Eq. 6-128 becomes

$$\mu = \frac{q(\mathbf{r} \times \mathbf{v})}{2} \qquad (6\text{-}129)$$

Note that Eq. 6-129 reduces to Eq. 6-128 for the case of a circular orbit. We can express μ in terms of angular momentum by using the fact that $\mathbf{L} = \mathbf{r} \times \mathbf{p}$ and $\mathbf{p} = m\mathbf{v}$, so that Eq. 6-129 becomes

$$\mu = \frac{q}{2m} \mathbf{L} \qquad (6\text{-}130)$$

Note that μ and $\mathbf{L}$ are perpendicular to the plane of the motion. For an electron, $q = -|e|$, and Eq. 6-130 becomes

$$\mu = -\frac{|e|}{2m_e} \mathbf{L} \qquad (6\text{-}131)$$

where m_e is the mass of the electron.

A magnetic dipole will interact with a magnetic field, and the potential energy of a magnetic dipole in a magnetic field is

$$U = -\boldsymbol{\mu} \cdot \mathbf{B} \tag{6-132}$$

where $\mathbf{B}$ is the strength of the magnetic field. The quantity $\mathbf{B}$ is defined through the equation

$$\mathbf{F} = q(\mathbf{v} \times \mathbf{B}) \tag{6-133}$$

where $\mathbf{F}$ is the force acting upon a charge q moving with a velocity $\mathbf{v}$ in a magnetic field of strength $\mathbf{B}$. The SI units of magnetic field strength are *tesla* (T). From Eq. 6-133, we see that one tesla is equal to one newton/ampere·meter. If, as usual, we take the magnetic field to be in the z direction, then Eq. 6-132 becomes

$$U = -\mu_z B_z \tag{6-134}$$

Using Eq. 6-131 for μ_z, we have

$$U = \frac{|e|B_z}{2m_e} L_z \tag{6-135}$$

If we replace L_z by its operator equivalent $\hat{L}_z$, then Eq. 6-135 gives the part of a hydrogen atom Hamiltonian that accounts for the external magnetic field. Thus, the Hamiltonian operator for a hydrogen atom in an external magnetic field is

$$\hat{H} = \hat{H}_0 + \frac{|e|B_z}{2m_e} \hat{L}_z \tag{6-136}$$

where $\hat{H}_0$ is the Hamiltonian in the absence of a magnetic field. The corresponding Schrödinger equation is

$$\hat{H}_0\psi + \frac{|e|B_z}{2m_e} \hat{L}_z\psi = E\psi \tag{6-137}$$

The hydrogen atomic wave functions are eigenfunctions of *both* $\hat{H}_0$ and $\hat{L}_z$, and so they are also eigenfunctions of $\hat{H}$ in Eq. 6-136. In particular, we have

$$\hat{H}_0 R_{nl}(r) Y_l^m(\theta, \phi) = -\frac{\mu e^4}{8\varepsilon_0^2 h^2 n^2} R_{nl}(r) Y_l^m(\theta, \phi)$$

and

$$\hat{L}_z R_{nl}(r) Y_l^m(\theta, \phi) = m\hbar R_{nl}(r) Y_l^m(\theta, \phi)$$

Therefore, the energy levels of a hydrogen atom in a magnetic field are

$$E = -\frac{\mu e^4}{8\varepsilon_0^2 h^2 n^2} + \beta m B_z \qquad \begin{array}{l} n = 1, 2, 3, \ldots \\ m = 0, \pm 1, \pm 2, \ldots, \pm l \end{array} \tag{6-138}$$

where β, defined as

$$\beta = \frac{|e|\hbar}{2m_e} \tag{6-139}$$

is called a *Bohr magneton*. Numerically, a Bohr magneton is given by

$$\beta = 9.274 \times 10^{-24} \ \text{J} \cdot \text{T}^{-1} \qquad (6\text{-}140)$$

Equation 6-138 shows that a state with given values of n and l is split into $2l + 1$ levels by an external magnetic field. For example, Figure 6-16 shows the results for the $1s$ and $2p$ states of atomic hydrogen. The $1s$ state is not split $(2l + 1 = 1)$, but the $2p$ state is split into three levels $(2l + 1 = 3)$. Figure 6-16 also shows that the $2p$ to $1s$ transition in atomic hydrogen will be split into three distinct transitions instead of just one.

Let us calculate the magnitude of the splitting shown in Figure 6-16. A typical magnetic field strength B_z is about 10 tesla. If we denote the splitting by ΔE, then

$$
\begin{aligned}
\Delta E &= \beta B_z \\
&= (9.274 \times 10^{-24} \ \text{J} \cdot \text{T}^{-1})(10 \ \text{T}) \\
&= (9.274 \times 10^{-23} \ \text{J}) \qquad (6\text{-}141)
\end{aligned}
$$

The energy difference between the unperturbed $1s$ and $2p$ levels is

$$E_{2p} - E_{1s} = -\frac{\mu e^4}{8\varepsilon_0^2 h^2}\left(\frac{1}{4} - \frac{1}{1}\right) = 1.63 \times 10^{-18} \ \text{J}$$

which shows numerically that the splitting is very small compared to the difference between the $1s$ and $2p$ levels. Consequently the three distinct transitions shown in Figure 6-16 lie very close together (Problem 38), and we say

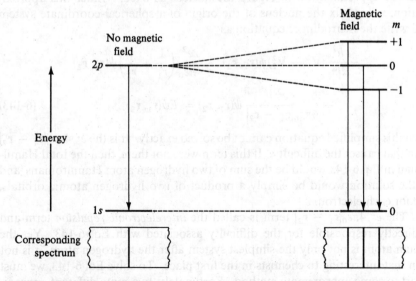

Figure 6-16. The splitting of the $2p$ state of the hydrogen atom in a magnetic field. The $2p$ state is split into three closely spaced levels. In a magnetic field, the $2p$ to $1s$ transition is split into three distinct transition frequencies.

that the 2p–1s transition that occurs in the absence of a magnetic field becomes a *triplet* in the presence of the field. The occurrence of such multiplets when atoms are placed in magnetic fields is known as the *Zeeman effect*.

6-12   *The Schrödinger Equation for the Helium Atom Cannot be Solved Exactly*

The next system to study is clearly the helium atom, whose Schrödinger equation is

$$
\left(-\frac{\hbar^2}{2M}\nabla^2 - \frac{\hbar^2}{2m_e}\nabla_1^2 - \frac{\hbar^2}{2m_e}\nabla_2^2 \right)\psi(\mathbf{R}, \mathbf{r}_1, \mathbf{r}_2)
$$

$$
+ \left(-\frac{2e^2}{4\pi\varepsilon_0|\mathbf{R}-\mathbf{r}_1|} - \frac{2e^2}{4\pi\varepsilon_0|\mathbf{R}-\mathbf{r}_2|} + \frac{e^2}{4\pi\varepsilon_0|\mathbf{r}_1-\mathbf{r}_2|} \right)\psi(\mathbf{R}, \mathbf{r}_1, \mathbf{r}_2) = E\psi(\mathbf{R}, \mathbf{r}_1, \mathbf{r}_2)
$$

$$(6\text{-}142)$$

In this equation, $\mathbf{R}$ is the position of the helium nucleus and $\mathbf{r}_1$ and $\mathbf{r}_2$ are the positions of the two electrons; M is the mass of the nucleus and m_e is the electronic mass; ∇^2 is the Laplacian operation with respect to the position of the nucleus and ∇_1^2 and ∇_2^2 are the Laplacian operators with respect to the electronic coordinates. Realize well that this is a three-body problem and *not* a two-body problem, and so the separation into center-of-mass and relative coordinates is more complicated than for hydrogen. However, because $M \gg m_e$, it is still an excellent approximation to regard the nucleus as fixed. Under this approximation, we can fix the nucleus at the origin of a spherical coordinate system and write the Schrödinger equation as

$$
-\frac{\hbar^2}{2m_e}(\nabla_1^2 + \nabla_2^2)\psi(\mathbf{r}_1, \mathbf{r}_2) - \frac{2e^2}{4\pi\varepsilon_0}\left(\frac{1}{r_1} + \frac{1}{r_2}\right)\psi(\mathbf{r}_1, \mathbf{r}_2)
$$

$$
+ \frac{e^2}{4\pi\varepsilon_0|\mathbf{r}_1 - \mathbf{r}_2|}\,\psi(\mathbf{r}_1, \mathbf{r}_2) = E\psi(\mathbf{r}_1, \mathbf{r}_2) \qquad (6\text{-}143)
$$

Even this simplified equation cannot be solved exactly. It is the $e^2/4\pi\varepsilon_0|\mathbf{r}_1 - \mathbf{r}_2|$ term that causes the difficulty. If this term were not there, then the total Hamiltonian in Eq. 6-143 would be the sum of two hydrogen atom Hamiltonians, and so the solution would be simply a product of two hydrogen atomic orbitals, one for each electron.

The $e^2/4\pi\varepsilon_0|\mathbf{r}_1 - \mathbf{r}_2|$ term is called the *interelectronic repulsion* term and is directly responsible for the difficulty associated with Eq. 6-143. Yet the helium atom is not only the simplest system after the hydrogen atom, it is not even that interesting to chemists in the first place. To solve Eq. 6-143, we must resort to some approximate method. Fortunately, two quite different approximate methods that can yield extremely good results have found wide use in quantum mechanics. These are called *perturbation theory* and the *variational method* and are presented in Chapter 7.

Summary

The problem of a particle confined to a rectangular parallelepiped is a simple extension of the problem of a particle in a one-dimensional box that was treated in Chapter 3. Because the Hamiltonian operator is separable, the three-dimensional problem essentially reduces to three separate one-dimensional problems. One new, interesting feature of the three-dimensional system is the occurrence of degenerate energies when the rectangular parallelepiped becomes a cube. Many three-dimensional quantum-mechanical systems are most conveniently described in terms of spherical coordinates. Two important examples are a rigid rotator and a hydrogen atom. A first step in formulating quantum-mechanical problems in spherical coordinates is to transform the Laplacian operator from Cartesian coordinates to spherical coordinates. The Schrödinger equation of a rigid rotator can be solved exactly. The eigenfunctions of a rigid rotator are spherical harmonics and the eigenvalues are given by $E = \hbar^2 l(l + 1)/2I$ with the quantum number l taking on the values $l = 0, 1, 2, \ldots$. The rigid rotator is a good approximation to a rotating diatomic or linear molecule and the predicted rotational spectrum, or microwave spectrum, is in good agreement with experimental observation. Microwave spectra yield values of bond lengths in molecules.

The Schrödinger equation of a hydrogen atom can be solved exactly. The hydrogen atomic wave functions are products of radial functions and spherical harmonics. The radial functions involve associated Laguerre polynomials. The complete wave functions are labeled by three quantum numbers. The principal quantum number n determines the energy of the electron in a hydrogen atom. The angular momentum quantum number l specifies the angular momentum of the electron. The magnetic quantum number m specifies a component of the angular momentum of the electron. Various sets of the three quantum numbers lead to the $1s, 2s, 2p_x, 3d_{z^2}$, etc., orbitals that are probably familiar from general chemistry (cf. Figures 6-12 and 6-13). It is interesting to note that the energy eigenvalues of the Schrödinger equation of a hydrogen atom are the same as those given by the Bohr model in Chapter 1.

Terms That You Should Know

degeneracy	microwave spectroscopy
separable Hamiltonian operator	rotational constant
Laplacian operator	Legendre's differential equation
plane polar coordinates	Legendre polynomials
spherical coordinates	associated Legendre functions
rigid rotator	spherical harmonics
selection rule	angular momentum operators

radial equation (of the hydrogen atom)   *d* orbital

associated Laguerre functions   virial theorem

principal quantum number   polar plot

angular momentum quantum number   Bohr magneton

magnetic quantum number   triplet

s orbital   Zeeman effect

p orbital   interelectronic repulsion term

Problems

1. Show that the normalization constant for a particle in a three-dimensional box is $(8/abc)^{1/2}$, where a, b, and c are the lengths of the sides of the box.

2. Show that the average momentum of a particle in a three-dimensional box is zero. Interpret this result.

3. Consider a particle confined to a cube of side a. Calculate the probability that the particle in its ground state is found in the subcube given by

$$\frac{a}{4} \le x \le \frac{3a}{4} \qquad \frac{a}{4} \le y \le \frac{3a}{4} \qquad \frac{a}{4} \le z \le \frac{3a}{4}$$

4. Consider a particle confined to the two-dimensional region defined by the rectangle

$$0 \le x \le a \qquad 0 \le y \le b$$

Show that the energy eigenfunctions of this system are given by

$$\psi_{n_x n_y}(x, y) = \left(\frac{4}{ab}\right)^{1/2} \sin \frac{n_x \pi x}{a} \sin \frac{n_y \pi y}{b} \qquad n_x, n_y = 1, 2, 3, \ldots$$

and that the allowed energies are given by

$$E_{n_x n_y} = \frac{h^2}{8m}\left(\frac{n_x^2}{a^2} + \frac{n_y^2}{b^2}\right)$$

Calculate the probability that the particle in its ground state is found within the region

$$\frac{a}{4} \le x \le \frac{3a}{4} \qquad \frac{b}{4} \le y \le \frac{3b}{4}$$

5. Using the results of Problem 4, calculate the probability that a particle is found in a region of a rectangle given in Figure 6-17(a). How do you think this result compares to the probability that the particle is found in the region described by Figure 6-17(b)?

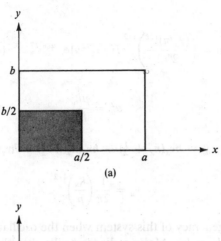

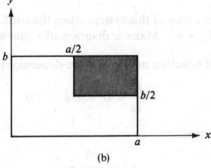

Figure 6-17. Regions of a rectangle that are referred to in Problem 5.

6. Sketch the first few energy eigenfunctions of a particle confined to a two-dimensional rectangular region given by $0 \le x \le a$ and $0 \le y \le b$ and compare these to those obtained for the normal modes of a vibrating rectangular membrane given in Figure 2-6.

7. Set up an energy-level diagram like Figure 6-2 for a particle confined to a square region whose sides are a.

8. Prove that if $\hat{H} = \hat{H}_1(Q_1) + \hat{H}_2(Q_2)$, where Q_1 and Q_2 are two independent sets of coordinates, then the eigenfunctions of $\hat{H}$ are $\psi(Q_1, Q_2) = \psi_1(Q_1)\psi_2(Q_2)$, where $\hat{H}_1\psi_1(Q_1) = E_1\psi_1(Q_1)$ and $\hat{H}_2\psi_2(Q_2) = E_2\psi_2(Q_2)$ and the eigenvalues of $\hat{H}$ are $E = E_1 + E_2$.

9. Show that the eigenfunctions and eigenvalues of a three-dimensional harmonic oscillator, whose potential energy is

$$U(x, y, z) = \tfrac{1}{2}k_x x^2 + \tfrac{1}{2}k_y y^2 + \tfrac{1}{2}k_z z^2$$

are

$$\psi_{n_x n_y n_z}(x, y, z) = \psi_{n_x}(x)\psi_{n_y}(y)\psi_{n_z}(z)$$

where

$$\psi_{n_u}(u) = \left(\frac{(\alpha_u/\pi)^{1/2}}{2^n n!}\right)^{1/2} H_n(\alpha_u^{1/2}u)e^{-\alpha_u u^2/2} \qquad (u = x, y, \text{ or } z)$$

and

$$\alpha_u^2 = \frac{\mu k_u}{\hbar^2}$$

and

$$E_{n_x n_y n_z} = h v_x(n_x + \tfrac{1}{2}) + h v_y(n_y + \tfrac{1}{2}) + h v_z(n_z + \tfrac{1}{2})$$

where

$$v_u = \frac{1}{2\pi}\left(\frac{k_u}{\mu}\right)^{1/2}$$

Discuss the degeneracy of this system when the oscillator is isotropic, that is, when $k_x = k_y = k_z$. Make a diagram like that shown in Figure 6-2.

10. The Schrödinger equation in two or three dimensions can be written as

$$-\frac{\hbar^2}{2\mu}\nabla^2\psi + U\psi = E\psi$$

where in two dimensions

$$\nabla^2 = \frac{\partial^2}{\partial x^2} + \frac{\partial^2}{\partial y^2} \tag{1}$$

$$U = U(x, y)$$

and in three dimensions

$$\nabla^2 = \frac{\partial^2}{\partial x^2} + \frac{\partial^2}{\partial y^2} + \frac{\partial^2}{\partial z^2}$$

$$U = U(x, y, z)$$

These equations are written in a form convenient only for a system that is best described by Cartesian coordinates. For systems with spherical symmetry or some other kind of symmetry, it is more convenient to express the Laplacian operator ∇^2 in terms of a coordinate system reflecting that symmetry. This problem is meant to illustrate the rather laborious conversion of ∇^2 from Cartesian coordinates to some other coordinates. In order to solve the Schrödinger equation for the case of a particle constrained to move on the circumference of a circle, it is necessary to express the two-dimensional Laplacian operator in polar coordinates, where in the particular case of a particle on a circle the radial coordinate r is fixed. Thus, we wish to transform the operator, Eq. 1,

$$\nabla^2 = \frac{\partial^2}{\partial x^2} + \frac{\partial^2}{\partial y^2}$$

into polar coordinates r and θ where

$$x = r \cos \theta \qquad y = r \sin \theta \tag{2}$$

To do this we must let the operator ∇^2 act upon an arbitrary function, say f, and use the fact that (this is called the *chain rule* of partial differentiation)

$$\left(\frac{\partial f}{\partial x}\right)_y = \left(\frac{\partial f}{\partial r}\right)_\theta \left(\frac{\partial r}{\partial x}\right)_y + \left(\frac{\partial f}{\partial \theta}\right)_r \left(\frac{\partial \theta}{\partial x}\right)_y \tag{3}$$

and

$$\left(\frac{\partial f}{\partial y}\right)_x = \left(\frac{\partial f}{\partial r}\right)_\theta \left(\frac{\partial r}{\partial y}\right)_x + \left(\frac{\partial f}{\partial \theta}\right)_r \left(\frac{\partial \theta}{\partial y}\right)_x \tag{4}$$

(We have included the first terms in Eq. 3 and 4 for completeness although they vanish when f is a function of only θ as it must be in this case because r is fixed.)

Now because

$$r = (x^2 + y^2)^{1/2} \quad \text{and} \quad \theta = \tan^{-1}\left(\frac{y}{x}\right)$$

show that

$$\left(\frac{\partial r}{\partial x}\right)_y = \cos \theta \qquad \left(\frac{\partial r}{\partial y}\right)_x = \sin \theta$$

$$\left(\frac{\partial \theta}{\partial x}\right)_y = -\frac{\sin \theta}{r} \qquad \left(\frac{\partial \theta}{\partial y}\right)_x = \frac{\cos \theta}{r} \tag{5}$$

and that

$$\left(\frac{\partial f}{\partial x}\right)_y = -\frac{\sin \theta}{r}\left(\frac{\partial f}{\partial \theta}\right)_r, \qquad \left(\frac{\partial f}{\partial y}\right)_x = \frac{\cos \theta}{r}\left(\frac{\partial f}{\partial \theta}\right)_r, \qquad [f(\theta) \text{ only}] \tag{6}$$

Now apply Eqs. 3 and 4 again to find

$$\frac{\partial^2 f}{\partial x^2} = \frac{\partial}{\partial x}\left(\frac{\partial f}{\partial x}\right)_y = \left[\frac{\partial}{\partial r}\left(\frac{\partial f}{\partial x}\right)_y\right]_\theta \left(\frac{\partial r}{\partial x}\right)_y + \left[\frac{\partial}{\partial \theta}\left(\frac{\partial f}{\partial x}\right)_y\right]_r \left(\frac{\partial \theta}{\partial x}\right)_y$$

$$= \left[\frac{\sin \theta}{r^2}\left(\frac{\partial f}{\partial \theta}\right)_r\right]\cos \theta + \left[-\frac{\cos \theta}{r}\left(\frac{\partial f}{\partial \theta}\right)_r - \frac{\sin \theta}{r}\left(\frac{\partial^2 f}{\partial \theta^2}\right)_r\right]\left(-\frac{\sin \theta}{r}\right)$$

$$= \frac{2 \sin \theta \cos \theta}{r^2}\left(\frac{\partial f}{\partial \theta}\right)_r + \frac{\sin^2 \theta}{r^2}\left(\frac{\partial^2 f}{\partial \theta^2}\right)_r \qquad [f(\theta) \text{ only}] \tag{7}$$

Similarly, show that

$$\frac{\partial^2 f}{\partial y^2} = \frac{\partial}{\partial y}\left(\frac{\partial f}{\partial y}\right)_x = \left[\frac{\partial}{\partial r}\left(\frac{\partial f}{\partial y}\right)_x\right]_\theta \left(\frac{\partial r}{\partial y}\right)_x + \left[\frac{\partial}{\partial \theta}\left(\frac{\partial f}{\partial y}\right)_x\right]_r \left(\frac{\partial \theta}{\partial y}\right)_x$$

$$= \left[-\frac{\cos \theta}{r^2}\left(\frac{\partial f}{\partial \theta}\right)_r\right]\sin \theta + \left[-\frac{\sin \theta}{r}\left(\frac{\partial f}{\partial \theta}\right)_r + \frac{\cos \theta}{r}\left(\frac{\partial^2 f}{\partial \theta^2}\right)_r\right]\left(\frac{\cos \theta}{r}\right)$$

$$= -\frac{2 \sin \theta \cos \theta}{r^2}\left(\frac{\partial f}{\partial \theta}\right)_r + \frac{\cos^2 \theta}{r^2}\left(\frac{\partial^2 f}{\partial \theta^2}\right)_r \qquad [f(\theta) \text{ only}] \tag{8}$$

Now add Eqs. 7 and 8 to obtain

$$\nabla^2 f = \frac{\partial^2 f}{\partial x^2} + \frac{\partial^2 f}{\partial y^2} = \frac{1}{r^2}\left(\frac{\partial^2 f}{\partial \theta^2}\right) \qquad \text{(constant } r\text{)}$$

or, as an operator,

$$\nabla^2 = \frac{1}{r^2}\frac{\partial^2}{\partial \theta^2} \qquad \text{(constant } r\text{)} \qquad (9)$$

Thus the Schrödinger equation in plane polar coordinates is

$$-\frac{\hbar^2}{2\mu r^2}\frac{\partial^2 \psi(\theta)}{\partial \theta^2} = E\psi(\theta) \qquad (10)$$

where r is the (fixed) circumference of the circle. The boundary condition in this case is that $\psi(\theta) = \psi(\theta + 2\pi)$. Show that the solutions to Eq. 10 can be written as

$$\psi(\theta) = Ae^{ik\theta} \qquad (11)$$

where $k = (2\mu r^2 E/\hbar^2)^{1/2}$. Show that the continuity condition on $\psi(\theta)$ requires that

$$k = m \qquad m = 0, \pm 1, \pm 2, \ldots$$

and that this condition leads to

$$E = \frac{m^2\hbar^2}{2\mu r^2} = \frac{m^2\hbar^2}{2I} \qquad m = 0, \pm 1, \pm 2, \ldots$$

where I is the moment of inertia.

The positive and negative integers correspond to rotation in opposite directions but with equal energies, and therefore all the levels except $m = 0$ (no rotation) are doubly degenerate. Lastly, show that the normalization constant in Eq. 11 is $(2\pi)^{-1/2}$ so that

$$\psi(\theta) = (2\pi)^{-1/2}e^{im\theta} \qquad m = 0, \pm 1, \pm 2, \ldots$$

Discuss how this result can be used as a free-electron model for the π electrons of benzene.

11. Generalize Problem 10 to the case of a particle moving in a plane under the influence of a central force; in other words, convert

$$\nabla^2 = \frac{\partial^2}{\partial x^2} + \frac{\partial^2}{\partial y^2}$$

to plane polar coordinates, this time without assuming that r is a constant. Use the method of separation of variables to separate the equation for this problem. Solve the angular equation.

12. Show that rotational transitions of a diatomic molecule occur in the micro-wave region or the far infrared region of the spectrum.

13. In the far infrared spectrum of $H^{79}Br$, there is a series of lines separated by 16.72 cm^{-1}. Calculate the moment of inertia and internuclear separation in $H^{79}Br$.

14. The $l = 0$ to $l = 1$ transition for carbon monoxide ($^{12}C^{16}O$) occurs at 1.153×10^5 MHz. Calculate the bond length in carbon monoxide.

15. In terms of the variable θ, Legendre's equation is

$$\sin \theta \frac{d}{d\theta} \left(\sin \theta \frac{d\Theta}{d\theta} \right) + (\beta \sin^2 \theta - m^2)\Theta = 0$$

Let $x = \cos \theta$ and $P(x) = \Theta(\theta)$ and show that

$$(1 - x^2)\frac{d^2P}{dx^2} - 2x\frac{dP}{dx} + \left(\beta - \frac{m^2}{1 - x^2} \right)P = 0$$

16. Show that the Legendre polynomials given in Table 6-1 satisfy Eq. 6-69 with $m = 0$.

17. Show that the orthogonality integral for the Legendre polynomials, Eq. 6-70, is equivalent to

$$\int_0^\pi P_l(\cos \theta)P_n(\cos \theta) \sin \theta \, d\theta = 0 \qquad l \neq n$$

18. Show that the Legendre polynomials satisfy the orthogonality and normalization conditions given by Eqs. 6-70 and 6-71.

19. Use Eq. 6-72 to generate the associated Legendre functions in Table 6-2.

20. Show that the first few associated Legendre functions given in Table 6-2 are solutions to Eq. 6-69 and that they satisfy the orthonormality condition, Eq. 6-74.

21. There are a number of recursion formulas for the associated Legendre functions. One that we shall have occasion to use in Section 10-14 is

$$(2l + 1)xP_l^{|m|}(x) = (l - |m| + 1)P_{l+1}^{|m|}(x) + (l + |m|)P_{l-1}^{|m|}(x)$$

Show that the first few associated Legendre functions in Table 6-2 satisfy this recursion relation.

22. Show that the first few spherical harmonics in Table 6-3 satisfy the ortho-normality condition, Eq. 6-77.

23. Using explicit expressions for $Y_l^m(\theta, \phi)$, show that

$$|Y_1^1(\theta, \phi)|^2 + |Y_1^0(\theta, \phi)|^2 + |Y_1^{-1}(\theta, \phi)|^2 = \text{constant}$$

This is a special case of the general theorem

$$\sum_{m=-l}^{+l} |Y_l^m(\theta, \phi)|^2 = \text{constant}$$

known as Unsöld's theorem.

24. In Cartesian coordinates

$$\hat{L}_z = -i\hbar\left(x\frac{\partial}{\partial y} - y\frac{\partial}{\partial x}\right)$$

Convert this to spherical coordinates, showing that

$$\hat{L}_z = -i\hbar\frac{\partial}{\partial \phi}$$

25. Convert $\hat{L}_x$ and $\hat{L}_y$ from Cartesian coordinates to spherical coordinates.

26. Prove that $\hat{L}^2$ commutes with $\hat{L}_x$, $\hat{L}_y$, and $\hat{L}_z$ but that

$$[\hat{L}_x, \hat{L}_y] = i\hbar\hat{L}_z \qquad [\hat{L}_y, \hat{L}_z] = i\hbar\hat{L}_x \qquad [\hat{L}_z, \hat{L}_x] = i\hbar\hat{L}_y$$

Hint: Use Cartesian coordinates.

27. It is a somewhat advanced exercise to prove generally that $\langle L_x \rangle = \langle L_y \rangle = 0$, but prove that they are zero at least for the first few l, m states by using the spherical harmonics given in Table 6-3.

28. Referring to Table 6-5, show that the first few hydrogen atomic wave functions are orthonormal.

29. Calculate the probability that a hydrogen $1s$ electron will be found within a distance $2a_0$ from the nucleus.

30. Calculate the radius of the sphere that encloses a 50% probability of finding a hydrogen $1s$ electron. Repeat the calculation for a 90% probability.

31. Many problems involving the calculation of average values for the hydrogen atom require doing integrals of the form

$$I_n = \int_0^\infty r^n e^{-\beta r}\, dr$$

This integral can be evaluated readily by starting with the elementary integral

$$I(\beta) = \int_0^\infty e^{-\beta r}\, dr = \frac{1}{\beta}$$

Show that the derivatives of $I(\beta)$ are

$$\frac{dI}{d\beta} = -\int_0^\infty re^{-\beta r}\, dr$$

$$\frac{d^2 I}{d\beta^2} = \int_0^\infty r^2 e^{-r\beta}\, dr$$

and so on. Using the fact that $I(\beta) = 1/\beta$, show that the values of these two integrals are $-1/\beta^2$ and $2/\beta^3$, respectively. Show that, in general,

$$\frac{d^n I}{d\beta^n} = (-1)^n \int_0^\infty r^n e^{-\beta r}\, dr$$

$$= (-1)^n \frac{n!}{\beta^{n+1}}$$

and that

$$I_n = \frac{n!}{\beta^{n+1}}$$

32. Prove that the average value of r in the $1s$ and $2s$ states is $\frac{3}{2}a_0$ and $6a_0$, respectively.

33. Prove that $\langle U \rangle = 2\langle E \rangle$ and, consequently, that $\langle \hat{K} \rangle = -\langle E \rangle$, for a $2s$ electron.

34. By evaluating the appropriate integrals, compute $\langle r \rangle$ in the $2s$, the $2p$, and the $3s$ states of the hydrogen atom; compare your results to the general formula

$$\langle r_{nl} \rangle = \frac{a_0}{2}[3n^2 - l(l+1)]$$

35. Use polar graph paper to plot the function $f(\theta) = \sin^2\theta$. Also plot $f(\theta) = \frac{1}{2}(5\cos^3\theta - 3\cos\theta)$.

36. Verify the contour lines in Figure 6-13(a).

37. Show that the first few hydrogen atomic orbitals in Table 6-6 are orthonormal.

38. Calculate the frequencies of the three $2p$ to $1s$ transitions for atomic hydrogen in an external magnetic field with a strength of 10 tesla.

39. Set up the Hamiltonian operator for the system of an electron interacting with a nucleus of atomic number Z. The simplest such system is singly ionized helium, where $Z = 2$. We shall call this a hydrogenlike system. Observe that the only difference between this Hamiltonian and the hydrogen atom Hamiltonian is the correspondence that e^2 for the hydrogen atom becomes Ze^2 for the hydrogenlike ion. Consequently, show that the energy becomes (cf. Eq. 6-99)

$$E_n = -\frac{\mu Z^2 e^4}{8\varepsilon_0^2 h^2 n^2} \qquad n = 1, 2, \ldots$$

Furthermore, now show that the solutions to the radial equation, Eq. 6-102, are

$$R_{nl}(r) = -\left\{\frac{(n-l-1)!}{2n[(n+l)!]^3}\right\}^{1/2}\left(\frac{2Z}{na_0}\right)^{l+3/2} r^l e^{-Zr/na_0} L_{n+l}^{2l+1}\left(\frac{2Zr}{na_0}\right)$$

Show that the 1s orbital for this system is

$$\psi_{1s} = \frac{1}{\sqrt{\pi}} \left(\frac{Z}{a_0} \right)^{3/2} e^{-Zr/a_0}$$

and show that it is normalized. Show that

$$\langle r \rangle = \frac{3a_0}{2Z}$$

and that

$$r_{mp} = \frac{a_0}{Z}$$

Lastly, calculate the ionization energy of a hydrogen atom and a singly ionized helium atom. Express your answer in electron volts.

40. In this problem we shall prove the quantum-mechanical virial theorem. Start with

$$\hat{H}\psi = E\psi$$

where

$$\hat{H} = -\frac{\hbar^2}{2m} \nabla^2 + U(x, y, z)$$

Using the fact that $\hat{H}$ is a Hermitian operator, show that

$$\int \psi^* [\hat{H}, \hat{A}] \psi \, d\tau = 0 \tag{1}$$

where $\hat{A}$ is any linear operator. Choose $\hat{A}$ to be

$$\hat{A} = -i\hbar \left(x \frac{\partial}{\partial x} + y \frac{\partial}{\partial y} + z \frac{\partial}{\partial z} \right) \tag{2}$$

and show that

$$[\hat{H}, \hat{A}] = i\hbar \left(x \frac{\partial U}{\partial x} + y \frac{\partial U}{\partial y} + z \frac{\partial U}{\partial z} \right) - \frac{i\hbar}{m} (\hat{P}_x^2 + \hat{P}_y^2 + \hat{P}_z^2)$$

$$= i\hbar \left(x \frac{\partial U}{\partial x} + y \frac{\partial U}{\partial y} + z \frac{\partial U}{\partial z} \right) - 2i\hbar \hat{K} \tag{3}$$

where $\hat{K}$ is the kinetic energy operator. Now use Eq. 1 and show that

$$\left\langle x \frac{\partial U}{\partial x} + y \frac{\partial U}{\partial y} + z \frac{\partial U}{\partial z} \right\rangle = 2\langle K \rangle \tag{4}$$

where the angular brackets denote the average

$$\langle B \rangle \equiv \int \psi^* \hat{B} \psi \, d\tau$$

Equation 4 is called the *quantum-mechanical virial theorem.*

Now show that if $U(x, y, z)$ is a Coulombic potential

$$U(x, y, z) = \frac{Ze^2}{4\pi\varepsilon_0(x^2 + y^2 + z^2)^{1/2}}$$

then

$$\langle U \rangle = -2\langle K \rangle = 2\langle E \rangle \tag{5}$$

where

$$\langle E \rangle = \langle K \rangle + \langle U \rangle$$

In Problem 33 we proved that this result is valid for the special case for a $2s$ electron. Although we have proved Eq. 5 only for the case of one electron in the field of one nucleus, Eq. 5 is valid for many-electron atoms and molecules. The proof is a straightforward extension of the proof developed in this problem.

41. Use the virial theorem (Problem 40) to prove that $\langle K \rangle = \langle U \rangle = E/2$ for a harmonic oscillator (cf. Problem 4 on p. 185 and Eqs. 5-58 and 5-59

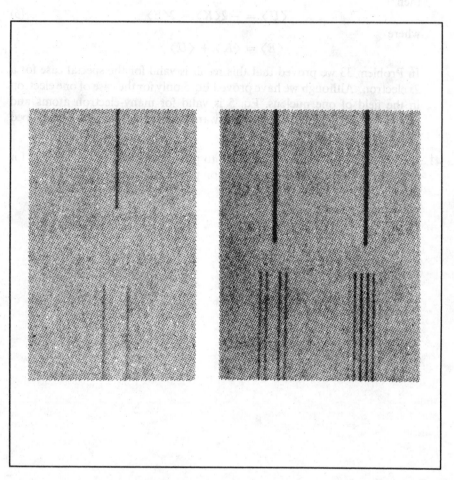

Spectral lines are split into several separate lines by an applied external magnetic field. This effect was first observed by Pieter Zeeman in 1896 and is called the Zeeman effect. The frequencies of the spectral lines in the Zeeman effect can be calculated using perturbation theory.

7

Approximate
Methods

WE have stated in Chapter 6 that it is
not possible to solve the Schrödinger equation exactly for any atom or molecule
more complicated than the hydrogen atom. It would appear at first thought
that this would certainly deprive quantum mechanics of any interest to chemists,
but fortunately there are approximate methods that can be used to solve the
Schrödinger equation to almost any accuracy desired. In this chapter we
shall discuss the two most widely used of these methods, perturbation theory
and the variational method. We shall develop the basic equations of perturbation theory and the variational method and then apply them to a variety of
problems.

7-1 Perturbation Theory Expresses the Solution to One Problem in Terms of Another Problem That Has Been Solved Previously

Suppose we wish to solve the Schrödinger equation

$$\hat{H}\psi = E\psi$$

for some particular system, but we are unable to find an exact solution like
we have done for the harmonic oscillator, the rigid rotator, and the hydrogen
atom in previous chapters. It turns out that most systems cannot be solved
exactly; two specific examples are a helium atom and an anharmonic oscillator.

255

We saw at the end of Chapter 6 that the Hamiltonian operator for a helium atom is

$$\hat{H} = -\frac{\hbar^2}{2m}(\nabla_1^2 + \nabla_2^2) - \frac{2e^2}{4\pi\varepsilon_0}\left(\frac{1}{r_1} + \frac{1}{r_2}\right) + \frac{e^2}{4\pi\varepsilon_0}\frac{1}{r_{12}} \tag{7-1}$$

Equation 7-1 can be written in the form

$$\hat{H} = \hat{H}_H(1) + \hat{H}_H(2) + \frac{e^2}{4\pi\varepsilon_0}\frac{1}{r_{12}} \tag{7-2}$$

where

$$\hat{H}_H(j) = -\frac{\hbar^2}{2m}\nabla_j^2 - \frac{2e^2}{4\pi\varepsilon_0}\frac{1}{r_j} \qquad j = 1 \text{ and } 2 \tag{7-3}$$

is the Hamiltonian operator for a single electron around a helium nucleus. Thus, $\hat{H}_H(1)$ and $\hat{H}_H(2)$ satisfy the equation

$$\hat{H}_H(j)\psi_H(r_j, \theta_j, \phi_j) = E_j\psi_H(r_j, \theta_j, \phi_j) \qquad j = 1 \text{ and } 2 \tag{7-4}$$

where $\psi_H(r_j, \theta_j, \phi_j)$ is a hydrogenlike wave function with $Z = 2$ (Table 6-6) and where the E_j are given by (Problem 6-39)

$$E_j = -\frac{Z^2\mu e^4}{8\varepsilon_0^2 h^2 n_j^2} \qquad j = 1 \text{ and } 2 \tag{7-5}$$

with $Z = 2$. Notice that if it were not for the interelectronic repulsion term $e^2/4\pi\varepsilon_0 r_{12}$ in Eq. 7-2, the Hamiltonian operator for a helium atom would be separable and the helium atomic wave functions would be products of hydrogen-like atomic wave functions.

Another example of a problem that could be solved readily if it were not for additional terms in the Hamiltonian is an anharmonic oscillator. Recall that the harmonic-oscillator potential arises naturally as the first term in a Taylor expansion of a general potential about the equilibrium nuclear separation. Consider an anharmonic oscillator whose potential energy is given by

$$U(x) = \tfrac{1}{2}kx^2 + \tfrac{1}{6}\gamma x^3 + \tfrac{1}{24}bx^4 \tag{7-6}$$

The Hamiltonian operator is

$$\hat{H} = -\frac{\hbar^2}{2\mu}\frac{d^2}{dx^2} + \frac{1}{2}kx^2 + \frac{1}{6}\gamma x^3 + \frac{1}{24}bx^4 \tag{7-7}$$

If $\gamma = b = 0$, Eq. 7-7 is the Hamiltonian operator for a harmonic oscillator, which was discussed in detail in Chapter 5.

These two examples, with their Hamiltonian operators given by Eqs. 7-1 and 7-7, introduce us to the basic idea behind perturbation theory. In both of these cases, the total Hamiltonian consists of two parts, one for which the Schrödinger equation can be solved exactly and an additional term, whose presence prevents an exact solution. We call the first term the *unperturbed Hamiltonian* and the additional term the *perturbation*. We shall denote the unperturbed Hamiltonian by $\hat{H}^{(0)}$ and the perturbation by $\hat{H}^{(1)}$ and write

$$\hat{H} = \hat{H}^{(0)} + \hat{H}^{(1)} \tag{7-8}$$

Associated with $\hat{H}^{(0)}$ is a Schrödinger equation, which we know how to solve, and so we have

$$\hat{H}^{(0)}\psi^{(0)} = E^{(0)}\psi^{(0)} \tag{7-9}$$

where $\psi^{(0)}$ and $E^{(0)}$ are the known eigenfunctions and eigenvalues of $\hat{H}^{(0)}$. Equation 7-9 specifies the unperturbed system. In the case of the helium atom we have

$$\hat{H}^{(0)} = \hat{H}_H(1) + \hat{H}_H(2)$$

$$\psi^{(0)} = \psi_H(r_1, \theta_1, \phi_1)\psi_H(r_2, \theta_2, \phi_2) \tag{7-10}$$

$$E^{(0)} = -\frac{4\mu e^4}{8\varepsilon_0^2 h^2 n_1^2} - \frac{4\mu e^4}{8\varepsilon_0^2 h^2 n_2^2}$$

and

$$\hat{H}^{(1)} = \frac{e^2}{4\pi\varepsilon_0 r_{12}}$$

In the case of an anharmonic oscillator, we have

$$\hat{H}^{(0)} = -\frac{\hbar^2}{2\mu}\frac{d^2}{dx^2} + \frac{1}{2}kx^2$$

$$\psi^{(0)} = \frac{(\alpha/\pi)^{1/4}}{(2^n n!)^{1/2}} e^{-\alpha x^2/2} H_n(\alpha^{1/2}x) \tag{7-11}$$

$$E^{(0)} = \left(n + \frac{1}{2}\right)h\nu$$

and

$$\hat{H}^{(1)} = \frac{\gamma}{6}x^3 + \frac{b}{24}x^4$$

You might expect intuitively that if the perturbation terms are not large in some sense, then the solution to the complete, perturbed problem should be close to the solution to the unperturbed problem. A simple example of this is if the anharmonicity terms $\gamma x^3/6$ and $bx^4/24$ are small. Thus, we are expecting that the unperturbed system is only perturbed and not altered drastically by the additional term.

7-2 *Perturbation Theory Consists of a Set of Successive Corrections to an Unperturbed Problem*

In this section, we shall derive the equations for perturbation theory. We shall derive them only in the lowest-level approximation, leaving the more complete derivation to Problem 24. The problem that we wish to solve is

$$\hat{H}\psi = E\psi \tag{7-12}$$

where

$$\hat{H} = \hat{H}^{(0)} + \hat{H}^{(1)} \tag{7-13}$$

and where the problem

$$\hat{H}^{(0)}\psi^{(0)} = E^{(0)}\psi^{(0)} \tag{7-14}$$

has been solved exactly previously, so that $\psi^{(0)}$ and $E^{(0)}$ are known. Assuming now that the effect of $\hat{H}^{(1)}$ is small, we write

$$\psi = \psi^{(0)} + \Delta\psi$$

and

$$E = E^{(0)} + \Delta E \tag{7-15}$$

where we assume that $\Delta\psi$ and ΔE are small. We substitute Eqs. 7-15 into Eq. 7-12 and obtain

$$\hat{H}^{(0)}\psi^{(0)} + \hat{H}^{(1)}\psi^{(0)} + \hat{H}^{(0)}\Delta\psi + \hat{H}^{(1)}\Delta\psi = E^{(0)}\psi^{(0)} + \Delta E\,\psi^{(0)} + E^{(0)}\Delta\psi + \Delta E\,\Delta\psi \tag{7-16}$$

The first terms on each side of Eq. 7-16 cancel because of Eq. 7-14. In addition, we shall neglect the last terms on each side because they represent the product of two small terms. Thus Eq. 7-16 becomes

$$\hat{H}^{(0)}\Delta\psi + \hat{H}^{(1)}\psi^{(0)} = E^{(0)}\Delta\psi + \Delta E\,\psi^{(0)} \tag{7-17}$$

Realize that $\Delta\psi$ and ΔE are the unknown quantities in this equation.

Note that all the terms in Eq. 7-17 are of the same order, in the sense that each is the product of an unperturbed term and a small term. We say that this equation is *first order* in the perturbation and that what we are doing here is *first-order perturbation theory*. The two terms that we have neglected in Eq. 7-16 are second-order terms and lead to second-order (and higher) corrections as shown in Problem 24.

Equation 7-17 can be simplified considerably by multiplying both sides from the left by $\psi^{(0)*}$ and integrating over all space. By doing this and rearranging slightly, we find

$$\int \psi^{(0)*}[\hat{H}^{(0)} - E^{(0)}]\Delta\psi\,d\tau + \int \psi^{(0)*}\hat{H}^{(1)}\psi^{(0)}\,d\tau = \Delta E \int \psi^{(0)*}\psi^{(0)}\,d\tau \tag{7-18}$$

The integral in the last term in Eq. 7-18 is unity because $\psi^{(0)}$ is taken to be normalized. More importantly, however, the first term on the left-hand side of Eq. 7-18 is zero. To see this, remember that $\hat{H}^{(0)} - E^{(0)}$ is Hermitian, and so we have that

$$\int \psi^{(0)*}[\hat{H}^{(0)} - E^{(0)}]\Delta\psi\,d\tau = \int \{[\hat{H}^{(0)} - E^{(0)}]\psi^{(0)}\}^* \,\Delta\psi\,d\tau \tag{7-19}$$

But according to Eq. 7-14, the integrand here vanishes. Thus, Eq. 7-18 becomes

$$\Delta E = \int \psi^{(0)*}\hat{H}^{(1)}\psi^{(0)}\,d\tau \tag{7-20}$$

Equation 7-20 is called the *first-order correction* to $E^{(0)}$. To first order, the energy is

$$E = E^{(0)} + \int \psi^{(0)*} \hat{H}^{(1)} \psi^{(0)} \, d\tau + \text{higher-order terms} \qquad (7\text{-}21)$$

In order to find a corresponding correction to $\psi^{(0)}$, we must refer to the more general derivation given in Problem 24. We shall need only Eq. 7-21 for the problems we shall discuss in this book.

Perhaps the simplest application of perturbation theory is to solve the problem of a particle in a one-dimensional box with a slanted bottom, as shown in Figure 7-1. In attempting to solve a problem by perturbation theory, the first and most important step is to formulate the problem into an unperturbed part and a perturbation or, in other words, to recognize what the unperturbed problem might be. In this case, the unperturbed problem is a particle in a box and so

$$\hat{H}^{(1)} = \frac{V}{a} x \qquad (7\text{-}22)$$

where V is a constant,

$$\psi^{(0)} = \left(\frac{2}{a}\right)^{1/2} \sin \frac{n\pi x}{a} \qquad (7\text{-}23)$$

and

$$E^{(0)} = \frac{n^2 h^2}{8ma^2} \qquad (7\text{-}24)$$

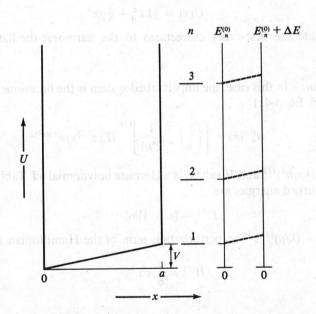

Figure 7-1. The potential well of a particle in a box with a slanted bottom. The unperturbed energies with their first-order corrections are shown. The perturbation potential is Vx/a, which represents the slanted bottom of the box shown above.

According to Eq. 7-20, the first-order correction to $E^{(0)}$ due to the perturbation given by Eq. 7-22 is

$$\Delta E = \int_0^a \psi^{(0)*} \left(\frac{x}{a} V \right) \psi^{(0)} dx$$

$$= \frac{2V}{a^2} \int_0^a x \sin^2 \frac{n\pi x}{a} dx$$

This integral occurs in Section 3-9 and is equal to $a^2/4$. Therefore, we find that

$$\Delta E = \frac{V}{2} \tag{7-25}$$

The energy levels are given by Eq. 7-21:

$$E = \frac{n^2 h^2}{8ma^2} + \frac{V}{2} + O(V^2) \qquad n = 1, 2, 3, \ldots \tag{7-26}$$

where the term $O(V^2)$ emphasizes that terms of order V^2 and higher have been dropped. Thus, we see in this case that each of the unperturbed energy levels is shifted by $V/2$ (cf. Figure 7-1).

EXAMPLE 7-1

Consider an anharmonic oscillator whose potential is

$$U(x) = \tfrac{1}{2}kx^2 + \tfrac{1}{6}\gamma x^3$$

Calculate the first-order corrections to the harmonic-oscillator energy levels.

Solution: In this case, the unperturbed system is the harmonic oscillator, with (cf. Eq. 5-41)

$$\psi_n^{(0)}(x) = \left[\left(\frac{\alpha}{\pi} \right)^{1/2} \frac{1}{2^n n!} \right]^{1/2} H_n(\alpha^{1/2} x) e^{-\alpha x^2/2}$$

where $\alpha = (k\mu/\hbar^2)^{1/2}$ and $H_n(\alpha^{1/2} x)$ is a Hermite polynomial (cf. Table 5-2). The unperturbed energies are

$$E^{(0)} = (n + \tfrac{1}{2})h\nu$$

where $2\pi\nu = (k/\mu)^{1/2}$. The perturbation term of the Hamiltonian is

$$\hat{H}^{(1)} = \frac{\gamma}{6} x^3$$

and so

$$\Delta E = \left[\left(\frac{\alpha}{\pi} \right)^{1/2} \frac{1}{2^n n!} \right] \frac{\gamma}{6} \int_{-\infty}^{\infty} H_n(\alpha^{1/2} x) x^3 H_n(\alpha^{1/2} x) e^{-\alpha x^2} dx$$

This integral can be evaluated for any value of n by remembering that the Hermite polynomials are either even or odd functions. Consequently, the integrand here is overall an odd function and so the integral itself vanishes, leaving us with

$$\Delta E = 0$$

and

$$E = (n + \tfrac{1}{2})h\nu + \text{higher-order terms}$$

Thus in this case there is no change in the energy up to first order. Note that if we had included a quartic term as well as the cubic term in the potential, we would have found that $\Delta E \neq 0$ (Problem 2).

EXAMPLE 7-2
Calculate the first-order correction to the ground-state energy of an anharmonic oscillator whose potential energy is

$$U(x) = \tfrac{1}{2}kx^2 + \tfrac{1}{6}\gamma x^3 + \tfrac{1}{24}bx^4$$

Solution: In this case, the perturbation is

$$\hat{H}^{(1)} = \tfrac{1}{6}\gamma x^3 + \tfrac{1}{24}bx^4$$

The ground-state wave function of a harmonic oscillator is

$$\psi_0(x) = \left(\frac{\alpha}{\pi}\right)^{1/4} e^{-\alpha x^2/2}$$

where $\alpha = (k\mu/\hbar^2)^{1/2}$. The first-order correction to the ground-state energy is given by

$$\Delta E = \left(\frac{\alpha}{\pi}\right)^{1/2} \int_{-\infty}^{\infty} (\tfrac{1}{6}\gamma x^3 + \tfrac{1}{24}bx^4)e^{-\alpha x^2}\, dx$$

The integral involving $\gamma x^3/6$ here vanishes because the integrand is odd. The remaining integral is

$$\Delta E = \frac{b}{12}\left(\frac{\alpha}{\pi}\right)^{1/2} \int_0^{\infty} x^4 e^{-\alpha x^2}\, dx$$

The integral here can be found in tables and is equal to $3\pi^{1/2}/8\alpha^{5/2}$, and so

$$\Delta E = \frac{b}{32\alpha^2}$$

$$= \frac{\hbar^2 b}{32k\mu}$$

The total ground-state energy is

$$E = \frac{h\nu}{2} + \frac{\hbar^2 b}{32k\mu} + \text{higher-order terms}$$

We shall apply perturbation theory to a helium atom in Chapter 8.

7-3   *The Variational Method Provides an Upper Bound to the Ground-State Energy of a System*

The second approximation method that we shall discuss is more useful than perturbation theory because it does not require that there be a similar problem that has been solved previously. This second approximation method is the *variational method*. We shall derive the variational method first and then illustrate it with a number of examples.

Consider the ground state of some particular arbitrary system. The ground-state wave function ψ_0 and energy E_0 satisfy the Schrödinger equation

$$\hat{H}\psi_0 = E_0\psi_0 \tag{7-27}$$

Multiply Eq. 7-27 from the left by ψ_0^* and integrate over all space to obtain

$$E_0 = \frac{\int \psi_0^* \hat{H}\psi_0 \, d\tau}{\int \psi_0^* \psi_0 \, d\tau} \tag{7-28}$$

where $d\tau$ represents the appropriate volume element. We have not set the denominator equal to unity in Eq. 7-28 in order to allow for the possibility that ψ_0 is not normalized beforehand. There is a beautiful theorem that says that if we substitute any other function for ψ_0 in Eq. 7-28 and calculate

$$E_\phi = \frac{\int \phi^* \hat{H}\phi \, d\tau}{\int \phi^* \phi \, d\tau} \tag{7-29}$$

then E_ϕ calculated through Eq. 7-29 will be greater than the ground-state energy E_0. In an equation, we have the *variational principle*

$$E_\phi \geq E_0 \tag{7-30}$$

The variational principle says that we can calculate an upper bound on E_0 by using any trial function we wish. The closer ϕ is to ψ_0 in some sense, the closer E_ϕ will be to E_0 (see Problem 9 for a more quantitative discussion of this point). We can choose ϕ such that it depends on some arbitrary parameters α, $\beta, \gamma, \ldots$, called *variational parameters*. The energy E_ϕ also will depend on these variational parameters and Eq. 7-30 will read

$$E_\phi(\alpha, \beta, \gamma, \ldots) \geq E_0 \tag{7-31}$$

Now we can minimize E_ϕ with respect to each of the variational parameters and thus approach the exact ground-state energy E_0.

As a specific example, consider the ground state of the hydrogen atom. Although we know from Chapter 6 that we can solve this problem exactly, let us assume that we cannot and use the variational method. We shall compare our variational result to the exact result. Because $l = 0$ in the ground state, the Hamiltonian operator is (cf. Eq. 6-98)

$$\hat{H} = -\frac{\hbar^2}{2\mu r^2}\frac{d}{dr}\left(r^2\frac{d}{dr}\right) - \frac{e^2}{4\pi\varepsilon_0 r} \tag{7-32}$$

As a *trial function*, we shall try a Gaussian function of the form $\phi(r) = e^{-\alpha r^2}$, where α is a variational parameter. It is straightforward calculation to show that (cf. Problem 10)

$$4\pi \int_0^\infty dr\, r^2 \phi^*(r)\hat{H}\phi(r) = \frac{3\hbar^2\pi^{3/2}}{4\sqrt{2}\mu\alpha^{1/2}} - \frac{e^2}{4\varepsilon_0\alpha}$$

and that

$$4\pi \int_0^\infty dr\, r^2 \phi^*(r)\phi(r) = \left(\frac{\pi}{2\alpha}\right)^{3/2} .$$

Therefore, from Eq. 7-29,

$$E(\alpha) = \frac{3\hbar^2\alpha}{2\mu} - \frac{e^2\alpha^{1/2}}{2^{1/2}\varepsilon_0\pi^{3/2}} \tag{7-33}$$

Now differentiate $E(\alpha)$ with respect to α and set the result equal to zero to find

$$\alpha = \frac{\mu^2 e^4}{18\pi^3\varepsilon_0^2\hbar^4} \tag{7-34}$$

as the value of α that minimizes $E(\alpha)$. Substituting Eq. 7-34 back into Eq. 7-33, we find that

$$E_{\min} = -\frac{4}{3\pi}\left(\frac{\mu e^4}{16\pi^2\varepsilon_0^2\hbar^2}\right) = -0.424\left(\frac{\mu e^4}{16\pi^2\varepsilon_0^2\hbar^2}\right) \tag{7-35}$$

compared to the exact value

$$E_0 = -\frac{1}{2}\left(\frac{\mu e^4}{16\pi^2\varepsilon_0^2\hbar^2}\right) = -0.500\left(\frac{\mu e^4}{16\pi^2\varepsilon_0^2\hbar^2}\right) \tag{7-36}$$

Note that $E_{\min} > E_0$, as the variational theorem assures us. Thus we see that the variational method gives a rather good result. We can obtain a better result by using a more flexible trial function. We shall see in Section 7-7 that one can approach the true ground-state energy quite well.

Now that we have illustrated the utility of the variational theorem by example, we shall prove it. Let

$$\hat{H}\psi_n = E_n\psi_n \tag{7-37}$$

be the problem of interest. Even though we do not know the ψ_n explicitly, we do know that we can expand any suitable arbitrary function ϕ in terms of the ψ_n and write

$$\phi = \sum_n c_n \psi_n \qquad (7\text{-}38)$$

If we substitute this into Eq. 7-29 and use the fact that the ψ_n are orthonormal, then we obtain

$$E_\phi = \frac{\sum_n c_n^* c_n E_n}{\sum_n c_n^* c_n} \qquad (7\text{-}39)$$

Subtract E_0 itself from the left-hand side and

$$\frac{E_0 \sum_n c_n^* c_n}{\sum_n c_n^* c_n}$$

from the right-hand side to find

$$E_\phi - E_0 = \frac{\sum_n c_n^* c_n (E_n - E_0)}{\sum_n c_n^* c_n} \qquad (7\text{-}40)$$

Now, by definition, E_0 is the ground-state energy. Consequently, $E_n - E_0 \geq 0$ for all values of n, and because all the $c_n^* c_n \geq 0$, Eq. 7-40 shows that

$$E_\phi - E_0 \geq 0 \qquad (7\text{-}41)$$

which is the variational theorem, Eq. 7-30.

As another example, consider the ground state of a harmonic oscillator. Even if we had not solved this problem exactly previously, we might expect that the ground-state wave function would be symmetric about $x = 0$. As a trial function, then, let us try

$$\phi = \cos \lambda x \qquad \left(-\frac{\pi}{2\lambda} < x < \frac{\pi}{2\lambda} \right) \qquad (7\text{-}42)$$

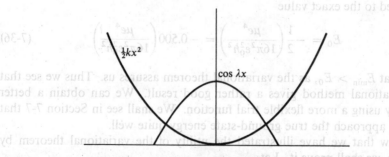

Figure 7-2. A harmonic-oscillator potential well and trial function of the form $\cos \lambda x$ with $-\pi/2\lambda < x < \pi/2\lambda$, where λ is a variational parameter.

where λ is a variational parameter. Equation 7-42 is plotted in Figure 7-2. The Hamiltonian operator for a harmonic oscillator is

$$\hat{H} = -\frac{\hbar^2}{2\mu}\frac{d^2}{dx^2} + \frac{k}{2}x^2$$

and so the numerator in Eq. 7-29 is

$$\text{numerator} = \int_{-\pi/2\lambda}^{\pi/2\lambda} \cos \lambda x \left(-\frac{\hbar^2}{2\mu}\frac{d^2}{dx^2} + \frac{k}{2}x^2\right)\cos \lambda x\, dx = \frac{\pi\hbar^2\lambda}{4\mu} + \left(\frac{\pi^3}{48} - \frac{\pi}{8}\right)\frac{k}{\lambda^3}$$

$$(7\text{-}43)$$

and the denominator in Eq. 7-29 is

$$\text{denominator} = \int_{-\pi/2\lambda}^{\pi/2\lambda} \cos^2 \lambda x\, dx = \frac{\pi}{2\lambda}$$

Equation 7-29 gives

$$E_\phi = \frac{\hbar^2\lambda^2}{2\mu} + \left(\frac{\pi^2}{24} - \frac{1}{4}\right)\frac{k}{\lambda^2}$$

Now, minimizing E_ϕ with respect to λ gives

$$E_{\min} = 2^{3/2}\left(\frac{\pi^2}{24} - \frac{1}{4}\right)^{1/2}\frac{1}{2}\hbar\left(\frac{k}{\mu}\right)^{1/2} = (1.14)\frac{1}{2}\hbar\omega \qquad (7\text{-}44)$$

compared to the exact value

$$E_0 = \tfrac{1}{2}\hbar\omega$$

Again, considering the simplicity of the trial function, we find quite good agreement with the exact result.

EXAMPLE 7-3
Use a trial function of the form $e^{-\alpha x^2/2}$ to calculate the ground-state energy of a quartic oscillator, whose potential is

$$U(x) = cx^4$$

Solution: The numerator of Eq. 7-29 is

$$\text{numerator} = \int_{-\infty}^{\infty} e^{-\alpha x^2/2}\left(-\frac{\hbar^2}{2\mu}\frac{d^2}{dx^2} + cx^4\right)e^{-\alpha x^2/2}\, dx$$

$$= \frac{\hbar^2}{4\mu}(\alpha\pi)^{1/2} + \frac{3c\pi^{1/2}}{4\alpha^{5/2}}$$

and the denominator of Eq. 7-29 is

$$\text{denominator} = \int_{-\infty}^{\infty} e^{-\alpha x^2}\, dx = \frac{\pi^{1/2}}{\alpha^{1/2}}$$

Therefore, E_ϕ is

$$E_\phi = \frac{\hbar^2 \alpha}{4\mu} + \frac{3c}{4\alpha^2}$$

If we differentiate E_ϕ with respect to α and set the result equal to zero, then we find that $\alpha = (6c\mu/\hbar^2)^{1/3}$ minimizes E_ϕ. The minimum value of E_ϕ is

$$E_{min} = \frac{3}{8}\left(\frac{6c\hbar^4}{\mu^2}\right)^{1/3}$$

7-4 *A Trial Function That Depends Linearly on the Variational Parameters Leads to a Secular Determinant*

As another example of the variational method, consider a particle in a one-dimensional box. Even without prior knowledge of the exact ground-state wave function, we should expect it to be symmetric about $x = a/2$ and go to zero at the walls. One of the simplest functions with this symmetry is $x^n(x - a)^n$ where n is an integer. Consequently, let us estimate E_0 by using

$$\phi = c_1 x(a - x) + c_2 x^2(a - x)^2 \tag{7-45}$$

as a trial function, where c_1 and c_2 are to be determined variationally, that is, where c_1 and c_2 are the variational parameters. If ϕ in Eq. 7-45 is used as a trial function, one finds after quite a lengthy but straightforward calculation that

$$E_{min} = 0.125002 \frac{h^2}{ma^2} \tag{7-46}$$

compared to

$$E_{exact} = \frac{h^2}{8ma^2} = 0.125000 \frac{h^2}{ma^2} \tag{7-47}$$

So we see that using a trial function with more than one parameter can produce impressive results. The price we pay is a correspondingly more lengthy, albeit straightforward, calculation. There is a systematic way to handle a trial function like Eq. 7-45. Note that Eq. 7-45 is a linear combination of functions. Such a trial function can be written generally as

$$\phi = \sum_{n=1}^{N} c_n f_n \tag{7-48}$$

where the c_n are variational parameters and the f_n are arbitrary known functions. We shall use such a trial function often. For simplicity, we shall assume that $N = 2$ in Eq. 7-48 and that the c_n and f_n are real. We relax these restrictions in Problem 16.

Consider

$$\phi = c_1 f_1 + c_2 f_2$$

Then

$$\int \phi \hat{H} \phi \, d\tau = \int (c_1 f_1 + c_2 f_2) \hat{H}(c_1 f_1 + c_2 f_2) \, d\tau$$

$$= c_1^2 \int f_1 \hat{H} f_1 \, d\tau + c_1 c_2 \int f_1 \hat{H} f_2 \, d\tau + c_1 c_2 \int f_2 \hat{H} f_1 \, d\tau + c_2^2 \int f_2 \hat{H} f_2 \, d\tau$$

$$= c_1^2 H_{11} + c_1 c_2 H_{12} + c_1 c_2 H_{21} + c_2^2 H_{22} \tag{7-49}$$

where

$$H_{ij} = \int f_i \hat{H} f_j \, d\tau \tag{7-50}$$

Because $\hat{H}$ is Hermitian, $H_{ij} = H_{ji}$, and so Eq. 7-49 becomes

$$\int \phi \hat{H} \phi \, d\tau = c_1^2 H_{11} + 2c_1 c_2 H_{12} + c_2^2 H_{22} \tag{7-51}$$

Similarly, we have

$$\int \phi^2 \, d\tau = c_1^2 S_{11} + 2c_1 c_2 S_{12} + c_2^2 S_{22} \tag{7-52}$$

where

$$S_{ij} = S_{ji} = \int \phi_i \phi_j \, d\tau \tag{7-53}$$

The quantities H_{ij} and S_{ij} are called *matrix elements*. By substituting Eqs. 7-51 and 7-52 into Eq. 7-29, we find

$$E(c_1, c_2) = \frac{c_1^2 H_{11} + 2c_1 c_2 H_{12} + c_2^2 H_{22}}{c_1^2 S_{11} + 2c_1 c_2 S_{12} + c_2^2 S_{22}} \tag{7-54}$$

where we emphasize here that E is a function of the variational parameters c_1 and c_2.

Before differentiating $E(c_1, c_2)$ in Eq. 7-54 with respect to c_1 and c_2, it is convenient to write Eq. 7-54 in the form

$$E(c_1, c_2)(c_1^2 S_{11} + 2c_1 c_2 S_{12} + c_2^2 S_{22}) = c_1^2 H_{11} + 2c_1 c_2 H_{12} + c_2^2 H_{22} \tag{7-55}$$

If we differentiate Eq. 7-55 with respect to c_1, we find

$$(2c_1 S_{11} + 2c_2 S_{12})E + \frac{\partial E}{\partial c_1}(c_1^2 S_{11} + 2c_1 c_2 S_{12} + c_2^2 S_{22}) = 2c_1 H_{11} + 2c_2 H_{12} \tag{7-56}$$

Because we are minimizing E, $\partial E/\partial c_1 = 0$ and so Eq. 7-56 becomes

$$c_1(H_{11} - ES_{11}) + c_2(H_{12} - ES_{12}) = 0 \tag{7-57}$$

Similarly, by differentiating $E(c_1, c_2)$ with respect to c_2 instead of c_1, we find that

$$c_1(H_{12} - ES_{12}) + c_2(H_{22} - ES_{22}) = 0 \tag{7-58}$$

Equations 7-57 and 7-58 constitute a pair of linear algebraic equations for c_1 and c_2. According to the theory of linear algebraic equations, there is a nontrivial solution, that is, a solution that is not simply $c_1 = c_2 = 0$, if and only if the determinant of the coefficients vanishes or if and only if

$$\begin{vmatrix} H_{11} - ES_{11} & H_{12} - ES_{12} \\ H_{12} - ES_{12} & H_{22} - ES_{22} \end{vmatrix} = 0 \qquad (7\text{-}59)$$

This determinant is called a *secular determinant*. When this 2×2 determinant is expanded, we obtain a quadratic equation in E, called the *secular equation*. The quadratic secular equation gives two values for E, and we take the smaller of the two solutions as our approximation for the ground-state energy.

To illustrate the use of Eq. 7-59, let us go back to solving the problem of a particle in a one-dimensional box variationally using Eq. 7-45 as a trial function. For convenience, we shall set $a = 1$. In this case

$$f_1 = x(1 - x) \quad \text{and} \quad f_2 = x^2(1 - x)^2 \qquad (7\text{-}60)$$

and the matrix elements (see Eqs. 7-50 and 7-53) are (see Problem 17)

$$H_{11} = \frac{\hbar^2}{6m} \qquad\qquad S_{11} = \frac{1}{30}$$

$$H_{12} = H_{21} = \frac{\hbar^2}{30m} \qquad\qquad S_{12} = S_{21} = \frac{1}{140}$$

$$H_{22} = \frac{\hbar^2}{105m} \qquad\qquad S_{22} = \frac{1}{630}$$

The secular determinant (Eq. 7-59) is

$$\begin{vmatrix} \dfrac{1}{6} - \dfrac{E'}{30} & \dfrac{1}{30} - \dfrac{E'}{140} \\ \dfrac{1}{30} - \dfrac{E'}{140} & \dfrac{1}{105} - \dfrac{E'}{630} \end{vmatrix} = 0$$

where $E' = Em/\hbar^2$.

The corresponding secular equation is

$$3E'^2 - 168E' + 756 = 0$$

whose roots are

$$E' = \frac{168 \pm \sqrt{19{,}152}}{6} = 51.065 \text{ and } 4.93487$$

We chose the smaller root and obtain

$$E_{min} = 0.125002 \frac{h^2}{m}$$

compared to (recall that $a = 1$)

$$E_{exact} = \frac{h^2}{8m} = 0.125000 \frac{h^2}{m}$$

The excellent agreement here is better than should be expected normally for such a simple trial function. Note that $E_{min} > E_{exact}$. One can also go back to the two simultaneous algebraic linear equations for c_1 and c_2 and determine c_1 and c_2 and hence ϕ itself, but we shall not do that in this chapter. We shall generally restrict ourselves to a determination of only the ground-state energy E_0.

If we use a linear combination of N functions instead of using a linear combination of two functions as we have done so far, we obtain an $N \times N$ secular determinant instead of a 2×2 secular determinant:

$$\begin{vmatrix} H_{11} - ES_{11} & H_{21} - ES_{21} & \cdots & H_{N1} - ES_{N1} \\ H_{12} - ES_{12} & H_{22} - ES_{22} & \cdots & H_{N2} - ES_{N2} \\ \vdots & \vdots & & \vdots \\ H_{1N} - ES_{1N} & H_{2N} - ES_{2N} & \cdots & H_{NN} - ES_{NN} \end{vmatrix} = 0 \qquad (7\text{-}61)$$

The secular equation associated with this secular determinant is an Nth-order polynomial in E. We choose the smallest root of the Nth-order secular equation as an approximation to the energy. The determination of the smallest root must usually be done graphically or numerically for values of N larger than two. This is actually a standard numerical problem and there are a number of packaged computer routines that do this.

7-5   *The Secular Determinant Simplifies If the Trial Function Is a Linear Combination of Orthonormal Functions*

It is often convenient to choose a trial function that is a linear combination of orthonormal functions. If this is done, then the $S_{ij} = \delta_{ij}$, and the secular determinant simplifies considerably. Equation 7-61 becomes (Problem 18)

$$\begin{vmatrix} H_{11} - E & H_{12} & H_{13} & \cdots & H_{1N} \\ H_{21} & H_{22} - E & H_{23} & \cdots & H_{2N} \\ \vdots & \vdots & \vdots & & \vdots \\ H_{N1} & H_{N2} & H_{N3} & \cdots & H_{NN} - E \end{vmatrix} = 0 \qquad (7\text{-}62)$$

EXAMPLE 7-4

Use the variational method to calculate the ground-state energy of a particle constrained to move within the region $0 \leq x \leq a$ in a potential given by

$$U(x) = V_1 x \qquad 0 \leq x \leq \frac{a}{2}$$

$$= V_1(a - x) \qquad \frac{a}{2} \leq x \leq a$$

As a trial function, use a linear combination of the first two particle-in-a-box wave functions.

$$\phi(x) = c_1 \left(\frac{2}{a}\right)^{1/2} \sin \frac{\pi x}{a} + c_2 \left(\frac{2}{a}\right)^{1/2} \sin \frac{2\pi x}{a}$$

Solution: The particle-in-a-box wave functions are orthonormal, and so we can use Eq. 7-62 with $N = 2$. We need to calculate the matrix elements H_{11}, $H_{12} = H_{21}$, and H_{22}. For example,

$$H_{11} = \frac{2}{a} \int_0^{a/2} \sin \frac{\pi x}{a} \left(-\frac{h^2}{2m} \frac{d^2}{dx^2} + V_1 x \right) \sin \frac{\pi x}{a} \, dx$$

$$+ \frac{2}{a} \int_{a/2}^{a} \sin \frac{\pi x}{a} \left[-\frac{h^2}{2m} \frac{d^2}{dx^2} + V_1(a - x) \right] \sin \frac{\pi x}{a} \, dx$$

The integrals here are straightforward. After some amount of algebra, we find

$$H_{11} = \frac{h^2}{8ma^2} + V_1 a \left(\frac{1}{4} + \frac{1}{\pi^2} \right)$$

Similarly, we find that

$$H_{12} = H_{21} = 0$$

and that

$$H_{22} = \frac{h^2}{2ma^2} + \frac{V_1 a}{4}$$

If we substitute these values of H_{11}, H_{12}, and H_{22} into Eq. 7-62, then we find

$$\begin{vmatrix} \dfrac{h^2}{8ma^2} + V_1 a \left(\dfrac{1}{4} + \dfrac{1}{\pi^2} \right) - E & 0 \\ 0 & \dfrac{h^2}{2ma^2} + \dfrac{V_1 a}{4} - E \end{vmatrix} = 0$$

The secular equation corresponding to this secular determinant is

$$\left(\frac{h^2}{8ma^2} + V_1 a \left(\frac{1}{4} + \frac{1}{\pi^2} \right) - E \right) \left(\frac{h^2}{2ma^2} + \frac{V_1 a}{4} - E \right) = 0$$

and so the two values of E are

$$E = \frac{h^2}{8ma^2} + V_1 a \left(\frac{1}{4} + \frac{1}{\pi^2} \right)$$

and

$$E = \frac{h^2}{2ma^2} + \frac{V_1 a}{4}$$

The smaller of these two roots depends upon the relative magnitude of h^2/ma^2 and $V_1 a$.

There are several comments to make about the result of Example 7-4. First, note that because $H_{12} = 0$, the resulting secular equation is automatically factored. Furthermore, the two roots can be written as

$$E = E_1 + V_1 a \left(\frac{1}{4} + \frac{1}{\pi^2} \right)$$

and

$$E = E_2 + \frac{V_1 a}{4}$$

where E_1 and E_2 are the first two energies of a particle in a box. The fact that $H_{12} = 0$ causes the lowest energy to be just the ground-state energy of a particle in a box with an added term $V_1 a/4$ which is the same result that we would obtain from perturbation theory (Problem 5). The second term in the trial function did not affect the result at all. We would have obtained the same result if we had used only the first term in the trial function. Clearly the fact that $H_{12} = 0$ has a profound affect on the result. Why did H_{12} turn out to be zero? To answer this question, note that

$$H_{12} = \frac{2}{a} \int_0^a \sin \frac{\pi x}{a} \left[-\frac{h^2}{2m} \frac{d^2}{dx^2} + U(x) \right] \sin \frac{2\pi x}{a} \, dx$$

The first term in H_{12} is zero because the second derivative of $\sin (2\pi x/a)$ gives $-(2\pi/a)^2 \sin (2\pi x/a)$, and the integral of the product of this and $\sin (\pi x/a)$ is zero because the particle-in-a-box wave functions are orthogonal. The second term in H_{12}, the one involving $U(x)$, is zero by symmetry; $U(x)$ is an even function about $x = a/2$, $\sin (\pi x/a)$ is an even function about $x = a/2$, and $\sin (2\pi x/a)$ is an odd function about $x = a/2$. Consequently, the entire integrand is an odd function about $x = a/2$, and so its integral from 0 to a vanishes. Thus, we see that the symmetry of the two terms in the trial function are responsible for the result that $H_{12} = 0$, which causes the final ground-state energy to be independent of the $\sin (2\pi x/a)$ term in the trial function. Problem 20 has you repeat the calculation with a trial function of the form

$$\phi(x) = c_1 \sin \frac{\pi x}{a} + c_2 \sin \frac{3\pi x}{a}$$

In this case both terms in the trial function are even functions about $x = a/2$, and so $H_{12} \neq 0$. The resulting ground-state energy is lower than $E_1 + V_1 a/4$. These considerations show that the symmetry of the terms in a trial function that is a linear combination are important. Only terms with the appropriate symmetry affect the final result.

As another application of Eq. 7-62, we shall calculate the polarizability of a hydrogen atom. The polarizability of an atom is a measure of the distortion of the electronic distribution of the atom when it is placed in an external electric field. When an atom is placed in an external electric field, the field induces a dipole moment in the atom. It is a good approximation to say that the magnitude of the induced dipole moment is proportional to the strength of the electric field. In an equation, we have

$$\mu = \alpha \mathscr{E} \tag{7-63}$$

where μ is the magnitude of the induced dipole moment, $\mathscr{E}$ is the strength of the electric field, and α is a proportionality constant called the *polarizability*. The value of α depends on the particular atom.

The energy required to induce a dipole moment is given by

$$E = -\int_0^{\mathscr{E}} \mu \, d\mathscr{E}' = -\int_0^{\mathscr{E}} \alpha \mathscr{E}' \, d\mathscr{E}'$$

$$= -\frac{\alpha \mathscr{E}^2}{2} \tag{7-64}$$

Equation 7-64 is the energy associated with a polarizable atom in an electric field.

Consider a hydrogen atom for simplicity. In a hydrogen atom, there is an instantaneous dipole moment pointing from the electron to the nucleus. This instantaneous dipole moment is given by $-e\mathbf{r}$ and interacts with an external electric field according to

$$E = -\boldsymbol{\mu} \cdot \boldsymbol{\mathscr{E}} = e\mathbf{r} \cdot \boldsymbol{\mathscr{E}} \tag{7-65}$$

If $\mathscr{E}$ is taken to be in the z direction, then Eq. 7-65 introduces a perturbation term to the Hamiltonian of the hydrogen atom that is of the form

$$\hat{H}^{(1)} = e\mathscr{E} r \cos \theta$$

and so the complete Hamiltonian operator is

$$\hat{H} = \hat{H}^{(0)} + e\mathscr{E} r \cos \theta \tag{7-66}$$

We can solve this problem using perturbation theory, but we shall use the variational method here to calculate the ground-state energy of a hydrogen atom in an external electric field.

Equation 7-62 shows that it is convenient to write a trial function as a linear combination of orthonormal functions. In particular, in this example it is convenient to choose the orthonormal functions to be the eigenfunctions of the unperturbed system. Because the field induces a dipole in the z direction, let us take

$$\phi = c_1\psi_{1s} + c_2\psi_{2p_z} \tag{7-67}$$

as our trial function. Because

$$\hat{H}^{(0)}\psi_{1s} = -\frac{e^2}{8\pi\varepsilon_0 a_0}\psi_{1s} \tag{7-68}$$

and

$$\hat{H}^{(0)}\psi_{2p_z} = -\frac{e^2}{32\pi\varepsilon_0 a_0}\psi_{2p_z} \tag{7-69}$$

the calculation is greatly simplified. Using the hydrogen atomic wave functions given in Table 6-6, it is straightforward to show that

$$H_{11} = -\frac{e^2}{2\kappa_0 a_0}$$

and

$$H_{22} = -\frac{e^2}{8\kappa_0 a_0} \tag{7-70}$$

and

$$H_{12} = \frac{8}{\sqrt{2}}\left(\frac{2}{3}\right)^5 e\mathscr{E} a_0$$

In Eqs. 7-70, we have let $\kappa_0 = 4\pi\varepsilon_0$. The two roots of the corresponding secular equation are

$$E = -\frac{5e^2}{16\kappa_0 a_0} \pm \frac{1}{2}\left[\left(\frac{3e^2}{8\kappa_0 a_0}\right)^2 + \frac{2^{17}}{3^{10}}e^2\mathscr{E}^2 a_0^2\right]^{1/2}$$

$$= -\frac{5e^2}{16\kappa_0 a_0} \pm \frac{3e^2}{16\kappa_0 a_0}\left(1 + \frac{2^{23}}{3^{12}}\frac{\mathscr{E}^2\kappa_0^2 a_0^4}{e^2}\right)^{1/2} \tag{7-71}$$

Now using the expansion

$$(1 + x)^{1/2} = 1 + \frac{x}{2} + \cdots \qquad x < 1 \tag{7-72}$$

we can expand the square-root term in parentheses in Eq. 7-71 to find

$$E \approx -\frac{e^2}{2\kappa_0 a_0} - \frac{2^{18}}{3^{11}}\kappa_0 a_0^3 \mathscr{E}^2 + \cdots$$

$$= -\frac{e^2}{2\kappa_0 a_0} - 2.96\kappa_0 a_0^3 \frac{\mathscr{E}^2}{2} + \cdots \tag{7-73}$$

By comparing this result to the macroscopic equation, Eq. 7-64, we see that the polarizability of a hydrogen atom is

$$\alpha = 2.96\kappa_0 a_0^3 \tag{7-74}$$

The exact value for the hydrogen atom is $9\kappa_0 a_0^3/2$. Although the numerical value is in error by 35%, we do see that the polarizability is proportional to a_0^3, or to a measure of the volume of the atom. This is a general result and can be used to estimate polarizabilities. Why is there no linear term in $\mathscr{E}$ in the above equation for E? What do you think a first-order perturbation calculation of the 1s state would give? (cf. Problem 4).

It is instructive to redo the calculation of the polarizability of a hydrogen atom using the trial function

$$\phi = c_1 \psi_{1s} + c_2 \psi_{3p_z} \tag{7-75}$$

This trial function has the same symmetry as Eq. 7-67, but it involves the ψ_{3p_z} orbital instead of the ψ_{2p_z}. Problem 22 has you show that in this case

$$E = -\frac{5e^2}{18\kappa_0 a_0} \pm \frac{1}{2}\left(\frac{16}{81}\frac{e^4}{\kappa_0^2 a_0^2} + \frac{3^6}{2^{11}}e^2\mathscr{E}^2 a_0^2\right)^{1/2}$$

$$= -\frac{5e^2}{18\kappa_0 a_0} \pm \frac{4e^2}{18\kappa_0 a_0}\left(1 + \frac{3^{10}}{2^{15}}\frac{\kappa_0^2 a_0^4 \mathscr{E}^2}{e^2}\right)^{1/2}$$

$$= -\frac{5e^2}{18\kappa_0 a_0} \pm \frac{4e^2}{18\kappa_0 a_0} \pm \frac{3^8}{2^{15}}\kappa_0 a_0^3 \mathscr{E}^2 + \cdots \tag{7.76}$$

or

$$E = -\frac{e^2}{2\kappa_0 a_0} - 0.200\kappa_0 a_0^3 \mathscr{E}^2 + \cdots$$

$$= -\frac{e^2}{2\kappa_0 a_0} - 0.400\kappa_0 a_0^3 \frac{\mathscr{E}^2}{2} \tag{7.77}$$

for a polarizability, $\alpha = 0.400\kappa_0 a_0^3$. Note that, in this case, the energy is quite a bit higher than that in Eq. 7-73, and in fact it is not very far from the 1s energy $-e^2/2\kappa_0 a_0$. This result suggests that the $3p_z$ orbital somehow does not play much of a role in the trial function, particularly compared to the trial function involving the 1s and $2p_z$ orbitals. These two calculations of the polarizability of a hydrogen atom illustrate a general principle that we shall now discuss.

7-6   *Terms in a Trial Function That Correspond to Progressively Higher Energies Contribute Progressively Less to the Ground-State Energy*

For algebraic simplicity, assume that the Hamiltonian can be written in the form

$$\hat{H} = \hat{H}^{(0)} + \hat{H}^{(1)} \tag{7-78}$$

and choose a trial function

$$\phi = c_1 \psi_1 + c_2 \psi_2 \tag{7-79}$$

where

$$\hat{H}^{(0)}\psi_j = E_j^{(0)}\psi_j \qquad j = 1, 2 \tag{7-80}$$

This is parallel to the case that we have just discussed for a hydrogen atom in an external electric field. The secular equation associated with the trial function is

$$\begin{vmatrix} H_{11} - E & H_{12} \\ H_{12} & H_{22} - E \end{vmatrix} = \begin{vmatrix} E_1^{(0)} + E_1^{(1)} - E & H_{12} \\ H_{12} & E_2^{(0)} + E_2^{(1)} - E \end{vmatrix} = 0 \quad (7\text{-}81)$$

where

$$E_j^{(1)} = \int \psi_j^* \hat{H}^{(1)} \psi_j \, d\tau \quad (7\text{-}82)$$

By solving Eq. 7-81 for E, we find that

$$E = \frac{E_1^{(0)} + E_1^{(1)} + E_2^{(0)} + E_2^{(1)}}{2} \pm \frac{1}{2}\{[E_1^{(0)} + E_1^{(1)} - E_2^{(0)} - E_2^{(1)}]^2 + 4H_{12}^2\}^{1/2}$$

$$(7\text{-}83)$$

If we arbitrarily assume that $E_1^{(0)} + E_1^{(1)} < E_2^{(0)} + E_2^{(1)}$, then we take the positive sign in Eq. 7-83 and write

$$E = \frac{E_1^{(0)} + E_1^{(1)} + E_2^{(0)} + E_2^{(1)}}{2} + \frac{E_1^{(0)} + E_1^{(1)} - E_2^{(0)} - E_2^{(1)}}{2}$$

$$\times \left\{ 1 + \frac{4H_{12}^2}{[E_1^{(0)} + E_1^{(1)} - E_2^{(0)} - E_2^{(1)}]^2} \right\}^{1/2}$$

$$= E_1^{(0)} + E_1^{(1)} + \frac{H_{12}^2}{[E_1^{(0)} + E_1^{(1)} - E_2^{(0)} - E_2^{(1)}]} + \cdots \quad (7\text{-}84)$$

Note that if $E_1^{(0)} + E_1^{(1)}$ and $E_2^{(0)} + E_2^{(1)}$ are widely separated, then the term involving H_{12}^2 in Eq. 7-84 is small. Therefore, the energy is simply that calculated using ψ_1 alone; the ψ_2 part of the trial function contributes little to the overall energy. The general result is that terms in a trial function that correspond to higher and higher energies contribute less and less to the total ground-state energy.

7-7   Trial Functions Can Be Linear Combinations of Functions That Also Contain Variational Parameters

It is fairly common in practice to use a trial function of the form

$$\phi = \sum_{j=1}^{N} c_j f_j$$

where the f_j themselves contain variational parameters. An example of such a trial function for the hydrogen atom is

$$\phi = \sum_{j=1}^{N} c_j e^{-\alpha_j r^2}$$

TABLE 7-1

The Ground-State Energy of a Hydrogen Atom Using a Trial Function of the Form

$$\phi = \sum_{j=1}^{N} c_j e^{-\alpha_j r^2}$$

where the c_j and the α_j Are Treated as Variational Parameters

N	$E_{min}/(\mu e^4/16\pi^2 \varepsilon_0^2 \hbar^2)$
1	-0.424413
2	-0.485813
3	-0.496967
4	-0.499276
5	-0.49976
6	-0.49988
8	-0.49992
16	-0.49998

We have seen in Section 7-3 that the use of one term gives an energy -0.424 $(\mu e^4/16\pi^2 \varepsilon_0^2 \hbar^2)$ compared to the exact value -0.500 $(\mu e^4/16\pi^2 \varepsilon_0^2 \hbar^2)$. Table 7-1 shows the results for taking more terms. One can see that the exact value is approached as N increases. It should be realized in this case, however, that one does not obtain a simple secular determinant, because ϕ is linear only in the c_j but not the α_j. The minimization of E with respect to the c_j and α_j is fairly involved, involving $2N$ parameters, and must be done numerically. Fortunately, there are a number of algorithms that can be used to do this.

Summary

Unlike the problems of a harmonic oscillator, a rigid rotator, and a hydrogen atom, most problems that occur in quantum mechanics or quantum chemistry cannot be solved exactly. There are approximate methods that can be used to obtain solutions to almost any degree of accuracy. One of these approximate methods is perturbation theory. The basic idea of perturbation theory is that the problem to be solved is similar to a problem that has already been solved. Perturbation theory is a systematic scheme that expresses the energies and wave functions of the perturbed system in terms of the (known) energies and wave functions of the unperturbed systems. The central perturbation theory result that we have derived in this chapter is that the first-order correction to the energy is given as an integral of the perturbation term of the Hamiltonian and the wave functions of the unperturbed system (cf. Eq. 7-20).

Another approximation method that is commonly used in quantum chemistry is the variational method. The variational method is based upon the variational principle. The variational principle says that the ground-state energy that is calculated using an arbitrary wave function is always equal to or greater than the energy that is calculated using the exact ground-state wave function. The variational principle is summarized by Eqs. 7-28 to 7-30. In practice, a trial function containing a number of parameters is used to calculate the energy, and then the energy is minimized with respect to these (variational) parameters in order to approach the ground-state energy as closely as possible. By using a more and more general trial function, the exact ground-state energy is approached more and more closely.

Terms That You Should Know

perturbation theory	variational parameter
unperturbed Hamiltonian	trial function
perturbation term	matrix element
first-order correction	secular determinant
variational method	secular equation
variational principle	polarizability

Problems

1. Identify $\hat{H}^{(0)}$, $\hat{H}^{(1)}$, $\psi^{(0)}$, and $E^{(0)}$ for the following problems.
   (a) An oscillator governed by the potential (cf. Problem 2)

$$U(x) = \frac{k}{2}x^2 + \frac{\gamma}{6}x^3 + \frac{b}{24}x^4$$

   (b) A particle constrained to move in the region $0 \leq x \leq a$ with the potential (cf. Problem 3)

$$U(x) = 0 \qquad 0 < x < \frac{a}{2}$$

$$= b \qquad \frac{a}{2} < x < a$$

   (c) A helium atom (Chapter 8).
   (d) A hydrogen atom in an electric field of strength $\mathscr{E}$. The Hamiltonian operator for this system is (Section 7-5)

$$\hat{H} = -\frac{\hbar^2}{2\mu}\nabla^2 - \frac{e^2}{4\pi\varepsilon_0 r} + e\mathscr{E}r\cos\theta$$

(e) A rigid rotator with a dipole moment μ in an electric field of strength $\mathcal{E}$. The Hamiltonian operator for this system is

$$\hat{H} = -\frac{\hbar^2}{2I}\nabla^2 + \mu\mathcal{E}\cos\theta$$

and where ∇^2 is given by Eq. 6-38.

2. Using a harmonic oscillator as the unperturbed problem, calculate the first-order correction to the energy of the $n = 1$ level for the system described in Problem 1a.

3. Using a particle in a box as the unperturbed problem, calculate the first-order correction to the ground-state energy for the system described in Problem 1b.

4. Using the result of Problem 1d, calculate the first-order correction to the ground-state energy of a hydrogen atom in an external electric field of strength $\mathcal{E}$.

5. Calculate the first-order correction to the energy of a particle constrained to move within the region $0 \le x \le a$ in the potential

$$U(x) = Vx \qquad 0 \le x \le \frac{a}{2}$$

$$= V(a - x) \qquad \frac{a}{2} \le x \le a$$

where V is a constant.

6. Calculate the first-order correction to the ground-state energy of a particle in a three-dimensional box with the perturbation

$$\hat{H}^{(1)} = V \qquad \frac{a}{4} \le x \le \frac{3a}{4}$$

$$\frac{b}{4} \le y \le \frac{3b}{4}$$

$$\frac{c}{4} \le z \le \frac{3c}{4}$$

$$= 0 \qquad \text{otherwise}$$

where V is a constant.

7. Use first-order perturbation theory to calculate the first-order correction to the ground-state energy of a quartic oscillator whose potential energy is

$$U(x) = cx^4$$

In this case, use a harmonic oscillator as the unperturbed system. What is the perturbing potential?

8. Certain dyes are a series of compounds of the type

$$H_2N-CH=CH-CH=\overset{+}{N}H_2$$

or

$$H_2N-CH=CH-CH=CH-CH=\overset{+}{N}H_2$$

We can apply the particle-in-a-box model to these compounds. If k is the number of carbon atoms in the molecule (an odd number), then the effective length of the box is given by

$$l = (k + 1)a$$

where a is about 1.4 Å.

It might be possible to improve the particle-in-a-box model by introducing a perturbing potential that tends to favor the ends of the box. Such a potential would be of the form

$$U(x) = A\left(x - \frac{l}{2}\right)^2$$

Determine the first-order correction to the energy levels of a particle in a box with this perturbing potential.

9. Prove that if a trial function and an exact wave function differ by $O(\varepsilon)$ over all space, then the approximate energy and the exact energy differ by $O(\varepsilon)$.

10. Using a Gaussian trial function $e^{-\alpha r^2}$ for the ground state of the hydrogen atom (see Eq. 7-32 for $\hat{H}$), show that

$$E(\alpha) = \frac{3\hbar^2\alpha}{2\mu} - \frac{e^2\alpha^{1/2}}{2^{1/2}\varepsilon_0\pi^{3/2}}$$

and that

$$E_{\min} = -\frac{4}{3\pi}\frac{\mu e^4}{16\pi^2\varepsilon_0^2\hbar^2}$$

11. Use a trial function $e^{-\alpha r}$ with α as a variational parameter to calculate the ground-state energy of a hydrogen atom. Compare your result to the exact ground-state energy. Why is the agreement so good?

12. Suppose one were to use a trial function of the form

$$\phi = c_1 e^{-\alpha r} + c_2 e^{-\beta r^2}$$

to carry out a variational calculation for the ground state of the hydrogen atom. Can you guess without doing any calculations what c_1, c_2, α, and $E_{\min}$ will come out to be? What about a trial function of the form

$$\phi = \sum_{k=1}^{5} c_k e^{-\alpha_k r - \beta_k r^2}$$

13. Use a trial function of the form $e^{-\beta x^2}$ with β as a variational parameter to calculate the ground-state energy of a harmonic oscillator. Compare your result with the exact energy $h\nu/2$. Why is the agreement so good?

14. Use a trial function $1/(x^2 + \alpha^2)$ with α as a variational parameter to calculate the ground-state energy of a harmonic oscillator. Compare to the exact value, $E_0 = h\nu/2$. You will need to refer to a good table of integrals to do this problem.

15. Consider a three-dimensional, spherically symmetric, isotropic harmonic oscillator, with $U(r) = kr^2/2$. Using a trial function $e^{-\alpha r^2}$ with α as a variational parameter, estimate the ground-state energy. Do the same using $e^{-\alpha r}$. Compare these two results to the exact ground-state energy, $E = \frac{3}{2}h\nu$. Why is one of these so much better than the other?

16. It is quite common to assume a trial function of the form

$$\phi = c_1\phi_1 + c_2\phi_2 + \cdots + c_n\phi_n$$

where the c_n are the variational parameters and the ϕ_n constitute any convenient set of functions. Using the simple, special case

$$\phi = c_1\phi_1 + c_2\phi_2$$

show that the variational method leads to

$$E_\phi = \frac{c_1^* c_1 H_{11} + c_1^* c_2 H_{12} + c_1 c_2^* H_{21} + c_2^* c_2 H_{22}}{c_1^* c_1 S_{11} + c_1^* c_2 S_{12} + c_1 c_2^* S_{21} + c_2^* c_2 S_{22}}$$

where

$$H_{ij} = \int \phi_i^* \hat{H}_j \phi_j d\tau = H_{ji}^*$$

$$S_{ij} = \int \phi_i^* \phi_j d\tau = S_{ji}^*$$

because $\hat{H}$ is Hermitian. Now write the above equation for E_ϕ as

$$c_1^* c_1 H_{11} + c_1^* c_2 H_{12} + c_1 c_2^* H_{21} + c_2^* c_2 H_{22}$$
$$= E_\phi(c_1^* c_1 S_{11} + c_1^* c_2 S_{12} + c_1 c_2^* S_{21} + c_2^* c_2 S_{22})$$

and show that if we set

$$\frac{\partial E_\phi}{\partial c_1^*} = 0 \quad \text{and} \quad \frac{\partial E_\phi}{\partial c_2^*} = 0$$

we obtain

$$(H_{11} - E_\phi S_{11})c_1 + (H_{12} - E_\phi S_{12})c_2 = 0$$
$$(H_{21} - E_\phi S_{21})c_1 + (H_{22} - E_\phi S_{22})c_2 = 0$$

There is a nontrivial solution to this pair of equations if and only if the determinant

$$\begin{vmatrix} (H_{11} - E_\phi S_{11}) & (H_{21} - E_\phi S_{21}) \\ (H_{12} - E_\phi S_{12}) & (H_{22} - E_\phi S_{22}) \end{vmatrix} = 0$$

which gives a quadratic equation for E_ϕ. We choose the smaller solution as an approximation to the ground-state energy.

17. Apply the result of Problem 16 to the case of a particle in a one-dimensional box, where

$$\phi = c_1 x(a - x) + c_2 x^2(a - x)^2$$

For simplicity, let $a = 1$, which amounts to measuring all distances in units of a. Show that

$$H_{11} = \frac{\hbar^2}{6m} \qquad\qquad S_{11} = \frac{1}{30}$$

$$H_{12} = H_{21} = \frac{\hbar^2}{30m} \qquad\qquad S_{12} = S_{21} = \frac{1}{140}$$

$$H_{22} = \frac{\hbar^2}{105m} \qquad\qquad S_{22} = \frac{1}{630}$$

and that the ground-state energy is approximated by the smaller root of

$$\begin{vmatrix} \dfrac{1}{6} - \dfrac{E'}{30} & \dfrac{1}{30} - \dfrac{E'}{140} \\[2mm] \dfrac{1}{30} - \dfrac{E'}{140} & \dfrac{1}{105} - \dfrac{E'}{630} \end{vmatrix} = 0$$

where $E' \equiv Em/\hbar^2$. It is convenient to multiply this determinant through by 1260 to eliminate all the denominators. Show that this gives

$$\begin{vmatrix} 210 - 42E' & 42 - 9E' \\[2mm] 42 - 9E' & 12 - 2E' \end{vmatrix} = 0$$

and so

$$E' = \frac{168 \pm \sqrt{19{,}152}}{6}$$

the smaller root being

$$E' = 4.93487$$

Recalling that $E' = Em/\hbar^2$, we have

$$E = 4.93487 \frac{\hbar^2}{m} \qquad (a = 1)$$

$$= 0.125002 \frac{\hbar^2}{m} \qquad (a = 1)$$

compared to

$$E_{\text{exact}} = \frac{\hbar^2}{8m} = 0.1250 \frac{\hbar^2}{m} \qquad (a = 1)$$

18. Suppose that a trial function is written as a linear combination of m ortho-normal functions ψ_n. Show that the ground-state energy is given as the smallest solution to the determinantal equation

$$
\begin{vmatrix}
H_{11} - E & H_{12} & \cdots & H_{1m} \\
H_{21} & H_{22} - E & \cdots & H_{2m} \\
\vdots & \vdots & & \vdots \\
H_{m1} & H_{m2} & \cdots & H_{mm} - E
\end{vmatrix} = 0
$$

Note that it is not necessary to evaluate a large number of S_{ij}; $S_{ij} = \delta_{ij}$ because we have chosen to write our trial function ϕ as a linear combination of *orthonormal* functions. Thus we have cut the necessary labor almost in half.

19. In Section 7-2 we showed that a particle in a box with a linear slanted bottom could be approximated by perturbation theory, and we found that

$$
E_0 \approx \frac{h^2}{8ma^2} + \frac{V}{2}
$$

to first order. Instead of using perturbation theory, we can use the variational method to treat this problem. Write the trial function as a linear combination of the first two orthonormal particle-in-a-box wave functions:

$$
\phi = c_1\psi_1 + c_2\psi_2
$$

$$
= c_1\left(\frac{2}{a}\right)^{1/2}\sin\frac{\pi x}{a} + c_2\left(\frac{2}{a}\right)^{1/2}\sin\frac{2\pi x}{a}
$$

Using this trial function and c_1 and c_2 as the variational parameters, calculate an upper bound to the ground-state energy of this problem. Compare this to the perturbation theory result. Clearly, this result can be successively improved by taking more and more terms in the linear combination. To keep the formulas simple, let $a = 1$, or, in other words, measure x in units of a.

20. Repeat the calculation in Example 7-4 using a trial function of the form

$$
\phi(x) = c_1\left(\frac{2}{a}\right)^{1/2}\sin\frac{\pi x}{a} + c_2\left(\frac{2}{a}\right)^{1/2}\sin\frac{3\pi x}{a}
$$

21. Consider a system subject to the potential

$$
U(x) = \frac{k}{2}x^2 + \frac{\gamma}{6}x^3 + \frac{\delta}{24}x^4
$$

Calculate the ground-state energy of this system using a trial function of the form

$$
\phi = c_1\psi_0(x) + c_2\psi_2(x)
$$

where $\psi_0(x)$ and $\psi_2(x)$ are the first two even wave functions of a harmonic oscillator.

22. Calculate the polarizability of a hydrogen atom using

$$\phi = c_1 \psi_{1s} + c_2 \psi_{3p_z}$$

as a trial function. Compare your result to the polarizability obtained using

$$\phi = c_1 \psi_{1s} + c_2 \psi_{2p_z}$$

as a trial function. What does this calculation illustrate?

23. There is a nice connection between perturbation theory and the variational method that is illustrated in this problem. Suppose that some Hamiltonian can be expressed as

$$\hat{H} = \hat{H}^{(0)} + \hat{H}^{(1)}$$

where

$$\hat{H}^{(0)} \psi_n^{(0)} = E_n^{(0)} \psi_n^{(0)}$$

is a previously solved problem. Instead of using perturbation theory, we can calculate the ground-state energy variationally using a trial function of the form

$$\phi = c_0 \psi_0^{(0)} + c_1 \psi_1^{(0)} + c_2 \psi_2^{(0)} + \cdots$$

To keep the algebra simple, let us limit our trial function to the first two terms. Show that the secular equation associated with this trial function is

$$\begin{vmatrix} E_0^{(0)} + E_0^{(1)} - E & H_{10} \\ H_{10} & E_1^{(0)} + E_1^{(1)} - E \end{vmatrix} = 0$$

where

$$E_j^{(1)} = \int \psi_j^{(0)*} \hat{H}^{(1)} \psi_j^{(0)} \, d\tau \qquad j = 0, 1$$

Choosing $E_0^{(0)} + E_0^{(1)}$ to be lower than $E_1^{(0)} + E_1^{(1)}$, show that

$$E = \frac{E_0^{(0)} + E_0^{(1)} + E_1^{(0)} + E_1^{(1)}}{2} + \frac{1}{2}[E_0^{(0)} + E_0^{(1)} - E_1^{(0)} - E_1^{(1)}]$$

$$\times \left\{ 1 + \frac{4H_{10}^2}{[E_0^{(0)} + E_0^{(1)} - E_1^{(0)} - E_1^{(1)}]^2} \right\}^{1/2}$$

Using the formula $(1 + x)^{1/2} = 1 + (x/2) + \cdots$ for $x \ll 1$ and assuming that $4H_{10}^2 < [E_0^{(0)} + E_0^{(1)} - E_1^{(0)} - E_1^{(1)}]^2$, show that

$$E = E_0^{(0)} + E_0^{(1)} + \frac{H_{10}^2}{[E_0^{(0)} + E_0^{(1)} - E_1^{(0)} - E_1^{(1)}]} + \cdots$$

We cannot identify the third term on the right-hand side here with the second-order energy because although the numerator is second order, the denominator is zero and first order. Using the fact that

$$\frac{1}{1 + x} = 1 - x + x^2 + \cdots \qquad x < 1$$

show that the second-order energy is

$$E_0^{(2)} = \frac{H_{10}^2}{E_0^{(0)} - E_1^{(0)}}$$

Compare this to Eq. 15 of Problem 24 and discuss what you think we would find for E if we used a trial function of the form

$$\phi = \sum_{j=0}^{\infty} c_j \psi_j^{(0)}$$

24. In this problem we shall derive the formulas of perturbation theory to second order in the perturbation. Suppose we wish to solve the equation

$$\hat{H}\psi_n = E_n\psi_n \tag{1}$$

and there is an equation for which we know the exact solutions,

$$\hat{H}^{(0)}\psi_n^{(0)} = E_n^{(0)}\psi_n^{(0)} \tag{2}$$

We assume that $\hat{H}$ and $\hat{H}^{(0)}$ satisfy the relation

$$\hat{H} = \hat{H}^{(0)} + \lambda\hat{H}^{(1)} \tag{3}$$

where λ is some parameter that represents the magnitude of the perturbation. The parameter λ might be the strength of an externally applied field, the magnitude of an anharmonic force constant, and so on.

Because $\hat{H}$ depends on λ, so do ψ_n and E_n in Eq. 1. We can write fairly generally that

$$\psi_n = \psi_n^{(0)} + \lambda\psi_n^{(1)} + \lambda^2\psi_n^{(2)} + \cdots \tag{4}$$

and that

$$E_n = E_n^{(0)} + \lambda E_n^{(1)} + \lambda^2 E_n^{(2)} + \cdots \tag{5}$$

The leading terms in these two equations are the unperturbed quantities because we require that $\psi_n \to \psi_n^{(0)}$ and $E_n \to E_n^{(0)}$ as $\lambda \to 0$. The other terms are first-order, second-order, and higher-order corrections.

Substitute Eqs. 4 and 5 into Eq. 1 and collect like powers of λ to obtain

$$\hat{H}^{(0)}\psi_n^{(0)} + \lambda[\hat{H}^{(0)}\psi_n^{(1)} + \hat{H}^{(1)}\psi_n^{(0)}] + O(\lambda^2)$$
$$= E_n^{(0)}\psi_n^{(0)} + \lambda[E_n^{(1)}\psi_n^{(0)} + E_n^{(0)}\psi_n^{(1)}] + O(\lambda^2) \tag{6}$$

Write out the λ^2 terms explicitly. If Eq. (6) is to be true for all values of λ, then we can equate like powers of λ to obtain

$$\hat{H}^{(0)}\psi_n^{(0)} = E_n^{(0)}\psi_n^{(0)}$$

and

$$\hat{H}^{(0)}\psi_n^{(1)} + \hat{H}^{(1)}\psi_n^{(0)} = E_n^{(1)}\psi_n^{(0)} + E_n^{(0)}\psi_n^{(1)} \tag{7}$$

and so on. These two equations are called the *zero-order* and *first-order equations*. Write out the second-order equation explicitly. Following the argument around Eq. 7-18, prove that

$$E_n^{(1)} = \int \psi_n^{(0)*} \hat{H}^{(1)} \psi_n^{(0)} \, d\tau \tag{8}$$

is the first-order correction to the energy.

If we substitute this result back into Eq. 7, then we obtain an equation in which the only unknown quantity is $\psi_n^{(1)}$. A standard way to solve the equation for $\psi_n^{(1)}$ is to expand the unknown $\psi_n^{(1)}$ in terms of the eigenfunctions of the unperturbed problem. Show that if we write

$$\psi_n^{(1)} = \sum_j a_{nj} \psi_j^{(0)} \tag{9}$$

substitute $\psi_n^{(1)}$ into Eq. 7, multiply by $\psi_k^{(0)*}$, and integrate, then we find

$$\sum_j a_{nj} \int \psi_k^{(0)*} [\hat{H}^{(0)} - E_n^{(0)}] \psi_j^{(0)} \, d\tau$$

$$= E_n^{(1)} \int \psi_k^{(0)*} \psi_n^{(0)} \, d\tau - \int \psi_k^{(0)*} \hat{H}^{(1)} \psi_n^{(0)} \, d\tau \tag{10}$$

There are two cases to consider here, $k = n$ and $k \neq n$. Show that when $k = n$, we obtain Eq. 8 again and that when $k \neq n$, we obtain

$$a_{nk} = \frac{\int \psi_k^{(0)*} \hat{H}^{(1)} \psi_n^{(0)} \, d\tau}{E_n^{(0)} - E_k^{(0)}} \qquad k \neq n \tag{11}$$

$$= \frac{H_{kn}^{(1)}}{E_n^{(0)} - E_k^{(0)}} \qquad k \neq n \tag{12}$$

where we have defined

$$H_{kn}^{(1)} = \int \psi_k^{(0)*} \hat{H}^{(1)} \psi_n^{(0)} \, d\tau \tag{13}$$

Thus we have determined all the a's in Eq. 9 except for a_{nn}. We can determine a_{nn} by requiring that ψ_n in Eq. (4) be normalized through first order or through terms linear in λ. Show that this requirement is equivalent to requiring that $\psi_n^{(0)}$ be orthogonal to $\psi_n^{(1)}$ and that it gives $a_{nn} = 0$. The complete wave function to first order then is

$$\psi_n = \psi_n^{(0)} + \lambda \sum_{j \neq n} \frac{H_{jn}^{(1)}}{E_n^{(0)} - E_j^{(0)}} \psi_j^{(0)} \tag{14}$$

Lastly, show that the second-order energy is

$$E_n^{(2)} = \sum_{j \neq n} \frac{H_{nj}^{(1)} H_{jn}^{(1)}}{E_n^{(0)} - E_j^{(0)}} \tag{15}$$

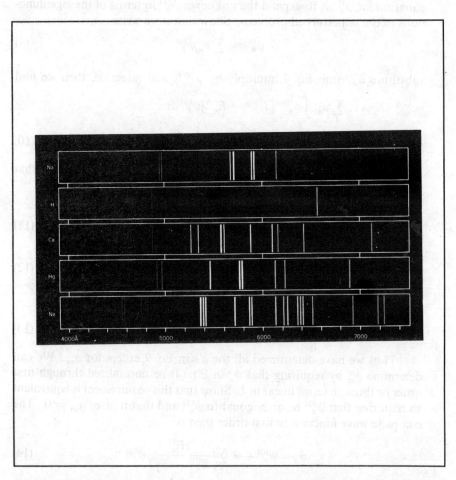

When an electric discharge passes through a vapor consisting of atoms, the electrons in the atoms are promoted to higher energy levels. As the atoms relax back to their ground state, radiation of certain characteristic frequencies is emitted. The result is a line spectrum which is characteristic of the element.

8

Atoms

WE concluded Chapter 6 with an introduction to the helium atom. We showed there that if we considered the nucleus to be fixed at the origin, then the Schrödinger equation has the form

$$\left\{ \hat{H}_H(1) + \hat{H}_H(2) + \frac{e^2}{4\pi\varepsilon_0 r_{12}} \right\} \psi(\mathbf{r}_1, \mathbf{r}_2) = E\psi(\mathbf{r}_1, \mathbf{r}_2) \qquad (8\text{-}1)$$

where $\hat{H}_H(j)$ is the hydrogenlike Hamiltonian of electron j. If it were not for the presence of the interelectronic repulsion term, Eq. 8-1 would be immediately solvable. Its eigenfunctions would be products of hydrogenlike wave functions and its eigenvalues would be sums of the hydrogenlike energies of the two electrons. Helium is our first complicated system, and although the helium atom may be of minimal interest to chemists, we shall discuss it in detail in this chapter because the solution of the helium atom illustrates the techniques that are used for more complex atoms. Then, after introducing the concept of electron spin and the Pauli Exclusion Principle, we shall discuss the Hartree-Fock theory of complex atoms, electron configurations and term symbols of atoms and ions, and atomic spectra.

8-1 Atomic and Molecular Calculations Are Expressed in Atomic Units

We shall apply both perturbation theory and the variational method to the helium atom, but before doing so we shall introduce a system of units, called *atomic units*, that is widely used in atomic and molecular calculations.

If we write Eq. 8-1 more explicitly, we have

$$\hat{H} = -\frac{\hbar^2}{2m}\nabla_1^2 - \frac{\hbar^2}{2m}\nabla_2^2 - \frac{Ze^2}{4\pi\varepsilon_0 r_1} - \frac{Ze^2}{4\pi\varepsilon_0 r_2} + \frac{e^2}{4\pi\varepsilon_0 r_{12}} \qquad (8\text{-}2)$$

If we introduce a set of units such that $\hbar = 1$, $m = 1$, $e = 1$, and $\kappa_0 = 4\pi\varepsilon_0 = 1$, then Eq. 8-2 becomes

$$\hat{H} = -\frac{1}{2}\nabla_1^2 - \frac{1}{2}\nabla_2^2 - \frac{Z}{r_1} - \frac{Z}{r_2} + \frac{1}{r_{12}} \qquad (8\text{-}3)$$

and is independent of any physical constants. For generality, we have written the Hamiltonian in Eq. 8-3 in terms of Z rather than letting Z be 2 for the specific case of helium.

It turns out that all other physical quantities can be expressed in terms of the above four basic units. For example, the Bohr radius a_0 is given by

$$a_0 = \frac{4\pi\varepsilon_0\hbar^2}{me^2} = 1 \qquad \text{(atomic units)} \qquad (8\text{-}4)$$

One atomic unit of length is called a *bohr*. By recalling Eq. 7-35 and 7-36, we see that the quantity $me^4/16\pi^2\varepsilon_0^2\hbar^2$ occurs as a "natural" energy, and so we

TABLE 8-1

Atomic Units and Their SI Equivalents

Quantity	Natural unit	SI equivalent
Mass	$m = 1$ (electron mass)	9.1091×10^{-31} kg
Charge	$|e| = 1$ (electronic charge)	1.6021×10^{-19} C
Angular momentum	$\hbar = 1$	1.0545×10^{-34} J·s
Permittivity	$\kappa_0 = 4\pi\varepsilon_0 = 1$	1.1126×10^{-10} C²·J⁻¹·m⁻¹
Length	$\kappa_0\hbar^2/me^2 = a_0 = 1$ (bohr) (Bohr radius)	5.29167×10^{-11} m
Energy	$me^4/\kappa_0^2\hbar^2 = e^2/\kappa_0 a_0 = 1$ (hartree) (twice the ionization energy of atomic hydrogen)	4.35944×10^{-18} J
Time	$\kappa_0^2\hbar^3/me^4 = 1$ (period of an electron in the first Bohr orbit)	2.41889×10^{-17} s
Speed	$e^2/\kappa_0\hbar = 1$ (speed of an electron in the first Bohr orbit)	2.18764×10^6 m·s⁻¹
Electric potential	$me^3/\kappa_0^2\hbar^2 = e/\kappa_0 a_0 = 1$ (potential energy of an electron in the first Bohr orbit)	27.211 V
Magnetic dipole moment	$e\hbar/m = 1$ (twice a Bohr magneton)	1.85464×10^{-23} J·T⁻¹

define the energy in atomic units to be

$$E = \frac{me^4}{16\pi^2\varepsilon_0^2\hbar^2} = 1 \qquad \text{(atomic units)} \qquad (8\text{-}5)$$

One atomic unit of energy is called a *hartree* and often is denoted by H. Note that in atomic units the ground-state energy of the hydrogen atom (in the fixed nucleus approximation) is $-\frac{1}{2}$ hartree. Equations 8-4 and 8-5 are called *derived units* because they are expressed in terms of the four base units, $\hbar$, m, e, and $\kappa_0 = 4\pi\varepsilon_0$. Table 8-1 lists a number of derived units, their names, and their SI equivalents; Problems 1 through 5 deal with conversions involving atomic units.

EXAMPLE 8-1

One hartree, the unit of energy in atomic units, is given by

$$\text{hartree} = \frac{me^4}{\kappa_0^2\hbar^2}$$

Express one hartree in units of joules (J), kilojoules per mole (kJ·mol^{-1}), wave numbers (cm^{-1}), and electron volts (eV).

Solution: To find one hartree expressed in joules, we substitute the SI values of m, e, κ_0, and $\hbar$ into the above equation. Using these values from Table 8-1, we find

$$\text{one hartree} = \frac{(9.1091 \times 10^{-31} \text{ kg})(1.6021 \times 10^{-19} \text{ C})^4}{(1.1126 \times 10^{-10} \text{ C}^2 \cdot \text{J}^{-1} \cdot \text{m}^{-1})^2 (1.0545 \times 10^{-34} \text{ J·s})^2}$$

$$= 4.3595 \times 10^{-18} \text{ J}$$

If we multiply this result by Avogadro's number, we obtain

$$\text{one hartree} = 2625 \text{ kJ·mol}^{-1}$$

To express one hartree in wave numbers (cm^{-1}), we use the equation

$$\bar{v} = \frac{1}{\lambda} = \frac{E}{ch} = \frac{(4.3595 \times 10^{-18} \text{ J})}{(2.9979 \times 10^8 \text{ m·s}^{-1})(6.6262 \times 10^{-34} \text{ J·s})}$$

$$= 2.195 \times 10^7 \text{ m}^{-1}$$

$$= 2.195 \times 10^5 \text{ cm}^{-1}$$

so that we can write

$$\text{one hartree} = 2.195 \times 10^5 \text{ cm}^{-1}$$

Lastly, to express one hartree in terms of electron volts, we use the conversion factor

$$1 \text{ eV} = 1.602 \times 10^{-19} \text{ J}$$

Using the value of one hartree in joules obtained previously, we have

$$\text{one hartree} = (4.3595 \times 10^{-18} \text{ J}) \left(\frac{1 \text{ eV}}{1.602 \times 10^{-19} \text{ J}} \right)$$

$$= 27.21 \text{ eV}$$

8-2 *Both Perturbation Theory and the Variational Method Can Yield Excellent Results for Helium*

The problem that we wish to solve is

$$\hat{H}\psi = E\psi \tag{8-6}$$

where $\hat{H}$ is given by Eq. 8-3. We can apply perturbation theory to this problem by considering the interelectronic repulsion term to be a perturbation. In this case

$$\hat{H}^{(0)} = -\frac{1}{2}\nabla_1^2 - \frac{Z}{r_1} - \frac{1}{2}\nabla_2^2 - \frac{Z}{r_2} \tag{8-7}$$

and so the zero-order ground-state wave function is

$$\psi^{(0)}(\mathbf{r}_1, \mathbf{r}_2) = \psi_{1s}(\mathbf{r}_1)\psi_{1s}(\mathbf{r}_2) \tag{8-8}$$

where

$$\psi_{1s}(\mathbf{r}_j) = \left(\frac{Z^3}{\pi} \right)^{1/2} e^{-Zr_j} \qquad j = 1 \text{ and } 2 \tag{8-9}$$

Because the ground-state energy of a hydrogenlike system is $-Z^2/2$, the energy $E^{(0)}$ is given by

$$E^{(0)} = -\frac{Z^2}{2} - \frac{Z^2}{2} = -Z^2 \text{ au} \tag{8-10}$$

The first-order perturbation theory correction to $E^{(0)}$ is given by (cf. Eq. 7-20)

$$E^{(1)} = \iint d\mathbf{r}_1 \, d\mathbf{r}_2 \, \psi^{(0)*}(\mathbf{r}_1, \mathbf{r}_2)\hat{H}^{(1)}\psi^{(0)}(\mathbf{r}_1, \mathbf{r}_2)$$

$$= \iint d\mathbf{r}_1 \, d\mathbf{r}_2 \, \psi_{1s}(\mathbf{r}_1)\psi_{1s}(\mathbf{r}_2) \frac{1}{r_{12}} \psi_{1s}(\mathbf{r}_1)\psi_{1s}(\mathbf{r}_2) \tag{8-11}$$

The evaluation of the integral in Eq. 8-11 is a little lengthy, but Problem 6 carries it through step by step. It is shown in Problem 6 that

$$E^{(1)} = \tfrac{5}{8}Z \text{ au} \tag{8-12}$$

and so the energy of a helium atom through first order is

$$E = E^{(0)} + E^{(1)} + \cdots$$

$$= -Z^2 + \tfrac{5}{8}Z + \cdots \tag{8-13}$$

For the helium atom, we set $Z = 2$ and find that

$$E = -\tfrac{11}{4} \text{ au} = -2.750 \text{ au}$$
$$= -74.83 \text{ eV} \tag{8-14}$$

where we have used the fact from Example 8-1 that 1 au = 27.21 eV. The experimental value of the energy is -79.00 eV or -2.9033 au, and so we see that first-order perturbation theory gives a result that is about 5% in error. Scheer and Knight (see Table 8-2) have calculated the energy through many orders of perturbation and find that

$$E = -Z^2 + \frac{5}{8} Z - 0.157666254 + \frac{0.008698679}{Z} + \frac{0.000888302}{Z^2} + \cdots$$

$$\tag{8-15}$$

Equation 8-15 yields a value of -2.9037 au, in good agreement with the experimental value, -2.9033 au.

TABLE 8-2
Ground-State Energies of the Helium Atom[a]

Method	Energy/au	Ionization energy/au
Perturbation calculations		
Complete neglect of the interelectronic repulsion term	−4.00	2.00
First-order perturbation theory	−2.75	0.75
Second-order perturbation theory	−2.91	0.91
Thirteenth-order perturbation theory[b]	−2.90372433	0.904
Variational calculations		
$(1s)^2$ with $\zeta = 1.6875$	−2.8477	0.848
$(ns)^2$ with $\zeta = 1.61162$ $n = 0.995$	−2.8542	0.854
Hartree-Fock[c]	−2.8617	0.862
Hylleras,[d] 10 parameters	−2.90363	0.904
Kinoshita,[e] 39 parameters	−2.9037225	0.904
Pekeris,[f] 1078 parameters	−2.903724375	0.904

[a] These are nonrelativistic, fixed-nucleus-approximation energies. Corrections for nuclear motion and relativistic corrections can be estimated to be about 10^{-4} au. The experimental result for the energy is -2.9033 au.
[b] C. W. Scheer and R. E. Knight, Rev. Mod. Phys. *35*, 426 (1963).
[c] C. C. J. Roothaan, L. M. Sachs, and A. W. Weiss, Rev. Mod. Phys. *32*, 186 (1960).
[d] E. A. Hylleras, Z. Physik *54*, 347 (1929).
[e] T. Kinoshita, Phys. Rev. *105*, 1490 (1957).
[f] C. L. Pekeris, Phys. Rev. *115*, 1216 (1959).

We can also use the variational method to calculate the ground-state energy of helium. For example, we can use Eq. 8-8 as a trial function with Z as a variational parameter. Thus we must evaluate

$$E = \int d\mathbf{r}_1 \, d\mathbf{r}_2 \, \psi \hat{H} \psi \tag{8-16}$$

with $\hat{H}$ given by Eq. 8-3 and ψ given by Eq. 8-8. Once again the integral is a little lengthy, albeit straightforward, to evaluate and is carried out step by step in Problem 7. The result is

$$E = Z^2 - \tfrac{27}{8}Z \tag{8-17}$$

If we minimize E with respect to Z, we find that $Z_{min} = \tfrac{27}{16}$ and that

$$E = -(\tfrac{27}{16})^2 = -2.8477 \text{ au} \tag{8-18}$$

compared to the first-order perturbation theory result of -2.7500 au and the higher-order result -2.9037 au. The value of Z that minimizes E can be interpreted as an *effective nuclear charge*. The fact that Z comes out to be less than 2 reflects the fact that each electron partially screens the nucleus from the other, so that the net effective nuclear charge is reduced from 2 to $\tfrac{27}{16}$.

The agreement that we have found between the first-order perturbation theory result or the variational result and the experimental result may appear to be quite good, but let us examine this agreement more closely. The ionization energy (IE) of helium is given by

$$\text{IE} = E_{\text{He}^+} - E_{\text{He}} \tag{8-19}$$

The energy of He^+ is $-Z^2/2$ (with $Z = 2$) in atomic units, and so we have

$$\text{IE} = -2 + \tfrac{11}{4} = 0.750 \text{ au} = 20.4 \text{ eV} \qquad \text{(first-order perturbation theory)}$$

or

$$\text{IE} = -2 + (\tfrac{27}{16})^2 = 0.848 \text{ au} = 23.1 \text{ eV} \qquad \text{(our variational result)}$$

whereas the experimental value of the ionization energy is 0.904 au, or 24.6 eV. Even the variational result, with its 2% discrepancy with the experimental total energy, is not too satisfactory if you realize that 1.5 eV is equivalent to $145 \text{ kJ} \cdot \text{mol}^{-1}$, which is the same order of magnitude as the strength of a chemical bond. Clearly, we must be able to do better.

One way to improve our results is to use a more general trial function than Eq. 8-8. Because a suitable trial function may be most any function, we are not restricted to choose a 1s hydrogenlike wave function. For example, in 1930 John Slater introduced a set of orbitals, now called *Slater orbitals*, which are of the form

$$S_{nlm}(r, \theta, \phi) = N_{nl} r^{n-1} e^{-\zeta r} Y_l^m(\theta, \phi) \tag{8-20}$$

where N_{nl} is a normalization constant and the Y_l^m are the spherical harmonics. The parameter ζ is taken to be arbitrary and is not necessarily equal to Z/n as in the hydrogenlike orbitals. If we use

$$\psi = S_{100}(r_1, \theta_1, \phi_1) S_{100}(r_2, \theta_2, \phi_2) \tag{8-21}$$

John C. Slater (1900–1976) received his Ph.D. in physics from Harvard University in 1923. He then studied at Cambridge and Copenhagen, and returned to Harvard in 1925. From 1930 to 1966, Slater was a professor of physics at the Massachusetts Institute of Technology. During the war years, he was involved in radar research at MIT and Bell Telephone Laboratories. From 1966 to 1976 Slater was research professor in physics and chemistry at the University of Florida.

as a trial function with ζ as the only variational parameter, we have seen above that $\zeta = 1.6875 = (\frac{27}{16})$ and $E = -2.8477$ au (see also Table 8-2). This value of E gives an ionization energy of 23.1 eV, compared to the experimental value of 24.6 eV. If we let n also be a variational parameter so that the trial function is

$$\psi = S_{n00}(r_1, \theta_1, \phi_1) S_{n00}(r_2, \theta_2, \phi_2) \qquad (8\text{-}22)$$

we find that $n = 0.995$, $\zeta = 1.6116$, and $E = -2.8542$ au, leading to an ionization energy of 23.2 eV.

If one uses a more flexible trial function of the form in which $\psi(\mathbf{r}_1, \mathbf{r}_2)$ is a product of one-electron functions, or *orbitals*,

$$\psi(\mathbf{r}_1, \mathbf{r}_2) = \phi(\mathbf{r}_1)\phi(\mathbf{r}_2) \qquad (8\text{-}23)$$

it turns out that one reaches a limit that is both practical and theoretical. In this limit, $E = -2.8617$ au and the ionization energy is 0.8617 au or 23.4 eV, compared to the best variational values 2.9037 au and 0.904 au, respectively. This limiting value is the best value of the energy that can be obtained using a trial function of the form of a product of one-electron wave functions (Eq. 8-23). This limit is called the *Hartree-Fock limit* and we shall discuss it more fully below. Note that the concept of electron orbitals is preserved in the *Hartree-Fock approximation*.

If one does not restrict the trial function to be a product of single-electron orbitals, then one can go on and obtain essentially the exact energy. It has been found to be advantageous to include terms containing the interelectronic distance r_{12} explicitly in the trial function. This was first done by Hylleras in 1930, who introduced a trial function of the form

$$\psi(r_1, r_2, r_{12}) = e^{-Zr_1}e^{-Zr_2}[1 + g(r_1, r_2, r_{12})] \qquad (8\text{-}24)$$

where g was chosen to be a polynomial in r_1, r_2, and r_{12}. For example, using simply

$$g = cr_{12}$$

and using Z and c as variational parameters, Hylleras obtained a value of $E = -2.8913$ au, within less than 0.5% of what is now accepted to be the exact value (Table 8-2). Using a polynomial of 14 terms for g, he obtained -2.9037 au, which is the exact result to five significant figures. With the advent of high-speed computers, this procedure can be carried out to a large number of terms, yielding an energy that is essentially exact. The most extensive such calculation was carried out in 1959 by Pekeris, who obtained $E = -2.903724375$ au using 1078 parameters. This result can be compared to Kinoshita's earlier result using 39 parameters ($E = -2.9037225$ au, Table 8-2).

Although these calculations do show that one can obtain essentially exact energies by using the variational method with r_{12} in the trial function explicitly, these calculations are quite difficult computationally and do not readily lend themselves to large atoms and molecules. Furthermore, we have abandoned the orbital concept altogether. The orbital concept has been of great use to chemists and so the trend nowadays is to find the Hartree-Fock orbitals mentioned above and to correct these by perturbation theory. It is instructive to outline the Hartree-Fock procedure for helium because the equations are fairly simple for this two-electron case and provide a nice physical interpretation.

8-3   *Hartree-Fock Equations Are Solved by the Self-Consistent Field Method*

The starting point of the Hartree-Fock procedure for helium is to write the two-electron wave function as a product of orbitals, as in Eq. 8-23.

$$\psi(\mathbf{r}_1, \mathbf{r}_2) = \phi(\mathbf{r}_1)\phi(\mathbf{r}_2) \qquad (8\text{-}25)$$

According to Eq. 8-25, the probability distribution of electron 2 is $\phi^*(\mathbf{r}_2)\phi(\mathbf{r}_2)\,d\mathbf{r}_2$. We can also interpret this probability distribution classically as a charge density, and so the potential energy that electron 1 experiences at the point $\mathbf{r}_1$ due to electron 2 is

$$U_1^{\text{eff}}(\mathbf{r}_1) = \int d\mathbf{r}_2\, \phi^*(\mathbf{r}_2)\frac{1}{r_{12}}\phi(\mathbf{r}_2) \qquad (8\text{-}26)$$

where the superscript eff emphasizes that $U_1^{\text{eff}}(\mathbf{r}_1)$ is an effective, or average, potential. We now define an effective one-electron Hamiltonian operator by

$$\hat{H}_1^{\text{eff}}(\mathbf{r}_1) = -\frac{1}{2}\nabla_1^2 - \frac{Z}{r_1} + U_1^{\text{eff}}(\mathbf{r}_1) \qquad (8\text{-}27)$$

The Schrödinger equation corresponding to this effective Hamiltonian is

$$\hat{H}_1^{\text{eff}}(\mathbf{r}_1)\phi(\mathbf{r}_1) = \varepsilon_1\phi(\mathbf{r}_1) \tag{8-28}$$

Equation 8-28 is the *Hartree-Fock equation* for a helium atom. The solution to Eq. 8-28 gives the best orbital wave function for helium.

Although we have deduced Eq. 8-28 by a physical argument, it is possible to derive Eq. 8-28 directly by applying the variational principle to the energy of a helium atom:

$$E = \iint d\mathbf{r}_1\, d\mathbf{r}_2\, \phi^*(\mathbf{r}_1)\phi^*(\mathbf{r}_2)\hat{H}\phi(\mathbf{r}_1)\phi(\mathbf{r}_2) \tag{8-29}$$

If we substitute Eq. 8-3 for $\hat{H}$ into Eq. 8-29, then we find (Problem 10)

$$E = I_1 + I_2 + J_{12} \tag{8-30}$$

where

$$I_j = \int d\mathbf{r}_j\, \phi^*(\mathbf{r}_j)\left[-\frac{1}{2}\nabla_j^2 - \frac{Z}{r_j}\right]\phi(\mathbf{r}_j) \tag{8-31}$$

and

$$J_{12} = \iint d\mathbf{r}_1\, d\mathbf{r}_2\, \phi^*(\mathbf{r}_1)\phi^*(\mathbf{r}_2)\frac{1}{r_{12}}\phi(\mathbf{r}_1)\phi(\mathbf{r}_2) \tag{8-32}$$

The integral J_{12} here is called a *Coulomb integral*. Equation 8-28 can be obtained by minimizing E with respect to ϕ.

Because $\hat{H}_1^{\text{eff}}$ in Eq. 8-28 is spherically symmetric, we write

$$\phi(\mathbf{r}) = R(r)Y_l^m(\theta, \phi) \tag{8-33}$$

where $R(r)$ is a radial function to be determined and $Y_l^m(\theta, \phi)$ is a spherical harmonic. If Eq. 8-33 is substituted into Eq. 8-28, we obtain (Problem 11)

$$\left[-\frac{1}{2r_1^2}\frac{d}{dr_1}\left(r_1^2\frac{d}{dr_1}\right) - \frac{Z}{r_1} + \frac{l(l+1)}{2r_1^2} + U_1^{\text{eff}}(r_1)\right]R(r_1) = \varepsilon R(r_1) \tag{8-34}$$

It appears now that we have an ordinary differential equation to solve here, but there is a catch. Recall that $U_1^{\text{eff}}(r_1)$ depends on $\phi(\mathbf{r}_2)$, or $R(r_2)$ (see Eq. 8-26). Thus, we must know the solution to Eq. 8-34 before we even know the operator. The method of solving an equation like Eq. 8-34 is by the *self-consistent field method*. We first guess the form of $\phi(r)$. We next use $\phi(r)$ to evaluate $U_1^{\text{eff}}(r_1)$ by Eq. 8-26 and then solve Eq. 8-34 for a new $\phi(r_1)$. Usually, after one cycle like this, the $\phi(r)$ that is used as input and the $\phi(r_1)$ obtained as output differ. We then use this new $\phi(r)$ as input by calculating $U_1^{\text{eff}}(r_1)$ with this new $\phi(r)$ and then solve Eq. 8-34 for a newer $\phi(r_1)$. This cyclic process is continued until the $\phi(r)$ used as input and the $\phi(r)$ obtained from Eq. 8-34 are sufficiently close, or are *self-consistent*. The orbitals obtained by this method are the *Hartree-Fock orbitals*.

In practice, one uses linear combinations of Slater orbitals for $\phi(r)$, varying the parameters in each Slater orbital and the number of Slater orbitals used until convergence is obtained. For helium, the result obtained by Enrico

Clementi of the IBM Research Laboratory is [IBM J. Res. Develop. 9, 2 (1965)]

$$\phi_{1s}(r_1) = \sum_{j=1}^{5} N_j c_j e^{-\zeta_j r_1} \qquad (8\text{-}35)$$

with an identical equation for $\phi_{1s}(r_2)$. In Eq. 8-35, the N_j are normalization constants and the c_j and ζ_j variational parameters, whose values are as follows:

j	c_j	ζ_j
1	0.78503	1.4300
2	0.20284	2.4415
3	0.03693	4.0996
4	−0.00293	6.4843
5	0.00525	0.7978

The method using linear combinations of Slater orbitals in Hartree-Fock calculations was developed by Professor C. Roothaan, of the University of Chicago. The *Hartree-Fock-Roothaan procedure* is widely used for the calculation of atomic orbitals. We shall discuss the Hartree-Fock-Roothaan method again in Section 8-7.

It is interesting to examine the physical significance of the eigenvalue ε in Eq. 8-28. The quantity ε is called the *orbital energy*. If we multiply Eq. 8-28 from the left by $\phi^*(r_1)$ and integrate, then we obtain

$$\int d\mathbf{r}_1 \, \phi^*(\mathbf{r}_1) \hat{H}_1^{\text{eff}}(\mathbf{r}_1) \phi(\mathbf{r}_1) = \varepsilon_1 \qquad (8\text{-}36)$$

Using Eq. 8-27 for $\hat{H}_1^{\text{eff}}$ and the definitions in Eqs. 8-31 and 8-32, we obtain

$$\varepsilon_1 = I_1 + J_{12} \qquad (8\text{-}37)$$

We first note that the total energy of a helium atom is *not* the sum of its orbital energies, because

$$\varepsilon_1 + \varepsilon_2 = (I_1 + J_{12}) + (I_2 + J_{12}) \neq E$$

(see Eq. 8-30). If we compare Eq. 8-37 and 8-30, then we see that

$$\varepsilon_1 = E - I_2 \qquad (8\text{-}38)$$

But according to Eq. 8-31, I_2 is the energy of a helium ion, calculated with the helium Hartree-Fock orbital $\phi(r)$. Thus, Eq. 8-38 suggests that the orbital energy ε_1 is an approximation to the ionization energy of a helium atom or that

$$\text{IE} \approx -\varepsilon_1 \qquad \text{(Koopmans' theorem)} \qquad (8\text{-}39)$$

Equation 8-39 is known as *Koopmans' theorem*. Even within the Hartree-Fock approximation, Koopmans' theorem is based on the approximation that the same orbitals can be used to calculate the energy of the neutral atom and the energy of the ion. The value of $-\varepsilon_1$ obtained by Clementi is 0.91796 au, compared to the experimental value of 0.904 au.

We can also calculate the ionization energy of a helium atom by using the exact value of E_{He^+}.

EXAMPLE 8-2

Calculate the ionization energy of a helium atom by using the Hartree-Fock energy of the helium atom and the exact energy of a helium ion.

Solution: The exact energy of a helium ion is

$$E_{He^+} = -\frac{Z^2}{2} = -2 \text{ au}$$

because $Z = 2$ for helium. The ionization energy is given by

$$IE = E_{He^+} - E_{He} = -2 + 2.86168$$
$$= 0.86168 \text{ au}$$

This is the Hartree-Fock value of the ionization energy given in Table 8-2. The experimental value is 0.904 au.

The Hartree-Fock method gives $E = -2.8617$ au compared to $E_{exact} = -2.9037$ au. This procedure yields the best value of the energy under the orbital approximation and the results seem to justify the use of the orbital concept for many-electron atoms (and molecules). It is interesting to investigate the discrepancy between the self-consistent field energy and the exact energy. Because $\psi(r_1, r_2) = \phi(r_1)\phi(r_2)$, the two electrons are taken to be independent of each other, or at least interacting only through some average, or effective, potential. We say, then, that the electrons are uncorrelated and we define a *correlation energy* (CE) by the equation

$$\text{correlation energy} = E_{exact} - E_{HF} \tag{8-40}$$

For helium, the correlation energy is

$$CE = (-2.9037 + 2.8617) \text{ au}$$
$$= -0.0420 \text{ au}$$

Although the Hartree-Fock energy in this case is almost 99% of the exact energy, the difference is greater than 1 eV or 110 kJ·mol^{-1}. The calculation of correlation energies and the inclusion of electron correlations in atomic and molecular wave functions is a problem of current and active interest. We shall say more about correlation energies in Section 8-7.

So much for the ground state of the helium atom. Let us go on and look at the lithium atom. Following Eq. 8-25, it would be "natural" to start a variational calculation with

$$\psi(r_1, r_2, r_3) = \phi_{1s}(r_1)\phi_{1s}(r_2)\phi_{1s}(r_3)$$

where ϕ_{1s} is a hydrogenlike or Slater 1s orbital, but we probably all know from general chemistry that you cannot put three electrons into a $1s$ orbital. This fact leads us to a discussion of the Pauli Exclusion Principle and to the spin of the electron.

8-4   *An Electron Has An Intrinsic Spin Angular Momentum*

As early as 1921, the American physicist Arthur H. Compton, who was studying the scattering of X rays from crystal surfaces, was led to conclude that "the electron itself, spinning like a tiny gyroscope, is probably the ultimate magnetic particle." The belief of the times, however, was that it was an entire atom or molecule that possessed a magnetic moment, because an enormous body of atomic spectroscopic data could be explained in this way. In 1922, two German physicists Otto Stern and Walter Gerlach passed a beam of silver atoms through an inhomogeneous magnetic field in order to split the beam into its $2l + 1$ space-quantized components. A homogeneous magnetic field will orient magnetic dipoles but not exert a translational force. An inhomogeneous magnetic field, however, will exert a translational force (Problem 13) and hence spatially separate magnetic dipoles that are oriented differently. Classically, a beam of magnetic dipoles will orient themselves through a continuous angle and so will become spread out in a continuous manner. Quantum mechanically, however, we have seen in Section 6-11 that a state with a given value of l will be restricted to $2l + 1$ discrete orientations, and so such a system will be split into $2l + 1$ components by an inhomogeneous magnetic field. Stern and Gerlach found the quite unexpected result that a beam of silver atoms splits into only two parts. Note that this corresponds to $2l + 1 = 2$, or to $l = \frac{1}{2}$. Up to now we have admitted only integer values of l.

Another similar observation is the so-called *doublet* that occurs in the spectra of alkali atoms (Section 8-11). These observations cannot be explained using the ideas and equations that we have developed up to now, and although there were indeed ingenious theories for all of these observations, the later contributions of a number of people made these explanations more and more tenuous. In addition, why all the electrons in the ground state of an atom do not occur in the innermost shell, which is the shell of lowest energy, was not understood. Niels Bohr had done a great deal of work on the periodic system of the elements and this was always an underlying nagging question.

In 1925, Wolfgang Pauli showed that all these observations could be explained with the postulate that an electron can exist in two distinct states. Pauli introduced a fourth quantum number in a rather ad hoc manner. This fourth quantum number, now called the *spin quantum number* m_s, is restricted to the two values $+\frac{1}{2}$ and $-\frac{1}{2}$. It is interesting that Pauli did not give any interpretation to this fourth quantum number. The existence of a fourth quantum number was somewhat of a mystery because the three spatial coordinates of an electron account for n, l, and m, but what is this fourth quantum number due to?

It was finally two Dutch physicists George Uhlenbeck and Samuel Goudsmit in 1925 who showed that the two intrinsic states of an electron could be

Wolfgang Pauli (1900–1958) received his Ph.D. at the University of Munich in 1921. He later worked with both Niels Bohr and Max Born. From 1928 until his death, Pauli held a position at the Eidgenossische Technische Hochschule (Federal Institute of Technology) at Zurich. Pauli mastered Einstein's papers on relativity while in high school and wrote a masterful monograph on the special and general theories of relativity when he was only 20 years old. Pauli later turned his considerable talent to nuclear physics, and predicted the existence of the neutrino. Pauli was famous for his sharp and critical judgment. He was awarded the Nobel Prize for physics in 1945.

George Uhlenbeck (b. 1900), *left*, and **Samuel Goudsmit** (1902–1978), *right*, were students together at the University of Leiden, and both received their Ph.D.'s in 1927. In that year they both were offered positions at the University of Michigan, where they remained until World War II. During World War II, they were involved in military radar research. After the war, Uhlenbeck returned to the University of Michigan, and Goudsmit went to the Brookhaven National Laboratory. In 1944 and 1945, Goudsmit accompanied the United States Army into newly liberated areas in order to learn what progress the Germans were making in nuclear research. Amazingly, neither ever received the Nobel Prize.

identified with two angular momenta, or spin, states. We have seen earlier that the orbital motion of electrons leads to an associated magnetic moment. In this case, it is the intrinsic spin of the electron that leads to a magnetic moment. It is as if the spinning electron produces an internal electric current, although this internal current is not observable, or real, in the classical sense.

We are going to simply graft the concept of spin onto the quantum theory and onto the postulates that we have developed earlier. This may appear to be a somewhat unsatisfactory way to proceed, but it turns out to be quite satisfactory for our purposes. In the early 1930s, Dirac developed a relativistic extension of quantum mechanics, and one of its greatest successes is that spin arose in a perfectly natural way. We shall introduce spin here, however, in an ad hoc manner.

We have seen from the Stern-Gerlach experiment that a beam of silver atoms splits into two components, implying that the magnetic moment of the electron and its associated angular momentum is described by an angular momentum quantum number $l = \frac{1}{2}$. Just as we have the eigenvalue equations for $\hat{L}^2$ and $\hat{L}_z$,

$$\hat{L}^2 Y_l^m(\theta, \phi) = \hbar^2 l(l + 1) Y_l^m(\theta, \phi) \tag{8-41}$$

and

$$\hat{L}_z Y_l^m(\theta, \phi) = m\hbar Y_l^m(\theta, \phi) \tag{8-42}$$

we define the spin operators $\hat{S}^2$ and $\hat{S}_z$ and their eigenfunctions α and β by the equations

$$\hat{S}^2 \alpha = \frac{1}{2}(\frac{1}{2} + 1)\hbar^2 \alpha \qquad \hat{S}^2 \beta = \frac{1}{2}(\frac{1}{2} + 1)\hbar^2 \beta$$

$$\hat{S}_z \alpha = \frac{1}{2}\hbar\alpha \qquad \hat{S}_z \beta = -\frac{1}{2}\hbar\beta \tag{8-43}$$

In a sense, $\alpha = Y_{1/2}^{1/2}$ and $\beta = Y_{1/2}^{-1/2}$, but this is a strictly *formal* association and α and β, and even $\hat{S}^2$ and $\hat{S}_z$ for that matter, do not have to be specified any further.

Just as we can write that the value of the orbital angular momentum of an electron in a hydrogen atom is given by

$$L = \hbar\sqrt{l(l + 1)} \tag{8-44}$$

we can say that the spin angular momentum of an electron is

$$S = \hbar\sqrt{s(s + 1)} \tag{8-45}$$

Unlike l, which can vary from 0 to ∞, s can have only the value $s = \frac{1}{2}$. Note that because s is not allowed to assume large values, the spin angular momentum can never assume classical behavior. Spin is strictly a nonclassical concept. The functions α and β in Eq. 8-43 are called *spin eigenfunctions*. We assume that α and β are orthonormal, which we write *formally as*

$$\int \alpha^* \alpha \, d\sigma = \int \beta^* \beta \, d\sigma = 1$$

$$\int \alpha^* \beta \, d\sigma = \int \alpha\beta^* \, d\sigma = 0 \tag{8-46}$$

where σ is called the *spin variable*. The spin variable has no classical analog.

Furthermore, for orbital angular momentum, we have the equations

$$\mu_L = -\frac{e}{2m_e}\,\mathbf{L}$$

or

$$\mu_L = -\frac{e\hbar}{2m_e}\sqrt{l(l+1)} = -\beta_0\sqrt{l(l+1)} \tag{8-47}$$

and

$$\mu_{zL} = -\frac{e}{2m_e}\,L_z = -\beta_0 m \tag{}$$

where β_0 is the Bohr magneton. For spin angular momentum, to obtain agreement with a number of experimental observations, we must assume or postulate that

$$\mu_s = -g\beta_0\sqrt{s(s+1)} \tag{8-48}$$

where $g = 2.0023$. For several years, g was called the "anomalous" spin factor, but it came as a natural result from Dirac's relativistic quantum theory. According to Eq. 8-48 then, we have

$$\mu_{zs} = -g\beta_0 m_s \approx \pm\beta_0 \tag{8-49}$$

In the Stern-Gerlach experiment, the two projections of the split beam occurred at positions consistent with magnetic moments $\pm\beta_0$, just as Eq. 8-49 predicts.

8-5   *Wave Functions Must Be Antisymmetric in the Interchange of Any Two Electrons*

We must now include the spin function with the spatial wave function. We postulate that the spatial and spin parts of a wave function are independent and so write

$$\Psi(x, y, z, \sigma) = \psi(x, y, z)\alpha(\sigma) \quad \text{or} \quad \psi(x, y, z)\beta(\sigma) \tag{8-50}$$

The complete one-electron wave function Ψ is called a *spin orbital*. Using the hydrogenlike wave functions as specific examples, the first two spin-orbitals of a hydrogenlike atom are

$$\Psi_{100\frac{1}{2}} = \left(\frac{Z^3}{\pi}\right)^{1/2} e^{-Zr}\alpha$$

$$\Psi_{100-\frac{1}{2}} = \left(\frac{Z^3}{\pi}\right)^{1/2} e^{-Zr}\beta \tag{8-51}$$

It follows that each of these spin orbitals is normalized because we can write

$$\int \Psi_{100\frac{1}{2}}^*(\mathbf{r}, \sigma)\Psi_{100\frac{1}{2}}(\mathbf{r}, \sigma)4\pi r^2\,dr\,d\sigma = \int_0^\infty \frac{Z^3}{\pi}e^{-2Zr}4\pi r^2\,dr \int \alpha^*\alpha\,d\sigma = 1 \tag{8-52}$$

where we have used Eq. 8-46. The spin orbitals are orthogonal to each other because

$$\int \Psi^*_{100\frac{1}{2}}(\mathbf{r}, \sigma)\Psi_{100-\frac{1}{2}}(\mathbf{r}, \sigma)\, d\mathbf{r}\, d\sigma = \int_0^\infty \frac{Z^3}{\pi} e^{-2Zr} 4\pi r^2\, dr \int \alpha^* \beta\, d\sigma = 0$$

$$(8\text{-}53)$$

Note that even though the "100" part in Eq. 8-53 is normalized, the two wave functions are orthogonal due to the spin parts.

You probably remember from general chemistry that no two electrons in an atom can have the same values of all four quantum numbers, n, l, m, and m_s. This restriction is called the *Pauli Exclusion Principle*. Note that the two wave functions given in Eq. 8-51 satisfy the Pauli Exclusion Principle. There is another more fundamental statement of the Exclusion Principle that restricts the form of a multielectron wave function. We shall present the Pauli Exclusion Principle as another postulate of quantum mechanics, but before doing so we must introduce the idea of an *antisymmetric wave function*. Let us go back to helium and write

$$\psi(1, 2) = 1s\alpha(1)1s\beta(2) \qquad (8\text{-}54)$$

where $1s\alpha$ and $1s\beta$ are shorthand notation for $\Psi_{100\frac{1}{2}}$ and $\Psi_{100-\frac{1}{2}}$, respectively, and where the arguments 1 and 2 denote all four coordinates $(x, y, z,$ and $\sigma)$ of electrons 1 and 2, respectively. Note that Eq. 8-54 corresponds to a product of the two wave functions given by Eq. 8-51. Because electrons are indistinguishable from each other and cannot really be labeled, the wave function

$$\psi(2, 1) = 1s\alpha(2)1s\beta(1) \qquad (8\text{-}55)$$

is equivalent to Eq. 8-54. Linear combinations of Eq. 8-54 and 8-55 are

$$\Psi_1 = \psi(1, 2) + \psi(2, 1) = 1s\alpha(1)1s\beta(2) + 1s\alpha(2)1s\beta(1) \qquad (8\text{-}56)$$

and

$$\Psi_2 = \psi(1, 2) - \psi(2, 1) = 1s\alpha(1)1s\beta(2) - 1s\alpha(2)1s\beta(1) \qquad (8\text{-}57)$$

Both Ψ_1 and Ψ_2 describe states in which there are two indistinguishable electrons; one electron is in the spin orbital $1s\alpha$ and the other is in $1s\beta$. Neither wave function specifies which electron is in each spin orbital, nor should they because the electrons are indistinguishable.

Both of the wave functions Ψ_1 and Ψ_2 appear to be acceptable wave functions for the ground state of a helium atom, but experimentally only the wave function Ψ_2 describes the ground state of a helium atom. Note that Ψ_2 has the property that it changes sign when the two electrons are interchanged, because

$$\Psi_2(1, 2) = \psi(1, 2) - \psi(2, 1)$$

and

$$\Psi_2(2, 1) = \psi(2, 1) - \psi(1, 2) = -\Psi_2(1, 2) \qquad (8\text{-}58)$$

We say that $\Psi_2(1, 2)$ is *antisymmetric* under the interchange of the two electrons. The generalization of the observation that the ground state of a helium atom described by only Ψ_2 is in accord with experimental data is the Pauli Exclusion

Principle, which says that

Postulate 6

All electronic wave functions must be antisymmetric under the interchange of any two electrons.

EXAMPLE 8-3

Show that Ψ_1 given by Eq. 8-56 is symmetric under the interchange of the two electrons and is not acceptable as an electronic wave function.

Solution: Equation 8-56 is

$$\Psi_1(1, 2) = \psi(1, 2) + \psi(2, 1)$$

If we interchange the two electrons, then we find

$$\Psi_1(2, 1) = \psi(2, 1) + \psi(1, 2) = \Psi_1(1, 2)$$

Thus we see that Ψ_1 is *symmetric* under the interchange of the two electrons. According to the Pauli Exclusion Principle, symmetric wave functions are not acceptable as electronic wave functions.

In Section 8-6, we shall show that Postulate 6 implies the more familiar statement of the Pauli Exclusion Principle, that no two electrons in an atom can have the same values of the four quantum numbers, n, l, m, and m_s.

8-6   *Antisymmetric Wave Functions Can Be Represented by Slater Determinants*

Now that we have introduced spin and have seen that we must use antisymmetric wave functions, we must ask why when we treated the helium atom in Section 8-2 we were able to ignore the spin part of the wave function. The reason is that Ψ_2 can be factored into a spatial part and a spin part. To see that this is so, notice that

$$\Psi_2 = 1s\alpha(1)1s\beta(2) - 1s\alpha(2)1s\beta(1)$$
$$= 1s(\mathbf{r}_1)1s(\mathbf{r}_2)[\alpha(\sigma_1)\beta(\sigma_2) - \alpha(\sigma_2)\beta(\sigma_1)] \qquad (8\text{-}59)$$

In Section 8-2 we used only the spatial part of Ψ_2, and the spatial part is just a product of two $1s$ Slater orbitals. If we use Ψ_2 to calculate the ground-state energy of a helium atom, then we obtain

$$E = \frac{\int d\mathbf{r}_1\, d\mathbf{r}_2\, d\sigma_1\, d\sigma_2\, \Psi_2^*(1, 2)\hat{H}\Psi_2(1, 2)}{\int d\mathbf{r}_1\, d\mathbf{r}_2\, d\sigma_1\, d\sigma_2\, \Psi_2^*(1, 2)\Psi_2(1, 2)} \qquad (8\text{-}60)$$

The numerator of Eq. 8-60 is

$$\int d\mathbf{r}_1 \, d\mathbf{r}_2 \, d\sigma_1 \, d\sigma_2 \, 1s^*(\mathbf{r}_1)1s^*(\mathbf{r}_2)[\alpha^*(\sigma_1)\beta^*(\sigma_2) - \alpha^*(\sigma_2)\beta^*(\sigma_1)]\hat{H}$$

$$\times \, 1s(\mathbf{r}_1)1s(\mathbf{r}_2)[\alpha(\sigma_1)\beta(\sigma_2) - \alpha(\sigma_2)\beta(\sigma_1)] \qquad (8\text{-}61)$$

Because the Hamiltonian does not contain any spin operators, it does not affect the spin functions and so we can factor the integral in Eq. 8-61 to give

$$\int d\mathbf{r}_1 \, d\mathbf{r}_2 \, 1s^*(\mathbf{r}_1)1s^*(\mathbf{r}_2)\hat{H}1s(\mathbf{r}_1)1s(\mathbf{r}_2)$$

$$\times \int d\sigma_1 \, d\sigma_2 \, [\alpha^*(\sigma_1)\beta^*(\sigma_2) - \alpha^*(\sigma_2)\beta^*(\sigma_1)][\alpha(\sigma_1)\beta(\sigma_2) - \alpha(\sigma_2)\beta(\sigma_1)] \quad (8\text{-}62)$$

The second integral here, the one over the spin variables σ_1 and σ_2, becomes the sum of four integrals when the two brackets are multiplied out. Two of these four integrals are

$$\int d\sigma_1 \, d\sigma_2 \, \alpha^*(\sigma_1)\beta^*(\sigma_2)\alpha(\sigma_1)\beta(\sigma_2) = \int d\sigma_1 \, \alpha^*(\sigma_1)\alpha(\sigma_1) \int d\sigma_2 \, \beta^*(\sigma_2)\beta(\sigma_2) = 1$$

and

$$\int d\sigma_1 \, d\sigma_2 \, \alpha^*(\sigma_1)\beta^*(\sigma_2)\beta(\sigma_1)\alpha(\sigma_2) = \int d\sigma_1 \, \alpha^*(\sigma_1)\beta(\sigma_1) \int d\sigma_2 \, \beta^*(\sigma_2)\alpha(\sigma_2) = 0$$

where we have used the orthonormality conditions of the spin functions, Eq. 8-46. The other two integrals in Eq. 8-62 are evaluated in exactly the same manner and give 0 and 1. Thus, the entire contribution of the integral over the spin variables is simply a factor of 2. It is a straightforward exercise (Problem 15) to show that the spin contribution to the denominator in Eq. 8-60 is also equal to 2 and so Eq. 8-60 becomes

$$E = \frac{\int d\mathbf{r}_1 \, d\mathbf{r}_2 \, \psi^*(\mathbf{r}_1, \mathbf{r}_2)\hat{H}\psi(\mathbf{r}_1, \mathbf{r}_2)}{\int d\mathbf{r}_1 \, d\mathbf{r}_2 \, \psi^*(\mathbf{r}_1, \mathbf{r}_2)\psi(\mathbf{r}_1, \mathbf{r}_2)} \qquad (8\text{-}63)$$

where $\psi(\mathbf{r}_1, \mathbf{r}_2)$ is just the spatial part of $\Psi_2(1, 2)$. Equation 8-63 is equivalent to Eq. 8-16 in Section 8-2. It is important to realize that a factorization into a spatial part and a spin part does not occur in general but that it does occur for two-electron systems.

It is fairly easy to write the antisymmetric two-electron wave function by inspection, but what if we have a set of N spin orbitals and we need to construct an antisymmetric N-electron wave function? In the early 1930s, Slater introduced the use of determinants to construct antisymmetric wave functions. If we use Eq. 8-59 as an example, then we see that we can write Ψ in the form

$$\Psi(1, 2) = \begin{vmatrix} 1s\alpha(1) & 1s\beta(1) \\ 1s\alpha(2) & 1s\beta(2) \end{vmatrix} \qquad (8\text{-}64)$$

The wave function $\Psi(1, 2)$ given by Eq. 8-64 is called a *determinantal wave function*. There are two properties of determinants that are of particular importance to us. The first property is that the sign of a determinant changes when we interchange any two rows or any two columns of the determinant. The second property is that a determinant is equal to zero if any two rows or any two columns are the same.

EXAMPLE 8-4

Evaluate the determinant

$$D = \begin{vmatrix} a & b \\ c & d \end{vmatrix}$$

and show that D changes sign if we interchange the rows or the columns. Show that $D = 0$ if the two columns are the same, that is, if $a = b$ and $c = d$.

Solution: By definition, the value of D is

$$D = ad - bc$$

If we interchange the rows of D, then we have

$$D_1 = \begin{vmatrix} c & d \\ a & b \end{vmatrix} = bc - ad = -D$$

If we interchange the columns of D, then we find

$$D_2 = \begin{vmatrix} b & a \\ d & c \end{vmatrix} = bc - ad = -D$$

If the two columns are the same, then

$$D_3 = \begin{vmatrix} a & a \\ c & c \end{vmatrix} = ac - ac = 0$$

Problem 16 extends these conclusions to a 3×3 determinant.

Notice that when we interchange the two electrons in the determinantal wave function $\Psi(1, 2)$, we interchange the two rows and so change the sign of $\Psi(1, 2)$. Furthermore, if we place both electrons into the same spin orbital, say the $1s\alpha$ spin orbital, then $\Psi(1, 2)$ becomes

$$\Psi(1, 2) = \begin{vmatrix} 1s\alpha(1) & 1s\alpha(1) \\ 1s\alpha(2) & 1s\alpha(2) \end{vmatrix} = 0$$

This determinant is equal to zero because the two columns are the same. Thus, we see that the determinantal representation of wave functions automatically satisfies the Pauli Exclusion Principle. Determinantal wave functions are always antisymmetric and vanish when any two electrons have the same four quantum numbers, that is, when both electrons occupy the same spin orbital.

We need to consider one more factor before our discussion of determinantal wave functions is complete. Let us evaluate the integral

$$I = \int d\mathbf{r}_1\, d\mathbf{r}_2\, d\sigma_1\, d\sigma_2\, \Psi^*(1, 2)\Psi(1, 2) \tag{8-65}$$

When we use Eq. 8-64 for $\Psi(1, 2)$ and multiply out the integrand in Eq. 8-65, then we see that I is the sum of four terms. The first term is

$$I_1 = \int 1s\alpha^*(1)1s\beta^*(2)1s\alpha(1)1s\beta(2)\, d\mathbf{r}_1\, d\mathbf{r}_2\, d\sigma_1\, d\sigma_2 \tag{8-66}$$

Using the fact that $1s\alpha^*(1) \equiv 1s^*(r_1)\alpha^*(\sigma_1)$, and so on, we can write Eq. 8-66 as

$$I_1 = \int d\mathbf{r}_1\, d\mathbf{r}_2\, d\sigma_1\, d\sigma_2\, 1s^*(r_1)\alpha^*(\sigma_1)1s^*(r_2)\beta^*(\sigma_2)1s(r_1)\alpha(\sigma_1)1s(r_2)\beta(\sigma_2)$$

$$= \int d\mathbf{r}_1\, d\mathbf{r}_2\, 1s^*(r_1)1s(r_1)1s^*(r_2)1s(r_2)\int d\sigma_1\, d\sigma_2\, \alpha^*(\sigma_1)\alpha(\sigma_1)\beta^*(\sigma_2)\beta(\sigma_2) \tag{8-67}$$

The spin part of I_1 here is unity, and so the entire integral is unity if we assume that the spatial part of the wave function is normalized. By continuing this argument, we find that two of the terms in Eq. 8-65 are unity and two are zero. Thus, we find that $I = 2$ in Eq. 8-65. Thus we see that (Problem 17)

$$\Psi(1, 2) = \frac{1}{\sqrt{2}}\begin{vmatrix} 1s\alpha(1) & 1s\beta(1) \\ 1s\alpha(2) & 1s\beta(2) \end{vmatrix} \tag{8-68}$$

is a *normalized* two-electron determinantal wave function. The factor of $1/\sqrt{2}$ assures that $\Psi(1, 2)$ is normalized.

We have developed the determinantal representation of wave functions using a two-electron system as an example. To generalize this development for an N-electron system, we use an $N \times N$ determinant. Furthermore, one can show (Problem 19) that the normalization constant is $1/\sqrt{N!}$, and so we have the N-electron determinantal wave function

$$\Psi(1, 2, \ldots, N) = \frac{1}{\sqrt{N!}}\begin{vmatrix} u_1(1) & u_2(1) & \cdots & u_N(1) \\ u_1(2) & u_2(2) & \cdots & u_N(2) \\ \vdots & \vdots & & \vdots \\ u_1(N) & u_2(N) & \cdots & u_N(N) \end{vmatrix} \tag{8-69}$$

where the u's in Eq. 8-69 are spin orbitals. Notice that $\Psi(1, 2, \ldots, N)$ changes sign whenever two electrons (rows) are interchanged and vanishes if any two electrons occupy the same spin orbital (two identical columns).

We are now ready to go back to the problem that led us to discuss spin, that is, the lithium atom. Note that we cannot put all three electrons into $1s$ orbitals because two columns in the determinantal wave function would be the same. Thus an appropriate wave function is

$$\Psi = \frac{1}{\sqrt{3!}}\begin{vmatrix} 1s\alpha(1) & 1s\beta(1) & 2s\alpha(1) \\ 1s\alpha(2) & 1s\beta(2) & 2s\alpha(2) \\ 1s\alpha(3) & 1s\beta(3) & 2s\alpha(3) \end{vmatrix} \tag{8-70}$$

The standard method for determining the best form of the spatial part of the spin orbitals in a determinantal wave function such as Eq. 8-69 or 8-70 is the Hartree-Fock self-consistent field method, which we outline in the next section.

8-7   *The Hartree-Fock Method Uses Antisymmetric Wave Functions*

Now that we have introduced spin into our atomic wave functions, we are ready to discuss the application of the Hartree-Fock method to more complex atoms. We discussed the Hartree-Fock method for helium in Section 8-3, but the application of the Hartree-Fock method to atoms that contain three or more electrons introduces new terms that occur because of the determinantal nature of the wave functions. For simplicity, we shall consider only closed-shell systems, in which the wave functions are represented by N doubly occupied spatial orbitals. In such cases, the atomic wave function is given by one Slater determinant. For open-shell systems, the wave function is usually a linear combination of Slater determinants (see Problem 23).

The Hamiltonian operator for a $2N$-electron atom is

$$\hat{H} = -\frac{1}{2}\sum_{j=1}^{2N} \nabla_j^2 - \sum_{j=1}^{2N} \frac{Z}{r_j} + \sum_{i=1}^{2N}\sum_{j>i} \frac{1}{r_{ij}} \qquad (8\text{-}71)$$

and the wave function is

$$\Psi(1, 2, \ldots, 2N) = \frac{1}{\sqrt{(2N)!}} \begin{vmatrix} \phi_1\alpha(1) & \phi_1\beta(1) & \cdots & \phi_N\alpha(1) & \phi_N\beta(1) \\ \phi_1\alpha(2) & \phi_1\beta(2) & \cdots & \phi_N\alpha(2) & \phi_N\beta(2) \\ \vdots & \vdots & & \vdots & \vdots \\ \phi_1\alpha(2N) & \phi_1\beta(2N) & \cdots & \phi_N\alpha(2N) & \phi_N\beta(2N) \end{vmatrix}$$

$$(8\text{-}72)$$

The energy is given by

$$E = \int d\mathbf{r}_1 \, d\sigma_1 \cdots d\mathbf{r}_{2N} \, d\sigma_{2N} \, \Psi^*(1, 2, \ldots, 2N)\hat{H}\Psi(1, 2, \ldots, 2N) \qquad (8\text{-}73)$$

It is a straightforward but worthwhile exercise (Problem 25) to show that Eq. 8-73 can be written as

$$E = 2\sum_{j=1}^{N} I_j + \sum_{i=1}^{N}\sum_{j=1}^{N} (2J_{ij} - K_{ij}) \qquad (8\text{-}74)$$

where

$$I_j = \int d\mathbf{r}_j \, \phi_j^*(\mathbf{r}_j)\left(-\frac{1}{2}\nabla_j^2 - \frac{Z}{r_j}\right)\phi_j(\mathbf{r}_j) \qquad (8\text{-}75)$$

$$J_{ij} = \iint d\mathbf{r}_1 \, d\mathbf{r}_2 \, \phi_i^*(\mathbf{r}_1)\phi_j^*(\mathbf{r}_2)\frac{1}{r_{12}}\phi_i(\mathbf{r}_1)\phi_j(\mathbf{r}_2) \qquad (8\text{-}76)$$

and

$$K_{ij} = \iint d\mathbf{r}_1 \, d\mathbf{r}_2 \, \phi_i^*(\mathbf{r}_1)\phi_j^*(\mathbf{r}_2)\frac{1}{r_{12}}\phi_i(\mathbf{r}_2)\phi_j(\mathbf{r}_1) \qquad (8\text{-}77)$$

The factors of 2 in Eq. 8-74 occur because we are considering a closed-shell system with $2N$ electrons, N of which have a spin function α and N of which have a spin function β. The J_{ij} integrals are called *Coulomb integrals* and the K_{ij} integrals are called *exchange integrals* if $i \neq j$. Note that $K_{ii} = J_{ii}$, however.

EXAMPLE 8-5

Show that Eq. 8-74 for a helium atom is the same as Eq. 8-30.

Solution: Realize that $N = 1$ in Eq. 8-74 for a helium atom. If we apply Eq. 8-74 to a helium atom, then Eq. 8-74 becomes

$$E = 2I_1 + 2J_{11} - K_{11}$$

From the definitions of J_{ij} (Eq. 8-76) and K_{ij} (Eq. 8-77), we see that $J_{11} = K_{11}$, and so we have

$$E = 2I_1 + J_{11}$$

But this equation is exactly Eq. 8-30 in different notation.

The spatial orbitals $\phi_i(\mathbf{r}_i)$ are determined by applying the variational principle to Eq. 8-73. When the variational principle is applied to Eq. 8-73, the following equations are obtained:

$$\hat{F}_i \phi_i = \varepsilon_i \phi_i \qquad i = 1, 2, \ldots, N \tag{8-78}$$

The operator $\hat{F}_i$, called the *Fock operator*, is given by

$$\hat{F}_i = \hat{f}_i + \sum_j (2\hat{J}_j - \hat{K}_j) \tag{8-79}$$

where

$$\hat{f}_i = -\frac{1}{2} \nabla_i^2 - \frac{Z}{r_i} \tag{8-80}$$

$$\hat{J}_j(\mathbf{r}_1) \phi_i(\mathbf{r}_1) = \phi_i(\mathbf{r}_1) \int d\mathbf{r}_2 \, \phi_j^*(\mathbf{r}_2) \frac{1}{r_{12}} \phi_j(\mathbf{r}_2) \tag{8-81}$$

and

$$\hat{K}_j(\mathbf{r}_1) \phi_i(\mathbf{r}_1) = \phi_j(\mathbf{r}_1) \int d\mathbf{r}_2 \, \phi_j^*(\mathbf{r}_2) \frac{1}{r_{12}} \phi_i(\mathbf{r}_2) \tag{8-82}$$

Recall that the Hartree-Fock equation for helium does not contain the exchange term K_j because the ground state of helium is a two-electron system with $\phi_i = \phi_j$. As in the case of helium, the Fock operator in Eq. 8-78 depends on all the orbitals and cannot be evaluated through Eq. 8-79 to 8-82 until all the orbitals are known. Thus, Eq. 8-78 represents a set of N *coupled* equations. These equations can be solved numerically by a self-consistent field procedure in which one assumes an initial set of orbitals $\phi_i(\mathbf{r}_i)$ and then calculates an initial set of Fock operators. Using these Fock operators, we can now solve Eq. 8-78 to find a new set of orbitals. These new orbitals are used to calculate a new set of Fock operators, which in turn are used to calculate a still new set of orbitals. This cyclic procedure is continued until the orbitals of one cycle are essentially the same as those of the next cycle or, in other words, until they are self-consistent.

8-8   *Hartree-Fock Calculations Give Good Agreement with Experimental Data*

The eigenvalues ε_i of the Hartree-Fock approximation are called *orbital energies*, and according to Koopmans' theorem the orbital energies are approximations for the ionization energy of an electron from the ith orbital ϕ_i. The accuracy of Koopmans' approximation rests upon the assumption that the removal of an electron from the ith orbital does not affect the other $N - 1$ orbitals. Under that approximation, you can show that (Problem 27)

$$E^+ - E = \text{IE} = -\varepsilon_i \qquad (8\text{-}83)$$

where E and E^+ are the Hartree-Fock energies of the neutral atom and the positive ion, respectively. Table 8-3 compares the ionization energies from various orbitals of Cu^+ obtained by Koopmans' theorem to experimental data obtained by X-ray spectroscopy. Table 8-4 compares some ionization energies of neon and argon obtained by using Koopmans' theorem and also obtained by subtracting the Hartree-Fock energy of the neutral atom from that of the ion. One can see from Table 8-4 that Koopmans' theorem gives results that are almost as good as the direct calculation. Figure 8-1 shows the ionization energies of the elements hydrogen through krypton plotted against atomic number. Both ionization energies obtained by Koopmans' theorem and experimental data are shown in the figure. This plot clearly shows the shell and subshell structure that one first learns in general chemistry. Given that there are no adjustable parameters involved in the calculated values in Figure 8-1, the agreement with experimental data is remarkable.

TABLE 8-3

Comparison of Hartree-Fock Orbital Energies with Experimental Data of Cu^+ (Energies Are in Atomic Units)

	Ionization energy	
Orbital	Hartree-Fock	X-ray value
1s	658.4	661.4
2s	82.3	81.0
2p	71.8	68.9
3s	10.6	8.9
3p	7.3	5.7
3d	1.6	0.4

TABLE 8-4

Ionization Energies (in Electron Volts) of Ne and Ar Obtained from Neutral Atom Orbital Energies (Koopmans' Theorem) and by Subtracting the Hartree-Fock Energy of the Neutral Atom from the Hartree-Fock Energy of the Appropriate State of the Positive Ion

			Ionization energies		
	Orbital occupancy	Ion	Koopmans' theorem	Direct Hartree-Fock calculations	Experiment
1s hole	$1s2s^2 2p^6$	Ne$^+$	891.7	868.6	870.3
2s hole	$1s^2 2s 2p^6$	Ne$^+$	52.5	49.3	48.5
2p hole	$1s^2 2s^2 2p^5$	Ne$^+$	23.1	19.8	21.6
1s hole	$1s2s^2 2p^6 3s^2 3p^6$	Ar$^+$	3227.4	3195.2	3206.3
2s hole	$1s^2 2s 2p^6 3s^2 3p^6$	Ar$^+$	335.3	324.8	—
2p hole	$1s^2 2s^2 2p^5 3s^2 3p^6$	Ar$^+$	260.4	248.9	248.5
3s hole	$1s^2 2s^2 2p^6 3s 3p^6$	Ar$^+$	34.8	33.2	29.2
3p hole	$1s^2 2s^2 2p^6 3s^2 3p^5$	Ar$^+$	16.1	14.8	15.8

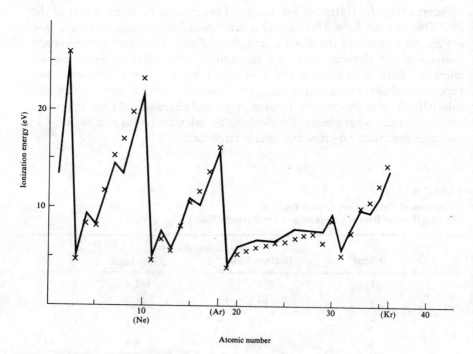

Figure 8-1. The ionization energies of neutral atoms of hydrogen through krypton plotted versus atomic number. The dots connected by straight lines are experimental data and the crosses are calculated according to Koopmans' theorem.

The self-consistent field (SCF) orbitals obtained from Eqs. 8-78 are called *Hartree-Fock orbitals*. Equations 8-78 are solved in practice by expressing the ϕ_i as linear combinations of Slater orbitals and treating the coefficients in the expansion and the exponential parameters in the Slater orbitals as variational parameters. This method was first introduced by Roothaan and is called the *Hartree-Fock-Roothaan method*. Hartree-Fock orbitals of many atoms and ions are available in the literature. Figure 8-2 shows the distribution of total electronic charge in an argon atom as a function of the distance from the nucleus. Note that the K, L, and M shells are clearly visible.

It is interesting to note that the order of the energies of the various subshells is in general agreement with observation for neutral atoms. Recall that the order for neutral atoms goes as $1s < 2s < 2p < 3s < 3p < 4s < 3d < 4p < 5s$, and so on. In particular, the energies of the $2s$ and $2p$ orbitals are not the same as they are in the case of the hydrogen atom. The degeneracy of the $2s$ and $2p$ orbitals or, more generally, the fact that the energy depends on only the principal quantum number is unique to the purely $1/r$ Coulombic potential in the hydrogen atom. In a Hartree-Fock calculation, the effective potential $U_j^{eff}(\mathbf{r}_j)$ is more complicated than $1/r$ and $U_j^{eff}(\mathbf{r}_j)$ breaks up the degeneracy that one finds in the hydrogen atom, giving us the familiar ordering of the orbital energies presented above and first learned in general chemistry.

We can deduce ground-state electron configurations of neutral atoms by starting with the $1s$ orbital and filling the orbitals up successively, placing 2 electrons in an s orbital, 6 electrons in the p orbitals, 10 electrons in the d orbitals, and so on. The ground-state electron configurations of the elements hydrogen through krypton are given in Table 8-5. Note that the first exception to the simple rule of filling orbitals successively occurs in chromium. Instead of having the electron configuration $[Ar]4s^2 3d^4$ as you might expect, it really is $[Ar]4s3d^5$ because half-filled and filled d orbitals have an extra degree of stability that

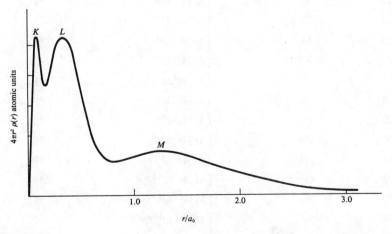

Figure 8-2. The distribution of electronic charge in an argon atom as a function of the distance from the nucleus.

TABLE 8-5

Ground State Electron Configurations and Term Symbols of the Elements Hydrogen through Krypton

Z	Atom	Electron configuration	Term symbol
1	H	$1s$	$^2S_{1/2}$
2	He	$1s^2$	$^1S_0$
3	Li	$[He]2s$	$^2S_{1/2}$
4	Be	$[He]2s^2$	$^1S_0$
5	B	$[He]2s^22p$	$^2P_{1/2}$
6	C	$[He]2s^22p^2$	$^3P_0$
7	N	$[He]2s^22p^3$	$^4S_{3/2}$
8	O	$[He]2s^22p^4$	$^3P_2$
9	F	$[He]2s^22p^5$	$^2P_{3/2}$
10	Ne	$[He]2s^22p^6$	$^1S_0$
11	Na	$[Ne]3s$	$^2S_{1/2}$
12	Mg	$[Ne]3s^2$	$^1S_0$
13	Al	$[Ne]3s^23p$	$^2P_{1/2}$
14	Si	$[Ne]3s^23p^2$	$^3P_0$
15	P	$[Ne]3s^23p^3$	$^4S_{3/2}$
16	S	$[Ne]3s^23p^4$	$^3P_2$
17	Cl	$[Ne]3s^23p^5$	$^2P_{3/2}$
18	Ar	$[Ne]3s^23p^6$	$^1S_0$
19	K	$[Ar]4s$	$^2S_{1/2}$
20	Ca	$[Ar]4s^2$	$^1S_0$
21	Sc	$[Ar]4s^23d$	$^2D_{3/2}$
22	Ti	$[Ar]4s^23d^2$	$^3F_2$
23	V	$[Ar]4s^23d^3$	$^4F_{3/2}$
24	Cr	$[Ar]4s3d^5$	$^7S_3$
25	Mn	$[Ar]4s^23d^5$	$^6S_{5/2}$
26	Fe	$[Ar]4s^23d^6$	$^5D_4$
27	Co	$[Ar]4s^23d^7$	$^4F_{9/2}$
28	Ni	$[Ar]4s^23d^8$	$^3F_4$
29	Cu	$[Ar]4s3d^{10}$	$^2S_{1/2}$
30	Zn	$[Ar]4s^23d^{10}$	$^1S_0$
31	Ga	$[Ar]4s^23d^{10}4p$	$^2P_{1/2}$
32	Ge	$[Ar]4s^23d^{10}4p^2$	$^3P_0$
33	As	$[Ar]4s^23d^{10}4p^3$	$^4S_{3/2}$
34	Se	$[Ar]4s^23d^{10}4p^4$	$^3P_2$
35	Br	$[Ar]4s^23d^{10}4p^5$	$^2P_{3/2}$
36	Kr	$[Ar]4s^23d^{10}4p^6$	$^1S_0$

can be achieved in this case by one of the $4s$ electrons going into the $3d$ orbital. This is seen also in the case of copper. Similar exceptions occur for heavier elements and in some cases the difference in energy between two different electronic configurations is so small that the exact specification of the ground state is uncertain.

Because the Hartree-Fock method uses determinantal wave functions, there is some correlation between electrons with the same spin. Two electrons with the same spin cannot occupy the same orbital. Electrons with different spins are uncorrelated, however, and so we define a correlation energy by (see Eq. 8-40)

$$\text{correlation energy} = E_{\text{exact}} - E_{\text{HF}}$$

For helium, the correlation energy is 0.042 au. Although correlation energies appear to be small, they are significant when we realize that many quantities of chemical interest are differences in energies (such as ΔH of a chemical reaction) and so small errors in E can become significant errors in ΔE. Consequently, much quantum-chemical research is directed toward the calculation of correlation energies. For example, perturbation schemes have been developed that treat the Hartree-Fock orbitals as the zero-order system, so that the correlation energy can be calculated by perturbation theory. Such calculations represent current quantum-chemical research.

8-9   *A Term Symbol Gives a Detailed Description of an Electron Configuration*

Many of the electron configurations in Table 8-5 are ambiguous in the sense that there are a number of sets of m and m_s consistent with the electron configuration. For example, consider the ground-state electron configuration of a carbon atom, $1s^2 2s^2 2p^2$. The two $2p$ electrons could be in any of the three $2p$ orbitals ($2p_x, 2p_y, 2p_z$) and have any spins consistent with the Pauli Exclusion Principle. The energies of these different states differ, and so we require a more detailed designation of the electronic states of atoms. The scheme that we shall present here is based upon the idea of determining the total orbital angular momentum **L** and the total spin angular momentum **S** and then adding **L** and **S** together to obtain the total angular momentum **J**. The result of such a calculation is presented as an *atomic term symbol*, which has the form

$$^{2S+1}L_J$$

In a term symbol, L is the total orbital angular momentum quantum number, S is the total spin quantum number, and J is the total angular momentum quantum number. We shall see that L will necessarily have values such as $0, 1, 2, \ldots$. Similar to assigning the letters s, p, d, f to the values $l = 0, 1, 2, 3$ of the orbital angular momentum in the case of the hydrogen atom, we shall make the correspondence

$$L = 0 \quad 1 \quad 2 \quad 3 \quad 4 \quad 5$$
$$ S \quad P \quad D \quad F \quad G \quad H$$

We shall also see that the total spin quantum number S will necessarily have values such as $0, \frac{1}{2}, 1, \frac{3}{2}, \ldots$, and so the $2S + 1$ left superscript on a term symbol will have values such as $1, 2, 3, \ldots$. Thus, ignoring for the time being the subscript J, term symbols will be of the type

$$^3S \quad ^2D \quad ^1P$$

A basic assumption in writing term symbols is that L and S are meaningful quantities. Realize that only the total angular momentum necessarily is conserved, which means that only J is a meaningful, or "good", quantum number. For light atoms, however, say with atomic number $Z < 40$, the total orbital angular momentum and the total spin angular momentum are almost separately conserved, and so L and S are almost "good" quantum numbers. The determination of **L** and **S** separately and then the coupling of **L** and **S** together to form **J** is called *spin-orbit coupling* or *Russell-Saunders coupling*. We shall discuss the justification for Russell-Saunders coupling more in Section 8-12, but now let us learn to deduce the possible atomic term symbols from electron configurations.

The total orbital angular momentum and the total spin angular momentum are given by

$$\mathbf{L} = \sum_i \mathbf{l}_i \qquad (8\text{-}84)$$

and

$$\mathbf{S} = \sum_i \mathbf{s}_i$$

where the summations are over the electrons in the atom. The z components of **L** and **S** are given by

$$L_z = \sum_i l_{zi} = \sum_i m_i = M \qquad (8\text{-}85)$$

$$S_z = \sum_i s_{zi} = \sum_i m_{is} = M_s \qquad (8\text{-}86)$$

Thus, although the angular momenta add vectorially as in Eq. 8-84, the z components add as scalars (Figure 8-3). Let us consider the electron configuration ns^2. There is only one set of possible values of m_1, m_{1s}, m_2, and m_{2s}

m_1	m_{1s}	m_2	m_{2s}	M	M_s
0	$+\frac{1}{2}$	0	$-\frac{1}{2}$	0	0

The fact that the only value of M is $M = 0$ implies that $L = 0$. Similarly, the fact that the only value of M_S is $M_S = 0$ implies that $S = 0$. The total angular momentum **J** is given by

$$\mathbf{J} = \mathbf{L} + \mathbf{S} \qquad (8\text{-}87)$$

and its z component is

$$J_z = L_z + S_z = (M + M_S) = M_J \qquad (8\text{-}88)$$

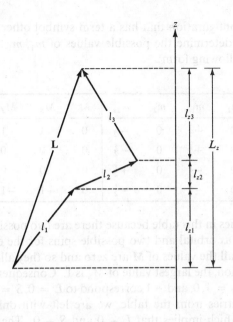

Figure 8-3. A schematic illustration of the addition of angular momentum vectors.

Because M and M_S above are equal only to zero, the only value of M_J is zero, which implies that $J = 0$. Consequently, for an ns^2 electron configuration, $L = 0$, $S = 0$, and $J = 0$. The value $L = 0$ is written as S in the term symbol, and so we find that the term symbol corresponding to an ns^2 electron configuration is $^1S_0$ (singlet S zero).

An np^6 electron configuration also will have a $^1S_0$ term symbol. To see this, realize that the three np orbitals have the quantum numbers $(n, 1, 1, \pm\frac{1}{2})$, $(n, 1, 0, \pm\frac{1}{2})$, and $(n, 1, -1, \pm\frac{1}{2})$. Therefore, $M = 0$ and $M_S = 0$ as for an ns^2 electron configuration, and we have $^1S_0$.

EXAMPLE 8-6

Show that the term symbol corresponding to an nd^{10} electron configuration is $^1S_0$.

Solution: The five d orbitals have the quantum numbers $(n, 2, 2, \pm\frac{1}{2})$, $(n, 2, 1, \pm\frac{1}{2})$, $(n, 2, 0, \pm\frac{1}{2})$, $(n, 2, -1, \pm\frac{1}{2})$, and $(n, 2, -2, \pm\frac{1}{2})$. Therefore, $M = 0$ and $M_S = 0$, as for the ns^2 and np^6 configurations, and the term symbol is $^1S_0$.

Notice that all completely filled subshells will necessarily have $M = 0$ and $M_S = 0$; thus, we can ignore the electrons in completely filled subshells when considering other electron configurations. We shall ignore the contributions of the $1s^2 2s^2$ orbitals to the $1s^2 2s^2 2p^2$ electron configurations of carbon when we discuss carbon later.

An electron configuration that has a term symbol other than $^1S_0$ is $nsn's$, where $n \neq n'$. To determine the possible values of m_1, m_{1s}, m_2, and m_{2s}, set up a table of the following form:

m_1	m_{1s}	m_2	m_{2s}	M	M_S	M_J
0	$+\frac{1}{2}$	0	$+\frac{1}{2}$	0	1	1
0	$+\frac{1}{2}$	0	$-\frac{1}{2}$	0	0	0
0	$-\frac{1}{2}$	0	$+\frac{1}{2}$	0	0	0
0	$-\frac{1}{2}$	0	$-\frac{1}{2}$	0	-1	-1

There are four entries in this table because there are two possible spins $(\pm\frac{1}{2})$ for the electron in the ns orbital and two possible spins for the electron in the $n's$ orbital. Note that all the values of M are zero and so they all must correspond to $L = 0$. In addition, the largest value of M_S is 1. Consequently, S must equal 1 and the values $M_S = 1, 0$, and -1 correspond to $L = 0, S = 1$. After eliminating these three entries from the table, we are left with only the entry with $M = 0$, $M_S = 0$, which implies that $L = 0$ and $S = 0$. These two pairs of L and S along with their possible values of M_J can be summarized as

$$L = 0, \quad S = 1 \qquad\qquad L = 0, \quad S = 0$$
$$M = 0, \quad M_S = 1, 0, -1 \qquad\qquad M = 0, \quad M_S = 0$$
$$M_J = M + M_S = 1, 0, -1 \qquad\qquad M_J = M + M_S = 0$$

The values of M_J here imply that $J = 1$ for the $L = 0, S = 1$ case and that $J = 0$ for the $L = 0, S = 0$ case. The two term symbols corresponding to the electron configuration $nsn's$ are

$$^3S_1 \quad \text{and} \quad {}^1S_0$$

The $^3S_1$ state is called a *triplet S state*. These two term symbols correspond to two different electronic states with different energies. In the triplet state ($^3S_1$), the two electrons have parallel spins; in the singlet state ($^1S_0$), the two electrons have opposite spins. We shall see below that the triplet state ($^3S_1$) has a lower energy than the singlet state ($^1S_0$).

As a final example of deducing atomic term symbols, we shall consider a carbon atom, whose electron configuration is $1s^2 2s^2 2p^2$. We have shown previously that we do not need to consider completely filled subshells because M and M_S are necessarily zero for completely filled subshells. Consequently, we can focus on the electron configuration np^2. As for the case of $nsn's$ above, we shall make a table of the possible values of m_1, m_{1s}, m_2, and m_{2s}. Before we do this, however, let us see how many entries there will be in the table for np^2. We are going to assign two electrons to two of six possible spin orbitals. There are 6 choices for the first spin orbital and 5 choices for the second, giving a total of $6 \times 5 = 30$ choices. It is important to realize, however, that the electrons are indistinguishable, so that the order of the two spin orbitals chosen is irrelevant. Thus, we should divide the 30 choices by a factor of 2, to give 15 as the number of distinct ways of assigning the two electrons to the six spin orbitals. Generally, the number of distinct ways to assign N electrons to G spin orbitals belonging to the same subshell (*equivalent orbitals*) is given by

$$\frac{G!}{N!(G-N)!} \qquad \text{(equivalent orbitals)} \qquad (8\text{-}89)$$

Note that Eq. 8-89 gives 15 if $G = 6$ and $N = 2$.

EXAMPLE 8-7

How many distinct ways are there of assigning six electrons to np orbitals? In other words, how many sets of m_i and m_{is} are there for an np^6 electron configuration?

Solution: There are three np orbitals, or six np spin orbitals. Thus, the number of distinct ways of placing six electrons in np orbitals is

$$\frac{6!}{6!0!} = 1$$

We had already deduced this result previously when we showed that $^1S_0$ is the term symbol for an np^6 electron configuration.

The 15 possible sets of m_1, m_{1s}, m_2, and m_{2s} for an np^2 electron configuration are as follows:

	m_1	m_{1s}	m_2	m_{2s}	M	M_S	M_J
1.	$+1$	$+\frac{1}{2}$	$+1$	$-\frac{1}{2}$	$+2$	0	$+2$
2.	$+1$	$+\frac{1}{2}$	0	$+\frac{1}{2}$	$+1$	$+1$	$+2$
3.	$+1$	$+\frac{1}{2}$	0	$-\frac{1}{2}$	$+1$	0	$+1$
4.	$+1$	$+\frac{1}{2}$	-1	$+\frac{1}{2}$	0	$+1$	$+1$
5.	$+1$	$+\frac{1}{2}$	-1	$-\frac{1}{2}$	0	0	0
6.	$+1$	$-\frac{1}{2}$	0	$+\frac{1}{2}$	$+1$	0	$+1$
7.	$+1$	$-\frac{1}{2}$	0	$-\frac{1}{2}$	$+1$	-1	0
8.	$+1$	$-\frac{1}{2}$	-1	$+\frac{1}{2}$	0	0	0
9.	$+1$	$-\frac{1}{2}$	-1	$-\frac{1}{2}$	0	-1	-1
10.	0	$+\frac{1}{2}$	0	$-\frac{1}{2}$	0	0	0
11.	0	$+\frac{1}{2}$	-1	$+\frac{1}{2}$	-1	$+1$	0
12.	0	$+\frac{1}{2}$	-1	$-\frac{1}{2}$	-1	0	-1
13.	0	$-\frac{1}{2}$	-1	$+\frac{1}{2}$	-1	0	-1
14.	0	$-\frac{1}{2}$	-1	$-\frac{1}{2}$	-1	-1	-2
15.	-1	$+\frac{1}{2}$	-1	$-\frac{1}{2}$	-2	0	-2

We must now deduce the possible values of L and S from the tabulated values of M and M_S. The largest value of M is 2, and this value occurs only with $M_S = 0$. Therefore, there must be a state with $L = 2$ and $S = 0$ (^1D). This ^1D state will account for the entries 1, 3, 5, 12, and 15 in the previous table. If we eliminate these entries, then we have the following.

	m_1	m_{1s}	m_2	m_{2s}	M	M_S	M_J
2.	$+1$	$+\frac{1}{2}$	0	$+\frac{1}{2}$	$+1$	$+1$	$+2$
4.	$+1$	$+\frac{1}{2}$	-1	$+\frac{1}{2}$	0	$+1$	$+1$
6.	$+1$	$-\frac{1}{2}$	0	$+\frac{1}{2}$	$+1$	0	$+1$
7.	$+1$	$-\frac{1}{2}$	0	$-\frac{1}{2}$	$+1$	-1	0
8.	$+1$	$-\frac{1}{2}$	-1	$+\frac{1}{2}$	0	0	0
9.	$+1$	$-\frac{1}{2}$	-1	$-\frac{1}{2}$	0	-1	-1
10.	0	$+\frac{1}{2}$	0	$-\frac{1}{2}$	0	0	0
11.	0	$+\frac{1}{2}$	-1	$+\frac{1}{2}$	-1	$+1$	0
13.	0	$-\frac{1}{2}$	-1	$+\frac{1}{2}$	-1	0	-1
14.	0	$-\frac{1}{2}$	-1	$-\frac{1}{2}$	-1	-1	-2

The largest value of M remaining is $M = 1$, implying $L = 1$, with $M = 0, \pm 1$. Each of these values of M occurs with a value of $M_S = 0$ or ± 1, and so we have a state with $L = 1$ and $S = 1$ (^3P). If we eliminate these nine entries from the table, then we are left with only the entry 10 with $M = 0$ and $M_S = 0$, which implies $L = 0$ and $S = 0$ (^1S).

To complete the specification of the term symbols, we must determine the possible values of J in each case. The values of M_J are given in the tables. For the five entries corresponding to the ^1D state, the values of M_J are 2, 1, 0, -1, and -2, which implies that $J = 2$. Thus, the complete term symbol of the ^1D state is $^1D_2$. The values of M_J for the nine entries for the ^3P state are 2, 1, 1, 0, 0, -1, 0, -1, and -2. We clearly have one set of 2, 1, 0, -1, -2 corresponding to $J = 2$. If we eliminate these five values, then we are left with 1, 0, 0, -1, which corresponds to $J = 1$ and $J = 0$. Thus, the ^3P state has three possible values of J, and so the term symbols are $^3P_2$, $^3P_1$, and $^3P_0$. The ^1S state must be $^1S_0$. In summary, then, the electronic states associated with an np^2 configuration are

$$^1D_2, \quad ^3P_0, \quad ^3P_1, \quad ^3P_2, \quad ^1S_0$$

The values of J for each term symbol can be determined in terms of the values of L and S if we recall that

$$\mathbf{J} = \mathbf{L} + \mathbf{S}$$

The largest value that J can have is in the case when both $\mathbf{L}$ and $\mathbf{S}$ are pointing in the same direction, so that $J = L + S$. The smallest value that J can have is when $\mathbf{L}$ and $\mathbf{S}$ are pointing in opposite directions, so that $J = |L - S|$. The values of J lying between $L + S$ and $|L - S|$ are obtained from

$$J = L + S, L + S - 1, L + S - 2, \dots, |L - S| \qquad (8\text{-}90)$$

If we apply Eq. 8-90 to the ^3P term symbol above, then we see that the values of J are given by

$$J = (1 + 1), (1 + 1) - 1, 0$$

and so $J = 2, 1, 0$, as we deduced above.

EXAMPLE 8-8

Use Eq. 8-90 to deduce the values of J associated with the term symbol ^3D.

Solution: For a ^3D state, $L = 2$ and $S = 1$. According to Eq. 8-90, the values of J will be 3, 2, and 1, and so the term symbols will be

$$^3D_1 \quad ^3D_2 \quad ^3D_3$$

Example 8-8 shows that the "L and S part" of a term symbol is sufficient to deduce the complete term symbol.

8-10 *Hund's Rules Are Used to Determine the Term Symbol of the Ground Electronic State*

Each of the states designated by a term symbol corresponds to a determinantal wave function that is an eigenfunction of $\hat{L}^2$ and $\hat{S}^2$, and each state corresponds to a certain energy. Although we could calculate the energy associated with each state, in practice the various states are ordered according to three empirical rules due to the German spectroscopist Frederick Hund. Hund's rules are as follows:

1. The state with the largest value of S is the most stable, and stability decreases with decreasing S.
2. For states with the same value of S, the state with the largest value of L is the most stable.
3. If the states have the same values of L and S, then, for a subshell that is less than half-filled, the state with the smallest value of J is the most stable; for a subshell that is more than half-filled, the state with the largest value of J is the most stable.

EXAMPLE 8-9

Use Hund's rules to deduce the lowest energy state of an $nsn's$ configuration and of an np^2 configuration.

Solution: The term symbols for a $nsn's$ configuration are

$$^3S_1 \quad \text{and} \quad ^1S_0$$

Friedrich Hund (b. 1896) received his Ph.D. in physics from the University of Göttingen in 1922. In 1926 he and Robert Mulliken worked together at Göttingen on the theory of molecular orbitals. Although Hund was not mentioned by the Nobel Prize committee, Mulliken has stated that he would have been glad to share the Nobel Prize with Hund. Hund was professor of theoretical physics at Rostock, Leipzig, Jena, Frankfurt, and Göttingen.

According to the first of Hund's rules, the more stable state is the $^3S_1$ state. The term symbols for an np^2 configuration are

$$^1S_0, \quad ^3P_0, \quad ^3P_1, \quad ^3P_2, \quad ^1D_2$$

According to the first of Hund's rules, the ground state is one of the ^3P states. According to Hund's third rule, the most stable state is the $^3P_0$ state.

8-11   *Atomic Term Symbols Are Used to Describe Atomic Spectra*

Atomic term symbols are sometimes called spectroscopic term symbols, because atomic spectral lines can be assigned to transitions between states that are described by atomic term symbols. For example, consider atomic hydrogen. In Chapter 6, we solved the Schrödinger equation for a hydrogen atom exactly and obtained the set of energy levels given by

$$E_n = -\frac{\mu e^4}{8\varepsilon_0^2 h^2 n^2} \qquad n = 1, 2, 3, \dots \qquad (8\text{-}91)$$

It is peculiar to the simple $1/r$ Coulombic potential of a hydrogen atom that the energy depends only on the principal quantum number n. An electron in a $3s$, $3p$, or $3d$ orbital, for example, has the same energy E_3 in Eq. 8-91. If we

TABLE 8-6
The First Few Electronic States of Atomic Hydrogen

Electron configuration	Term symbol	Energy/cm^{-1}
$1s$	$1s\ ^2S_{1/2}$	0.00
$2p$	$2p\ ^2P_{1/2}$	82,258.917
$2s$	$2s\ ^2S_{1/2}$	82,258.942
$2p$	$2p\ ^2P_{3/2}$	82,259.272
$3p$	$3p\ ^2P_{1/2}$	97,492.198
$3s$	$3s\ ^2S_{1/2}$	97,492.208
$3p, 3d$	$3p\ ^2P_{3/2}, 3d\ ^2D_{3/2}$	97,492.306
$3d$	$3d\ ^2D_{5/2}$	97,492.342
$4p$	$4p\ ^2P_{1/2}$	102,823.835
$4s$	$4s\ ^2S_{1/2}$	102,823.839
$4p, 4d$	$4p\ ^2P_{3/2}, 4d\ ^2D_{3/2}$	102,823.881
$4d, 4f$	$4d\ ^2D_{5/2}, 4f\ ^2F_{5/2}$	102,823.896
$4f$	$4f\ ^2F_{7/2}$	102,823.904

From C. E. Moore, "Atomic Energy Levels," Natl. Bur. Std. Circ. No. 467 (U.S. Government Printing Office, Washington, D.C., 1949).

include the effect of spin-orbit coupling in a hydrogen atom, however, states with different values of J will have different energies according to Hund's third rule. The electron configurations and the corresponding term symbols for the various states of atomic hydrogen are given in Table 8-6. Except for a small difference between the various $^2S_{1/2}$ and $^2P_{1/2}$ states, which is due to a subtle quantum-electrodynamic effect, the energies for each value of n depend on only J. This J dependence is due to spin-orbit coupling.

Let us use Table 8-6 to take a closer look at the atomic hydrogen spectrum. In particular, let us look at the Lyman series, which is the series of transitions from the $n = 1$ state to states of higher n (see Figure 1-10). As we did in Chapter 1, we can use the Rydberg formula to calculate the frequencies of the lines in the Lyman series. The frequencies of the lines in the Lyman series are given by

$$\bar{v} = 109,677.58\left(1 - \frac{1}{n^2}\right) \text{cm}^{-1} \qquad n = 2, 3, \dots \qquad (8\text{-}92)$$

If we express our result in terms of wave numbers, we obtain the following:

Transition	Frequency/cm^{-1}
$1 \rightarrow 2$	82,258.20
$1 \rightarrow 3$	97,491.18
$1 \rightarrow 4$	102,822.73
$1 \rightarrow 5$	105,290.48

If we use Table 8-6, we see that there are three states for $n = 2$ (two states, ignoring the very small difference between the $^2S_{1/2}$ and $^2P_{1/2}$ states), and so we do not know which state to use to calculate the transition frequency into the ground state, $1s\ ^2S_{1/2}$. To determine which states make transitions into which states, we must appeal to *selection rules*. Selection rules are restrictions that govern the possible, or *allowed*, transitions from one state to another. In the case of atomic spectra, the selection rules that concern us here are that

$$\Delta L = \pm 1$$

and
$$\Delta J = 0, \pm 1$$

(8-93)

In the $\Delta J = 0$ case, the transition from a state with $J = 0$ to another state with $J = 0$ is *forbidden*. The selection rules given by Eq. 8-93 have been deduced experimentally and corroborated theoretically. We shall derive some spectroscopic selection rules in Chapter 10, but here we shall just accept them. The selection rules given in Eq. 8-93 tell us that $^2P \rightarrow\ ^2S$ transitions are allowed, but that $^2S \rightarrow\ ^2D$ transitions and $^2F \rightarrow\ ^2P$ transitions are not allowed, because $\Delta L = \pm 2$, respectively, in these transitions. Thus, if we look closely at the Lyman series of atomic hydrogen, then we see that the allowed transitions are

$$np\ ^2P_{1/2} \rightarrow 1s\ ^2S_{1/2}$$

or
$$np\ ^2P_{3/2} \rightarrow 1s\ ^2S_{1/2}$$

(8-94)

No other transitions into the $1s\ ^2S_{1/2}$ ground state are allowed. The frequencies associated with the $2 \rightarrow 1$ transitions given in Eq. 8-94 can be computed from Table 8-6; their values are

$$\bar{v} = (82{,}258.917 - 0.00)\ \mathrm{cm}^{-1} = 82{,}258.917\ \mathrm{cm}^{-1}$$

and
$$\bar{v} = (82{,}259.272 - 0.00)\ \mathrm{cm}^{-1} = 82{,}259.272\ \mathrm{cm}^{-1}$$

(8-95)

respectively. We see that the $n = 2$ to $n = 1$ transition, which occurs at a frequency $\bar{v} = 82{,}258.20\ \mathrm{cm}^{-1}$ if we ignore spin-orbit coupling, consists of two closely spaced lines whose frequencies are given by Eq. 8-95. This closely spaced pair of lines is called a *doublet*, and so we see that under high resolution, the first line of the Lyman series is a doublet. Table 8-6 shows that all the lines of the Lyman series are doublets and that the separation of the doublet lines decreases with increasing n. The increased spectral complexity caused by spin-orbit coupling is called *fine structure*.

EXAMPLE 8-10

Calculate the frequencies of the lines in the $3d\ ^2D$ to $2p\ ^2P$ transition for atomic hydrogen.

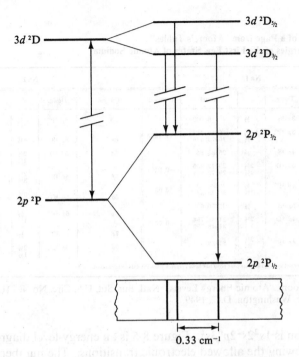

Figure 8-4. The fine structure of the spectral line associated with the $3d\ ^2D \to 2p\ ^2P$ transition in atomic hydrogen.

Solution: There are two $2p\ ^2P$ states in atomic hydrogen, $2p\ ^2P_{1/2}$ and $2p\ ^2P_{3/2}$. The transitions from the $3d\ ^2D$ states into the $2p\ ^2P_{1/2}$ state are

$$3d\ ^2D_{3/2} \to 2p\ ^2P_{1/2} \qquad \bar{v} = (97,492.306 - 82,258.917)\ \text{cm}^{-1}$$
$$= 15,233.389\ \text{cm}^{-1}$$

and the $3d\ ^2D \to 2p\ ^2P_{3/2}$ transitions are

$$3d\ ^2D_{3/2} \to 2p\ ^2P_{3/2} \quad \bar{v}=(97,492.306-82,259.272)\ \text{cm}^{-1}=15,233.034\ \text{cm}^{-1}$$
$$3d\ ^2D_{5/2} \to 2p\ ^2P_{3/2} \quad \bar{v}=(97,492.342-82,259.272)\ \text{cm}^{-1}=15,233.070\ \text{cm}^{-1}$$

These three transitions are illustrated in Figure 8-4. Note that the $3d\ ^2D_{5/2} \to 2p\ ^2P_{1/2}$ transition is not allowed because $\Delta J = 2$ is not allowed.

The type of data presented in Table 8-6 for atomic hydrogen have been tabulated for many atoms and ions in a United States Government publication, "Atomic Energy Levels" by Charlotte E. Moore (National Bureau of Standards Circular No. 467, U.S. Government Printing Office, 1949). These tables are usually referred to as "Moore's tables." Table 8-7 is a direct copy of the energy-level data for the first few levels of atomic sodium, whose ground-state electron

TABLE 8-7

A Photograph of a Page from "Moore's Tables"
Giving the Energies of the First Few States of Atomic Sodium

Na I					Na I				
Config.	Desig.	J	Level	Interval	Config.	Desig.	J	Level	Interval
3s	3s ²S	½	0. 000		5p	5p ²P°	½	35040. 27	2. 52
3p	3p ²P°	½	16956. 183	17. 1963			1½	35042. 79	
		1½	16973. 379		6s	6s ²S	½	36372. 647	
4s	4s ²S	½	25739. 86		5d	5d ²D	2½	37036. 781	−0. 0230
3d	3d ²D	2½	29172. 855	−0. 0494			1½	37036. 805	
		1½	29172. 904		5f	5f ²F°	{ 2½, 3½ }	37057. 6	
4p	4p ²P°	½	30266. 88	5. 63	5g	5g ²G	{ 3½, 4½ }	37060. 2	
		1½	30272. 51		6p	6p ²P°	½	37296. 51	1. 25
5s	5s ²S	½	33200. 696				1½	37297. 76	
4d	4d ²D	2½	34548. 754	−0. 0346	7s	7s ²S	½	38012. 074	
		1½	34548. 789		6d	6d ²D	2½	38387. 287	=0. 0124
4f	4f ²F°	{ 2½, 3½ }	34588. 6				1½	38387. 300	

*The last 14 members are not included because page proof had been prepared when the data were received.

From C. E. Moore, "Atomic Energy Levels," Natl. Bur. Std. U.S. Circ. No. 467 (U.S. Government Printing Office, Washington, D.C., 1949.

configuration is $1s^2 2s^2 2p^6 3s^1$. Figure 8-5 is an energy-level diagram of atomic sodium, showing the allowed electronic transitions. The numbers on the lines connecting various states are the wavelengths of the lines associated with these transitions.

EXAMPLE 8-11

Use Table 8-7 to calculate the wavelengths of the two lines in the doublet associated with the $3p\ ^2P \rightarrow 3s\ ^2S$ transition in sodium, and compare your results to Figure 8-5.

Solution: The two transitions are

$$3p\ ^2P_{1/2} \rightarrow 3s\ ^2S_{1/2} \qquad \bar{\nu} = 16,956.183 \text{ cm}^{-1}$$

$$3p\ ^2P_{3/2} \rightarrow 3s\ ^2S_{1/2} \qquad \bar{\nu} = 16,973.379 \text{ cm}^{-1}$$

The wavelengths are given by $\lambda = 1/\bar{\nu}$, or

$$\lambda = 5897.6 \text{ Å} \quad \text{and} \quad 5891.6 \text{ Å}$$

If we compare these wavelengths to those in Figure 8-5, then we see that there is a small discrepancy. This discrepancy is due to the fact that wavelengths determined experimentally are measured in air, whereas the calculations using Table 8-7 provide wavelengths in vacuum. We use the index of refraction of air (1.00029) to convert from one wavelength to another:

$$\lambda_{\text{vac}} = 1.00029\lambda_{\text{air}}$$

If we divide each of the wavelengths that we have obtained above by

1.00029, we obtain

$$\lambda_{\text{expt}} = 5895.9 \text{ Å and } 5889.9 \text{ Å}.$$

in perfect agreement with Figure 8-5. These wavelengths occur in the
yellow region of the spectrum and account for the intense yellow doublet,
called the *sodium* D *line*, that is characteristic of the emission spectrum
of sodium.

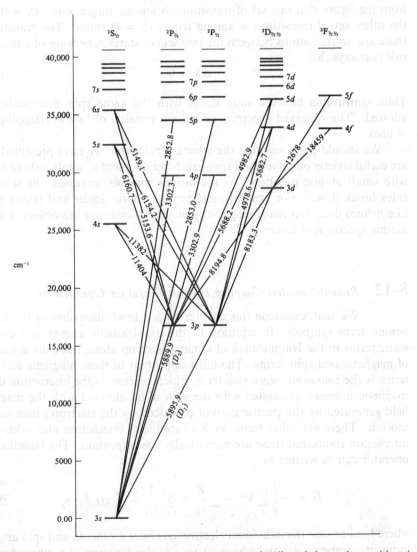

Figure 8-5. Energy-level diagram of atomic sodium, showing the allowed electronic transitions in
atomic sodium. The numbers on the lines are the wavelengths in angstroms (Å) of the transitions.

We can use Moore's tables to investigate the magnitude of the spin-orbit splitting of atomic energy levels. From Table 8-7, we see that the spin-orbit splitting of the np ^2P states of sodium are 17.2 cm^{-1} for $n = 3$, 5.63 cm^{-1} for $n = 4$, 2.52 cm^{-1} for $n = 5$, and 1.25 cm^{-1} for $n = 6$. The results for all the alkali metals, which have similar sets of energy states, are given in Table 8-8. We can see from the table that the splitting decreases with the principal quantum number n and increases with atomic number.

Figure 8-6 shows the energy-level diagram of helium at a resolution where the spin-orbit splittings are not significant. The principal feature of the helium energy-level diagram is that it indicates two separate sets of transitions. Notice from the figure that one set of transitions is among singlet states ($S = 0$) and the other set of transitions is among triplet ($S = 1$) states. The reason that there are no transitions between the two sets of states is because of a selection rule that says that

$$\Delta S = 0 \tag{8-96}$$

Thus, transitions between only states with the same spin multiplicity are allowed. The observed spectrum of helium consists of two overlapping sets of lines.

We should point out that the selection rules that we have presented here are useful strictly only for small spin-orbit coupling and so apply only to atoms with small atomic numbers. As the atomic number increases, the selection rules break down. For example, mercury has both singlet and triplet states like helium does, but many singlet-triplet state transitions are observed in the atomic spectrum of mercury.

8-12   *Russell-Saunders Coupling Is Most Useful for Light Atoms*

We shall conclude this chapter with a brief discussion of the theory behind term symbols. In addition to the usual kinetic energy and electrostatic terms in the Hamiltonian of a many-electron atom, there are a number of magnetic and spin terms. The most important of these magnetic and spin terms is the *spin-orbit interaction* term, which represents the interaction of the magnetic moment associated with the spin of an electron with the magnetic field generated by the electric current produced by the electron's own orbital motion. There are other terms such as spin-spin interaction and orbit-orbit interaction terms, but these are numerically less important. The Hamiltonian operator can be written as

$$\hat{H} = -\frac{1}{2}\sum_j \nabla_j^2 - \sum_j \frac{Z}{r_j} + \sum_{i<j} \frac{1}{r_{ij}} + \sum_j \xi(r_j)\mathbf{l}_j \cdot \mathbf{s}_j \tag{8-97}$$

where $\mathbf{l}_j$ and $\mathbf{s}_j$ are the individual electronic orbital momenta and spin angular momenta, respectively, and where $\xi(r_j)$ is a scalar function of r_j whose form is

TABLE 8-8

The Spin-Orbit Splitting of the np ^2P States in the Alkali Metals.
The Entries in the Table Are the Differences in the Energies (Wavenumbers)
of the np $^2P_{3/2}$ and np $^2P_{1/2}$ States

Alkali metal	3	4	5	6	7
Na	17.2	5.63	2.52	1.25	0.74
K		57.7	18.76	8.41	4.48
Rb			238	77.5	
Cs				554	181

From C. E. Moore, "Atomic Energy Levels," Natl. Bur. Std. Circ. No. 467, (U.S. Government Printing Office, Washington, D.C., 1949).

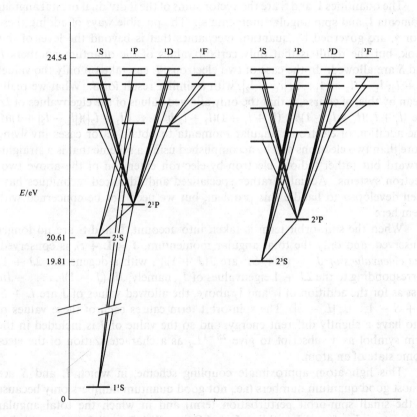

Figure 8-6. The energy-level diagram of helium, showing the two separate sets of singlet and triplet states.

not necessary here. We can abbreviate Eq. 8-97 by writing

$$\hat{H} = \hat{H}_0 + \hat{H}_{ee} + \hat{H}_{so} \qquad (8\text{-}98)$$

where $\hat{H}_0$ represents the first two terms (no interelectronic interactions), $\hat{H}_{ee}$ represents the third term (interelectronic repulsion), and $\hat{H}_{so}$ represents the fourth term (spin-orbit coupling) in Eq. 8-97.

For light atoms ($Z < 40$), $\hat{H}_{so}$ is small enough to be considered a small perturbation. If $\hat{H}_{so}$ is neglected altogether, then it can be shown that the total orbital angular momentum **L** and the total spin angular momentum **S** are conserved separately. However, in this case, the individual orbital angular momenta and spin angular momenta are not conserved and so are not useful concepts. The eigenvalues of the square of the total orbital angular momentum operator $\hat{L}^2$ and the square of the total spin angular momentum operator $\hat{S}^2$ are $L(L + 1)\hbar^2$ and $S(S + 1)\hbar^2$, respectively.

The quantities **L** and **S** are the vector sums of the individual orbital angular momenta $\mathbf{l}_j$ and spin angular momenta $\mathbf{s}_j$. The possible ways of adding these $\mathbf{l}_j$ or $\mathbf{s}_j$ are governed by quantum mechanics that is beyond the level of this book, but the result is that only certain values of the quantum numbers L and S are allowed. In the case of two electrons, L can take on only the values $l_1 + l_2, l_1 + l_2 - 1, \ldots, |l_1 - l_2|$, with a similar result for S. What we really mean by this, of course, is that the only allowed values of the eigenvalues of $\hat{L}^2$ are $(l_1 + l_2)(l_1 + l_2 + 1)\hbar^2$, $(l_1 + l_2 - 1)(l_1 + l_2)\hbar^2, \ldots, (|l_1 - l_2|)(|l_1 - l_2| + 1)\hbar^2$. The addition of electronic angular momenta to obtain L for cases involving more than two electrons can be accomplished using a scheme that is a straightforward but rather tedious electron-by-electron extension of the above two-electron systems. Actually, rather specialized and advanced techniques have been developed to handle this problem, but we need not be concerned with them here.

When the spin-orbit term is taken into account, **L** and **S** are no longer conserved, and only the total angular momentum, $\mathbf{J} = \mathbf{L} + \mathbf{S}$, is conserved. *The eigenvalues of $\hat{J}^2 = (\hat{L} + \hat{S})^2$ are $J(J + 1)\hbar^2$, with a degeneracy $2J + 1$,* corresponding to the $2J + 1$ eigenvalues of $\hat{J}_z$, namely, $J\hbar, (J - 1)\hbar, \ldots, -J\hbar$. Just as for the addition of $\mathbf{l}_1$ and $\mathbf{l}_2$ above, the allowed values of J are $L + S$, $L + S - 1, \ldots, |L - S|$. The spin-orbit term causes each of these values of J to have a slightly different energy, and so the value of J is included in the term symbol as a subscript to give $^{2S+1}L_J$ as a characterization of the electronic state of an atom.

This light-atom approximate coupling scheme, in which L and S are almost good quantum numbers (i.e., not good quantum numbers only because of the small spin-orbit perturbation term) and in which the total angular momentum **J** is found by adding **L** and **S**, is called *Russell-Saunders coupling* or *L-S coupling*. As the atomic number of the atom becomes larger, the spin-orbit term becomes larger than the interelectronic repulsion term, and H_{ee} can be considered to be a small perturbation on the others. In this case L and S are no longer meaningful, and the individual total angular momenta, $\mathbf{j}_i = \mathbf{l}_i + \mathbf{s}_i$, become the approximately conserved quantities. One then couples the

j's to obtain the total angular momentum. This scheme is called *j-j coupling* and is applicable to heavier atoms. In spite of the deterioration of *L-S* coupling as Z increases, it is still approximately useful, and so the electronic states of even heavy atoms are designated by term symbols of the form $^{2S+1}L_J$.

Let us go on now to discuss molecules. One of the great achievements of quantum mechanics is a detailed explanation of the stability of the chemical bond, such as in H_2. Because H_2 is the simplest molecule, we shall discuss it in some quantitative detail like we did helium in this chapter and then discuss the results of similar calculations for more complicated molecules more qualitatively.

Summary

Although the Schrödinger equation for a hydrogen atom can be solved analytically and hence exactly, the Schrödinger equation of even a helium atom must be solved by approximate methods. Both perturbation theory and the variational method can yield excellent results for helium, but in general both methods become cumbersome as the number of electrons in the atom increases. A common, and useful, simplifying approximation is to write the N-electron atomic wave function in terms of N single-electron wave functions, or orbitals. Electron spin is incorporated in the formalism by using spin orbitals, which are products of spatial orbitals and spin eigenfunctions. Spin orbitals are described by the four quantum numbers, n, l, m, and m_s. The Pauli Exclusion Principle requires that electronic wave functions be antisymmetric under the interchange of the coordinates of any two electrons. In the orbital, or spin-orbital, approximation, the required antisymmetry is achieved by writing a wave function as a determinant of spin orbitals, called a *Slater determinant*. The best wave function that can be obtained under the orbital approximation is called a *Hartree-Fock wave function* and the best energy is called the *Hartree-Fock energy*. The procedure for determining a Hartree-Fock wave function and a Hartree-Fock energy involves solving a set of coupled effective Schrödinger equations by an iterative method called the *self-consistent field method*. Hartree-Fock atomic energies are within a percent or two of exact energies for atoms with atomic number less than 40 or so, and many other properties are in satisfactory agreement with experiment (cf. Figure 8-1). The agreement can be improved by a variety of methods, including perturbation theory.

Atomic energy states are designated by atomic term symbols. Atomic spectra can be described as transitions between atomic energy states, and the term symbols can be used to predict which transitions are allowed and which transitions are forbidden. A study of atomic spectra yields information concerning the set of energy states of a given atom. Such information is summarized by a table such as Table 8-7 or a figure such as Figure 8-5 for a sodium atom.

Terms That You Should Know

atomic units	spin eigenfunction
bohr	spin variable
hartree	spin orbital
effective nuclear charge	Pauli Exclusion Principle
Slater orbitals	antisymmetric wave function
orbital	determinantal wave function
Hartree-Fock limit	exchange integral
Hartree-Fock approximation	Fock operator
Hartree-Fock equation	atomic term symbol
Coulomb integral	spin-orbit coupling
self-consistent field method	Russell-Saunders coupling
Hartree-Fock orbitals	Hund's rules
Hartree-Fock-Roothan procedure	selection rule
orbital energy	doublet
Koopmans' theorem	fine structure
correlation energy	Moore's tables
Stern-Gerlach experiment	L-S coupling
spin quantum number	j-j coupling
electron spin	

Problems

1. Show that the ground-state energy of a helium ion in atomic units is -2 au.

2. The electric potential at a distance r from a charge q is

$$V = \frac{q}{4\pi\varepsilon_0 r} = \frac{q}{\kappa_0 r}$$

Show that the atomic unit of potential is the potential at a distance of one Bohr radius from an electron (see Table 8-1).

3. Show that the speed of an electron in the first Bohr orbit is $e^2/4\pi\varepsilon_0\hbar = e^2/\kappa_0\hbar = 2.188 \times 10^6$ m/sec. This speed is the unit of speed in atomic units (see Table 8-1).

4. Show that the time for an electron to go one radian in the first Bohr orbit is $T = (4\pi\varepsilon_0)^2\hbar^3/me^4 = \kappa_0^2\hbar^3/me^4$. Because $\hbar = m = |e| = \kappa_0 = 1$ in atomic units, T is the unit of time in atomic units. Show that $T = 2.418 \times 10^{-17}$ s.

5. Show that the speed of light in atomic units is equal to 137 au.

6. In applying first-order perturbation theory to the helium atom, we must evaluate the integral (Eq. 8-11)

$$E^{(1)} = \iint d\mathbf{r}_1 d\mathbf{r}_2 \, \psi_{1s}^*(\mathbf{r}_1)\psi_{1s}^*(\mathbf{r}_2)\frac{1}{r_{12}}\psi_{1s}(\mathbf{r}_1)\psi_{1s}(\mathbf{r}_2)$$

where

$$\psi_{1s}(\mathbf{r}_j) = \left(\frac{Z^3}{\pi}\right)^{1/2} e^{-Zr_j}$$

and $Z = 2$ for the helium atom. This same integral occurs in a variational treatment of helium, where in that case the value of Z is left arbitrary. This problem proves that

$$E^{(1)} = \tfrac{5}{8}Z \text{ au}$$

Let $\mathbf{r}_1$ and $\mathbf{r}_2$ be the radius vectors of electron 1 and 2, respectively, and let θ be the angle between these two vectors. Now this is generally *not* the θ of spherical coordinates, but if we choose one of the radius vectors, say $\mathbf{r}_1$, to be the z axis, then the two θ's are the same. Using the law of cosines,

$$r_{12} = (r_1^2 + r_2^2 - 2r_1r_2 \cos \theta)^{1/2}$$

show that $E^{(1)}$ becomes

$$E^{(1)} = \frac{Z^6}{\pi^2} \int_0^\infty e^{-2Zr_1}4\pi r_1^2 \, dr_1 \int_0^\infty e^{-2Zr_2}r_2^2 \, dr_2$$

$$\times \int_0^{2\pi} d\phi \int_0^\pi \frac{\sin \theta \, d\theta}{(r_1^2 + r_2^2 - 2r_1r_2 \cos \theta)^{1/2}}$$

Letting $x = \cos \theta$, show that the integral over θ is

$$\int_0^\pi \frac{\sin \theta \, d\theta}{(r_1^2 + r_2^2 - 2r_1r_2 \cos \theta)^{1/2}} = \int_{-1}^1 \frac{dx}{(r_1^2 + r_2^2 - 2r_1r_2 x)^{1/2}}$$

$$= \frac{2}{r_1} \qquad r_1 > r_2$$

$$= \frac{2}{r_2} \qquad r_1 < r_2$$

Substituting this result into $E^{(1)}$, show that

$$E^{(1)} = 16Z^6 \int_0^\infty e^{-2Zr_1}r_1^2 \, dr_1 \left(\frac{1}{r_1}\int_0^{r_1} e^{-2Zr_2}r_2^2 dr_2 + \int_{r_1}^\infty e^{-2Zr_2}r_2 \, dr_2\right)$$

$$= 4Z^3 \int_0^\infty e^{-2Zr_1}r_1^2 \, dr_1 \left[\frac{1}{r_1} - e^{-2Zr_1}\left(Z + \frac{1}{r_1}\right)\right]$$

$$= \frac{5}{8}Z$$

Show that the energy through first order is

$$-Z^2 + \tfrac{5}{8}Z = -\tfrac{11}{4} \text{ au} = -2.75 \text{ au}$$

compared to the exact result, $E_{\text{exact}} = -2.9037$ au.

7. This problem fills in the steps of the variational treatment of helium. We use a trial function of the form

$$\psi(\mathbf{r}_1, \mathbf{r}_2) = \frac{Z^3}{\pi} e^{-Z(r_1 + r_2)}$$

with Z as an adjustable parameter. The Hamiltonian of the helium atom is

$$\hat{H} = -\frac{1}{2}\nabla_1^2 - \frac{1}{2}\nabla_2^2 - \frac{2}{r_1} - \frac{2}{r_2} + \frac{1}{r_{12}}$$

We now evaluate

$$E(Z) = \int d\mathbf{r}_1 \, d\mathbf{r}_2 \, \psi^* \hat{H} \psi$$

The evaluation of this integral is greatly simplified if you recall that $\phi(r_j) = (Z^3/\pi)^{1/2} e^{-Zr_j}$ is an eigenfunction of a hydrogenlike Hamiltonian, one for which the nucleus has a charge Z. Thus, it is convenient to write the helium atom Hamiltonian as

$$\hat{H} = -\frac{1}{2}\nabla_1^2 - \frac{Z}{r_1} - \frac{1}{2}\nabla_2^2 - \frac{Z}{r_2} + \frac{(Z-2)}{r_1} + \frac{(Z-2)}{r_2} + \frac{1}{r_{12}}$$

where

$$\left(-\frac{1}{2}\nabla^2 - \frac{Z}{r}\right)\left(\frac{Z^3}{\pi}\right)^{1/2} e^{-Zr} = -\frac{Z^2}{2}\left(\frac{Z^3}{\pi}\right)^{1/2} e^{-Zr}$$

Show that

$$E(Z) = \frac{Z^6}{\pi^2} \iint e^{-Z(r_1+r_2)}\left[-\frac{Z^2}{2} - \frac{Z^2}{2} + \frac{(Z-2)}{r_1} + \frac{(Z-2)}{r_2} + \frac{1}{r_{12}}\right] e^{-Z(r_1+r_2)} \, d\mathbf{r}_1 \, d\mathbf{r}_2$$

$$= -Z^2 + 2(Z-2)\frac{Z^3}{\pi}\int d\mathbf{r}\,\frac{e^{-2Zr}}{r} + \frac{5}{8}Z$$

$$= -Z^2 + 2(Z-2)Z + \frac{5}{8}Z$$

$$= Z^2 - \frac{27}{8}Z$$

Now minimize E with respect to Z and show that

$$E = -\left(\tfrac{27}{16}\right)^2 \text{ au} = -2.8477 \text{ au}$$

Interpret the value of Z that minimizes E.

8. Show that the normalization constant for the radial part of Slater orbitals is $(2\zeta)^{n+\frac{1}{2}}/[(2n)!]^{1/2}$.

9. Show that the radial parts of the few first Slater orbitals are not orthogonal to each other. Give a general argument for this result.

10. Prove that the Hartree-Fock energy of a helium atom is given by

$$E = I_1 + I_2 + J_{12}$$

where I_1, I_2, and J_{12} are given by Eqs. 8-31 and 8-32.

11. Show that the substitution $\phi(\mathbf{r}) = R(r)Y_l^m(\theta, \phi)$ into Eq. 8-28 yields Eq. 8-34 for $R(r)$.

12. Prove that the orbital energy in the Hartree-Fock approximation for helium is given by

$$\varepsilon = I_1 + J_{12}$$

and prove that the total energy is *not* the sum of the two orbital energies.

13. Consider a molecule with dipole moment μ in an electric field $\mathbf{E}$ (see Figure 8-7). For convenience, we take the field to be in the z direction. We picture the dipole moment as a positive charge of magnitude q and a negative charge of magnitude q separated by a vector $\mathbf{l}$. The field E_z causes the dipole to rotate into a direction parallel with E_z. Therefore, it requires work to rotate the dipole to an angle θ to E_z. The force causing the molecule to rotate is actually a torque (torque is the angular analog of force) and is given by $l/2$ times the force perpendicular to $\mathbf{l}$ at each end of $\mathbf{l}$. Show that the force perpendicular to $\mathbf{l}$ is $qE_z \sin \theta$ and that the torque is $2(l/2)qE_z \sin \theta = \mu E_z \sin \theta$. The energy required to rotate the dipole from 0 to some angle θ is

$$\varepsilon = \int_0^\theta \mu E_z \sin \theta' \, d\theta'$$

Now show that if one takes the arbitrary zero of energy to be when the dipole is perpendicular to the field, then the energy of a dipole in an electric field is

$$\varepsilon = -\mu E_z \cos \theta = -\mu_z E_z \qquad (8\text{-}99)$$

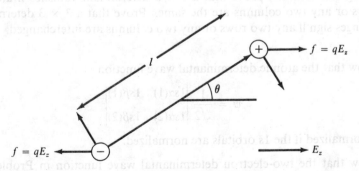

Figure 8-7. The torque acting upon a dipole moment in an electric field E_z. The length of the dipole is l and the charges at each end are $+q$ and $-q$.

where μ_z is the z component of μ. If the field were not necessarily in the z direction, then Eq. 8-99 would be $\varepsilon = -\boldsymbol{\mu} \cdot \mathbf{E}$. If we have a magnetic dipole $\mathbf{m}$ in a magnetic field $\mathbf{B}$, the energy is given by a similar expression

$$\varepsilon = -\mathbf{m} \cdot \mathbf{B} \qquad (8\text{-}100)$$

Thus we see that a dipole moment tends to be oriented in a uniform external field but that there is no translational force exerted on it.

14. Just as electrons have intrinsic magnetic moments, nuclei do also, and the magnitude of a nuclear moment is given by

$$\mu = g \frac{e}{2m_N} \mathbf{S}$$

where g is a factor characteristic of the particular nucleus, m_N is the mass of the nucleus, and $\mathbf{S}$ is the spin angular momentum of the nucleus. For example, a proton has a spin $= \frac{1}{2}$ and $g = 5.5849$. In a nuclear magnetic resonance experiment involving protons, the protons undergo transitions between the states $s_z = -\frac{1}{2}$ and $s_z = +\frac{1}{2}$. Calculate the frequency of radiation for such an experiment in a magnetic field of 2.0 tesla.

15. Given that $\Psi = 1s\alpha(1)1s\beta(2) - 1s\alpha(2)1s\beta(1)$, prove that

$$\int \Psi^*(1, 2)\Psi(1, 2)\,d\tau_1\,d\tau_2 = 2$$

if the spatial part is normalized.

16. One way to evaluate a 3×3 determinant is by the equation

$$\begin{vmatrix} a_{11} & a_{12} & a_{13} \\ a_{21} & a_{22} & a_{23} \\ a_{31} & a_{32} & a_{33} \end{vmatrix} = a_{11} \begin{vmatrix} a_{22} & a_{23} \\ a_{32} & a_{33} \end{vmatrix} - a_{12} \begin{vmatrix} a_{21} & a_{23} \\ a_{31} & a_{33} \end{vmatrix} + a_{13} \begin{vmatrix} a_{21} & a_{22} \\ a_{31} & a_{32} \end{vmatrix}$$

Note that the 2×2 determinants here are obtained by striking out the row and the column containing the a_{ij} factor in front of each 2×2 determinant and that the sign of each term is $(-1)^{i+j}$ if a_{ij} denotes the factor in front. Using this formula, prove that a 3×3 determinant vanishes if any two rows or any two columns are the same. Prove that a 3×3 determinant changes sign if any two rows or any two columns are interchanged.

17. Show that the atomic determinantal wave function

$$\psi = \frac{1}{\sqrt{2}} \begin{vmatrix} 1s\alpha(1) & 1s\beta(1) \\ 1s\alpha(2) & 1s\beta(2) \end{vmatrix}$$

is normalized if the $1s$ orbitals are normalized.

18. Show that the two-electron determinantal wave function in Problem 17 factors into a spatial part and a spin part.

19. Argue that the normalization constant of an $N \times N$ Slater determinant of orthonormal spin orbitals is $1/\sqrt{N!}$.

20. The total z component of the spin angular momentum for an n-electron system is

$$S_{z, \text{total}} = \sum_{j=1}^{n} S_{zj}$$

Show that both

$$\psi = \frac{1}{\sqrt{2}} \begin{vmatrix} 1s\alpha(1) & 1s\beta(1) \\ 1s\alpha(2) & 1s\beta(2) \end{vmatrix}$$

and

$$\psi = \frac{1}{\sqrt{3!}} \begin{vmatrix} 1s\alpha(1) & 1s\beta(1) & 2s\alpha(1) \\ 1s\alpha(2) & 1s\beta(2) & 2s\alpha(2) \\ 1s\alpha(3) & 1s\beta(3) & 2s\alpha(3) \end{vmatrix}$$

are eigenfunctions of $\hat{S}_{z, \text{total}}$. What are the eigenvalues in each case?

21. Consider the determinantal atomic wave function

$$\Psi = \frac{1}{\sqrt{2}} \begin{vmatrix} \psi_{211}\alpha(1) & \psi_{21-1}\beta(1) \\ \psi_{211}\alpha(2) & \psi_{21-1}\beta(2) \end{vmatrix}$$

where $\psi_{21\pm1}$ is a hydrogenlike wave function. Show that Ψ is an eigenfunction of

$$\hat{L}_{z, \text{total}} = \hat{L}_{z1} + \hat{L}_{z2}$$

and

$$\hat{S}_{z, \text{total}} = \hat{S}_{z1} + \hat{S}_{z2}$$

What are the eigenvalues?

22. For a two-electron system there are four possible spin functions:

1. $\alpha(1)\alpha(2)$
2. $\beta(1)\alpha(2)$
3. $\alpha(1)\beta(2)$
4. $\beta(1)\beta(2)$

The concept of indistinguishability forces us to consider only linear combinations of 2 and 3,

$$\psi_{\pm} = \frac{1}{\sqrt{2}} [\alpha(1)\beta(2) \pm \beta(1)\alpha(2)]$$

instead of 2 and 3 separately. Show that of the four acceptable spin functions, 1, 4, and $\psi_{\pm}$, three are symmetric and one is antisymmetric.

Now for a two-electron system, we can combine spatial wave functions with spin functions. Show that this leads to only four allowable combinations:

$$[\psi(1)\phi(2) + \psi(2)\phi(1)] \frac{1}{\sqrt{2}} [\alpha(1)\beta(2) - \alpha(2)\beta(1)]$$

$$[\psi(1)\phi(2) - \psi(2)\phi(1)][\alpha(1)\alpha(2)]$$

$$[\psi(1)\phi(2) - \psi(2)\phi(1)][\beta(1)\beta(2)]$$

$$[\psi(1)\phi(2) - \psi(2)\phi(1)] \frac{1}{\sqrt{2}} [\alpha(1)\beta(2) + \alpha(2)\beta(1)]$$

where ψ and ϕ are two spatial wave functions. Show that $M_s = m_{1s} + m_{2s}) = 0$ for the first of these and that $M_s = 1, -1$, and 0 for the next three, respectively.

Consider the first excited state of a helium atom, in which $\psi = 1s$ and $\phi = 2s$. The first one of the four wave functions above, with the symmetric spatial part, will give a higher energy than the remaining three, which form a degenerate set of three. The first state is a singlet state and the degenerate set of three represents a triplet state. Because M_s equals zero and only zero for the singlet state, the singlet state corresponds to $S = 0$. The other three, with $M_s = \pm 1, 0$, correspond to $S = 1$. Note that the degeneracy is $2S + 1$ in each case.

Putting all this into a more mathematical form, given that $\hat{S}_{total} = \hat{S}_1 + \hat{S}_2$, it can be shown that

$$\hat{S}^2_{total}[\alpha(1)\beta(2) - \alpha(2)\beta(1)] = 0$$

corresponding to $S = 0$ and that

$$\hat{S}^2_{total} \begin{bmatrix} \alpha(1)\alpha(2) \\ \frac{1}{\sqrt{2}} [\alpha(1)\beta(2) + \alpha(2)\beta(1)] \\ \beta(1)\beta(2) \end{bmatrix} = 2\hbar^2 \begin{bmatrix} \alpha(1)\alpha(2) \\ \frac{1}{\sqrt{2}} [\alpha(1)\beta(2) + \alpha(2)\beta(1)] \\ \beta(1)\beta(2) \end{bmatrix}$$

corresponding to $S = 1$.

23. Consider a helium atom in an excited state in which one of its $1s$ electrons is raised to the $2s$ level, so that its electron configuration is $1s2s$. Argue that because the two orbitals are different, there are four possible determinantal wave functions for this system:

$$\phi_1 = \frac{1}{\sqrt{2}} \begin{vmatrix} 1s\alpha(1) & 2s\alpha(1) \\ 1s\alpha(2) & 2s\alpha(2) \end{vmatrix}$$

$$\phi_2 = \frac{1}{\sqrt{2}} \begin{vmatrix} 1s\beta(1) & 2s\beta(1) \\ 1s\beta(2) & 2s\beta(2) \end{vmatrix}$$

$$\phi_3 = \frac{1}{\sqrt{2}} \begin{vmatrix} 1s\alpha(1) & 2s\beta(1) \\ 1s\alpha(2) & 2s\beta(2) \end{vmatrix}$$

$$\phi_4 = \frac{1}{\sqrt{2}} \begin{vmatrix} 1s\beta(1) & 2s\alpha(1) \\ 1s\beta(2) & 2s\alpha(2) \end{vmatrix}$$

To calculate the energy of the $1s2s$ configuration, assume the variational function

$$\psi = c_1\phi_1 + c_2\phi_2 + c_3\phi_3 + c_4\phi_4$$

Show that the secular equation associated with this linear combination trial function is (this is the only lengthy part of this problem and at least you have the answer in front of you; be sure to remember that the $1s$ and $2s$ orbitals here are eigenfunctions of the hydrogenlike Hamiltonian operator)

$$\begin{vmatrix} E_0 + J - K - E & 0 & 0 & 0 \\ 0 & E_0 + J - K - E & 0 & 0 \\ 0 & 0 & E_0 + J - E & -K \\ 0 & 0 & -K & E_0 + J - E \end{vmatrix} = 0$$

where

$$J = \iint d\tau_1\, d\tau_2\, 1s(1)1s(1)\left(\frac{1}{r_{12}}\right)2s(2)2s(2)$$

$$K = \iint d\tau_1\, d\tau_2\, 1s(1)2s(1)\left(\frac{1}{r_{12}}\right)1s(2)2s(2)$$

and E_0 is the energy without the $1/r_{12}$ term in the helium atom Hamiltonian. Show that

$$E_0 = -\tfrac{5}{2}\ \text{au}$$

Explain why J is called an atomic Coulomb integral and K is called an atomic exchange integral.

Even though the above secular determinant is 4×4 and appears to give a fourth-degree polynomial in E, note that it really consists of two 1×1 blocks and a 2×2 block. Show that this symmetry in the determinant reduces the determinantal equation to

$$(E_0 + J - K - E)^2 \begin{vmatrix} E_0 + J - E & -K \\ -K & E_0 + J - E \end{vmatrix} = 0$$

and that this equation gives the four roots

$$E = E_0 + J - K \quad \text{(twice)}$$
$$= E_0 + J \pm K$$

Show that the wave function corresponding to the positive sign in
E in the $E_0 + J \pm K$ is

$$\psi_3 = \frac{1}{\sqrt{2}}(\phi_3 - \phi_4)$$

and that corresponding to the negative sign in $E_0 + J \pm K$ is

$$\psi_4 = \frac{1}{\sqrt{2}}(\phi_3 + \phi_4)$$

Now show that both ψ_3 and ψ_4 can be factored into a spatial part and a
spin part, even though ϕ_3 and ϕ_4 separately cannot. Furthermore, let

$$\psi_1 = \phi_1 \quad \text{and} \quad \psi_2 = \phi_2$$

and show that both of these can be factored also. Using the argument
given in Problem 22, group these four wave functions ($\psi_1, \psi_2, \psi_3, \psi_4$) into
a singlet state and a triplet state.

Now calculate the energy of the singlet and triplet states in terms of
E_0, J, and K. Argue that $J > 0$. Given that $K > 0$ also, does the singlet
state or the triplet state have the lower energy? The values of J and K
when hydrogenlike wave functions with $Z = 2$ are used are $J = \frac{10}{27}$ au and
$K = 32/(27)^2$ au. Using the ground-state wave function

$$\psi = \frac{1}{\sqrt{2}} \begin{vmatrix} 1s\alpha(1) & 1s\beta(1) \\ 1s\alpha(2) & 1s\beta(2) \end{vmatrix}$$

show that the first-order perturbation theory result is $E = -11/4$ au if
hydrogenlike wave functions with $Z = 2$ are used. Use this value of E to
calculate the energy difference between the ground state and the first
excited singlet state and the first triplet state of helium. The experimental
values are 19.8 eV and 20.6 eV, respectively (cf. Figure 8-6).

24. Show that the Slater determinantal wave function for the ground state of
lithium takes the form $1/\sqrt{3!}$ times

$$\Psi = [1s(1)1s(2)2s(3) - 2s(1)1s(2)1s(3)]\alpha(1)\beta(2)\alpha(3)$$
$$+ [1s(1)2s(2)1s(3) - 1s(1)1s(2)2s(3)]\beta(1)\alpha(2)\alpha(3)$$
$$+ [2s(1)1s(2)1s(3) - 1s(1)2s(2)1s(3)]\alpha(1)\alpha(2)\beta(3)$$

Show that Ψ is an eigenfunction of the total $\hat{S}_z$. What is the eigenvalue?

25. Show that the energy associated with the wave function in Eq. (8-72) is

$$E = 2 \sum_{j=1}^{N} I_j + \sum_{i=1}^{N} \sum_{j=1}^{N} (2J_{ij} - K_{ij})$$

26. Why are the J_{ij} terms in the Hartree-Fock method called Coulomb integrals? Why are the K_{ij} terms called exchange integrals?

27. Prove that the Hartree-Fock orbital energies ε_i are given by

$$\varepsilon_i = E - E^+$$

where E and E^+ are the Hartree-Fock energies of the neutral atom and ion, respectively.

28. Prove that the total Hartree-Fock energy is not given by a sum of the orbital energies. Show that the total Hartree-Fock energy is given by

$$E = \sum (I_i + \varepsilon_i)$$

29. Determine the term symbols associated with an np^1 electron configuration. Show that these term symbols are the same as for an np^5 electron configuration. Which term symbol represents the ground state?

30. Show that the term symbols for an np^4 electron configuration are the same as for an np^2 electron configuration.

31. Show that the number of sets of magnetic quantum numbers (m) and spin quantum numbers (m_s) associated with any term symbol is equal to $(2L + 1)(2S + 1)$. Apply this result to the np^2 case discussed in Section 8-9 and show that the term symbols ^1S, ^3P, and ^1D account for all the possible sets of magnetic quantum numbers and spin quantum numbers.

32. Calculate the number of sets of magnetic quantum numbers (m) and spin quantum numbers (m_s) there are for an nd^8 electron configuration. Prove that the term symbols ^1S, ^1D, ^3P, ^3F and ^1G account for all the possible term symbols.

33. Determine the term symbols for the electron configuration $nsnp$. Which term symbol corresponds to the lowest energy?

34. How many sets of magnetic quantum numbers (m) and spin quantum numbers (m_s) are there for an $nsnd$ electron configuration? What are the term symbols? Which term symbol corresponds to the lowest energy?

35. The term symbols for an nd^2 electron configuration are ^1S, ^1D, ^1G, ^3P, and ^3F. Calculate the values of J associated with each of these term symbols. Which term symbol represents the ground state?

36. The term symbols for an np^3 electron configuration are ^2P, ^2D, and ^4S. Calculate the values of J associated with each of these term symbols. Which term symbol represents the ground state?

37. What is the electron configuration of a magnesium atom in its ground state, and what is its ground-state term symbol?

38. Given that the ground-state electronic configuration of a zirconium atom is $[Kr](4d)^2(5s)^2$, what is the ground-state term symbol for Zr?

39. Given that the ground-state electronic configuration of a palladium atom is $[Kr](4d)^{10}$, what is the ground-state term symbol for Pd?

40. Use Table 8-6 to calculate the separation of the doublets that occur in the Lyman series of atomic hydrogen.

41. Use Table 8-7 to calculate the wavelength of the $4f\ ^2F \rightarrow 3d\ ^2D$ transition in atomic sodium and compare your result to that given in Figure 8-5. Be sure to use the relation $\lambda_{vac} = 1.00029\lambda_{air}$ (see Example 8-11).

42. The orbital designations s, p, d, and f come from an analysis of the spectrum of atomic sodium. The series of lines due to $ns\ ^2S \rightarrow 3p\ ^2P$ transitions is is called the *sharp* (s) series; the series of lines due to $np\ ^2P \rightarrow 3s\ ^2S$ transitions is called the *principal* (p) series; the series of lines due to $nd\ ^2D \rightarrow 3p\ ^2P$ transitions is called the *diffuse* (d) series; and the series of lines due to $nf\ ^2F \rightarrow 3d\ ^2D$ transitions is called the *fundamental* (f) series. Identify each of these series in Figure 8-5 and tabulate the wavelengths of the first few lines in each series.

43. Problem 42 defines the sharp, principal, diffuse, and fundamental series in the spectrum of atomic sodium. Use Table 8-7 to calculate the wavelengths of the first few lines in each series and compare your results to Figure 8-5. Be sure to use the relation $\lambda_{vac} = 1.00029\lambda_{air}$ (see Example 8-11).

44. In Problem 6 we evaluated the integral that occurs in the first-order perturbation theory treatment of helium (see Eq. 8-11). In this problem we shall evaluate the integral by another method, one that uses an expansion for $1/r_{12}$ that is useful in many applications. It is possible to write $1/r_{12}$ as an expansion in terms of spherical harmonics

$$\frac{1}{r_{12}} = \frac{1}{|\mathbf{r}_1 - \mathbf{r}_2|} = \sum_{l=0}^{\infty} \sum_{m=-l}^{+l} \frac{4\pi}{2l+1} \frac{r_<^l}{r_>^{l+1}} Y_l^m(\theta_1, \phi_1)\, Y_l^{m*}(\theta_2, \phi_2)$$

where θ_i and ϕ_i are the angles that describe $\mathbf{r}_i$ in a spherical coordinate system and $r_<$ and $r_>$ are, respectively, the smaller and larger values of r_1 and r_2. In other words, if $r_1 < r_2$, then $r_< = r_1$ and $r_> = r_2$. Substitute $\psi_{1s}(r_i) = (Z^3/\pi)^{1/2}e^{-Zr_i}$ and the above expansion for $1/r_{12}$ into Eq. 8-11, integrate over the angles, and show that all the terms except for the $l = 0$, $m = 0$ term vanish. Show that

$$E^{(1)} = 16Z^6 \int_0^\infty dr_1 r_1^2 e^{-2Zr_1} \int_0^\infty dr_2 r_2^2 \frac{e^{-2Zr_2}}{r_>}$$

Now show that

$$E^{(1)} = 16Z^6 \int_0^\infty dr_1 r_1 e^{-2Zr_1} \int_0^{r_1} dr_2 r_2^2 e^{-2Zr_2}$$
$$+ 16Z^6 \int_0^\infty dr_1 r_1^2 e^{-2Zr_1} \int_{r_1}^\infty dr_2 r_2 e^{-2Zr_2}$$
$$= -4Z^3 \int_0^\infty dr_1 r_1 e^{-2Zr_1}[e^{-2Zr_1}(2Z^2 r_1^2 + 2Zr_1 + 1) - 1]$$
$$+ 4Z^4 \int_0^\infty dr_1 r_1^2 e^{-2Zr_1}[e^{-2Zr_1}(2Zr_1 + 1)]$$

$$= -4Z^6 \int_0^\infty dr_1 e^{-4Zr_1} \left[\frac{r_1^2}{Z^2} + \frac{r_1}{Z^3} \right] + 4Z^3 \int_0^\infty dr_1 r_1 e^{-2Zr_1}$$

$$= \frac{5}{8} Z$$

as in Problem 6.

An oxygen molecule in its ground electronic state has two unpaired electrons, and so has a net electronic spin. This net spin causes an oxygen molecule to act as a tiny magnet. Consequently, oxygen is a magnetic substance and is attracted to a region between the poles of a magnet as shown above.

9

Molecules

ONE of the great early achievements of quantum mechanics was a description of the chemical bond by Heitler and London in 1927. Prior to this time, it was impossible to explain why two hydrogen atoms come together to form a stable chemical bond. We shall see in this chapter that the existence of a stable chemical bond is a quantum-mechanical effect. Because H_2 is the simplest molecule or chemical bond, we shall discuss H_2 in detail like we did for a helium atom in Chapter 8. Many of the ideas and techniques that we shall develop for H_2 will be applicable to more complex molecules. After discussing H_2 in some detail, we then shall learn how to construct molecular orbitals for diatomic molecules. We shall place electrons into molecular orbitals in accord with the Pauli Exclusion Principle just as we placed electrons into atomic orbitals in Chapter 8. We shall conclude the chapter with a discussion of hybrid orbitals and with a simple theory of conjugated and aromatic hydrocarbons.

9-1 The Born-Oppenheimer Approximation Simplifies Molecular Hamiltonian Operators

The Hamiltonian operator for a hydrogen molecule is

$$\hat{H} = -\frac{\hbar^2}{2M}(\nabla_A^2 + \nabla_B^2) - \frac{\hbar^2}{2m}(\nabla_1^2 + \nabla_2^2) - \frac{Ze^2}{4\pi\varepsilon_0 r_{1A}} - \frac{Ze^2}{4\pi\varepsilon_0 r_{1B}}$$

$$- \frac{Ze^2}{4\pi\varepsilon_0 r_{2A}} - \frac{Ze^2}{4\pi\varepsilon_0 r_{2B}} + \frac{e^2}{4\pi\varepsilon_0 r_{12}} + \frac{Z^2 e^2}{4\pi\varepsilon_0 R} \tag{9-1}$$

J. Robert Oppenheimer (1904–1967). After graduating from Harvard, Oppenheimer traveled and studied in Europe and received a Ph.D. in 1927 from the University of Göttingen, where he studied at the invitation of Max Born. In 1928 he received a joint appointment at California Institute of Technology and the University of California at Berkeley. In 1943 Oppenheimer was named director of the nuclear research laboratories at Los Alamos, New Mexico. From 1947 to 1966 he was director of the Institute of Advanced Studies at Princeton University. Oppenheimer was chairman of the general advisory committee to the Atomic Energy Commission from 1947 to 1953, when he was denied access to classified information. Oppenheimer has been the subject of several biographies.

In Eq. 9-1, M is the mass of a hydrogen nucleus, m is the electronic mass, Z is the atomic number of the nucleus ($Z = 1$ for hydrogen), ∇_A^2 and ∇_B^2 are the Laplacian operators with respect to the positions of nuclei A and B, ∇_1^2 and ∇_2^2 are the Laplacian operators for the positions of electrons 1 and 2, and the various distances are illustrated in Figure 9-1.

As in the case of the helium atom in Chapter 8, we assume that because the nuclei are so much more massive than the electrons, the nuclei can be considered to be fixed relative to the motion of the electrons. Thus, we neglect the terms

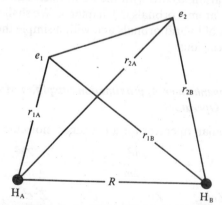

Figure 9-1. Definition of the distances involved in the Hamiltonian for a hydrogen molecule, Eq. 9-1.

involving ∇_A^2 and ∇_B^2 in Eq. 9-1 and write Eq. 9-1 as

$$\hat{H} = -\frac{\hbar^2}{2m}(\nabla_1^2 + \nabla_2^2) - \frac{Ze^2}{4\pi\varepsilon_0 r_{1A}} - \frac{Ze^2}{4\pi\varepsilon_0 r_{1B}} - \frac{Ze^2}{4\pi\varepsilon_0 r_{2A}} - \frac{Ze^2}{4\pi\varepsilon_0 r_{2B}} + \frac{e^2}{4\pi\varepsilon_0 r_{12}} + \frac{Z^2 e^2}{4\pi\varepsilon_0 R}$$

$$\text{(9-2)}$$

The approximation of neglecting the nuclear motion is called the *Born-Oppenheimer approximation*. The Born-Oppenheimer approximation can be corrected systematically by perturbation theory, using the ratio m/M as the small expansion parameter.

As usual we shall express all our equations in atomic units, and so Eq. 9-2 becomes for $Z = 1$ (Problem 1)

$$\hat{H} = -\frac{1}{2}(\nabla_1^2 + \nabla_2^2) - \frac{1}{r_{1A}} - \frac{1}{r_{1B}} - \frac{1}{r_{2A}} - \frac{1}{r_{2B}} + \frac{1}{r_{12}} + \frac{1}{R} \qquad \text{(9-3)}$$

9-2   *The Valence-Bond Treatment of a Hydrogen Molecule Was The First Successful Description of a Chemical Bond*

The first satisfactory explanation of the stability of the chemical bond, and of H_2 in particular, was given by Heitler and London in 1927. Their method has been extended to more complicated molecules and is known as the *valence-bond method*. As we did for the case of the helium atom, we shall ignore spin for the moment and then include it later. We have seen in Chapter 8 that a two-electron wave function can be factored into a spatial part and a spin part.

Consider two hydrogen atoms, each with its "own" electron. If the hydrogen atoms are in their ground state and are sufficiently far apart, then the wave function for the two hydrogen atoms is

$$\psi_1 = 1s_A(1)1s_B(2) \qquad \text{(9-4)}$$

where $1s_A$ denotes a $1s$ hydrogen orbital centered on nucleus A, that is, with nucleus A serving as the origin of the spherical coordinate system in which the $1s$ orbital is expressed. Similarly, $1s_B$ denotes the same thing but with nucleus B serving as the origin. Because the electrons are indistinguishable, the wave function

$$\psi_2 = 1s_A(2)1s_B(1) \qquad \text{(9-5)}$$

is equally valid. Following Heitler and London, then, we take the linear combination

$$\psi = c_1\psi_1 + c_2\psi_2 \qquad \text{(9-6)}$$

as a trial function. The determinantal secular equation associated with Eq. 9-6 is (Problem 2)

$$\begin{vmatrix} H_{11} - ES_{11} & H_{12} - ES_{12} \\ H_{12} - ES_{12} & H_{22} - ES_{22} \end{vmatrix} = 0 \qquad \text{(9-7)}$$

Let us look at each of the elements of this determinant. For example,

$$S_{11} = \iint d\mathbf{r}_1\, d\mathbf{r}_2\, 1s_A(1)1s_B(2)1s_A(1)1s_B(2)$$

$$= \int d\mathbf{r}_1\, 1s_A(1)1s_A(1) \int d\mathbf{r}_2\, 1s_B(2)1s_B(2)$$

$$= 1 \times 1 = 1 \tag{9-8}$$

because the $1s$ orbitals are normalized. Similarly, it is easy to show that $S_{22} = 1$. The evaluation of S_{12}, however, is a little more complicated. We have that

$$S_{12} = \iint d\mathbf{r}_1\, d\mathbf{r}_2\, 1s_A(1)1s_B(2)1s_A(2)1s_B(1)$$

$$= \int d\mathbf{r}_1\, 1s_A(1)1s_B(1) \int d\mathbf{r}_2\, 1s_B(2)1s_A(2) \tag{9-9}$$

Both of the integrals in Eq. 9-9 are the same. Let us denote each of these integrals by S, so that we have

$$S_{12} = S^2 \tag{9-10}$$

where

$$S = \int d\mathbf{r}_1\, 1s_A(1)1s_B(1) \tag{9-11}$$

Realize that this integral is not the same as those that appear in S_{11} in Eq. 9-8, because in Eq. 9-11 one of the $1s$ orbitals is centered on nucleus A and the other is centered on nucleus B. These two orbitals are shown schematically in Figure 9-2. Note that the integrand in Eq. 9-11 is nonzero only when $1s_A$ and $1s_B$ are *simultaneously* nonzero, which according to Figure 9-2 occurs only for regions in which the two orbitals overlap with each other. Because the magnitude of the integral S given by Eq. 9-11 depends on the extent of overlap of the two orbitals $1s_A$ and $1s_B$, it is called an *overlap integral*. An overlap integral is a direct measure of the extent of the overlap of the orbitals centered on two different nuclei. Again referring to Figure 9-2, one can see that the value of S depends on the internuclear distance R and, in fact, we have the inequality

$$0 \le S(R) \le 1 \tag{9-12}$$

The explicit evaluation of $S(R)$ is a little bit lengthy and is discussed in Problem 3.

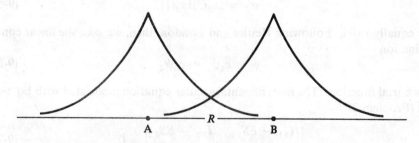

Figure 9-2. The overlap of $1s$ orbitals centered on hydrogen nuclei located at A and B.

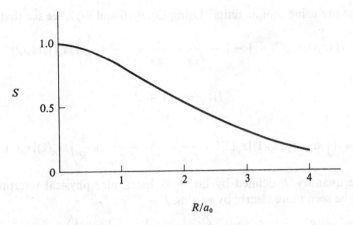

Figure 9-3. The overlap integral S for two hydrogen atom 1s orbitals plotted versus the internuclear separation in atomic units.

The result, however, is that

$$S(R) = e^{-R}\left(1 + R + \frac{R^2}{3}\right) \tag{9-13}$$

Equation 9-13 is plotted versus R in Figure 9-3.

9-3 The Valence-Bond Energy of H₂ Is Given in Terms of a Coulomb Integral, an Exchange Integral, and an Overlap Integral

We must now evaluate the other elements in Eq. 9-7. Let us consider H_{11}, which is given by

$$H_{11} = \iint d\mathbf{r}_1\, d\mathbf{r}_2\, 1s_A(1)1s_B(2)\hat{H}1s_A(1)1s_B(2) \tag{9-14}$$

where (see Eq. 9-3)

$$\hat{H} = -\frac{1}{2}(\nabla_1^2 + \nabla_2^2) - \frac{1}{r_{1A}} - \frac{1}{r_{1B}} - \frac{1}{r_{2A}} - \frac{1}{r_{2B}} + \frac{1}{r_{12}} + \frac{1}{R} \tag{9-15}$$

Because the 1s orbitals are eigenfunctions of the hydrogen atom Hamiltonian, we note that

$$\left(-\frac{1}{2}\nabla_1^2 - \frac{1}{r_{1A}}\right)1s_A(1) = -\frac{1}{2}1s_A(1) \tag{9-16}$$

and

$$\left(-\frac{1}{2}\nabla_2^2 - \frac{1}{r_{2B}}\right)1s_B(2) = -\frac{1}{2}1s_B(2) \tag{9-17}$$

where we are using atomic units. Using Eq. 9-16 and 9-17, we see that

$$\hat{H}1s_A(1)1s_B(2) = \left(-1 - \frac{1}{r_{1B}} - \frac{1}{r_{2A}} + \frac{1}{r_{12}} + \frac{1}{R}\right)1s_A(1)1s_B(2) \quad (9\text{-}18)$$

and that

$$H_{11} = -1 + J \quad (9\text{-}19)$$

where

$$J = \iint d\mathbf{r}_1\, d\mathbf{r}_2\, 1s_A(1)1s_B(2)\left(-\frac{1}{r_{1B}} - \frac{1}{r_{2A}} + \frac{1}{r_{12}} + \frac{1}{R}\right)1s_A(1)1s_B(2) \quad (9\text{-}20)$$

The quantity J, defined by Eq. 9-20, has a nice physical interpretation that can be seen more clearly by writing J as

$$J = \iint d\mathbf{r}_1\, d\mathbf{r}_2\, [1s_A(1)]^2\left(-\frac{1}{r_{1B}} - \frac{1}{r_{2A}} + \frac{1}{r_{12}} + \frac{1}{R}\right)[1s_B(2)]^2 \quad (9\text{-}21)$$

Now J can be written as the sum of four terms:

$$J = -\int \frac{d\mathbf{r}_1\, [1s_A(1)]^2}{r_{1B}} - \int \frac{d\mathbf{r}_2\, [1s_B(2)]^2}{r_{2A}} + \iint d\mathbf{r}_1\, d\mathbf{r}_2\, \frac{[1s_A(1)]^2[1s_B(2)]^2}{r_{12}} + \frac{1}{R}$$

$$(9\text{-}22)$$

where in the first integral, for example, we have carried out the integration over the coordinates of electron 2 and have used the fact that the $1s$ orbitals are normalized. The first term in Eq. 9-22 can be interpreted as the charge density of electron 1 around nucleus A interacting with nucleus B via the Coulombic potential; the second term is the Coulombic energy of interaction of the charge density of electron 2 around B with nucleus A; the third term is the mutual Coulombic interaction energy of the two electronic charge densities; and the fourth term is simply the nuclear-nuclear Coulombic interaction. Thus, each of the four terms in Eq. 9-22 can be interpreted as a classical Coulomb interaction, and so J is called a *Coulomb integral*. The value of J depends on the internuclear separation, and its evaluation is a somewhat tedious exercise. The evaluation of J is discussed in Problem 4, and it is shown there that

$$J = e^{-2R}\left(\frac{1}{R} + \frac{5}{8} - \frac{3}{4}R - \frac{R^2}{6}\right) \quad (9\text{-}23)$$

Equation 9-23 is plotted versus R in Figure 9-4.

It is straightforward to show that $H_{22} = H_{11}$ (Problem 5). In order to evaluate H_{12}, we start with

$$H_{12} = \iint d\mathbf{r}_1\, d\mathbf{r}_2\, 1s_A(1)1s_B(2)\hat{H}1s_B(1)1s_A(2) \quad (9\text{-}24)$$

and use the fact that

$$\left(-\frac{1}{2}\nabla_1^2 - \frac{1}{r_{1B}}\right)1s_B(1) = -\frac{1}{2}1s_B(1) \quad (9\text{-}25)$$

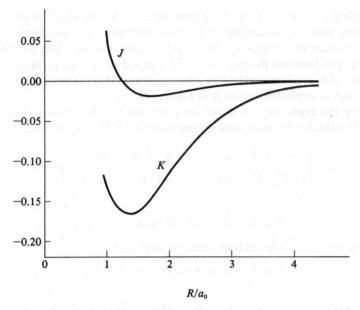

Figure 9-4. The Heitler-London valence-bond Coulomb (J) and exchange (K) integrals as a function of internuclear separation R. All quantities are expressed in atomic units.

and

$$\left(-\frac{1}{2}\nabla_2^2 - \frac{1}{r_{2A}}\right)1s_A(2) = -\frac{1}{2}\,1s_A(2) \qquad (9\text{-}26)$$

to write

$$\hat{H}1s_B(1)1s_A(2) = \left(-1 - \frac{1}{r_{1A}} - \frac{1}{r_{2B}} + \frac{1}{r_{12}} + \frac{1}{R}\right)1s_B(1)1s_A(2) \qquad (9\text{-}27)$$

If we now multiply Eq. 9-27 by $1s_A(1)1s_B(2)$ and integrate over the coordinates of both electrons, then we obtain

$$H_{12} = -S^2 + K \qquad (9\text{-}28)$$

where

$$K = \iint d\mathbf{r}_1\,d\mathbf{r}_2\,1s_A(1)1s_B(2)\left(-\frac{1}{r_{1A}} - \frac{1}{r_{2B}} + \frac{1}{r_{12}} + \frac{1}{R}\right)1s_B(1)1s_A(2) \qquad (9\text{-}29)$$

It is interesting to note that K does *not* lend itself to the same type of interpretation that we have discussed previously for J. If we write K in the form

$$K = \iint d\mathbf{r}_1\,d\mathbf{r}_2\,[1s_A(1)1s_B(1)]\left(-\frac{1}{r_{1A}} - \frac{1}{r_{2B}} + \frac{1}{r_{12}} + \frac{1}{R}\right)[1s_A(2)1s_B(2)]$$

then we see that we have a factor like $1s_A(1)1s_B(1)$ instead of $[1s_A(1)]^2$ as we have in J. A detailed analysis (Problem 6) shows that K arises only because we are using a wave function of the form of Eq. 9-6, one which explicitly recognizes the indistinguishability of the two electrons. Consequently, K is a strictly quantum-mechanical quantity, and because it arises when the electrons are exchanged between the two nuclei, K is called the *exchange integral*. The evaluation of K as a function of R involves functions that are beyond the level of this text, but K is plotted versus R in Figure 9-4.

Using the expressions that we have derived for the various elements in Eq. 9-7, the Heitler-London secular determinant for H_2, Eq. 9-7, becomes

$$\begin{vmatrix} -1 + J - E & -S^2 + K - ES^2 \\ -S^2 + K - ES^2 & -1 + J - E \end{vmatrix} = 0 \tag{9-30}$$

or

$$(E + 1 - J)^2 = (-S^2 + K - ES^2)^2$$

By taking the square root of both sides, we find that

$$E + 1 - J = \pm(-S^2 + K - ES^2)$$

or that

$$E(1 \pm S^2) = -1 + J \pm (K - S^2) = -(1 \pm S^2) + J \pm K$$

By dividing through by $1 \pm S^2$, we obtain

$$E_\pm = -1 + \frac{J \pm K}{1 \pm S^2} \tag{9-31}$$

By identifying the -1 in Eq. 9-31 as the energy of two isolated ground-state hydrogen atoms, we can write

$$\Delta E_\pm = \frac{J \pm K}{1 \pm S^2} \tag{9-32}$$

for the energy of H_2 *relative* to two isolated hydrogen atoms.

9-4   *The Exchange Integral Accounts for the Stability of the Chemical Bond in H_2*

Equation 9-32 gives two values of the energy of a hydrogen molecule. Thus, we expect that one of these two values, the one of lower energy, represents the binding energy of H_2. By substituting E_+ into either one of the algebraic equations that led to the secular determinant Eq. 9-7, that is, into either

$$c_1(H_{11} - ES_{11}) + c_2(H_{12} - ES_{12}) = 0 \tag{9-33}$$

or

$$c_1(H_{12} - ES_{12}) + c_2(H_{22} - ES_{22}) = 0 \tag{9-34}$$

one finds that (using Eq. 9-33)

$$c_1(-1 + J - E_+) + c_2(-S^2 + K - E_+ S^2) = 0$$

or that (Problem 7)

$$c_1 = c_2 \tag{9-35}$$

Thus, the Heitler-London wave function corresponding to E_+, or ΔE_+, is

$$\psi = c_1(\psi_1 + \psi_2)$$

where ψ_1 and ψ_2 are given by Eqs. 9-4 and 9-5. The value of c_1 can be found by requiring that ψ be normalized:

$$c_1^2 \iint d\mathbf{r}_1 \, d\mathbf{r}_2 \, (\psi_1^2 + 2\psi_1\psi_2 + \psi_2^2) = 1$$

This normalization condition gives

$$c_1^2(1 + 2S^2 + 1) = 1$$

or finally

$$c_1 = \frac{1}{\sqrt{2(1 + S^2)}} \tag{9-36}$$

Thus, the normalized Heitler-London wave function for H_2 is

$$\psi_+ = \frac{1}{\sqrt{2(1 + S^2)}} (\psi_1 + \psi_2) \tag{9-37}$$

We have subscripted ψ with a $+$ to indicate that this wave function is symmetric under the interchange of the (spatial) coordinates of the two electrons.

EXAMPLE 9-1

Determine the wave function that corresponds to E_-.

Solution: To find c_1 and c_2, we substitute E_- from Eq. 9-31 into either Eq. 9-33 or 9-34. Using Eq. 9-33, we find

$$c_1(-1 + J - E_-) + c_2(-S^2 + K - E_-S^2) = 0$$

$$c_1\left(J - \frac{J - K}{1 - S^2}\right) + c_2\left(+K - \frac{(J - K)S^2}{1 - S^2}\right) = 0$$

$$c_1\left(\frac{K - JS^2}{1 - S^2}\right) + c_2\left(\frac{K - JS^2}{1 - S^2}\right) = 0$$

or $c_2 = -c_1$. Thus, we have

$$\psi_- = c_1(\psi_1 - \psi_2)$$

We evaluate c_1 by requiring that ψ_- be normalized, and so

$$c_1^2(1 - 2S^2 + 1) = 1$$

or that

$$c_1 = \frac{1}{\sqrt{2(1 - S^2)}}$$

Finally, then, we find that

$$\psi_- = \frac{1}{\sqrt{2(1 - S^2)}} (\psi_1 - \psi_2) \qquad (9\text{-}38)$$

Note that ψ_- is antisymmetric under the interchange of the coordinates of the two electrons.

Figure 9-4 shows $J(R)$ and $K(R)$ plotted as functions of R. Remembering that negative values of energy represent stability, one can see from Figure 9-4 that it is $K(R)$, the exchange integral, that confers the stability to H_2. Because the exchange integral is a strictly quantum-mechanical quantity, we say that the stability or even the existence of the chemical bond is a quantum-mechanical effect.

Figure 9-5 shows ΔE_+ and ΔE_- plotted versus R. One can see from this figure that ΔE_+ describes a stable chemical bond because the energy is less than that of two isolated hydrogen atoms, whereas ΔE_- describes a state that is stable for no values of R. The ΔE_+ curve is the type of curve that we might

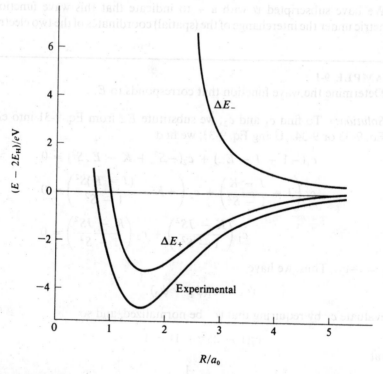

Figure 9-5. The internuclear potential energy curves of H_2 calculated by the Heitler-London valence-bond method.

TABLE 9-1

Results of Various Calculations for H₂

Wave function	Effective nuclear charge	Total energy/au	Dissociation energy/au	Bond length/au	Vibrational frequency/10^3 cm^{-1}
(VB)[a] $1s_A(1)1s_B(2) + 1s_B(1)1s_A(2)$	1.000	-1.1160	0.1160	1.64	4.08
(VB)[b] $1s_A(1)1s_B(2) + 1s_B(1)1s_A(2)$	1.166	-1.1389	0.1389	1.39	4.18
(MO)[c] $[1s_A(1) + 1s_B(1)][1s_A(2) + 1s_B(2)]$	1.000	-1.0990	0.0990	1.61	4.16
(MO)[c] $[1s_A(1) + 1s_B(1)][1s_A(2) + 1s_B(2)]$	1.197	-1.1282	0.1282	1.38	4.58
Hartree-Fock[d]	—	-1.1336	0.1336	1.40	—
(VB + ionic)[e] $c[1s_A(1)1s_B(2) + 1s_B(1)1s_A(2)]$ $+ [1s_A(1)1s_A(2) + 1s_B(1)1s_B(2)]$	1.000	-1.1187	0.1187	1.67	
(VB + ionic)[e] $c[1s_A(1)1s_B(2) + 1s_B(1)1s_A(2)]$ $+ [1s_A(1)1s_A(2) + 1s_B(1)1s_B(2)]$	1.193	-1.1478	0.1478	1.43	4.75
(VB)[f] $\phi_A(1)\phi_B(2) + \phi_B(1)\phi_A(2)$ $\phi = 1s + \lambda 2p_z$	1.19	-1.1484	0.1484	1.416	
(VB + ionic)[e] $c[\phi_A(1)\phi_B(2) + \phi_B(1)\phi_A(2)]$ $+ [1s_A(1)1s_A(2) + 1s_B(1)1s_B(2)]$ $\phi = 1s + \lambda 2p_z$	1.190	-1.1514	0.1514	1.41	
Equation 9-95 13 terms[g]		-1.1735	0.1735	1.40	
Equation 9-95 100 terms[h]	1.072	-1.174475	0.174475	1.40	4.385
MO-CI 28 configurations[i]		-1.16724	0.16724	1.40	
experimental[j]		-1.174	0.174	1.4006	4.401

[a] W. Heitler and F. London, Z. Physik 44, 455 (1927).
[b] S. C. Wang, Phys. Rev. 31, 579 (1928).
[c] C. A. Coulson, Trans. Far. Soc. 33, 1479 (1937).
[d] W. Kolos and C. C. J. Roothaan, Rev. Mod. Phys. 32, 219 (1960).
[e] S. Weinbaum, J. Chem. Phys. 1, 593 (1933).
[f] N. Rosen, Phys. Rev. 38, 2099 (1931).
[g] H. M. James and A. S. Coolidge, J. Chem. Phys. 1, 825 (1933).
[h] W. Kolos and L. Wolniewicz, J. Chem. Phys. 41, 3663 (1964); 49, 404 (1968).
[i] S. Hagstrom and H. Shull, Rev. Mod. Phys. 35, 624 (1963).
[j] G. Herzberg, J. Mol. Spectroscopy 33, 147 (1970).
See also A. D. McLean, A. Weiss, and M. Yoshimine, Rev. Mod. Phys. 32, 211 (1960).

expect for the interatomic interaction leading to a stable chemical bond. The two atoms attract each other as they approach but eventually pass through a minimum and begin to repel each other as they approach too closely. The minimum in the curve represents the stable equilibrium position, because the force, that is, $d\,\Delta E_+/dR$, is equal to zero at the minimum. The value of ΔE_+ at this minimum represents the dissociation energy of the hydrogen molecule and the value of R at the minimum represents the equilibrium bond length. The determination of these quantities must be done numerically, but it turns out that $E_{\text{dissociation}} = 0.116$ au $= 3.15$ eV $= 305$ kJ/mol and that $R_{\text{min}} = 1.6$ au $= 0.087$ nm, compared to the experimental values of 4.75 eV and 0.074 nm (see Table 9-1). Thus, we see that although the Heitler-London treatment gives a stable chemical bond, its quantitative predictions are not too accurate.

Recall from Chapter 5 that the force constant, and hence the fundamental vibrational frequency, is determined from the curvature of the energy curve at its minimum. For this case, one finds that $\bar{v} = 4.08 \times 10^3$ cm^{-1} versus the experimental value of 4.40×10^3 cm^{-1}.

In the conventional Heitler-London treatment that we have presented here, the wave function is built up from hydrogen $1s$ orbitals with $Z = 1$ in the exponent. It is a straightforward matter to allow the orbital exponent to vary instead of fixing it at unity, and if one chooses Z to minimize the energy, then one finds that $Z_{\text{optimum}} = 1.166$ and $E_{\text{dissociation}} = 0.1389$ au $= 3.80$ eV, $R_{\text{min}} = 1.39$ au $= 0.076$ nm, and $\bar{v} = 4.18 \times 10$ cm^{-1} (see Table 9-1).

9-5 *The Two States of H$_2$ Given by the Heitler-London Theory Are a Singlet State and a Triplet State*

Before going on to study other treatments of the chemical bond, it is interesting and instructive to return to Figure 9-5 and inquire about the meaning of the curve given by ΔE_-. In order to ascertain the nature of the state described by ΔE_-, we must include spin in our wave functions. For a two-electron system, there are four possible spin functions:

$$\alpha(1)\alpha(2)$$

$$\beta(1)\beta(2)$$

$$\alpha(1)\beta(2) \tag{9-39}$$

$$\alpha(2)\beta(1)$$

The first two of these four spin functions represent states with parallel spins (both $+\frac{1}{2}$ or both $-\frac{1}{2}$) and the other two represent states with antiparallel spins. The fact that electrons are fundamentally indistinguishable, however, forces us to consider the two linear combinations

$$\frac{1}{\sqrt{2}}\left[\alpha(1)\beta(2) \pm \alpha(2)\beta(1)\right] \tag{9-40}$$

instead of the last two of Eq. 9-39. The factor of $\sqrt{2}$ in Eq. 9-40 is a normalization constant (Problem 10). Of the four allowable spin functions, three are symmetric,

$$\alpha(1)\alpha(2)$$

$$\beta(1)\beta(2)$$

$$\frac{1}{\sqrt{2}}\left[\alpha(1)\beta(2) + \alpha(2)\beta(1)\right] \tag{9-41}$$

and one is antisymmetric,

$$\frac{1}{\sqrt{2}}\left[\alpha(1)\beta(2) - \alpha(2)\beta(1)\right] \tag{9-42}$$

Now for a two-electron system, we can simply multiply the spatial wave functions (Eqs. 9-37 and 9-38) and the spin functions (Eqs. 9-41 and 9-42) to obtain complete wave functions that are antisymmetric under the interchange of the spatial *and* spin coordinates of the two electrons. To do this, we multiply the symmetric spatial wave function ψ_+ by the one antisymmetric spin function (Eq. 9-42) and the antisymmetric spatial wave function ψ_- by any of the three symmetric spin functions (Eq. 9-41). Thus, we find that there are four allowable complete wave functions, given by

$$\frac{1}{\sqrt{2(1 + S^2)}}(\psi_1 + \psi_2)\left\{\frac{1}{\sqrt{2}}\left[\alpha(1)\beta(2) - \alpha(2)\beta(1)\right]\right\} \tag{9-43}$$

and

$$\frac{1}{\sqrt{2(1 - S^2)}}(\psi_1 - \psi_2)\left\{\begin{array}{c} \alpha(1)\alpha(2) \\ \beta(1)\beta(2) \\ \frac{1}{\sqrt{2}}\left[\alpha(1)\beta(2) + \alpha(2)\beta(1)\right] \end{array}\right. \tag{9-44}$$

Because the Hamiltonian does not depend on spin (to the approximation that we are considering in most of this text), the energy is determined entirely by the spatial parts of the wave functions, and so Eq. 9-43 corresponds to E_+ and Eq. 9-44 corresponds to E_-.

EXAMPLE 9-2

Show that the spin function associated with ψ_+ has $M_S = 0$ and that the spin functions associated with ψ_- have $M_S = 1, 0,$ and -1.

Solution: Recall that the spin functions α and β satisfy the relations

$$\hat{S}_z\alpha = \frac{\hbar}{2}\alpha$$

and

$$\hat{S}_z\beta = -\frac{\hbar}{2}\beta$$

Therefore, for the spin function in Eq. 9-43,

$$\hat{S}_z\left\{\frac{1}{\sqrt{2}}[\alpha(1)\beta(2) - \alpha(2)\beta(1)]\right\}$$

$$= \frac{1}{\sqrt{2}}(\hat{S}_{z1} + \hat{S}_{z2})[\alpha(1)\beta(2) - \alpha(2)\beta(1)]$$

$$= \frac{1}{\sqrt{2}}[(\hat{S}_{z1} + \hat{S}_{z2})\alpha(1)\beta(2) - (\hat{S}_{z1} + \hat{S}_{z2})\alpha(2)\beta(1)]$$

$$= \frac{1}{\sqrt{2}}\left[\left(\frac{\hbar}{2} - \frac{\hbar}{2}\right)\alpha(1)\beta(2) - \left(-\frac{\hbar}{2} + \frac{\hbar}{2}\right)\alpha(2)\beta(1)\right]$$

$$= 0$$

For the first spin function in Eq. 9-44, we have

$$\hat{S}_z\alpha(1)\alpha(2) = (\hat{S}_{z1} + \hat{S}_{z2})\alpha(1)\alpha(2) = \left(\frac{\hbar}{2} + \frac{\hbar}{2}\right)\alpha(1)\alpha(2) = \hbar\alpha(1)\alpha(2)$$

Similarly, for the third spin function in Eq. 9-44, we have

$$\hat{S}_z\beta(1)\beta(2) = (\hat{S}_{z1} + \hat{S}_{z2})\beta(1)\beta(2) = \left(-\frac{\hbar}{2} - \frac{\hbar}{2}\right)\beta(1)\beta(2) = -\hbar\beta(1)\beta(2)$$

For the second spin function in Eq. 9-44,

$$\hat{S}_z\left\{\frac{1}{\sqrt{2}}[\alpha(1)\beta(2) + \alpha(2)\beta(1)]\right\}$$

$$= \frac{1}{\sqrt{2}}(\hat{S}_{z1} + \hat{S}_{z2})[\alpha(1)\beta(2) + \alpha(2)\beta(1)]$$

$$= \frac{1}{\sqrt{2}}[(\hat{S}_{z1} + \hat{S}_{z2})\alpha(1)\beta(2) + (\hat{S}_{z1} + \hat{S}_{z2})\alpha(2)\beta(1)]$$

$$= \frac{1}{\sqrt{2}}\left[\left(\frac{\hbar}{2} - \frac{\hbar}{2}\right)\alpha(1)\beta(2) + \left(-\frac{\hbar}{2} + \frac{\hbar}{2}\right)\alpha(2)\beta(1)\right]$$

$$= 0$$

Example 9-2 shows that the three spin functions combined with ψ_- have values of M_S equal to $+1$, -1, and 0 and the spin function combined with ψ_+ has $M_S = 0$. Thus, we can associate the three spin functions in Eq. 9-44 with a spin state with total spin angular momentum $S_{\text{total}} = 1$ with its three possible projections $M_S = 0, \pm 1$. Similarly, we can associate the one spin function in Eq. 9-43 with a spin state with $S_{\text{total}} = 0$, and consequently $M_S = 0$. It would be more direct to show that these wave functions are eigenfunctions of $\hat{S}^2$ with eigenvalues $S_{\text{total}}(S_{\text{total}} + 1)\hbar^2$ with $S_{\text{total}} = 0$ and 1. This is possible to do but is beyond the level of our discussion. Because the degeneracy of these spin states is $2S_{\text{total}} + 1$, we call the state described by Eq. 9-43 a *singlet state* and that described by Eq. 9-44 a *triplet state*. Thus, we see that the ground state of H_2 is a singlet state and that the triplet state is an excited state that is everywhere repulsive.

We have just shown that the state corresponding to ΔE_- is a triplet state by considering the four possible spin states and by combining these spin states with the two spatial wave functions so that the overall product is antisymmetric under the interchange of the spatial *and* spin coordinates of the two electrons. We were able to consider the spatial and spin wave functions separately because we are considering a two-electron system, where the spatial and spin parts of the complete wave function factor. This factorization does not occur in general, and perhaps we should have started our discussion by using determinantal wave functions built up of spin orbitals at the outset. It is a straightforward but lengthy exercise (Problem 11) to show that if we start with

$$\psi_1 = \begin{vmatrix} 1s_A\alpha(1) & 1s_B\beta(1) \\ 1s_A\alpha(2) & 1s_B\beta(2) \end{vmatrix} \tag{9-45}$$

and

$$\psi_2 = \begin{vmatrix} 1s_A\beta(1) & 1s_B\alpha(1) \\ 1s_A\beta(2) & 1s_B\alpha(2) \end{vmatrix} \tag{9-46}$$

and use

$$\psi = c_1\psi_1 + c_2\psi_2$$

then we obtain

$$\psi_s = \frac{1}{\sqrt{2(1 + S^2)}}\left(\frac{1}{\sqrt{2}}\psi_1 - \frac{1}{\sqrt{2}}\psi_2\right) \qquad E = E_+ \tag{9-47}$$

and

$$\psi_t = \frac{1}{\sqrt{2(1 - S^2)}}\left(\frac{1}{\sqrt{2}}\psi_1 + \frac{1}{\sqrt{2}}\psi_2\right) \qquad E = E_- \tag{9-48}$$

Note that both ψ_s and ψ_t are antisymmetric because ψ_1 and ψ_2 are antisymmetric. It is straightforward to show that both ψ_s and ψ_t are eigenfunctions of $\hat{S}_{z,\text{total}}$ with eigenvalue zero (Problem 12). In addition, although we cannot prove it here, both ψ_s and ψ_t are eigenfunctions of $\hat{S}^2_{\text{total}}$ with eigenvalues $S(S + 1)\hbar^2$ with $S = 0$ in the case of ψ_s and $S = 1$ in the case of ψ_t. The subscripts s and t then denote *singlet* and *triplet*. The other two members of the triplet are

$$\psi_t = \frac{1}{\sqrt{2(1 - S^2)}} \begin{vmatrix} 1s_A\alpha(1) & 1s_B\alpha(1) \\ 1s_A\alpha(2) & 1s_B\alpha(2) \end{vmatrix} \tag{9-49}$$

$$\psi_t = \frac{1}{\sqrt{2(1 - S^2)}} \begin{vmatrix} 1s_A\beta(1) & 1s_B\beta(1) \\ 1s_A\beta(2) & 1s_B\beta(2) \end{vmatrix} \tag{9-50}$$

Robert S. Mulliken (b. 1896) received his Ph.D. in physical chemistry from the University of Chicago in 1921, and then did postgraduate study at Chicago, Harvard and Göttingen, where he met Friedrich Hund. He returned to the University of Chicago in 1928 with a joint appointment in the departments of physics and chemistry. Although Mulliken does not perform experiments himself, he considers himself to be a middleman between experiment and theory. Mulliken was awarded the Nobel Prize for chemistry in 1966.

The valence-bond method of Heitler and London was developed and extended to larger molecules by Pauling and Slater. It would appear to be natural to discuss this extension at this time, but instead we shall discuss an alternative method developed in the early 1930s by Hund, Mulliken, and others. This method is called *molecular-orbital theory* and is rather similar to the way that one builds helium and other atomic wave functions by using products of hydrogenlike, or single-electron, wave functions.

9-6 *The Simple Molecular-Orbital Treatment of H_2^+ Yields a Bonding Orbital and an Antibonding Orbital*

In the molecular-orbital method, we write molecular wave functions as products of single-electron molecular wave functions, or *molecular orbitals*. To derive a set of molecular orbitals that is analogous to the set of hydrogen atomic orbitals, we must consider the simplest single-electron molecular species, H_2^+, the hydrogen molecular ion. The Hamiltonian operator for H_2^+ is

$$\hat{H} = -\frac{1}{2}\nabla^2 - \frac{1}{r_A} - \frac{1}{r_B} + \frac{1}{R} \qquad (9\text{-}51)$$

where ∇^2 is the Laplacian operator on the coordinates of the electron, r_A is the distance of the electron from nucleus A, r_B is the distance of the electron from nucleus B, and R is the nuclear-nuclear separation. It so happens that it is possible to solve the Schrödinger equation for H_2^+ exactly, but the solutions are quite complicated and not easy to use. Instead, it is more convenient to solve H_2^+ approximately and to use the resultant approximate molecular orbitals to build molecular wave functions. Although this may seem like a terribly crude way to proceed, we shall see below that it can be suitably refined to yield very satisfactory results.

As a trial function for H_2^+, consider the linear combination

$$\psi = c_1 1s_A + c_2 1s_B \tag{9-52}$$

In a sense, Eq. 9-52 is a one-electron analog of Eq. 9-6 and is motivated by the success of the Heitler-London theory. The secular equation associated with the wave function given by Eq. 9-52 is

$$\begin{vmatrix} H_{AA} - E & H_{AB} - ES \\ H_{AB} - ES & H_{BB} - E \end{vmatrix} = 0 \tag{9-53}$$

where

$$H_{AA} = \int d\mathbf{r}\, 1s_A \hat{H} 1s_A = H_{BB} \tag{9-54}$$

$$H_{AB} = \int d\mathbf{r}\, 1s_A \hat{H} 1s_B = \int d\mathbf{r}\, 1s_B \hat{H} 1s_A \tag{9-55}$$

$$S = \int d\mathbf{r}\, 1s_A 1s_B \tag{9-56}$$

Using the fact that

$$\left(-\frac{1}{2}\nabla^2 - \frac{1}{r_A}\right)1s_A = -\frac{1}{2} 1s_A \tag{9-57}$$

and

$$\left(-\frac{1}{2}\nabla^2 - \frac{1}{r_B}\right)1s_B = -\frac{1}{2} 1s_B \tag{9-58}$$

it is straightforward to show that

$$H_{AA} = -\tfrac{1}{2} + J' \tag{9-59}$$

where

$$J' = \int d\mathbf{r}\, 1s_A\left(-\frac{1}{r_B} + \frac{1}{R}\right)1s_A \tag{9-60}$$

and to show that

$$H_{AB} = -\frac{S}{2} + K' \tag{9-61}$$

where

$$K' = \int d\mathbf{r}\, 1s_A\left(-\frac{1}{r_A} + \frac{1}{R}\right)1s_B \tag{9-62}$$

Similarly to the Heitler-London treatment, J' and K' are called a Coulomb integral and an exchange integral, respectively.

If we write out Eq. 9-53, then we obtain

$$(H_{AA} - E)^2 - (H_{AB} - ES)^2 = 0$$

or

$$E_{\pm} = \frac{H_{AA} \pm H_{AB}}{1 \pm S} \tag{9-63}$$

Substituting Eqs. 9-59 and 9-61 into Eq. 9-63, we have

$$E_{\pm} = -\frac{1}{2} + \frac{J' \pm K'}{1 \pm S} \tag{9-64}$$

By identifying $-\frac{1}{2}$ in Eq. 9-64 as the ground-state energy of an isolated hydrogen atom and a bare proton, we can write Eq. 9-64 in the form

$$\Delta E_{\pm} = \frac{J' \pm K'}{1 \pm S} \tag{9-65}$$

where ΔE is the energy of H_2^+ relative to a separated proton and a hydrogen atom.

The integrals J', K', and S are fairly easy to evaluate (Problem 14), and the result is

$$S = e^{-R}\left(1 + R + \frac{R^2}{3}\right) \tag{9-66}$$

$$J' = e^{-2R}\left(1 + \frac{1}{R}\right) \tag{9-67}$$

$$K' = \frac{S}{R} - e^{-R}(1 + R) \tag{9-68}$$

If Eqs. 9-66 through 9-68 are substituted into Eq. 9-65, then we obtain the curves that are presented in Figure 9-6. The energy ΔE_{+} describes a stable molecular species whose dissociation energy is 0.065 au = 1.77 eV and whose equilibrium bond length is 2.49 au = 0.132 nm, compared to the experimental values of 0.102 au = 2.78 eV and 2.00 au = 0.106 nm, respectively. If we simply use $1s$ orbitals with the exponent as a variational parameter, then we obtain a dissociation energy of 0.083 au = 2.25 eV and a bond length of 2.00 au = 0.106 nm.

Although we could obtain increasingly better values of the energy and bond length of H_2^+, we are primarily interested in the corresponding wave functions.

EXAMPLE 9-3

Determine the molecular orbitals that correspond to the energies E_{+} and E_{-} in Eq. 9-64.

Solution: To determine the coefficients c_1 and c_2 in Eq. 9-52, we must use the algebraic equations that lead to the secular determinant in Eq. 9-53. These equations are

$$c_1(H_{AA} - E) + c_2(H_{AB} - ES) = 0$$

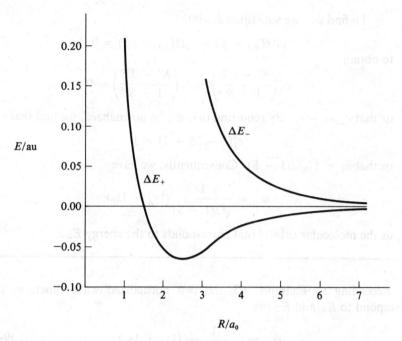

Figure 9-6. The energy as a function of internuclear separation for the H_2^+ molecular ion according to Eq. 9-65. All quantities are given in atomic units.

and

$$c_1(H_{AB} - ES) + c_2(H_{BB} - E) = 0$$

with H_{AA} and H_{AB} given by Eqs. 9-59 and 9-61, respectively. If we substitute E_+ from Eq. 9-64 into either of the above equations, say the first, then we obtain

$$c_1\left(J' - \frac{J' + K'}{1 + S}\right) + c_2\left[K' - \frac{(J' + K')S}{1 + S}\right] = 0$$

or

$$c_1\left(\frac{J'S - K'}{1 + S}\right) + c_2\left(\frac{K' - J'S}{1 + S}\right) = 0$$

or that $c_1 = c_2$. Consequently, the molecular orbital corresponding to E_+ is

$$\psi_+ = c_1(1s_A + 1s_B)$$

By requiring ψ_+ to be normalized, we find that

$$c_1^2(1 + 2S + 1) = 1$$

or that $c_1 = 1/\sqrt{2(1 + S)}$. Finally, then, we have

$$\psi_+ = \frac{1}{\sqrt{2(1 + S)}}(1s_A + 1s_B)$$

To find ψ_-, we substitute E_- into

$$c_1(H_{AA} - E) + c_2(H_{AB} - ES) = 0$$

to obtain

$$c_1\left(\frac{K' - JS'}{1 - S}\right) + c_2\left(\frac{K' - J'S}{1 - S}\right) = 0$$

or that $c_2 = -c_1$. By requiring that ψ_- be normalized, we find that

$$c_1^2(1 - 2S + 1) = 1$$

or that $c_1 = 1/\sqrt{2(1 - S)}$. Consequently, we have

$$\psi_- = \frac{1}{\sqrt{2(1 - S)}}(1s_A - 1s_B)$$

as the molecular orbital that corresponds to the energy E_-.

According to Example 9-3, the two normalized wave functions that correspond to E_+ and E_- are

$$\psi_{\pm} = \frac{1}{\sqrt{2(1 \pm S)}}(1s_A \pm 1s_B) \qquad (9\text{-}69)$$

These two wave functions and their squares are plotted in Figure 9-7. Note that ψ_+, the one that corresponds to the bound state, shows electron density piled up between the two nuclei; whereas ψ_-, the wave function that corresponds to the unbound state, has a node between the two nuclei and, consequently, a lack of electron density between the nuclei. Because ψ_+ describes a state that exhibits a stable chemical bond, ψ_+ is called a *bonding orbital*; because ψ_- describes a state that is everywhere repulsive, ψ_- is called an *antibonding orbital*. We shall indicate whether an orbital is a bonding orbital or an antibonding orbital by using a b or an a subscript; therefore, we write

$$\psi_b = \psi_+ = \frac{1}{\sqrt{2(1 + S)}}(1s_A + 1s_B) \qquad (9\text{-}70)$$

and

$$\psi_a = \psi_- = \frac{1}{\sqrt{2(1 - S)}}(1s_A - 1s_B) \qquad (9\text{-}71)$$

The bonding orbital ψ_b describes the ground state of H_2^+ and the antibonding orbital ψ_a describes an excited state.

Note that the simple approach that we have used to derive molecular orbitals has led to only two molecular orbitals, ψ_b and ψ_a. We stated previously that we are discussing H_2^+ in order to find a set of molecular orbitals out of which to build molecular wave functions much like we did in Chapter 8, where we built atomic wave functions from products of hydrogenlike orbitals. One may wonder why in the atomic case we have an infinite set of atomic orbitals

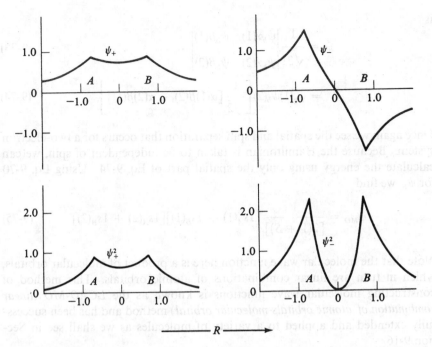

Figure 9-7. The molecular orbitals ψ_+ and ψ_- from Eq. 9-69 and their squares plotted along the internuclear axis.

(e.g., the hydrogenlike atomic orbitals), whereas in the molecular case we have only two H_2^+ molecular orbitals. It is important to realize that we obtained only two molecular orbitals because we used a linear combination of only two atomic orbitals as our trial function (Eq. 9-52). This was done solely for simplicity, and one could have just as well used a linear combination such as

$$\psi = c_1 1s_A + c_2 2s_A + c_3 2p_{zA} + c_4 1s_B + c_5 2s_B + c_6 2p_{zB} \qquad (9\text{-}72)$$

This particular choice would lead to a 6×6 secular determinant with six energies and six molecular orbitals instead of just two. Clearly there is no limit to this procedure and we could generate a large set of molecular orbitals. For pedagogical reasons, however, we shall develop a molecular-orbital theory of H_2 using just Eq. 9-70 and 9-71.

9-7 The Simple Valence-Bond Theory Ignores Ionic Terms and the Simple Molecular-Orbital Theory Overemphasizes Ionic Terms

Because ψ_b is the molecular orbital corresponding to the ground-state energy, we can describe the ground state of H_2 by placing two electrons with opposite spins in ψ_b. The Slater determinant corresponding to this assignment is

$$\psi = \frac{1}{\sqrt{2!}} \begin{vmatrix} \psi_b\alpha(1) & \psi_b\beta(1) \\ \psi_b\alpha(2) & \psi_b\beta(2) \end{vmatrix} \tag{9-73}$$

$$= \psi_b(1)\psi_b(2)\left[\frac{1}{\sqrt{2}}\left[\alpha(1)\beta(2) - \alpha(2)\beta(1)\right]\right] \tag{9-74}$$

Once again we see the spatial and spin separation that occurs for a two-electron system. Because the Hamiltonian is taken to be independent of spin, we can calculate the energy using only the spatial part of Eq. 9-74. Using Eq. 9-70 for ψ_b, we find

$$\psi_{MO} = \frac{1}{[2(1 + S)]}\left[1s_A(1) + 1s_B(1)\right]\left[1s_A(2) + 1s_B(2)\right] \tag{9-75}$$

Note that the molecular wave function here is a product of molecular orbitals, which in turn are linear combinations of atomic orbitals. This method of constructing molecular wave functions is known as the *LCAO-MO* (*linear combination of atomic orbitals-molecular orbital*) method and has been successfully extended and applied to a variety of molecules as we shall see in Section 9-16.

If we substitute the normalized LCAO-MO wave function, Eq. 9-75, into

$$E = \int \psi \hat{H} \psi \, d\mathbf{r}_1 \, d\mathbf{r}_2 \tag{9-76}$$

to find $E_{MO}(R)$, then the resulting integrals are similar to those that we encountered in the Heitler-London valence-bond method. The integrals can be evaluated analytically, but they result in functions that are somewhat advanced. If $E_{MO}(R)$ is plotted versus R, then one finds $E_{dissociation} = 0.099$ au $= 2.70$ eV, $R_{min} = 1.61$ au $= 0.085$ nm, and a fundamental vibrational frequency $\bar{v} = 4.16 \times 10^3$ cm^{-1}. The experimental values of these quantities are given in Table 9-1 along with the results obtained from Eq. 9-75 when the orbital exponent in the 1s orbital is allowed to vary.

The valence-bond method and the molecular-orbital method may appear to be two rather different approaches to chemical bonding or to H_2 in particular. Although the two methods appear to be quite different and in a sense competitive, they actually are closely related to each other. To see their relation, consider the (unnormalized) molecular-orbital wave function

$$\psi_{MO} = \left[1s_A(1) + 1s_B(1)\right]\left[1s_A(2) + 1s_B(2)\right]$$
$$= 1s_A(1)1s_B(2) + 1s_B(1)1s_A(2) + 1s_A(1)1s_A(2) + 1s_B(1)1s_B(2) \tag{9-77}$$

The first two terms here are just ψ_{VB}, our valence-bond wave function for H_2. What do the second two terms correspond to? These terms represent the electron configurations in which both electrons are on one atom. We can describe these two terms by the electron-dot formulas

$$H_A: \quad H_B \quad \text{and} \quad H_A \quad :H_B$$

or as

$$H_A^- H_B^+ \quad \text{and} \quad H_A^+ H_B^-$$

Thus, we see that third and fourth terms in Eq. 9-77 represent ionic structures for H_2.

If we let

$$\psi_{ionic} = 1s_A(1)1s_A(2) + 1s_B(1)1s_B(2) \tag{9-78}$$

then we can write Eq. 9-77 as

$$\psi_{MO} = \psi_{VB} + \psi_{ionic} \tag{9-79}$$

Equation 9-79 suggests that ψ_{MO} overemphasizes ionic terms, whereas ψ_{VB} underemphasizes (ignores) them.

We can develop a method intermediate to the VB and MO methods by using a linear combination of the form

$$\psi = c_1 \psi_{VB} + c_2 \psi_{ionic} \tag{9-80}$$

This was done by Weinbaum in 1933, who found $R_{min} = 1.67$ au $= 0.088$ nm and $E_{dissociation} = 0.1187$ au $= 3.23$ eV with $Z = 1$, and $R_{min} = 1.43$ au $= 0.076$ nm and $E_{dissociation} = 0.1478$ au $= 4.03$ eV when Z was allowed to vary. In addition, Weinbaum found that $c_2/c_1 = 0.16$ at R_{min} for the $Z = 1$ case. Some people would say that this implies that there is 0.16 or really $(0.16)^2 = 0.03$ ionic character in H_2, but this is a shaky interpretation. For instance, Weinbaum also found that $c_2/c_1 = 0.26$ for the optimum value of Z, and so we see that the ratio depends on the functions used in ψ_{VB} and ψ_{ionic}. In fact, as we have discussed briefly earlier, one does not need to use simple $1s$ orbitals. For example, it is clear that the electron distributions in each hydrogen atom do not remain spherical as the two atoms approach each other. If we let the internuclear axis be the z axis, then we might try constructing our valence-bond orbitals out of a linear combination of a $1s$ orbital and a $2p_z$ orbital

$$\phi = 1s + \lambda 2p_z \tag{9-81}$$

instead of from just a $1s$ orbital. In this case, we would have

$$\psi_{VB} = \phi_A(1)\phi_B(2) + \phi_B(1)\phi_A(2) \tag{9-82}$$

where ϕ_A and ϕ_B are given by Eq. 9-81. Equation 9-82 was used by Rosen in 1931 (see Table 9-1), and ionic terms were included 2 years later by Weinbaum (see Table 9-1). If this procedure is carried to its extreme, then we include more and more terms in Eq. 9-81 and will eventually reach the Hartree-Fock limit like we did in the atomic case. We shall discuss the Hartree-Fock method for molecules in Section 9-16.

9-8 *Valence-Bond Theory Plus Ionic Terms Are Formally Identical to Molecular-Orbital Theory with Configuration Interaction*

The relation between the valence-bond theory and molecular-orbital theory is even more complete than we have shown up to now. Consider our simple LCAO treatment of H_2^+, in which we obtained the (unnormalized) molecular orbitals

$$\phi_b = 1s_A + 1s_B$$
$$\phi_a = 1s_A - 1s_B$$

(9-83)

In our molecular-orbital discussion, we used

$$\psi = \begin{vmatrix} \phi_b\alpha(1) & \phi_b\beta(1) \\ \phi_b\alpha(2) & \phi_b\beta(2) \end{vmatrix}$$

(9-84)

or simply its spatial part, $\phi_b(1)\phi_b(2)$. However, we can extend our molecular-orbital treatment by using the antibonding molecular orbital ϕ_a as well. Considering only spatial parts for simplicity, we can form

$$\psi_1 = \phi_b(1)\phi_b(2)$$
$$\psi_2 = \phi_b(1)\phi_a(2) + \phi_a(1)\phi_b(2)$$
$$\psi_3 = \phi_b(1)\phi_a(2) - \phi_a(1)\phi_b(2)$$
$$\psi_4 = \phi_a(1)\phi_a(2)$$

(9-85)

We should take a linear combination of these four wave functions as a trial function and obtain a 4×4 determinant, but it is algebraically easier to start with ψ_1 and to add in each wave function in turn. Consider just ψ_1 and ψ_2 first. In this case, then

$$\psi = c_1\psi_1 + c_2\psi_2$$

and

$$\begin{vmatrix} H_{11} - ES_{11} & H_{12} - ES_{12} \\ H_{12} - ES_{12} & H_{22} - ES_{22} \end{vmatrix} = 0$$

(9-86)

where

$$H_{12} = \iint \psi_1 \hat{H} \psi_2 \, d\mathbf{r}_1 \, d\mathbf{r}_2$$
$$= \iint \phi_b(1)\phi_b(2)\hat{H}[\phi_b(1)\phi_a(2) + \phi_a(1)\phi_b(2)] \, d\mathbf{r}_1 \, d\mathbf{r}_2$$

(9-87)

Consider now the integral

$$I = \int \phi_b(2)\hat{H}\phi_a(2) \, d\mathbf{r}_2$$
$$= \int [1s_A(2) + 1s_B(2)]\hat{H}[1s_A(2) - 1s_B(2)] \, d\mathbf{r}_2$$

(9-88)

Note that this integral appears in H_{12} in Eq. 9-87. It is possible to show that I vanishes without doing any intergrations at all. We simply shall appeal to a symmetry argument. The subscripts A and B denote the labels of the two hydrogen nuclei. The Hamiltonian is symmetric in A and B, in the sense that it does not change if we relabel the two nuclei by replacing A by B and B by A. Thus, if we interchange A and B in Eq. 9-88, then we find that $I = -I$. The fact that $I = -I$ implies that $I = 0$ and eventually that $H_{12} = 0$ in Eq. 9-87. Similarly, it is straightforward to show that $S_{12} = 0$ (Problem 16), and so Eq. 9-86 becomes

$$\begin{vmatrix} H_{11} - E & 0 \\ 0 & H_{22} - E \end{vmatrix} = 0 \qquad (9\text{-}89)$$

The two roots to Eq. 9-89 are simply H_{11} and H_{22}, which are the results that we would have obtained if we had used ψ_1 and ψ_2 separately. Thus, we see that the two states described by ψ_1 and ψ_2 have no influence on each other. We say that ψ_1 and ψ_2 do not interact or mix.

Now let us consider a linear combination of ψ_1 and ψ_3 in Eq. 9-85. By a similar analysis (Problem 17), we find that ψ_1 and ψ_3 do not interact or mix. The only wave function in Eq. 9-85 that interacts with ψ_1 is ψ_4.

EXAMPLE 9-4

Show that the symmetry argument that we used to show that ψ_1 does not mix with ψ_2 and ψ_3 does *not* imply that ψ_1 does not mix with ψ_4.

Solution: The integral of interest here is H_{14}, because if $H_{14} = 0$, then ψ_1 and ψ_4 do not mix, and if $H_{14} \neq 0$, then ψ_1 and ψ_4 do mix. The integral H_{14} is

$$H_{14} = \iint dr_1\, dr_2\, \phi_b(1)\phi_b(2)\hat{H}\phi_a(1)\phi_a(2)$$

The argument that we have used to show that H_{12} and H_{13} equal zero is based upon the fact that $\phi_a \to -\phi_a$ when nuclei A and B are interchanged. For example (see Eq. 9-87),

$$H_{12} = \iint dr_1\, dr_2\, \phi_b(1)\phi_b(2)\hat{H}\phi_b(1)\phi_a(2) + \iint dr_1\, dr_2\, \phi_b(1)\phi_b(2)\hat{H}\phi_a(1)\phi_b(2)$$

When the two nuclei are interchanged, ϕ_b and $\hat{H}$ remain unchanged, but $\phi_a \to -\phi_a$ in each of the two integrals in H_{12}. Thus, we find that $H_{12} = -H_{12}$, which implies that $H_{12} = 0$.

Note that H_{14}, however, contains two factors of ϕ_a, the two factors being $\phi_a(1)$ and $\phi_a(2)$. Thus, H_{14} does *not* change sign upon the interchange of the two nuclei. Consequently, we cannot conclude from a symmetry argument that H_{14} equals zero, and in fact H_{14} does not equal zero.

The linear combination

$$\psi_{CI} = c_1\psi_1 + c_4\psi_4$$
$$= c_b\phi_b(1)\phi_b(2) + c_a\phi_a(1)\phi_a(2) \qquad (9\text{-}90)$$

describes the ground state of H_2. Equation 9-90 is a ground-state molecular-orbital wave function with an excited-state configuration mixed in. The extension of simple molecular-orbital theory to include excited-state configurations is called *configuration interaction*. The CI subscript in Eq. 9-90 denotes that ψ_{CI} is a configuration interaction wave function.

Let us look at ψ_{CI} given by Eq. 9-90 in more detail. Equation 9-90 can be written out as

$$\psi_{CI} = c_b[1s_A(1)1s_A(2) + 1s_A(1)1s_B(2) + 1s_B(1)1s_A(2) + 1s_B(1)1s_B(2)]$$
$$+ c_a[1s_A(1)1s_A(2) - 1s_A(1)1s_B(2) - 1s_B(1)1s_A(2) + 1s_B(1)1s_B(2)]$$
$$= (c_b - c_a)\psi_{VB} + (c_b + c_a)\psi_{ionic} \qquad (9\text{-}91)$$

Thus, we see that molecular-orbital theory with configuration interaction is exactly the same as valence-bond theory with ionic terms included. Both methods become exact in the limit of including more and more covalent and ionic terms or more and more excited-state configurations. In practice, however, one does not use the complete limit and so the two methods do differ. Each method has its advantages in certain applications, but molecular-orbital theory plus configuration interaction is much more widely used.

Before finishing our discussion of H_2, we should discuss briefly the early work of James and Coolidge (1933) and the more recent work of Kolos and Wolniewicz (1968). We saw in Chapter 8 that Hylleras was able to obtain essentially the exact ground-state energy of the helium atom by including the interelectronic distance r_{12} explicitly in the trial wave function. A similar approach was applied to H_2 with equal success by James and Coolidge as early as 1933.

When discussing the hydrogen molecule and evaluating the various integrals that occur, it is natural to use a coordinate system called *elliptic coordinates* (see also Problem 3). The three coordinates used to specify the location of a point in elliptic coordinates are

$$\lambda = \frac{r_A + r_B}{R_{AB}} \qquad \mu = \frac{r_A - r_B}{R_{AB}} \qquad (9\text{-}92)$$

and ϕ, which is the angle of the (r_A, r_B, R_{AB}) triangle about the interfocal axis. For the two electrons in H_2 we have

$$\lambda_1 = \frac{r_{1A} + r_{1B}}{R_{AB}} \qquad \lambda_2 = \frac{r_{2A} + r_{2B}}{R_{AB}}$$

$$\mu_1 = \frac{r_{1A} - r_{1B}}{R_{AB}} \qquad \mu_2 = \frac{r_{2A} - r_{2B}}{R_{AB}} \qquad (9\text{-}93)$$

In addition to these four coordinates, James and Coolidge also introduced a fifth coordinate

$$\rho = \frac{r_{12}}{R_{AB}} \tag{9-94}$$

and used a spatially symmetric trial function of the form

$$\psi = e^{-\alpha(\lambda_1 + \lambda_2)} \sum_{m,n,j,k,p} c_{mnjkp} (\lambda_1^m \lambda_2^n \mu_1^j \mu_2^k \rho^p + \lambda_1^n \lambda_2^m \mu_1^k \mu_2^j \rho^p) \tag{9-95}$$

where α and the c_{mnjkp}'s are variational parameters. Using 13 terms in this expansion, James and Coolidge found $E_{\text{dissociation}} = 0.1735$ au $= 4.72$ eV and $R_{\min} = 1.40$ au $= 0.074$ nm, in excellent agreement with the experimental values (see Table 9-1). A more recent calculation by Kolos and Wolniewicz in 1968 gave a dissociation energy of 0.1745 au $= 4.75$ eV, in complete agreement with experiment.

We can see in Table 9-1 that the dissociation energy and the equilibrium bond distance obtained by James and Coolidge or by Kolos and Wolniewicz are in excellent accord with the experiment values. The calculation of James and Coolidge represents one of the great early achievements of quantum mechanics as applied to chemistry.

9-9 *Molecular Orbitals Can Be Ordered According to Their Energies*

We can use either the valence-bond theory or the molecular-orbital theory to treat molecules that are more complicated than H_2. A great advantage of the molecular-orbital theory is that we can construct a set of molecular orbitals into which we can place electrons in accord with the Pauli Exclusion Principle. The assignment of electrons to molecular orbitals will allow us to introduce electron configurations for molecules just as we did for atoms in Chapter 8. To do this, we must construct sets of molecular orbitals. We shall construct molecular orbitals for homonuclear diatomic molecules in some detail and then just present some results for heteronuclear diatomic molecules and polyatomic molecules.

We shall use the LCAO-MO approximation, in which we form molecular orbitals as linear combinations of atomic orbitals. In the simplest case, we have only one atomic orbital centered on each atom and, as in the molecular-orbital treatment of H_2 discussed in Section 9-7, the two molecular orbitals are

$$\psi_{\pm} = 1s_A \pm 1s_B$$

if we start with a $1s$ orbital on each atom. These two molecular orbitals are shown in Figure 9-8. Note that ψ_+ concentrates electron density in the region

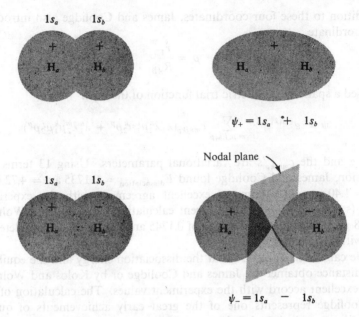

Figure 9-8. The linear combinations of two $1s$ atomic orbitals to give the bonding ($\sigma 1s$ or $\sigma_g 1s$) and antibonding ($\sigma^* 1s$ or $\sigma_u 1s$) molecular orbitals.

between the two nuclei, whereas ψ_- excludes electron density from the region between the two nuclei and even has a nodal plane between the two nuclei. Consequently, ψ_+ is a bonding orbital and ψ_- is an antibonding orbital. There are several notations to denote these two molecular orbitals. Because the electron density is symmetric about the internuclear axis, both ψ_+ and ψ_- are called σ _orbitals_, much like a spherically symmetric atomic orbital is called an _s orbital_. Because these σ orbitals are made out of s orbitals, and $1s$ orbitals in particular, they are denoted by $\sigma 1s$. There are two common notations to distinguish a bonding orbital from an antibonding orbital. One of these notations is to denote the bonding orbital by $\sigma 1s$ and to denote the antibonding orbital by $\sigma^* 1s$. The other way is to indicate the symmetry of the molecular orbital under an inversion of the wave function through the point midway between the two nuclei. If the wave function does not change its sign under this inversion, then we label the wave function _gerade_ after the German word for _even_, and we subscript the molecular orbital with a g. Referring to either Figure 9-8 or 9-7, we see that ψ_+ does not change its sign under inversion, and so we denote ψ_+ by $\sigma_g 1s$. We see from either Figure 9-8 or 9-7 that ψ_- changes sign under inversion, and we denote ψ_- by $\sigma_u 1s$, where the u stands for _ungerade_, the German word for _odd_. Thus, we have two designations of these orbitals: $\sigma 1s$ and $\sigma^* 1s$, or $\sigma_g 1s$ and $\sigma_u 1s$. Both of these designations are commonly used.

We can construct molecular orbitals out of other kinds of atomic orbitals in a similar way. In a first approximation, only orbitals of close energies combine (Problem 18), and so we consider combinations such as $2s_A \pm 2s_B$. The two molecular orbitals look like the two molecular orbitals in Figure 9-8 but are larger in extent. Following the notation we have developed, we shall designate the two molecular orbitals $2s_A \pm 2s_B$ by $\sigma 2s$ and σ^*2s, or by $\sigma_g 2s$ and $\sigma_u 2s$. Because a 2s atomic orbital is associated with a higher energy than a 1s orbital, we expect that the energy of the $\sigma 2s$ orbitals will be higher than that of the $\sigma 1s$ orbitals. In addition, because bonding orbitals have a lower energy than antibonding orbitals, we have the energy ordering $\sigma 1s < \sigma^*1s < \sigma 2s < \sigma^*2s$.

We can go on now and consider linear combinations of p orbitals. Although p orbitals have the same energy as s orbitals in the case of the hydrogen atom, that is not so for other atoms, and so we expect that molecular orbitals built up from p orbitals will have a higher energy than $\sigma 2s$ orbitals. If we let the internuclear axis be the z axis, then we can see from Figures 9-9 and 9-10 that the p_z orbitals combine to give a different molecular orbital than the p_x or p_y give. In fact, we see from Figure 9-9 that the molecular orbitals $2p_{zA} \pm 2p_{zB}$ are symmetric about the internuclear axis and so are σ orbitals. Once again, we find a bonding and antibonding situation and we designate these bonding and antibonding orbitals by $\sigma 2p_z$ and σ^*2p_z or by $\sigma_g 2p_z$ and $\sigma_u 2p_z$.

The p_x or p_y orbitals combine to give molecular orbitals that are not symmetric about the internuclear axis. Figure 9-10 shows that the y-z plane is a nodal plane in both the bonding and antibonding combinations of p_x orbitals. In the atomic case, orbitals with one nodal plane are called *p orbitals*, and so in the molecular case orbitals with one nodal plane are called *π orbitals*. The π^*2p_x has another nodal plane perpendicular to the internuclear axis. Consequently, the π^*2p_x orbital is an antibonding orbital. The $\pi 2p_x$ orbital does not have a nodal plane perpendicular to the internuclear axis, and so the $\pi 2p_x$ orbital is a bonding orbital. Note, however, that unlike the σ orbitals the bonding orbital changes sign upon inversion through the origin, whereas the

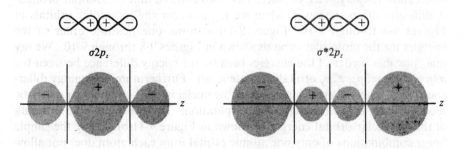

Figure 9-9. The $\sigma 2p_z$ and σ^*2p_z molecular orbitals formed from linear combinations of $2p_z$ atomic orbitals. Another notation for these molecular orbitals is $\sigma_g 2p_z$ and $\sigma_u 2p_z$ for the bonding and antibonding orbitals, respectively.

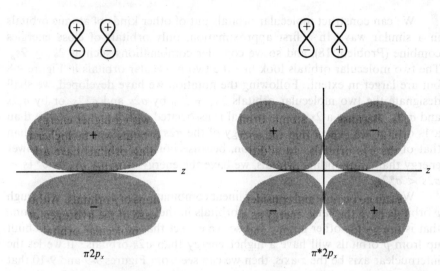

Figure 9-10. The $\pi 2p_x$ and π^*2p_x molecular orbitals formed from linear combinations of $2p_x$ atomic orbitals. Another notation for these molecular orbitals is $\pi_u 2p_x$ and $\pi_g 2p_x$ for the bonding and antibonding orbitals, respectively.

antibonding orbital remains unchanged upon inversion. Thus, for π orbitals the bonding orbital is *ungerade* and the antibonding orbital is *gerade*, leading us to the notation $\pi 2p_x$ and π^*2p_x' or $\pi_u 2p_x$ and $\pi_g 2p_x$. The p_y orbitals combine in a similar manner and the resultant molecular orbitals look like those in Figure 9-10 but are directed along the y axis instead of along the x axis as in Figure 9-10. The x-z plane is the nodal plane for π^*2p_y orbitals. Because the $\pi 2p_x$ and the $\pi 2p_y$ orbitals differ only in their spatial orientation, we expect that these sets of orbitals will be doubly degenerate. Figures like Figures 9-8 through 9-10 appear in most general chemistry texts.

Now that we have developed a set of molecular orbitals by combining atomic orbitals, we wish to determine the order of these molecular orbitals with respect to energy. We can then place electrons two at a time into the molecular orbitals just as we placed electrons two at a time into atomic orbitals. A difficulty arises, however, when we try to order the molecular orbitals in Figures 9-8 through 9-10. Figure 9-11(a) shows one possible order of the energies for the molecular orbitals shown in Figures 9-8 through 9-10. We say one "possible" order of the energies because the energy difference between the $\sigma 2p$ and the $\pi 2p_x$, $\pi 2p_y$ orbitals is quite small. Furthermore, the energy difference varies with the atomic number of the nuclei in the homonuclear diatomic molecule and with the internuclear separation. The other possible ordering of the molecular-orbital energies is shown in Figure 9-11(b). Using the simple linear combinations of only one atomic orbital from each atom does not allow us to distinguish between the two schemes in Figure 9-11. Fortunately, however, many of the predictions of the two schemes in Figure 9-11 are the same, and many of these predictions are of real chemical interest. We shall discuss the results of more extensive LCAO's in Section 9-14.

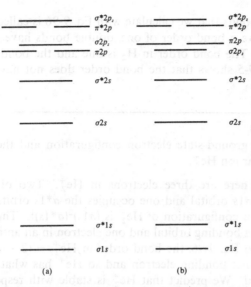

Figure 9-11. Two possible energy-level diagrams for homonuclear diatomic molecules. The separation between the $\pi 2p$ and $\sigma 2p_z$ orbitals not only is very small but varies with the atomic number of the nuclei and the internuclear separation. Thus, it is difficult to know beforehand which scheme applies to a given homonuclear diatomic molecule.

9-10   *Molecular-Orbital Theory Predicts That Diatomic Helium Does Not Exist*

We shall predict electron configurations of homonuclear diatomic molecules by placing electrons into the molecular orbitals in accord with the Pauli Exclusion Principle. Let us consider H_2 first. According to the Pauli Exclusion Principle, we place two electrons of opposite spin in the $\sigma 1s$ orbital and write the electron configuration of H_2 as $(\sigma 1s)^2$. The two electrons in the bonding orbital constitute a bonding pair of electrons and account for the single bond of H_2. Now consider He_2. The species He_2 has four electrons. Two of the electrons occupy the $\sigma 1s$ orbital and two occupy the $\sigma^* 1s$ orbital. The ground-state electron configuration of He_2 is $(\sigma 1s)^2(\sigma^* 1s)^2$. This assignment for He_2 gives two electrons in a bonding orbital and two electrons in an antibonding orbital. Electrons in a bonding orbital tend to draw the nuclei together, whereas electrons in an antibonding orbital tend to draw the nuclei apart. These two effects cancel each other and the result is that an antibonding electron cancels the effect of a bonding electron. In the case of He_2, the two antibonding electrons cancel the bonding of the two bonding electrons, and so there is no net bonding in He_2. This is in nice accord with the fact that the species He_2 has never been observed experimentally.

We can formalize the above result by the formula

$$\text{number of bonds} = \frac{\left(\begin{array}{c}\text{number of electrons} \\ \text{in bonding orbitals}\end{array}\right) - \left(\begin{array}{c}\text{number of electrons} \\ \text{in antibonding orbitals}\end{array}\right)}{2} \quad (9\text{-}96)$$

The number of bonds that we calculate with Eq. 9-96 is called the *bond order*. Single bonds have a bond order of one, double bonds have a bond order of two, and so on. The bond order in H_2 is one and the bond order in He_2 is zero. Example 9-5 shows that the bond order does not have to be a whole number.

EXAMPLE 9-5

Deduce the ground-state electron configuration and the bond order of the molecular ion He_2^+.

Solution: There are three electrons in He_2^+. Two of these electrons occupy the $\sigma 1s$ orbital and one occupies the $\sigma^* 1s$ orbital. The ground-state electron configuration of He_2^+ is $(\sigma 1s)^2(\sigma^* 1s)^1$. Thus there are two electrons in a bonding orbital and one electron in an antibonding orbital. According to Eq. 9-96, the bond order in $He_2^+ = (2 - 1)/2 = \frac{1}{2}$. There is only one net bonding electron and so He^+ has what is called a *one-electron bond*. We predict that He_2^+ is stable with respect to separated He and He^+. The bond length in He_2^+ is 108 pm and the bond energy is 251 kJ·mol^{-1}.

Table 9-2 summarizes the properties of H_2^+, H_2, He_2^+, and He_2.

TABLE 9-2
Molecular Properties of H_2^+, H_2, He_2^+, and He_2.

Species	Number of electrons	Ground-state electron configuration	Bond order	Bond length/pm	Bond energy/ kJ·mol^{-1}
H_2^+	1	$(\sigma 1s)^1$	$\frac{1}{2}$	106	255
H_2	2	$(\sigma 1s)^2$	1	74	431
He_2^+	3	$(\sigma 1s)^2(\sigma^* 1s)^1$	$\frac{1}{2}$	108	251
He_2	4	$(\sigma 1s)^2(\sigma^* 1s)^2$	0	Not observed	

9-11 *Molecular Electron Configurations Are Obtained by Placing Electrons into Molecular Orbitals in Accord with the Pauli Exclusion Principle*

Let us go on now and discuss the homonuclear diatomic molecules Li_2 through Ne_2. Each lithium atom has three electrons, and so Figure 9-11 gives the ground-state electron configuration, $(\sigma 1s)^2(\sigma^* 1s)^2(\sigma 2s)^2$. The bond

TABLE 9-3

Properties of the Diatomic Molecules
of Elements in the Second Row of the Periodic Table

Species	Ground-state electron configuration	Bond order	Bond length/pm	Bond energy/ $kJ \cdot mol^{-1}$
Li_2	$KK(\sigma 2s)^2$	1	267	105
Be_2	$KK(\sigma 2s)^2(\sigma *2s)^2$	0	Not observed	
B_2	$KK(\sigma 2s)^2(\sigma *2s)^2(\pi 2p)^2$	1	159	289
C_2	$KK(\sigma 2s)^2(\sigma *2s)^2(\pi 2p)^4$	2	124	599
N_2	$KK(\sigma 2s)^2(\sigma *2s)^2(\pi 2p)^4(\sigma 2p_z)^2$	3	110	942
O_2	$KK(\sigma 2s)^2(\sigma *2s)^2(\pi 2p)^4(\sigma 2p_z)^2(\pi *2p)^2$	2	121	494
F_2	$KK(\sigma 2s)^2(\sigma *2s)^2(\pi 2p)^4(\sigma 2p_z)^2(\pi *2p)^4$	1	141	154
Ne_2	$KK(\sigma 2s)^2(\sigma *2s)^2(\pi 2p)^4(\sigma 2p_z)^2(\pi *2p)^4(\sigma *2p_z)^2$	0	Not observed	

order in Li_2 is one. Thus we predict that Li_2 is stable relative to two separated lithium atoms. Lithium vapor is known to contain diatomic lithium molecules. Table 9-3 shows that Li_2 has a bond length of 267 pm and a bond energy of 105 $kJ \cdot mol^{-1}$.

Contour maps of the electron density in the individual molecular orbitals and the total electron density in Li_2 are shown in Figure 9-12. These contour maps have been obtained by detailed computer solution of the Schrödinger equation for Li_2. Figure 9-12 shows clearly that there is little difference between the electron densities in the $\sigma 1s$ and $\sigma *1s$ molecular orbitals of Li_2 and the electron densities in the two $1s$ atomic orbitals of the individual lithium atoms. This observation justifies the usual assumption that only the electrons in the valence shell need be included in discussions of chemical bonding. The $1s$ electrons are held tightly about each nucleus and do not participate in the bonding. Therefore, the ground-state electron configuration of Li_2 can be written as $KK(\sigma 2s)^2$, where K represents the filled K shell ($n = 1$ shell) on each lithium atom.

The nuclear charges of the atoms beyond lithium in the periodic table are greater than the nuclear charge of lithium, and so the $1s$ electrons in these atoms are held even more tightly than are the $1s$ electrons in lithium. Thus we consider only the valence electrons in writing electron configurations of molecules. Valence electrons occupy the molecular orbitals starting with the $\sigma 2s$ orbital in Figure 9-11. The $\sigma 1s$ and $\sigma *1s$ orbitals are equivalent to the filled K shell on each atom. We can illustrate this procedure with Be_2. Each beryllium atom has two valence electrons, and so Be_2 has a total of four valence electrons. Two of the valence electrons in Be_2 occupy the $\sigma 2s$ orbital and two of the electrons occupy the $\sigma *2s$ orbital, giving the ground-state electron

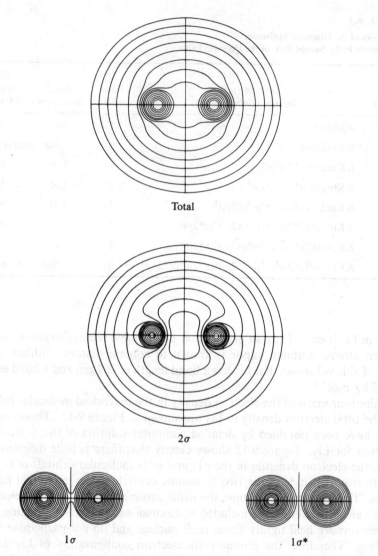

Total

2σ

1σ $1\sigma^*$

Figure 9-12. Electron-density contours of the molecule Li_2. Note that the electrons in the $\sigma 1s$ and $\sigma^* 1s$ orbitals are held tightly around the nucleus and do not really participate in the bonding. It is the electrons in the 2σ orbital that are responsible for the bonding in Li_2. [From A. C. Wahl, Science *151*, 961 (1966). Copyright 1966 by the American Association for the Advancement of Science.]

configuration $KK(\sigma 2s)^2(\sigma^* 2s)^2$. Thus, Be_2 has no net bonding electrons. The Be_2 molecule has never been observed experimentally. The vapor phase of beryllium consists of beryllium atoms. Note that this conclusion is independent of whether we use the energy scheme in Figure 9-11(a) or (b).

Each boron atom has three valence electrons, giving a total of six valence electrons in B_2. The B_2 molecule is the first case for which we find a disagreement between the predictions of Figure 9-11(a) and (b). The two possible electron configurations of B_2 are $KK(\sigma 2s)^2(\sigma^* 2s)^2(\pi 2p_x)^1(\pi 2p_y)^1$ or $KK(\sigma 2s)^2(\sigma^* 2s)^2(\sigma 2p_z)^2$. As in the atomic case, we apply Hund's rule to the first possible electron configuration and place one electron into each $\pi 2p$ orbital such that the electrons have parallel spins. We shall return to a discussion of B_2 later and determine which of the ground-state electron configurations of B_2 is correct.

Diatomic carbon exists in flames and arcs and is another case where we have two possibilities for the ground-state electron configuration. According to Figure 9-11, we have the two possibilities: $KK(\sigma 2s)^2(\sigma^* 2s)^2(\pi 2p_x)^2(\pi 2p_y)^2$ or $KK(\sigma 2s)^2(\sigma^* 2s)^2(\sigma 2p_z)^2(\pi 2p_x)^1(\pi 2p_y)^1$. Once again, we shall return to this case later.

9-12   *Photoelectron Spectra Demonstrate the Existence of Molecular Orbitals*

The ground-state electron configuration of N_2, $KK(\sigma 2s)^2(\sigma^* 2s)^2(\sigma 2p_z)^2$ $(\pi 2p_x)^2(\pi 2p_y)^2$, is the same for both schemes of Figure 9-11. The bond order of N_2 is three, indicating a triple bond in N_2. The Lewis formula, $:N\equiv N:$, is in nice accord with a bond order of three. The triple bond in N_2 accounts for its short bond length (110 pm) and its large bond energy (942 kJ·mol^{-1}). The bond in N_2 is the second strongest known bond.

To many students the idea of atomic orbitals and molecular orbitals is rather abstract and sometimes appears to be far removed from "reality." It so happens, however, that the electron configurations of molecules can be verified experimentally. In Chapter 1, we discussed the photoelectric effect. Ultraviolet radiation directed at a metallic surface can eject electrons from the metallic surface, and the kinetic energy of the ejected electrons can be measured experimentally. It is possible to carry out similar experiments with gases rather than with metallic surfaces. If high-energy electromagnetic radiation, such as X radiation, is directed into a gas, then electrons are ejected from the molecules of the gas. The energy required to eject an electron from a molecule in the gas is a direct measure of how strongly the electron is bound within the molecule. The energy with which an electron is bound in a molecule is called the *binding energy* of that electron. The binding energy of an electron within a molecule depends on which molecular orbital the electron occupies. The lower the energy of the molecular orbital that the electron occupies, the more energy it takes to remove the electron from the molecule.

The measurement of the energies of the electrons ejected by radiation incident to gaseous molecules is called *photoelectron spectroscopy*. A *photoelectron spectrum* of N_2 is shown in Figure 9-13. The peaks in this figure correspond to the molecular-orbital energies indicated in Figure 9-11. Also note that the 1s electrons in N_2 are much more tightly bound than the valence electrons. Photoelectron spectra provide a striking experimental verification of the molecular-orbital picture that we are developing here.

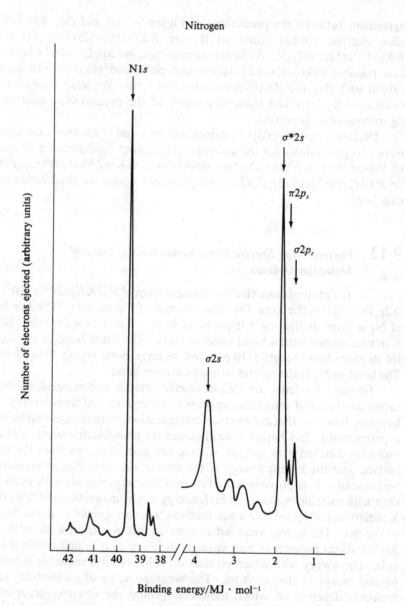

Figure 9-13. Photoelectron spectrum of N_2. The peaks in the above plot are due to electrons being ejected from various molecular orbitals. The peaks that are not labeled are due to impurities. [Redrawn from *ESCA Applied to Free Molecules* by K. Seigbahn et al. (Amsterdam: North-Holland Publishing Company, 1969).]

9-13 Molecular-Orbital Theory Correctly Predicts That Oxygen Molecules Are Paramagnetic and That Diatomic Neon Does Not Exist

The prediction of the electron configuration of an oxygen molecule is one of the most impressive successes of molecular-orbital theory. Oxygen molecules are *paramagnetic*. This means that oxygen is attracted to a region between the poles of a magnet.

The ground-state electron configuration of O_2 is $KK(\sigma 2s)^2(\sigma^* 2s)^2(\pi 2p_x)^2$ $(\pi 2p_y)^2(\sigma 2p_z)^2(\pi^* 2p_x)^1(\pi^* 2p_y)^1$. According to Hund's rule, the $\pi^* 2p_x$ and $\pi^* 2p_y$ orbitals are occupied by one electron such that the spins of the electrons are parallel. Thus, an oxygen molecule has a net electron spin and so is paramagnetic.

The amount of oxygen in air can be monitored by measuring the paramagnetism of a sample of air. Because oxygen is the only component in air that is paramagnetic, the measured paramagnetism of air is directly proportional to the amount of oxygen present. Linus Pauling utilized the paramagnetism of O_2 to develop a method that was used to monitor oxygen levels in the atmospheres of submarines in World War II. This method is still used by physicians to monitor the oxygen content in blood during anesthesia.

We can use molecular-orbital theory to predict relative bond lengths and bond energies.

Linus Pauling (b. 1901) received his Ph.D. in chemistry from the California Institute of Technology in 1925, and then taught there for many years. Pauling's book *The Nature of the Chemical Bond*, first published in 1939, is one of the most influential chemistry texts of the twentieth century. During the 1950s, Pauling was in the forefront of the fight against nuclear testing. He recently has become embroiled in the controversy of advocating the use of Vitamin C as protection against the common cold and other maladies. Pauling was awarded the Nobel Prize for chemistry in 1954 and the Nobel Peace Prize in 1963.

EXAMPLE 9-6

Discuss the relative bond lengths and bond energies of O_2^+, O_2, O_2^-, and O_2^{2-}.

Solution: We have seen above that O_2 has 12 valence electrons. According to Figure 9-11, the ground-state electron configurations and bond orders for these species are as follows:

	Ground-state electron configuration	Bond order
O_2^+	$KK(\sigma 2s)^2(\sigma^*2s)^2(\pi 2p_x)^2(\pi 2p_y)^2(\sigma 2p_z)^2(\pi^*2p_x)^1$	$2\frac{1}{2}$
O_2	$KK(\sigma 2s)^2(\sigma^*2s)^2(\pi 2p_x)^2(\pi 2p_y)^2(\sigma 2p_z)^2(\pi^*2p_x)^1(\pi^*2p_y)^1$	2
O_2^-	$KK(\sigma 2s)^2(\sigma^*2s)^2(\pi 2p_x)^2(\pi 2p_y)^2(\sigma 2p_z)^2(\pi^*2p_x)^2(\pi^*2p_y)^1$	$1\frac{1}{2}$
O_2^{2-}	$KK(\sigma 2s)^2(\sigma^*2s)^2(\pi 2p_x)^2(\pi 2p_y)^2(\sigma 2p_z)^2(\pi^*2p_x)^2(\pi^*2p_y)^2$	1

We predict that the bond lengths decrease and that the bond energies increase with increasing bond order. This is in nice agreement with the experimental values, which follow:

	Bond length/pm	Bond energy/$kJ \cdot mol^{-1}$
O_2^+	112	643
O_2	121	494
O_2^-	135	395
O_2^{2-}	149	

The diatomic molecule F_2 has 14 valence electrons and the ground-state configuration $KK(\sigma 2s)^2(\sigma^*2s)^2(\pi 2p_x)^2(\pi 2p_y)^2(\sigma 2p_z)^2(\pi^*2p_x)^2(\pi^*2p_y)^2$. The bond order of F_2 is one. The Lewis formula for F_2 is in good agreement with this result.

The neon diatomic molecule would have 16 valence electrons, and so the electron configuration would be

$$KK(\sigma 2s)^2(\sigma^*2s)^2(\pi 2p_x)^2(\pi 2p_y)^2(\sigma 2p_z)^2(\pi^*2p_x)^2(\pi^*2p_y)^2(\sigma^*2p_z)^2$$

giving no net bonding electrons. The Ne_2 species has never been observed experimentally. The theoretical predictions of molecular-orbital theory for the homonuclear diatomic molecules formed from the elements across the second row of the periodic table are in excellent agreement with observation. For example, molecular-orbital theory predicts that the species Be_2 and Ne_2 do not occur and predicts that O_2 is paramagnetic.

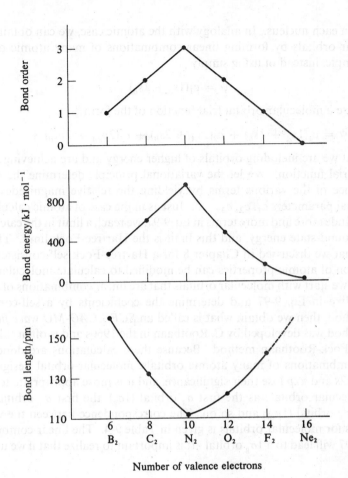

Figure 9-14. A plot of bond properties versus the number of valence electrons for the homonuclear diatomic molecules B_2 through Ne_2.

The results for the diatomic molecules of the elements in the second row of the periodic table are summarized in Table 9-3. Figure 9-14 illustrates the correlation between the predicted bond orders and bond lengths and bond energies.

9-14   An SCF-LCAO-MO Wave Function Is a Molecular Orbital That Is Formed from a Linear Combination of Atomic Orbitals Where the Coefficients Are Determined by a Self-Consistent Field Method

The molecular-orbital scheme that we have presented in the previous sections is the simplest possible molecular-orbital treatment. Each of the molecular orbitals in Figures 9-8 through 9-10 is formed from just one atomic orbital on each nucleus. In analogy with the atomic case, we can obtain better molecular orbitals by forming linear combinations of many atomic orbitals. For example, instead of using simply

$$\psi = c_1(1s_A + 1s_B)$$

we can use a molecular-orbital trial function of the form

$$\psi = c_1(1s_A + 1s_B) + c_2(2s_A + 2s_B) + c_3(2p_{zA} + 2p_{zB}) + \cdots \quad (9\text{-}97)$$

Note that we are including orbitals of higher energy and are achieving a more flexible trial function. We let the variational principle determine the relative importance of the various terms by yielding the relative magnitudes of the variational parameters $c_1, c_2, c_3, \ldots$. Just as in the case of atomic calculations, as we include more and more terms in Eq. 9-97, we reach a limit in the calculation of the ground-state energy, and this limit is the Hartree-Fock limit. The procedure that we discussed in Chapter 8 for a Hartree-Fock self-consistent field calculation of atomic properties can be modified to calculate molecular properties. If we start with molecular orbitals that are linear combinations of atomic orbitals like in Eq. 9-97 and determine the coefficients by a self-consistent field method, then we obtain what is called an *SCF-LCAO-MO wave function*. This method was developed by C. Roothaan in the 1960s and is often called the Hartree-Fock-Roothaan method. Because these calculations are done using linear combinations of many atomic orbitals, molecular-orbital designations such as $\sigma 2s$ and $\pi 2p$ lose their significance, and it is more appropriate to designate molecular orbitals as the first σ_g orbital ($1\sigma_g$), the first σ_u orbital ($1\sigma_u$), the first π_u orbital ($1\pi_u$), and so on. The correspondence between the various notations for molecular orbitals is given in Table 9-4. The linear combination in Eq. 9-97 will lead to a $1\sigma_g$ orbital. It is important to realize that if we use only

TABLE 9-4

The Correspondence between the Various Notations for Molecular Orbitals

Simple LCAO-MO		*SCF-LCAO-MO*
$\sigma 1s$	$\sigma_g 1s$	$1\sigma_g$
$\sigma^* 1s$	$\sigma_u 1s$	$1\sigma_u$
$\sigma 2s$	$\sigma_g 2s$	$2\sigma_g$
$\sigma^* 2s$	$\sigma_u 2s$	$2\sigma_u$
$\pi 2p_x$	$\pi_u 2p_x$	$1\pi_u$
$\pi 2p_y$	$\pi_u 2p_y$	$1\pi_u$
$\sigma 2p_z$	$\sigma_g 2p_z$	$3\sigma_g$
$\pi^* 2p_x$	$\pi_g 2p_x$	$1\pi_g$
$\pi^* 2p_y$	$\pi_g 2p_y$	$1\pi_g$
$\sigma^* 2p_z$	$\sigma_u 2p_z$	$3\sigma_u$

TABLE 9-5

An Illustration of the Convergence to the Hartree-Fock Limit for H_2

LCAO-MO	Effective nuclear charge	Total energy/au	Dissociation energy/au	Bond length/au
$1s_A + 1s_B$	1.000	-1.0990	0.0990	1.61
$1s_A + 1s_B$	1.197	-1.1282	0.1282	1.38
Equation 9-97	1.231	-1.1321	0.1321	1.40
Equation 9-97	$Z(1s) = 1.378$ $Z(2s) = 1.176$ $Z(2p) = 1.820$	-1.1335	0.1335	1.40
Hartree-Fock limit		-1.1336	0.1336	1.40

a few terms in the LCAO-MO and determine all the coefficients self-consistently, then we may not necessarily achieve or reach the Hartree-Fock limit. Thus, an SCF-LCAO-MO molecular orbital is not necessarily the same as a Hartree-Fock orbital. They are the same only if the SCF-LCAO-MO molecular orbitals contain enough terms so that the Hartree-Fock limit is reached.

We can use Eq. 9-97 to illustrate the difference between an SCF-LCAO-MO calculation and a Hartree-Fock calculation. If $c_2 = c_3 = 0$ in Eq. 9-97, and only c_1 is varied, then we have the result that we obtained in Section 9-7. The energy and bond length are the first MO entry in Table 9-1 and given again in Table 9-5. If we allow nuclear charge Z in the $1s$ orbitals to vary, then we obtain the second MO entry in Tables 9-1 and 9-5. Now consider the LCAO-MO given by Eq. 9-97 where the atomic orbitals are Slater orbitals (Eq. 8-20):

$$\psi_{nlm}(r, \theta, \phi) = N_{nl} r^{n-1} e^{-\zeta r} Y_l^m(\theta, \phi)$$

If c_1, c_2, c_3, and ζ are taken to be variational parameters, then the dissociation energy is 0.1321 au and the bond length is 1.40 au (Table 9-5). If the values of ζ in the $1s$, $2s$, and $2p$ orbitals are varied independently, then the dissociation energy is 0.1335 au and the bond length is 1.40 au. This is still not the Hartree-Fock limit. If more terms are included in Eq. 9-97, then eventually (about nine terms) the Hartree-Fock limit of a dissociation energy of 0.1336 au and a bond length of 1.40 au is reached. Hartree-Fock wave functions have been calculated for many diatomic molecules. Figure 9-15 shows the contour diagrams of the total electron density and for the individual molecular orbitals for the homonuclear diatomic molecules H_2 through F_2. The ground-state configurations of H_2 through F_2 are also given in Figure 9-15. All of these electron configurations are consistent with the ordering given in Figure 9-11(a), but this is a fortuitous result.

Molecular-orbital theory can also be applied to *heteronuclear diatomic molecules*, that is, diatomic molecules in which the two nuclei are different. As

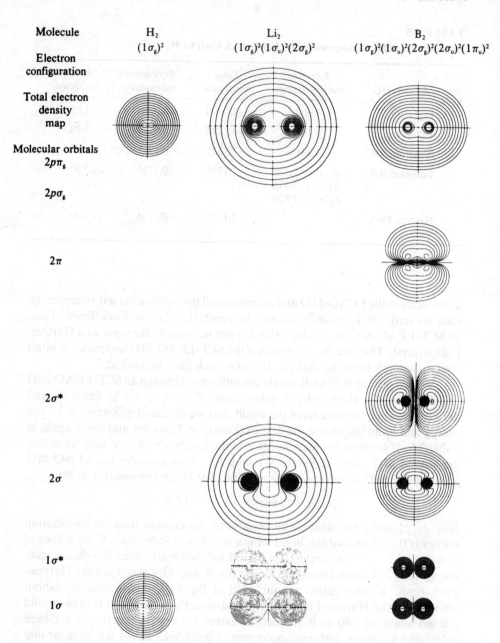

Molecule	H_2	Li_2	B_2
	$(1\sigma_g)^2$	$(1\sigma_g)^2(1\sigma_u)^2(2\sigma_g)^2$	$(1\sigma_g)^2(1\sigma_u)^2(2\sigma_g)^2(2\sigma_u)^2(1\pi_u)^2$
Electron configuration			
Total electron density map			
Molecular orbitals $2p\pi_g$			
$2p\sigma_g$			
2π			
$2\sigma^*$			
2σ			
$1\sigma^*$			
1σ			

Figure 9-15. Contour maps of the various molecular orbitals and the total electron density of the homonuclear diatomic molecules H_2 through F_2. [From A. C. Wahl, Science *151*, 961 (1966). Copyright 1966 by the American Association for the Advancement of Science.]

C_2 N_2 O_2 F_2

$(1\sigma_g)^2(1\sigma_u)^2(2\sigma_g)^2(2\sigma_u)^2(1\pi_u)^4$ $(1\sigma_g)^2(1\sigma_u)^2(2\sigma_g)^2(2\sigma_u)^2(1\pi_u)^4(3\sigma_g)^2(1\pi_g)^2$

$(1\sigma_g)^2(1\sigma_u)^2(2\sigma_g)^2(2\sigma_u)^2(1\pi_u)^4(3\sigma_g)^2$ $(1\sigma_g)^2(1\sigma_u)^2(2\sigma_g)^2(2\sigma_u)^2(1\pi_u)^4(3\sigma_g)^2(1\pi_g)^2(1\pi_g)^4$

Atomic
orbitals

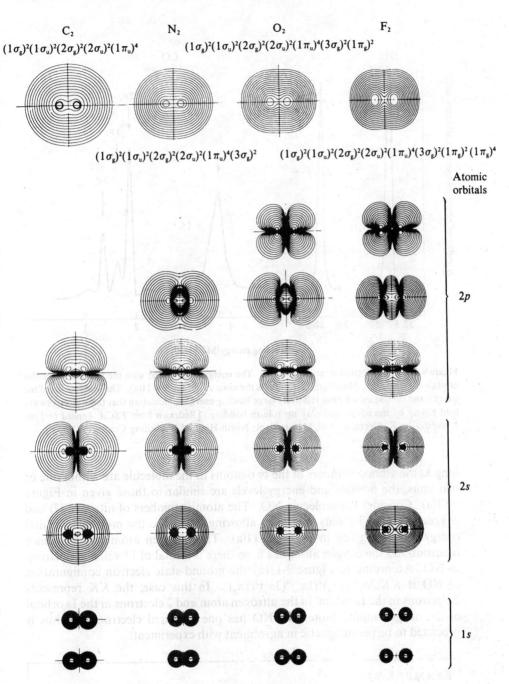

$2p$

$2s$

$1s$

Figure 19-15 (continued)

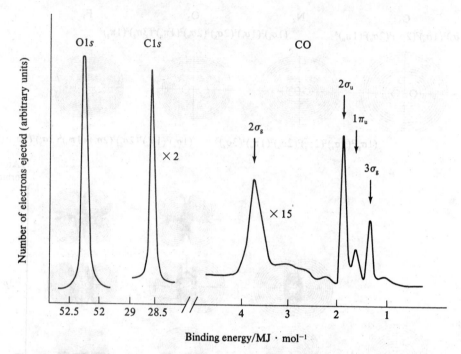

Figure 9-16. Photoelectron spectrum of CO. The energies associated with the various molecular orbitals are identified. Note that their order is the same as in Figure 9-11(a). The 1s electrons of the oxygen and carbon atoms have relatively large binding energies, indicating that these electrons are held tightly by the nuclei and play no role in bonding. [Redrawn from *ESCA Applied to Free Molecules* by K. Siegbahn et al. (Amsterdam: North-Holland Publishing Company, 1969).]

long as the atomic numbers of the two atoms in the molecule are within one or two units, the orbitals and energy levels are similar to those given in Figure 9-11(a). Consider the molecule NO. The atomic numbers of nitrogen (7) and oxygen (8) differ by only one unit, allowing us to use the molecular-orbital energy diagram given in Figure 9-11(a). The nitrogen atom has 5 valence electrons and the oxygen atom has 6, so there is a total of 11 valence electrons in NO. According to Figure 9-11(a), the ground-state electron configuration of NO is $KK(2\sigma_g)^2(2\sigma_u)^2(1\pi_u)^4(3\sigma_g)^2(1\pi_g)^1$. In this case, the KK represents 2 electrons in the 1s orbital of the nitrogen atom and 2 electrons in the 1s orbital of the oxygen atom. Note that NO has one unpaired electron and thus is predicted to be paramagnetic in agreement with experiment.

EXAMPLE 9-7

Discuss the bonding in the carbon monoxide molecule, CO.

Solution: There is a total of 10 valence electrons in the CO molecule. Note that CO is *isoelectronic* with N_2. Using the same energy levels as in Figure 9-11(a), the ground-state electron configuration of CO is

$KK(2\sigma_g)^2(2\sigma_u)^2(1\pi_u)^4(3\sigma_g)^2$. The bond order is three. Because both N_2 and CO have triple bonds and because a nitrogen atom, a carbon atom, and an oxygen atom are approximately the same size, we expect that the bond length and bond energy of CO are comparable to those of N_2. The experimental values follow:

	Bond length/pm	Bond energy/kJ·mol⁻¹
N_2	110	942
CO	113	1071

The bond energy of CO is the largest known bond energy. The photo-electron spectrum of CO given in Figure 9-16 clearly shows the 1s electrons on the carbon and oxygen atoms. This is another verification that the 1s electrons do not play any role in the bonding in these molecules.

9-15 The Electronic States of Diatomic Molecules Are Designated by Molecular Term Symbols

We have seen in Section 8-9 that the electronic states of atoms are designated by term symbols. The electronic states of molecules are also designated by term symbols. Molecular term symbols are easier to determine than atomic term symbols. In order to determine molecular term symbols, one first determines

$$M_L = m_{l_1} + m_{l_2} + \cdots \tag{9-98}$$

where $m_l = 0$ for a σ orbital, $m_l = \pm 1$ for a π orbital, and so on. Then one determines

$$M_S = m_{s_1} + m_{s_2} + \cdots \tag{9-99}$$

The possible values of M_L and M_S are then arranged into a table as shown below. From the table, one associates pairs of M_L and S and, given these two values, the term symbol is represented by

$$^{2S+1}|M_L|$$

The various values of $|M_L|$ are associated with capital Greek letters according to

$|M_L|$	Letter
0	Σ
1	Π
2	Δ
3	Φ

Note that these Greek letters correspond to S, P, D, and F in the atomic case. Thus, molecular term symbols are of the form $^1\Sigma$, $^3\Pi$, and $^2\Delta$. The determination of molecular term symbols from molecular-orbital electron configurations is best illustrated by examples.

Consider the simplest case, H_2, first. The electron configuration is $(1\sigma_g)^2$, and so $m_l = 0$ for each of the occupied σ orbitals. Therefore

$$M_L = 0 + 0 = 0$$

The spins of the two electrons must be opposite in order to satisfy the Pauli Exclusion Principle, and so we have that

$$M_S = +\tfrac{1}{2} - \tfrac{1}{2} = 0$$

Because we have only one possible value of M_S, then S must equal zero and so the term symbol for H_2 is $^1\Sigma$ (a singlet sigma state).

Consider now He_2^+. The ground-state electron configuration of He_2^+ is $(1\sigma_g)^2(1\sigma_u)^1$. We can construct a table of the possible values of m_{l_1}, m_{s_1}, m_{l_2}, m_{s_2}, m_{l_3}, and m_{s_3}.

m_{l_1}	m_{s_1}	m_{l_2}	m_{s_2}	m_{l_3}	m_{s_3}	M_L	M_S
0	$+\tfrac{1}{2}$	0	$-\tfrac{1}{2}$	0	$\pm\tfrac{1}{2}$	0	$\pm\tfrac{1}{2}$

The fact that $M_L = 0$ says that we have a Σ state. The $M_S = \pm\tfrac{1}{2}$ corresponds to the two projections of $S = \tfrac{1}{2}$, and so the term symbol of He_2^+ is $^2\Sigma$ (a doublet sigma state).

Neither of the two examples that we have discussed thus far actually requires the construction of a table because there has been only one possible value of S. Thus, it is easy to deduce the term symbol. The next example, B_2, is a little more complicated and illustrates the scheme to be used for general cases. The electron configuration of B_2 is $(1\sigma_g)^2(1\sigma_u)^2(2\sigma_g)^2(2\sigma_u)^2(1\pi_u)^2$.

The first four molecular orbitals in B_2 have $M_L = 0$ and $M_S = 0$, and so we need consider only the last two electrons. Each of these electrons is in a π orbital, which can have $m_l = \pm 1$ and $m_s = \pm\tfrac{1}{2}$. We construct a table of the possible values of m_{l_1}, m_{s_1}, m_{l_2}, and m_{s_2}. We can calculate why there are six

	m_{l_1}	m_{s_1}	m_{l_2}	m_{s_2}	M_L	M_S
1.	$+1$	$+\tfrac{1}{2}$	$+1$	$-\tfrac{1}{2}$	2	0
2.	$+1$	$+\tfrac{1}{2}$	-1	$+\tfrac{1}{2}$	0	1
3.	$+1$	$+\tfrac{1}{2}$	-1	$-\tfrac{1}{2}$	0	0
4.	$+1$	$-\tfrac{1}{2}$	-1	$+\tfrac{1}{2}$	0	0
5.	$+1$	$-\tfrac{1}{2}$	-1	$-\tfrac{1}{2}$	0	-1
6.	-1	$+\tfrac{1}{2}$	-1	$-\tfrac{1}{2}$	-2	0

entries in this table. There are four possible pairs of values (m_{l_1}, m_{s_1}), and because of the Pauli Exclusion Principle the pair (m_{l_2}, m_{s_2}) must be different from the pair (m_{l_1}, m_{s_1}), and so there are only three possible pairs of values of (m_{l_2}, m_{s_2}). So far, then, we have $4 \times 3 = 12$ possible combinations of (m_{l_1}, m_{s_1}) and (m_{l_2}, m_{s_2}). We must realize, however, that electrons are indistinguishable, and so we must divide the 12 combinations by two to obtain six entries in the previous table. This type of calculation is similar to the one we did for the atomic case in Section 8-9.

Entries 1 and 6 in the table correspond to $|M_L| = 2$ and $M_S = 0$, and so we find a $^1\Delta$ (singlet delta) state. Entries 2, 3, and 5 correspond to $M_L = 0$ and $S = 1$, and so we have a $^3\Sigma$ (triplet sigma) state. The remaining entry has $M_L = 0$ and $M_S = 0$ and so corresponds to a $^1\Sigma$ state. Thus we see that we have three possible molecular states, with term symbols $^3\Sigma$, $^1\Sigma$, and $^1\Delta$ for B_2. Hund's rules apply to molecular electronic states as well as to atomic electronic states and say that the state with the largest spin multiplicity will be the ground state of B_2. Thus, we predict that the ground state of B_2 is a $^3\Sigma$ state.

EXAMPLE 9-8

Determine the term symbol of the ground state of C_2, whose electron configuration is $(1\sigma_g)^2(1\sigma_u)^2(2\sigma_g)^2(2\sigma_u)^2(1\pi_u)^4$.

Solution: There is only one set of m_l and m_s that satisfy the Pauli Exclusion Principle:

m_{l_1}	m_{s_1}	m_{l_2}	m_{s_2}	m_{l_3}	m_{s_3}	m_{l_4}	m_{s_4}	M_L	M_S
$+1$	$+\frac{1}{2}$	$+1$	$-\frac{1}{2}$	-1	$+\frac{1}{2}$	-1	$-\frac{1}{2}$	0	0

Thus, we see that the term symbol for the ground state of C_2 is $^1\Sigma$.

TABLE 9-6
The Ground-State Electron Configurations and Term Symbols for the First-Row Homonuclear Diatomic Molecules

H_2^+	$(1\sigma_g)^1$	$^2\Sigma$
H_2	$(1\sigma_g)^2$	$^1\Sigma$
He_2^+	$(1\sigma_g)^2(1\sigma_u)^1$	$^2\Sigma$
Li_2	$(1\sigma_g)^2(1\sigma_u)^2(2\sigma_g)^2$	$^1\Sigma$
B_2	$(1\sigma_g)^2(1\sigma_u)^2(2\sigma_g)^2(2\sigma_u)^2(1\pi_u)^2$	$^3\Sigma$
C_2	$(1\sigma_g)^2(1\sigma_u)^2(2\sigma_g)^2(2\sigma_u)^2(1\pi_u)^4$	$^1\Sigma$
N_2^+	$(1\sigma_g)^2(1\sigma_u)^2(2\sigma_g)^2(2\sigma_u)^2(1\pi_u)^4(3\sigma_g)^1$	$^2\Sigma$
N_2	$(1\sigma_g)^2(1\sigma_u)^2(2\sigma_g)^2(2\sigma_u)^2(1\pi_u)^4(3\sigma_g)^2$	$^1\Sigma$
O_2^+	$(1\sigma_g)^2(1\sigma_u)^2(2\sigma_g)^2(2\sigma_u)^2(1\pi_u)^4(3\sigma_g)^2(1\pi_g)^1$	$^2\Pi$
O_2	$(1\sigma_g)^2(1\sigma_u)^2(2\sigma_g)^2(2\sigma_u)^2(1\pi_u)^4(3\sigma_g)^2(1\pi_g)^2$	$^3\Sigma$
F_2	$(1\sigma_g)^2(1\sigma_u)^2(2\sigma_g)^2(2\sigma_u)^2(1\pi_u)^4(3\sigma_g)^2(1\pi_g)^4$	$^1\Sigma$

We should point out that molecular term symbols are more involved than we have indicated in this section. Molecular term symbols also indicate the symmetry of the corresponding wave function under certain symmetry operations, but we shall neglect this extra information here.

Table 9-6 lists the term symbols of the ground states of a number of homonuclear diatomic molecules and Problem 27 involves the determination of these term symbols.

9-16   *It Is Possible to Calculate Molecular Properties to a High Degree of Accuracy*

In Section 9-14, we pointed out that there is a difference between an SCF-LCAO-MO calculation and a Hartree-Fock calculation. If one uses only a few terms in the LCAO-MO, then one may determine all the coefficients self-consistently but not achieve or reach the Hartree-Fock limit. The set of atomic orbitals in an LCAO-MO is called a *basis set*. The accuracy or reliability of a quantum-chemical calculation depends on the size of the basis set used. Thus, there is a spectrum of SCF-LCAO-MO calculations in the quantum-chemical literature. These calculations range from those using as few atomic orbitals as possible (such a calculation is referred to as a *minimal basis set calculation*) to calculations involving very large basis sets. The Hartree-Fock limit is approached as the size of the basis set is increased. Strictly speaking, calculations using large basis sets are called *near Hartree-Fock* calculations. The difference between a near Hartree-Fock calculation and a full Hartree-Fock calculation is that in a full Hartree-Fock calculation the Hartree-Fock equations are solved numerically without recourse to an expansion in a basis set. Nevertheless, the terms *near Hartree-Fock* and *Hartree-Fock* are often used interchangeably. Because of the great range of SCF-LCAO-MO calculations, one must examine closely any particular set of calculations before one can assess its quality.

Near Hartree-Fock calculations have been carried out for a large number of molecules. There are computer programs that are available that can be used to calculate ground-state geometries to a high degree of accuracy. Table 9-7 shows some results of John Pople and his group at Carnegie-Mellon University. You can see from Table 9-7 that the agreement with experimental data is truly impressive. Table 9-8 summarizes the mean deviations of the theoretical predictions from the observed values of bond lengths and bond angles for a large number of molecules. Note that the calculated bond lengths are good to a few picometers and that the bond angles are good to a degree or two. The agreement is all the more impressive if you realize that there are no adjustable parameters in these calculations. Such calculations are called *ab initio calculations*. Professor Pople has been one of the pioneers of the calculation of molecular properties and has made his computer programs available through an organization called the Quantum Chemistry Program

TABLE 9-7
**Theoretical and Experimental Structures of Some One-Heavy-Atom
Molecules and Some Two-Heavy-Atom Molecules. All Bond Lengths Are in Picometers***

Molecule	Geometrical parameter	Near Hartree-Fock	Improved Hartree-Fock	Experimental
H—H	r(HH)	73.0	73.8	74.1
Li—H	r(LiH)	163.6	164.0	159.5
Be—H	r(BeH)	138.3	138.5	134.3
B—H	r(BH)	122.5	123.3	123.0
C—H	r(CH)	110.8	112.0	112.0
N—H	r(NH)	102.4	103.9	104.5
O—H	r(OH)	95.8	97.9	97.1
F—H	r(FH)	91.1	93.4	91.7
Li—Li	r(LiLi)	280.7	277.2	267
Li—F	r(LiF)	156.6	157.0	156.4
HC≡CH	r(CC)	118.5	121.7	120.3
	r(CH)	105.7	106.3	106.1
HC≡N	r(CN)	113.2	117.8	115.3
	r(CH)	105.9	106.9	106.5
HN≡C	r(NC)	115.4	118.7	116.5
	r(NH)	98.5	100.2	99.4
$^-$C≡O$^+$	r(CO)	111.4	115.2	112.8
O=O	r(OO)	116.8	124.5	120.7
F—F	r(FF)	134.5	142.4	141.7
H₂C (bent CH₂)	r(CH)	109.6	110.9	111.1
	∠(HCH)	103.0	102.1	102.4
pyramidal CH₃	r(CH)	107.3	107.9	107.9
CH₄ (tetrahedral)	r(CH)	108.4	109.0	108.6
H₂N (bent NH₂)	∠(HNH)	104.3	103.3	103.4
pyramidal NH₃	r(NH)	100.2	101.7	101.2
		107.2	106.4	106.7

(continued)

TABLE 9-7 (continued)

Molecule	Geometrical parameter	Near Hartree-Fock	Improved Hartree-Fock	Experimental
H₂O (water)	$r(OH)$	94.7	96.9	95.9
	$\angle(HOH)$	105.5	104.0	103.9
H₂C=CH₂ (ethylene)	$r(CC)$	131.7	133.5	133.9
	$r(CH)$	107.6	108.5	108.5
	$\angle(HCH)$	116.4	116.5	117.8
H₃C—CH₃ (ethane)	$r(CC)$	152.7	152.7	152.6
	$r(CH)$	108.6	109.4	108.8
	$\angle(HCH)$	107.7	107.7	107.4
H₂C=O (formaldehyde)	$r(CO)$	118.4	122.0	120.8
	$r(CH)$	109.2	110.4	111.6
	$\angle(HCH)$	115.7	115.6	116.5
H₃C—F	$r(CF)$	136.4	139.2	138.3
	$\angle(FCH)$	108.2	109.3	110.0
	$\angle(HCH)$	109.8	109.7	110.6
HN=NH (diazene)	$r(NN)$	121.5	126.7	125.2
	$r(NH)$	101.4	103.6	102.8
	$\angle(NNH)$	107.4	105.4	106.9
H₂N—NH₂ (hydrazine)	$r(NN)$	141.4	144.0	144.7
	$r(NH_a)$	99.9	101.6	100.8
	$r(NH_b)$	100.2	102.1	100.8
	$\angle(NNH_a)$	107.9	106.3	109.2
	$\angle(NNH_b)$	112.2	111.4	109.2
	$\angle(H_aNH_b)$	108.2	106.9	113.3
HN=O	$r(NO)$	117.4	123.8	121.2
	$r(NH)$	103.1	105.8	106.3
	$\angle(ONH)$	108.8	107.4	108.6
H—O—F	$r(OF)$	137.5	144.4	144.2
	$r(OH)$	95.2	97.9	96.4
	$\angle(HOF)$	99.8	97.2	97.2
H—O—O—H	$r(OO)$	139.3	146.7	147.5
	$r(OH)$	94.9	97.6	95.0
	$\angle(OOH)$	102.2	98.7	94.8
	$\angle(HOOH)$	115.2	121.3	120

* Reprinted with permission from D. J. DeFrees et al., J. Am. Chem. Soc. *101*, 4085 (1979). Copyright 1979 American Chemical Society.

TABLE 9-8

The Average of the Absolute Values of the Deviations between the Calculated Structural Parameters and the Experimental Structural Parameters in Table 9-7*

Structural parameter	Number of comparisons	Average deviation near Hartree-Fock	Improved Hartree-Fock
		One-Heavy-Atom Molecules	
AH bond lengths/pm	17	1.3	1.1
HAH bond angles	7	2.2	1.4
		Two-Heavy-Atom Molecules	
AH bond lengths/pm	23	1.1	0.8
AB bond lengths/pm	23	3.6	1.7
HAH bond angles	11	1.0	1.4
HAB bond angles	13	1.8	1.4

* Reprinted with permission from D. J. DeFrees et al., J. Am. Chem. Soc. *101*, 4085 (1979). Copyright 1979 American Chemical Society.

Exchange (QCPE) at Indiana University. The QCPE acts as a central library of quantum-chemical computer programs.

There is another column in Table 9-7 in which the agreement with experimental data is even better than for the (near) Hartree-Fock calculations. Recall that Hartree-Fock wave functions do not include correlation of electrons in different orbitals. Electron correlation can be included by configuration interaction or by perturbation theory. The column headed by improved Hartree-Fock in Table 9-7 contains values of bond lengths and bond angles that were obtained by a perturbation scheme that used Hartree-Fock wave functions as the starting point. Hartree-Fock wave functions can also be improved by configuration interaction. Table 9-9 gives the dipole moments of the first-row hydrides calculated by configuration interaction. The agreement with experimental data is excellent and is typical of CI calculations.

With the constant development in computer speed and capacity, reliable quantum-chemical calculations are becoming available for a large variety of molecules. Near Hartree-Fock calculations have been carried out for portions of proteins to investigate substrate-enzyme interactions, for studies of base-pair interactions in DNA and for many other interesting systems. Some areas of current research in quantum chemistry are the calculation of the ground-state properties of transition-metal complexes, the calculation of excited states of molecules, and the description of molecular collisions as when molecules come together to react.

Although it is possible to carry out Hartree-Fock calculations for many molecules, it is still useful to have simple qualitative theories of structure and bonding that can be used as an aid to chemical intuition. We shall conclude this chapter with a discussion of some simple, intuitive theories of chemical bonding and molecular structure.

TABLE 9-9

Dipole Moments (in Debyes) of the First-Row
Hydrides Calculated by Configuration Interaction

	Near Hartree-Fock	CI	Experiment
LiH	6.002	5.853	5.82
BeH	0.282	0.248	
BH	-1.733	-1.470	
CH	-1.570	-1.427	-1.40
NH	-1.627	-1.587	
OH	-1.780	-1.633	-1.66
FH	-1.942	-1.816	-1.82

From C. F. Bender and E. R. Davidson, Phys. Rev. *183*, 21 (1969).

9-17 *The Valence-Bond Theory Has a Direct Relation to Lewis Formulas*

In this section we shall discuss valence-bond theory. Although the valence-bond theory is not often used anymore, it serves as a background for the idea of localized bonds and hybrid orbitals, which are discussed in Section 9-18. In addition, the valence-bond theory can be used to formalize chemists' intuitive ideas regarding Lewis formulas, resonance formulas, and so on. Recall that we discussed the application of the valence-bond theory to H_2 in Section 9-5. We showed that

$$\psi_1 = \begin{vmatrix} 1s_A\alpha(1) & 1s_B\beta(1) \\ 1s_A\alpha(2) & 1s_B\beta(2) \end{vmatrix}$$

and

$$\psi_2 = \begin{vmatrix} 1s_A\beta(1) & 1s_B\alpha(1) \\ 1s_A\beta(2) & 1s_B\alpha(2) \end{vmatrix}$$

both represent H_2 with one electron on each hydrogen atom. If we use

$$\psi = c_1\psi_1 + c_2\psi_2$$

as a trial function and minimize the energy with respect to c_1 and c_2, then we find that

$$\psi_s = \frac{1}{\sqrt{4(1 + S^2)}}(\psi_1 - \psi_2)$$

is the ground-state wave function of H_2.

Now consider the molecule LiH. In the ground state of the lithium atom there are two $1s$ electrons and one $2s$ electron, and in a hydrogen atom there is the one $1s$ electron. One of the (unnormalized) Slater determinants in the valence-bond wave function of LiH is of the form

$$\psi_1 = \begin{vmatrix} \psi_{1sLi}\alpha(1) & \psi_{1sLi}\beta(1) & \psi_{2sLi}\alpha(1) & \psi_{1sH}\beta(1) \\ \psi_{1sLi}\alpha(2) & \psi_{1sLi}\beta(2) & \psi_{2sLi}\alpha(2) & \psi_{1sH}\beta(2) \\ \psi_{1sLi}\alpha(3) & \psi_{1sLi}\beta(3) & \psi_{2sLi}\alpha(3) & \psi_{1sH}\beta(3) \\ \psi_{1sLi}\alpha(4) & \psi_{1sLi}\beta(4) & \psi_{2sLi}\alpha(4) & \psi_{1sH}\beta(4) \end{vmatrix} \quad (9\text{-}100)$$

After you write many Slater determinants like Eq. 9-100, you welcome any abbreviation that can be used. Note that each row in a Slater determinant has the same form and differs only in the number labeling the electron. Thus, we can represent such a Slater determinant uniquely by noting only the diagonal elements and writing

$$\psi_1 = |\psi_{1sLi}\alpha(1)\psi_{1sLi}\beta(2)\psi_{2sLi}\alpha(3)\psi_{1sH}\beta(4)| \quad (9\text{-}101)$$

This abbreviated notation for Slater determinants is very commonly used. The other terms in the valence-bond wave function describing the covalent bond in LiH are

$$\psi_2 = |\psi_{1sLi}\beta(1)\psi_{1sLi}\alpha(2)\psi_{2sLi}\alpha(3)\psi_{1sH}\beta(4)|$$

$$\psi_3 = |\psi_{1sLi}\alpha(1)\psi_{1sLi}\beta(2)\psi_{2sLi}\beta(3)\psi_{1sH}\alpha(4)|$$

$$\psi_4 = |\psi_{1sLi}\beta(1)\psi_{1sLi}\alpha(2)\psi_{2sLi}\beta(3)\psi_{1sH}\alpha(4)|$$

and the valence-bond wave function for the covalent bond of LiH can be written as the linear combination

$$\psi_{cov} = c_1\psi_1 + c_2\psi_2 + c_3\psi_3 + c_4\psi_4 \quad (9\text{-}102)$$

We should note, however, that ψ_1 and ψ_2 differ by only a sign because they differ by only an interchange of the two unbonded Li $1s$ electrons. Similarly, ψ_3 and ψ_4 differ for the same reason and so the valence-bond wave function for the covalent bond in LiH really consists of only two terms:

$$\psi_{cov} = c_1\psi_1 + c_3\psi_3 \quad (9\text{-}103)$$

Generally, when an atomic orbital is doubly occupied, it is not necessary to consider the interchange of the two electrons because it does not contribute a new term to the valence-bond wave function for the covalent bond. The parameters c_1 and c_3 in Eq. 9-103 are determined variationally and, just as in the case of H_2 above, one finds that $c_1 = -c_3$, and so we have

$$\psi_{cov} = |\psi_{1sLi}\alpha(1)\psi_{1sLi}\beta(2)\psi_{2sLi}\alpha(3)\psi_{1sH}\beta(4)|$$
$$- |\psi_{1sLi}\alpha(1)\psi_{1sLi}\beta(2)\psi_{2sLi}\beta(3)\psi_{1sH}\alpha(4)| \quad (9\text{-}104)$$

for our valence-bond wave function for the covalent bond in LiH. Using Hartree-Fock atomic orbitals for the lithium atom and the $1s$ orbital for the hydrogen atom, we can use ψ_{cov} in Eq. 9-104 to determine the bond length and the energy of LiH. The calculated values are 3.01 au and -215.98 au versus the experimental values 3.02 au and -219.71 au. One reason for the poor agreement in the energy is that we have not allowed for any ionic character in our valence-bond wave function. So far we have described only a purely covalent bond.

We can include the ionic structure Li^+H^- into our valence-bond treatment by using

$$\psi_{ionic} = |\psi_{1sLi}\alpha(1)\psi_{1sLi}\beta(2)\psi_{1sH}\alpha(3)\psi_{1sH}\beta(4)| \qquad (9\text{-}105)$$

Note that ψ_{ionic} describes Li^+H^- in that there are two electrons on Li^+ and two electrons on H^-. We now take a linear combination of ψ_{cov} (Eq. 9-104) and ψ_{ionic} (Eq. 9-105) and write

$$\psi_{VB} = c_{cov}\psi_{cov} + c_{ionic}\psi_{ionic} \qquad (9\text{-}106)$$

The inclusion of the ionic term in Eq. 9-106 gives an energy of -217.0 au.

Because the two $1s$ electrons in the lithium atom do not play a great role in the formation of the bond in LiH, it is a convenient, common approximation to ignore inner-core electrons in the valence-bond wave function and to consider only the bonding, or valence, electrons. In this approximation, then, we would have

$$\psi_{cov} = |\psi_{2sLi}\alpha(1)\psi_{1sH}\beta(2)| - |\psi_{2sLi}\beta(1)\psi_{1sH}\alpha(2)| \qquad (9\text{-}107)$$

and

$$\psi_{ionic} = |\psi_{1sH}\alpha(1)\psi_{1sH}\beta(2)| \qquad (9\text{-}108)$$

The neglect of inner-core electrons is not an important or particularly useful approximation for LiH, because LiH is only a four-electron problem and can be solved to a high degree of accuracy by an SCF-CI method. Nevertheless, the ideas presented here for LiH do become very useful when discussing larger systems.

For another example of the construction of a valence-bond wave function, consider the molecule hydrogen fluoride, HF. In this case, the bonding electrons are the $1s$ electron of hydrogen and the unpaired $2p$ electron of fluorine. For simplicity we shall consider only the bonding electrons (Problem 30 asks you to include the other electrons) and write

$$\psi_{cov} = |\psi_{1sH}\alpha(1)\psi_{2p_zF}\beta(2)| - |\psi_{1sH}\beta(1)\psi_{2p_zF}\alpha(2)| \qquad (9\text{-}109)$$

where, as is customarily done, we have taken the internuclear axis to be the z axis, so that the $2p_z$ orbital of fluorine is the bonding orbital. You learned in general chemistry that hydrogen fluoride has a large dipole moment and so we should include ionic character in our valence-bond wave function. The wave function corresponding to the ionic form H^+F^- is

$$\psi_{ionic} = |\psi_{2p_zF}\alpha(1)\psi_{2p_zF}\beta(2)| \qquad (9\text{-}110)$$

and the total valence-bond wave function is

$$\psi_{VB} = c_1\psi_{cov} + c_2\psi_{ionic} \qquad (9\text{-}111)$$

The relative magnitudes of c_1^2 and c_2^2 give an indication of the relative degree of ionic and covalent character in the molecule, but as we have discussed on page 365, one must treat this interpretation carefully. The precise values of c_1 and c_2 depend on the atomic orbitals that are used for fluorine, but generally c_1 and c_2 are approximately equal, as one might expect intuitively.

The idea of introducing ionic terms into valence-bond wave functions nicely illustrates the concept of resonance that you learned in general chemistry and organic chemistry. Quantum mechanically, we see that if we can write two or more sensible Lewis structural formulas for a molecule, then the wave function of that molecule is a linear combination of these structures and the "true" picture is some intermediate structure. The variational principle, which dictates the numerical values of the coefficients in the linear combination, gives us an indication of the relative importance of various possible Lewis formulas.

The extension of the construction of valence-bond wave functions to nonlinear or polyatomic molecules is straightforward in principle. Consider the molecule H_2O. The electron configuration of the oxygen atom is $1s^2 2s^2 2p_x^2 2p_y^1 2p_z^1$, suggesting that the unpaired $2p_y$ and $2p_z$ electrons are available for bonding with the hydrogen atoms. We have shown in Problem 8 that a maximum overlap of atomic orbitals leads to a lowering of the energy, and in order to maximize the overlap between the hydrogen atom orbitals and the $2p_y$ and $2p_z$ orbitals of the oxygen atom, the two hydrogen atoms will lie along the y and z axes (Figure 9-17). Thus, we see that a simple valence-bond picture predicts an H—O—H bond angle of 90°, compared to the experimental value of 104°. If one introduces ionic terms, however, the two hydrogen atoms will acquire some positive character, repel each other, and give a bond angle closer to 104°. For the corresponding molecules H_2S, H_2Se, and H_2Te, however, the electronegativities of the sulfur, selenium, and tellurium atoms are such that ionic

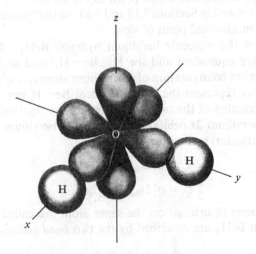

Figure 9-17. An illustration of the formation of the two O—H bonds in H_2O by overlapping hydrogen $1s$ orbitals with two of the $2p$ orbitals on the oxygen atom.

terms contribute less significantly as one goes from H_2S to H_2Te, and so the predicted 90° becomes progressively better in accord with experiment.

The covalent contribution to the valence-bond wave function for H_2O can be determined by the variational method to be

$$
\begin{aligned}
\psi = \quad & |\psi_{2p_xO}\alpha(1)\psi_{1sA}\beta(2)\psi_{2p_yO}\alpha(3)\psi_{1sB}\beta(4)| \\
- \; & |\psi_{2p_xO}\alpha(1)\psi_{1sA}\beta(2)\psi_{2p_yO}\beta(3)\psi_{1sB}\alpha(4)| \\
- \; & |\psi_{2p_xO}\beta(1)\psi_{1sA}\alpha(2)\psi_{2p_yO}\alpha(3)\psi_{1sB}\beta(4)| \\
+ \; & |\psi_{2p_xO}\beta(1)\psi_{1sA}\alpha(2)\psi_{2p_yO}\beta(3)\psi_{1sB}\alpha(4)|.
\end{aligned}
\tag{9-112}
$$

Note that each of the 4×4 determinants in Eq. 9-112 gives 24 terms when it is expanded, and so there is a total of 96 terms in Eq. 9-112, and this is just the covalent contribution to ψ_{VB}. This is one reason why valence-bond calculations have lost favor to molecular-orbital calculations.

9-18   *sp Hybrid Orbitals Are Equivalent and Are Directed 180° from Each Other*

If we consider ammonia, NH_3, then a simple valence-bond picture predicts that the H—N—H bond angles are 90°, compared to the experimental value of 107°. Once again the situation can be improved by introducing ionic terms, but this approach fails us when we consider methane, CH_4. Certainly the electron configuration $1s^2 2s^2 2p_x^1 2p_y^1$ of the carbon atom does not explain the well-known tetrahedral bonding in methane and other saturated hydrocarbons. You probably have learned in organic chemistry that what happens is that one of the $2s$ electrons is promoted to the $2p_z$ orbital ($1s^2 2s^2 2p_x^1 2p_y^1 \rightarrow 1s^2 2s^1 2p_x^1 2p_y^1 2p_z^1$) and then the four singly occupied orbitals hybridize into four equivalent sp^3 hybrid orbitals, which point to the corners of a regular tetrahedron. In this section and in Sections 9.19 and 9.20, we shall discuss hybridization from a quantum-mechanical point of view.

Consider first the molecule beryllium hydride, BeH_2. The two Be—H bonds in BeH_2 are equivalent and the H—Be—H bond angle is 180°. The ground-state electron configuration of a beryllium atom is $(1s)^2(2s)^2$. The question is how can we represent the two equivalent Be—H bonds in BeH_2. To obtain the directionality of the two Be—H bonds, we shall take a linear combination of the beryllium $2s$ orbital and one of the beryllium $2p$ orbitals (the $2p_z$ orbital, in particular) and write

$$
\begin{aligned}
\xi &= a_1 2s_{Be} + b_1 2p_{zBe} \\
\xi' &= a_2 2s_{Be} + b_2 2p_{zBe}
\end{aligned}
\tag{9-113}
$$

Linear combinations of orbitals on the same atom are called *hybrid orbitals*. The two bonds in BeH_2 are described by the two *bond orbitals*

$$
\begin{aligned}
\phi &= c_1 1s_A + c_2 \xi \\
\phi' &= c_1' 1s_B + c_2' \xi'
\end{aligned}
\tag{9-114}
$$

where $1s_A$ and $1s_B$ are the $1s$ orbitals of the two hydrogen atoms. We now shall determine the forms of the two hybrid orbitals ξ and ξ', so that ϕ and ϕ' describe two equivalent bond orbitals that are directed $180°$ from each other. We can approximate the $2s$ and $2p_z$ orbitals of the beryllium atom by the Slater orbitals

$$\psi_{2s} = \left(\frac{1}{4\pi}\right)^{1/2} R(r)$$

$$\psi_{2p_z} = \left(\frac{3}{4\pi}\right)^{1/2} R(r) \cos \theta$$

(9-115)

where, for simplicity, we have assumed the same functional form of the radial function in the two orbitals. The factors of $(1/4\pi)^{1/2}$ and $(3/4\pi)^{1/2}$ in Eq. 9-115 are normalization factors. If we substitute Eq. 9-115 into Eq. 9-113, then we have

$$\xi = \frac{R(r)}{\sqrt{4\pi}} (a_1 + \sqrt{3}b_1 \cos \theta)$$

(9-116)

If a_1 and b_1 are both positive, then ξ is directed along the positive z axis. The other hybrid orbital, ξ' in Eq. 9-115, is

$$\xi' = \frac{R(r)}{\sqrt{4\pi}} (a_2 + \sqrt{3}b_2 \cos \theta)$$

(9-117)

It is convenient to require that ξ and ξ' be orthogonal, in which case we have

$$\int_0^\infty \int_0^\pi 2\pi r^2 \sin \theta \, dr \, d\theta \, \xi(r, \theta)\xi'(r, \theta) = 0$$

(9-118)

We assume that the radial function in Eq. 9-115 is normalized, so that

$$\int_0^\infty R^2(r)r^2 \, dr = 1$$

Therefore, Eq. 9-118 reads

$$\int_0^\pi d\theta \sin \theta (a_1 + b_1\sqrt{3} \cos \theta)(a_2 + b_2\sqrt{3} \cos \theta) = 0$$

(9-119)

The evaluation of the integral in Eq. 9-119 is elementary and gives $a_1a_2 + b_1b_2 = 0$. Because we have taken a_1 and b_1 to be both positive, then a_2 and b_2 must have opposite signs, and so ξ' is directed along the negative z axis. Because the two Be—H bonds in BeH_2 are equivalent, we shall require that the two hybrid orbitals have the same shape. Thus, we require that $a_1 = a_2$ and that $b_1 = -b_2$. Furthermore, because $a_1a_2 + b_1b_2 = 0$, we find that $a = \pm b$. Lastly, if the two equivalent orbitals are normalized, then

$$\xi = \frac{1}{\sqrt{2}} (2s + 2p_z)$$

(9-120)

and

$$\xi' = \frac{1}{\sqrt{2}} (2s - 2p_z)$$

(9-121)

Because these hybrid orbitals are made up of a $2s$ orbital and one $2p$ orbital, ζ and ζ' are called *sp hybrid orbitals*. A contour map of an sp hybrid orbital is shown in Figure 9-18, and the two hybrid orbitals are illustrated in Figure 9-19. The BeH_2 molecule is formed by overlapping a hydrogen $1s$ orbital with each of the sp hybrid orbitals as illustrated in Figure 9-20. The electron

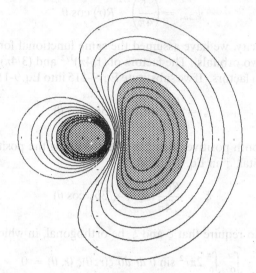

Figure 9-18. A contour map of an sp hybrid orbital. The two sp hybrid orbitals are equivalent and are directed 180° from each other. [From G. Gerhold et al., Am. J. Phys. *40*, 988 (1972).]

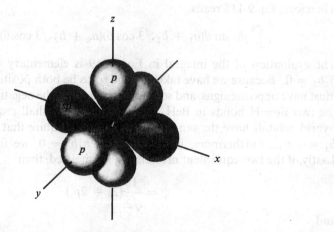

Figure 9-19. An illustration of sp orbitals. The two sp orbitals are directed 180° from each other as shown above. The two remaining $2p$ orbitals are perpendicular to each other and to the line formed by the sp orbitals.

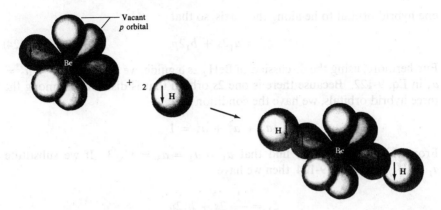

Figure 9-20. The formation of the two equivalent localized bond orbitals in BeH_2. Each bond orbital is formed by the overlap of a beryllium sp orbital and a hydrogen $1s$ orbital. There are four valence electrons in BeH_2, two from the beryllium atom and one from each of the two hydrogen atoms. The four valence electrons occupy the two localized bond orbitals, forming the two localized beryllium-hydrogen bonds in BeH_2.

configuration of BeH_2 in this bond-orbital description is $K(\phi)^2(\phi')^2$, where ϕ and ϕ' are the bond orbitals given in Eq. 9-114. In this picture, a chemical bond is described as two electrons of opposite spin occupying a bond orbital.

9-19   *sp² Hybrid Orbitals Are Equivalent, Lie in a Plane, and Are Directed 120° from Each Other*

Consider the molecule BH_3. The three B—H bonds in BH_3 are equivalent and lie in a plane, directed 120° from each other. In this section, we shall construct hybrid orbitals that can describe the bonding in BH_3. To describe the three equivalent bonds in BH_3, we must construct three hybrid orbitals on the boron atom. Let these three hybrid orbitals be given by

$$\xi_1 = a_1 2s + b_1 2p_z + c_1 2p_x$$
$$\xi_2 = a_2 2s + b_2 2p_z + c_2 2p_x \qquad (9\text{-}122)$$
$$\xi_3 = a_3 2s + b_3 2p_z + c_3 2p_x$$

where the $2s$ and $2p_z$ orbitals on the boron atom are Slater orbitals given by Eq. 9-115 and $2p_x$ is a Slater orbital given by

$$\psi_{2p_x} = \left(\frac{3}{4\pi}\right)^{1/2} R(r) \sin\theta \cos\phi \qquad (9\text{-}123)$$

Because these hybrid orbitals are constructed from one $2s$ orbital and two $2p$ orbitals, they are *sp² hybrid orbitals*. Without any loss of generality, we take one hybrid orbital to lie along the z axis, so that

$$\xi_1 = a_1 2s + b_1 2p_z \qquad (9\text{-}124)$$

Furthermore, using the discussion of BeH_2 as a guide, we shall take $a_1 = a_2 = a_3$ in Eq. 9-122. Because there is one $2s$ orbital that is distributed among the three hybrid orbitals, we have the condition

$$a_1^2 + a_2^2 + a_3^2 = 1$$

From this condition, we find that $a_1 = a_2 = a_3 = 1/\sqrt{3}$. If we substitute $a_1 = 1/\sqrt{3}$ into Eq. 9-124, then we have

$$\xi_1 = \frac{1}{\sqrt{3}} 2s + b_1 2p_z$$

Because ξ_1 is normalized, we have that

$$\tfrac{1}{3} + b_1^2 = 1$$

or that

$$b_1 = \sqrt{\tfrac{2}{3}}$$

Thus,

$$\xi_1 = \frac{1}{\sqrt{3}} 2s + \sqrt{\frac{2}{3}} 2p_z \qquad (9\text{-}125)$$

The second hybrid orbital is

$$\xi_2 = \frac{1}{\sqrt{3}} 2s + b_2 2p_z + c_2 2p_x \qquad (9\text{-}126)$$

If we require that ξ_1 and ξ_2 be orthogonal, then we have (Problem 32)

$$\tfrac{1}{3} + b_2 \sqrt{\tfrac{2}{3}} = 0$$

or that $b_2 = -1/\sqrt{6}$. Thus,

$$\xi_2 = \frac{1}{\sqrt{3}} 2s - \frac{1}{\sqrt{6}} 2p_z + c_2 2p_x \qquad (9\text{-}127)$$

Now if we require that ξ_2 be normalized, we obtain

$$\tfrac{1}{3} + \tfrac{1}{6} + c_2^2 = 1$$

or that $c_2 = 1/\sqrt{2}$ and that

$$\xi_2 = \frac{1}{\sqrt{3}} 2s - \frac{1}{\sqrt{6}} 2p_z + \frac{1}{\sqrt{2}} 2p_x \qquad (9\text{-}128)$$

It is interesting to compare the directional properties of ξ_1 and ξ_2. The hybrid orbital ξ_1 is directed along the positive z axis, or along the line $\theta = 0$. Let us see in which direction ξ_2 points. The $2p_x$ orbital lies in the x-z plane, and so we shall set $\phi = 0$ in Eq. 9-123 to write

$$\xi_2 = \frac{R(r)}{(4\pi)^{1/2}} \left(\frac{1}{\sqrt{3}} - \frac{\sqrt{3}}{\sqrt{6}} \cos\theta + \frac{\sqrt{3}}{\sqrt{2}} \sin\theta \right)$$

If we maximize ξ_2 with respect to θ to find the direction of maximum ξ_2, then we find that

$$\frac{d\xi_2}{d\theta} = \frac{\sqrt{3}}{\sqrt{6}} \sin\theta + \frac{\sqrt{3}}{\sqrt{2}} \cos\theta = 0$$

or that

$$\tan\theta = -\sqrt{3}$$

or that $\theta = 120°$. Thus, the orbital ξ_2 and ξ_1 lie in a plane and ξ_2 is directed 120° from ξ_1.

If we go on to investigate

$$\xi_3 = \frac{1}{\sqrt{3}} 2s + b_3 2p_z + c_3 2p_x$$

then we find that

$$\xi_3 = \frac{1}{\sqrt{3}} 2s - \frac{1}{\sqrt{6}} 2p_z - \frac{1}{\sqrt{2}} 2p_x \qquad (9\text{-}129)$$

Example 9-9 shows that ξ_3 is directed 240° from ξ_1.

EXAMPLE 9-9

Show that ξ_3 is directed 240° from ξ_1.

Solution: Using the Slater orbitals for $2s$, $2p_z$, and $2p_x$ (with $\phi = 0$), ξ_3 becomes

$$\xi_3 = \frac{R(r)}{(4\pi)^{1/2}} \left(\frac{1}{\sqrt{3}} - \frac{\sqrt{3}}{\sqrt{6}} \cos\theta - \frac{\sqrt{3}}{\sqrt{2}} \sin\theta \right)$$

To find the direction of maximum ξ_3, we maximize ξ_3 with respect to θ to obtain

$$\frac{d\xi_3}{d\theta} = \frac{\sqrt{3}}{\sqrt{6}} \sin\theta - \frac{\sqrt{3}}{\sqrt{2}} \cos\theta = 0$$

or that $\tan\theta = \sqrt{3}$, or $\theta = 240°$.

As Example 9-9 shows, ξ_3 is directed 240° from ξ_1, and so the three hybrid orbitals ξ_1, ξ_2, and ξ_3 are equivalent; lie in a single plane; and are directed 120° from each other. An electron-density contour map of an sp^2 orbital is shown in Figure 9-21. The sp^2 hybrid orbitals are shown together in Figure 9-22. The molecule BH_3 is formed by overlapping a hydrogen $1s$ orbital with each of the sp^2 hybrid orbitals as shown in Figure 9-23.

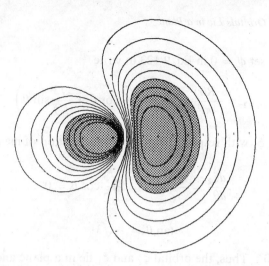

Figure 9-21. An electron-density contour map of an sp^2 hybrid orbital. [From G. Gerhold et al., Am. J. Phys. *40*, 988 (1972).]

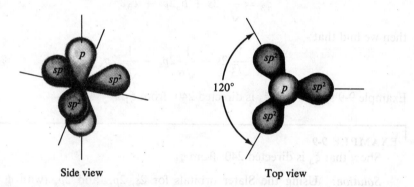

Side view   Top view

Figure 9-22. The geometry associated with sp^2 orbitals. The three sp^2 orbitals lie in a plane and point to the vertices of an equilateral triangle. The remaining $2p$ orbital is perpendicular to the plane formed by the three sp^2 orbitals.

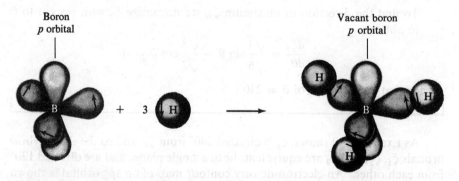

Figure 9-23. A schematic illustration of the bonding in BH_3. Each of the three boron-hydrogen bond orbitals is formed by the overlap of a boron sp^2 orbital and a hydrogen $1s$ orbital.

9-20 *sp³ Hybrid Orbitals Are Directed Toward the Vertices of a Regular Tetrahedron*

As our final example of the construction of hybrid orbitals, let us consider methane, CH_4. The four C—H bonds in methane are equivalent and are directed toward the vertices of a regular tetrahedron. In the case of CH_4, the molecular bond orbitals corresponding to Eq. 9-114 are

$$\phi_1 = c_1 1s_A + d_1 \xi_1$$
$$\phi_2 = c_2 1s_B + d_2 \xi_2$$
$$\phi_3 = c_3 1s_C + d_3 \xi_3 \tag{9-130}$$
$$\phi_4 = c_4 1s_D + d_4 \xi_4$$

Following Eq. 9-113, we can write the hybrid orbitals on the carbon atom in methane as

$$\xi_1 = a_1 2s_C + b_1 2p_{xC} + c_1 2p_{yC} + d_1 2p_{zC}$$
$$\xi_2 = a_2 2s_C + b_2 2p_{xC} + c_2 2p_{yC} + d_2 2p_{zC}$$
$$\xi_3 = a_3 2s_C + b_3 2p_{xC} + c_3 2p_{yC} + d_3 2p_{zC} \tag{9-131}$$
$$\xi_4 = a_4 2s_C + b_4 2p_{xC} + c_4 2p_{yC} + d_4 2p_{zC}$$

Because these hybrid orbitals are formed from one $2s$ orbital and three $2p$ orbitals, they are called sp^3 *hybrid orbitals.* By requiring these four hybrid orbitals to be equivalent, we have that $a_1 = a_2 = a_3 = a_4$. Using the condition $a_1^2 + a_2^2 + a_3^2 + a_4^2 = 1$, we find that $a_1 = a_2 = a_3 = a_4 = 1/\sqrt{4}$. Without loss of generality, we take one of the C—H bonds to be directed along the positive z axis. Because the $2p_x$ and $2p_y$ orbitals are directed along only the x and y axes, respectively, then b_1 and c_1 are zero in one of Eq. 9-131. If we let this orbital be ξ_1, then

$$\xi_1 = \frac{1}{\sqrt{4}} 2s + d_1 2p_z$$

By requiring that ξ_1 be normalized, we have that

$$\tfrac{1}{4} + d_1^2 = 1$$

or that $d_1 = \sqrt{\tfrac{3}{4}}$. Therefore, ξ_1 becomes

$$\xi_1 = \frac{1}{\sqrt{4}} 2s + \sqrt{\frac{3}{4}} 2p_z \tag{9-132}$$

Equation 9-132 is the first of the four sp^3 hybrid orbitals that describe the bonding in methane. An electron-density contour map of an sp^3 orbital is shown in Figure 9-24.

Without any loss of generality, we take the second hybrid orbital to lie in the x-z plane, so that

$$\xi_2 = \frac{1}{\sqrt{4}} 2s + b_2 2p_x + d_2 2p_z \tag{9-133}$$

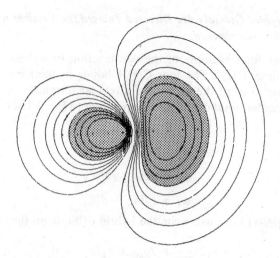

Figure 9-24. An electron-density contour map of an sp^3 hybrid orbital. [From G. Gerhold et al., *Am. J. Phys.* **40**, 988 (1972).]

If we require ξ_2 to be orthogonal to ξ_1, then we find

$$\tfrac{1}{4} + d_2\sqrt{\tfrac{3}{4}} = 0$$

or that $d_2 = -1/\sqrt{12}$. Equation 9-133 for ξ_2 now is

$$\xi_2 = \frac{1}{\sqrt{4}}\, 2s + b_2 2p_x - \frac{1}{\sqrt{12}}\, 2p_z$$

Now if we require that ξ_2 be normalized, then we have

$$\tfrac{1}{4} + b_2^2 + \tfrac{1}{12} = 1$$

or that $b_2 = \sqrt{2/3}$. Thus, the second sp^3 orbital is

$$\xi_2 = \frac{1}{\sqrt{4}}\, 2s + \sqrt{\frac{2}{3}}\, 2p_x - \frac{1}{\sqrt{12}}\, 2p_z \tag{9-134}$$

We can determine the direction in which ξ_2 points by differentiating ξ_2 with respect to θ. Using Eqs. 9-115 and 9-123 for the Slater orbitals in Eq. 9-134, we have (with $\phi = 0$)

$$\xi_2 = \frac{R(r)}{\sqrt{4\pi}}\left(\frac{1}{\sqrt{4}} + \sqrt{2}\sin\theta - \frac{\sqrt{3}}{\sqrt{12}}\cos\theta\right)$$

and so

$$\frac{d\xi_2}{d\theta} = 0 = \sqrt{2}\cos\theta + \frac{\sqrt{3}}{\sqrt{12}}\sin\theta$$

or that

$$\tan\theta = -\sqrt{8} \tag{9-135}$$

The value of θ given by Eq. 9-135 is $\theta = 109°28'$, the well-known tetrahedral

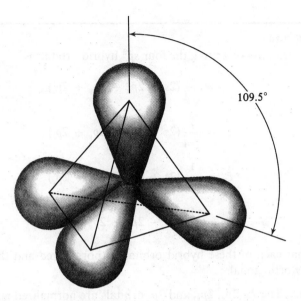

Figure 9-25. The geometry associated with sp^3 orbitals. The four sp^3 orbitals point toward the vertices of a tetrahedron. The angle between sp^3 orbitals is the tetrahedral bond angle 109.5°.

bond angle in methane. If we go on to determine ξ_3 and ξ_4, then we shall find that ξ_1, ξ_2, ξ_3, and ξ_4 are directed toward the vertices of a regular tetrahedron as shown in Figure 9-25. The methane molecule is described by overlapping a hydrogen $1s$ orbital with each of the sp^3 hybrid orbitals as shown in Figure 9-26. The electron configuration of methane in this localized orbital picture is $K(\phi_1)^2(\phi_2)^2(\phi_3)^2(\phi_4)^2$, where the ϕ's are the four localized bond orbitals in Eq. 9-121.

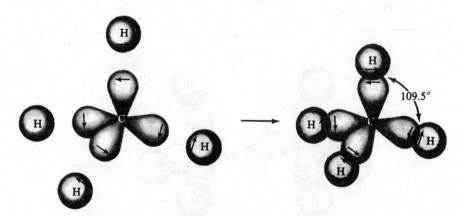

Figure 9-26. An illustration of the formation of four equivalent localized bond orbitals in CH_4 by overlapping the four carbon sp^3 orbitals and the hydrogen $1s$ orbitals. The eight valence electrons in CH_4 (four from the carbon atom and one from each hydrogen atom) occupy the four bond orbitals, accounting for the four localized carbon-hydrogen bonds in CH_4.

EXAMPLE 9-10

A symmetric way of writing the four sp^3 hybrid orbitals is

$$\xi_1 = \frac{1}{\sqrt{4}}(2s + 2p_x + 2p_y + 2p_z)$$

$$\xi_2 = \frac{1}{\sqrt{4}}(2s - 2p_x - 2p_y + 2p_z)$$

$$\xi_3 = \frac{1}{\sqrt{4}}(2s + 2p_x - 2p_y - 2p_z)$$

$$\xi_4 = \frac{1}{\sqrt{4}}(2s - 2p_x + 2p_y - 2p_z)$$

Show that each of these hybrid orbitals is normalized and that they are mutually orthogonal.

Solution: The $2s$, $2p_x$, $2p_y$, and $2p_z$ orbitals are normalized and mutually orthogonal. Consequently,

$$\int \xi_1^2 \, d\tau = \tfrac{1}{4} + \tfrac{1}{4} + \tfrac{1}{4} + \tfrac{1}{4} = 1$$

Because the coefficients in the other three hybrid orbitals are ± 1, they are also normalized. The orthogonality condition is obtained by making an analogy of the ξ with vectors and forming the dot product. For example,

$$\int \xi_1 \xi_2 \, d\tau = \tfrac{1}{4}(1 - 1 - 1 + 1) = 0$$

Similarly,

$$\int \xi_1 \xi_3 \, d\tau = \tfrac{1}{4}(1 + 1 - 1 - 1) = 0$$

and so on.

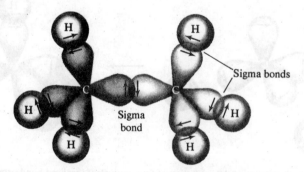

Figure 9-27. A schematic representation of the bonding in ethane, CH_3CH_3. The seven bond orbitals in ethane result from the overlap of sp^3 orbitals on the carbon atoms and $1s$ orbitals on the hydrogen atoms. There are 14 valence electrons in ethane. Each of the seven bond orbitals is occupied by 2 valence electrons of opposite spins, accounting for the seven bonds in ethane. The electrons are depicted by arrows in the above figure.

The sp^3 hybrid orbitals are used to describe the bonding in saturated hydrocarbons. Figure 9-27 is an illustration of the bonding in ethane, C_2H_6. The bonding in other saturated hydrocarbons is a straightforward extension of the bonding shown in Figure 9-27.

9-21   *Conjugated Hydrocarbons and Aromatic Hydrocarbons Can Be Treated by a π-Electron Approximation*

Our discussion of hybrid orbitals leads us naturally to a discussion of unsaturated hydrocarbons. For example, ethylene, C_2H_4, is a planar unsaturated hydrocarbon, all of whose bond angles are 120°. One can describe the structure of ethylene by saying that the carbon atoms form sp^2 hybrid orbitals as in Figure 9-28. The C—H bonds in ethylene result from the overlap of a $1s$ hydrogen orbital with an sp^2 carbon hybrid orbital. Part of the C—C bond in ethylene is due to the overlap of an sp^2 orbital from each carbon atom as shown in Figure 9-28. Because each of the bonds shown in Figure 9-28 is a σ bond, the representation in Figure 9-28 is called the *σ-bond framework* of the ethylene molecule. If we say that this σ framework lies in the x-y plane, implying that the $2p_x$ and $2p_y$ orbitals were used to construct the sp^2 hybrid orbitals, then the $2p_z$ orbital on each carbon atom is still available for bonding. Because these $2p_z$ orbitals are perpendicular to the x-y plane, we have the situation pictured in Figure 9-29, where an additional contribution to the C—C bond results from the overlap of the $2p_z$ orbitals. The charge distribution along the C—C bond due to the overlap of the $2p_z$ orbitals produces a π bond. We are developing here a σ-π description of unsaturated hydrocarbons. We shall see that it is a fairly good approximation to treat the π electrons as moving in some fixed, effective, electrostatic potential due to the electrons in the σ framework. This approximation is called the *π-electron approximation*. The π-electron approximation can be developed formally by starting with the

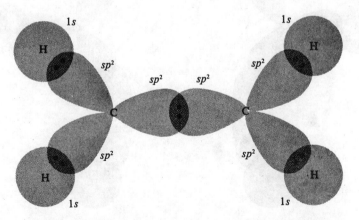

Figure 9-28. The σ-orbital framework of the ethylene molecule.

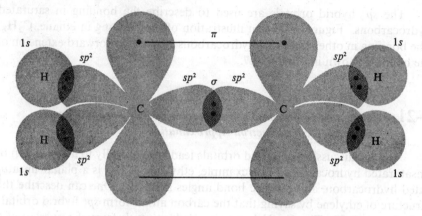

Figure 9-29. A schematic representation of the π bond in the ethylene molecule.

Schrödinger equation, but we shall simply accept the π-electron approximation here as a physically intuitive scheme.

The benzene molecule is described nicely by a σ-π approximation. The σ framework is formed by the overlap of sp^2 hybrid orbitals and the $1s$ hydrogen orbitals as shown in Figure 9-30. The π orbitals are formed from the overlap

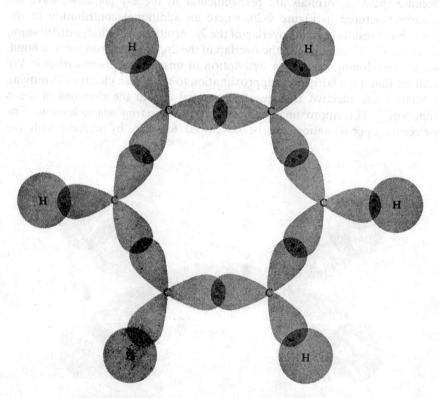

Figure 9-30. The σ-orbital framework of the benzene molecule.

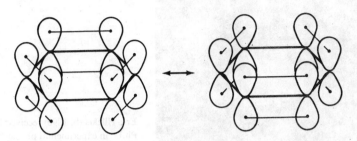

Figure 9-31. The two Kekulé structures of the benzene molecule.

of the $2p_z$ orbital from each carbon atom as shown in Figure 9-31. The two Kekulé structures

that are usually assigned to the benzene molecule imply that the bond lengths around the ring should alternate from those of a single bond to a double bond. This prediction is not in accord with the experimental fact that the benzene ring is a regular hexagon and has none of the chemical properties of a double-bonded system. This fact is reconciled readily by the valence-bond theory by writing the wave function for benzene as

$$\psi = c_A\psi_A + c_B\psi_B \tag{9-136}$$

where ψ_A and ψ_B are the valence-bond wave functions of the two Kekulé structures just shown. Thus, the predicted structure of benzene is intermediate between the two Kekulé resonance structures, and Eq. 9-136 predicts that all the C—C bond distances are equal and lie between that of a C—C single bond and a C—C double bond.

The two Kekulé structures for benzene have the same energy, and $c_A = c_B$ in Eq. 9-136. The energy calculated from ψ is less than that calculated from either ψ_A or ψ_B separately. This difference in energy is called the *resonance energy* of the benzene molecule. We shall calculate the resonance energy of benzene in Section 9-23.

9-22   *The Energies in Hückel Molecular-Orbital Theory Are Expressed in Terms of an Empirical Parameter β*

Although one can apply the valence-bond method to benzene and other aromatic hydrocarbons, the calculations are somewhat involved and are not presented here. Instead, we shall conclude this chapter with a simple treatment of conjugated molecules and aromatic molecules due to Hückel in 1930, which, along with various extensions and modifications, has found wide success in organic chemistry. This theory is referred to as *Hückel molecular-orbital theory*. One of the principal assumptions of Hückel molecular-orbital

Eric Hückel (b. 1896) received his
Ph.D. in experimental physics in 1921
at the University of Göttingen. After
spending a year with David Hilbert in
mathematics and Max Born, he left
Göttingen for a position at the ETH
Federal Institute of Technology) in
Zurich with Peter Debye. While at
Zurich, Hückel and Debye developed
the Debye-Hückel theory of strong
electrolytes. In 1930 Hückel received
an appointment in chemical physics
at the Technical Institute in Stuttgart.
In 1937 he was appointed a professor
of theoretical physics at the University of Marburg, where he remained until his retirement in 1962.

theory is that the π electrons move in a fixed, electrostatic, effective potential
due to the σ framework of the molecule. The σ electrons are described in terms
of localized hybrid bond orbitals and the π electrons are described by molecular
wave functions that extend over each of the atoms that contributes a π electron.
Thus, the π electrons are *delocalized*.

We shall illustrate the additional simplifications used in Hückel theory by
considering some specific examples. Let us consider the simple case of ethylene
first. The σ framework of ethylene is shown in Figure 9-28. Each carbon atom
contributes a $2p_z$ orbital to the delocalized π orbital, and as in the case of the
molecular orbital treatment of H_2 we write

$$\psi_\pi = c_1\chi_1 + c_2\chi_2 \tag{9-137}$$

where χ_1 and χ_2 are the carbon $2p_z$ orbitals. Realize that the Hamiltonian
operator in this theory involves the effective potential due to the electrons in
the σ framework of the molecule and so itself is an effective Hamiltonian. A
principal appeal of the Hückel theory is that it is not necessary ever to specify
this effective Hamiltonian.

The secular determinantal equation associated with Eq. 9-137 is

$$\begin{vmatrix} H_{11} - ES_{11} & H_{12} - ES_{12} \\ H_{12} - ES_{12} & H_{22} - ES_{22} \end{vmatrix} = 0 \tag{9-138}$$

where the H_{ij} are integrals involving the effective Hamiltonian. Because the carbon atoms in ethylene are equivalent, $H_{11} = H_{22}$. These diagonal elements of the secular determinant, called *Coulomb integrals*, are customarily denoted by α. The off-diagonal H's in Eq. 9-138 are called *resonance integrals* or exchange integrals and are customarily denoted by β. Note that β is a two-center integral because it involves the atomic orbitals from two different carbon atoms. Although it is not necessary, one often neglects the overlap integrals in Hückel theory and so the S_{ij} in Eq. 9-138 are given by

$$S_{ij} = 0 \quad \text{if } i \neq j$$
$$= 1 \quad \text{if } i = j \qquad (9\text{-}139)$$

Thus, the Hückel secular determinantal equation describing the ethylene molecule is

$$\begin{vmatrix} \alpha - E & \beta \\ \beta & \alpha - E \end{vmatrix} = 0 \qquad (9\text{-}140)$$

The two roots of this secular determinant are $E = \alpha \pm \beta$.

To evaluate α and β, we would have to know the effective Hamiltonian operator. Fortunately, we do not have to do this because α and β are assigned empirical values. Because α is essentially the energy of an electron in an isolated carbon $2p_z$ orbital, we can use α to set our zero of energy. The quantity β has been determined from a consideration of a variety of data and can be assigned a value of approximately $-75 \text{ kJ} \cdot \text{mol}^{-1}$.

There are two π electrons in ethylene. In the ground state of ethylene, both electrons occupy the orbital of lowest energy. Because β is negative, the lowest energy is $E = \alpha + \beta$. An energy-level diagram showing the ground state of ethylene is

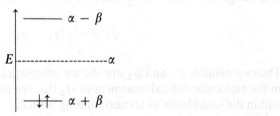

The π-electronic energy of ethylene is $E_\pi = 2\alpha + 2\beta$. Because α is used to specify the zero of energy, the two energies $E = \alpha \pm \beta$ must correspond to bonding and antibonding orbitals.

Let us determine the Hückel molecular orbitals. Recall that the secular determinantal equation originates from the pair of linear algebraic equations for c_1 and c_2 in Eq. 9-137 and in particular that we have

$$c_1(H_{11} - ES_{11}) + c_2(H_{12} - ES_{12}) = 0$$
$$c_1(H_{12} - ES_{12}) + c_2(H_{22} - ES_{22}) = 0$$

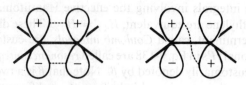

Figure 9-32. The bonding and antibonding orbitals in the simple Hückel molecular-orbital treatment of ethylene.

Upon specifying the Hückel approximations for the H_{ij} and S_{ij}, we have (see Eq. 9-140)

$$c_1(\alpha - E) + c_2\beta = 0$$
$$c_1\beta + c_2(\alpha - E) = 0 \tag{9-141}$$

To find the c's associated with each value of E, we substitute one value of E into either of Eq. 9-141. For example, for the value $E = \alpha + \beta$, either of Eq. 9-141 yields $c_1 = c_2$, so that

$$\psi_1 = c_1(\chi_1 + \chi_2)$$

The value of c_1 is found by requiring that ψ_1 be normalized. Because we are using $S_{12} = 0$, then we find that $c = 1/\sqrt{2}$. Consequently,

$$\psi_1 = \frac{1}{\sqrt{2}}(\chi_1 + \chi_2) \tag{9-142}$$

It is straightforward to show that the root $E = \alpha - \beta$ yields

$$\psi_2 = \frac{1}{\sqrt{2}}(\chi_1 - \chi_2) \tag{9-143}$$

The two orbitals ψ_1 and ψ_2 are shown schematically in Figure 9-32. Note as in the molecular-orbital treatment of H_2 that the molecular orbital with a node within the bond leads to an antibonding orbital.

EXAMPLE 9-11

Generalize our Hückel molecular-orbital treatment of ethylene to include overlap of χ_1 and χ_2 in Eq. 9-138.

Solution: If we do not assume that the S_{ij} in Eq. 9-138 are given by Eq. 9-139, then Eq. 9-140 becomes

$$\begin{vmatrix} \alpha - E & \beta - ES \\ \beta - ES & \alpha - E \end{vmatrix} = 0$$

The two roots of this secular determinantal equation are

$$E = \frac{\alpha \pm \beta}{1 \pm S}$$

The two molecular orbitals are determined by

$$c_1(\alpha - E) + c_2(\beta - ES) = 0$$

or

$$c_1(\beta - ES) + c_2(\alpha - E) = 0$$

Substitution of $E_+ = (\alpha + \beta)/(1 + S)$ into either of these equations gives $c_1 = c_2$, and so

$$\psi_+ = c_1(\chi_1 + \chi_2)$$

The normalization condition on ψ_+ gives

$$c_1^2(1 + 2S + 1) = 1$$

or that $c_1 = 1/\sqrt{2(1 + S)}$. Therefore,

$$\psi_+ = \frac{1}{\sqrt{2(1 + S)}}(\chi_1 + \chi_2)$$

Similarly, if we use the root $E_- = (\alpha - \beta)/(1 - S)$, then we find that

$$\psi_- = \frac{1}{\sqrt{2(1 - S)}}(\chi_1 - \chi_2)$$

9-23   Butadiene Is Stabilized by a Delocalization Energy

The case of butadiene is more interesting than ethylene. Although butadiene exists in a *cis* or *trans* configuration, we shall ignore that and picture the butadiene molecule as simply a linear sequence of four carbon atoms, each of which contributes a $2p_z$ orbital to a π-electron orbital (Figure 9-33). Because we have a linear combination of four atomic orbitals, we are going to have a 4×4 secular determinant, four different energies, and four different π-molecular

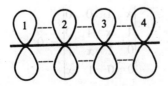

Figure 9-33. A highly schematic representation of the $2p_z$ orbitals on each of the carbon atoms in the butadiene molecule.

orbitals. Thus, we introduce the notation

$$\psi_i = \sum_{n=1}^{4} c_{in}\chi_n \tag{9-144}$$

where c_{in} is the coefficient of the atomic orbital of the nth atom in the ith molecular orbital. We are going to use these coefficients in several applications, and so it is important to understand this notation.

The secular determinantal equation for the butadiene molecule is

$$\begin{vmatrix} H_{11} - ES_{11} & H_{12} - ES_{12} & H_{13} - ES_{13} & H_{14} - ES_{14} \\ H_{12} - ES_{12} & H_{22} - ES_{22} & H_{23} - ES_{23} & H_{24} - ES_{24} \\ H_{13} - ES_{13} & H_{23} - ES_{23} & H_{33} - ES_{33} & H_{34} - ES_{34} \\ H_{14} - ES_{14} & H_{24} - ES_{24} & H_{34} - ES_{34} & H_{44} - ES_{44} \end{vmatrix} = 0 \tag{9-145}$$

Because we are taking the four carbon atoms in the butadiene molecule to be equivalent, all the H_{ii} in Eq. 9-145 are equal. As in the case of ethylene, we shall denote the H_{ii} by α. The H_{ij}, on the other hand, are two-center integrals. They involve the $2p_z$ orbital centered on carbons i and j. In the simplest version of Hückel theory, one sets $H_{ij} = \beta$ if the i and j carbon atoms are adjacent and sets $H_{ij} = 0$ if the i and j carbon atoms are not adjacent. The justification for this is that the overlap of the $2p_z$ orbitals from two carbon atoms decreases with their separation. Following this argument, one might set $S_{ij} = S$ for adjacent carbon atoms and $S_{ij} = 0$ for nonadjacent carbon atoms. In the simplest version of Hückel theory, one goes even one step further and sets $S = 0$.

Under these approximations and assumptions, the Hückel theory secular determinantal equation for butadiene becomes

$$\begin{vmatrix} \alpha - E & \beta & 0 & 0 \\ \beta & \alpha - E & \beta & 0 \\ 0 & \beta & \alpha - E & \beta \\ 0 & 0 & \beta & \alpha - E \end{vmatrix} = 0 \tag{9-146}$$

If we factor β from each column and let $x = (\alpha - E)/\beta$, then Eq. 9-146 becomes

$$\begin{vmatrix} x & 1 & 0 & 0 \\ 1 & x & 1 & 0 \\ 0 & 1 & x & 1 \\ 0 & 0 & 1 & x \end{vmatrix} = 0 \tag{9-147}$$

If this determinant is expanded, then the secular equation is (Problem 36)

$$x^4 - 3x^2 + 1 = 0$$

We can solve this equation for x^2 to obtain

$$x^2 = \frac{3 \pm \sqrt{5}}{2}$$

Therefore, we find the four roots

$$x = \pm 1.61804$$
$$= \pm 0.61804 \tag{9-148}$$

Recalling that $x = (\alpha - E)/\beta$ and that β is a negative quantity, we can construct a Hückel theory energy-level diagram for butadiene. There are four π electrons in butadiene. In the ground state, these four π electrons occupy the two orbitals of lowest energy as in

$$
\begin{array}{ll}
\underline{} & \alpha - 1.618\beta \\
\underline{} & \alpha - 0.618\beta \\
E \cdots\cdots\cdots\cdots & \alpha \\
\underline{\uparrow\downarrow} & \alpha + 0.618\beta \\
\underline{\uparrow\downarrow} & \alpha + 1.618\beta
\end{array}
$$

The total π-electronic energy of butadiene is

$$E_\pi = 2(\alpha + 1.618\beta) + 2(\alpha + 0.618\beta)$$
$$= 4\alpha + 4.472\beta \tag{9-149}$$

It is interesting to compare the energy given by Eq. 9-149 to the energy of the localized structure in which the two double bonds are localized between carbon atoms 1 and 2 and carbon atoms 3 and 4 in butadiene. In the simple Hückel theory, this localized structure is equivalent to two isolated ethylene molecules. We have shown above that $E_\pi = 2\alpha + 2\beta$ for ethylene, and so we can define a *delocalization energy* by

$$DE = E_\pi(\text{butadiene}) - 2E_\pi(\text{ethylene})$$
$$= 0.472\beta \tag{9-150}$$

If β is given the value $-75 \text{ kJ} \cdot \text{mol}^{-1}$, then we see that the delocalization energy in butadiene is about $-35 \text{ kJ} \cdot \text{mol}^{-1}$. This is the energy by which butadiene is stabilized relative to two isolated double bonds or the stability that butadiene derives because its π electrons are delocalized over the entire length of the molecule instead of being localized to the two end bonds.

EXAMPLE 9-12
The Hückel secular determinant for benzene

is

$$\begin{vmatrix} \alpha - E & \beta & 0 & 0 & 0 & \beta \\ \beta & \alpha - E & \beta & 0 & 0 & 0 \\ 0 & \beta & \alpha - E & \beta & 0 & 0 \\ 0 & 0 & \beta & \alpha - E & \beta & 0 \\ 0 & 0 & 0 & \beta & \alpha - E & \beta \\ \beta & 0 & 0 & 0 & \beta & \alpha - E \end{vmatrix} = 0$$

This 6×6 secular determinant leads to a sixth-degree polynomial for E. The six roots of the polynomial for E are

$$E_1 = \alpha + 2\beta$$

$$E_2 = E_3 = \alpha + \beta$$

$$E_4 = E_5 = \alpha - \beta$$

$$E_6 = \alpha - 2\beta$$

Construct a Hückel energy-level diagram for benzene and calculate the delocalization energy for benzene.

Solution: The Hückel energy-level diagram of benzene is

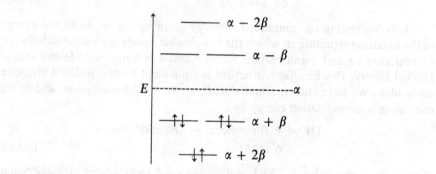

We have placed the six π electrons in benzene into the lowest three molecular orbitals.

The total π-electronic energy in benzene is

$$E_\pi = 2(\alpha + 2\beta) + 4(\alpha + \beta)$$

$$= 6\alpha + 8\beta$$

If the six π electrons were localized to three double bonds, then the π-electronic energy would be equal to the energy of three ethylene molecules. The π-electronic energy of three ethylene molecules is

$$E_\pi = 3(2\alpha + 2\beta) = 6\alpha + 6\beta$$

Therefore, the delocalization (or resonance) energy in benzene is

$$DE = E_\pi(\text{benzene}) - 3E_\pi(\text{ethylene})$$
$$= 2\beta$$

Thus, Hückel molecular-orbital theory predicts that benzene is stabilized by about $150 \text{ kJ} \cdot \text{mol}^{-1}$.

9-24 · The Coefficients in Hückel Molecular Orbitals Can Be Used to Calculate Charge Distributions and Bond Orders

Associated with each of the four molecular-orbital energies of butadiene that we have found is a molecular orbital. The molecular orbitals are given by

$$\psi_i = \sum_{n=1}^{4} c_{in}\chi_n$$

where the c_{in} are determined by the set of linear algebraic equations that lead to the secular determinantal equation. We determined molecular orbitals for ethylene because the algebra was simple, but in the case of butadiene the algebra is quite a bit lengthier (although certainly straightforward). The resulting wave functions for butadiene are

$$\psi_1 = 0.3717\chi_1 + 0.6015\chi_2 + 0.6015\chi_3 + 0.3717\chi_4$$

$$\psi_2 = 0.6015\chi_1 + 0.3717\chi_2 - 0.3717\chi_3 - 0.6015\chi_4$$

$$\psi_3 = 0.6015\chi_1 - 0.3717\chi_2 - 0.3717\chi_3 + 0.6015\chi_4 \qquad (9\text{-}151)$$

$$\psi_4 = 0.3717\chi_1 - 0.6015\chi_2 + 0.6015\chi_3 - 0.3717\chi_4$$

These butadiene molecular orbitals are presented schematically in Figure 9-34. Notice that the energy increases as the number of nodes increases.

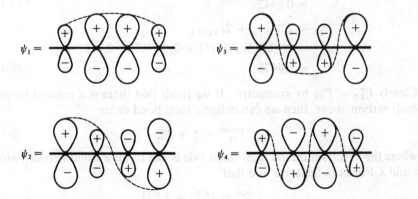

Figure 9-34. The four molecular orbitals obtained in the simple Hückel molecular-orbital treatment of butadiene.

Because we have set $S_{ij} = \delta_{ij}$ in Eq. 9-146, we have in effect assumed that the χ_n are orthonormal. Using this fact, one can see that

$$\sum_{n=1}^{4} c_{in}^2 = 1 \qquad i = 1, 2, 3, 4 \tag{9-152}$$

Equation 9-152 allows us to interpret c_{in}^2 as the fractional π-electronic charge on the nth carbon atom due to an electron in the ith molecular orbital. Thus, the total π-electronic charge on the nth carbon atom is

$$q_n = \sum_i n_i c_{in}^2 \tag{9-153}$$

where n_i is the number of electrons in the ith molecular orbital. For butadiene, for example,

$$\begin{aligned} q_1 &= 2c_{11}^2 + 2c_{21}^2 + 0c_{31}^2 + 0c_{41}^2 \\ &= 2(0.3717)^2 + 2(0.6015)^2 \\ &= 1.000 \end{aligned} \tag{9-154}$$

The other q's are also equal to unity, indicating that the π electrons in butadiene are uniformly distributed over the molecule.

Another interesting quantity that can be defined in terms of the c_{in} is the π-bond order. We can interpret the product $c_{ir}c_{is}$ as the π-electron charge in the ith molecular orbital between the adjacent carbon atoms r and s. We define the π-*bond order* between the adjacent carbon atoms r and s by

$$P_{rs}^\pi = \sum_i n_i c_{ir} c_{is} \tag{9-155}$$

where n_i is the number of π electrons in the ith molecular orbital. For butadiene, we have

$$\begin{aligned} P_{12}^\pi &= 2c_{11}c_{12} + 2c_{21}c_{22} + 0c_{31}c_{32} + 0c_{41}c_{42} \\ &= 2(0.3717)(0.6015) + 2(0.6015)(0.3717) \\ &= 0.8942 \end{aligned} \tag{9-156}$$

$$\begin{aligned} P_{23}^\pi &= 2c_{12}c_{13} + 2c_{22}c_{23} \\ &= 2(0.6015)(0.6015) + 2(0.3717)(-0.3717) \\ &= 0.4473 \end{aligned} \tag{9-157}$$

Clearly $P_{12}^\pi = P_{34}^\pi$ by symmetry. If we recall that there is a σ bond between each carbon above, then we can define a total bond order

$$P_{rs}^{\text{total}} = 1 + P_{rs}^\pi \tag{9-158}$$

where the first term on the right-hand side is due to the σ bond between atoms r and s. For butadiene, we find that

$$P_{12}^{\text{total}} = P_{34}^{\text{total}} = 1.894$$
$$P_{23}^{\text{total}} = 1.447 \tag{9-159}$$

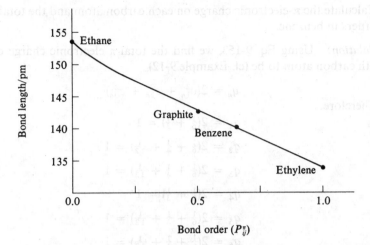

Figure 9-35. The correlation of experimental carbon-carbon bond lengths with π-electron bond orders.

Equations 9-159 are in excellent agreement with the experimental observations involving the reactivity of these bonds in butadiene. Figure 9-35 shows the correlation of experimental carbon-carbon bond lengths with the total bond order calculated from Hückel theory.

EXAMPLE 9-13

The Hückel molecular orbitals of benzene are

$$\psi_1 = \frac{1}{\sqrt{6}}(\chi_1 + \chi_2 + \chi_3 + \chi_4 + \chi_5 + \chi_6) \qquad E = \alpha + 2\beta$$

$$\psi_2 = \frac{1}{\sqrt{4}}(\chi_2 + \chi_3 - \chi_5 - \chi_6)$$

$$\psi_3 = \frac{1}{\sqrt{3}}\left(\chi_1 + \frac{1}{2}\chi_2 - \frac{1}{2}\chi_3 - \chi_4 - \frac{1}{2}\chi_5 + \frac{1}{2}\chi_6\right) \left.\begin{array}{c} \\ \\ \\ \end{array}\right\} E = \alpha + \beta$$

$$\psi_4 = \frac{1}{\sqrt{4}}(\chi_2 - \chi_3 + \chi_5 - \chi_6)$$

$$\psi_5 = \frac{1}{\sqrt{3}}\left(\chi_1 - \frac{1}{2}\chi_2 - \frac{1}{2}\chi_3 + \chi_4 - \frac{1}{2}\chi_5 - \frac{1}{2}\chi_6\right) \left.\begin{array}{c} \\ \\ \\ \end{array}\right\} E = \alpha - \beta$$

$$\psi_6 = \frac{1}{\sqrt{6}}(\chi_1 - \chi_2 + \chi_3 - \chi_4 + \chi_5 - \chi_6) \qquad E = \alpha - 2\beta$$

Calculate the π-electronic charge on each carbon atom and the total bond orders in benzene.

Solution: Using Eq. 9-153, we find the total π-electronic charge on the nth carbon atom to be (cf. Example 9-12)

$$q_n = 2(c_{1n}^2 + c_{2n}^2 + c_{3n}^2)$$

Therefore,

$$q_1 = 2(\tfrac{1}{6} + \tfrac{1}{3}) = 1$$
$$q_2 = 2(\tfrac{1}{6} + \tfrac{1}{4} + \tfrac{1}{12}) = 1$$
$$q_3 = 2(\tfrac{1}{6} + \tfrac{1}{4} + \tfrac{1}{12}) = 1$$
$$q_4 = 2(\tfrac{1}{6} + \tfrac{1}{3}) = 1$$
$$q_5 = 2(\tfrac{1}{6} + \tfrac{1}{4} + \tfrac{1}{12}) = 1$$
$$q_6 = 2(\tfrac{1}{6} + \tfrac{1}{4} + \tfrac{1}{12}) = 1$$

Thus, we see that the π electrons are distributed uniformly around the benzene ring.

Using Eq. 9-155 for the π-bond orders, we have

$$P_{rs}^\pi = 2(c_{1r}c_{1s} + c_{2r}c_{2s} + c_{3r}c_{3s})$$

Therefore,

$$P_{12}^\pi = 2(\tfrac{1}{6} + \tfrac{1}{6}) = \tfrac{2}{3}$$
$$P_{23}^\pi = 2(\tfrac{1}{6} + \tfrac{1}{4} - \tfrac{1}{12}) = \tfrac{2}{3}$$
$$P_{34}^\pi = 2(\tfrac{1}{6} + \tfrac{1}{6}) = \tfrac{2}{3}$$
$$P_{45}^\pi = 2(\tfrac{1}{6} + \tfrac{1}{6}) = \tfrac{2}{3}$$
$$P_{56}^\pi = 2(\tfrac{1}{6} + \tfrac{1}{4} - \tfrac{1}{12}) = \tfrac{2}{3}$$
$$P_{61}^\pi = 2(\tfrac{1}{6} + \tfrac{1}{6}) = \tfrac{2}{3}$$

Thus, we find that all the bonds in benzene are equivalent, in nice agreement with the chemical properties of benzene.

Hückel molecular-orbital theory has been applied to a great variety of organic molecules with some success and has been refined and extended in a number of ways so that it is now a useful tool and guide in organic chemistry.

Summary

In 1927 Heitler and London formulated the valence-bond treatment of molecules and presented the first successful description of a chemical bond. As applied to H_2, the valence-bond theory uses a molecular wave function of the form

$$\psi = c_1 1s_A(1)1s_B(2) + c_2 1s_A(2)1s_B(1)$$

When c_1 and c_2 are determined variationally, the resulting energy shows a minimum when the energy is plotted versus the internuclear separation (cf. Figure 9-5). This minimum in $E(R)$ corresponds to the formation of a covalent bond in H_2. An analysis of the equations of the valence-bond treatment of H_2 shows that the minimum in $E(R)$ is due to the antisymmetry of the H_2 molecular wave function and shows that the formation of a covalent bond is a strictly quantum-mechanical effect. Another description of the formation of chemical bonds is molecular-orbital theory, which was developed by Hund and Mulliken in the early 1930s. The wave functions of molecular-orbital theory are single-electron wave functions that extend over an entire molecule. Consequently, these wave functions are called *molecular orbitals*. For a given molecule there is a set of molecular orbitals, just as there is a set of atomic orbitals for a given atom. Electrons occupy molecular orbitals in accord with the Pauli Exclusion Principle, resulting in an electronic description in terms of molecular electron configurations. An even more detailed description of the electronic state of a molecule is given by its molecular term symbol. The application of molecular-orbital theory to homonuclear diatomic molecules predicts that He_2 and Ne_2 are unstable and that O_2 is paramagnetic. In practice, molecular orbitals are written as linear combinations of atomic (Slater) orbitals and the variational parameters are determined by a self-consistent field solution of the Hartree-Fock equations. Such a calculation is called an *SCF-LCAO-MO calculation* and the resulting orbitals are called *SCF-LCAO-MO orbitals*. The optimum molecular orbitals are (near) Hartree-Fock orbitals. Hartree-Fock calculations have been carried out for many molecules and the agreement of Hartree-Fock calculations with experimental data is very good (cf. Table 9-7). The bonding in many molecules can be described in terms of localized bond orbitals that are formed from hybrid orbitals. Hybrid orbitals are linear combinations of orbitals on the same atom and have specific directional properties. For example, the four sp^3 hybrid orbitals are directed toward the vertices of a regular tetrahedron and describe the geometry of methane and other saturated hydrocarbons. The bonding in unsaturated hydrocarbons is described in terms of σ bonds and π bonds. For example, the double bond in ethylene can be described as the overlap of an sp^2 hybrid orbital on each carbon atom and the overlap of an atomic p orbital from each carbon atom. This picture nicely accounts for the planar geometry of ethylene. Hückel molecular-orbital theory is a semiempirical scheme that is used to describe the delocalized π-electron distribution in conjugated and aromatic hydrocarbons.

Terms That You Should Know

Born-Oppenheimer approximation	exchange integral
valence-bond theory	singlet state
overlap integral	triplet state
Coulomb integral	molecular-orbital theory

molecular orbitals

bonding orbital

antibonding orbital

LCAO-MO

configuration interaction

elliptic coordinates

σ orbital

gerade

ungerade

π orbitals

bond order

photoelectron spectroscopy

binding energy

paramagnetic

Hartree-Fock limit

SCF-LCAO-MO

Hartree-Fock-Roothan method

molecular term symbol

basis set

minimal basis set

near Hartree-Fock calculation

ab initio calculation

QCPE

hybrid orbital

bond orbital

sp orbital

*sp*² orbital

*sp*³ orbital

σ-bond framework

π-electron approximation

resonance energy

Hückel molecular-orbital theory

resonance integral

delocalization energy

π-bond order

Problems

1. Express the Hamiltonian operator for a hydrogen molecule in atomic units.

2. Show that the determinantal secular equation associated with $\psi = c_1\psi_1 + c_2\psi_2$ is given by Eq. 9-7.

3. The overlap integral, Eq. 9-11, and other integrals that arise in two-center problems like H_2 are called *two-center integrals*. Two-center integrals are most easily evaluated by using a coordinate system called *elliptic coordinates*. In this coordinate system (Figure 9-36), there are two fixed points, separated by a distance R. A point P is given by the three coordinates

$$\lambda = \frac{r_A + r_B}{R}$$

$$\mu = \frac{r_A - r_B}{R}$$

and the angle ϕ, which is the angle that the (r_A, r_B, R) triangle makes about

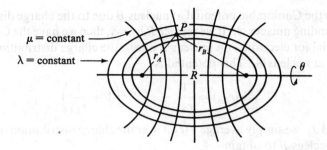

Figure 9-36. Elliptic coordinates.

the interfocal axis. The differential volume element in elliptic coordinates is

$$d\mathbf{r} = \frac{R^3}{8}(\lambda^2 - \mu^2)\,d\lambda\,d\mu\,d\phi$$

Given the above definitions of λ, μ, and ϕ, show that

$$1 \le \lambda \le \infty$$
$$-1 \le \mu \le 1$$
$$0 \le \phi \le 2\pi$$

Now use elliptic coordinates to evaluate the overlap integral, Eq. 9-11,

$$S = \int 1s_A 1s_B\,d\mathbf{r}$$
$$= \frac{Z^3}{\pi}\int e^{-Zr_A}e^{-Zr_B}\,d\mathbf{r}$$

4. The Coulomb integral that arises in the valence-bond treatment of H_2 can be written as (see Eq. 9-22)

$$J = J_1 - 2J_2 + \frac{1}{R}$$

where

$$J_1 = \iint d\mathbf{r}_1\,d\mathbf{r}_2\,\frac{[1s_A(1)]^2[1s_B(2)]^2}{r_{12}}$$

and

$$J_2 = \int \frac{d\mathbf{r}_1\,[1s_A(1)]^2}{r_{1B}}$$

Using elliptic coordinates (Problem 3), show that

$$J_2 = \frac{1}{R} - e^{-2R}\left(1 + \frac{1}{R}\right)$$

This is the Coulombic potential at nucleus B due to the charge distribution surrounding nucleus A. If we replace R by r_{2A}, then we have the Coulombic potential for electron 2 on nucleus B due to the charge distribution of electron 1 at nucleus A. This potential is

$$V(r_{2A}) = \frac{1}{r_{2A}} - e^{-2r_{2A}}\left(1 + \frac{1}{r_{2A}}\right)$$

To find J_1, we simply average $V(r_{2A})$ over the charge distribution of electron 2 on nucleus B to obtain

$$J_1 = \frac{1}{\pi}\int d\tau \, e^{-2r_{2B}} V(r_{2A})$$

Using elliptic coordinates, show that

$$J_1 = \frac{1}{R} - e^{-2R}\left(\frac{1}{R} + \frac{11}{8} + \frac{3R}{4} + \frac{R^2}{6}\right)$$

and finally derive Eq. 9-23.

5. Prove that $H_{11} = H_{22}$ in the Heitler-London valence-bond treatment of H_2.

6. Prove that the exchange integral arises in the Heitler-London treatment of H_2 only because a wave function of the form of Eq. 9-6 is used as the starting point. Show that either term in Eq. 9-6 used separately will not lead to an exchange integral.

7. Show that $c_1 = c_2$ in the ground-state Heitler-London wave function of H_2.

8. Show that ΔE_+ in the Heitler-London valence-bond treatment of H_2 can be written in the form

$$\Delta E_+ = \frac{J + (ab|ab) - 2S(a|ab) + (S^2/R)}{1 + S^2}$$

where

$$(ab|ab) = \iint 1s_A(1)1s_B(1)\frac{1}{r_{12}}1s_A(2)1s_B(2)\,d\mathbf{r}_1\,d\mathbf{r}_2$$

and

$$(a|ab) = \iint 1s_A(1)1s_B(1)\frac{d\mathbf{r}_1}{r_{A1}}$$

This is an instructive form in which to write ΔE_+ because it turns out numerically that the $-2S(a|ab)$ term, proportional to the overlap integral S, is the term predominantly responsible for the stability of H_2. Thus, we see that, other things being equal, the larger the value of S, the greater the stability. This is the origin of the intuitive idea that greater overlap leads to stability.

9. The internuclear potential energy of the hydrogen molecule is shown in Figure 9-37. Figure 9-37 is typical of many diatomic molecules, and there have been many attempts to find simple, empirical or semiempirical formulas to represent such curves. One of the more widely used is due to Morse in 1929 and is called the *Morse potential*:

$$u(r) = D_e[1 - e^{-a(r-r_e)}]^2$$

where D_e is the depth of the well, r_e is the equilibrium internuclear separation, and a is an empirical constant. Show that $u(r)$ has the form shown in Figure 9-37. Argue that the observed dissociation energy of the molecule is

$$D_0 = D_e - \tfrac{1}{2}h\nu$$

where ν is the fundamental vibrational frequency of the molecule. Recall now that ν is given in the harmonic oscillator approximation through the force constant and the reduced mass μ. Show that

$$u(r) = \frac{1}{2}\left(\frac{d^2u}{dr^2}\right)_{r=r_e}(r - r_e)^2 + \cdots$$

$$= \frac{k}{2}(r - r_e)^2 + \cdots$$

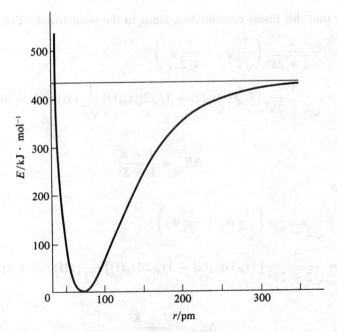

Figure 9-37. The potential energy of the hydrogen molecule in the ground electronic state.

for values of r close to r_e. Find k in terms of a and D_e and show that

$$v = \frac{1}{2\pi}\left(\frac{k}{\mu}\right)^{1/2}$$

$$= \frac{a}{\pi}\left(\frac{D_e}{2\mu}\right)^{1/2}$$

where μ is the reduced mass. Notice, then, that v is determined by the curvature of $u(r)$ at its minimum. Given that, for H_2, $r_e = 0.749$ Å, $D_e = 456$ kJ·mol^{-1}, and $a = 1.963 \times 10^8$ cm^{-1}, calculate the fundamental vibrational frequency of H_2 and compare it to the experimental value of 4.40×10^3 cm^{-1}.

10. Prove that $(1/\sqrt{2})\left[\alpha(1)\beta(2) \pm \alpha(2)\beta(1)\right]$ is normalized.

11. Carry through the Heitler-London valence-bond treatment of H_2 starting with

$$\psi = c_1\psi_1 + c_2\psi_2$$

where

$$\psi_1 = \begin{vmatrix} 1s_A\alpha(1) & 1s_B\beta(1) \\ 1s_A\alpha(2) & 1s_B\beta(2) \end{vmatrix}$$

$$\psi_2 = \begin{vmatrix} 1s_A\beta(1) & 1s_B\alpha(1) \\ 1s_A\beta(2) & 1s_B\alpha(2) \end{vmatrix}$$

Show that this linear combination leads to the normalized wave function

$$\psi_+ = \frac{1}{\sqrt{2 + 2S^2}}\left(\frac{1}{\sqrt{2}}\psi_1 - \frac{1}{\sqrt{2}}\psi_2\right)$$

$$= \frac{1}{\sqrt{2 + 2S^2}}\left[1s_A(1)1s_B(2) + 1s_A(2)1s_B(1)\right]\frac{1}{\sqrt{2}}\left[\alpha(1)\beta(2) - \alpha(2)\beta(1)\right]$$

with

$$\Delta E_+ = \frac{J + K}{1 + S^2}$$

and to

$$\psi_- = \frac{1}{\sqrt{2 - 2S^2}}\left(\frac{1}{\sqrt{2}}\psi_1 + \frac{1}{\sqrt{2}}\psi_2\right)$$

$$= \frac{1}{\sqrt{2 - 2S^2}}\left[1s_A(1)1s_B(2) - 1s_A(2)1s_B(1)\right]\frac{1}{\sqrt{2}}\left[\alpha(1)\beta(2) + \alpha(2)\beta(1)\right]$$

with

$$\Delta E_- = \frac{J - K}{1 - S^2}$$

Show that ψ_- is also normalized. Lastly, show that

$$\psi_3 = \frac{1}{\sqrt{2 - 2S^2}} \begin{vmatrix} 1s_A\alpha(1) & 1s_B\alpha(1) \\ 1s_A\alpha(2) & 1s_B\alpha(2) \end{vmatrix}$$

$$\psi_4 = \frac{1}{\sqrt{2 - 2S^2}} \begin{vmatrix} 1s_A\beta(1) & 1s_B\beta(1) \\ 1s_A\beta(2) & 1s_B\beta(2) \end{vmatrix}$$

give ΔE_-, thus showing that ψ_-, ψ_3, and ψ_4 represent a triplet state (cf. Problem 12).

12. Show that ψ_s given by Eq. 9-47 and ψ_t given by Eq. 9-48 are eigenfunctions of $\hat{S}_z$ with zero eigenvalue. Show that ψ_t given by Eqs. 9-49 and 9-50 are eigenfunctions of S_z with eigenvalues $+\hbar$ and $-\hbar$, respectively.

13. Show that

$$H_{AA} = H_{BB} = -\tfrac{1}{2} + J'$$

and that

$$H_{AB} = -\frac{S}{2} + K'$$

in the simple molecular-orbital treatment of H_2^+. The quantities J' and K' are given by Eqs. 9-60 and 9-62, respectively.

14. Use the elliptic coordinate system of Problem 3 to derive analytic expressions for S, J', and K' for the simple molecular-orbital treatment of H_2^+.

15. Prove for H_2 that the VB wave function with covalent and ionic terms is identical to the MO-CI wave function; that is, prove that

$$\psi_{VB} = c_n[1s_A(1)1s_B(2) + 1s_A(2)1s_B(1)] + c_i[1s_A(1)1s_A(2) + 1s_B(1)1s_B(2)]$$

and

$$\psi_{MO} = c_b[1s_A(1) + 1s_B(1)][1s_A(2) + 1s_B(2)] + c_a[1s_A(1) - 1s_B(1)][1s_A(2) - 1s_B(2)]$$

are identical. Derive a relation between c_i/c_n and c_a/c_b. Clearly c_n, c_i, c_b, and c_a depend on R. Given that $c_i/c_n = 0.16$ and that $c_a/c_b = -0.73$ at $R = R_{eq}$ if simple $1s$ hydrogen orbitals are used to calculate E, then show that the values of c_i/c_n and c_a/c_b are consistent.

16. Use a symmetry argument to show that the off-diagonal elements in Eq. 9-86 vanish.

17. Prove that if we use the following wave function for H_2

$$\psi = c_1\psi_1 + c_3\psi_3$$

where

$$\psi_1 = \phi_b(1)\phi_b(2)$$

and

$$\psi_3 = \phi_b(1)\phi_a(2) - \phi_a(1)\phi_b(2)$$

where

$$\phi_b = 1s_A + 1s_B$$

and

$$\phi_a = 1s_A - 1s_B$$

then the energy is the same as that calculated from ψ_1 and ψ_3 separately. Why is this so?

18. When we built up the molecular orbitals for diatomic molecules, we combined only those orbitals with the same energy since we said that only those with similar energies mix well. This problem is meant to illustrate this idea. Consider two atomic orbitals χ_A and χ_B. Show that a linear combination of these orbitals leads to the secular determinant

$$\begin{vmatrix} \alpha_A - E & \beta - ES \\ \beta - ES & \alpha_B - E \end{vmatrix} = 0$$

where

$$\alpha_A = \int \chi_A h^{\text{eff}} \chi_A \, d\tau$$

$$\alpha_B = \int \chi_B h^{\text{eff}} \chi_B \, d\tau$$

$$\beta = \int \chi_B h^{\text{eff}} \chi_A \, d\tau = \int \chi_A h^{\text{eff}} \chi_B \, d\tau$$

$$S = \int \chi_A \chi_B \, d\tau$$

where h^{eff} is some effective one-electron Hamiltonian for the electron that occupies the molecular orbital ϕ. Show that

$$(1 - S^2)E^2 + [2\beta S - \alpha_A - \alpha_B]E + \alpha_A\alpha_B - \beta^2 = 0$$

It is usually a satisfactory first approximation to neglect S. Doing this, show that

$$E_\pm = \frac{\alpha_A + \alpha_B \pm [(\alpha_A - \alpha_B)^2 + 4\beta^2]^{1/2}}{2}$$

Now if χ_A and χ_B have the same energy, show that $\alpha_A = \alpha_B = \alpha$ and that

$$E_\pm = \alpha \pm \beta$$

giving one level of β units below α and one level of β units above α, that is, one level of β units more stable than the isolated orbital energy and one level of β units less stable. Now investigate the case where $\alpha_A \neq \alpha_B$, say $\alpha_A < \alpha_B$. Show that

$$E_\pm = \frac{\alpha_A + \alpha_B}{2} \pm \frac{(\alpha_A - \alpha_B)}{2}\left[1 + \frac{4\beta^2}{(\alpha_A - \alpha_B)^2}\right]^{1/2}$$

$$= \frac{\alpha_A + \alpha_B}{2} \pm \frac{(\alpha_A - \alpha_B)}{2}\left[1 + \frac{2\beta^2}{(\alpha_A - \alpha_B)^2} - \frac{2\beta^4}{(\alpha_A - \alpha_B)^4} + \cdots\right]$$

$$E_\pm = \frac{\alpha_A + \alpha_B}{2} \pm \frac{(\alpha_A - \alpha_B)}{2} \pm \frac{\beta^2}{(\alpha_A - \alpha_B)} + \cdots$$

where we have assumed that $\beta^2 < (\alpha_A - \alpha_B)^2$ and have used the expansion

$$(1 + x)^{1/2} = 1 + \frac{x}{2} - \frac{x^2}{8} + \cdots$$

Show that

$$E_+ = \alpha_A + \frac{\beta^2}{\alpha_A - \alpha_B} + \cdots$$

$$E_- = \alpha_B - \frac{\beta^2}{\alpha_A - \alpha_B} + \cdots$$

Using this result, discuss the stabilization-destabilization of α_A and α_B versus the case above in which $\alpha_A = \alpha_B$. For simplicity, initially assume that $\alpha_A - \alpha_B$ is large.

19. Use molecular-orbital theory to explain why the dissociation energy of N_2 is greater than that of N_2^+, but the dissociation energy of O_2^+ is greater than that of O_2.

20. Discuss the bond properties of F_2 and F_2^+ using molecular-orbital theory.

21. Predict the relative stabilities of the species N_2^+, N_2, and N_2^-.

22. Predict the relative bond strengths and bond lengths of diatomic carbon, C_2, and the acetylide ion, C_2^{2-}.

23. Write out the MO electron configurations for Na_2 through Ar_2. Would you predict a stable Mg_2 molecule?

24. Determine the ground-state electron configurations of NO^+ and NO. Compare the bond orders of these two species.

25. Determine the bond order in a cyanide ion.

26. Show that filled orbitals can be ignored in the determination of molecular term symbols.

27. Deduce the ground-state term symbols of all the diatomic molecules given in Table 9-6.

28. Determine the ground-state molecular term symbols of O_2, N_2, N_2^+, and O_2^+.

29. The highest occupied molecular orbitals for an excited electronic configuration of the oxygen molecule are

$$[1\pi_g]^1[3\sigma_u]^1$$

What are the molecular term symbols for oxygen with this electronic configuration?

30. Construct a covalent valence-bond wave function for HF, including the $1s$, $2s$, and all the $2p$ electrons of fluorine.

31. Construct a valence-bond wave function for NH_3.

32. Given that one sp^2 hybrid orbital is

$$\xi_1 = \frac{1}{\sqrt{3}} 2s + \sqrt{\frac{2}{3}} 2p_z$$

construct a second hybrid orbital of the form

$$\xi_2 = \frac{1}{\sqrt{3}} 2s + b_2 2p_z + c_2 2p_x$$

by requiring that ξ_2 be orthogonal to ξ_1 and that ξ_2 be normalized.

33. Derive the third sp^2 hybrid orbital given that

$$\xi_1 = \frac{1}{\sqrt{3}} 2s + \sqrt{\frac{2}{3}} 2p_z$$

and that

$$\xi_2 = \frac{1}{\sqrt{3}} 2s - \frac{1}{\sqrt{6}} 2p_z + \frac{1}{\sqrt{2}} 2p_x$$

34. In Section 9-20, it was shown that the tetrahedral bond angle satisfies the relation $\tan \theta = -\sqrt{8}$. Show that this relation is equivalent to $\cos \theta = -\frac{1}{3}$.

35. In our derivation of the sp^3 hybrid orbitals of carbon, we found the first one (Eq. 9-132) to be

$$\xi_1 = \frac{1}{2} 2s + \frac{\sqrt{3}}{2} 2p_z$$

Prove that the second orbital can be taken to lie in the x-z plane without loss of generality and that

$$\xi_2 = a_2 2s + b_2 2p_x + d_2 2p_z$$

Furthermore, because the angle ϕ equals zero in the x-z plane, show that we can write $2p_x$ as

$$\psi_{2p_x} = \left(\frac{3}{4\pi}\right)^{1/2} R(r) \sin \theta$$

Now show that if we require ξ_1 and ξ_2 to be orthogonal, then $a_2 = -\sqrt{3}d_2$. In addition, show that if we require ξ_2 to be normalized, then $b_2 = (1 - 4d_2^2)^{1/2}$, and so

$$\xi_2 = \left(\frac{3}{4\pi}\right)^{1/2} R(r)[-d_2 + (1 - 4d_2^2)^{1/2} \sin \theta + d_2 \cos \theta]$$

Now show that maximizing ξ_2 with respect to both d_2 and θ gives

$$\tan \theta = \frac{(1 - 4d_2^2)^{1/2}}{d_2}$$

and

$$-1 - \frac{4d_2}{(1 - 4d_2^2)^{1/2}} \sin \theta + \cos \theta = 0$$

Substitute the first of these into the second to prove that $\cos \theta = -\frac{1}{3}$ or that $\theta = 109°28'$, the well-known tetrahedral bond angle.

36. Show that

$$\begin{vmatrix} x & 1 & 0 & 0 \\ 1 & x & 1 & 0 \\ 0 & 1 & x & 1 \\ 0 & 0 & 1 & x \end{vmatrix} = 0$$

gives the algebraic equation

$$x^4 - 3x^2 + 1 = 0$$

37. Calculate the Hückel π-electron energies of cyclobutadiene. What do Hund's rules say about the ground state of cyclobutadiene? Compare the stability of cyclobutadiene to two isolated ethylene molecules.

38. Calculate the Hückel π-electron energy of trimethylenemethane

$$\underset{\underset{CH_2}{\overset{\|}{C}}}{CH_2 \quad CH_2}$$

Compare the π-electron energy of trimethylenemethane to two isolated ethylene molecules.

39. Calculate the π-electronic energy levels and the total π-electronic energy of bicyclobutadiene

40. Calculate the delocalization energy, the charge on each carbon atom, and the bond orders for the allyl radical, carbonium ion, and carbanion. Sketch the molecular orbitals for the allyl systems.

41. Show that the Hückel molecular orbitals of benzene given in Example 9-13 are orthonormal.

42. Set up, but do not try to solve, the Hückel molecular-orbital theory determinantal equation for naphthalene.

43. A Hückel calculation for naphthalene, $C_{10}H_{10}$, gives the molecular-orbital energy levels $E_i = \alpha + m_i\beta$, where the 10 values of m_i are 2.3028, 1.6180, 1.3029, 1.0, 0.6180, -0.6180, -1.0, -1.3029, -1.6180, -2.3028. Calculate the ground-state π-electron energy of naphthalene.

44. The total π- electron energy of naphthalene is

$$E_\pi = 10\alpha + 13.68\beta$$

Calculate the delocalization energy of naphthalene.

45. Calculate the π-electron charge on each carbon atom in a butadiene cation, $C_4H_6^+$, and in a butadiene anion, $C_4H_6^-$.

46. Prove that

$$E_\pi = \sum_n q_n\alpha_n + 2\sum_n\sum_{m>n} P^\pi_{nm}\beta_{nm}$$

where α_n is the Coulomb integral associated with the nth atom and β_{nm} is the exchange integral between atoms n and m. This relation serves as a good check on the calculated energy levels, the q_n and the P^π_{nm}.

47. Using Hückel MO theory, determine whether the linear state ($H—H—H^+$) or the triangular state

$$\left[\begin{array}{c} H \\ \diagup \;\; \diagdown \\ H—H \end{array}\right]^+$$

of H_3^+ is the more stable state. Repeat the calculation for H_3 and H_3^-.

48. Set up a Hückel theory secular determinant for pyridine.

49. In the Born-Oppenheimer approximation, we assume that because the nuclei are so much more massive than the electrons, the electrons can essentially instantaneously adjust to any nuclear motion, and hence we have a unique and well-defined $E(R)$. Under this same approximation, $E(R)$ is the internuclear potential and so is the potential field in which the nuclei vibrate. Argue, then, that under the Born-Oppenheimer approximation, the force constant is independent of isotopic substitution. Using the above ideas, given that the dissociation energy for H_2 is $D_0 = 4.46$ eV and that the fundamental vibrational frequency v is 1.32×10^{14} s^{-1}, calculate D_0 and v for deuterium, D_2. Realize that the observed dissociation energy is given by

$$D_0 = D_e - \tfrac{1}{2}hv$$

where D_e is the value of $E(R)$ at R_{eq}.

Gerhard Herzberg was born in Hamburg, Germany, in 1904. He received a Doctor of Engineering degree from the Technical University at Darmstadt in 1928. After spending a year with Max Born at Göttingen, Herzberg returned to Darmstadt. In 1935 he was forced to emigrate from Germany and received an appointment at the University of Saskatchewan as a research professor in physics. In 1948 Herzberg was appointed director of the Pure Physics Division of the National Research Council of Canada, and in 1969 he was appointed as Distinguished Research Scientist at the Herzberg Institute of Astrophysics of the National Research Council of Canada. His three comprehensive volumes, Molecular Spectra and Molecular Structure: I. Spectra of Diatomic Molecules; II. Infrared and Raman Spectra of Polyatomic Molecules; *and* III. Electronic Spectra and Electronic Structure of Polyatomic Molecules, *are classic books in spectroscopy. Herzberg was awarded the Nobel Prize in chemistry in 1971.*

436

10

Molecular
Spectroscopy

THE INTERACTION of electromagnetic radiation with atoms and molecules is one of the richest probes into atomic and molecular structure. We shall see in this chapter that radiation from various regions of the electromagnetic spectrum yields different molecular information. For example, microwave radiation is used to investigate the rotation of molecules and yields moments of inertia and bond lengths. Infrared radiation is used to study the vibrations of molecules and yields information concerning the stiffness or rigidity of chemical bonds. We have already discussed the quantum-mechanical properties of a rigid rotator (Section 6-4) and a harmonic oscillator (Chapter 5), which are simple models for molecular rotations and vibrations, respectively. We shall review these models in this chapter and extend them and compare their predictions to experimental data. We shall discuss rotational and vibrational-rotational spectra in some detail and discuss electronic spectra only briefly. For simplicity, most of our discussion will be limited to diatomic molecules.

The latter sections of the chapter deal with the quantum-mechanical foundations of the results presented in the earlier sections. We shall discuss the Born-Oppenheimer approximation and the separation of a molecular Schrödinger equation into its rotational, vibrational, and electronic parts. Then we shall use time-dependent perturbation theory to derive the various spectroscopic selection rules.

TABLE 10-1
Regions of the Electromagnetic Spectrum and the Corresponding Molecular Processes

Region	Frequency/Hz	Wavelength/m	Wave number/cm^{-1}	Energy/$J \cdot molecule^{-1}$	Molecular process
Microwave	10^9–10^{11}	3×10^{-1}–3×10^{-3}	0.033–3.3	6.6×10^{-25}–6.6×10^{-23}	Rotation of polyatomic molecules
Far infrared	10^{11}–10^{13}	3×10^{-3}–3×10^{-5}	3.3–330	6.6×10^{-23}–6.6×10^{-21}	Rotation of small molecules
Infrared	10^{13}–10^{14}	3×10^{-5}–3×10^{-6}	330–3300	6.6×10^{-21}–6.6×10^{-20}	Vibration of flexible bonds
Visible and ultraviolet	10^{14}–10^{16}	3×10^{-6}–3×10^{-8}	3300–3.3×10^5	6.6×10^{-20}–6.6×10^{-18}	Electronic transitions

10-1 Different Regions of the Electromagnetic Spectrum Are Used to Investigate Different Molecular Processes

The features of the electromagnetic spectrum that we shall use in this chapter are summarized in Table 10-1. The absorption of microwave radiation is due to transitions between rotational energy levels; the absorption of infrared radiation is due to transitions between vibrational levels, accompanied by transitions between rotational energy levels; and the absorption of visible and ultraviolet radiation is due to transitions between electronic energy levels, accompanied by simultaneous transitions between vibrational and rotational levels. The frequency of the radiation absorbed is given by

$$\Delta E = E_u - E_l = h\nu \tag{10-1}$$

where E_u and E_l are the energies of the upper and lower states, respectively.

EXAMPLE 10-1

Calculate ΔE for radiation of wave number, $\bar{\nu} = 1.00 \text{ cm}^{-1}$. To what type of molecular process will this radiation correspond?

Solution: Recall that wave number is given by reciprocal wavelength or that

$$\bar{\nu} = \frac{1}{\lambda}$$

Therefore, ΔE is related to $\bar{\nu}$ by

$$\Delta E = h\nu = \frac{hc}{\lambda} = hc\bar{\nu}$$

and so

$$\Delta E = hc\bar{\nu} = (6.626 \times 10^{-34} \text{ J·s})(3.00 \times 10^8 \text{ m·s}^{-1})(100 \text{ m}^{-1})$$
$$= 1.99 \times 10^{-23} \text{ J}$$

According to Table 10-1, this value of energy corresponds to rotational transitions.

10-2 A Rigid Rotator Is the Simplest Model of Molecular Rotation

We discussed the quantum-mechanical properties of a diatomic rigid rotator in Section 6-4, but we shall review those results here. The classical energy of a rigid rotator is all kinetic energy and is given by

$$K = \tfrac{1}{2}I\omega^2 \tag{10-2}$$

where ω is the angular velocity (radians/second) and I is the moment of inertia

$$I = \mu R_0^2 \qquad (10\text{-}3)$$

where μ is the reduced mass $[\mu = m_1 m_2/(m_1 + m_2)]$ and R_0 is the bond length. The classical angular momentum is

$$L = I\omega \qquad (10\text{-}4)$$

and so the energy can be written as

$$K = \frac{L^2}{2I} \qquad (10\text{-}5)$$

The Hamiltonian operator is the kinetic energy operator

$$\hat{H} = -\frac{\hbar^2}{2I}\nabla^2 = \frac{\hat{L}^2}{2I} \qquad (10\text{-}6)$$

where

$$\hat{L}^2 = -\hbar^2\left[\frac{1}{\sin\theta}\frac{\partial}{\partial\theta}\left(\sin\theta\frac{\partial}{\partial\theta}\right) + \frac{1}{\sin^2\theta}\frac{\partial^2}{\partial\phi^2}\right] \qquad (10\text{-}7)$$

The eigenvalues of $\hat{H}$ are

$$E_J = \frac{\hbar^2}{2I}J(J + 1) \qquad J = 0, 1, 2, \ldots \qquad (10\text{-}8)$$

with a degeneracy

$$g_J = 2J + 1 \qquad (10\text{-}9)$$

The eigenfunctions of $\hat{H}$ and $\hat{L}^2$ are the spherical harmonics $Y_J^M(\theta, \phi)$

$$\hat{H}Y_J^M(\theta, \phi) = \frac{\hbar^2 J(J + 1)}{2I} Y_J^M(\theta, \phi) \qquad (10\text{-}10)$$

$$\hat{L}^2 Y_J^M(\theta, \phi) = \hbar^2 J(J + 1)Y_J^M(\theta, \phi) \qquad (10\text{-}11)$$

where (Eq. 6-76 and Table 6-3)

$$Y_J^M(\theta, \phi) = (-1)^{|M|}\left[\frac{2J + 1}{4\pi}\frac{(J - |M|)!}{(J + |M|)!}\right]^{1/2} P_J^{|M|}(\cos\theta)e^{iM\phi} \qquad (10\text{-}12)$$

Recall that M is restricted to the $2J + 1$ values, $-J, -J + 1, \ldots, J - 1, J$.

The transitions between the various rotational energy levels are governed by a selection rule, which states that $\Delta J = \pm 1$ and that the molecule must have a permanent dipole moment.

EXAMPLE 10-2

Show that the rotational absorption predicted by the rigid rotator model consists of a series of equally spaced lines in the microwave region.

Solution: The energy levels are given by Eq. 10-8. According to the selection rule for rotational transitions, $\Delta J = +1$ for absorption. The energy change for a rotational transition is

$$\Delta E = E_{J+1} - E_J = \frac{h^2}{2I}(J + 1)(J + 2) - \frac{h^2}{2I}J(J + 1)$$

$$= \frac{h^2}{2I}[(J + 1)(J + 2) - J(J + 1)]$$

$$= \frac{h^2}{I}(J + 1) \qquad J = 0, 1, 2, \ldots \qquad (10\text{-}13)$$

Using Eq. 10-1,

$$\nu = \frac{\Delta E}{h} = \frac{h}{4\pi^2 I}(J + 1) \qquad J = 0, 1, 2, \ldots \qquad (10\text{-}14)$$

The spectrum consists of a series of equally spaced lines whose frequencies are integral multiples of $h/4\pi^2 I$. Using an atomic mass of 40×10^{-27} kg and a bond length of 200 pm, we find

$$I = \mu R_0^2 = \left(\frac{m_1 m_2}{m_1 + m_2}\right) R_0^2 = \frac{(40 \times 10^{-27} \text{ kg})^2}{(40 + 40) \times 10^{-27} \text{ kg}}(2 \times 10^{-10} \text{ m})^2$$

$$= 8 \times 10^{-46} \text{ kg} \cdot \text{m}^2$$

The corresponding frequencies, then, are integral multiples of $h/4\pi^2 I$, or

$$\nu = \frac{h}{4\pi^2 I}(J + 1) = \frac{(6.626 \times 10^{-34} \text{ J} \cdot \text{s})}{4\pi^2(8 \times 10^{-46} \text{ kg} \cdot \text{m}^2)}(J + 1)$$

$$= 2.1 \times 10^{10}(J + 1) \text{ Hz} \qquad J = 0, 1, 2, \ldots$$

According to Table 10-1, these lines occur in the microwave region.

EXAMPLE 10-3

It is customary to write Eq. 10-8 in the form

$$\bar{E}_J = \bar{B}J(J + 1) \qquad (10\text{-}15)$$

where $\bar{B}$ is called the *rotational constant* of the molecule. Derive an equation for $\bar{B}$ in units of wave numbers.

Solution: From Eq. 10-8,

$$E_J = \frac{h^2}{2I}J(J + 1)$$

where E_J is expressed in joules. The relation between energy and wave numbers is given by $E = hc\bar{v}$, and so

$$\bar{v} = \frac{E_J}{hc} = \frac{\hbar^2}{2hcI} J(J+1)$$

$$= \frac{h}{8\pi^2 cI} J(J+1)$$

Comparing this result with Eq. 10-15, we see that

$$\bar{B} = \frac{h}{8\pi^2 cI} \tag{10-16}$$

Typical values of $\bar{B}$ for diatomic molecules are of the order of 1 cm^{-1} (cf. Table 10-4).

Using the results of Example 10-2, we find that the rotational spectrum consists of a series of equally spaced lines separated by $2\bar{B}$. From the observed microwave spectrum, one can determine $\bar{B}$, then I by Eq. 10-16, and finally R_0 by Eq. 10-3. Thus we see that bond distances can be determined from observed microwave spectra (cf. Problems 1 and 2).

10-3   *The Harmonic Oscillator Is the Simplest Model of Molecular Vibrations*

The quantum-mechanical properties of a harmonic oscillator were developed in Chapter 5. Recall that the Hamiltonian operator of a diatomic harmonic oscillator is

$$\hat{H} = -\frac{\hbar^2}{2\mu}\frac{d^2}{dx^2} + \frac{k}{2}x^2 \tag{10-17}$$

where k is the force constant of the molecule. The eigenvalues of $\hat{H}$ are nondegenerate and are

$$E_n = (n + \tfrac{1}{2})h\nu \qquad n = 0, 1, 2, \ldots \tag{10-18}$$

where

$$\nu = \frac{1}{2\pi}\left(\frac{k}{\mu}\right)^{1/2} \tag{10-19}$$

is the fundamental vibrational frequency of the oscillator. The eigenfunctions of $\hat{H}$ are (cf. Eq. 5-41)

$$\psi_n(x) = \left(\frac{1}{2^n n!}\right)^{1/2}\left(\frac{\alpha}{\pi}\right)^{1/4} H_n\left[\left(\frac{k\mu}{\hbar^2}\right)^{1/4}x\right]e^{-(k\mu/\hbar^2)^{1/2}x^2/2} \tag{10-20}$$

where the H_n are the Hermite polynomials.

Transitions among the vibrational levels are subject to a selection rule that states that $\Delta n = \pm 1$ and that the dipole moment must vary during a vibration.

EXAMPLE 10-4

Show that the vibrational absorption spectrum of a diatomic molecule in the harmonic-oscillator approximation consists of just one line whose frequency is given by Eq. 10-19.

Solution: From Eq. 10-18,

$$E_n = (n + \tfrac{1}{2})h\nu \qquad n = 0, 1, 2, \ldots$$

According to the selection rule, $\Delta n = +1$ for absorption. The vibrational energy change for absorption is

$$\Delta E = \dot{E}_{n+1} - E_n = \left(n + 1 + \frac{1}{2}\right)h\nu - \left(n + \frac{1}{2}\right)h\nu$$

$$= h\nu = \frac{h}{2\pi}\left(\frac{k}{\mu}\right)^{1/2}$$

Thus, the spectrum consists of a single line whose frequency is

$$\nu_{\text{obs}} = \frac{\Delta E}{h} = \frac{1}{2\pi}\left(\frac{k}{\mu}\right)^{1/2} \tag{10-21}$$

Using Eq. 10-21, the observed infrared frequency can yield the force constant k, which is a direct measure of the stiffness of the bond (cf. Problems 7 and 8).

10-4 Most Diatomic Molecules Are in the n = 0 Vibrational State at Room Temperature

The quantum-mechanical systems that we have studied in this book have in common the property that their energy levels are quantized. Let the set of energies available to a system be $\{E_j\}$. A question of practical importance is how the molecules of a gas are distributed over these available levels; if there are N molecules in the gas, then how many are in level 0, how many in level 1, and so on? The answer to this question comes from the kinetic theory of gases and says that if N_i is the number of molecules with energy E_i, then

$$N_i \propto e^{-E_i/k_B T}$$

where k_B is the Boltzmann constant and T is the absolute temperature. In terms of an equation, we have

$$N_i = ce^{-E_i/k_B T} \tag{10-22}$$

where c is a proportionality constant. Equation 10-22 is called the *Boltzmann distribution* and governs how the energy levels are populated at any temperature. We can determine c by summing both sides of Eq. 10-22 over i and using the fact that $\sum_i N_i = N$:

$$\sum_i N_i = N = c \sum_j e^{-E_i/k_BT}$$

or

$$c = \frac{N}{\sum_i e^{-E_i/k_BT}}$$

Substitute this back into Eq. 10-22 and obtain f_i, the fraction of molecules in the ith energy level:

$$f_i = \frac{N_i}{N} = \frac{e^{-E_i/k_BT}}{\sum_i e^{-E_i/k_BT}} \tag{10-23}$$

Let us apply Eq. 10-23 to the case of a harmonic oscillator. The energies are given by $E_i = (i + \frac{1}{2})hv$ with $i = 0, 1, 2, \ldots$, and so

$$f_i = \frac{\exp\left[\dfrac{-(i + \frac{1}{2})hv}{k_BT}\right]}{\displaystyle\sum_{i=0}^{\infty} \exp\left[\dfrac{-(i + \frac{1}{2})hv}{k_BT}\right]} = \frac{e^{-ihv/k_BT}}{\displaystyle\sum_{i=0}^{\infty} e^{-ihv/k_BT}} \tag{10-24}$$

The denominator on the right-hand side of this equation can be easily evaluated by recognizing it to be a geometric series

$$\sum_{i=0}^{\infty} x^i = \frac{1}{1 - x}$$

with $x \equiv e^{-hv/k_BT}$. Thus we can write

$$\sum_{i=0}^{\infty} e^{-ihv/k_BT} = \frac{1}{1 - e^{-hv/k_BT}}$$

If we substitute this into Eq. 10-24, we obtain the fraction of molecules in the ith vibrational state:

$$f_i = (1 - e^{-hv/k_BT})e^{-ihv/k_BT} \tag{10-25}$$

We can use Eq. 10-25 to calculate the fraction of diatomic molecules that are in their lowest vibrational energy level. If we let $i = 0$ in Eq. 10-25, then we find

$$f_0 = 1 - e^{-hv/k_BT} \tag{10-26}$$

A typical vibrational frequency of a diatomic molecule is 5×10^{13} Hz. Therefore at 25°C

$$\frac{hv}{k_BT} = \frac{(6.626 \times 10^{-34}\ \text{J·s})(5 \times 10^{13}\ \text{s}^{-1})}{(1.38 \times 10^{-23}\ \text{J·K}^{-1})(298\ \text{K})} = 8$$

and

$$f_0 = 0.9997$$

Thus we see that nearly all the molecules are in the ground vibrational state at 25°C. Figure 10-1 shows f_i versus i for NO at 1000 K and 2000 K.

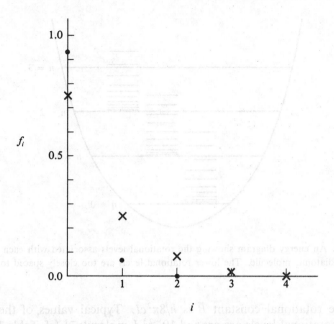

Figure 10-1. The fraction of NO molecules in the ith vibrational state. The dots are the fractions at 1000 K and the crosses are the fractions at 2000 K. At 300 K, the fraction of NO molecules in the ground vibrational state is 0.99989.

EXAMPLE 10-5

Calculate the fraction of HBr molecules in the ground vibrational state at 300 K and 2000 K. The fundamental vibrational frequency of HBr is 7.7×10^{13} Hz.

Solution: The ratio $h\nu/k_B T$ is 12.3 at 300 K and 1.8 at 2000 K. Using Eq. 10-26, we find that

$$f_0 = 1 - e^{-12.3} \approx 1 \quad \text{at} \quad 300 \text{ K}$$

$$f_0 = 1 - e^{-1.8} = 0.83 \quad \text{at} \quad 2000 \text{ K}$$

Thus, even at 2000 K, 83% of the HBr molecules are in their ground vibrational state.

10-5 *Rotational Transitions Accompany Vibrational Transitions*

Within the rigid rotator-harmonic oscillator approximation, the rotational and vibrational energy of a diatomic molecule is

$$E_{\text{vib,rot}} = (n + \tfrac{1}{2})h\nu_0 + hc\bar{B}J(J + 1) \qquad \begin{aligned} n &= 0, 1, 2, \ldots \\ J &= 0, 1, 2, \ldots \end{aligned} \qquad (10\text{-}27)$$

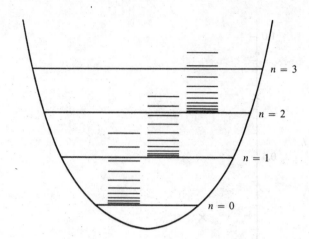

Figure 10-2. An energy diagram showing the rotational levels associated with each vibrational state for a diatomic molecule. The lower rotational levels are too closely spaced to be shown.

where the rotational constant $\bar{B}$ is $h/8\pi^2 cI$. Typical values of the spacing between rotational levels are around 10^{-23} J·molecule^{-1} (cf. Table 10-1) and of those of vibrational levels are around 10^{-21} J·molecule^{-1} (cf. Table 10-1). This result is shown schematically in Figure 10-2 (cf. Problem 13). When a molecule absorbs infrared radiation, the vibrational transition is accompanied by a rotational transition. The selection rules for absorption of infrared radiation are

$$\Delta n = +1 \quad \text{(absorption)}$$
$$\Delta J = \pm 1 \tag{10-28}$$

The frequency v_{obs} associated with the absorption is

$$v_{\text{obs}} = v_0 + c\bar{B}[J'(J' + 1) - J(J + 1)]$$

where J' can be either $J + 1$ or $J - 1$. If $J' = J + 1$, then

$$v_{\text{obs}}(\Delta J = +1) = v_0 + 2c\bar{B}(J + 1) \quad J = 0, 1, 2, \ldots \tag{10-29}$$

If $J' = J - 1$, then

$$v_{\text{obs}}(\Delta J = -1) = v_0 - 2c\bar{B}J \quad J = 1, 2, 3, \ldots \tag{10-30}$$

In both Eq. 10-29 and 10-30, J is the initial rotational quantum number. Typically, $c\bar{B} \approx 10^{11}$ Hz and $v_0 \approx 10^{13}$ Hz, and so the spectrum predicted by Eqs. 10-29 and 10-30 typically contains lines at 10^{13} Hz $\pm$ integral multiples of 10^{11}Hz. Notice that there is no line at v_0. The rotational-vibrational spectrum of HBr(g) is shown in Figure 10-3. The gap centered around 2560 cm^{-1} corresponds to the missing line at v_0. On each side of the gap is a series of lines whose spacing is about 10 cm^{-1}. The series toward the high-frequency side is called the *R branch* and is due to rotational transitions with $\Delta J = +1$. The series toward the low frequencies is called the *P branch* and is due to rotational transitions with $\Delta J = -1$.

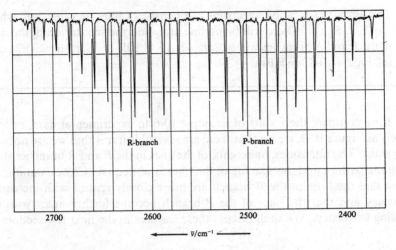

Figure 10-3. The rotational-vibrational spectrum of the $0 \to 1$ vibrational transition of HBr(g). The R branch and the P branch are indicated in the figure. (From *Introduction to Molecular Spectroscopy* by Gordon Barrow. Used with the permission of McGraw-Hill Book Company.)

EXAMPLE 10-6

The bond length in $C^{12}N^{14}$ is 117 pm and its force constant is 1630 N·m^{-1}. Predict the vibration-rotation spectrum of $C^{12}N^{14}$.

Solution: First we must calculate the fundamental frequency v_0 (Eq. 10-21) and the rotational constant $\bar{B}$ (Eq. 10-16). Both quantities require the reduced mass, which is

$$\mu = \frac{(12.0 \text{ amu})(14.0 \text{ amu})}{(12.0 + 14.0) \text{ amu}} (1.66 \times 10^{-27} \text{ kg·amu}^{-1}) = 1.07 \times 10^{-26} \text{ kg}$$

Using Eq. 10-21 for v_0,

$$v_0 = \frac{1}{2\pi}\left(\frac{k}{\mu}\right)^{1/2} = \frac{1}{2\pi}\left(\frac{1630 \text{ N·m}^{-1}}{1.07 \times 10^{-26} \text{ kg}}\right)^{1/2}$$

$$= 6.20 \times 10^{13} \text{ s}^{-1} = 2.07 \times 10^{3} \text{ cm}^{-1}$$

Using Eq. 10-16 for $\bar{B}$,

$$\bar{B} = \frac{h}{8\pi^2 cI} = \frac{h}{8\pi^2 c\mu R_0^2}$$

$$= \frac{(6.626 \times 10^{-34} \text{ J·s})}{8\pi^2 (3.00 \times 10^8 \text{ m·s}^{-1})(1.07 \times 10^{-26} \text{ kg})(117 \times 10^{-12} \text{ m})^2}$$

$$= 1.91 \text{ cm}^{-1} = 5.73 \times 10^{10} \text{ s}^{-1}$$

The vibration-rotation spectrum will consist of lines at $v_0 \pm 2c\bar{B}j$ where $j = 1, 2, 3, \ldots$. There will be no line at v_0 and the separation of the lines in the P and R branches will be $2c\bar{B} = 1.15 \times 10^{11} \text{ s}^{-1}$, or $2\bar{B} = 3.82 \text{ cm}^{-1}$ (cf. Figure 10-3 for HBr).

If we compare the results of Example 10-6 to experimental data, or look closely at Figure 10-3, we see that there are several features that we are not able to explain. The intensities, or heights, of the lines in the P and R branches show a definite pattern and the spacing of the lines is not equal. Close examination shows that the lines in the R branch are more closely spaced with increasing frequency and that the lines of the P branch become further apart with decreasing frequency. We shall discuss these features in the next few sections.

10-6 *The Intensities of the Lines in the P and R Branches in a Vibration-Rotation Spectrum Are Explained By a Rotational Boltzmann Distribution*

If we assume that the intensities of the rotational lines in a vibration-rotation spectrum are proportional to the fraction of molecules in the rotational level from which the transition occurs, then we can use the Boltzmann distribution of rotational energies to explain the observed intensities. We cannot use Eq. 10-22 directly because the rotational energy levels are $(2J + 1)$-fold

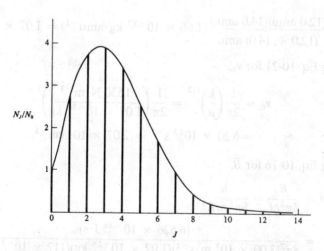

Figure 10-4. The relative populations of the rotational levels of HCl(g) at 300 K.

degenerate. If the ith level has a degeneracy g_i, then Eq. 10-22 becomes

$$N_i = cg_i e^{-E_i/k_B T} \tag{10-31}$$

For rotational energies, we have

$$N_J = c(2J + 1) \exp\left[\frac{-\bar{B}J(J + 1)}{k_B T}\right] \tag{10-32}$$

Instead of evaluating the proportionality constant by summing over J as we did in the case of a harmonic oscillator, it is easier in this case to evaluate c in Eq. 10-32 by letting $J = 0$ to obtain

$$N_0 = c$$

Thus, Eq. 10-32 can be written in the form

$$\frac{N_J}{N_0} = (2J + 1) \exp\left[\frac{-\bar{B}J(J + 1)}{k_B T}\right] \tag{10-33}$$

Note that N_J/N_0 is *not* the fraction of molecules in the Jth energy level, but it is the number in the Jth level relative to the number in the ground state. Equation 10-33 is plotted in Figure 10-4 for HCl ($\bar{B} = 10.6 \text{ cm}^{-1}$) at 300 K. Note that the envelope of the lines in Figure 10-4 is similar to the envelope of the lines of the P and R branches in Figure 10-3. Thus we see that the shape of the P and R branches reflects the population of the rotational energy levels.

10-7   The Lines in a Rotational Spectrum Are Not Equally Spaced

Table 10-2 lists some of the observed lines in the rotational spectrum of $H^{35}Cl$. The differences listed in the third column clearly show that the lines are not exactly equally spaced as the rigid rotator approximation predicts. The discrepancy can be resolved by realizing that a chemical bond is not truly rigid. As the molecule rotates faster and faster (increasing J), the centrifugal force causes the bond to stretch. The extent of the stretching of the bond can be determined by balancing the Hooke's law force $[k(R - R_0)]$ and the centrifugal force ($\mu R\omega^2$):

$$k(R - R_0) = \mu R\omega^2 \tag{10-34}$$

In this equation, R_0 is the bond length when there is no rotation ($J = 0$). Solving Eq. 10-34 for R, we find that the stretched bond length is

$$R = \frac{kR_0}{k - \mu\omega^2} \tag{10-35}$$

The total energy of the rotator is made up of a kinetic energy part and a potential energy part:

$$E = \tfrac{1}{2}I\omega^2 + \tfrac{1}{2}k(R - R_0)^2$$

TABLE 10-2

The Rotational Absorption Spectrum of H³⁵Cl

Transition	$\bar{v}_{obs}/cm^{-1}$	$\Delta\bar{v}_{obs}/cm^{-1}$	$\begin{array}{c}\bar{v}_{calc}=2\bar{B}(J+1)\\ \bar{B}=10.34\ cm^{-1}\end{array}$	$\begin{array}{c}\bar{v}_{calc}=2\bar{B}(J+1)-4\bar{D}(J+1)^3\\ \bar{B}=10.395\ cm^{-1}\\ \bar{D}=0.0004\ cm^{-1}\end{array}$
3 → 4	83.03		82.72	83.06
		21.07		
4 → 5	104.10		103.40	103.75
		20.20		
5 → 6	124.30		124.08	124.39
		20.73		
6 → 7	145.03		144.76	144.98
		20.48		
7 → 8	165.51		165.44	165.50
		20.35		
8 → 9	185.86		186.12	185.94
		20.52		
9 → 10	206.38		206.80	206.30
		20.12		
10 → 11	226.50		227.48	226.56

If we substitute Eq. 10-34 into the potential energy term here, then we find

$$E = \frac{1}{2}I\omega^2 + \frac{\mu^2 R^2\omega^4}{2k}$$

$$= \frac{L^2}{2I} + \frac{L^4}{2I^2 kR^2} \tag{10-36}$$

where we have used the relation $L = I\omega = \mu R^2\omega$. We can convert the classical energy given by Eq. 10-36 into the quantum-mechanical energy by substituting the quantum condition $L^2 = \hbar^2 J(J + 1)$ into Eq. 10-36 and obtain

$$E_J = \frac{\hbar^2}{2I}J(J + 1) + \frac{\hbar^4}{2I^2 kR^2}J^2(J + 1)^2 \tag{10-37}$$

Lastly, we replace R (remember that $I = \mu R^2$) by Eq. 10-35. To do this we write Eq. 10-35 as

$$\frac{1}{R^2} = \frac{[1 - (\mu\omega^2/k)]^2}{R_0^2} = \frac{1}{R_0^2}\left(1 - \frac{2\mu\omega^2}{k} + \frac{\mu^2\omega^4}{k^2}\right)$$

$$= \frac{1}{R_0^2}\left(1 - \frac{2L^2}{\mu kR_0^4} + \frac{L^4}{\mu^2 k^2 R_0^8}\right)$$

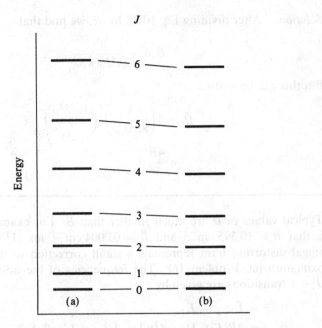

Figure 10-5. The energy levels of (a) a rigid rotator and (b) a nonrigid rotator.

Replace each factor of L^2 by $\hbar^2 J(J + 1)$, and substitute the result into Eq. 10-37 to obtain

$$E_J = \frac{\hbar^2}{2I_0} J(J + 1) - \frac{\hbar^4}{2I_0^2 k R_0^2} J^2(J + 1)^2 + \cdots \qquad (10\text{-}38)$$

where $I_0 = \mu R_0^2$ and where we have neglected the term in $J^3(J + 1)^3$. It is customary to write Eq. 10-38 in units of wave numbers by dividing by hc.

$$\bar{E}_J \equiv \frac{E_J}{hc} = \bar{B}J(J + 1) - \bar{D}J^2(J + 1)^2 \qquad (10\text{-}39)$$

where $\bar{D}$ is defined by this equation. The quantity $\bar{D}$ is called the *centrifugal distortion constant*. Rigid rotator and nonrigid rotator energy levels are sketched in Figure 10-5.

EXAMPLE 10-7
  Show that

$$\bar{D} = \frac{4\bar{B}^3}{\bar{\nu}^2} \qquad (10\text{-}40)$$

where $\bar{\nu}$ is the fundamental vibrational frequency in wave numbers, or

$$\bar{\nu} = \frac{1}{2\pi c} \left(\frac{k}{\mu} \right)^{1/2}$$

Solution: After dividing Eq. 10-38 by hc, we find that

$$\bar{D} = \frac{h^3}{32\pi^4 I_0^2 ckR_0^2}$$

But this can be written as

$$\bar{D} = 4\left(\frac{h}{8\pi^2 I_0 c}\right)^3 \left(\frac{4\pi^2 c^2 \mu}{k}\right)$$

$$= \frac{4\bar{B}^3}{\bar{\nu}^2}$$

Typical values of $\bar{D}$ are much smaller than $\bar{B}$. For example, Table 10-2 shows that $\bar{B} = 10.395\ \text{cm}^{-1}$ and $\bar{D} = 0.0004\ \text{cm}^{-1}$ for $H^{35}Cl$, and so the centrifugal distortion term represents a small correction to the rigid-rotator approximation (cf. Problem 16). The frequencies of the absorption due to $J \to J + 1$ transitions are given by

$$\bar{\nu} = \bar{E}_{J+1} - \bar{E}_J$$

$$= 2\bar{B}(J + 1) - 4\bar{D}(J + 1)^3 \qquad J = 0, 1, 2, \ldots \qquad (10\text{-}41)$$

The predictions of this equation are given in Table 10-2.

10-8   *Overtones Are Observed in Vibrational Spectra*

Thus far we have treated the vibrational motion of a diatomic molecule by means of a harmonic-oscillator model. We saw in Chapter 5, however, that the internuclear potential energy is not a simple parabola but is more like that illustrated in Figure 5-5 (cf. also Figure 10-6). The dashed line in either of these figures depicts the harmonic oscillator. Recall from Section 5-4 (Eq. 5-29) that the potential energy $U(R)$ may be expanded in a Taylor series about R_e, the value of R at the minimum of $U(R)$, to give

$$U(R) - U(R_e) = \frac{1}{2!}\left(\frac{d^2 U}{dR^2}\right)_{R=R_e} (R - R_e)^2 + \frac{1}{3!}\left(\frac{d^3 U}{dR^3}\right)_{R=R_e} (R - R_e)^3 + \cdots$$

$$= \frac{k}{2}x^2 + \frac{\gamma_3}{6}x^3 + \frac{\gamma_4}{24}x^4 + \cdots \qquad (10\text{-}42)$$

where x is the displacement of the nuclei from their equilibrium separation, k is the force constant, and $\gamma_j \equiv (d^j U/dR^j)_{R=R_e}$.

The harmonic-oscillator approximation consists of keeping only the quadratic term in Eq. 10-42. The harmonic-oscillator approximation predicts that there be only one line in the vibrational spectrum of a diatomic molecule. Experimentally it is found that there is indeed one dominant line (called the *fundamental*), but in addition there are lines of weaker intensity at almost integral

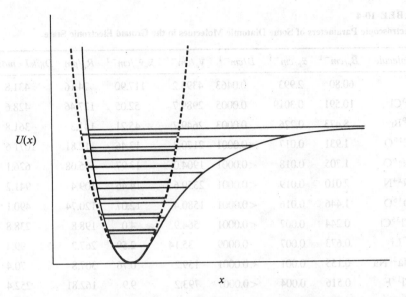

$U(x)$

x

Figure 10-6. The energy states of a harmonic oscillator and an anharmonic oscillator superimposed on a harmonic-oscillator potential and a more realistic internuclear potential.

multiples of the fundamental. These lines are called *overtones* (Table 10-3). If the anharmonic terms in Eq. 10-42 are included in the Hamiltonian operator for the vibrational motion of a diatomic molecule, then the Schrödinger equation can be solved by perturbation theory to give

$$E_n = \bar{v}_e(n + \tfrac{1}{2}) - \bar{x}_e\bar{v}_e(n + \tfrac{1}{2})^2 + \cdots \qquad n = 0, 1, 2, \ldots \qquad (10\text{-}43)$$

where $\bar{x}_e$ is called the *anharmonicity constant*. The anharmonic correction in Eq. 10-43 is much smaller than the harmonic term because $\bar{x}_e \ll 1$ (cf. Table 10-4 and Problem 21).

TABLE 10-3
The Vibrational Spectrum of $H^{35}Cl$

		$\bar{v}_{calc}/cm^{-1}$	
Transition	$\bar{v}_{obs}/cm^{-1}$	Harmonic oscillator $\bar{v} = 2885.90n$	Anharmonic oscillator $\bar{v} = 2988.90n - 51.60n(n+1)$
$0 \to 1$ (fundamental)	2885.9	2885.9	2885.7
$0 \to 2$ (first overtone)	5668.0	5771.8	5668.2
$0 \to 3$ (second overtone)	8347.0	8657.7	8347.5
$0 \to 4$ (third overtone)	10,923.1	11,543.6	10,923.6
$0 \to 5$ (fourth overtone)	13,396.5	14,429.5	13,396.5

TABLE 10-4

Spectroscopic Parameters of Some Diatomic Molecules in the Ground Electronic State

Molecule	$\bar{B}_e/cm^{-1}$	$\bar{\alpha}_e/cm^{-1}$	$\bar{D}/cm^{-1}$	$\bar{v}_e/cm^{-1}$	$\bar{x}_e\bar{v}_e/cm^{-1}$	R_e/pm	$D_0/kJ\cdot mol^{-1}$
H_2	60.80	2.993	0.0463	4395.2	117.90	74.16	431.8
$H^{35}Cl$	10.591	0.3019	0.0005	2989.7	52.05	127.46	428.6
$H^{79}Br$	8.473	0.226	0.0003	2649.7	45.21	141.3	361.8
$^{12}C^{16}O$	1.931	0.017	<0.0001	2170.2	13.46	112.81	1071.6
$^{14}N^{16}O$	1.705	0.018	<0.0001	1904.0	13.97	115.08	626.1
$^{14}N^{14}N$	2.010	0.019	<0.0001	2359.6	14.46	109.4	941.2
$^{16}O^{16}O$	1.446	0.016	<0.0001	1580.4	12.07	120.74	490.1
$^{35}Cl^{35}Cl$	0.244	0.002	<0.0001	564.9	4.0	198.8	238.8
$^7Li^7Li$	0.673	0.007	0.0009	35.14	2.59	267.2	99.4
$^{23}Na^{23}Na$	0.155	0.001	<0.0001	159.2	0.76	307.8	70.4
$^{35}Cl^{19}F$	0.516	0.004	<0.0001	793.2	9.9	162.81	252.4
^{23}NaH	4.901	0.135	<0.0001	1172.2	19.72	188.73	202

Figures 10-6 and 10-7 show the levels given by Eq. 10-43. Notice that the levels are not equally spaced as they are for a harmonic oscillator and, in fact, that their separation decreases with increasing n. For larger energies, the amplitude of vibration is larger than that of the harmonic-oscillator approximation and so the energy is less than the corresponding harmonic-oscillator energy (Figure 10-6). [Recall from the simple model of a particle in a box (Section 3.5) that the energy is inversely proportional to the distance over which the particle can move (Problem 28)]. Notice also from Figure 10-6 that the harmonic-oscillator approximation is best for small values of n, which are the most important values at room temperature.

The selection rule for an anharmonic oscillator is that Δn can have any integral value, although the intensities of the $\Delta n = \pm 2, \pm 3, \ldots$ transitions are much less than for the $\Delta n = \pm 1$ transitions. If we recognize that most diatomic molecules are in the ground vibrational state at room temperature, then the frequencies of the observed $0 \rightarrow n$ transitions will be given by

$$\bar{v}_{obs} = \bar{E}_n - \bar{E}_0 = \bar{v}_e n - \bar{x}_e\bar{v}_e n(n + 1) \qquad n = 1, 2, \ldots \qquad (10\text{-}44)$$

The application of Eq. 10-44 to the spectrum of $H^{35}Cl$ is given in Table 10-3. It can be seen that the agreement with experimental data is a substantial improvement over the harmonic-oscillator approximation.

EXAMPLE 10-8

Given that $\bar{v}_e = 536.10 \text{ cm}^{-1}$ and $\bar{x}_e\bar{v}_e = 3.83 \text{ cm}^{-1}$ for $^{23}Na^{19}F$, calculate the frequencies of the first and second overtones of the $0 \rightarrow 1$ transition.

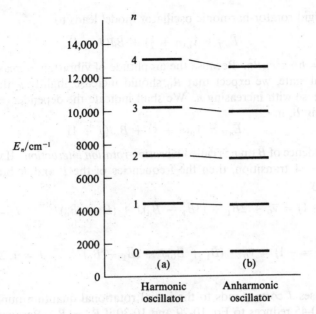

Figure 10-7. The vibrational energy states of $H^{35}Cl(g)$ calculated (a) in the harmonic-oscillator approximation and (b) with a correction for anharmonicity.

Solution: We use Eq. 10-44:

$$\bar{\nu}_{obs} = \bar{\nu}_e n - \bar{x}_e \bar{\nu}_e n(n + 1) \qquad n = 1, 2, \ldots$$

The fundamental is given by letting $n = 1$ and the first two overtones are given by letting $n = 2$ and 3.

Fundamental: $\bar{\nu}_{obs} = \bar{\nu}_e - 2\bar{x}_e\bar{\nu}_e = 528.44$ cm^{-1}

First overtone: $\bar{\nu}_{obs} = 2\bar{\nu}_e - 6\bar{x}_e\bar{\nu}_e = 1049.22$ cm^{-1}

Second overtone: $\bar{\nu}_{obs} = 3\bar{\nu}_e - 12\bar{x}_e\bar{\nu}_e = 1562.34$ cm^{-1}

Note that the overtones are not integral multiples of the fundamental frequency.

10-9   *Vibration-Rotation Interaction Accounts for the Unequal Spacing of the Lines in the P Branch and R Branch of a Vibration-Rotation Spectrum*

Although the extensions that we have considered in Sections 10-7 and 10-8 are important for pure rotational and vibrational spectra, there is another extension that is more important for vibrational-rotational spectra. Recall that the rigid rotator-harmonic oscillator model leads to

$$\bar{E}_{n,J} = \bar{v}_0(n + \tfrac{1}{2}) + \bar{B}J(J + 1)$$

where $\bar{B} = h/8\pi^2 c\mu R_0^2$. Because the amplitude of vibration increases with the vibrational state, we expect that R_0 should increase slightly with n, causing $\bar{B}$ to decrease with increasing n. We shall indicate the dependence of $\bar{B}$ upon n by writing $\bar{B}_n$ in

$$\bar{E}_{n,J} = \bar{v}_0(n + \tfrac{1}{2}) + \bar{B}_n J(J + 1)$$

The dependence of $\bar{B}$ on n is called *vibration-rotation interaction.* If we consider an $n = 0 \to 1$ transition, then the frequencies of the P and R branches will be given by

$$\bar{v}_R(\Delta J = +1) = \bar{v}_0 + 2\bar{B}_1 + (3\bar{B}_1 - \bar{B}_0)J + (\bar{B}_1 - \bar{B}_0)J^2 \qquad J = 0, 1, 2, \ldots$$
$$(10\text{-}45\text{a})$$

$$\bar{v}_P(\Delta J = -1) = \bar{v}_0 - (\bar{B}_1 + \bar{B}_0)J + (\bar{B}_1 - \bar{B}_0)J^2 \qquad J = 1, 2, 3, \ldots$$
$$(10\text{-}45\text{b})$$

In both cases J corresponds to the initial rotational quantum number. Note that Eq. 10-45 reduces to Eq. 10-29 and 10-30 if $\bar{B}_1 = \bar{B}_0$. Because $\bar{B}_1 < \bar{B}_0$, the spacing between the lines in the R branch decrease and the spacing between the lines in the P branch increase with increasing J. This behavior can be seen in Figure 10-3.

EXAMPLE 10-9

The lines in the R and P branches are labeled by the initial value of the rotational quantum number giving rise to the lines. Thus, the lines given by Eq. 10-45a are $R(0)$, $R(1)$, $R(2)$, ... and those given by Eq. 10-45b are $P(1)$, $P(2)$, ... Given the following data,

Line	Frequency/cm^{-1}
$R(0)$	4178.98
$R(1)$	4218.32
$P(1)$	4096.88
$P(2)$	4054.12

calculate $\bar{B}_0$ and $\bar{B}_1$ and R_0 and R_1. Take the reduced mass of the molecule to be 1.58×10^{-27} kg.

Solution: Using Eq. 10-45a with $J = 0$ and 1 and Eq. 10-45b with $J = 1$ and 2, we have

$$\left.\begin{array}{l} 4178.98 \text{ cm}^{-1} = \bar{v}_0 + 2\bar{B}_1 \\ 4218.32 \text{ cm}^{-1} = \bar{v}_0 + 6\bar{B}_1 - 2\bar{B}_0 \end{array}\right\} R \text{ branch}$$

and

$$4096.88 \text{ cm}^{-1} = \bar{v}_0 - 2\bar{B}_0$$
$$4054.12 \text{ cm}^{-1} = \bar{v}_0 + 2\bar{B}_1 - 6\bar{B}_0 \bigg\} P \text{ branch}$$

If we subtract the first line of the P branch from the second line of the R branch, we find

$$121.44 \text{ cm}^{-1} = 6\bar{B}_1$$

or $\bar{B}_1 = 20.24 \text{ cm}^{-1}$. If we subtract the second line of the P branch from the first line of the R branch, we find

$$124.86 \text{ cm}^{-1} = 6\bar{B}_0$$

or $\bar{B}_0 = 20.81 \text{ cm}^{-1}$. Using the fact that $\bar{B}_n = h/8\pi^2 c\mu R_n^2$, we obtain $R_0 = 92.3$ pm and $R_1 = 93.6$ pm.

The dependence of $\bar{B}_n$ on n is usually expressed as

$$\bar{B}_n = \bar{B}_e - \bar{\alpha}_e(n + \tfrac{1}{2}) \tag{10-46}$$

Values of $\bar{B}_e$ and $\bar{\alpha}_e$ as well as other spectroscopic parameters of some diatomic molecules are given in Table 10-4.

10-10 *The Vibrations of Polyatomic Molecules Are Represented by Normal Coordinates*

Up to this point we have considered only diatomic molecules in this chapter. The rotational spectra of (nonlinear) polyatomic molecules are somewhat complex even in the rigid-rotator approximation, but the vibrational spectra turn out to be easily understood in the harmonic-oscillator approximation. The key point is the introduction of normal coordinates, which we discuss in this section.

Consider a molecule containing N nuclei. A complete specification of this molecule in space requires $3N$ coordinates, three Cartesian coordinates for each nucleus. We say that the N-atomic molecule has a total of $3N$ *degrees of freedom*. Of these $3N$ coordinates, three can be used to specify the center of mass of the molecule. Motion along these three coordinates corresponds to translational motion of the center of mass of the molecule, and so we call these three coordinates *translational degrees of freedom*. It requires two coordinates to specify the orientation of a linear molecule about its center of mass and three coordinates to specify the orientation of a nonlinear molecule about its center of mass. Because motion along these coordinates corresponds to rotational motion, we say that a linear molecule has two *degrees of rotational freedom* and that a nonlinear molecule has three degrees of rotational freedom. The remaining coordinates ($3N - 5$ for a linear molecule and $3N - 6$ for a nonlinear molecule) specify the relative positions of the N nuclei. Because motion along these coordinates corresponds to vibrational motion, we say

TABLE 10-5

**The Number of Various Degrees of Freedom
of a Polyatomic Molecule Containing N Atoms**

	Linear	Nonlinear
Translational degrees of freedom	3	3
Rotational degrees of freedom	2	3
Vibrational degrees of freedom	$3N - 5$	$3N - 6$

that a linear molecule has $3N - 5$ *vibrational degrees of freedom* and that a nonlinear molecule has $3N - 6$ vibrational degrees of freedom. These results are summarized in Table 10-5.

EXAMPLE 10-10

Determine the number of various degrees of freedom of HCl, CO_2, H_2O, NH_3, and CH_4.

Solution:

	Total	Translational	Rotational	Vibrational
HCl	6	3	2	1
CO_2 (linear)	9	3	2	4
H_2O	9	3	3	3
NH_3	12	3	3	6
CH_4	15	3	3	9

The potential energy of a polyatomic molecule is a function of the $3N - 5$ or $3N - 6$ vibrational coordinates. If we let the displacements about the equilibrium values of these coordinates be denoted by $q_1, q_2, \ldots, q_{N_{vib}}$, then the potential energy is

$$\Delta U \equiv U(q_1, q_2, \ldots, q_{N_{vib}}) - U(0, 0, \ldots, 0) = \frac{1}{2} \sum_{i=1}^{N_{vib}} \sum_{j=1}^{N_{vib}} \left(\frac{\partial^2 U}{\partial q_i \, \partial q_j} \right) q_i q_j + \cdots$$

$$= \frac{1}{2} \sum_{i=1}^{N_{vib}} \sum_{j=1}^{N_{vib}} f_{ij} q_i q_j + \cdots \tag{10-47}$$

The presence of the cross terms in Eq. 10-47 makes the solution of the corresponding Schrödinger equation very difficult to obtain. There is a theorem of classical mechanics, however, that allows us to eliminate all the cross terms. The details are too specialized to go into here, but there is a straightforward procedure using matrix algebra that can be used to find a new set of coordinates $\{Q_j\}$, such that

$$\Delta U = \frac{1}{2} \sum_{j=1}^{N_{\text{vib}}} F_j Q_j^2 \qquad (10\text{-}48)$$

Note that there are no cross terms in this expression. These new coordinates are called *normal coordinates* or *normal modes*. In terms of normal coordinates, the vibrational Hamiltonian operator is

$$\hat{H}_{\text{vib}} = -\sum_{j=1}^{N_{\text{vib}}} \frac{\hbar^2}{2\mu_j} \frac{d^2}{dQ_j^2} + \frac{1}{2} \sum_{j=1}^{N_{\text{vib}}} F_j Q_j^2 \qquad (10\text{-}49)$$

Recall from Section 6-2 that if a Hamiltonian operator can be written as a sum of independent terms, then the wave function is a product and the energy is a sum of independent energies. Applying this to Eq. 10-49, we have

$$\hat{H}_{\text{vib}} = \sum_{j=1}^{N_{\text{vib}}} \hat{H}_{\text{vib}, j} = \sum_{j=1}^{N_{\text{vib}}} \left(-\frac{\hbar^2}{2\mu_j} \frac{d^2}{dQ_j^2} + \frac{1}{2} F_j Q_j^2 \right)$$

$$\psi_{\text{vib}}(Q_1, Q_2, \dots, Q_{N_{\text{vib}}}) = \prod_{j=1}^{N_{\text{vib}}} \psi_{\text{vib}, j}(Q_j) \qquad (10\text{-}50)$$

and

$$E_{\text{vib}} = \sum_{j=1}^{N_{\text{vib}}} h\nu_j(n_j + \tfrac{1}{2}) \qquad \text{each } n_j = 0, 1, 2, \dots \qquad (10\text{-}51)$$

The practical consequence of Eqs. 10-49 through 10-51 is that under the harmonic-oscillator approximation, the vibrational motion of a polyatomic molecule appears as N_{vib} independent harmonic oscillators, each with its own characteristic fundamental frequency ν_j. For example, H_2O has three degrees of vibrational freedom and so has three normal modes:

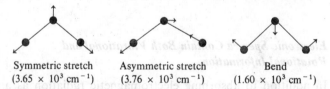

Symmetric stretch   Asymmetric stretch   Bend
($3.65 \times 10^3 \text{ cm}^{-1}$)   ($3.76 \times 10^3 \text{ cm}^{-1}$)   ($1.60 \times 10^3 \text{ cm}^{-1}$)

The dipole moment varies in each of these normal modes and so there are three fundamental lines in the infrared spectrum of $H_2O(g)$. The three normal modes of $H_2O(g)$ are said to be *infrared active*. For CO_2, there are four normal modes:

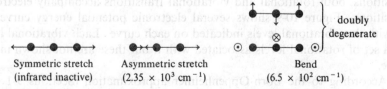

doubly
degenerate

Symmetric stretch   Asymmetric stretch   Bend
(infrared inactive)   ($2.35 \times 10^3 \text{ cm}^{-1}$)   ($6.5 \times 10^2 \text{ cm}^{-1}$)

There is no change in dipole moment during the symmetric stretch of CO_2 and so this mode does not lead to absorption in the infrared. This mode is

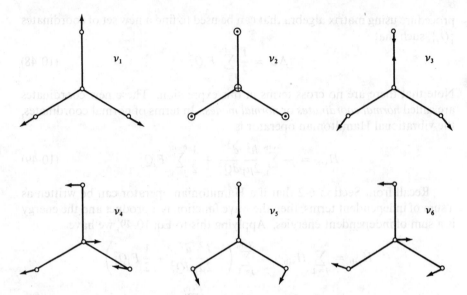

Figure 10-8. The normal modes of a planar XY_3 molecule. All the normal modes are nondegenerate, giving a total of $3N - 6 = 6$ normal modes.

said to be *infrared inactive*. Even though the permanent dipole moment of CO_2 is zero when the nuclei are in their equilibrium positions, the asymmetric stretch and bending modes lead to an oscillating dipole. Although CO_2 has four normal modes, there are only two fundamental lines in its infrared spectrum. The normal coordinates of a few other molecules are illustrated in Figure 10-8.

10-11   *Electronic Spectra Contain Both Vibrational and Rotational Information*

In addition to absorbing electromagnetic radiation as a result of rotational and vibrational transitions, molecules can absorb electromagnetic radiation as a result of electronic transitions. The difference in energies between electronic levels are usually such that the radiation absorbed falls in the visible or ultraviolet regions. Just as rotational transitions accompany vibrational transitions, both rotational and vibrational transitions accompany electronic transitions. Figure 10-9 shows several electronic potential energy curves of O_2 with the vibrational levels indicated on each curve. Each vibrational level has a set of rotational levels associated with it but these are not shown in the figure.

According to the Born-Oppenheimer approximation (Sections 9-1 and 10-12), the electronic energy is independent of the vibrational-rotational energy. If we use the anharmonic oscillator-rigid rotator approximation, the total

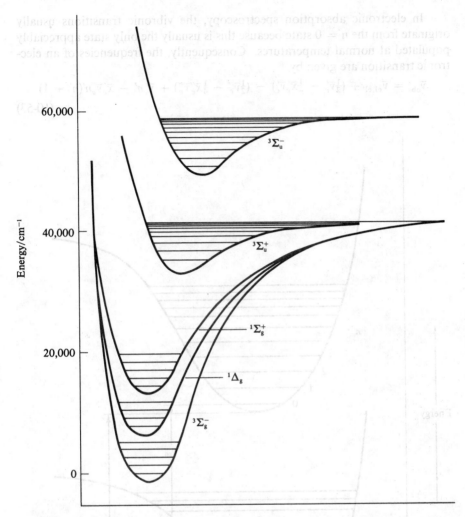

Figure 10-9. A potential energy diagram of O_2, showing the vibrational states associated with the various electronic states.

energy of a diatomic molecule, excluding translational energy, is

$$\bar{E}_{\text{total}} = \bar{v}_{\text{el}} + \bar{v}_e(n + \tfrac{1}{2}) - \bar{x}_e\bar{v}_e(n + \tfrac{1}{2})^2 + \bar{B}J(J + 1) \qquad (10\text{-}52)$$

where $\bar{v}_{\text{el}}$ is the energy at the minimum of the electronic potential energy curve. The selection rule for *vibronic transitions* (vibrational transitions in electronic spectra) allows Δn to take on any integral value, unlike the case of vibrational-rotational transitions where $\Delta n = \pm 1$. Because rotational energies are usually much smaller than vibrational energies, we shall first ignore the rotational term in Eq. 10-52 and investigate only the vibrational substructure of electronic spectra.

In electronic absorption spectroscopy, the vibronic transitions usually originate from the $n = 0$ state because this is usually the only state appreciably populated at normal temperatures. Consequently, the frequencies of an electronic transition are given by

$$\bar{\nu}_{obs} = \bar{\nu}_{el,el} + (\tfrac{1}{2}\bar{\nu}'_e - \tfrac{1}{4}\bar{x}'_e\bar{\nu}'_e) - (\tfrac{1}{2}\bar{\nu}''_e - \tfrac{1}{4}\bar{x}''_e\bar{\nu}''_e) + \bar{\nu}'_e n' - \bar{x}'_e\bar{\nu}'_e n'(n' + 1)$$

$$(10\text{-}53)$$

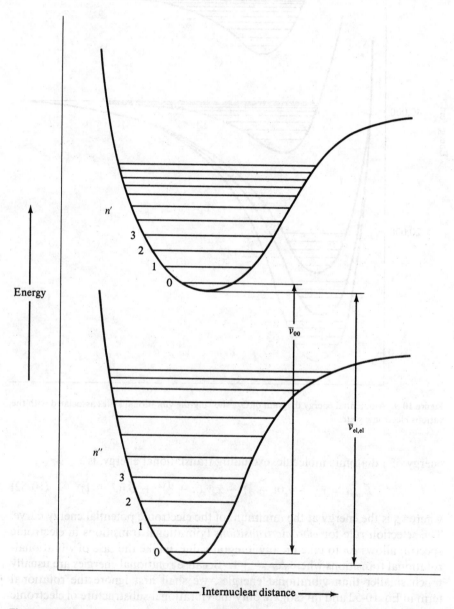

Figure 10-10. Two electronic states of a diatomic molecule, illustrating the two quantities $\bar{\nu}_{el,el}$ and $\bar{\nu}_{00}$.

The term $\bar{v}_{el,el}$ is the difference in energies of the minima of the two electronic potential energy curves (cf. Figure 10-10) and the single primes and double primes indicate the upper electronic state and lower electronic state, respectively. Realize that $\bar{v}_e$ and $\bar{x}_e\bar{v}_e$ depend on the shape of the electronic potential energy curve at its minimum and so should differ for each electronic state.

The two terms in parentheses in Eq. 10-53 are the zero-point energies of the upper and lower states. Therefore, the quantity $\bar{v}_{00}$ defined by

$$\bar{v}_{00} = \bar{v}_{el,\,el} + (\tfrac{1}{2}\bar{v}_e' - \tfrac{1}{4}\bar{x}_e'\bar{v}_e') - (\tfrac{1}{2}\bar{v}_e'' - \tfrac{1}{4}\bar{x}_e''\bar{v}_e'')$$

corresponds to the energy of the $0 \to 0$ vibronic transition. Introducing $\bar{v}_{00}$ into Eq. 10-53, we obtain

$$\bar{v}_{obs} = \bar{v}_{00} + \bar{v}_e'n' - \bar{x}_e'\bar{v}_e'n'(n' + 1) \qquad n' = 0, 1, 2, \ldots \qquad (10\text{-}54)$$

As n' takes on successive values in Eq. 10-54, the vibronic spacing becomes progressively smaller, until the spectrum is essentially continuous as shown in Figures 10-11 and 10-12. Example 10-11 illustrates how experimental data like that in Figure 10-12 can be used to determine the vibrational parameters of excited electronic states.

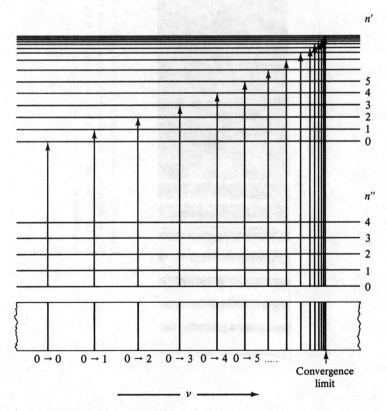

Figure 10-11. The electronic spectrum due to $n'' = 0$ to $n' = 0, 1, 2, \ldots$, transitions. Such a set of transitions is called an n' progression.

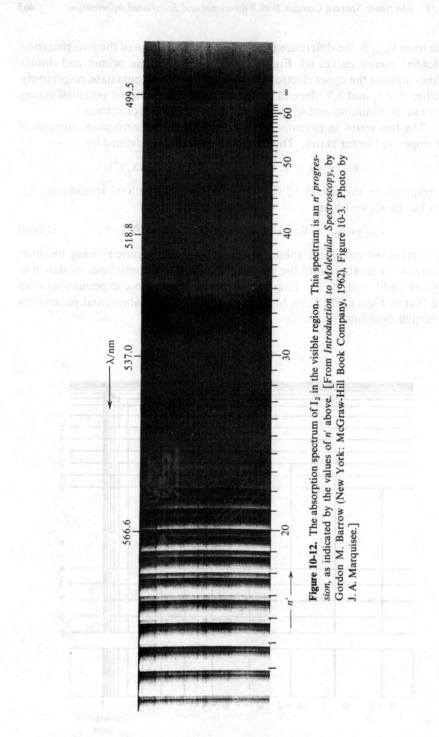

λ/nm

499.5 518.8 537.0 566.5

n' →

Figure 10-12. The absorption spectrum of I_2 in the visible region. This spectrum is an n' *progression*, as indicated by the values of n' above. [From *Introduction to Molecular Spectroscopy*, by Gordon M. Barrow (New York: McGraw-Hill Book Company, 1962), Figure 10-3. Photo by J. A. Marquisee.]

EXAMPLE 10-11

The frequencies of the first few vibronic transitions to an excited electronic state of PN follow:

Vibronic transition	$\bar{\nu}_{obs}/cm^{-1}$
$0 \rightarrow 0$	39,699.10
$0 \rightarrow 1$	40,786.80
$0 \rightarrow 2$	41,858.90

Use these data to calculate $\bar{\nu}_e$ and $\bar{x}_e\bar{\nu}_e$ for the excited electronic state of PN.

Solution: Using Eq. 10-54 with $n' = 0, 1,$ and 2, we have

$$39,699.10 = \bar{\nu}_{00}$$

$$40,786.80 = \bar{\nu}_{00} + \bar{\nu}'_e - 2\bar{x}'_e\bar{\nu}'_e$$

$$41,858.90 = \bar{\nu}_{00} + 2\bar{\nu}'_e - 6\bar{x}'_e\bar{\nu}'_e$$

By subtracting the first equation from the second and third, we find

$$1087.70 \text{ cm}^{-1} = \bar{\nu}'_e - 2\bar{x}'_e\bar{\nu}'_e$$

$$2159.80 \text{ cm}^{-1} = 2\bar{\nu}'_e - 6\bar{x}'_e\bar{\nu}'_e$$

Solving these two equations for $\bar{\nu}'_e$ and $\bar{x}'_e\bar{\nu}'_e$, we find

$$\bar{\nu}'_e = 1103.3 \text{ cm}^{-1} \qquad \bar{x}'_e\bar{\nu}'_e = 7.80 \text{ cm}^{-1}$$

Analysis of electronic spectra yields structural information of excited electronic states that would be difficult to obtain otherwise.

Figure 10-13 shows part of the emission spectrum of N_2. An examination of the spectrum in Figure 10-13 shows that each vibronic transition has a substructure that is due to accompanying rotational transitions. This rotational fine structure is shown in Figure 10-14. For a given vibronic band, Eq. 10-52 gives

$$\bar{\nu}_{obs} = \bar{\nu}_{el, vib} + [\bar{B}'J'(J' + 1) - \bar{B}''J''(J'' + 1)]$$

where, once again, the single primes and double primes denote upper and lower states, respectively. The rotational selection rules depend on the electronic states involved. For electronic transitions between $^1\Sigma$ states (cf. Section 9-15), $\Delta J = \pm 1$. The frequencies for the $R(\Delta J = +1)$ and $P(\Delta J = -1)$ branches are

$$\bar{\nu}_R(\Delta J = +1) = \bar{\nu}_{el, vib} + 2\bar{B}' + (3\bar{B}' - \bar{B}'')J + (\bar{B}' - \bar{B}'')J^2 \qquad J = 0, 1, 2, \ldots \quad (10\text{-}55)$$

$$\bar{\nu}_P(\Delta J = -1) = \bar{\nu}_{el, vib} - (\bar{B}' + \bar{B}'')J + (\bar{B}' - \bar{B}'')J^2 \qquad J = 1, 2, 3, \ldots \quad (10\text{-}56)$$

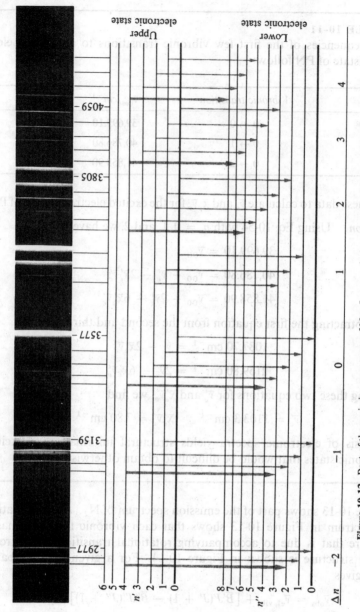

Figure 10-13. Part of the emission spectrum of N_2. In an emission spectrum, the transitions occur from the upper electronic state to the lower electronic state. The indicated wavelengths are in angstrom units. [From *Introduction to Molecular Spectroscopy* by Gordon M. Barrow (New York: McGraw-Hill Book Company, 1962), Figure 10-4. Photo by J. A. Marquisee.]

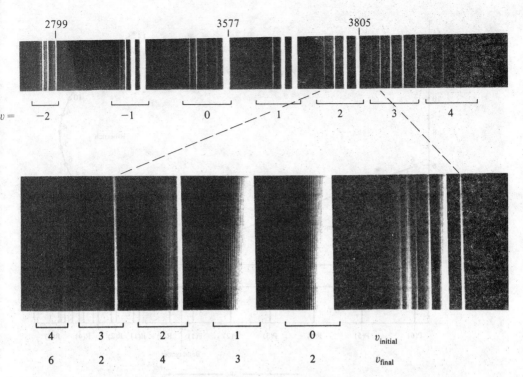

Figure 10-14. The rotational fine structure in the emission spectrum of N_2. The indicated wavelengths are in angstrom units. [From *Advanced Physical Chemistry* by Jeff C. Davis (New York: Ronald Press, 1965). Photo by J. A. Marquisee. Reprinted by permission of John Wiley & Sons, Inc.]

These equations are similar to the equations for the vibrational-rotational spectra (Eqs. 10-45), but there is a significant difference. The equilibrium nuclear separations in different electronic states are often quite different, and so $\bar{B}'$ and $\bar{B}''$ can also be quite different. In most cases, the equilibrium nuclear separation is greater for an excited electronic state than for the ground electronic state, and thus $\bar{B}' < \bar{B}''$. The quadratic term in Eq. 10-55 is negative, causing the R branch to reverse in direction toward lower frequencies for large J. In the P branch, the frequencies simply decrease in a nonlinear fashion as J increases. This behavior is shown in Figure 10-15. A plot of J versus $\bar{\nu}_{obs}$ for the R and P branches, as in Figure 10-15, is called a *Fortrat diagram*. The frequency at which the reversal in the R branch occurs is called the *band head*. Figure 10-16 shows an experimental observation of a band head in the spectrum of CuH.

The analysis of electronic spectra provides an exceedingly rich view of molecular structure. As we have seen, structural information of excited electronic states as well as ground electronic states can be obtained. In addition, the selection rules do not require the molecule to have a permanent dipole moment, nor must there be a change in dipole moment upon vibration. Thus,

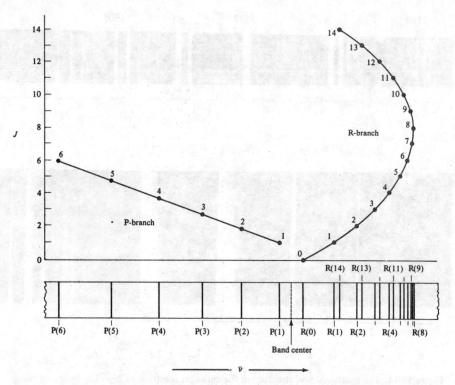

Figure 10-15. A Fortrat diagram, which is a plot of J versus $\bar{\nu}_R$ and $\bar{\nu}_P$ from Eqs. 10-55 and 10-56. Note the occurrence of the band head in the R branch. The band head occurs because $\bar{B}' < \bar{B}''$.

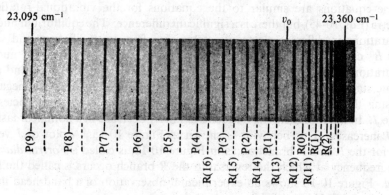

Figure 10-16. The fine structure of the CuH band at 4280 nm, showing the band head in the R branch as depicted in Figure 10-15. [From *Molecular Spectra and Molecular Structure, I. Spectra of Diatomic Molecules* by Gerhard Herzberg (Princeton, N.J.: D. Van Nostrand, 1950.]

electronic spectroscopy yields information about homonuclear diatomic molecules (such as I_2 in Figure 10-12) that cannot be obtained from either rotational or vibrational spectroscopy. All the parameters given in Table 10-4 can be obtained from electronic spectra.

10-12   *The Born-Oppenheimer Approximation Factors a Molecular Wave Function into an Electronic Part and a Nuclear Part*

In the remainder of this chapter we shall discuss the basis of the spectroscopic material that we have covered thus far. Up to now we have introduced rotational, vibrational, and electronic spectroscopy as somewhat separate topics. In this section we shall show how a total molecular Schrödinger equation can be approximately separated into an equation for the motion of the electrons and a separate equation for the motion of the nuclei. In Section 10-13, we shall show how the equation for the nuclear motion may be further separated into an equation for rotational motion and one for vibrational motion.

Let us consider H_2 for simplicity. The molecular Schrödinger equation for H_2 is

$$\hat{H}\psi(\mathbf{r}_1, \mathbf{r}_2, \mathbf{R}_A, \mathbf{R}_B) = E\psi(\mathbf{r}_1, \mathbf{r}_2, \mathbf{R}_A, \mathbf{R}_B) \tag{10-57}$$

where $\hat{H}$ is given by Eq. 9-1:

$$\hat{H} = -\frac{\hbar^2}{2M}\left(\nabla_A^2 + \nabla_B^2\right) - \frac{\hbar^2}{2m}\left(\nabla_1^2 + \nabla_2^2\right) - \frac{e^2}{4\pi\varepsilon_0 r_{1A}}$$

$$-\frac{e^2}{4\pi\varepsilon_0 r_{1B}} - \frac{e^2}{4\pi\varepsilon_0 r_{2A}} - \frac{e^2}{4\pi\varepsilon_0 r_{2B}} + \frac{e^2}{4\pi\varepsilon_0 r_{12}} + \frac{e^2}{4\pi\varepsilon_0 R}$$

We argued at the beginning of Chapter 9 that because the nuclei are so much more massive than the electrons, the electrons adjust essentially instantaneously to any motion of the nuclei. Thus we may consider the nuclei to be fixed at some internuclear separation R and solve the electronic Schrödinger equation with R as a parameter. The electronic Schrödinger equation is simply

$$\hat{H}_{el}\psi_{el}(\mathbf{r}_1, \mathbf{r}_2; R) = E_{el}(R)\psi_{el}(\mathbf{r}_1, \mathbf{r}_2; R) \tag{10-58}$$

where $\hat{H}_{el}$ is given by Eq. 9-1 without the first term, which represents the kinetic energy of the two nuclei, now considered to be fixed. In Eq. 10-58 the notation emphasizes the dependence on the nuclear separation R as a parameter. The electronic energies $E_{el}(R)$ will be functions of R similar to those shown in Figure 10-9 for the first few electronic states.

A systematic treatment of a molecular Schrödinger equation assumes that

$$\psi(\mathbf{r}_1, \mathbf{r}_2, \mathbf{R}_A, \mathbf{R}_B) \approx \psi_{el}(\mathbf{r}_1, \mathbf{r}_2; R)\psi_n(\mathbf{R}_A, \mathbf{R}_B) \tag{10-59}$$

If Eq. 10-59 is substituted into Eq. 10-57 and terms of order m/M are neglected, then two separate equations can be obtained (Problem 37). One of these equations represents the motion of the electrons and is identical with Eq. 10-58. The other represents the motion of the nuclei and is

$$-\frac{\hbar^2}{2M}(\nabla_A^2 + \nabla_B^2)\psi_n(\mathbf{R}_A, \mathbf{R}_B) + E_{\text{el}}(R)\psi_n(\mathbf{R}_A, \mathbf{R}_B) = E\psi_n(\mathbf{R}_A, \mathbf{R}_B) \quad (10\text{-}60)$$

Notice that the nuclei move in the potential energy $E_{\text{el}}(R)$ set up by the electrons. The approximate separation of a molecular Schrödinger equation such as Eq. 10-57 into one for the electronic motion (Eq. 10-58) and one for the nuclear motion (Eq. 10-60) is called the *Born-Oppenheimer approximation*. The essence of the Born-Oppenheimer approximation is Eq. 10-59, which assumes that the complete molecular wave function can be factored into an electronic part and a nuclear part. Although we have discussed the application of the Born-Oppenheimer equation only to the case of H_2, its extension to other molecules is straightforward.

10-13　*The Schrödinger Equation for Nuclear Motion Can Be Factored Approximately into a Rotational Part and a Vibrational Part*

Equation 10-60 can be simplified further by introducing center-of-mass and relative coordinates. Under this transformation the problem separates into one for the translational motion and one for the internal motion of the nuclei (Problem 41). The resulting equations are

$$E = E_{\text{trans}} + E_{\text{int}} \quad (10\text{-}61)$$

and

$$\psi_n(\mathbf{R}_A, \mathbf{R}_B) = \psi_{\text{trans}}(\mathbf{R}_{\text{CM}})\psi_{\text{int}}(\mathbf{R}) \quad (10\text{-}62)$$

where ψ_{trans} and ψ_{int} satisfy the separate equations

$$-\frac{\hbar^2}{2M}\nabla_{R_{\text{CM}}}^2\psi_{\text{trans}}(\mathbf{R}_{\text{CM}}) = E_{\text{trans}}\psi_{\text{trans}}(\mathbf{R}_{\text{CM}}) \quad (10\text{-}63)$$

and

$$-\frac{\hbar^2}{2\mu}\nabla_R^2\psi_{\text{int}}(\mathbf{R}) + E_{\text{el}}(R)\psi_{\text{int}}(\mathbf{R}) = E_{\text{int}}\psi_{\text{int}}(\mathbf{R}) \quad (10\text{-}64)$$

In these equations, $\mathbf{R}_{\text{CM}} = (m_1\mathbf{R}_A + m_2\mathbf{R}_B)/M$, $\mathbf{R} = \mathbf{R}_A - \mathbf{R}_B$, $R = |\mathbf{R}_A - \mathbf{R}_B|$, M is the total mass $(m_1 + m_2)$, and μ is the reduced mass. Equation 10-63 is the equation for a free particle or a particle in a box and is of no consequence for spectroscopy. Equation 10-64 represents both the rotational and vibrational motion of the nuclei.

We have already studied an equation very similar to Eq. 10-64 in Section 6-8 (cf. Eq. 6-94). The only difference is the functional form of $E_{\text{el}}(R)$. Following the development in Section 6-8, we introduce spherical coordinates and write

(cf. Eq. 6-96)

$$-\hbar^2 \frac{\partial}{\partial R}\left(R^2 \frac{\partial \psi_{int}}{\partial R}\right) + \hat{L}^2 \psi_{int}(R, \theta, \phi) + 2\mu R^2 [E_{el}(R) - E_{int}]\psi_{int}(R, \theta, \phi) = 0$$

$$(10\text{-}65)$$

Recall that the eigenfunctions of $\hat{L}^2$ are the spherical harmonics (cf. Section 6-6)

$$\hat{L}^2 Y_J^M(\theta, \phi) = \hbar^2 J(J + 1) Y_J^M(\theta, \phi) \qquad (10\text{-}66)$$

This suggests that we write $\psi_{int}(R, \theta, \phi)$ as

$$\psi_{int}(R, \theta, \phi) = \psi_{vib}(R) Y_J^M(\theta, \phi) \qquad (10\text{-}67)$$

If we substitute this into Eq. 10-65, use Eq. 10-66, and divide by $Y_J^M(\theta, \phi)$, then we obtain

$$-\frac{\hbar^2}{2\mu R^2}\frac{d}{dR}\left(R^2\frac{d\psi_{vib}}{dR}\right) + E_{el}(R)\psi_{vib}(R) + \frac{\hbar^2 J(J+1)}{2\mu R^2}\psi_{vib}(R) = E_{int}\psi_{vib}(R) \quad (10\text{-}68)$$

The third term in this equation is the rotational kinetic energy of the molecule. The factor of $\hbar^2 J(J + 1)$ accounts for the fact that the angular momentum of the system is conserved. The rotational energy is not conserved, however, as it varies with R.

Equation 10-68 represents the nuclear motion along the internuclear separation, or vibrational motion. At this point, the rotational and vibrational motions are coupled. We now recognize that the vibrational amplitudes of most diatomic molecules are fairly small and so we replace R in the denominator of the rotational kinetic energy term in Eq. 10-68 by R_e, the equilibrium nuclear separation. By introducing this approximation, then, we have

$$E_{rot} = \frac{\hbar^2 J(J + 1)}{2\mu R_e^2} \qquad (10\text{-}69)$$

and Eq. 10-68 becomes

$$-\frac{\hbar^2}{2\mu R^2}\frac{d}{dR}\left(R^2\frac{d\psi_{vib}}{dR}\right) + E_{el}(R)\psi_{vib}(R) + E_{rot}\psi_{vib}(R) = E_{int}\psi_{vib}(R)$$

$$-\frac{\hbar^2}{2\mu R^2}\frac{d}{dR}\left(R^2\frac{d\psi_{vib}}{dR}\right) + E_{el}(R)\psi_{vib}(R) = (E_{int} - E_{rot})\psi_{vib}(R)$$

$$= E_{vib}\psi_{vib}(R) \qquad (10\text{-}70)$$

Thus far, then, we have

$$E_{int} = E_{vib} + E_{rot}$$

$$\psi_{int}(R, \theta, \phi) = \psi_{vib}(R)\psi_{rot}(\theta, \phi)$$

where $\psi_{rot}(\theta, \phi) = Y_J^M(\theta, \phi)$. If we let $\psi_{vib}(R) = S_{vib}(R)/R$ in Eq. 10-70 and next let $q = R - R_e$, then we find

$$-\frac{\hbar^2}{2\mu}\frac{d^2 S_{\text{vib}}}{dq^2} + E_{\text{el}}(q)S_{\text{vib}}(q) = E_{\text{vib}}S_{\text{vib}}(q) \qquad (10\text{-}71)$$

This is the equation of an anharmonic oscillator in the potential $E_{\text{el}}(q)$. If we expand $E_{\text{el}}(q)$ about $q = 0$ and keep only the quadratic term, we obtain the equation of a harmonic oscillator, and $S_{\text{vib}}(R)$ are the harmonic-oscillator wave functions.

   In summary, by starting with a molecular Schrödinger equation and introducing a series of well-defined approximations, we have shown that

$$E \approx E_{\text{el}} + E_{\text{trans}} + E_{\text{rot}} + E_{\text{vib}} \qquad (10\text{-}72)$$

and that

$$\psi \approx \psi_{\text{el}}\psi_{\text{trans}}\psi_{\text{rot}}\psi_{\text{vib}} \qquad (10\text{-}73)$$

$$\approx \psi_{\text{trans}}(\mathbf{R}_{\text{CM}})\frac{S_{\text{vib}}(R)}{R} Y_J^M(\theta, \phi)\psi_{\text{el}}(\{\mathbf{r}_j\}; R) \qquad (10\text{-}74)$$

where the notation $\{\mathbf{r}_j\}$ in ψ_{el} denotes the set of electron coordinates. By proceeding in a systematic manner, we can introduce corrections for each of these approximations by means of perturbation theory and derive the equations such as Eq. 10-39 and 10-43 for the more refined models. We shall use Eq. 10-74 to determine the selection rules in electronic spectroscopy, but first we must derive formulas for the selection rules. To do this, we must introduce time-dependent perturbation theory.

10-14   *Selection Rules Are Derived from Time-Dependent Perturbation Theory*

   The spectroscopic selection rules determine which transitions from one state to another are possible. The very nature of transitions implies a time-dependent phenomenon, and so we consider the time-dependent Schrödinger equation (Eq. 4-13)

$$\hat{H}\Psi = i\hbar \frac{\partial \Psi}{\partial t} \qquad (10\text{-}75)$$

We showed in Section 4-3 that if $\hat{H}$ does not depend explicitly on time, then

$$\Psi_n(\mathbf{r}, t) = \psi_n(\mathbf{r})e^{-iE_n t/\hbar}$$

where $\psi_n(\mathbf{r})$ satisfies the equation

$$\hat{H}\psi_n(\mathbf{r}) = E_n\psi_n(\mathbf{r})$$

If the system is in a state described by $\psi_n(\mathbf{r})$, then $\Psi_n^*\Psi_n = \psi_n^*\psi_n$ is independent of time. The states described by ψ_n are called *stationary states* (cf. Section 4-3).

   The idea of stationary states applies to isolated systems. Consider now a molecule interacting with electromagnetic radiation. The electromagnetic field may be written approximately as

$$\mathbf{E} = \mathbf{E}_0 \cos 2\pi vt \qquad (10\text{-}76)$$

where v is the frequency of the radiation. If $\boldsymbol{\mu}$ is the dipole moment of the molecule, then the interaction energy is

$$\hat{H}^{(1)} = -\boldsymbol{\mu} \cdot \mathbf{E} = -\boldsymbol{\mu} \cdot \mathbf{E}_0 \cos 2\pi vt \qquad (10\text{-}77)$$

Thus we must solve

$$\hat{H}\Psi = i\hbar \frac{\partial \Psi}{\partial t} \qquad (10\text{-}78)$$

where

$$\hat{H} = \hat{H}_0 - \boldsymbol{\mu} \cdot \mathbf{E}_0 \cos 2\pi vt \qquad (10\text{-}79)$$

and $\hat{H}_0$ is the Hamiltonian of the isolated molecule. We shall see below that the time-dependent term can induce transitions from one stationary state to another.

To solve Eq. 10-78, we shall treat the time-dependent term in $\hat{H}$ as a small perturbation. This procedure is called *time-dependent perturbation theory*. Although an isolated molecule generally has an infinite number of stationary states, for simplicity of notation we shall consider only a two-state system. For such a system

$$\hat{H}_0\Psi = i\hbar \frac{\partial \Psi}{\partial t} \qquad (10\text{-}80)$$

where there are only two stationary states, ψ_1 and ψ_2, with

$$\Psi_1(t) = \psi_1 e^{-iE_1 t/\hbar} \quad \text{and} \quad \Psi_2(t) = \psi_2 e^{-iE_2 t/\hbar}$$

EXAMPLE 10-12

Show that Ψ_1 and Ψ_2 given above satisfy Eq. 10-80.

Solution: Substitute $\Psi_1(t) = \psi_1 e^{-iE_1 t/\hbar}$ into Eq. 10-80:

$$\hat{H}_0\Psi_1 = \hat{H}_0\psi_1 e^{-iE_1 t/\hbar} = E_1 \psi_1 e^{-iE_1 t/\hbar}$$

$$= i\hbar \frac{\partial \Psi_1}{\partial t} = i\hbar\psi_1 \frac{d}{dt} e^{-iE_1 t/\hbar} = E_1 \psi_1 e^{-iE_1 t/\hbar}$$

where we have used the fact that ψ_1 is a stationary state or that $\hat{H}_0\psi_1 = E_1\psi_1$. The proof that Ψ_2 is also a solution is similar.

Assume now that initially the system is in state 1. We let the perturbation begin at $t = 0$ and assume that

$$\Psi(t) = a_1(t)\Psi_1(t) + a_2(t)\Psi_2(t) \qquad (10\text{-}81)$$

where $a_1(t)$ and $a_2(t)$ are to be determined. Because the system is initially in state 1,

$$a_1(0) = 1 \qquad a_2(0) = 0 \tag{10-82}$$

We substitute Eq. 10-81 into Eq. 10-78 to obtain

$$a_1(t)\hat{H}_0\Psi_1 + a_2(t)\hat{H}_0\Psi_2 + a_1(t)\hat{H}^{(1)}\Psi_1 + a_2(t)\hat{H}^{(1)}\Psi_2$$

$$= i\hbar\Psi_1\frac{da_1}{dt} + i\hbar\Psi_2\frac{da_2}{dt} + i\hbar a_1\frac{\partial\Psi_1}{\partial t} + i\hbar a_2\frac{\partial\Psi_2}{\partial t} \tag{10-83}$$

We are able to cancel the terms in Eq. 10-83 because Ψ_1 and Ψ_2 are solutions of Eq. 10-80. Multiply Eq. 10-83 by ψ_2^*, integrate over spatial coordinates, and use the fact that Ψ_1 and Ψ_2 are orthogonal to obtain

$$i\hbar\frac{da_2}{dt} = a_1(t)\exp\left[\frac{-i(E_1 - E_2)t}{\hbar}\right]\int\psi_2^*\hat{H}^{(1)}\psi_1\,d\tau + a_2(t)\int\psi_2^*\hat{H}^{(1)}\psi_2\,d\tau \tag{10-84}$$

From Eq. 10-82, $a_1(0) = 1$ and $a_2(0) = 0$. Because $\hat{H}^{(1)}$ is considered to be a small perturbation, there are not enough transitions out of state 1 that a_1 and a_2 differ appreciably from their initial values. Thus, as an approximation, we may replace $a_1(t)$ and $a_2(t)$ in the right-hand side of Eq. 10-84 by their initial values and find

$$i\hbar\frac{da_2}{dt} = \exp\left[\frac{-i(E_1 - E_2)t}{\hbar}\right]\int\psi_2^*\hat{H}^{(1)}\psi_1\,d\tau \tag{10-85}$$

For convenience only, we take the electric field to be in the z direction and write

$$\hat{H}^{(1)} = -\mu_z E_{0z}\cos 2\pi vt$$

$$= -\frac{\mu_z E_{0z}}{2}(e^{i2\pi vt} + e^{-i2\pi vt})$$

We substitute this into Eq. 10-85 and obtain

$$\frac{da_2}{dt} \propto (\mu_z)_{21}E_{0z}\left\{\exp\left[\frac{i(E_2 - E_1 + hv)t}{\hbar}\right] + \exp\left[\frac{i(E_2 - E_1 - hv)t}{\hbar}\right]\right\} \tag{10-86}$$

where

$$(\mu_z)_{21} = \int\psi_2^*\mu_z\psi_1\,d\tau \tag{10-87}$$

The quantity $(\mu_z)_{21}$ is the z component of the *dipole transition moment* between states 1 and 2. Note that if $(\mu_z)_{21} = 0$, then $da_2/dt = 0$ and so there will be no transitions out of state 1 into state 2. It is the dipole transition moment that underlies the various selection rules. Transitions occur only between states for which the transition moment is nonzero. We shall derive various selection rules in the next few sections, but before doing so let us integrate Eq. 10-86 between 0 and t to obtain

$$a_2(t) \propto (\mu_z)_{21}E_{0z}$$

$$\times\left\{\frac{1 - \exp\left[i(E_2 - E_1 + hv)t/\hbar\right]}{E_2 - E_1 + hv} + \frac{1 - \exp\left[i(E_2 - E_1 - hv)t/\hbar\right]}{E_2 - E_1 - hv}\right\} \tag{10-88}$$

Because $E_2 > E_1$, the so-called *resonance denominators* in Eq. 10-88 cause the second term in this equation to become much larger than the first term and be of major importance in determining $a_2(t)$ when

$$E_2 - E_1 = h\nu$$

which is the *Bohr frequency condition:* When a system makes a transition from one state to another, it absorbs (or emits) a photon whose energy is equal to the difference in the energies of the two states.

10-15   *The Selection Rule in the Rigid Rotator Approximation Is* $\Delta J = \pm 1$

We can use Eq. 10-87 and the properties of the spherical harmonics to derive the selection rule for a rigid rotator. The dipole transition moment between any two states in the rigid rotator approximation is

$$(\mu_z)_{J,M;J',M'} = \int_0^{2\pi} d\phi \int_0^{\pi} d\theta \, \sin\theta \, Y_{J'}^{M'}(\theta, \phi)^* \mu_z Y_J^M(\theta, \phi)$$

$$= \mu \int_0^{2\pi} d\phi \int_0^{\pi} d\theta \, \sin\theta \cos\theta \, Y_{J'}^{M'}(\theta, \phi)^* Y_J^M(\theta, \phi) \quad (10\text{-}89)$$

Notice that μ must be nonzero for the transition moment to be nonzero. Thus, we see that a molecule must have a permanent dipole moment for it to have a pure rotational spectrum, at least in the rigid rotator approximation.

We can also determine for which values of J, M, J', and M' the integral in Eq. 10-89 will be nonzero. Recall that (Eq. 6-76)

$$Y_J^M(\theta, \phi) = N_{JM}P_J^{|M|}(\cos\theta)e^{iM\phi} \qquad (10\text{-}90)$$

where N_{JM} is a normalization constant. Substitute Eq. 10-90 into Eq. 10-89 and let $x = \cos\theta$ to obtain

$$(\mu_z)_{J,M;J',M'} = \mu N_{JM}N_{J'M'}\int_0^{2\pi} d\phi \, e^{i(M-M')\phi} \int_{-1}^1 dx \, xP_{J'}^{|M'|}(x)P_J^{|M|}(x) \quad (10\text{-}91)$$

The integral over ϕ is zero unless $M = M'$, and so we find that $\Delta M = 0$ is part of the rigid rotator selection rule. Integration over ϕ for $M = M'$ gives a factor of 2π, and so we have

$$(\mu_z)_{J,J',M} = 2\pi\mu N_{JM}N_{J'M}\int_{-1}^1 dx \, xP_{J'}^{|M|}(x)P_J^{|M|}(x) \qquad (10\text{-}92)$$

We can evaluate this integral in general by using (Problem 21 on p. 249)

$$(2J+1)xP_J^{|M|}(x) = (J-|M|+1)P_{J+1}^{|M|}(x) + (J+|M|)P_{J-1}^{|M|}(x)$$

By using this relation in Eq. 10-92, we obtain

$$(\mu_z)_{J,J',M} = 2\pi\mu N_{JM}N_{J'M}\int_{-1}^1 dx \, P_{J'}^{|M|}(x)$$

$$\times \left[\frac{(J-|M|+1)}{2J+1}P_{J+1}^{|M|}(x) + \frac{(J+|M|)}{2J+1}P_{J-1}^{|M|}(x)\right]$$

Using the orthogonality relation for the $P_J^M(x)$ (Eq. 6-74), we find that the above integral will vanish unless $J' = J + 1$ or $J' = J - 1$. This leads to the selection rule $J' = J \pm 1$, or $\Delta J = \pm 1$. Thus we have shown in this section that the selection rule for pure rotational spectra in the rigid rotator approximation is that the molecule must have a permanent dipole moment and that $\Delta J = \pm 1$ and $\Delta M = 0$.

EXAMPLE 10-13

Using the explicit formulas for the spherical harmonics given in Table 6-3, show that the rotational transition $J = 0 \rightarrow J = 1$ is allowed, but $J = 0 \rightarrow J = 2$ is forbidden in microwave spectroscopy (in the rigid rotator approximation).

Solution: Referring to Eq. 10-89, we see that we must show that the integral

$$I_{0 \rightarrow 1} = \int_0^{2\pi} d\phi \int_0^\pi d\theta \sin\theta \cos\theta\, Y_1^M(\theta, \phi) Y_0^0(\theta, \phi)$$

can be nonzero and that

$$I_{0 \rightarrow 2} = \int_0^{2\pi} d\phi \int_0^\pi d\theta \sin\theta \cos\theta\, Y_2^M(\theta, \phi) Y_0^0(\theta, \phi)$$

can never be nonzero. In either case, it is easy to see that the integral over ϕ will be zero unless $M = 0$ and so we shall concentrate only on the θ integration. For $I_{0 \rightarrow 1}$, we have

$$I_{0 \rightarrow 1} = 2\pi \int_0^\pi d\theta \sin\theta \cos\theta \left(\frac{3}{4\pi}\right)^{1/2} \cos\theta \left(\frac{1}{4\pi}\right)^{1/2}$$

$$= \frac{\sqrt{3}}{2} \int_{-1}^1 dx\, x^2 = \frac{1}{\sqrt{3}} \neq 0$$

For $I_{0 \rightarrow 2}$, we have

$$I_{0 \rightarrow 2} = 2\pi \int_0^\pi d\theta \sin\theta \cos\theta \left(\frac{5}{16\pi}\right)^{1/2} (3\cos^2\theta - 1)\left(\frac{1}{4\pi}\right)^{1/2}$$

$$= \frac{\sqrt{5}}{4} \int_{-1}^1 dx (3x^3 - x) = 0$$

10-16   *The Harmonic-Oscillator Selection Rule Is $\Delta n = \pm 1$*

Using Eq. 10-87 and the fact that the harmonic-oscillator wave functions are (Eq. 5-41)

$$\psi_n(q) = N_n H_n(\alpha^{1/2} q) e^{-\alpha q^2/2} \tag{10-93}$$

where $\alpha = (k\mu/\hbar^2)^{1/2}$, the dipole transition moment is

$$(\mu_z)_{nn'} = \int_{-\infty}^{\infty} N_n N_{n'} H_{n'}(\alpha^{1/2}q)e^{-\alpha q^2/2}\mu_z(q)H_n(\alpha^{1/2}q)e^{-\alpha q^2/2}dq \tag{10.94}$$

Now expand $\mu_z(q)$ about the equilibrium nuclear separation

$$\mu_z(q) = \mu_0 + \left(\frac{d\mu}{dq}\right)_0 q + \cdots \tag{10-95}$$

If we substitute this into Eq. 10-94, then we have two terms:

$$(\mu_z)_{nn'} = N_n N_{n'}\mu_0 \int_{-\infty}^{\infty} H_{n'}(\alpha^{1/2}q)H_n(\alpha^{1/2}q)e^{-\alpha q^2}dq$$

$$+ N_n N_{n'}\left(\frac{d\mu}{dq}\right)_0 \int_{-\infty}^{\infty} H_{n'}(\alpha^{1/2}q)qH_n(\alpha^{1/2}q)e^{-\alpha q^2}dq \tag{10-96}$$

The first integral here vanishes if $n \neq n'$ due to the orthogonality of the harmonic-oscillator wave functions.

The second integral can be evaluated in general by using the relation (Eq. 5-97)

$$\xi H_n(\xi) = nH_{n-1}(\xi) + \tfrac{1}{2}H_{n+1}(\xi) \tag{10-97}$$

If we substitute this into Eq. 10-96, letting $\alpha^{1/2}q = \xi$, then we obtain

$$(\mu_z)_{nn'} = \frac{N_n N_{n'}}{\alpha}\left(\frac{d\mu}{dq}\right)_0 \int_{-\infty}^{\infty} H_{n'}(\xi)\left[nH_{n-1}(\xi) + \frac{1}{2}H_{n+1}(\xi)\right]e^{-\xi^2}d\xi \tag{10-98}$$

Using now the orthogonality property of the Hermite polynomials, we see that $(\mu_z)_{nn'}$ vanishes unless $n' = n \pm 1$. Thus the selection rule for vibrational transitions under the harmonic-oscillator approximation is that $\Delta n = \pm 1$. In addition, the factor of $(d\mu/dq)_0$ in front of the transition moment integral implies that the dipole moment of the molecule must vary during a vibration.

EXAMPLE 10-14

Using the explicit formulas for the harmonic-oscillator wave functions given in Table 5-2, show that a $0 \to 1$ vibrational transition is allowed and that a $0 \to 2$ transition is forbidden.

Solution: From Table 5-2, we have

$$\psi_0(\xi) = \left(\frac{\alpha}{\pi}\right)^{1/4} e^{-\xi^2/2}$$

$$\psi_1(\xi) = \sqrt{2}\left(\frac{\alpha}{\pi}\right)^{1/4} \xi e^{-\xi^2/2}$$

$$\psi_2(\xi) = \frac{1}{\sqrt{2}}\left(\frac{\alpha}{\pi}\right)^{1/4} (2\xi^2 - 1)e^{-\xi^2/2}$$

The integral to be studied is

$$I_{0\to n} \propto \int_{-\infty}^{\infty} \psi_n(\xi)\xi\psi_0(\xi)\,d\xi$$

For $n = 1$, we have

$$I_{0\to 1} \propto \left(\frac{2\alpha}{\pi}\right)^{1/2} \int_{-\infty}^{\infty} \xi^2 e^{-\xi^2}\,d\xi \neq 0$$

because the integrand is everywhere positive. For $n = 2$,

$$I_{0\to 2} \propto \left(\frac{\alpha}{2\pi}\right)^{1/2} \int_{-\infty}^{\infty} (2\xi^3 - \xi)e^{-\xi^2}\,d\xi = 0$$

because the integrand is an odd function and the limits go from $-\infty$ to $+\infty$.

10-17 *The Selection Rule in Electronic Spectroscopy Is Less Restrictive Than for Pure Rotational or Vibrational Spectroscopy*

According to Eq. 10-74,

$$\psi_{\text{mol}} \simeq \psi_{\text{trans}}(\mathbf{R}_{\text{CM}})\frac{S_{\text{vib}}(R)}{R} Y_J^M(\theta, \phi)\psi_{\text{el}}(\{\mathbf{r}_j\}; R) \qquad (10\text{-}99)$$

Generally the dipole moment of a diatomic molecule is given by

$$\mu = Z_1 e\mathbf{R}_1 + Z_2 e\mathbf{R}_2 - \sum_j e\mathbf{r}_j$$

$$= \mu_n + \mu_{\text{el}} \qquad (10\text{-}100)$$

where μ_n is the dipole moment due to the positions of the nuclei and μ_{el} is that due to the positions of the electrons. If we substitute Eqs. 10-99 and 10-100 into the integral for a dipole transition moment (cf. Eq. 10-87), then we obtain

$$I = \int \psi_{\text{mol}}^{\prime *}\mu_n\psi_{\text{mol}}\,d\tau + \int \psi_{\text{mol}}^{\prime *}\mu_{\text{el}}\psi_{\text{mol}}\,d\tau$$

$$= \int \psi_{\text{trans}}^{\prime *}\frac{S_{\text{vib}}^{\prime *}}{R} Y_{J'}^{M'*}\psi_{\text{el}}^{\prime *}\mu_n\psi_{\text{trans}}\frac{S_{\text{vib}}}{R} Y_J^M\psi_{\text{el}}\,d\tau$$

$$+ \int \psi_{\text{trans}}^{\prime *}\frac{S_{\text{vib}}^{\prime *}}{R} Y_{J'}^{M'*}\psi_{\text{el}}^{\prime *}\mu_{\text{el}}\psi_{\text{trans}}\frac{S_{\text{vib}}}{R} Y_J^M\psi_{\text{el}}\,d\tau \qquad (10\text{-}101)$$

where $d\tau$ is shorthand for all the appropriate volume elements.

Because μ_n does not depend on the electronic coordinates, the integral containing μ_n is zero due to the orthogonality of the electronic wave functions.

Thus

$$I = \int \psi_{\text{trans}}'^* \frac{S_{\text{vib}}'^*}{R} Y_{J'}^{M'^*} \psi_{\text{el}}'^* \mu_{\text{el}} \psi_{\text{trans}} \frac{S_{\text{vib}}}{R} Y_J^M \psi_{\text{el}} \, d\tau \qquad (10\text{-}102)$$

Because of the orthogonality of the translational wave functions, the integral over the center-of-mass coordinates

$$\int \psi_{\text{trans}}'^*(\mathbf{R}_{\text{CM}}) \psi_{\text{trans}}(\mathbf{R}_{\text{CM}}) \, d\mathbf{R}_{\text{CM}}$$

is zero unless the two translational states are the same. Translational spectra are not observed. Furthermore, if we consider the z component of μ_{el} for concreteness, we see that the integral over the rotational coordinates is the same as in Section 10-15. Thus, the selection rule for rotational transitions in electronic spectroscopy is that $\Delta J = \pm 1$ and $\Delta M = 0$. This is the same as for pure rotational spectroscopy, except that it is no longer required that the molecule have a permanent dipole moment.

Thus far, then, we have

$$I = \int \psi_{\text{el}}'^* \mu_{\text{el}} \psi_{\text{el}} \, d\tau_e \int \frac{S_{\text{vib}}'^* S_{\text{vib}}}{R^2} R^2 \, dR \qquad (10\text{-}103)$$

The first integral here is called the *electronic transition moment* and its value depends on the two electronic states. A complete discussion of its dependence on ψ_{el} and ψ_{el}' and, in particular, the symmetry of these wave functions is beyond the scope of this chapter. We shall discuss the second integral in Eq. 10-103, however. In this case, the integral involving the vibrational wave functions is *not* zero unless $\Delta n = \pm 1$ because S_{vib}' and S_{vib} are the vibrational wave functions in different electronic states, with different potential energy curves and so different force constants, for example. Thus, $\Delta n = 0, \pm 1, \pm 2, \pm 3, \ldots$ in electronic spectroscopy. The intensities of vibronic transitions are governed by the value of

$$I \propto \int S_{\text{vib}}'^* S_{\text{vib}} \, dR \qquad (10\text{-}104)$$

which is called the *vibrational overlap integral*, the square of which is called the *Franck-Condon factor*.

10-18 The Franck-Condon Principle Predicts the Relative Intensities of Vibronic Transitions

Equation 10-104 has a nice pictorial interpretation. Figure 10-17 shows two electronic potential energy curves with the vibrational states associated with each electronic energy state indicated. In each vibrational state, the harmonic-oscillator probability densities are plotted (cf. Figure 5-7). Notice that except for the ground vibrational state, the most likely internuclear separation occurs at the extreme of a vibration, which is called a *classical turning point* because the vibrational motion changes direction at that point. Because electrons are so much less massive than nuclei, the motion of electrons

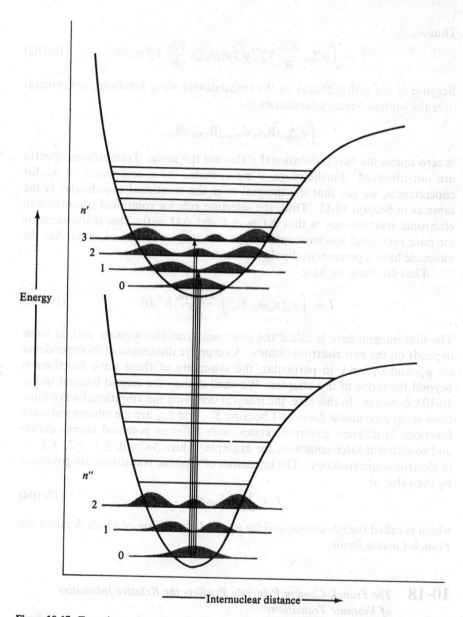

Figure 10-17. Two electronic potential energy curves showing the vibrational states associated with each electronic state. The minimum of the upper curve lies almost directly over the minimum of the lower curve. The shaded areas represent the harmonic-oscillator probability densities for each vibrational state. The vertical lines represent a series of $0 \rightarrow n'$ vibronic transitions.

is almost instantaneous relative to the motion of nuclei. Consequently, when an electron makes a transition from one electronic state to another, the nuclei do not move appreciably during the transition. Electronic transitions can be depicted as vertical lines in a diagram such as in Figure 10-17. This argument can be made rigorous and is known as the *Franck-Condon principle*. The Franck-Condon principle and Eq. 10-104 allow us to estimate relative intensities of vibronic transitions. In Figure 10-17, the minima of the two electronic states lie very nearly above each other. According to Eq. 10-104, the relative intensity of a $0 \rightarrow n'$ transition is proportional to the overlap of the harmonic-oscillator wave functions in the two vibrational states. Figure 10-17 shows that the wave functions in the upper and lower vibronic states overlap less and less as n' increases. Thus we obtain a distribution of intensities like that shown in Figure 10-18(a).

Figure 10-19 shows another commonly occurring case, where the minimum of the upper potential energy curve lies at a somewhat greater value of the internuclear separation than for the lower curve. In this case, the $0 \rightarrow 0$ transition is not the most intense transition. The most intense transition as shown in Figure 10-19 is the $0 \rightarrow 1$ transition, and the distribution of intensities for this case is like that given in Figure 10-18(b). Performing a detailed analysis of the intensities of such vibronic transitions yields much information of the shapes of electronic potential energy curves.

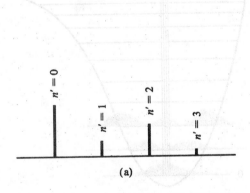

(a)

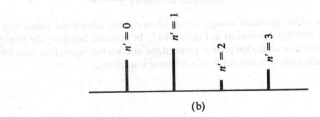

(b)

Figure 10-18. The distribution of the intensities of the vibronic transitions for the case shown in (a) Figure 10-17 and (b) Figure 10-19.

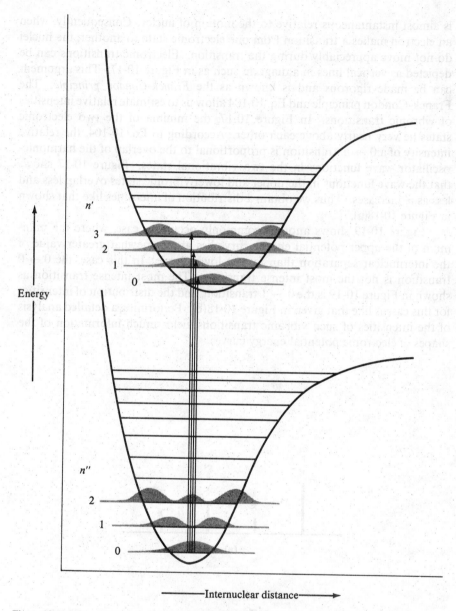

Figure 10-19. Two electronic potential energy curves showing the vibrational states and the harmonic-oscillator probability densities as in Figure 10-17. In this case, however, the minimum of the upper curve occurs at a somewhat greater value of the internuclear separation than for the lower curve. The vertical lines represent the $0 \rightarrow n'$ vibronic transitions.

Summary

The interaction of electromagnetic radiation with molecules is called *molecular spectroscopy*. Molecular spectroscopy is a rich source of information concerning the size, shape, and electron distribution within molecules. The simplest models of the rotation and the vibrations of molecules are the rigid-rotator model and the harmonic-oscillator model. The rigid-rotator model predicts that the rotational spectrum of a diatomic or linear molecule consists of a series of equally spaced lines in the microwave region. The spacing of these lines gives the bond lengths in the molecule. Although the lines in the microwave spectrum of a molecule are almost equally spaced, closer examination shows that the lines are not quite equally spaced. The modification of the rigid rotator model by including centrifugal distortion accounts well for the details of the rotational spectra of diatomic molecules.

The harmonic-oscillator approximation predicts that the vibrational spectrum of a diatomic molecule consists of just a single line in the infrared. The frequency of this line gives the force constant of the molecule. Closer examination of the infrared spectrum of a diatomic molecule shows that there are weak overtones, whose frequencies are almost, but not quite, integral multiples of the frequency of the fundamental line. The extension of the harmonic-oscillator approximation by the inclusion of anharmonic terms explains the occurrence of the weak overtones that are found. Under higher resolution, the line in the vibrational spectrum of a diatomic molecule is seen to consist of a number of closely spaced lines. The structure of this spectrum is due to the rotational transitions that accompany the vibrational transition. The rotational-vibrational spectrum consists of an R branch and a P branch. The rigid rotator-harmonic oscillator approximation predicts that the lines in the R branch and P branch are equally spaced, but closer examination shows that this is not so (cf. Figure 10-3). The discrepancy between the predictions of the rigid rotator-harmonic oscillator model and experimental data can be accounted for by realizing that the average bond length increases slightly with vibrational energy. Although most of the chapter deals with the spectra of diatomic molecules, the discussion of Section 10-10 shows that the vibrational motion of a polyatomic molecule can be expressed in terms of normal modes, at least in the harmonic-oscillator approximation.

Electronic spectra occur in the visible and ultraviolet regions. Electronic spectra of diatomic molecules are somewhat complicated because they contain both vibrational and rotational fine structure (cf. Figures 10-12 to 10-14). Electronic spectra particularly useful for homonuclear diatomic molecules. The selection rules for rotational and rotational-vibrational spectroscopy are such that a homonuclear molecule will not have a pure rotational spectrum nor a rotational-vibrational spectrum. The selection rules in electronic spectroscopy are less restrictive, however, and so electronic spectra are a source of the rotational and the vibrational properties of homonuclear diatomic molecules.

The Born-Oppenheimer approximation can be used to factor a molecular wave function into an electronic part and a nuclear part; and then the Schrödinger equation for the nuclear motion can be factored further into a rotational part and a vibrational part. Thus a molecular wave function can be written approximately as a product of an electronic wave function, a vibrational wave function, and a rotational wave function. The molecular wave function can be used along with time-dependent perturbation theory to derive the selection rules that we have used without proof in many sections of the book. The selection rules are expressed in terms of a dipole transition moment. Rotational transitions, vibrational transitions, and electronic transitions have different selection rules.

Terms That You Should Know

electromagnetic spectrum	vibration-rotation interaction
microwave region	translational degrees of freedom
far infrared region	rotational degrees of freedom
infrared region	vibrational degrees of freedom
visible region	normal coordinates
ultraviolet region	normal modes
rigid rotator	infrared active
selection rule	infrared inactive
moment of inertia	vibronic transition
rotational constant	n' progression
harmonic oscillator	Fortrat diagram
force constant	band head
Boltzmann distribution	Born-Oppenheimer approximation
geometric series	time-dependent perturbation theory
rigid rotator-harmonic	dipole transition moment
oscillator approximation	Bohr frequency condition
R branch	selection rule
P branch	electronic transition moment
nonrigid rotator	vibrational overlap integral
centrifugal force	Franck-Condon factor
centrifugal distortion constant	classical turning point
anharmonicity constant	Franck-Condon principle
overtone	

Problems

1. The spacing between the lines in the microwave spectrum of $H^{35}Cl$ is 6.350×10^{11} Hz. Calculate the bond length of $H^{35}Cl$.

2. The microwave spectrum of $^{39}K^{127}I$ consists of a series of lines whose spacing is almost constant at 3634 MHz. Calculate the bond length of $^{39}K^{127}I$.

3. The equilibrium internuclear distance of $H^{127}I$ is 160.4 pm. Calculate B in wave numbers and megahertz.

4. Assuming that the rotation of a diatomic molecule in the $J = 10$ state may be approximated by classical mechanics, calculate how many revolutions per second $^{23}Na^{35}Cl$ makes in the $J = 10$ rotational state? The rotational constant of $^{23}Na^{35}Cl$ is 6500 MHz.

5. The results that we have derived for a rigid rotator apply to linear poly-atomic molecules as well as to diatomic molecules. Given that the moment of inertia I for $H^{12}C^{14}N$ is 1.89×10^{-46} kg·m^2 (cf. Problem 6), predict the microwave spectrum of $H^{12}C^{14}N$.

6. This problem involves the calculation of the moment of inertia of a linear triatomic molecule such as $H^{12}C^{14}N$ (cf. Problem 5). The moment of inertia of any set of point masses is

$$I = \sum_j m_j r_j^2$$

where r_j is the distance of the jth mass from the center of mass. Thus, the moment of inertia of $H^{12}C^{14}N$ is

$$I = m_H r_H^2 + m_C r_C^2 + m_N r_N^2$$

Show that this can be written as

$$I = \frac{m_H m_C r_{HC}^2 + m_H m_N r_{HN}^2 + m_C m_N r_{CN}^2}{m_H + m_C + m_N}$$

where the r's are the various internuclear distances. Given that $r_{HC} = 106.8$ pm and $r_{CN} = 115.6$ pm, calculate I and compare the result to that given in Problem 5.

7. In the far infrared spectrum of $^{39}K^{35}Cl$ there is an intense line at 378.0 cm^{-1}. Calculate the force constant and the period of vibration of $^{39}K^{35}Cl$.

8. The force constant of $^{79}Br^{79}Br$ is 240 N·m^{-1}. Calculate the fundamental vibrational frequency and the zero-point energy of $^{79}Br_2$.

9. Prove that

$$\langle x^2 \rangle = \frac{\hbar}{(\mu k)^{1/2}} \left(n + \frac{1}{2} \right)$$

486 10 Molecular Spectroscopy

for a harmonic oscillator. Use this equation to calculate the root-mean-square amplitude of $^{14}N_2$ in its ground vibrational state (cf. Section 5-10). Use $k = 2260$ N·m^{-1} for $^{14}N_2$.

10. Given that $\bar{v} = 2330.70$ cm^{-1} for N_2, plot the fraction of N_2 molecules in the nth vibrational state at 300 K and 1000 K.

11. Calculate the fraction of molecules in the ground vibrational state of H_2 at 300 K, which has a relatively large value of $\bar{v}$ (4159.2 cm^{-1}) and NaCl at 300 K, which has a relatively small value of $\bar{v}$ (378.0 cm^{-1}).

12. Given that $B = 56,000$ MHz and $\bar{v}_e = 2143.0$ cm^{-1} for CO, calculate the frequencies of the first few lines of the R and P branches in the vibration-rotation spectrum of CO.

13. Given that $R_0 = 156$ pm and $k = 250$ N·m^{-1} for ^{6}LiF, use the rigid rotator-harmonic oscillator approximation to construct to scale an energy-level diagram for the first five rotational levels in the $n = 0$ and $n = 1$ vibrational states. Indicate the allowed transitions in an absorption experiment and calculate the frequencies of the first few lines in the R and P branches of the vibration-rotation spectrum of ^{6}LiF.

14. Plot N_J/N_0 versus J for $^{14}N_2$ at 25°C. The rotational constant of $^{14}N_2$ is 60,260 MHz.

Treating J as a continuous parameter, show that the value of J in the most populated rotational state is the nearest integer to

$$J_{max} = \frac{1}{2}\left[\left(\frac{2k_BT}{B}\right)^{1/2} - 1\right]$$

Calculate J_{max} for H^{35}Cl ($\bar{B} = 10.60$ cm^{-1}) and ^{127}I^{35}Cl ($\bar{B} = 0.114$ cm^{-1}) at 300 K.

15. The summation that occurs in the rotational Boltzmann distribution (Eq. 10-33) can be evaluated approximately by converting the summation to an integral. Show that

$$\sum_{J=0}^{\infty}(2J+1)\exp\left[\frac{-\bar{B}J(J+1)}{k_BT}\right] \approx \int_0^{\infty}\exp\left[\frac{-\bar{B}J(J+1)}{k_BT}\right]d[J(J+1)]$$

$$= \frac{k_BT}{\bar{B}} = \frac{8\pi^2 cIk_BT}{h}$$

This is an excellent approximation for values of $\bar{B}/k_BT$ less than 0.05 or so. Using this result, calculate and plot the fraction of ^{127}I^{35}Cl molecules in the Jth rotational state versus J at 25°C. ($\bar{B} = 0.114$ cm^{-1}).

16. Use the data in Table 10-4 to calculate the ratio of centrifugal distortion energy to the total rotational energy of H^{35}Cl and ^{35}Cl^{35}Cl in the $J = 10$ state.

17. The frequencies of the rotational transitions in the nonrigid-rotator approximation are given by Eq. 10-41. Show how both $\bar{B}$ and $\bar{D}$ may be obtained by plotting $\bar{\nu}/(J + 1)$ versus $(J + 1)^2$. Use this method and the data in Table 10-2 to determine $\bar{B}$ and $\bar{D}$ for $H^{35}Cl$.

18. The following data are obtained in the microwave spectrum of $^{12}C^{16}O$. Use the method of Problem 17 to determine $\bar{B}$ and $\bar{D}$ from these data.

Transition	Frequency/cm^{-1}
$0 \rightarrow 1$	3.84540
$1 \rightarrow 2$	7.69060
$2 \rightarrow 3$	11.53550
$3 \rightarrow 4$	15.37990
$4 \rightarrow 5$	19.22380
$5 \rightarrow 6$	23.06685

19. Using the parameters given in Table 10-2, calculate the frequencies (in cm^{-1}) of the $0 \rightarrow 1$, $1 \rightarrow 2$, $2 \rightarrow 3$, and $3 \rightarrow 4$ rotational transitions in the ground vibrational state of $H^{35}Cl$ in the nonrigid-rotator approximation.

20. Using the development in Section 10-7, show that

$$R = R_0 + \frac{\hbar^2 J(J + 1)}{\mu k R_0^3} + \cdots$$

21. Calculate the fraction of vibrational energy that is due to the anharmonic term for $H^{35}Cl$ in the vibrational states $n = 0, 5,$ and 10.

22. A simple function that is a good representation of an internuclear potential is the Morse potential

$$U(q) = D_e(1 - e^{-\beta q})^2$$

where q is $R - R_e$. Show that the force constant calculated for a Morse potential is given by

$$k = 2D_e\beta^2$$

Given that $D_e = 7.31 \times 10^{-19}$ J·molecule^{-1} and $\beta = 1.83 \times 10^{10}$ m^{-1} for HCl, calculate k.

23. The Morse potential is presented in Problem 22. Given that $D_e = 8.16 \times 10^{-19}$ J·molecule^{-1}, $\bar{\nu}_e = 1580.0$ cm^{-1}, and $R_e = 121$ pm for O_2, plot a Morse potential for O_2. Plot the corresponding harmonic-oscillator potential on the same graph.

24. The fundamental line for $^{12}C^{16}O$ occurs at 2143.0 cm^{-1} and the first overtone occurs at 4260.0 cm^{-1}. Calculate $\bar{\nu}_e$ and $\bar{x}_e\bar{\nu}_e$ for $^{12}C^{16}O$.

25. Using the parameters given in Table 10-4, calculate the fundamental and the first three overtones of $H^{79}Br$.

26. The frequencies of the vibrational transitions in the anharmonic-oscillator approximation are given by Eq. 10-44. Show how both $\bar{v}_e$ and $\bar{x}_e\bar{v}_e$ may be obtained by plotting $\bar{v}_{obs}/n$ versus $(n + 1)$. Use this method and the data in Table 10-3 to determine $\bar{v}_e$ and $\bar{x}_e\bar{v}_e$ for $H^{35}Cl$.

27. The following data are obtained from the infrared spectrum of $^{127}I^{35}Cl$. Using the method of Problem 26, determine $\bar{v}_e$ and $\bar{x}_e\bar{v}_e$ from these data.

Transition	Frequency/cm^{-1}
$0 \rightarrow 1$	381.20
$0 \rightarrow 2$	759.60
$0 \rightarrow 3$	1135.00
$0 \rightarrow 4$	1507.40
$0 \rightarrow 5$	1877.00

28. Use the energy levels of a particle in a one-dimensional box to argue that the energy levels of an oscillator in a potential well like in Figure 10-6 should bunch closer together as n increases.

29. Using the values of $\bar{v}_e$, $\bar{x}_e\bar{v}_e$, $\bar{B}_e$, and $\bar{\alpha}_e$ given in Table 10-4, construct to scale an energy-level diagram for the first five rotational levels in the $n = 0$ and $n = 1$ vibrational states for $H^{35}Cl$. Indicate the allowed transitions in an absorption experiment and calculate the frequencies of the first few lines in the R and P branches.

30. The following data are obtained for the vibration-rotation spectrum of $H^{127}I$. Determine $\bar{B}_0$, $\bar{B}_1$, $\bar{B}_e$, and $\bar{\alpha}_e$ from these data.

Line	Frequency/cm^{-1}
$R(0)$	2242.6
$R(1)$	2254.8
$R(2)$	2266.6
$P(1)$	2217.1
$P(2)$	2203.8
$P(3)$	2190.2

31. Determine the number of translational, rotational, and vibrational degrees of freedom in
    (a) CH_3Cl (b) OCS
    (c) C_6H_6 (d) $H-C\equiv C-H$
    (e) H_2CO (f) cyclopropane

32. The normal modes of GaI_3 are similar to those shown in Figure 10-8. Which of the modes are infrared active? Which are infrared inactive?

33. The values of $\bar{\nu}_e$ and $\bar{x}_e\bar{\nu}_e$ of $^{12}C^{16}O$ are 2170.21 cm^{-1} and 13.46 cm^{-1} in the ground electronic state and 1514.10 cm^{-1} and 17.40 cm^{-1} in the first excited electronic state. If the $0 \rightarrow 0$ vibronic transition occurs at 6.47514×10^4 cm^{-1}, calculate $\bar{\nu}_{el, el}$, the energy difference between the minima of the potential curves of the two electronic states.

34. Given the following parameters for $^{12}C^{16}O$,

$$\bar{\nu}_{el,el} = 6.508043 \times 10^4 \text{ cm}^{-1}$$

$$\bar{\nu}'_e = 1514.10 \text{ cm}^{-1}$$

$$\bar{x}'_e\bar{\nu}'_e = 17.40 \text{ cm}^{-1}$$

$$\bar{\nu}''_e = 2170.21 \text{ cm}^{-1}$$

$$\bar{x}''_e\bar{\nu}''_e = 13.46 \text{ cm}^{-1}$$

construct to scale an energy-level diagram of the first two electronic states, showing the first five vibrational states in each electronic state. Indicate the allowed transitions from $n'' = 0$ and calculate the frequencies of these transitions. Also calculate the zero-point vibrational energy in each electronic state.

35. An analysis of the electronic spectrum of $^{12}C^{32}S$ gives the following results:

n	B_n/cm^{-1}
0	0.81708
1	0.81116
2	0.80524
3	0.79932

Determine $\bar{B}_e$ and $\bar{\alpha}_e$ from these data.

36. Suppose that $\bar{B}' = 9.80$ cm^{-1} and $\bar{B}'' = 11.25$ cm^{-1} in two electronic states of a given molecule. Construct a Fortrat diagram by plotting J versus $\bar{\nu}_{obs} - \bar{\nu}_{el, el}$ for both the R and P branches as in Figure 10-15. Use the Fortrat diagram to determine the frequency (relative to $\bar{\nu}_{el, el}$) at the band head.

37. Substitute Eq. 10-59 into Eq. 10-57 and use Eq. 10-58 to obtain

$$\left[-\frac{\hbar^2}{2M} (\nabla_A^2 + \nabla_B^2) + E_{el}(R) \right] \psi_{el}(\mathbf{r}_1, \mathbf{r}_2; R)\psi_n(\mathbf{R}_A, \mathbf{R}_B)$$

$$= E\psi_{el}(\mathbf{r}_1, \mathbf{r}_2; R)\psi_n(\mathbf{R}_A, \mathbf{R}_B)$$

Now argue that

$$\nabla_A^2 \psi_{el}\psi_n \simeq \psi_{el}\nabla_A^2 \psi_n$$

$$\nabla_B^2 \psi_{el}\psi_n \simeq \psi_{el}\nabla_B^2 \psi_n$$

and derive Eq. 10-60.

38. Explain why the force constants and the equilibrium nuclear separations of H_2, HD, and D_2 are the same under the Born-Oppenheimer approximation. Are the fundamental vibrational frequencies the same? Are the rotational constants the same?

39. Given that the fundamental vibrational frequency of $H^{35}Cl$ is 2990.0 cm^{-1}, estimate the fundamental vibrational frequency of $D^{35}Cl$.

40. Given that $\bar{\nu}_e = 4395.20$ cm^{-1} for H_2, calculate $\bar{\nu}_e$ for HD and D_2. Given that $\bar{B}_0 = 59.31$ cm^{-1} for H_2, calculate $\bar{B}_0$ for HD and D_2.

41. Show that Eq. 10-60 can be separated into an equation for center-of-mass motion and an equation for internal motion by introducing center-of-mass and relative coordinates. For simplicity, work only in one dimension.

42. The vibrational Schrödinger equation derived in Section 10-13 in the harmonic-oscillator approximation is

$$-\frac{\hbar^2}{2\mu}\frac{d^2 S_{vib}}{dq^2} + \frac{k}{2}q^2 S_{vib}(q) = E_{vib}S_{vib}(q)$$

where $q = R - R_e$ and $\psi_{vib}(R) = S_{vib}(R - R_e)/R$. According to the above equation, the $S_{vib}(q)$ are the harmonic-oscillator wave functions. The $\psi_{vib}(R)$ are orthogonal. What is the orthogonality integral for the $S_{vib}(R)$? What is the volume element? What about the lower limit (cf. Eq. 10-103)?

43. Calculate the ratio of the dipole transition moments for the $0 \rightarrow 1$ and $1 \rightarrow 2$ rotational transitions in the rigid-rotator approximation.

44. Calculate the ratio of the dipole transition moments for the $0 \rightarrow 1$ and $1 \rightarrow 2$ vibrational transitions in the harmonic-oscillator approximation.

45. Determine the selection rules for Δl and Δm in the spectrum of atomic hydrogen.

A

Derivation of the Classical Wave Equation

IN CHAPTER 2, WE present and discuss the classical wave equation. In one dimension, the classical wave equation is

$$\frac{\partial^2 u}{\partial x^2} = \frac{1}{v^2}\frac{\partial^2 u}{\partial t^2}$$

This equation governs the small vibrations of an elastic string that is stretched to a length l and then fixed at the endpoints. The dependent variable $u(x, t)$ represents the displacement of the string at a point x at a time t from its equilibrium position (see Figure 2-1). We shall derive the one-dimensional classical wave equation in this appendix.

We shall assume that the string is homogeneous; that is, we shall assume that the mass of the string per unit length is a constant. We shall denote the mass of the string per unit length by ρ. We also shall assume that the string undergoes only small vertical displacements from its equilibrium position.

To derive an equation for the displacement $u(x, t)$, consider Figure A-1. The quantities T_1 and T_2 in Figure A-1 are the tensions at the points P and Q on the string. Both T_1 and T_2 are tangential to the curve of the string. Because there is only vertical motion of the string, the horizontal components of the tensions at all points along the string must be equal. Using the notation presented in Figure A-1, we have that

$$T_1 \cos \alpha = T_2 \cos \beta = T = \text{constant} \qquad \text{(A-1)}$$

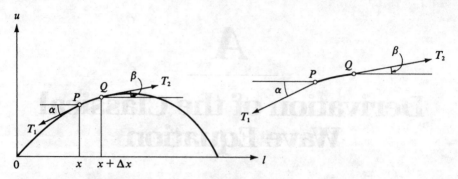

Figure A-1. A vibrating string at an instant of time. The quantities shown in the figure are used in the derivation of the wave equation for a vibrating string.

There is a net force in the vertical direction that causes the vertical motion of the string. Again, using the notation in Figure A-1, we find that the net vertical force is

$$\text{net vertical force} = T_2 \sin \beta - T_1 \sin \alpha \qquad \text{(A-2)}$$

By Newton's second law, this net force is equal to the mass $\rho \, \Delta x$ along the segment PQ times the acceleration of the string $(\partial^2 u/\partial t^2)$. Thus, we write

$$T_2 \sin \beta - T_1 \sin \alpha = \rho \, \Delta x \, \frac{\partial^2 u}{\partial t^2} \qquad \text{(A-3)}$$

Dividing Eq. A-3 by Eq. A-1 gives

$$\frac{T_2 \sin \beta}{T_2 \cos \beta} - \frac{T_1 \sin \alpha}{T_1 \cos \alpha} = \tan \beta - \tan \alpha = \frac{\rho \, \Delta x}{T} \frac{\partial^2 u}{\partial t^2} \qquad \text{(A-4)}$$

But $\tan \beta$ and $\tan \alpha$ are the slopes of the curve of the string at x and $x + \Delta x$, and so (cf. Figure A-1)

$$\tan \alpha = \left(\frac{\partial u}{\partial x}\right) \quad \text{at } x$$

$$= u_x(x) \qquad \text{(A-5)}$$

where u_x denotes $\partial u/\partial x$. Similarly,

$$\tan \beta = \left(\frac{\partial u}{\partial x}\right) \quad \text{at } x + \Delta x$$

$$= u_x(x + \Delta x) \qquad \text{(A-6)}$$

If we substitute Eqs. A-5 and A-6 into Eq. A-4 and then divide both sides by Δx, then we obtain

$$\frac{1}{\Delta x} [u_x(x + \Delta x) - u_x(x)] = \frac{\rho}{T} \frac{\partial^2 u}{\partial t^2} \qquad \text{(A-7)}$$

If we let Δx approach zero, the left-hand side of Eq. A-7 is, by definition, the derivative of u_x. The derivative of $u_x \equiv \partial u/\partial x$ is $\partial^2 u/\partial x^2$, and so Eq. A-7 becomes

$$\frac{\partial^2 u}{\partial x^2} = \frac{\rho}{T}\frac{\partial^2 u}{\partial t^2} \tag{A-8}$$

If we define v as $(T/\rho)^{1/2}$, then Eq. A-8 is

$$\frac{\partial^2 u}{\partial x^2} = \frac{1}{v^2}\frac{\partial^2 u}{\partial t^2} \tag{A-9}$$

which is the one-dimensional classical wave equation. Note that the speed with which a disturbance propagates along a stretched string depends on the tension in the string and the linear mass density of the string.

B

Complex Numbers

THERE ARE MANY algebraic equations such as

$$x^2 + 4 = 0 \quad \text{and} \quad x^2 + 2x + 10 = 0$$

that are not satisfied by any real number. Seeking the solutions of such equations leads to *imaginary numbers and complex numbers.* An imaginary number is of the form iy, where y is a real number and $i^2 = -1$. The symbol i is called the *imaginary unit.* The solutions to the first of the above two equations are $\pm 2i$. The sum of a real number and an imaginary number is a complex number, $x + iy$, where x and y are real numbers. The solutions to the second of the above two equations are $-1 \pm 3i$. It is customary to write complex numbers as

$$z = x + iy \qquad \text{(B-1)}$$

We say that x is the *real part* of z and that y is the *imaginary part* of z. We often write

$$\text{Re } z = x \qquad \text{Im } z = y \qquad \text{(B-2)}$$

Complex numbers and complex functions occur frequently in quantum mechanics, and so it is necessary for us to become familiar with the properties and the algebraic manipulations associated with complex numbers.

A complex number can be represented as a point in an x-y Cartesian coordinate system as in Figure B-1. The x-y plane in Figure B-1 is called the *complex plane.* The x axis is called the *real axis* and the y axis is called the *imaginary axis.* Two complex numbers are equal if and only if they are re-

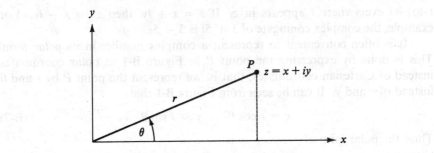

Figure B-1. The representation of a complex number as a point in an *x-y* Cartesian coordinate system.

presented by the same point in the complex plane. Therefore,

$$z_1 = z_2 \quad \text{if and only if} \quad x_1 = x_2 \quad and \quad y_1 = y_2 \qquad \text{(B-3)}$$

Two complex numbers are added by adding the real parts and the imaginary parts of the two complex numbers; that is,

$$z_1 + z_2 = (x_1 + x_2) + i(y_1 + y_2) \qquad \text{(B-4)}$$

Similarly,

$$z_1 - z_2 = (x_1 - x_2) + i(y_1 - y_2) \qquad \text{(B-5)}$$

The product of z_1 and z_2 is formed by multiplying z_1 and z_2 together and letting $i^2 = -1$ wherever i^2 occurs. In other words,

$$z_1 z_2 = (x_1 + iy_1)(x_2 + iy_2) = x_1 x_2 + i x_2 y_1 + i x_1 y_2 + i^2 y_1 y_2$$
$$= (x_1 x_2 - y_1 y_2) + i(x_2 y_1 + x_1 y_2) \qquad \text{(B-6)}$$

EXAMPLE B-1

Given $z_1 = -2 + i$ and $z_2 = 1 - 2i$, calculate $z_1 + z_2$, $z_1 - z_2$, and $z_1 z_2$.

Solution: Using Eqs. B-4 through B-6, we have

$$z_1 + z_2 = (-2 + 1) + i(1 - 2) = -1 - i$$

$$z_1 - z_2 = (-2 - 1) + i(1 + 2) = -3 + 3i$$

$$z_1 z_2 = (-2 + i)(1 - 2i) = -2 + i + 4i - 2i^2$$
$$= 0 + 5i = 5i$$

The product $z_1 z_2$ is said to be *pure imaginary*.

An important quantity associated with any complex number z is its *complex conjugate z^**. The complex conjugate of z is obtained by changing *i* to $-i$ everywhere *i* appears in *z*. If $z = x + iy$, then $z^* = x - iy$. For example, the complex conjugate of $3 + 5i$ is $3 - 5i$.

It is often convenient to represent a complex number in its *polar form*. This is done by expressing the point *P* in Figure B-1 in polar coordinates instead of Cartesian coordinates; that is, we represent the point *P* by *r* and θ instead of *x* and *y*. It can be seen from Figure B-1 that

$$x = r \cos \theta \qquad y = r \sin \theta \qquad \text{(B-7)}$$

Thus, the polar form of $z = x + iy$ is

$$z = r(\cos \theta + i \sin \theta) \qquad \text{(B-8)}$$

The value of *r* in Eq. B-8 is called the *absolute value* or the *modulus* of *z*. The angle θ in Eq. B-8 is called the *phase angle* of *z*. The absolute value of *z* is often denoted by $|z|$ and is given by (see Figure B-1)

$$|z| = (x^2 + y^2)^{1/2} \qquad \text{(B-9)}$$

An important expression for $|z|$ is $|z| = (zz^*)^{1/2}$. To see that $|z| = (zz^*)^{1/2}$, consider

$$zz^* = (x + iy)(x - iy) = x^2 - i^2 y^2 = x^2 + y^2$$

Therefore,

$$|z| = (x^2 + y^2)^{1/2} = (zz^*)^{1/2} \qquad \text{(B-10)}$$

EXAMPLE B-2
Calculate the absolute value of $-4 + 3i$.

Solution: Using Eq. B-10, we have

$$|z| = [(-4 + 3i)(-4 - 3i)]^{1/2} = (16 + 9)^{1/2} = 5$$

Note that the absolute magnitude of a complex number is always a positive number. Geometrically, the absolute value of *z* is the distance of the point (x, y) from the origin in Figure B-1.

It is often convenient to express a complex number in an exponential form. To find the exponential form of a complex number, consider the three Maclaurin expansions:

$$e^x = 1 + x + \frac{x^2}{2!} + \frac{x^3}{3!} + \frac{x^4}{4!} + \frac{x^5}{5!} + \cdots$$

$$\cos x = 1 - \frac{x^2}{2!} + \frac{x^4}{4!} - \cdots$$

$$\sin x = x - \frac{x^3}{3!} + \frac{x^5}{5!} - \cdots$$

If we replace x by $i\theta$ in e^x, then we find

$$e^{i\theta} = 1 + i\theta + \frac{i^2\theta^2}{2!} + \frac{i^3\theta^3}{3!} + \frac{i^4\theta^4}{4!} + \frac{i^5\theta^5}{5!} + \cdots$$

$$= 1 + i\theta - \frac{\theta^2}{2!} - \frac{i\theta^3}{3!} + \frac{\theta^4}{4!} + \frac{i\theta^5}{5!} + \cdots$$

$$= \left(1 - \frac{\theta^2}{2!} + \frac{\theta^4}{4!} - \cdots\right) + i\left(\theta - \frac{\theta^3}{3!} + \frac{\theta^5}{5!} - \cdots\right)$$

The power series in parentheses here are $\cos\theta$ and $\sin\theta$, and so we have just shown that

$$e^{i\theta} = \cos\theta + i\sin\theta \qquad (B-11)$$

Equation B-11 is known as *Euler's formula* and is an important formula. If we substitute Eq. B-11 into Eq. B-8, then we obtain the *exponential form* of z:

$$z = re^{i\theta} \qquad (B-12)$$

Note that

$$z^* = re^{-i\theta}$$

and that

$$|z| = (zz^*)^{1/2} = (re^{i\theta}re^{-i\theta})^{1/2} = r = (x^2 + y^2)^{1/2}$$

EXAMPLE B-3

Show that $e^{-i\theta} = \cos\theta - i\sin\theta$. Now use this result and the polar representation of z (Eq. B-8) to show that $|e^{i\theta}| = 1$.

Solution: To prove that $e^{-i\theta} = \cos\theta - i\sin\theta$, we use Eq. B-11 and the fact that $\cos\theta$ is an even function of θ [$(\cos(-\theta)) = \cos\theta$] and that $\sin\theta$ is an odd function of θ [$\sin(-\theta) = -\sin\theta$].

$$e^{-i\theta} = \cos(-\theta) + i\sin(-\theta) = \cos\theta - i\sin\theta$$

$$|e^{i\theta}| = [(\cos\theta + i\sin\theta)(\cos\theta - i\sin\theta)]^{1/2}$$

$$= (\cos^2\theta + \sin^2\theta)^{1/2} = 1$$

The following problems are meant to provide practice for the manipulation of complex numbers.

Problems

1. Find the real and imaginary parts of the following quantities:
   (a) $(2 - i)^3$ (b) $e^{\pi i/2}$

(c) $e^{-2+i\pi/2}$ (d) $(\sqrt{2} + 2i)e^{-i\pi/2}$

(e) $(1 - i)(2 + 3i)(-2 + i)$

2. Prove that

$$\text{Re } z = \frac{1}{2}(z + z^*)$$

$$\text{Im } z = \frac{1}{2i}(z - z^*)$$

3. If $z = x + 2iy$, then find
(a) Re z^* (b) Re z^2
(c) Im z^2 (d) Re (zz^*)
(e) Im (zz^*)

4. Find the absolute magnitude and the phase angle for each of the following complex numbers:
(a) $6i$ (b) $4 - \sqrt{2}i$
(c) $-1 - 2i$ (d) $\pi + ei$
(e) -3 (f) $\sqrt{5} - 2i$

5. Prove that $e^{i\pi} = -1$. Comment on the nature of the numbers in this relation.

6. Show that

$$\cos \theta = \frac{e^{i\theta} + e^{-i\theta}}{2}$$

and that

$$\sin \theta = \frac{e^{i\theta} - e^{-i\theta}}{2i}$$

7. Use Eqs. B-8 and B-11 to derive

$$z^n = r^n (\cos \theta + i \sin \theta)^n = r^n (\cos n\theta + i \sin n\theta)$$

and from this, the *formula of De Moivre:*

$$(\cos \theta + i \sin \theta)^n = \cos n\theta + i \sin n\theta$$

8. Use the formula of De Moivre to derive the trigonometric identities

$$\cos 2\theta = \cos^2 \theta - \sin^2 \theta$$

$$\sin 2\theta = 2 \sin \theta \cos \theta$$

$$\cos 3\theta = \cos^3 \theta - 3 \cos \theta \sin^2 \theta$$

$$= 4 \cos^3 \theta - 3 \cos \theta$$

$$\sin 3\theta = 3 \cos^2 \theta \sin \theta - \sin^3 \theta$$

$$= 3 \sin \theta - 4 \sin^3 \theta$$

9. Consider the set of functions

$$\Phi_m(\phi) = \frac{1}{\sqrt{2\pi}} e^{im\phi} \qquad \begin{aligned} &m = 0, \pm1, \pm2, \ldots \\ &0 \le \phi \le 2\pi \end{aligned}$$

First show that

$$\int_0^{2\pi} d\phi \, \Phi_m(\phi) = 0 \qquad \text{for all values of } m \ne 0$$

$$= \sqrt{2\pi} \qquad m = 0$$

Now show that

$$\int_0^{2\pi} d\phi \, \Phi_m^*(\phi)\Phi_n(\phi) = 0 \qquad m \ne n$$

$$= 1 \qquad m = n$$

10. This problem offers an alternative derivation of Euler's formula. Start with

$$f(\theta) = \ln (\cos \theta + i \sin \theta) \tag{1}$$

Show that

$$\frac{df}{d\theta} = i \tag{2}$$

Now integrate both sides of Eq. 2 to obtain

$$\ln (\cos \theta + i \sin \theta) = i\theta + c \tag{3}$$

where c is a constant of integration. Show that $c = 0$ and then exponentiate Eq. 3 to obtain Euler's formula.

Solutions to Problems

Chapter 1

1. $\lambda = 2000$ Å

$$v = \frac{c}{\lambda} = \frac{3.0 \times 10^8 \text{ m}\cdot\text{s}^{-1}}{2000 \times 10^{-10} \text{ m}} = 1.5 \times 10^{15} \text{ s}^{-1}$$

$$\bar{v} = \frac{1}{\lambda} = 5.0 \times 10^6 \text{ m}^{-1} = 5.0 \times 10^4 \text{ cm}^{-1}$$

$$\varepsilon = \frac{hc}{\lambda} = 9.9 \times 10^{-19} \text{ J}$$

2. $\bar{v} = 10^3 \text{ cm}^{-1}$
   $\lambda = 10^{-3} \text{ cm} = 10^{-5} \text{ m}$
   $v = c\bar{v} = 3.0 \times 10^{13} \text{ s}^{-1}$
   $\varepsilon = hv = 2.0 \times 10^{-20} \text{ J}$

3. $v = 2.0 \times 10^4 \text{ MHz} = 2.0 \times 10^{10} \text{ s}^{-1}$

$$\bar{v} = \frac{v}{c} = 67 \text{ m}^{-1} = 0.67 \text{ cm}^{-1}$$

$$\lambda = \frac{c}{v} = 1.5 \times 10^{-2} \text{ m}$$

$$\varepsilon = hv = 1.32 \times 10^{-23} \text{ J}$$

5. $x = \dfrac{hc}{\lambda_{max}kT} = 4.965$ gives that $\lambda_{max}T = 2.90 \times 10^{-3} \text{ m}\cdot\text{K}$.

6. $\lambda_{max}T = 2.90 \times 10^{-3} \text{ m}\cdot\text{K}$
   $\lambda_{max} = 9.67 \times 10^{-6}$ m at 300 K
   $\quad\quad = 9.67 \times 10^{-7}$ m at 3000 K
   $\quad\quad = 2.90 \times 10^{-7}$ m at 10,000 K

7. $T = 1.1 \times 10^4$ K

8. $\lambda_{max} = 2.90 \times 10^{-10}$ m $= 2.90$ Å   (X rays)

9. $\sigma = 5.6703 \times 10^{-8} \text{ J}\cdot\text{m}^{-2}\cdot\text{K}^{-4}\cdot\text{s}^{-1}$

11. kinetic energy $= 1.80$ eV
$$= 2.89 \times 10^{-19} \text{ J}$$
$$V_s = 1.80 \text{ V}$$

12. $\phi = 4.59$ V
$$v_0 = 1.11 \times 10^{15} \text{ s}^{-1}$$

14. $\text{J} \cdot \text{s} = (\text{kg} \cdot \text{m}^2 \cdot \text{s}^{-2}) \cdot \text{s} = \text{kg} \cdot \text{m}^2 \cdot \text{s}^{-1}$

15. $v = 3.29 \times 10^{15} \text{ s}^{-1}$
$$\lambda = 9.12 \times 10^{-8} \text{ m}$$
$$\text{Ryd} = 1.31 \times 10^3 \text{ kJ} \cdot \text{mol}^{-1} = 13.6 \text{ eV}$$

16. $\mu = 1.162 \times 10^{-26}$ kg (N_2)
$$= 1.627 \times 10^{-27} \text{ kg} \quad (\text{HCl})$$

17. $I = 5.362 \times 10^{-47}$ kg·m^2
$$r = 1.82 \times 10^{-10} \text{ m} = 182 \text{ pm}$$

18. $R_H = 109{,}680$ cm^{-1} 19. See Eq. 1-48.   21. IE $= 54.4$ eV

22. $\mu = 1.69 \times 10^{-28}$ kg $r = 0.284$ pm $v = 4.60 \times 10^{17}$ s^{-1} $E = -4.06 \times 10^{-16}$ J
$$\Delta E = 3.045 \times 10^{-16} \text{ J}$$

23. (a) 1.23×10^{-10} m   (b) 9.05×10^{-14} m   (c) 3.33×10^{-10} m

24. (a) $E = 1.602 \times 10^{-17}$ J $\lambda = 1.23 \times 10^{-10}$ m   (b) 6.02×10^{-18} J

25. 82 mV   26. $E = 8$ eV $= 1.28 \times 10^{-18}$ J $\lambda = 5.06 \times 10^{-12}$ m

27. $v(n = 1) = 2.19 \times 10^6$ m·s^{-1} $v(n = 2) = 1.09 \times 10^6$ m·s^{-1} $v(n = 3) = 0.73 \times 10^6$ m·s^{-1}

Chapter 2

1. (a) $y(x) = c_1 e^x + c_2 e^{3x}$
(b) $y(x) = c_1 + c_2 e^{-6x}$
(c) $y(x) = ce^{-3x}$
(d) $y(x) = e^{-x}(c_1 e^{\sqrt{2}x} + c_2 e^{-\sqrt{2}x})$
(e) $y(x) = c_1 e^x + c_2 e^{2x}$

2. (a) $y(x) = 2e^{2x}$
(b) $y(x) = 2e^{3x} - 3e^{2x}$
(c) $y(x) = 2e^{2x}$

4. (a) $x(t) = \dfrac{v_0}{\omega} \sin \omega t$

(b) $x(t) = \dfrac{v_0}{\omega} \sin \omega t + A \cos \omega t$

5. $c_1 = A \sin \phi$ $c_1 = B \cos \psi$
$c_2 = A \cos \phi$ $c_2 = -B \sin \psi$

6. (a) $y(x) = e^{-x}(c_1 \cos x + c_2 \sin x)$ (b) $y(x) = e^{3x}(c_1 \cos 4x + c_2 \sin 4x)$
(c) $y(x) = e^{-\beta x}(c_1 \cos \omega x + c_2 \sin \omega x)$ (d) $y(x) = e^{-2x}(\cos x - \sin x)$

7. The motion is oscillatory with frequency $(1/2\pi)(k/m)^{1/2}$ and amplitude $v_0 (m/k)^{1/2}$.

8. $\xi(t) = e^{-\gamma t/2m} \cos(\omega' t + \phi)$ with $\omega' = \sqrt{4km - \gamma^2}/2m = \sqrt{(k/m) - (\gamma/2m)^2}$. The motion is oscillatory with an amplitude that decreases with time according to $e^{-\gamma t/2m}$.

10. $\psi(x) = A \sin \dfrac{n\pi x}{a}$ $n = 1, 2, \ldots$ 13. See Eq. 2-29.

16. $\psi(x, y) = A \sin \dfrac{n_x \pi x}{a} \sin \dfrac{n_y \pi y}{b}$ $n_x = 1, 2, \ldots$
$n_y = 1, 2, \ldots$

17. $\psi(x, y, z) = A \sin \dfrac{n_x \pi x}{a} \sin \dfrac{n_y \pi y}{b} \sin \dfrac{n_z \pi z}{c}$ $\begin{array}{l} n_x = 1, 2, \ldots \\ n_y = 1, 2, \ldots \\ n_z = 1, 2, \ldots \end{array}$ $E = \dfrac{h^2}{8m}\left(\dfrac{n_x^2}{a^2} + \dfrac{n_y^2}{b^2} + \dfrac{n_z^2}{c^2}\right)$

18. $x(t) = -\frac{1}{2}gt^2 - v_0 t + x_0$ 19. $x(t) = -\frac{1}{2}gt^2 + v_0 t$ 20. natural frequency $= \dfrac{1}{2\pi}\left(\dfrac{g}{l}\right)^{1/2}$

$$t_{\text{return}} = \dfrac{2v_0}{g}$$

21. $\theta(t) = A_0 e^{-\lambda t/2m} \cos(\omega t + \phi)$ where $\omega = \sqrt{(g/l) - (\lambda/2m)^2}$. If $\lambda^2 > 4m^2 g/l$, then solution is
$\theta(t) = e^{-\lambda t/2m}(c_1 e^{\alpha t} + c_2 e^{-\alpha t})$, where $\alpha = \sqrt{(\lambda/2m)^2 - (g/l)}$ is real. Therefore, there is no
oscillatory motion if $\lambda^2 > 4m^2 g/l$.

23. $m\ddot{\xi} = -m\omega_0^2\xi - 2k\xi = -(m\omega_0^2 + 2k)\xi$
$m\ddot{\eta} = -m\omega_0^2\eta$

$\xi(t) = A\cos(\omega t + \phi)$ $\omega^2 = \omega_0^2 + \dfrac{2k}{m}$

$\eta(t) = A'\cos(\omega' t + \phi)$ $\omega' = \omega_0$

Chapter 3

1. (a) $\pm x^2$ (b) $(x^3 - \alpha^3)e^{-\alpha x}$ (c) $\frac{9}{4}$ (d) $6xy^2z^4 + 2x^3z^4 + 12x^3y^2z^2$
2. (a) nonlinear   (b) nonlinear   (c) linear   (d) nonlinear   (e) linear   (f) nonlinear
3. (a) $-\omega^2$ (b) $i\omega$ (c) $\alpha^2 + 2\alpha + 3$ (d) 6
4. The eigenvalue is $-(a^2 + b^2 + c^2)$.

5. (a) $\dfrac{d^4}{dx^4}$ (b) $\dfrac{d^2}{dx^2} + 2x\dfrac{d}{dx} + x^2 + 1$ (c) $\dfrac{d^4}{dx^4} - 4x\dfrac{d^3}{dx^3} + (4x^2 - 2)\dfrac{d^2}{dx^2} + 1$

6. (a) commute   (b) do not commute
     (c) do not commute (watch $\pm$ signs)   (d) commute
7. $(\hat{P} + \hat{Q})(\hat{P} - \hat{Q}) = \hat{P}^2 - \hat{Q}^2 + \hat{Q}\hat{P} - \hat{P}\hat{Q}$
    Same result as ordinary algebra only if $\hat{P}$ and $\hat{Q}$ commute.
9. $(3 \times 1.35) + (2 \times 1.54) + 1.54 = 8.67$ Å
    Transition is an $n = 3$ to $n = 4$ transition.
    $\Delta E = 8.015 \times 10^{-20}(16 - 9)\,\text{J} = 5.61 \times 10^{-19}\,\text{J} = 2.82 \times 10^4\,\text{cm}^{-1}$

11. $\langle x \rangle = 0.30$ **12.** $\langle n \rangle = \lambda$ **13.** $c = \lambda$
    $\langle x^2 \rangle = 5.80$ $\langle n^2 \rangle = \lambda^2 + \lambda$
    $\sigma^2 = 5.71 > 0$ $\sigma^2 = \lambda$ $\langle x \rangle = \dfrac{1}{\lambda}$

$$\langle x^2 \rangle = \frac{2}{\lambda^2}$$

$$\sigma^2 = \frac{1}{\lambda^2}$$

$$\text{Prob}\,[x \geq a] = e^{-\lambda a}$$

14. A Gaussian probability density is an even function of x, and so the integrand for any odd moment of x will be an odd function of x. The limits are from $-\infty$ to $+\infty$, and so the integral vanishes.

$$\langle x^4 \rangle = 3\sigma^4 \quad \text{(see Example 3.12)}$$

16. $\langle x \rangle = \dfrac{2}{a}\displaystyle\int_0^a x\sin^2\dfrac{n\pi x}{a}\,dx = \dfrac{a}{2}$ for $n = 1, 2, \dots$

17. $\sigma_x = a\left(\dfrac{2\pi^2 n^2 - 12}{24\pi^2 n^2}\right)^{1/2} < a$ for all n **20.** Use Euler's formula.

22. Use the fact that an integral of $\cos x$ or $\sin x$ vanishes over a complete cycle.
29. In the classical case $\langle x \rangle = a/2$ and $\langle x^2 \rangle = a^2/3$, and so $\sigma^2 = \langle x^2 \rangle - \langle x \rangle^2 = a^2/12$.

Chapter 4

1. (a) normalizable, $(2/\pi)^{1/4}e^{-x^2}$ **2.** (a) not acceptable (not normalizable)
    (b) not normalizable   (b) acceptable
    (c) normalizable, $(2\pi)^{-1/2}e^{i\theta}$ (c) not acceptable (not normalizable)

(d) not normalizable

(e) normalizable, $2xe^{-x}$

(d) acceptable

(e) not acceptable (not single valued)

3. $v_1 \cdot v_2 = 3$

$|v_1| = \sqrt{14}$

$|v_2| = \sqrt{6}$

$\theta = \cos^{-1}(0.327) = 70.89°$

4. $v_1 \times v_2 = -7i + j + 5k$

$\theta = \sin^{-1}\left(\dfrac{\sqrt{75}}{\sqrt{14}\sqrt{6}}\right) = 70.89°$

7. $r \times F$ is a torque. The direction of l is perpendicular to the plane formed by r and p.

8. $\langle E \rangle = \dfrac{6h^2}{ma^2}$

$\langle E^2 \rangle = \dfrac{126h^4}{m^2 a^4}$

$\sigma_E^2 = \dfrac{90h^4}{m^2 a^4}$

10. $\langle p \rangle = 0$

$\langle p^2 \rangle = \dfrac{h^2}{4}\left(\dfrac{n_x^2}{a^2} + \dfrac{n_y^2}{b^2}\right)$

$\sigma_p^2 = \langle p^2 \rangle$

11. $\langle E \rangle = \dfrac{5h^2}{m}\left(\dfrac{1}{a^2} + \dfrac{1}{b^2}\right)$

13. d/dx is not Hermitian.

id/dx is Hermitian.

d^2/dx^2 is Hermitian.

id^2/dx^2 is not Hermitian.

xd/dx is not Hermitian.

x is Hermitian.

19. $f_0(x) = 1$

$f_1(x) = \sqrt{3}(1 - 2x)$

$f_2(x) = \sqrt{5}(1 - 6x + 6x^2)$

24. (a) $2\dfrac{d}{dx}$ (b) 2 (c) $\hat{A}\hat{B}f = f(x) - f(0)$ (d) $4x\dfrac{d}{dx} + 3$

$\hat{B}\hat{A}f = f(x)$

$[\hat{A}, \hat{B}]f(x) = -f(0)$

27. $e^{\hat{A}+\hat{B}} = e^{\hat{A}}e^{\hat{B}}$ only if $\hat{A}$ and $\hat{B}$ commute.

28. Both E and A have sharp values and can be measured simultaneously with infinite precision.

Chapter 5

3. $2\pi\left(\dfrac{m}{k}\right)^{1/2}$

5. (a) $x(t) = \dfrac{1}{2}gt^2 + v_0 t$

$K = \dfrac{1}{2}m\dot{x}^2 = \dfrac{m}{2}(gt + v_0)^2 = \dfrac{1}{2}mg^2t^2 + mgv_0 t + \dfrac{1}{2}mv_0^2$

$U = mg(x_0 - x) = mgx_0 - \dfrac{1}{2}mg^2t^2 - mgv_0 t$

$K + U = \dfrac{1}{2}mv_0^2 + mgx_0 = \text{total initial energy}$

(b) $x(t) = -\frac{1}{2}gt^2 - v_0 t + x_0$

$K = \frac{1}{2}m\dot{x}^2 = \frac{1}{2}mg^2t^2 + mgv_0 t + \frac{1}{2}mv_0^2$

$U = mgx = -\frac{1}{2}mg^2t^2 - mgv_0 t + mgx_0$

$K + U = \frac{1}{2}mv_0^2 + mgx_0 = \text{total initial energy}$

8. $484\ \text{N}\cdot\text{m}^{-1}$

9. $393\ \text{N}\cdot\text{m}^{-1}, 1.30 \times 10^{-14}\ \text{s}^{-1}$

10. $\bar{v} = 320 \text{ cm}^{-1}$ $E_0 = 3.19 \times 10^{-21} \text{ J}$

18. 8.82 pm (H_2)
4.14 pm ($^{35}Cl^{35}Cl$)
3.20 pm ($^{14}N^{14}N$)

Chapter 6

3. $\left(\dfrac{1}{2} + \dfrac{1}{\pi}\right)^3 = 0.548$

4. $\left(\dfrac{1}{2} + \dfrac{1}{\pi}\right)^2 = 0.670$

5. $\frac{1}{4}$, the probabilities are the same.

13. $I = 3.35 \times 10^{-47} \text{ kg·m}^2$
$\mu = 1.64 \times 10^{-27} \text{ kg}$
$r = 143 \text{ pm}$

14. $I = 1.46 \times 10^{-46} \text{ kg·m}^2$
$\mu = 1.14 \times 10^{-26} \text{ kg}$
$r = 113 \text{ pm}$

29. $1 - 13e^{-4} = 0.762$

30. Prob $= 1 - e^{-2D}(2D^2 + 2D + 1)$ where D is the distance (in units of a_0) of the electron from the nucleus. $D = 1.339$ when Prob $= 0.50$ and $D = 2.66$ when Prob $= 0.90$.

34. $\langle r \rangle_{2s} = 6a_0$
$\langle r \rangle_{2p} = 5a_0$
$\langle r \rangle_{3s} = \frac{27}{2}a_0$

36. See answer to Problem 30.

38. $\Delta E = (1.63 \times 10^{-18} + 9.27 \times 10^{-23}m) \text{ J}$ $m = 0, \pm 1$
$v = (2.46 \times 10^{15} + 1.40 \times 10^{11}m) \text{ s}^{-1}$

39. IE $= 13.6$ eV for H and 54.4 eV for He.

Chapter 7

1. (a) $\hat{H}^{(0)}$, $\psi^{(0)}$, and $E^{(0)}$ are given by the harmonic-oscillator solutions (Chapter 5) and $\hat{H}^{(1)} = (\gamma/6)x^3 + (b/24)x^4$.
(b) $\hat{H}^{(0)}$, $\psi^{(0)}$, and $E^{(0)}$ are given by particle-in-a-box solutions (Chapter 3) and

$$\hat{H}^{(1)} = 0 \qquad 0 < x < \frac{a}{2}$$

$$= b \qquad \frac{a}{2} < x < a$$

(c) $\hat{H}^{(0)} = \hat{H}_H(1) + \hat{H}_H(2)$
$\psi^{(0)} = \psi_H(1)\psi_H(2)$
$E^{(0)} = E_H(1) + E_H(2)$

$$\hat{H}^{(1)} = \frac{e^2}{4\pi\varepsilon_0 r_{12}}$$

(d) $\hat{H}^{(0)}$, $\psi^{(0)}$, and $E^{(0)}$ are given by the hydrogen atom solutions (Chapter 6) and $\hat{H}^{(1)} = e\mathscr{E}r\cos\theta$.
(e) $\hat{H}^{(0)}$, $\psi^{(0)}$, and $E^{(0)}$ are given by rigid-rotator solutions (Chapter 6) and $\hat{H}^{(1)} = \mu\mathscr{E}\cos\theta$.

2. $\psi_1^{(0)}(x) = (2\alpha)^{1/2}\left(\dfrac{\alpha}{\pi}\right)^{1/4} xe^{-\alpha x^2/2}$

3. $\Delta E = \dfrac{b}{2}$

4. $\Delta E = 0$

$$\hat{H}^{(1)} = \frac{\gamma}{6}x^3 + \frac{b}{24}x^4$$

$$\Delta E = 0 + \frac{5}{32}\frac{b}{\alpha^2}$$

5. $\Delta E = \dfrac{Va}{4} + \dfrac{Va}{2n^2\pi^2}(1 - \cos n\pi)$

6. $\Delta E = 0.548$ V (see Problem 3 on p. 244)

7. $\hat{H}^{(1)} = cx^4 - \dfrac{k}{2}x^2$

$\Delta E = \dfrac{3c}{4\alpha^2} - \dfrac{k}{4\alpha}$

8. $\Delta E = A\left(\langle x^2 \rangle - l\langle x \rangle + \dfrac{l^2}{4}\right)$

$= A\left(\dfrac{l^2}{12} - \dfrac{l^2}{2\pi^2 n^2}\right) = \dfrac{Al^2}{12}\left(1 - \dfrac{6}{\pi^2 n^2}\right)$

10. $\alpha = \dfrac{\mu^2 e^4}{18\pi^3\varepsilon_0^2 h^4}$ $E_{\min} = -\dfrac{\mu e^4}{12\pi^2\varepsilon_0^2 h^2}$

11. The variational method gives the exact ground-state energy in this case because the trial function happens to have the same functional form as the exact ground-state wave function.

12. The value of c_2 will come out to be zero because the first term has the same functional form as the exact ground-state wave function. The first term will come out to be $(\pi a_0^3)^{-1/2} e^{-r/a_0}$ after it is normalized and $E_{\min}$ will be the exact ground-state energy.
In the second trial function, $c_2 = c_3 = c_4 = c_5 = 0$.

13. This trial function gives the exact ground-state energy because the trial function has the same functional form as the exact ground-state wave function. The parameter β comes out to be $(\mu k/4h^2)^{1/2}$.

14. $\alpha^2 = \dfrac{h}{(2\mu k)^{1/2}}$ $E_{\min} = \dfrac{1}{\sqrt{2}}h\left(\dfrac{k}{\mu}\right)^{1/2}$

15. $\alpha^2 = \dfrac{(3\mu k)^{1/2}}{h}$ $E_{\min} = \sqrt{3}h\left(\dfrac{k}{\mu}\right)^{1/2}$ for $e^{-\alpha r}$

The trial function $e^{-\alpha r^2}$ gives the exact ground-state energy because it has the same functional form as the exact ground-state wave function.

19. $H_{11} = \dfrac{h^2}{8m} + \dfrac{V}{2}$ $H_{22} = \dfrac{4h^2}{8m} + \dfrac{V}{2}$ $H_{12} = H_{21} = -\dfrac{16V}{9\pi^2}$

20. $H_{11} = \dfrac{h^2}{8ma^2} + 0.35V_1 a$ $H_{22} = \dfrac{9h^2}{8ma^2} + 0.26V_1 a$ $H_{12} = H_{21} = -\dfrac{V_1 a}{\pi^2}$

21. $\psi_0(x) = \left(\dfrac{\alpha}{\pi}\right)^{1/4} e^{-\alpha x^2/2}$

$\psi_2(x) = \left(\dfrac{1}{8}\right)^{1/2}\left(\dfrac{\alpha}{\pi}\right)^{1/4}(4\alpha x^2 - 2)e^{-\alpha x^2/2}$

$H_{11} = E_0 + \dfrac{\delta}{24}\langle x^4 \rangle_{00} = E_0 + \dfrac{\delta}{24}\left(\dfrac{3}{4\alpha^2}\right)$

$H_{22} = E_2 + \dfrac{\delta}{24}\langle x^4 \rangle_{22} = E_2 + \dfrac{\delta}{24}\left(\dfrac{39}{4\alpha^2}\right)$

$H_{12} = 0 + \dfrac{\delta}{24}\langle x^4 \rangle_{02} = \dfrac{\delta}{24}\left(\dfrac{3}{\sqrt{2\alpha^2}}\right)$

Chapter 8

1. $E = -(Z^2/2) = -2$ au when $Z = 2$.

5. The atomic unit of speed is 2.18764×10^6 m·s^{-1}. The ratio of c to this value is 137.

7. The value of Z that minimizes E is an effective nuclear charge.

8. Use the fact that

$$\int_0^\infty r^{2n} e^{-2\zeta r} \, dr = \frac{(2n)!}{(2\zeta)^{2n+1}}$$

9. The radial part of Slater orbitals are everywhere positive and so the integral of their product can never be zero.

11. Recall that the angular part of ∇^2 is $\hat{L}^2$ and that the $Y_l^m(\theta, \phi)$ are eigenfunctions of $\hat{L}^2$.

14. The two states involved in the transition have spin angular momenta $\pm \hbar/2$, and so $\Delta E = g(e/2m_p)\hbar B_z = (2.821 \times 10^{-26} \text{ J} \cdot \text{T}^{-1})(2.0 \text{ T}) = 5.642 \times 10^{-26}$ J. The frequency of the radiation that is absorbed is $\nu = \Delta E/h = 85.15$ MHz.

18. $\psi = \dfrac{1}{\sqrt{2}}\{1s(1)1s(2)[\alpha(1)\beta(2) - \alpha(2)\beta(1)]\}$

19. The expansion of an Nth-order determinant has $N!$ terms. Each term will contribute unity if the individual spin orbitals are normalized.

20. 0 and $\frac{1}{2}$ 21. The eigenvalues are zero.

23. $E_0 = E_{1s} + E_{2s} = -\dfrac{Z^2}{2} - \dfrac{Z^2}{8} = -\dfrac{5}{2}$ when $Z = 2$

See Section 8.2 for the proof that $E = -\frac{11}{4}$ for the ground state of helium.

$$E(\text{triplet}) = E_0 + J - K = -\frac{5}{2} + \frac{10}{27} - \frac{32}{(27)^2} = -2.174 \text{ au}$$

$$E(\text{singlet}) = E_0 + J + K = -\frac{5}{2} + \frac{10}{27} + \frac{32}{(27)^2} = -2.086 \text{ au}$$

$$\Delta E(\text{triplet to ground state}) = -2.174 + \frac{11}{4} = 0.576 \text{ au} = 15.7 \text{ eV}$$

$$\Delta E(\text{singlet to ground state}) = -2.086 + \frac{11}{4} = 0.664 \text{ au} = 18.1 \text{ eV}$$

24. The eigenvalue is $\frac{1}{2}$.   29. $^2P_{3/2}$ and $^2P_{1/2}$; the ground state is $^2P_{1/2}$.

30. $^3P_2, \, ^3P_1, \, ^3P_0, \, ^1D_2, \, ^1S_0$ 31. $(1 \times 1) + (3 \times 3) + (1 \times 5) = 15$

32. 45; $(1 \times 1) + (1 \times 5) + (3 \times 3) + (3 \times 7) + (1 \times 9) = 45$

33. $^3P_2, \, ^3P_1, \, ^3P_0, \, ^1P_1$; the state of lowest energy is $^3P_0$.

34. 20; $^3D_3, \, ^3D_2, \, ^3D_1, \, ^1D_2$; the state of lowest energy is $^3D_1$.

35. $^1S_0, \, ^1D_2, \, ^1G_4, \, ^3P_2, \, ^3P_1, \, ^3P_0, \, ^3F_4, \, ^3F_3, \, ^3F_2$; the state of lowest energy is $^3F_2$.

36. $^2P_{3/2}, \, ^2P_{1/2}, \, ^2D_{5/2}, \, ^2D_{3/2}, \, ^4S_{3/2}$;   37. [Ne]$3s^2$; $^1S_0$ 38. $^3F_2$ 39. $^1S_0$

40. $2p \rightarrow 1s$ $\Delta E = 82,259.272 - 82,258.917 = 0.355 \text{ cm}^{-1}$
    $3p \rightarrow 1s$ $\Delta E = 97,492.306 - 97,492.198 = 0.108 \text{ cm}^{-1}$
    $4p \rightarrow 1s$ $\Delta E = 102,823.881 - 102,823.835 = 0.046 \text{ cm}^{-1}$

41. From Table 8-7, $\Delta E = 5415.7 \text{ cm}^{-1}$. $\lambda_{\text{vac}} = 18,465$ Å and $\lambda_{\text{air}} = 18,459$ Å, in excellent agreement with Figure 8-5.

Chapter 9

1. $\hat{H} = -\dfrac{1}{2}(\nabla_1^2 + \nabla_2^2) - \dfrac{1}{r_{A1}} - \dfrac{1}{r_{A2}} - \dfrac{1}{r_{B1}} - \dfrac{1}{r_{B2}} + \dfrac{1}{r_{12}} + \dfrac{1}{R_{AB}}$

3. $S(R) = e^{-ZR}(1 + ZR + \frac{1}{3}Z^2 R^2)$ 9. $k = 2a^2 D_e$

$$\bar{\nu} = \frac{a}{\pi c}\left(\frac{D_e}{2\mu}\right)^{1/2} = 4430 \text{ cm}^{-1}$$

14. $J' = e^{-2R}\left(1 + \dfrac{1}{R}\right)$

$K' = \dfrac{S}{R} - e^{-R}(1 + R)$

15. $c_n = c_b - c_a$ and $c_i = c_b + c_a$
and so

$$\dfrac{c_i}{c_n} = \dfrac{c_b + c_a}{c_b - c_a} = \dfrac{1 + (c_a/c_b)}{1 - (c_a/c_b)}$$

17. ψ_1 and ψ_3 do not mix because of symmetry.

19. The bond orders of N_2 and N_2^+ are 3 and $2\frac{1}{2}$, respectively. Thus the dissociation energy of N_2 is greater than that of N_2^+. Similarly, the bond orders of O_2^+ and O_2 are $2\frac{1}{2}$ and 2, respectively, and so the dissociation energy of O_2^+ is greater than that of O_2.

20. The ground-state electron configurations are
F_2 $KK(\sigma 2s)^2(\sigma^* 2s)^2(\pi 2p)^4(\sigma 2p_z)^2(\pi^* 2p)^4$
F_2^+ $KK(\sigma 2s)^2(\sigma^* 2s)^2(\pi 2p)^4(\sigma 2p_z)^2(\pi^* 2p)^3$
F_2^+ has one less antibonding electron than F_2, and so F_2^+ has a greater bond strength and a shorter bond than F_2.

21. $N_2 > N_2^+ \approx N_2^-$

22. C_2^{2-} has two more bonding electrons than C_2, and so C_2^- has a stronger bond and a shorter bond length.

23. Na_2 $KKLL(\sigma 3s)^2$
Mg_2 $KKLL(\sigma 3s)^2(\sigma^* 3s)^2$
   (not stable)
Al_2 $KKLL(\sigma 3s)^2(\sigma^* 3s)^2(\pi 3p)^2$
Si_2 $KKLL(\sigma 3s)^2(\sigma^* 3s)^2(\pi 3p)^4$

P_2 $KKLL(\sigma 3s)^2(\sigma^* 3s)^2(\pi 3p)^4(\sigma 3p_z)^2$
S_2 $KKLL(\sigma 3s)^2(\sigma^* 3s)^2(\pi 3p)^4(\sigma 3p_z)^2(\pi^* 3p)^2$
Cl_2 $KKLL(\sigma 3s)^2(\sigma^* 3s)^2(\pi 3p)^4(\sigma 3p_z)^2(\pi^* 3p)^4$
Ar_2 $KKLL(\sigma 3s)^2(\sigma^* 3s)^2(\pi 3p)^4(\sigma 3p_z)^2(\pi^* 3p)^4(\sigma^* 3p_z)^2$
   (not stable)

24. NO^+ $KK(\sigma 2s)^2(\sigma^* 2s)^2(\pi 2p)^4(\sigma 2p_z)^2$
NO $KK(\sigma 2s)^2(\sigma^* 2s)^2(\pi 2p)^4(\sigma 2p_z)^2(\pi^* 2p)^1$
The bond orders of NO^+ and NO are 3 and $2\frac{1}{2}$, respectively.

25. CN^- is isoelectronic with CO. The bond order is three.

27. See Table 9.6.   **28.** See Table 9.6.   **29.** $^1\Pi$ or $^3\Pi$

31. In contrast to the valence-bond wave function of H_2O given by Eq. 9-112, the valence-bond wave function of NH_3 will have eight terms. A typical term is

$$|\psi_{2p_xN}\alpha(1)\psi_{1sA}\beta(2)\psi_{2p_yN}\alpha(3)\psi_{1sB}\beta(4)\psi_{2p_zN}\alpha(5)\psi_{1sC}\beta(6)|$$

Note that the bonding is described by the overlap of a hydrogen 1s orbital with each of the 2p orbitals on the nitrogen atom. Each bond consists of two electrons of opposite spin.

32. $\xi_2 = \dfrac{1}{\sqrt{3}}2s - \dfrac{1}{\sqrt{6}}2p_z + \dfrac{1}{\sqrt{2}}2p_x$ **33.** $\xi_3 = \dfrac{1}{\sqrt{3}}2s - \dfrac{1}{\sqrt{6}}2p_z - \dfrac{1}{\sqrt{2}}2p_x$

34. $\tan\theta = \dfrac{\sin\theta}{\cos\theta} = \dfrac{\sqrt{1-\cos^2\theta}}{\cos\theta} = -\sqrt{8}$

or

$\dfrac{1-\cos^2\theta}{\cos^2\theta} = 8$

which gives $\cos\theta = -\frac{1}{3}$.

36. If we expand about the first row, then we obtain $x(x^3 - 2x) - (x^2 - 1) = x^4 - 3x^2 + 1$.

37. $\begin{vmatrix} x & 1 & 0 & 1 \\ 1 & x & 1 & 0 \\ 0 & 1 & x & 1 \\ 1 & 0 & 1 & x \end{vmatrix} = x^4 - 4x^2 = 0$

$x = 2, 0, 0, -2$
$E = \alpha + 2\beta, \alpha, \alpha, \alpha - 2\beta$
$E_\pi = 2(\alpha + 2\beta) + 2\alpha = 4\alpha + 4\beta$
The ground state is predicted to be a triplet. Cyclobutadiene has no delocalization energy.

38.

$$\begin{vmatrix} x & 0 & 0 & 1 \\ 0 & x & 0 & 1 \\ 0 & 0 & x & 1 \\ 1 & 1 & 1 & x \end{vmatrix} = x^4 - 3x^2 = 0$$

$x = \sqrt{3}, 0, 0, -\sqrt{3}$

$E = \alpha + \sqrt{3}\beta, \alpha, \alpha, \alpha - \sqrt{3}\beta$

$E_\pi = 2(\alpha + \sqrt{3}\beta) + 2\alpha = 4\alpha + 2\sqrt{3}\beta$

For two isolated ethylene molecules, $E_\pi = 4\alpha + 4\beta$.

39.

$$\begin{vmatrix} x & 1 & 1 & 1 \\ 1 & x & 0 & 1 \\ 1 & 0 & x & 1 \\ 1 & 1 & 1 & x \end{vmatrix} = x^4 - 5x^2 + 4x = 0$$

$x = 1, 0, -\frac{1}{2} \pm \frac{1}{2}\sqrt{17}$

$E_\pi = 2(\alpha + 2.5615\beta) + 2\alpha = 4\alpha + 5.123\beta$

$DE = 1.123\beta$

40. $E_1 = \alpha + \sqrt{2}\beta \qquad \psi_1 = \frac{1}{2}\chi_1 + \frac{\sqrt{2}}{2}\chi_2 + \frac{1}{2}\chi_3$

$\qquad E_2 = \alpha \qquad\qquad \psi_2 = \frac{1}{\sqrt{2}}\chi_1 - \frac{1}{\sqrt{2}}\chi_3$

$\qquad E_3 = \alpha - \sqrt{2}\beta \qquad \psi_3 = \frac{1}{2}\chi_1 - \frac{\sqrt{2}}{2}\chi_2 + \frac{1}{2}\chi_3$

For the allyl radical,

$DE = 2(\alpha + \sqrt{2}\beta) + \alpha - (3\alpha + 2\beta) = 0.828\beta$

$q_1 = q_2 = q_3 = 1.0$

$P_{12}^\pi = P_{23}^\pi = 0.707$

For the allyl carbonium ion,

$DE = 2(\alpha + \sqrt{2}\beta) - 2(\alpha + \beta) = 0.828\beta$

$q_1 = q_3 = \frac{1}{2} \qquad q_2 = 1$

$P_{12}^\pi = P_{23}^\pi = 0.707$

For the allyl carbanion,

$DE = 2(\alpha + \sqrt{2}\beta) + 2\alpha - (4\alpha + 2\beta) = 0.828\beta$

$q_1 = q_3 = \frac{3}{2} \qquad q_2 = 1$

$P_{12}^\pi = P_{23}^\pi = 0.707$

42.

$$\begin{vmatrix} x & 0 & 0 & 0 & 0 & 0 & 0 & 1 & 1 & 0 \\ 0 & x & 1 & 0 & 0 & 0 & 0 & 0 & 1 & 0 \\ 0 & 1 & x & 1 & 0 & 0 & 0 & 0 & 0 & 0 \\ 0 & 0 & 1 & x & 1 & 0 & 0 & 0 & 0 & 0 \\ 0 & 0 & 0 & 1 & x & 0 & 0 & 0 & 0 & 1 \\ 0 & 0 & 0 & 0 & 0 & x & 1 & 0 & 0 & 1 \\ 0 & 0 & 0 & 0 & 0 & 1 & x & 1 & 0 & 0 \\ 1 & 0 & 0 & 0 & 0 & 0 & 1 & x & 0 & 0 \\ 1 & 1 & 0 & 0 & 0 & 0 & 0 & 0 & x & 1 \\ 0 & 0 & 0 & 0 & 1 & 1 & 0 & 0 & 1 & x \end{vmatrix}$$

43. $E_\pi = 2(\alpha + 2.3028\beta) + 2(\alpha + 1.6180\beta) + 2(\alpha + 1.3029\beta) + 2(\alpha + \beta) + 2(\alpha + 0.6180\beta)$
$= 10\alpha + 13.68\beta$

44. $DE = 10\alpha + 13.68\beta - 10(\alpha + \beta)$
$= 3.68\beta$

45. Use Eq. 9-151.
For the butadiene cation,
$q_1 = q_4 = 2(0.3717)^2 + (0.6015)^2 = 0.6381$
$q_2 = q_3 = 2(0.6015)^2 + (0.3717)^2 = 0.8617$
For the butadiene anion,
$q_1 = q_4 = 2(0.3717)^2 + 2(0.6015)^2 + (0.6015)^2 = 1.362$
$q_2 = q_3 = 2(0.6015)^2 + 2(0.3717)^2 + (0.3717)^2 = 1.138$

47. For the triangular geometry,

$$\begin{vmatrix} x & 1 & 1 \\ 1 & x & 1 \\ 1 & 1 & x \end{vmatrix} = x^3 - 3x + 2 = 0$$

$x = 1, 1, -2$
$E_{H_3^+} = 2\alpha + 4\beta \qquad E_{H_3} = 3\alpha + 3\beta \qquad E_{H_3^-} = 4\alpha + 2\beta$
For the linear geometry,

$$\begin{vmatrix} x & 1 & 0 \\ 1 & x & 1 \\ 0 & 1 & x \end{vmatrix} = x^3 - 2x = 0$$

$x = 0, \pm\sqrt{2}$
$E_{H_3^+} = 2\alpha + 2\sqrt{2}\beta \qquad E_{H_3} = 3\alpha + 2\sqrt{2}\beta \qquad E_{H_3^-} = 4\alpha + 2\sqrt{2}\beta$
The triangular geometry is more stable for H_3^+; the linear geometry is more stable for H_3^-;
and the two geometries have almost the same energy for H_3.

48.

$$\begin{vmatrix} \alpha_N - E & \beta_{CN} & 0 & 0 & 0 & \beta_{CN} \\ \beta_{CN} & \alpha_C - E & \beta_{CC} & 0 & 0 & 0 \\ 0 & \beta_{CC} & \alpha_C - E & \beta_{CC} & 0 & 0 \\ 0 & 0 & \beta_{CC} & \alpha_C - E & \beta_{CC} & 0 \\ 0 & 0 & 0 & \beta_{CC} & \alpha_C - E & \beta_{CC} \\ \beta_{CN} & 0 & 0 & 0 & \beta_{CC} & \alpha_C - E \end{vmatrix}$$

49. $D_e = 7.58 \times 10^{-19}$ J
$k = 570$ N·m^{-1}
$\nu_{D_2} = 9.34 \times 10^{13}$ s^{-1}
$D_0 = 7.27 \times 10^{-19}$ J

Chapter 10

1. $I = 2.64 \times 10^{-47}$ kg·m^2
$r = 1.28 \times 10^{-10}$ m $= 128$ pm

2. $I = 4.62 \times 10^{-45}$ kg·m^2
$r = 3.04 \times 10^{-10}$ m $= 304$ pm

3. $B = 1.97 \times 10^{11}$ s^{-1} $= 1.97 \times 10^5$ MHz
$\bar{B} = 6.56$ cm^{-1}

4. Use the relation $\frac{1}{2}I\omega^2 = hc\bar{B}J(J + 1)$, relate I to B, and derive the relation $\omega = 4\pi B\sqrt{J(J + 1)}$.
For $J = 10$, $\omega = 8.57 \times 10^{11}$ radians·s^{-1}

5. The spectrum is predicted to be a series of equally spaced lines whose frequencies are multiples of $v = 8.88 \times 10^{10}$ s^{-1}.

6. $I = 1.90 \times 10^{-46}$ kg·m^2

7. $k = 156$ N·m^{-1}
$T = 8.82 \times 10^{-14}$ s

8. $v = 9.60 \times 10^{12}$ s$^{-1} = 320$ cm^{-1}
$E_0 = 3.18 \times 10^{-21}$ J

9. $x_{rms} = 3.21$ pm

10. At 300 K, $f_0 \approx 1$, $f_1 = 1.4 \times 10^{-5}$.
At 1000 K, $f_0 = 0.965$, $f_1 = 3.4 \times 10^{-2}$.

11. H$_2$, $f_0 \approx 1$; NaCl, $f_0 = 0.84$

12. P branch, $v_{obs}/$cm$^{-1} = 2143 - 3.74J$ $J = 1, 2, 3, \ldots$
R branch, $v_{obs}/$cm$^{-1} = 2143 + 3.74(J + 1)$ $J = 0, 1, 2, \ldots$

13. P branch, $v_{obs}/$cm$^{-1} = 961.2 - 1.51J$ $J = 1, 2, \ldots$
R branch, $v_{obs}/$cm$^{-1} = 961.2 + 1.51(J + 1)$ $J = 0, 1, 2, \ldots$

14. $J_{max} \approx 2$ to 3 for H^{35}Cl and $J_{max} \approx 30$ for ^{127}I^{35}Cl at 300 K.

15. $f_J = \dfrac{(2J + 1)\exp[-BJ(J + 1)/k_B T]}{k_B T/B}$

16. ratio $= \dfrac{\bar{D}J^2(J + 1)^2}{BJ(J + 1) - \bar{D}J^2(J + 1)^2}$
For H^{35}Cl, ratio $= 5 \times 10^{-3}$.

18. $\bar{B} = 1.923$ cm^{-1}
$\bar{D} \approx 10^{-5}$ cm^{-1}

19. Using the $\bar{B}$ and $\bar{D}$ given in Table 10-2, $\bar{v}_{obs} = 20.788$ cm^{-1}, 41.567 cm^{-1}, 62.327 cm^{-1}, 83.057 cm^{-1}.

21. fraction $= \dfrac{\bar{x}_e \bar{v}_e (n + \frac{1}{2})^2}{\bar{v}_e(n + \frac{1}{2}) - \bar{x}_e \bar{v}_e(n + \frac{1}{2})^2}$
$= 0.0088(n = 0), 0.106(n = 5), 0.224(n = 10)$

22. $k = 490$ N·m^{-1}

24. $\bar{v}_e = 2156.0$ cm^{-1} $\bar{x}_e \bar{v}_e = 6.5$ cm^{-1}

25. $\bar{v}_{obs} = 2559.3$ cm^{-1}, 5028.1 cm^{-1}, 7406.6 cm^{-1}, 9694.6 cm^{-1}

27. $\bar{v}_e = 384.1$ cm^{-1} $\bar{x}_e \bar{v}_e = 1.45$ cm^{-1}

28. As n increases, the size of the effective box increases, and so the energies are spaced closer together.

29. $\bar{v}_R/$cm$^{-1} = 2885.6 + 20.28 + 19.97J - 0.30J^2$ $J = 0, 1, 2, \ldots$
$\bar{v}_P/$cm$^{-1} = 2885.6 - 20.58J - 0.30J^2$ $J = 1, 2, 3, \ldots$

30. $\bar{B}_0 = 6.47$ cm^{-1} $\bar{B}_1 = 6.28$ cm^{-1}
$\bar{B}_e = 6.56$ cm^{-1} $\bar{\alpha}_e = 0.19$ cm^{-1}

31. (a) 3, 3, 9   (b) 3, 2, 4
(c) 3, 3, 30   (d) 3, 2, 7
(e) 3, 3, 6   (f) 3, 3, 21

32. All are infrared active except v_1.

33. $\bar{v}_{el,el} = 6.50804 \times 10^4$ cm^{-1}

34. $E_0' = 752.70$ cm^{-1} $E_0'' = 1081.74$ cm^{-1}
$\bar{v}_{obs}(0 \to 0) = 6475.4$ cm^{-1} $\bar{v}_{obs}(0 \to 1) = 66,230.7$ cm^{-1}
$\bar{v}_{obs}(0 \to 2) = 67,675.2$ cm^{-1} $\bar{v}_{obs}(0 \to 3) = 69,084.9$ cm^{-1}
$\bar{v}_{obs}(0 \to 4) = 70,459.8$ cm^{-1}

35. $\bar{B}_e = 0.82004$ cm^{-1} and $\bar{\alpha}_e = 0.00592$ cm^{-1}

38. The force constants are the same because the internuclear potential energy curve is the same under the Born-Oppenheimer approximation. The fundamental vibrational frequencies and the rotational constants are not the same because the reduced masses are different.

39. $\dfrac{v_1}{v_2} = \left(\dfrac{\mu_2}{\mu_1}\right)^{1/2}$ (Born-Oppenheimer approximation)
$v(D^{35}Cl) = 2143.4$ cm^{-1}

40. $\bar{v}_e(HD) = 3806.4$ cm^{-1} $\bar{B}_0(HD) = 44.48$ cm^{-1}
$\bar{v}_e(D_2) = 3107.9$ cm^{-1} $\bar{B}_0(D_2) = 29.66$ cm^{-1}

42. The volume element for the orthogonality of the $S_{vib}(R)$ is simply dR. It is not $R^2\, dR$ because $\psi_{vib}(R) = S_{vib}(R)/R$.

43. $0 \rightarrow 1$ transition $\sim \dfrac{1}{\sqrt{3}}$ (see Example 10.13)

    $1 \rightarrow 2$ transition $\sim \dfrac{2}{\sqrt{15}}$

    ratio $= \dfrac{\sqrt{5}}{2}$

44. $0 \rightarrow 1$ transition $\sim \dfrac{1}{\sqrt{2}}$

    $1 \rightarrow 2$ transition ~ 1

    ratio $= \dfrac{1}{\sqrt{2}}$

45. $\Delta l = \pm 1 \qquad \Delta m = 0 \quad (\mu_z) \quad \text{and} \quad = \pm 1 \quad (\mu_x \text{ and } \mu_y)$

Appendix B

1. (a) $2 - 11i$
   (b) i
   (c) $e^{-2}i$
   (d) $2 - \sqrt{2}i$
   (e) $-11 + 3i$

3. (a) x
   (b) $x^2 - 4y^2$
   (c) $4xy$
   (d) $x^2 + 4y^2$
   (e) 0

4. (a) $|z| = 6 \qquad \phi = 90°$
   (b) $|z| = 3\sqrt{2} \qquad \phi = -19.5°$
   (c) $|z| = \sqrt{5} \qquad \phi = 243.4°$
   (d) $|z| = \sqrt{\pi^2 + e^2} \qquad \phi = 40.9°$
   (e) $|z| = 3 \qquad \phi = 180°$
   (f) $|z| = 3 \qquad \phi = -41.8°$

5. $e^{i\pi} = \cos \pi + i \sin \pi = -1$
   e and π are irrational numbers; yet $e^{i\pi} = -1$.

43. $0 \leftarrow 1$ transition $\sim \dfrac{1}{\sqrt{3}}$ (see Example 10.13) 44. $0 \leftarrow 1$ transition $\sim \dfrac{1}{\sqrt{2}}$

Index

Ab initio calculation, 390
Absolute value, 496
Acetylene, 391
Addition of angular momenta, 315, 328
Allyl species, 434
Ammonia, Hartree-Fock calculation, 391, 433
Amplitude, 53, 155
  quantum-mechanical, 173–175
  root-mean-square, 173–175, 188, 486
Angstrom unit, *inside back cover*
Angular momentum
  addition of, 315, 328
  in atoms, 313ff
  classical, 22, 116, 207, 440
  commutation relations, 220, 250
  conservation of, 144
  operators, 217–220
  quantum mechanical, 117, 207, 217–220, 250, 440
  quantum number, 225
Anharmonic oscillator, 260, 261, 265, 277, 452ff, 472, 488
Anharmonic terms, 162, 452
Anharmonicity constant, 453, 454(t), 461–465, 487, 488, 489
Anomalous spin factor, 301
Antibonding orbitals, 362, 370ff, 415
Antisymmetric wave function, 302, 335, 336
Associated Laguerre functions, 223(t) 251
Associated Legendre functions, 215, 475, 214(t)
Asymptotic behavior, 175–177
Asymptotic solution, 175–177, 188
Atomic spectrum, 16ff, 286, 320–327
Atomic term symbol, 313ff, 320ff, 312(t), 339
Atomic units, 289–290, 330, 331, 345
Average value, 90

Balmer, J. J., 17
Balmer formula, 18
Balmer series, 18
Band head, 467–469
Basis set, 390
Bender, C. F., 394
Benzene, 410, 411, 417, 420, 422, 423, 434
Beryllium hydride, 398–400

Beryllium molecule, 375
Bicyclobutadiene, 434
Blackbody radiation, 5ff
Bohr, N., 23
Bohr formula, 24, 25, 26, 29, 42
Bohr frequency condition, 25, 163, 211, 439, 475
Bohr magneton, 241, 288, 301
Bohr orbit, 24, 42, 330
Bohr radius of the hydrogen atom, 288
Bohr theory of the hydrogen atom, 22ff
Bohr unit, 288
Boltzmann distribution
  rotational, 448–449, 486
  vibrational, 443–445, 486
Bond orbital, 398ff, 401, 405, 408, 410
Bond order, 374ff, 432
Bonding orbitals, 362, 370ff, 415
Born, M. 84
Born-Oppenheimer approximation, 345, 434, 460, 469, 470, 489, 490
Born postulate, 84
Boron hydride, 402ff
Boron molecule, 376, 377, 388, 389
Boundary conditions, 85, 111
Butadiene, 415–421, 434

Carbon molecule, 377, 375, 389, 432
Cathode rays, 4
Center-of-mass coordinate, 74, 159, 202, 470, 490
Central force, 144
Centrifugal distortion constant, 451, 454(t), 486, 487
Chain rule, 247
Classical harmonic oscillator, 66, 67, 153–162
Classical mechanics, 114
Classical physics, 4
Classical wave equation, 48, 58, 491–493
Classically forbidden region, 173
Clementi, E., 296
Commutation relations
  angular momentum, 150, 250
  coordinates and momenta, 137
Commutator, 136

Commuting operators, eigenfunctions of, 138
Complementary error function, 173
Complex conjugate, 495
Complex numbers, 494–499
Complex plane, 494–495
Configuration interaction, 366, 368, 391, 429
Conjugated molecules, 415ff
Conservative system, 155ff
Contour graph, 233, 234, 386, 387, 400, 404, 407
Conversion factors, table of, *inside front cover*
Coolidge, A. S., 353, 368
Correlation energy, 297, 313, 391
Correspondence between dynamical variables and operators, 117(t)
Coulomb integral, 295, 308, 337, 338, 348, 349, 359, 413, 425, 426
Coulomb's law, 23
Coulson, C. A., 353
Coupled pendulums, 73
Crooke's tube, 4
Cross product of vectors, 143
Cyanide ion, 431
Cyclobutadiene, 433

d orbitals, 232, 234, 236, 237
Davidson, E. R., 394
de Broglie, L., 30
de Broglie wavelength, 31ff, 42, 103
De Frees, D. J., 391–393
Degeneracy
  in hydrogen atom, 225
  particle in a cube, 198, 199
  rigid rotator, 440
  vibrating membrane, 62
Degrees of freedom, 74, 457–458, 488
Delocalization energy, 417, 418, 419, 420
Delocalized electrons, 412ff
Determinantal wave function, 304, 334, 335, 338
Determinants, 305, 334, 418, 419
Differential equations, power-series solution of, 191
Dipole moment
  electric, 272, 278, 333, 391, 394, 478, 479
  function, 478
  magnetic, 334
Dipole transition moment, 474–479, 490
Dirac, P. A. M., 300, 301
Dissociation energy, 454(t)
Dot product of vectors, 143
Doublet, 298, 322, 340
Dulong and Petit, law of, 15
Dynamical variable, 113

Effective nuclear charge, 292
Ehrenfest's theorem, 151
Eigenfunction
  angular momentum, 217–220
  of commuting operators, 138
  definition, 81

Eigenfunction (*continued*)
  harmonic oscillator, 165–166
  of Hermitian operators, 126ff
  hydrogen atom, 224, 238
  of momentum operator, 111
  particle in a box, 88
  rigid rotator, 215, 216
Eigenvalue
  angular momentum, 218, 219
  definition, 81
  harmonic oscillator, 163
  of Hermitian operators, 124
  hydrogen atom, 222
  momentum, 111
  particle in a box, 85
  rigid rotator, 209, 216
Einstein, A., 15
Electric dipole moment, 272, 278, 333, 391, 394, 478, 479
Electromagnetic spectrum, 40, 438
Electron configurations
  atoms, 312
  homonuclear diatomic molecules, 375, 380, 390(t), 432, 433
  heteronuclear diatomic molecules, 384
Electron diffraction, 33
Electron volt, 13, 289
Electronic spectra, 460–469, 489
Electronic transition moment, 479
Elliptic coordinates, 368, 424, 425, 429
Emission spectrum, 16
Energy levels
  free particle, 111
  harmonic oscillator, 163
  hydrogen atom, 222
  particle in a box, 85
  rigid rotator, 209–212, 216
Equivalent orbitals, 401, 405, 408
Ethane, 392, 408
Ethylene, 392, 410, 411, 412–415
Euler's formula, 52, 497, 499
Even function, 94, 168
Exchange integral, 308, 337, 338, 349, 350, 359, 427
Excited-state helium atom, 336ff
Exclusion principle, Pauli, 302ff, 374, 389
Expansion of functions, 129
Expectation value, 90

Far-infrared radiation, 40, 438
Fine structure, 322
First harmonic, 56
First-order perturbation theory, 258
Fluorine molecule, 375, 380, 391, 432,
Fock operator, 308
Force constant, 66, 122, 154, 164, 165, 187, 429, 485
Formula of DeMoivre, 498
Fortrat diagram, 467–468, 489
Foucault pendulum, 152
Fourier series, 57, 129, 147

Franck-Condon factor, 479
Franck-Condon principle, 481
Free-electron model, 87, 103, 107, 279
Free particle, 84, 100, 110
Fundamental mode, 56
Fundamental vibrational frequency, 164, 165, 442, 452, 454(t)

Gaussian distribution, 93ff, 104, 112, 192
geométric series, 444
gerade, 370, 371
Gerhold, G., 234, 400, 404, 407
Goudsmit, S., 299
Gram-Charlier series, 192
Group theory, 108

Hagstrom, S., 353
Hamiltonian operator, 82
Harmonic, 56, 57
Harmonic oscillator
    classical, 66, 67, 153–162, 190
    energy levels, 163, 442
    quantum, 122, 162–183, 442–445
    selection rule, 163, 442
    wave functions, 165, 442
Hartree-Fock equations, 295, 307–309
Hartree-Fock limit, 293, 382, 383, 390ff
Hartree-Fock method
    for atoms, 294–298, 307–309
    for diatomic molecules, 382ff, 390ff
Hartree-Fock orbital, 295, 311, 333
    energy, 296, 309, 339
Hartree-Fock-Roothaan method
    atoms, 311
    diatomic molecules, 382ff
Hartree unit, 288, 289
Heisenberg, W., 36
Heisenberg uncertainty principle, 36ff, 96ff, 105, 138ff, 163, 170–172, 220
Heitler, W., 345, 353
Heitler-London treatment of H_2, 345–358, 426, 428
Helium atom, 290–298, 291(t)
Helium molecule, 373
Hermite polynomials, 165, 166(t), 167, 442
Hermite's differential equation, 177, 188, 189
Hermitian operators, 123ff, 146, 150
Herzberg, G., 353, 436
Hooke's law, 66, 70, 153ff, 449
Hückel, E., 412
Hückel molecular-orbital theory, 411–422, 433–434
Hückel secular determinant, 413–419, 434
Hund, F., 320, 358
Hund's rules, 319ff, 339, 377, 379
Hybrid orbitals, 398–409, 432, 433
Hybridization, 398–410
Hydrogen fluoride, 391, 396, 432
Hydrogen molecule, 343, 358
    ion, 358–363, 430

Hydrogenlike atomic energy levels, 251
Hydrogenlike atomic wave functions
    complex form, 224(t)
    real form, 238(t)
Hydrogenlike orbitals,
    complex form, 224
    real form, 238
Hylleras, E., 291, 294

Imaginary number, 494
Imaginary part, 494
Imaginary unit, 494
Index of refraction of air, 324, 340
Induced dipole moment, 272
Infrared active, 459, 488
Infrared inactive, 460, 488
Infrared radiation, 40, 438
Infrared spectrum, 488
Intensity of a wave, 109
Ionic structures, 365, 396, 397
Ionization energy, 26, 292, 296, 297, 309, 310

James, H. M., 353, 368
j-j coupling, 329

Kekulé structures, 411
Kinetic-energy operator, 82, 252
Kinoshita, T., 291, 294
Knight, R. E., 291
Kolos, W., 353, 368
Koopmans' theorem, 296, 309, 310
Kronecker delta, 106, 127, 147

Laplacian operator, 103, 203–206, 246–248
LCAO-MO, 364, 382
Legendre polynomials, 213(t), 214, 215
Legendre's equation, 213, 249
Line spectrum, 16
Linear differential equation, 49
Linear operators, 80
Linear variational functions, 266ff
Lithium atom, 306
Lithium hydride
    Hartree-Fock calculation, 391
    valence-bond treatment, 394ff
Lithium molecule, 375, 391
Localized orbitals, 399ff, 401, 405, 408, 410
London, F., 345, 353
L-S coupling, 313ff, 327ff
Lyman series, 19, 20, 41, 321, 340

Maclaurin expansion, 273, 444, 452, 496, 497
McLean, A. D., 353
Magnesium molecule, 432
Magnetic dipole, 237ff, 334
Magnetic moment, 334
    and spin, 334
Magnetic quantum number, 225
Matrix elements, 267
Mesonic atom, 42

Methane
  SCF-MO treatment, 391
  valence-bond treatment, 405–409
Microwave radiation, 438
Microwave spectrum, 211, 212, 440–442, 485, 487
Millikan, R. A., 5
Minimal basis set, 390
Modern physics, 4
Molecular-orbital (MO) theory
  for diatomic molecules, 369ff, 432, 433
  for H_2^+, 358ff, 430
  for H_2, 363ff
  and the valence bond method, 363ff, 430
Moment of inertia, 21, 28, 90, 207, 485
Momentum eigenfunction, 111
Momentum operator, 81, 137, 198
Moore's tables, 321, 323, 324, 327
Morse potential, 186, 427, 487
Mulliken, R. S., 358

n' progression, 463, 464
Naphthalene, 434
Near Hartree-Fock calculation, 390ff
Neon molecule, 375, 380
Nitrogen molecule, 375, 377, 432
Nodal line, 61
Node, 56, 69
Nonrigid rotator, 449ff, 487
Normal coordinates, 459, 460, 488
Normal mode, 55ff, 61, 62, 68, 69, 74, 459–460, 488
Normalization
  of associated Laguerre functions, 223
  of associated Legendre functions, 215
  constant, 88
  of spherical harmonics, 215

Observable, 114
Odd function, 94, 168
Oil-drop experiment, 5
One-electron bond, 374
Operand, 79
Operators
  angular momentum, 117
  commutation of, 83
  definition, 79
  Hamiltonian, 82, 117
  Hermitian, 123ff
  linear, 80
  momentum, 81
  potential-energy, 117
  quantum-mechanical, 116
Oppenheimer, J. R., 344
Orbital
  atomic, 228–236, 293
  bond, 399ff, 401, 405, 408, 410
  equivalent, 401, 405, 408
  Hartree-Fock, 295, 311, 333
  hybrid, 398–410, 433, 434

Orbital (*continued*)
  localized, 399ff, 401, 405, 408, 410
  molecular, 369ff.
Orbital exponent, 292–293
Orthogonality,
  of associated Legendre functions, 215
  definition, 106, 126
  of eigenfunctions, 169
  of Hermite polynomials, 169, 476–478
  of Hückel molecular orbitals, 434
  of hybrid orbitals, 398ff, 433
  of hydrogen atomic orbitals, 223
  of Legendre polynomials, 214, 249
  of spin functions, 300
Orthonormality, 106, 127, 499
  of associated Legendre functions, 215
  of Hermite polynomials, 169
  of Hückel molecular orbitals, 434
  of hydrogen atomic orbitals, 223
Overlap integral, 346, 414, 416, 417, 426, 428
Overtone, 56, 452–455, 487
Oxygen molecule, 342, 375, 379, 380, 391 432, 433

P branch, 446–449, 455–457, 465–469, 486, 488
p orbital, 230–233
Paramagnetism of O_2, 342, 379ff
Particle in a box
  one-dimensional, 85ff
  three-dimensional, 195ff
Particle-in-a-box energy levels, 85(1D), 224(2D), 197(3D)
Particle-in-a-box wave functions, 85(1D), 224(2D), 197(3D)
Pauli, W., 299
Pauli exclusion principle, 302ff, 374, 389
Pauling, L., 379
Pekeris, C. L., 291, 294
Permittivity of free space, 23, 221
Perturbation theory, time-independent, 255–262
Photoelectric effect, 12ff
Photoelectron spectra, 377, 378, 386
Photon, 13
Physical constants, table of, *inside front cover*
Pi bond, 410ff
  order, 420–423
Pi-electron approximation, 409ff
Pi-electron bond order, 420–423
Pi-electron charge distribution, 420–423
Pi-electron energy, 415, 418, 419, 420, 434, 435
Pi orbitals, 371, 417
Planck, M., 7
Planck's constant, 9
Planck's distribution law, 9
Plane polar coordinates, 204
Polar graph paper, 230, 231, 235
Polar plot, 230, 231, 235
Polarizability, 272–274
Pople, J. A., 390

Postulates of quantum mechanics, 140–142, 303
Potential-energy curve for molecules, 161, 352, 461, 462, 480, 482
Principal quantum number, 225
Probability, 88–95
Pyridine, 434

Quadratically integrable, 115
Quantum Chemistry Program Exchange, 390, 391

R branch, 446–449, 455–457, 465–469, 486, 488
Radial function (hydrogen atom) 225–228
Radial Schrödinger equation, 222
Rayleigh-Jeans law, 7
Real part, 494
Recursion relation,
  associated Legendre functions, 249, 475
  definition, 178
  Hermite polynomials, 182, 189, 477
  three-term, 190
Reduced mass, 28, 41, 158, 160, 186, 206, 207, 440, 470
Relative coordinates, 74, 159, 186, 202, 470, 490
Resonance, 397, 411, 412
  denominator, 475
  energy, 411
  integral, 413ff
Rigid rotator, 206–221, 439–442
  degeneracy, 440
  energy levels, 216, 440
  selection rule, 440, 475–476
  wave functions, 216, 440
  harmonic-oscillator approximation, 445–449, 486
Ritz combination rule, 20
Röentgen, W., 5
Roothaan, C. C. J., 291, 296, 353, 382
Root-mean-square amplitude, 173–175, 188, 486
Rosen, N., 353, 365
Rotational constant, 42, 211, 441, 454(T)
Rotational fine structure, 467
Rotational spectrum, 440–442, 450
Russell-Saunders coupling, 313ff, 327ff
Rydberg constant, 19, 29, 42
Rydberg formula, 19, 321
Rydberg unit, 41

s orbitals, 225–230
Sachs, L. M., 291
Scalar product of vectors, 143
SCF-LCAO-MO, 381ff, 390ff
SCF method
  atoms, 295, 308, 311
  diatomic molecules, 382ff
Scherr, C. W., 291

Schmidt orthogonalization, 129, 147
Schrödinger, E., 76, 85
Schrödinger equation:
  time-dependent, 120ff, 472ff
  time-independent, 47, 79ff, 121
Schwartz inequality, 139, 150
Second harmonic, 56
Second-order perturbation theory, 284–285
Second overtone, 56
Secular determinant, 268, 269
Secular equation, 268, 418
Selection rules,
  atomic hydrogen, 322, 490
  electronic, 478–479
  harmonic-oscillator, 163, 442, 476–478, 490
  rigid-rotator, 210, 211, 440, 475–476, 490
Self-consistent field method
  atoms, 295, 308, 311
  diatomic molecules, 382ff
Separable Hamiltonian operator, 199–202, 245
Separation of variables, 49ff, 59ff
Series expansion, 273, 444, 452, 496, 497
Series limit, 19
Series method, 191
  Hermite's equation, 177–181
Shull, H., 353
SI units, *inside back cover*
Sigma bond framework, 409, 410
Sigma orbitals, 370
Simple pendulum, 71–73
Simultaneous linear equations, 267–268
Sirius, 10, 41
Slater, J. C., 293
Slater determinant, 303ff, 335, 395ff
Slater orbitals, 292, 295, 296, 311, 332, 333, 383, 399ff
Sodium D line, 325
Solar radiation, 10
Solvay conference, 141
sp hybrid orbitals, 398–401
sp² hybrid orbitals, 401–404, 410ff, 432
sp³ hybrid orbitals, 405–409, 432, 433
Spectroscopic parameters, table of, 454
Spherical coordinates, 205, 206, 216
Spherical harmonics, 216(t), 440, 477
Spin, 298ff
Spin eigenfunctions, 300
Spin magnetic moment, 298–301
Spin-orbit coupling, 314, 327ff
Spin-orbit splitting, 326, 327
Spin orbitals, 301
Spin quantum number, 225, 298, 300
Spin variable, 300
Square integrable, 115
Standing wave, 46, 56, 57, 58
Stationary state, 472ff
Stationary-state wave function 121
Stefan-Boltzmann constant, 11, 41
Stefan-Boltzmann law, 11

Stern-Gerlach experiment, 298–300, 301
Stopping potential, 12
Symmetry argument, 108, 367
Term symbol,
  atomic, 313ff, 320ff, 312(t), 339
  molecular, 387ff, 431, 432
Tesla, 240
Tetrahedron, 405ff, 433
Thomson, G. P., 35
Thomson, J. J., 4
Threshold frequency, 12
Time-dependent perturbation theory, 472–475
Time-dependent Schrödinger equation,
  120ff, 472ff
Time-dependent wave function, 472–475
Time-independent Schrödinger equation,
  79, 82
Trajectory, 70, 71, 72, 114
Transition moment, 474–479
Translational wave function, 202, 203
Traveling wave, 57, 58, 69
Trial function, 263
Triatomic hydrogen, 434
Trimethylenemethane, 433
Triplet, 241, 242, 354
Tunnel effect, 173
Two-body problem, 27ff
Two-center integral, 424

Uhlenbeck, G., 299
Ultraviolet catastrophe, 7
Ultraviolet radiation, 40, 438
Uncertainty principle
  for angular momentum, 220
  for coordinates and momenta, 96ff
  for electrons in nucleii, 105
  harmonic oscillator, 163, 170–172
  proof of, 138ff
ungerade, 370–371
Unperturbed Hamiltonian operator, 256, 257
Unsöld's theorem, 250

Valence-bond (VB) method
  for H_2, 345ff
  ionic structures in, 365
  and molecular orbital theory, 363ff, 430
  for polyatomic molecules, 394ff, 433

Valence-electron approximation, 377
Valence electrons, 377, 376, 401, 408, 410
Variance, 89, 90
Variational method, 262–276
Variational parameters, 262
Variational principle, 262–264
Vectors, 143
Vibration-rotation interaction, 455ff, 471, 488
Vibrational overlap integral, 479
Vibrational-rotational spectrum, 446–449.
Vibrational spectrum, 443, 453, 455–457,
  486, 488
Vibrating membrane, 58ff
Vibrating string, 491–493
Vibronic transition, 461ff, 489
Virial theorem, 229, 252, 253
Visible radiation, 40, 438

Wahl, A. C., 376, 384, 385
Wang, S. C., 353
Water
  Hartree-Fock calculation, 392
  valence bond method, 397, 398
Wave function
  conditions on, 115
  harmonic-oscillator, 165
  hydrogen atom, 224(t), 238(t)
  interpretation of, 115
  particle-in-a-box, 86, 88, 126, 197, 244
  rigid-rotator, 440
  stationary state, 79, 121
Wave number, 17, 439
Wave-particle duality, 31
Weinbaum, S., 353, 365
Weiss, A. W., 291, 353
Well-behaved function, 115
Wien's displacement law, 10
Wolniewicz, L., 353, 368
Work function, 13

X-ray spectroscopy, 309

Yoshimine, M., 353

Zeeman, P., 239
Zeeman effect, 242, 254
Zero-point energy, 162, 463, 485, 489

ATOMIC UNITS AND THEIR SI EQUIVALENTS

Quantity	Atomic unit	SI equivalent
Mass	$m = 1$ (electron mass)	9.1091×10^{-31} kg
Charge	$|e| = 1$ (electron charge)	1.6021×10^{-19} C
Angular momentum	$\hbar = 1$	1.0545×10^{-34} J s
Permittivity	$\kappa_0 = 4\pi\varepsilon_0 = 1$	1.1126×10^{-10} C^2 J^{-1} m^{-1}
Length	$\kappa_0\hbar^2/me^2 = a_0 = 1$ (bohr) (Bohr radius)	5.2917×10^{-11} m
Energy	$me^4/\kappa_0^2\hbar^2 = e^2/\kappa_0 a_0 = 1$ (hartree) (twice the ionization energy of atomic hydrogen)	4.3594×10^{-18} J
Time	$\kappa_0^2\hbar^3/me^4 = 1$ (period of an electron in the first Bohr orbit)	2.4189×10^{-17} s
Speed	$e^2/\kappa_0\hbar = 1$ (speed of an electron in the first Bohr orbit)	2.1877×10^6 m s^{-1}
Electric potential	$me^3/\kappa_0^2\hbar^2 = e/\kappa_0 a_0 = 1$ (potential energy of an electron in the first Bohr orbit)	27.211 V
Magnetic dipole moment	$e\hbar/m = 1$ (twice a Bohr magneton)	1.8564×10^{-23} J T^{-1}

Fraction	Prefix	Symbol	Multiple	Prefix	Symbol
10^{-1}	deci	d	10	deka	da
10^{-2}	centi	c	10^2	hecto	h
10^{-3}	milli	m	10^3	kilo	k
10^{-6}	micro	μ	10^6	mega	M
10^{-9}	nano	n	10^9	giga	G
10^{-12}	pico	p	10^{12}	tera	T
10^{-15}	femto	f	10^{15}	peta	P
10^{-18}	atto	a	10^{18}	exa	E

Greek alphabet

Alpha	A	α	Iota	I	ι	Rho	P	ρ
Beta	B	β	Kappa	K	κ	Sigma	Σ	σ
Gamma	Γ	γ	Lambda	Λ	λ	Tau	T	τ
Delta	Δ	δ	Mu	M	μ	Upsilon	Υ	υ
Epsilon	E	ε	Nu	N	ν	Phi	Φ	ϕ
Zeta	Z	ζ	Xi	Ξ	ξ	Chi	X	χ
Eta	H	η	Omicron	O	o	Psi	Ψ	ψ
Theta	Θ	θ	Pi	Π	π	Omega	Ω	ω

ATOMIC UNITS AND THEIR SI EQUIVALENTS

Quantity	Atomic unit	SI equivalent
Mass	$m = 1$ (electron mass)	9.1091×10^{-31} kg
Charge	$|e| = 1$ (electron charge)	1.6021×10^{-19} C
Angular momentum	$\hbar = 1$	1.0545×10^{-34} J·s
Permittivity	$\kappa_0 = 4\pi\varepsilon_0 = 1$	1.1126×10^{-10} C^2·J^{-1}·m^{-1}
Length	$\kappa_0\hbar^2/me^2 = a_0 = 1$ (bohr) (Bohr radius)	5.29177×10^{-11} m
Energy	$me^4/\kappa_0^2\hbar^2 = e^2/\kappa_0 a_0 = 1$ (hartree) (twice the ionization energy of atomic hydrogen)	4.35944×10^{-18} J
Time	$\kappa_0^2\hbar^3/me^4 = 1$ (period of an electron in the first Bohr orbit)	2.41889×10^{-17} s
Speed	$e^2/\kappa_0\hbar = 1$ (speed of an electron in the first Bohr orbit)	2.18764×10^6 m·s^{-1}
Electric potential	$me^3/\kappa_0^2\hbar^2 = e/\kappa_0 a_0 = 1$ (potential energy of an electron in the first Bohr orbit)	27.211 V
Magnetic dipole moment	$e\hbar/m = 1$ (twice a Bohr magneton)	1.85464×10^{-23} J·T^{-1}

Fraction	Prefix	Symbol	Prefix	Multiple	Symbol
10^{-1}	deci	d	deka	10	da
10^{-2}	centi	c	hecto	10^2	h
10^{-3}	milli	m	kilo	10^3	k
10^{-6}	micro	μ	mega	10^6	M
10^{-9}	nano	n	giga	10^9	G
10^{-12}	pico	p	tera	10^{12}	T
10^{-15}	femto	f	peta	10^{15}	P
10^{-18}	atto	a	exa	10^{18}	E

Greek alphabet

Alpha	A	α	Iota	I	ι	Rho	P	ρ
Beta	B	β	Kappa	K	κ	Sigma	Σ	σ
Gamma	Γ	γ	Lambda	Λ	λ	Tau	T	τ
Delta	Δ	δ	Mu	M	μ	Upsilon	Υ	υ
Epsilon	E	ε	Nu	N	ν	Phi	Φ	ϕ
Zeta	Z	ζ	Xi	Ξ	ξ	Chi	X	χ
Eta	H	η	Omicron	O	o	Psi	Ψ	ψ
Theta	Θ	θ	Pi	Π	π	Omega	Ω	ω